# ORACLE® DATABASE

## Construction Kit

# ORACLE®
# DATABASE
# Construction Kit

John Palinski

# Oracle Database Construction Kit



Library of Congress Catalog No.: 97-68697

ISBN: 0-7897-1419-1



99 98 97 6 5 4 3 2 1

Interpretation of the printing code: the rightmost double-digit number is the year of the book's printing; the rightmost single-digit number, the number of the book's printing. For example, a printing code of 97-1 shows that the first printing of the book occurred in 1997.



Screen reproductions in this book were created by using Collage Plus from Inner Media, Inc., Hollis, NH.

# Contents at a Glance

# Table of Contents

## III PL/SQL Oracle's Procedure Language

# IV Oracle's User Interface (Oracle Forms 4.5)

# V Oracle's Report Writer: Oracle Reports 2.5

# Credits

**PRESIDENT**
Roland Elgey

**SENIOR VICE PRESIDENT/PUBLISHING**
Don Fowley

**SENIOR TITLE MANAGER**
Bryan Gambrel

**GENERAL MANAGER**
Joe Muldoon

**MANAGING EDITOR**
Caroline D. Roop

**DIRECTOR OF ACQUISITIONS**
Cheryl Willoughby

**ACQUISITIONS EDITOR**
Tracy Dunkelberger

**SENIOR EDITOR**
Mike La Bonne

**EDITORS**
Keith Cline
Judith Goode

**PRODUCT MARKETING MANAGER**
Kourtnaye Sturgeon

**ASSISTANT PRODUCT MARKETING MANAGER/ DESIGN**
Gretchen Schlesinger

**TECHNICAL EDITOR**
Steve Tallon

**SOFTWARE SPECIALIST**
Brandon Penticuff

**SOFTWARE COORDINATOR**
Andrea Duvall

**ACQUISITIONS COORDINATOR**
Carmen Krikorian

**SOFTWARE RELATIONS COORDINATOR**
Susan D. Gallagher

**EDITORIAL ASSISTANTS**
Travis Bartlett
Jeff Chandler

**BOOK DESIGNERS**
Ruth Harvey

**COVER DESIGNER**
Jay Corpus

**PRODUCTION TEAM**
DiMonique Ford
Tony McDonald
Nicole Ruessler
Julie Searls
Paul Wilson

**INDEXER**
Joe Long

Composed in *Century Old Style* and *ITC Franklin Gothic* by Que Corporation.

*I dedicate this book to my lovely wife Linda. She has been my constant companion and best friend for over a quarter of a century. I couldn't do it without her and wouldn't want to.*

# About the Author

**John Palinski** has been employed by his company, a utility, for the past 22 years. His current position is Supervisor, Computer Applications in the Engineering Division. He manages all computing projects that affect his division. He has been project manager of several large-scale projects. One is the T & D Work Management System, the first work management system developed in a relational database by a utility. He also managed a Streetlight Information Management project that developed streetlight facility and billing applications in an AM/FM/GIS system. He also oversaw the inventory and entry into the AM/FM landbase of 60,000 streetlights in his company's service area. John has developed numerous Oracle applications over the past nine years. He is currently teaching Oracle database development at a local community college. He has a BA in history, a BS in Business Administration, and an MBA.

# Acknowledgments

There are a number of people I want to acknowledge. The first is **Norm Firkins**. He introduced me to Oracle and empowered me with the tools to develop databases. This allowed me to accomplish work and develop skills I continue to use today. I also thank **Jim Larrick**. He taught me the use of triggers and showed me how to keep Version 2.0 master/detail blocks in synch. I also thank **Dick Liebentritt** and **Terry Pirruccello** for allowing me to attend continuing Oracle training.

A special thanks to **Dennis Kirlin** of Iowa Western. He gave me my first teaching position and opened the doors to new career horizons. Two other people deserve special mention. First is my son **Matthew**, who set up my new PC and taught me how to use Windows 95. He had as much patience training me as I have helping him with his homework. Second is **Steve Aarhus**. Without Steve's expertise, I would still be trying to unencode the nondisclosure form sent by Que.

I also acknowledge **Rush Limbaugh**. He has constantly reminded me that America is loaded with opportunity. In order to gain this opportunity, people have to make the effort to grab it. If they wait for it to come to them, someone else will grab it.

## We'd Like to Hear from You!

As part of our continuing effort to produce books of the highest possible quality, Que would like to hear your comments. To stay competitive, we *really* want you to let us know what you like or dislike most about this book or other Que products.

Please send your comments, ideas, and suggestions for improvement to:


The Expert User Team

E-mail: **euteam@que.mcp.com**

Fax: (317) 581-4663

Our mailing address is:

Expert User Team
Que Corporation
201 West 103rd Street
Indianapolis, IN 46290-1097


You can also visit our Team's home page on the World Wide Web at:

**http://www.mcp.com/que/developer_expert**

Thank you in advance. Your comments will help us to continue publishing the best books available in today's market.

Thank You,

The Expert User Team

# Introduction

The idea for this book first occurred to me in the summer of 1996. I was searching for a textbook to use in an Oracle database development course I planned to teach in the fall at Iowa Western Community College (IWCC). This course would be the first regular semester Oracle database development course taught at an academic institution in the Omaha area, or in the Midwest as far as I knew. Of all the books available on Oracle system development, I couldn't find one that covered the areas I felt were necessary. I searched the local bookstores, the Internet, and talked to other Oracle developers. I finally found a book that covered the various Oracle products I was interested in, but the book was so general that it could not be used as a reference for student homework or doing real work in the workplace. I used the book, but was forced to prepare and distribute a large amount of supplementary material to my students. My students found the supplements extremely useful, but commented on the ineffectiveness of the book. The extra work and my students' complaints caused me to continue my search. ■

I've been developing Oracle systems for the past 10 years. During that period I've amassed many books and training manuals about the various Oracle products I use. Whenever I have a problem with PL/SQL syntax, or have trigger errors, or a question on data format, or myriad other problems, I need to search a number of books. Unfortunately, the books are usually on someone else's desk. Most of my reference books are instruction books purchased directly from Oracle. They mainly consist of the Help screen in paperbound form. Since these sets cost several hundred dollars each and are not user-friendly, I have been reluctant to buy a set for each of my employees. For some time, I've wanted a relatively low-cost reference manual that covers the proper areas of development and database commands.

With these two problems in mind and no solution in the marketplace, I decided to write my own book. This book would cover the development of an Oracle database from initial design to Web enabling the applications. I approached Que with my idea of developing a book that would cover the flagship Oracle database and system development products. The products would include the Oracle7 database (Oracle Server) and Oracle's Developer 2000 development tools.

More specifically, the book would also thoroughly cover SQL*PLUS. This product executes commands and instructions against the Oracle7 or Oracle 8 database. The book also would cover PL/SQL, which is Oracle's procedure language. This language is used in most of the other Oracle products to perform specialized functions. Another product the book would cover was SQL*LOADER, which is Oracle's product to load data into the database for ASCII files. A major portion of the book is coverage of Oracle Forms 4.5. This product is Oracle's main user interface development tool. It is used to develop graphic user interface (GUI) forms. Finally, the book would cover Oracle Reports 2.5, which is Oracle's report writer.

Que bought the idea and you hold the result in your hands. This book, as did my IWCC course, targets several groups, from novice to advanced users. I want the novice to be able to gain the skills required to successfully develop a relational database and applications. The book will also enable the experienced developer new to Oracle to acquire the skills necessary to develop systems by using the Oracle products. Finally, I want the book to serve as the single-source reference book for all areas of Oracle development. I want the book to be **the** source that experienced Oracle developers, such as myself or members of my staff, use in the future.

If you're a novice developer, you'll find that this book is strong in the concepts and techniques of database and application design. Each chapter presents concepts you need to develop a database. At the end of each chapter are problems for you to solve that help you practice the skills learned in the chapter. You also have the opportunity to develop an employee database from scratch. At the end of each Part, you'll be given a series of tasks to perform. The results of the tasks will be a completed system, which can be used as a prototype for other systems you may develop. I identified the template for this system 10 years ago. I've used this design in every system I've developed since then.

The book also contains much reference material. I identified the areas in which I often sought technical specifications, and then included those materials in the book. They should come in handy for the experienced developer. In fact, I used completed portions of this book as a source in my work before it was published. The book may not be the definitive source for obscure areas of the Oracle database, but I believe experienced programmers will find it a good source of information to keep close to their computers.

Finally, I've developed a number of systems in the past 12 years. In these projects, I have made a lot of mistakes and identified what users seem to like about a system. Interspersed throughout the book are discussions of the various problems I've encountered and system development techniques I've learned over the years. I've tried to include some of these personal observations and sincerely hope these add a special element to the book.

## How This Book Is Organized

The book is organized in parts and each part covers a specific area of the database development cycle or specific Oracle tools. The order of the parts follows the normal development cycle of the database. At the end of each chapter are problems you can use to practice the techniques discussed. The answers to the problems are in Appendix E, "Answers to Practice Problems," and on the CD-ROM enclosed with the book. In addition, throughout the book, you'll see the various steps needed to develop an employee database system you can use as a template for other systems. At the end of each part, you'll find a series of tasks you need to complete this database. The completion of the tasks will bring you one step closer to developing the book's template system. The answers to the tasks are in Chapter 20, "Developing a Template Employee Information System." Finally, the book has appendixes that contain information on triggers, system variables, and built-in functions.

The following parts and chapters are included in this book:

### Part I: Designing Your Database Objects

This part introduces you to the Oracle Corporation and its various products. You learn about the major relational database objects such as tablespaces, tables, indexes, views, and database design concepts and techniques such as data normalization. This part includes Chapter 1, "Introduction to Oracle Tools," Chapter 2, "Designing Your Database," and Chapter 3, "Acquiring Data by Using the Select Statement."

At the end of Part I are two employee project tasks. The first asks you to identify the data elements used in the database and their attributes, and the second asks you to normalize the data and document the tables in a table relationship diagram.

### Part II: Using SQL*PLUS to Access the Database

This part discusses Oracle's SQL *PLUS product, which interfaces with the Oracle7 and Oracle 8 database products. The first several chapters cover the various aspects of the `SELECT` statement, which is used to acquire and display data from the database. You learn about the data definition language (DDL) statements used to create, alter, and delete database objects such as tables. The part also shows data manipulation (DML) commands used to add, update, and delete records. Finally, the part describes how SQL*PLUS acquires data and produces formatted reports. This part includes Chapter 4, "Formatting Reports in SQL*PLUS," Chapter

5, "Combining Tables and Rows," Chapter 6, "Defining the Database Objects," and Chapter 7, "Modifying Your Tables with DML Commands."

The project tasks at the end of Part II set up the employee database objects. This includes creating the tablespace, tables, and indexes, and creating a user account and granting privileges.

### Part III: PL/SQL Oracle's Procedure Language

This part covers PL/SQL Oracle's procedure language. PL/SQL is used in SQL*PLUS to modify tables. It is used by SQL Forms to control form behavior and process form data. It is also used by Oracle Reports to compute values. The final portion of PART III covers the SQL*LOADER, which loads ASCII text files into an Oracle table. This part includes Chapter 8, "Creating Your First PL/SQL Program," Chapter 9, "Increasing the Power of Your PL/SQL Blocks," and Chapter 10, "Using SQL*LOADER."

At the end of Part III, you are asked to load the tables created in Part II with data by using SQL*LOADER.

### Part IV: Oracle's User Interface (Oracle Forms 4.5)

Part IV covers all of the components of the Oracle Forms 4.5 application development product, which develops forms or screens used to add, update, delete, and view database records. This part include Chapter 11, "Using an Oracle Form," Chapter 12, "Using Object Navigator to Create Your First Oracle Form," Chapter 13, "Formatting Your Form," Chapter 14, "Creating and Modifying Master-Detail Forms," Chapter 15, "Using Triggers and Modifying Classes," and Chapter 16, "Calling Other Forms and Using Menus."

The project tasks at the end of the part ask you to develop a security update application, employee update application, department update application, employee directory, and a system menu.

### Part V: Oracle's Report Writer: Oracle Reports 2.5

Part V covers the Oracle Reports product, which is a powerful report writer used to develop highly formatted reports. This part includes Chapter 17, "Creating Your First Report," and Chapter 18, "Customizing Reports and Advanced Report Functions."

The project task asks you to develop an employee report and integrate it into the applications developed in Part IV.

### Part VI: Moving Your Application to the Web

This Part covers Chapter 19, "Moving Oracle Applications to the Web," which discusses the Layout Editor and its menu options, tools, and object properties. It also discusses reports and summary and formula columns.

### Part VII: Complete Template System

This part covers Chapter 20, "Developing a Template Employee Information System," which discusses designing a normalized relational database, creating employee system database objects, loading database tables, designing forms menus, and designing various reports.

### Appendixes

The book has five appendixes that cover the following topics: Appendix A, "Built-In Subprograms," discusses procedures developed for use in Oracle Forms. The procedures perform functions such as navigating to the next record. Appendix B, "Triggers," covers tools that cause Oracle Forms to execute PL/SQL statements at special times such as before inserting a record into the database. Appendix C, "System Variables," covers variables used to monitor and control Runtime Forms. Appendix D, "Practice Database Installation Instructions," covers the procedures to install the Oracle database used for the book's examples and exercises. Appendix E, "Answers to the Practice Problems," contains the answers to the exercises at the end of each chapter.

PART I

# Designing Your Database Objects

CHAPTER 1

# Introduction to Oracle Tools

This chapter introduces you to the Oracle Corporation and its main development products: the Oracle7 database and the Developer 2000 Tools Set. They are the main tools for developing an Oracle relational database. ■

# Oracle the Company

Oracle began in the early 1980s as a relational database company with very few software products. At the time, relational databases were in their infancy. The pioneers that formed Oracle foresaw that the computing industry would move toward relational databases. During this period, IBM (Big Blue) dominated the industry with a very good relational database called DB2, but it operated only on their hardware. Since Oracle was a competitor, it was forced to take a different strategy. Oracle developed an open-system concept whereby the Oracle database could be used on virtually any computer. This was an attractive option for the non-IBM vendors of hardware and software. It also was attractive to the customers in the industry that didn't like being locked into IBM.

Today, Oracle is one of the largest companies in the industry. It has a wealth of products that revolve around their Oracle7 database product. Their main products are the Oracle7 database, Developer 2000, and Designer 2000. Oracle also provides consulting services for the planning, development, and implementation of systems.

The company is based in Redwood, California. It does business in more than 90 countries and has software that runs on scores of computers. Oracle also is a major player on the information highway.

# Oracle7—Oracle's Database Product

Oracle7 is Oracle's relational database product. The product runs on scores of computer platforms and is the database of choice for many software vendors. Oracle7 supports several configurations and can be used in a host-based configuration where the user is connected to the same computer that contains the database. Mainframe applications would be an example of this type of configuration. The mainframe contains the database and the software. A dumb terminal or a PC acting as a terminal accesses the mainframe. In contrast, Oracle7 also supports client/server applications where the database is contained on a server and the applications on a different platform. The application software and the database are accessed through the use of a network. Oracle7 also supports the distributed processing configuration, which means that the database may be spread across multiple platforms. For instance, part of the database is located in Los Angeles and the other part in Portland, Maine. These last two configurations are powerful features in an era of rightsizing computers and distributed data processing.

Oracle7 also has a number of significant features, including extensive security mechanisms—sensitive data can be safeguarded through the use of privileges. Also, the database administrator can grant privileges to view, update, or delete records. There are myriad other privileges available to the administrator to control access to the database.

The database also has sophisticated backup and recovery procedures that minimize the chance for data loss. Every transaction made against the database is stored in archive files. Thus, when the need arises, Oracle can restore the database. Oracle7 also has flexible space management tools that allow the database administrator to place limits on the size a database can grow. Finally, the Oracle7 database supports open connectivity, which means that you can access other vendors' databases through the product. Oracle7 can access databases such as DB2, Sybase, or Microsoft's Access. In addition, Visual Basic and a myriad of other software products can use Oracle7. The ability of multiple software packages accessing a commom database is an important feature for a company that does not want to worry about being locked into a product.

Oracle7 has a number of important components, one of which is PL/SQL, or Oracle's procedure language. PL/SQL performs functions similar to other languages, such as C, FORTRAN, COBOL, and BASIC. PL/SQL is a very easy and powerful language to learn. I often use it to convert data from one system to another.

The Oracle7 database provides you with tools to develop stored procedures. These procedures, stored in the database itself, consist of PL/SQL programs or scripts that perform specialized functions such as printing a letter to customers thanking them for subscribing to a service. These procedures are triggered or initiated by transactions that occur in the database.

Another component is database triggers, which isPL/SQL code stored in the database that is fired when events such as inserting, deleting, or updating records occurs. Oracle7 also allows you to group procedures into packages. The procedures also are stored in the database.

The database also has a distributed option that allows the data to reside in numerous locations. This makes the location of the data transparent to the user. In addition, there is a parallel server option. Some computers are clustered, which means that they each have their own memory, but have a common storage device. This option allows Oracle7 to operate within this configuration.

## Oracle8—The Next Generation

Oracle8 is Oracle's next generation database that will eventually replace the Oracle7 installations. It is an object-relational database, which means the database is a relational database with object-oriented properties. This type of database allows developers to migrate their existing applications without rewriting them. When the time is ready, the applications can be converted to use the new object technology. This makes Oracle8 upward compatible with existing databases. This is a safe approach by Oracle. A drastic shift from the mainstay relational database would likely cause Oracle to loose market share. I believe that people like to play it safe and loathe uncertainty. Object-oriented technology offers some excellent benefits for the future and I applaud Oracle's position of gradually moving the industry in this direction.

This book is primarily a development book. It follows the traditional relational database design used for many years. The concepts are employed by using an Oracle7 database. They will also be valid using the Oracle8 database. At key places in the book, I will explain some of the new features of Oracle8. The most important of these features are new datatypes that allow the database to hold new objects such as images, video, and spatial data. Oracle8 also has capabilities for the support of database warehouses. These features do not play a role in this book. The purpose of this book is to identify and discuss the tools needed to develop the normal everyday type of system commonly used in a place of business. These are the types of systems a developer will spend most of the time implementing.

The comments on Oracle8 will occur during Part I and II of the book. This is the portion of the book that will discuss database design. Later parts of the book will include information on expected changes to Developer 2000.

### SQL*PLUS—Oracle's Database Language

SQL*PLUS uses the SQL language. SQL stands for Structure Query Language, and is the industry standard adopted by all database vendors. SQL defines database objects such as tables, indexes, views, and synonyms. It also allows you to manipulate the data through various commands. Commands you learn for Oracle may also be used against a DB2 or Access database. SQL is ANSI compliant. The Oracle7 database understands only the SQL language.

### Other Oracle Products

Developer 2000 is a suite of tools that allow you to develop, implement, and maintain the software for the Oracle7 database. It consists of Oracle Forms 4.5, a robust product that allows you to develop Windows-type screens to manipulate data. This is Oracle's front-end product and provides for rapid application development. Another important product is Oracle Reports 2.5, which is Oracle's main report writing product. It allows for the development of highly formatted reports. The tool suite also includes Oracle Graphics, a product that enables you to develop display modules. A module may be a chart that you derive from the database or a graphic representation that has no bearing on the database. Oracle Browser is another tool in the suite that allows the user to develop simple queries. This is an ideal tool for the casual user that wants to have a tool to perform an ad hoc query, but does not want to develop a report.

Oracle Book, which is an on-line document viewing facility for sharing text across Oracle products, is also included in the set. Other products include SQL*NET and Oracle Procedure Builder.

### Designer 2000

Designer 2000 is Oracle's case tool product, which consists of the Case Dictionary, Oracle Forms Generator, Oracle Reports Generator, and Case Designer.

### Personal Oracle7

Personal Oracle7 is Oracle's database for the personal computer. It operates in both DOS and Windows. Most of the topics that apply to the Oracle7 database also apply to this product.

## Conventions and Techniques Used Throughout this Book

This book uses several conventions. Key words or technical jargon explained in a section are italicized. Tips and notes are placed throughout the book. These items are contained in frames that denote their purpose. The tips are based upon the past experiences of the author.

The book contains many listings and examples. The code for these listings and examples can be found on the CD. The listings begin with the letter l followed by the number of the chapter and the listing number. This name can be used to identify the file on the CD.

The names of the forms used as examples are identified in the chapter. Each chapter has a completed form that contains the modifications discussed in the chapter. This form may be used as a practice form for the techniques discussed in the following chapter.

At the end of most of the chapters are exercises. The answers to these exercises can be found in Appendix E and on the CD.

## Summary

The purpose of this book is to provide you with a guide and reference manual to develop an Oracle database by using the Developer 2000 Tool Set. The book is divided into parts that follow the steps in the development of the application. At the end of each part, you can develop several of the components of the Employee Database project.

The examples in this book require the use of an Oracle database. Appendix D contains instructions for installing this database. The database can be installed on your PC by using a copy of Oracle's Personnel Oracle7. The database may also be installed on your university or company's server. The same instructions and programs may be used regardless of where the database is installed.

Oracle has an excellent Web site. The address is **www.oracle.com**. From this address, you can navigate to other pages. At the time of this writing, Oracle has an excellent trial product program. You may download products for evaluation free of charge. You may also get a CD of the products for a nominal price.

In addition to the Oracle Web site, there are many local Oracle user groups that can be used for product information or answering questions. Many of these groups have pages on the Web that can be used to contact them.

A group that I belong to is the Oracle Developer Tools User Group. This is an organization that has strong ties to The Oracle Tool Development group. They offer members Beta copies of software. They also provide several excellent seminars. The Web site for this organization is **www.odtug.com/index/shtm**.

Like all software and hardware vendors, Oracle is constantly developing and releasing new products. It is a real challenge to write a book for the latest product. Generally, the new releases look similar to the old releases. They do have a few new wrinkles. Throughout this book, I will try to offer some information about future releases of Oracle8 and Developer 2000 2.0. This information is based on available periodicals and other sources. ●

CHAPTER 2

# Designing Your Database

**What is a relational database?**

This section discusses the differences between relational and hierarchical databases. It also discusses why the industry has chosen databases such as Oracle7 over other types.

**Database components**

This section covers the various database components. It explains tablespaces, tables, fields or table items, views, synonyms, indexes, grants, and roles.

**Relational database design**

This section exposes you to some fundamental principles of database design. It covers database terminology, describing your design, and normalizing the data.

A *database* is a collection of data and the applications that use the data. Without the applications, you cannot collect and store data; without the data, you have no reason to use your applications. Oracle7 really combines the applications and data by enabling you to define procedures (code) and triggers within the relational database management system (RDBMS or Oracle7). Actions that occur in the database itself execute these triggers and procedures. ■

**NOTE** This definition of a database surprised me when I first discovered it. I had always thought the database consisted of the data and the objects that hold the data. I never thought of the applications as part of the database. In my mind, they were external to the database because it only consisted of the data. I like this definition because it shows the interdependence of the applications and the data. ■

This chapter discusses the database objects that reside in Oracle7 or any other RDBMS. To successfully design database applications in Oracle Forms 4.5 or any other product, it is important to understand "what's under the hood." The setup of the data affects the way your applications work and how they ultimately support your users. A badly designed database causes badly designed applications.

**NOTE** Oracle Forms 4.5 is the product used to develop and execute GUI forms. The forms are used by an operator to manage and view the data. ■

If you have a good background in relational database design, you may want to move on to Chapter 3. If you are new to database design and terminology, this chapter gives you the background to understand the engine that drives the applications. This chapter explains what a relational database is, what its components are, and how to design the tables.

The first installment of the Employee Information System Project appears at the end of this chapter. This installment introduces you to the project requirements. The goal of this installment is to develop a model of the database tables. This model contains the specifications for the database objects you will create in the second installment at the end of Part II.

# What Is a Relational Database?

A *relational database* is a set of tables or holders of records that are "related" to each other by a common value. Think of two index card files that you have in a cabinet. The first file contains a record for each employee. This information consists of data unique to the employee. It contains a payroll number, address, phone number, department number, and a Social Security Number. The second file contains a record for each tool purchase the employee made. Records in this table contain the employee's payroll number and information pertinent to the tool purchase. Each of the two files contains different information, but are "related" through their one common piece of data, payroll number (see Figure 2.1).

**FIG. 2.1**
Two sets of employee index cards containing tool information.

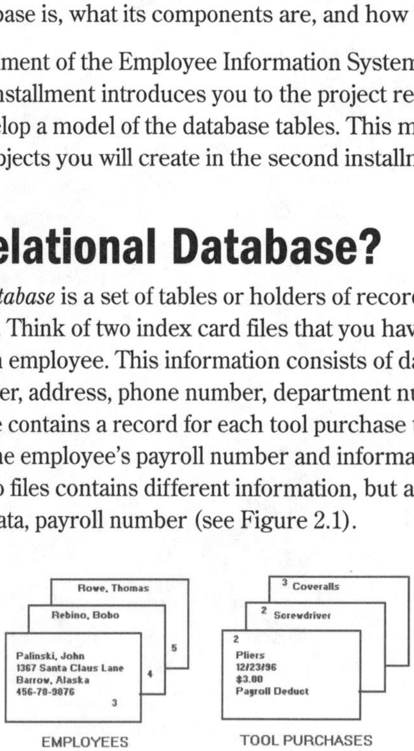

Figure 2.1 shows two sets of index cards that are related to each other. The tool purchase records are sorted by employee number. If you want to find the tool records for "Palinski," you must first go to the employees file, identify the payroll number, and find the tool records that contain the payroll number. Without the common payroll number values on the records of each file, you could not use the two files together, and the tool purchase file would need to contain information from the employees file. To retrieve records from the tool purchase file by using the last name of the employee, each record in the tool purchase file needs to have the information in the related employees file. This causes redundant data to exist in the files. It is much more efficient to use the two files together to store and retrieve information.



When the data is placed in a relational database management system (RDBMS) such as Oracle7, the structure is much the same. The index card files would be *tables*, the records in the files would be called *records* or *rows*, and each data value on the record would be called an *item* or *field*. The two tables would be "related" by a payroll_number field that existed in each table.

Before relational databases, database developers used hierarchical data structures. They consist of a file comprised of segments. Each segment is comparable to a table in a relational database, except the segment does not contain a common value with its parent and children segments. The parent knows the children through the use of a pointer. In Figure 2.2, the parent segment contains the unique information about the employee. The children segments contain records for tool purchases and glasses. Because the segments do not contain common values with their parents, they must use positional pointers to determine where the record exists. A pointer exists for each child record, telling the parent the disk location of the record.

**FIG. 2.2**
A hierarchical data structure.

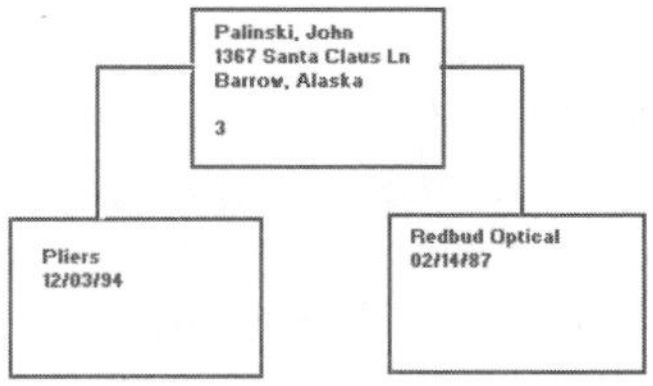


**NOTE** A parent segment contains records that must exist before the records in a child segment can be created. For example, an employee record must exist before employee tool purchase records can be created.

This type of structure works fairly well until you have to add items to the segment. This causes problems; old database structures and software are very positional. In a sequential file, the programmer knows exactly where each record starts and stops. As Figure 2.3 shows, the first record begins at position 1 and ends at position 68. The next record begins at position 69 and ends at position 136. Each subsequent record begins 67 positions or bytes later. The code is written with this positioning in mind.

**FIG. 2.3**
Changes in the position of records due to a field addition.

| | ORIGINAL | | MODIFIED | |
|---|---|---|---|---|
| | RECORD 1 | RECORD2 | RECORD1 | RECORD2 |
| LAST_NAME | 1-20 | 69-88 | 1-20 | 76-95 |
| ADDRESS | 21-39 | 89-107 | 21-39 | 96-114 |
| CITY | 40-50 | 108-118 | 40-50 | 115-125 |
| STATE | 51-52 | 119-120 | 51-52 | 126-127 |
| HOME_PHONE | 53-60 | 121-128 | 53-60 | 128-135 |
| WORK_PHONE | 61-68 | 129-136 | 61-68 | 136-143 |
| NEW COLUMN (FAX #) | | | 69-76 | |

The problems occur when you add a column to the file. This changes the starting position of the second and subsequent records. The application will no longer display the proper values because the application no longer knows where the records begin and end. To correct this problem, you need to change the software. This change is labor intensive and risky because errors can be introduced to the applications. In addition, you must restructure the data in the database file. To avoid this mess, developers tack on segments in different places, causing redundant data to exist within the database.

Because of these problems, relational databases swept the industry. Relational tables enable the developer to add a column to the table without any worry to the existing applications. Because relational databases are not position-oriented, none of the existing software needs to be rewritten. In addition, there is no restructuring of the database. This makes relational databases the database type of choice.

# Database Components

Various components comprise a relational database management system such as Oracle7. This discussion begins with the objects that hold data. Database objects have a similarity to the devices that store manual records. In Oracle7, all database objects must have an owner. Ownership is determined through a *user account* or *id*. Before any database object can be built, the database administrator creates a user account or id. Database items are tied to the user id.

**NOTE** I store records in three drawers in my desk. My desk is very much like a database. To begin with, the desk is mine. Because I am the owner, I can put index cards into it or rubber bands or any other objects I choose. You can think of the drawers in my desk as the database. Drawers separate the records in my desk. Oracle7 also has objects similar to my desk drawers. They are called tablespaces. Within the tablespaces, you can create datafiles. Datafiles are very similar to partitions in my desk drawer reserved to hold my index cards. ■

At the highest level, a database consists a number of tablespaces. *Tablespaces* reserve sections of the disk for record retention. Each tablespace contains one or more datafiles. The *datafile* has a defined amount of disk space. The size of the tablespace equals the aggregate size of the datafiles. Although the datafiles fill up with data and database objects, you can always increase the size of the tablespace by adding another datafile to the tablespace.

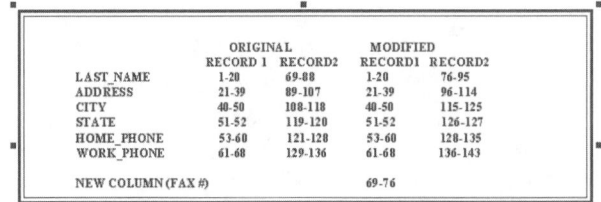

One of the main objects within the tablespace is the table. A table is comparable to a set of index cards. Each card in the set is the same as a row or record in the table. You can also think of tables as spreadsheets. A spreadsheet contains one or more rows that have one of more columns of data. Figure 2.4 illustrates table columns and rows.

**FIG. 2.4**
Row and columns in a table.

| | A | B | C | D |
|---|---|---|---|---|
| 1 | Kennedy | John | 1/20/61 | |
| 2 | Johnson | Lyndon | 11/23/63 | |
| 3 | Eisenhower | Dwight | 1/20/53 | |
| 4 | Truman | Harry | 4/13/45 | |
| 5 | Roosevelt | Franklin | 1/20/32 | |
| 6 | | | | |
| 7 | | | | |



The spreadsheet contains five records or rows, and each record contains three *columns*. Table columns are also called *fields* or *items*. Columns contain similar bits of information. Column A contains the employee last names. The row is used to relate the set of columns. All the data contained in the row pertain to one *instance* of the table entity. In row 4, each column contains information that pertains to employee "Harry Truman." None of the values in the record pertain to any of the other employees contained in the spreadsheet.

**NOTE** One of the differences between the records in my desk drawer and records stored in an electronic database is that each of the items in the database has a unique name. Everything needs a name because you need a way to tell the database manager which record you want, and the database manager needs a way to identify the record you want. ■

The records illustrated in Figure 2.4 are part of a set of records contained in a table called Employee. The first column is called last_name, the second first_name, and the third employment_date. The table is contained in the tablespace Emp. You can obtain Truman's employment date by telling Oracle7 to open an Oracle session using an Oracle user id that has appropriate privileges, locate the Employee file in the Emp tablespace, obtain the fourth record, and display the employment_date column.

## Tablespaces

Oracle7 uses several different kinds of tablespaces. The tablespace used in the preceding example is a *data* tablespace. It holds data and the objects used to control the data. Another tablespace is the *system* tablespace. This area is an area where Oracle7 stores information it needs to perform its functions. Normally, you won't be concerned with this area.

A third tablespace is the *temporary* tablespace. This is where Oracle stores temporary information it needs to record. A fourth tablespace is the *tool* tablespace. Oracle7 stores the database objects related to the various tools in this space. These tools consist of products such as Oracle Forms 4.5. A fifth tablespace is a *rollback* tablespace. When you make changes to a database, these changes are not made permanent until you issue a special command called *commit*. The transactions are saved in the temporary tablespace and the rollback tablespaces. Thus Oracle7 enables you to restore the database to its condition before the changes were made. This protects against erroneous changes. In addition, if you are using a program to modify data, and the program stops abnormally, all changes made by the program are rolled back.

TIP

I get concerned with tablespaces under two circumstances. The first is when the tablespace gets filled and I can't save any additional data. This causes me to add a new datafile to the tablespace. The second and more common problem occurs when I am performing data conversion routines on large files. The temporary and rollback tablespaces have a tendency to fill up with these updates because they are not committed until the program is done executing.

The program stops abnormally when these tablespaces are filled. All the new changes are then lost. To avoid this situation, you may want to divide the data into smaller sections. This division enables you to commit the changes and free up space in the tablespaces.

## Tables and Fields

Tables and fields are the most common database objects you will probably use. *Tables* are sets of records that contain various values called *fields*. When creating a table, you must include the names and characteristics of the fields in the definition.

There are three types of fields. The first type of data is called *character*. Character fields can hold alphanumeric values such as letters of the alphabet, numbers, or special characters. The second type of data is *numeric*. Numeric fields hold a number such as an integer or decimal. The third data type is *date*. This data type holds a calendar date. Dates are a special type of data. The value is stored in the database as a number and is displayed as a set of characters. An example of Oracle's default date display is "08-APR-51". Dates are stored in the table as a number because of the necessity to perform mathematical calculations using the fields. Table 2.1 contains a list of the data types used in table definitions.

**Table 2.1 Data Types**

| Data Type | Description |
|---|---|
| char(*len*) | Defines an alphanumeric field with a total fixed length of *len*. The maximum length of a char field is 255 characters. |
| varchar2(len) | Defines an alphanumeric field with a total variable length of len. The maximum length of a varchar2 field is 2,000 characters. |
| number(*len*, *prec*) | Defines a numeric field with a length of *len* and a precision of *prec*. Precision indicates the number of decimal positions the number may have. Monetary values generally contain a precision of 2. |
| date | Defines a date format field. This field can hold date information that ranges from January 1, 4712 B.C. to December 31, 4712 A.D. |

A second characteristic of a field is the length. Each field, except date fields, may contain a length specification. The number data type contains two settings: maximum length of the number, and amount of decimal positions or precision.

The char data type is a fixed length field. This means that the field uses the maximum defined number of bytes of storage even if the field is not fully filled with characters. *White space*, similar to spaces caused by a space bar, fills the positions in the field that do not contain characters. The *varchar2* data type is variable length. This means the field only uses the number of bytes equal to the actual characters contained in the field. The positions in the field that do not contain characters contain null values. Null means blank or unknown. The char data type is often used for fields that always contain the same number of characters. Examples include payroll ids, model numbers, or ZIP Codes. Varchar2 fields are used for addresses or text.



## Indexes

Indexes are comparable to indexes in a book. The index at the back of this book contains key words used throughout the book. Each reference has an associated page number used to locate the passage that discusses the key word. Indexes help the reader quickly identify the location of information. Database indexes perform the same function. They are mini-tables that contain a subset of the table's data and are used to rapidly locate records.

Database indexes increase the speed of record retrieval because they avoid tablespace scans. When the database manager tries to retrieve records from a table that does not contain an index, it must read each record in the table. This scanning of the table from the first byte to the last is called a ***tablespace scan***. Developers try to avoid them as much as possible because reading records on the hard disk is a slow process. *Indexes* are mini-tables that contain the values from one or more of the table's columns and the location of the associated record. They eliminate the need to perform tablespace scans by allowing the database manager to read them rather than the table to obtain the record location.

Figure 2.5 illustrates the differences in size. If the Customer Information Table is unindexed and you try to find a record for an account number, Oracle7 must perform a tablespace scan. The database manager must read 80,000,000 bytes to obtain the records. When an index is created on the account number field, the database manager uses the index to locate the record. The index is only 2,000,000 bytes. This is 40 times less data through which the database manager must search.

**FIG. 2.5**
Comparison of the sizes of the Customer Information Table and an index on the Customer Account Number Field.

CUSTOMER INFORMATION TABLE

200,000 records * 400 bytes each = 80,0000,000 bytes

INDEX ON THE ACCOUNT NUMBER FIELD ONLY

200,000 records * 10 bytes each = 2,000,000 bytes

Indexes have other features as well that aid the retrieval of records. The first feature is that the records are sorted. This means the database manager does not have to continue reading the index after finding the desired record because it knows a record with the same value cannot exist somewhere else in the index. This sorting property also allows the database manager to perform special searches, eliminating the need to scan the entire index. The manager can read the middle record first. The record is likely to be lesser or greater than the value contained in this index record. After determining this, the manager has eliminated half of the records in the index. The next record read is at the end of the first quarter or third quarter of the index. The manager then determines whether the value in the record is higher or lower than the desired value. By repeating this process, the database manager can obtain the location of the desired records after reading a small number of index records.

Good database practice requires each record in a table to have a field(s) that makes that record unique to any other record in the table. Indexes provide the database manager with the mechanism to maintain this uniqueness. Oracle7 enables the developer to define ***unique indexes***. This type of index allows only one occurrence of a particular value in a column. Before a record is added to the table, the value in the indexed field(s) are checked against the index. If the value matches an existing record, the database manager stops the transaction. If the value does not match, the transaction completes.

**TIP** You will find that indexes are one of the most important objects in a database for the enhancement of database performance. Whenever you are having performance trouble with a query, form, or report, the first place to look is the existing indexes.

## Views

A database ***view*** is similar to a window. It enables the user to see or access a portion of the database. A view is, in reality, a predefined query that produces a virtual or temporary set of records or table when executed. Because a view defines how data is to be assembled, views do not have any impact on the database unless executed.

Views do have several advantages. Views enable the developer to hide portions of the table from others. To do this, you exclude these fields from the view definition. Views also enable you to hide data complexity from the user. In relational databases, information is seldom held in one table; it is contained in several related tables. The developer defines the complex logic of assembling data into the view. You can then use the view as a tablename in a query. You do not need to include the complex logic in the query. The user never knows whether he is using a view or a table (see Figure 2.6).

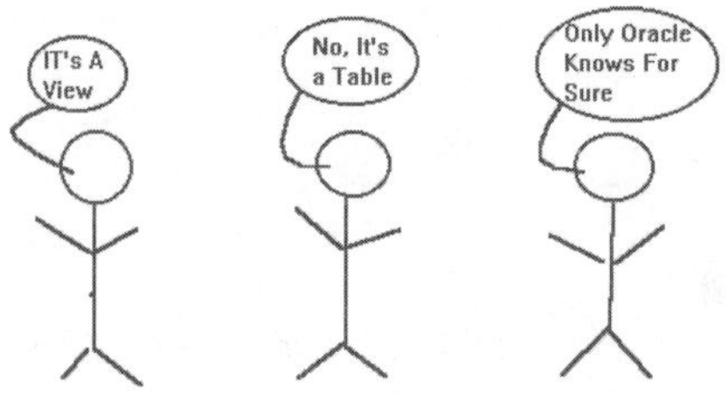


**FIG. 2.6**
It's a view.

Views enable the developer to define custom names for the columns. This creates an element of user-friendliness in the database because the columns can conform to user desires rather than corporate naming standards.

A special advantage of views is that you can use them as a tablename in an Oracle Form. You will understand this more after reading about Oracle Forms 4.5 in Part IV of this book.



## Synonyms

A *synonym* is another name for an Oracle table or view. Synonyms enable a developer to create simpler names for these objects.

**NOTE** At the company that I work for, our data administrators like to give tables descriptive names. One of the tables that I use contains electrical equipment called CTPS. This name is an acronym, so the data administrator decided to use the real equipment name for the table. The table was named T_and_D_Cable_Terminal_Poles (see Figure 2.7). Every time I use this name in a query, form, or report, I need to type 28 characters. I generally make a mistake typing that many characters, so I asked the DBA to create a synonym called CTPS for the table. This greatly increased the usability of the table.

**FIG. 2.7**
What's that table's name? Oracle Forms 4.5 is the product used to develop and execute GUI forms. The forms are used by an operator to manage and view the data.

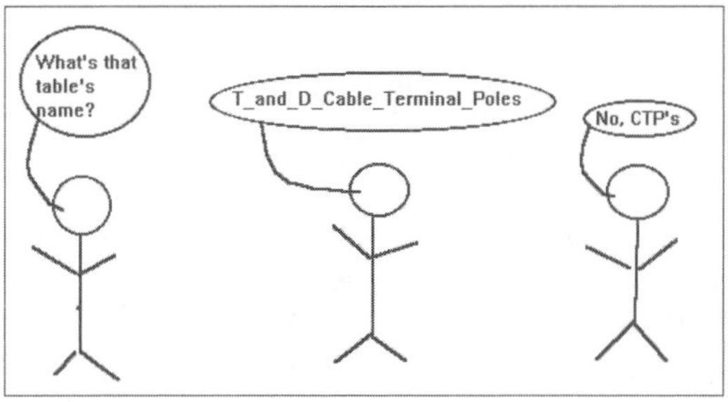


Synonyms are also useful when the table is in a remote database. Remote database tables require some extra characters at the end of the tablename. The characters tell Oracle where the table is located. You can use a synonym to mask these characters. Users can then use the table as if it is located in their own user id.

## Grants and Roles

Before Oracle allows you to establish a session, create a database object, or perform any database function, you must be *granted a privilege*. Privileges enable the developer to perform a large array of functions. You can find definitions of these *privileges* in Chapter 6, "Defining the Database Objects."

When a lot of privileges are granted to many users, it may be easier to create a *role* and grant the privileges to the role. The user is then given the role. When new privileges are needed, the role is granted the privileges. By default, each user that is assigned the role gets the new privilege. This decreases the DBA overhead in managing the database.

# Relational Database Design

This section defines some relational database terms, and then describes how databases are designed and how to graphically portray them. It is important to understand these concepts (including the database objects information discussed in the preceding section), because they are used throughout the remainder of this book. The database design section of the chapter illustrates the Rules of Normalization. This technique is also used to determine the design of the Employee Information System project. The remainder of the book illustrates how to create the database objects and applications that manipulate the data in the objects.

## Database Terminology

Databases are generally modeled to represent a single real-world object. This object can be a transformer, customer, or as in the case of this book an employee. This object is called an *entity*. In a database, the entity is represented by a number of tables and the business rules that pertain to the entity. These rules form the table relationship and the validation procedures contained in the application.

Figure 2.8 illustrates the employee entity, and contains an instance of the entity. An *instance* is one of the objects that comprise the entity. Instances have various properties. These properties are called *attributes*.

**FIG. 2.8**
I'm Harry Truman!

In this example, you can identify a number of significant attributes about the employee. The employee's first name is "Harry," the last "Truman." He started work in the "POL" department on April 13, 1945 and has purchased several pairs of glasses. In the database table, each of these attributes would be recorded in a field or column. The sum of the attributes is a representation of the entity.

Each attribute has a *data type*. This means the attribute can be a number, integer, a set of characters, or even a date. The database developer needs to determine the data type values along with the size of the values. You need to determine the possible range of values, which is called the *attribute domain*. If the employee entity has a gender attribute, for example, you want only values of "M" or "F" in the field in the table. Oracle7 and Oracle Forms have built-in devices that help the developer to protect the database from containing data outside the attribute domains.

After you identify the entities' attributes, data types, and domains, you group them into logical sets of data. These groupings eventually become your tables, after the normalization process described at the end of the chapter. In Figure 2.9, you have a logical grouping of the attributes illustrated in Figure 2.8. The grouping is the beginning of Employee table definition. Each of the attributes has a name, a data type, and a size value.



**FIG. 2.9**
The Employee table attributes.

| | |
|---|---|
| last_name | varchar(15) |
| first_name | varchar(12) |
| dept | char(3) |
| employment_date | date |
| glasses_purchase1 | date |
| glasses_purchase2 | date |

One major problem exists with the Employee table attribute definition. None of the attributes uniquely identify the employee. It is a common occurrence for two employees to have the same first and last name. Good table design requires that each record must have an identifier that differentiates the record from all other records in the table. This identifier is called a *primary key*. A likely attribute to uniquely identify an employee is a payroll number or possibly a Social Security Number. If you add one of these attributes, each record would have a primary key.

The majority of the attributes in the definition are unique to the employee. This means the particular attribute cannot have two or more values. The employee cannot have two last names or be in two or more departments. Tables that contain unique information about the entity and have the unique information (primary key) to identify the entity instance are called *base tables*. All entities have one of these tables.

Two attributes in the definition are not really unique: glasses_purchase1, and glasses_purchase2. These attributes hold the dates of eyeglass purchases by the employee. The table can hold dates for two purchases, but has problems when the third and subsequent purchases occur. The table does not have fields to contain these values. You can resolve this problem by identifying an employee eyeglass purchase entity and creating another table to hold these records. By placing these purchase records in their own table, you can record as many purchases as necessary. This type of table is called a *relation table*.

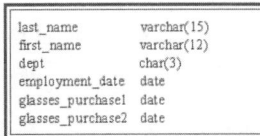

Relation tables do not have any real significance without a tie to a base table. This means that each record in the relation table must have the primary key attribute from the base table. This enables you to determine which base table record is related to the relation table record. This primary key attribute in the relation table is called a *foreign key*. Relation tables always have foreign key fields and a foreign key is part of their primary key. In Figure 2.9, the primary key of the relation table is the combination of payroll_number and purchase_date. You need two fields because one employee may make multiple purchases, and several employees can make purchases on the same date. It is unlikely that one employee will make two purchases on the same day. The combination of the two fields make this a good unique key to the table. One final word, when the unique key to a table consists of more than one field, it is called a *composite key*. Relation tables always have composite primary keys.

## Documenting the Design of the Database

Before you can begin to design the database, you must understand how to describe the design. Although you can use a number of different mechanisms such as entity relationship diagrams, this discussion uses a *table relationship diagram*. The diagram uses boxes to denote tables, and lines between the boxes to denote relationships. At the end of the lines, symbols denote the type of relationship that exists between the tables. Figure 2.10 illustrates the various diagrams used to depict table relationships. The symbols used in the diagrams are **1**, **O**, and **M**. The **1** symbol means one record. The **M** symbol means many records, and the **O** means the relation is optional. When a relation is optional, the table does not have to contain a record(s) to match the record at the other end of the relationship.

**FIG. 2.10**
Table relationship diagram symbols

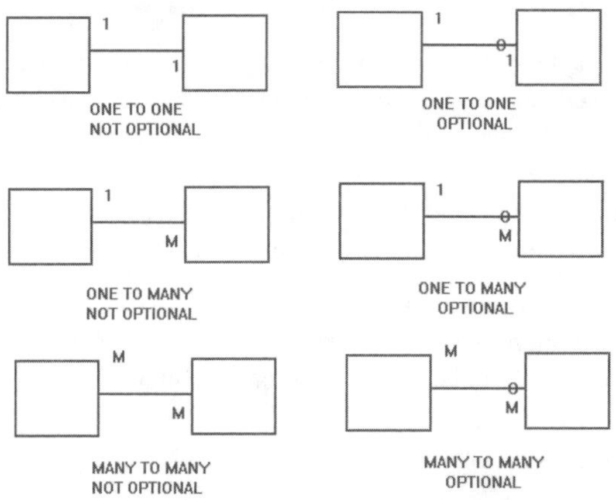


The top-left diagram is the *one to one not optional* relationship. This relationship is used when the record in the first table must have only one record in the second table. When the second table does not have to have a matching record, the **O** symbol is placed on the line next to the optional table. This relationship is called *one to one optional*.

The *one to many not optional* diagram is located in the middle left. This relationship is used when one record in the first table must have one or more records in the second table. The adjacent diagram depicts the relationship when it is optional. Master detail relationships are usually *one to many optional*, with the single record table the master or base table and the many table the detail or relation table.

The *many to many not optional* relationship at the bottom left means many records in the first table are related to many records in the second table. This relationship is not very common and generally means the table design is poor. When you use this type of relationship to relate records, you are not certain which record is the one you want.

In the depicted relationships, remember that the primary key in the first table is the foreign key in the second table.

Figure 2.11 depicts a simplified version of a table relationship diagram. It illustrates the concepts discussed in this section of the book. The diagram contains two entities: manufacturers and transformers. There are many transformers for one manufacturer, but there does not have to be a transformer record for each manufacturer. The Manufacturer table contains records for other electrical equipment manufacturers, and not all manufacturers build transformers.

**FIG. 2.11**
Table relationship diagram depicting a transformer database.

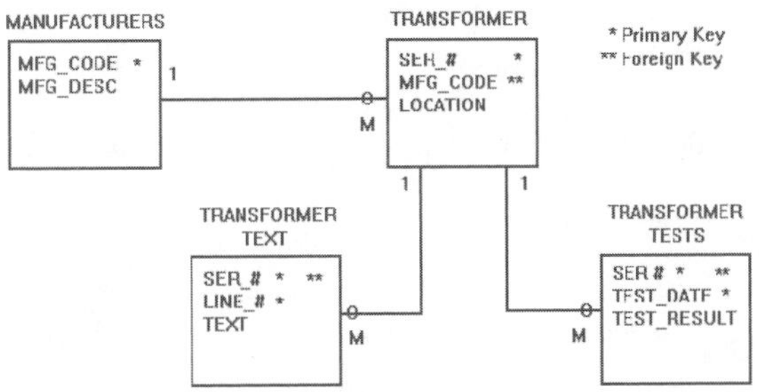


The primary key for the Manufacturers table is the mfg_code field. To relate the table to Transformers, the mfg_code is included in the table. Mfg_code is a foreign key in the table. The primary key of the Transformers table is Ser_#. This table has a one to many but optional relationship to the Transformer Text and Transformer Test tables. The relationships are optional because the transformer does need to have text recorded or a test performed. It is not optional the other way. A transformer does have to exist in order for text to be recorded about it or a test performed.

The Ser_# field, which is the primary key in the Transformers table, is a foreign key in the Transformer Text and Transformer Tests tables. Each of these tables has a composite primary key. The primary key in the Transformer Text table consists of Ser_# and Line_#. Transformer_Tests has a primary key of Ser_# and Test_date.

Now that you have learned some of the database terms you are ready to discuss design principles. The next section covers relational database design principles and normalizing data.

# Database Tables

A properly designed set of database tables makes the applications easier to build, improves the quality of the data, and makes the maintenance of the data easier for the user. You should keep some important things in mind when you are designing the database tables and applications. The first and most important is: Will the database support the business needs of the organization? If it doesn't, it should not be built. Does the system allow the applications to quickly access the data? Have you built constraints into the database that protect the data? Do the tables contain redundant data? Does the organization have similar databases? Is the data protected against unauthorized persons? Some of these issues require political decision within the organization. Groups often resist when attempts to combine databases occur. Fortunately, Oracle7 and the Developer 2000 product has many features that nullify many of these concerns. These features, such as the database constraints, are discussed in later chapters in this book.

When designing your database tables structure, you should take the following steps:

1. Decide what your database represents. For example, is the intent of the database to model transformers, or is it to model all electrical equipment with transformers being one of many types of equipment?
2. Identify the entities in your database. Examples of an entity is a transformer, customer, or a vehicle.
3. Identify the characteristics or attributes of the entities in the database. This includes size of the values and whether they are alphanumeric or numeric. If they are numeric, do the values contain decimals? Do the attributes contain specific values such as male or female?
4. Place the attributes into logical sets. Place the unique attributes of the object into a base table and attributes that can be repeated into related tables. A unique attribute is the last name of the employee. A repeating attribute is the instances of sick leave taken by the employee.
5. Decide how the various sets of data are related. Be certain that the sets have a value(s) that makes the record unique. The sets in the related tables should have values that relate the record to the base table.
6. Perform a normalization exercise on the sets of data and establish your tables. See next section for the Rules of Normalization used to normalize the database
7. Identify the fields that will be indexed. All primary key and foreign key fields should be indexed. You should also identify the fields that are not keys but are often used to identify the record. An example of this type of field is the location of a transformer. This attribute is often used to identify the particular transformer at that location. The identified nonkey fields that are often used should also be indexed. This will increase the performance of your queries.
8. Identify fields that must always contain a value of a field that contains specific values. The primary keys are always fields that must contain a value. They are called "not null" fields because they cannot contain null or empty values. An example of a primary key is a payroll number. A field such as gender is an example of a field that contains specific values. This step will help you to identify constraints that can be placed on the data base.
9. Prepare a table relationship diagram of the tables. Figure 2.11 contains an example of a simplified diagram.
10. Study the diagram carefully. Think about the queries the users will execute against the tables. Queries are SELECT statements that retrieve data from the database. They are discussed in the next chapter. Complex queries will cause users a trouble. Think about complexities in the data structure that will cause application development problems. This step can cause you to avoid problems later on in the application development cycle. It is much easier to change your database design now rather than when you have several applications developed.

When you are satisfied with the table design, create the tables and begin application development.

## Normalizing Your Data

*Normalization* is a procedure where the developer analyzes the data and establishes the table structure. Completion of the exercise ensures that redundant data is eliminated, the files will be as small as possible, and the records will be easy to identify. You normalize your data by using the Rules of Normalization. This consists of several steps. Each step places the data into a specific *form* or *format*. The data is rearranged during each step to meet the criteria of the form.



The normalization procedures are as follows:

**First Normal Form** Analyze your unnormalized data and identify the attributes that will repeat. Remove these rows from the table and place them in their own tables. Figure 2.12 illustrates this procedure. The unnormalized set of data has two fields for eyeglass purchases. These attributes are removed and placed in a table of their own called Eyeglasses Purchase. The table needs to have a payroll_number field that relates the records back to the Employee table.

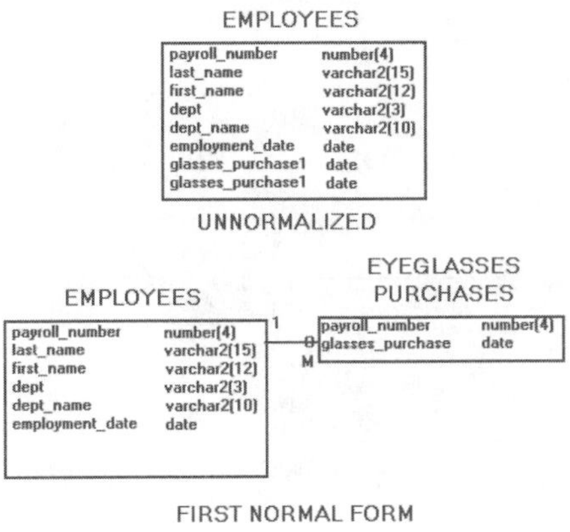


**FIG. 2.12**
Normalizing data to the first normal form.

This step alleviates the database of some potential problems. Inexperienced developers often create this repeating row feature in databases. They don't understand the techniques used to combine data from multiple tables, so they try to create one table that can be used for all the data. Consider, for example, a secretary using a table that has 50 fields used to record past employee wage increases. Every time an employee receives a raise, the secretary runs a program that places the value in raise field 49 into raise field 50, and continues the chain until raise field 1 is empty. She then enters the new information into raise field 1.

This procedure is bad because the secretary needs to run a complex, time-consuming program to perform a simple data entry function. Secondly, many of the fields in the employee records do not contain values because the records were established to hold increases over a 25-year period. These blank records take up space in the database that would be better used for other purposes.

By normalizing the secretary's employee file to the first normal form, you can alleviate all of these problems.

**Second Normal Form** This step looks at the keys to the tables. You must verify that all the fields in the table are dependent on the entire key. If you find fields that are not, these fields should be placed in their own table. In Figure 2.12 the Employees table contains a field for the department name. The department name is not dependent on the primary key, payroll_number. Department name is dependent on dept field. This violates the rule that all values must be dependent on the key. To achieve the second normal form, you should remove the dept_name field from the Employee table and create a new table called Departments. The primary key to the Departments table is dept. The Employee table is related to the Departments table by the common dept field. Figure 2.13 shows the database after the above has been performed. The database is now in second normal form.

**FIG. 2.13**
Normalizing data to the second normal form.

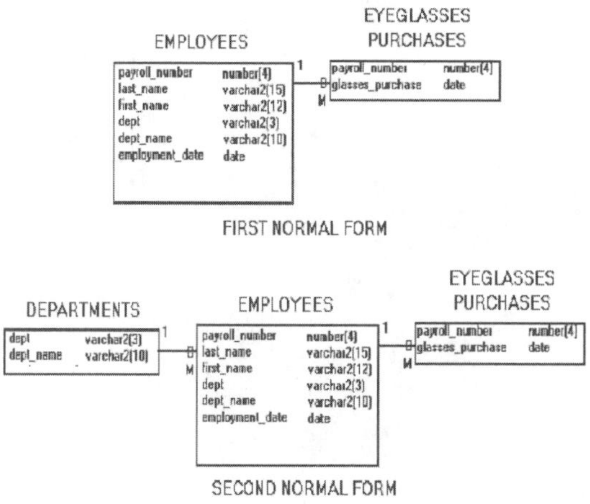


Performing this step in the normalization process removes redundant or excess data from the database. In the first normal form, the department name is carried in each employee record. The department name is only recorded once in the second normal form. It is recorded in the department's record only.

**Third Normal Form** Normalizing the data to the third normal form means that all the nonkey columns of a table must be dependent on the primary key and are independent of each other. The model in this discussion meets this criteria.

Performing the Rules of Normalization helps you ensure the proper setup of your database.

**Rules of Normalization**

The database design approach based on the Rules of Normalization is the time-tested method of designing a relational database. Now that Oracle8 is ready to enter the business computing environment with its new object technology, changes to design approach will likely occur. In the relational approach the entity and its attributes are identified. These attributes are then placed in a series of related tables. The developer worried about data redundancy, minimizing disk space usage, and data integrity. The result of the procedure is a set of tables related by primary and foreign keys.

As you will see in the next several chapters, acquiring and modifying data from multiple tables can be complex. Novice users sometimes have difficulty writing the script or statements needed to retrieve the data from multiple tables. A database based on objects eliminates some of these difficulties for the user and developer.

When designing a database based upon an object, the developer does not have to worry about multiple tables and their relationships. The developer identifies the attributes needed by the object. These objects are linked together through the definition of the object. When the object is created, Oracle places the attributes in different areas. They are related through a pointer rather than primary and foreign keys. The attributes in the database can be identified and extracted through the use of a common object. This reduces the complexity of data retrieval for the user and developer. The user and developer no longer need to know the names of the tables and how they are related. The developer does not use the Rules of Normalization and does not create related tables. Oracle8 may do this, but it is transparent to the developer. The retrieval query and update scripts will become less complex as a result.

The problem with the object approach is maintenance of the database. A true relational database such as Oracle7 is very forgiving to the designer. If the designer forgets a field, it is very easy to add it to the table. Oracle8 is reintroducing the pointer. The pointer is similar to the one used in heirarchial databases. This possibly reintroduces into Oracle8 some of the problems caused by hierarchial databases. It is my belief that DBA's and developers will have a much more difficult time restructuring the database by using Oracle8. This does not mean I am not anxious to use the object-oriented features of Oracle8. It does mean that we as designers and developers need to do our homework up front.

The purpose of this book is to offer a practical approach to the design of an Oracle database. This approach is the one portrayed in this chapter that uses the Rules of Normalization. When Oracle8 begins to enter the mainstream computing environment, I believe you will see more emphasis of object-oriented design. Until then, it is best for the novice developer to stick with proven methods.

A database consists of the database objects and the applications that affect them. There are a large variety of database objects. The tablespace defines the amount of disk storage allowed. The table contains a record for each instance or occurrence of the entity. The record contains a number of attributes that have a specified data type and length.

Databases use mini-tables called indexes to enforce uniqueness and increase performance. Other useful database objects are views, which are virtual database tables, and synonyms, which are alternate names for a table. Before a user can create any of these items, a user account must be created and privileges granted to the user account.

Relational database table records have unique keys that make the record unique from all others in the database. This unique key is called a primary key. If the primary key contains more than one field, it is also called a composite key. Fields that have a corresponding value that is a primary key in another table are called foreign keys.

To design a database, you must take a number of steps. You identify the entities and their associated attributes, place the attributes into logical sets, perform a normalization exercise, and then document the results.

# From Here...

In this chapter, you learned database terminology, the steps in designing a database, how to normalize the data, and how to graphically represent the design. In the next chapter, you will begin to learn the SQL language. This language is the heart and soul of all the Designer 2000 products. Before you proceed to that chapter, you may want to set up the tables used in the exercises. Appendix D, "Practice Database Installation Instructions," contains the steps to perform this task.

# Review Exercises

Figure 2.14 depicts a Transformer database composed of one table. The table contains both current and historical records. The current records pertain to the current location of the transformer. The historic records record previous locations of the transformer. The current record is identified by a status of "CURRENT." Previous location records have a status of "HISTORY."

**FIG. 2.14**
Existing transformer records.

TRANSFORMER DATA FILE

| TRF# | INSTALL DATE | MFG | MODEL | STATUS | WEIGHT | LOCATION | TEST DATE1 | TEST RESULT1 | TEST DATE2 | TEST RESULT2 |
|---|---|---|---|---|---|---|---|---|---|---|
| A100 | 09-JUL-85 | W | GO-5A | HISTORY | 1000 | 9311 Monroe | 08-JUL-85 | 70 | | |
| B670 | 10-SEP-86 | GE | W-97 | CURRENT | 2000 | 1719 Taylor | | | | |
| A101 | 12-SEP-91 | W | GO-5 | CURRENT | 1000 | 9311 Monroe | 10-SEP-91 | 72 | | |
| A100 | 12-SEP-91 | W | GO-5 | CURRENT | 100 | STORES | 12-SEP-91 | 73 | | |
| B979 | 12-SEP-91 | GE | W-97 | CURRENT | 2000 | 8742 Pine | 11-SEP-91 | 94 | 11-OCT-91 | 76 |

When the transformer is moved to a new location, the clerk creates a new record and copies information from the previous record into the new one. Transformers are periodically tested. The table has fields for two of these tests. A novice developer that did not understand relational databases designed this database. You should analyze this database. Identify problems with the current design, opinion, and offer an alternate design.

## EMPLOYEE DATABASE PRACTICE PROJECT INSTALLMENT 1

The Greater Midwest Utility District has an existing employee database developed in a software product that is obsolete. You have been asked to develop an Oracle system to replace the existing system. The Employee system is used to record basic information about each of GMUD's employees. The old system tracks historic and current records for appraisals, promotions, annual cost-of-living raises, and safety eyeglass and tool purchases.

GMUD has two types of employees: exempt and contract. Exempt employees consist of management and registered professional engineers. The remainder of the personnel are considered contract personnel because they fall under the union contract. All employees receive an annual performance appraisal. This occurs within 30 days of the anniversary of their hiring date. All the employees receive an annual cost-of-living raise. Exempt personnel get their raises in April, and the contract personnel get theirs in June.

Contract employees are assigned to a classification. Each classification has a series of pay steps. Journeyman electrician has five steps. The electrician has to progress through the five steps to receive the top pay in the classification. Each step takes six months. At the end of two and one-half years, the journeyman electrician will receive top pay.

The company requires all employees to wear safety eyeglasses. Those employees that wear prescription glasses can purchase them from an optician at the company's expense. The company will only purchase one pair every two years. Employees may purchase their tools through the company. The employee has the option to pay immediately or on payroll deduction.

System Requirements:

- A set of Oracle Forms applications to record basic employee information, past appraisals, past wage increases, past promotions, and tool purchases and eyeglass purchases.
- A report listing the employees that require a performance appraisal in the next 30 days.
- A report listing the tool payment that must be deducted from each employee's pay that payday. Employees are paid bi-weekly. The deduction is the same for all paydays except the last, which is used to adjust.
- A report listing employees that reached the top of their classifications and the date they are eligible to be promoted to the next classification. Employees below journeyman electrician and senior clerk are eligible for promotion one year after reaching the top step of the classification. Journeyman electrician and senior clerk are the only top classifications. All other classifications are below them.
- A PL/SQL program that updates the current wages with the cost-of-living increases. It also stores the previous wage in a historic classification record.

Data:

The old system was designed by a clerk in the Human Relations department. It consisted of one table. It had multiple fields to contain tool, eyeglass, and classification information. The data fields are shown in Table 2.2.

**Table 2.2 Current Employee Database Items**

| Item Description | Data Type | Length |
|---|---|---|
| Payroll number | Number | 4 |
| Last name | Character | 15 |
| First name | Character | 15 |
| Absences | Number | 2 |
| Wages | Number | 8,2 |
| Street | Character | 20 |
| City | Character | 15 |
| State | Character | 2 |
| Phone | Character | 13 |
| Soc. Sec. # | Character | 11 |
| Employment date | Date | |
| Birth date | Date | |
| Classification | Character | 15 |
| Class date | Date | |
| Department # | Character | 3 |
| Dept name | Character | 15 |
| The following set of eyeglass fields are repeated four times in the table to accommodate multiple eyeglass purchases. | | |
| Eyeglass purchase date | Date | |
| Optician | Character | 20 |
| Eyeglass cost | Number | 5 |
| Check number | Character | 10 |
| The following set of tool purchase fields are repeated eight times in the table to accommodate multiple tool purchases. | | |
| Tool purchase date | Date | |
| Payroll deduct | Character | 1 |
| Tool name | Character | 15 |
| Tool cost | Number | 5 |
| Payment amount | Number | 5 |

| Item Description | Data Type | Length |
|---|---|---|
| Last payment amount | Number | 5 |
| First payment date | Date | |
| Last payment date | Date | |
| The following set of historical classification fields are repeated 20 times in the table to accommodate multiple classification changes. | | |
| Department # | Character | 4 |
| Classification | Character | 15 |
| Classification date | Date | |
| Wages | Number | 8 |
| Comments | Character | 20 |

Your Assignment: Normalize the preceding data and make a table relationship diagram.

The answer to this installment is in Chapter 20, "Developing a Template Employee Information System." ●

CHAPTER 3

# Acquiring Data by Using the *Select* Statement

SQL*PLUS is Oracle's core product; it gives developers direct access to the Oracle7 database. Developers can perform an array of functions with this product. This includes retrieving data, modifying the database, and managing the database objects. The commands and functions available for use with this product are based on the SQL language. These commands and functions are used extensively in the Developer 2000 products, especially Oracle Forms and Oracle Report Writer.

The designer/developer uses this product to retrieve data and modify the database. Generally, the database objects are managed by a database administrator. In order to perform the database functions, you must learn how to execute commands in SQL*PLUS. You must also become familiar with the SQL language. The easiest way to learn SQL and SQL*PLUS is to begin with the `SELECT` command. In this chapter, you learn how to retrieve data in the SQL*PLUS environment. Subsequent chapters will increase the complexity of the SQL. You learn to retrieve records from multiple tables through the use of a join. The

**Logging on and using the editor**

This section helps you to log on to SQL*PLUS and the Oracle7 database. It also teaches you the methods of editing SQL statements by using the SQL*PLUS editor or an external editor.

**Selecting, ordering, and identifying the records**

This section teaches you the basic format of the `SELECT` statement used to acquire data from the database. This section also discusses SELECT statement options that can be used to limit the records retrieved and to order the data.

**Column arithmetic, date arithmetic, and null values**

This section teaches you how to perform mathematical functions on expressions in the `SELECT` statement. The section also discusses how to perform date arithmetic and the effect of Null values in calculations.

**Performing functions**

This section teaches you about the functions available for use in the `SELECT` statement. These functions modify character strings, decode values, and perform statistical computations. The section also covers date pictures used to format dates.

final two chapters of this part cover data definition language (DDL) and data modification language (DML) commands. DDL consists of commands used to maintain the database objects. DML commands are used to add, update, and delete database records.

The examples and exercises in the remainder of the book were executed against an Oracle7 database. This database is contained in Appendix D, which contains instructions for two different installation methods. The database may be installed in any Oracle7 product. It can be loaded on a server at your place of employment or on your PC by using a copy of Personnel Oracle7. If you have access to Oracle7 on a server at school or work, contact the DBA to gain a user id. If you do not have access to Oracle7, Oracle has been willing to supply a 60-day trial copy of the Oracle7 database and Developer 2000 product. Oracle may be contacted on its web site at **www.oracle.com**. ■

# Logging On SQL*PLUS

Logging on to SQL*PLUS is as simple as double-clicking the SQL*PLUS icon. As Figure 3.1 shows, the SQL*PLUS icon is located in the Oracle Icons group on your PC.

**FIG. 3.1**
The Oracle Icons Group, which contains the SQL*PLUS icon.

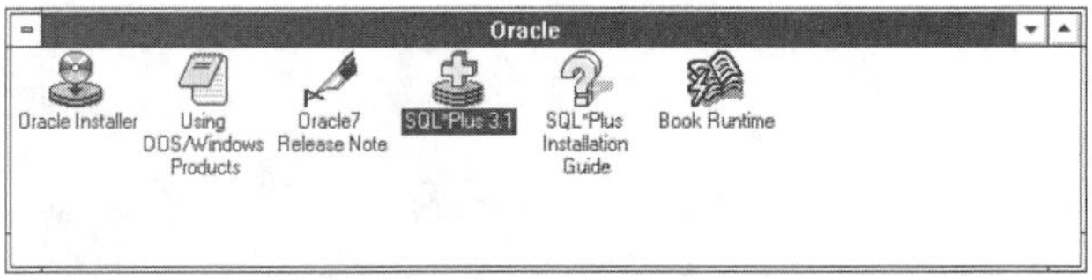


This causes a password entry dialog box to appear (see Figure 3.2). Enter your user id in the top box, your password in the middle box, and your connect string in the bottom box. The host or connect string tells Oracle on which server your id is located.

**FIG. 3.2**
The SQL*PLUS Log On dialog box.

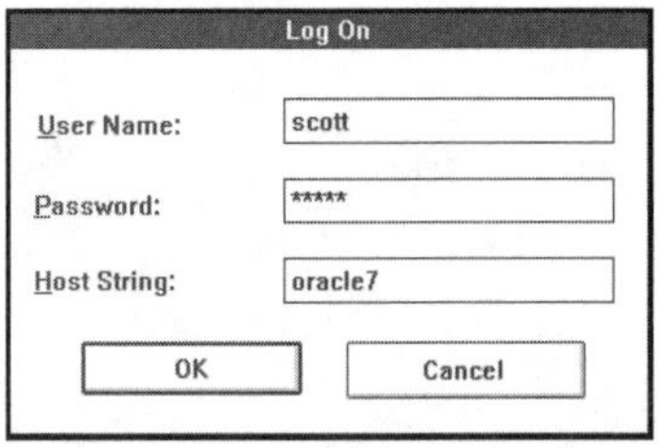


**NOTE** The user id and connect string depends upon where the database is installed. If you are using the trial Personnel Oracle7 database, the default user id/password is "scott/tiger." The DBA id on the Personnel Oracle7 database is "system/manager." The connect string is needed only if the database is located on a remote server. When this has occurred, a DBA probably created the user id and established a database. The DBA will know the parameters to log on to the database. ■

After successfully entering the security requirements, the SQL*PLUS environment appears. You know when you are in this product when the sql> appears (see Figure 3.3).

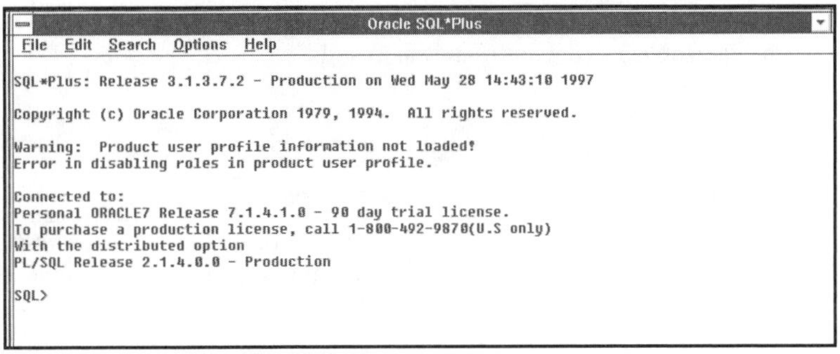

Oracle SQL*Plus
File Edit Search Options Help
SQL*Plus: Release 3.1.3.7.2 - Production on Wed May 28 14:43:10 1997
Copyright (c) Oracle Corporation 1979, 1994. All rights reserved.
Warning: Product user profile information not loaded!
Error in disabling roles in product user profile.
Connected to:
Personal ORACLE7 Release 7.1.4.1.0 - 90 day trial license.
To purchase a production license, call 1-800-492-9870(U.S only)
With the distributed option
PL/SQL Release 2.1.4.0.0 - Production
SQL>


**FIG. 3.3**
The SQL*PLUS Prompt and Editor.



# The SQL*PLUS Editor

Now that you have logged on to SQL*PLUS, you need to learn how to enter and run commands. Two editors are available in SQL*PLUS. The first is the *buffer editor*. This editor enables you to enter and change commands interactively from the sql> prompt. The second is any external editing product such as Windows Notepad. The two editing environments work together. A script is a block of SQL statements. Scripts developed and saved in the external editor may be loaded into the buffer and edited through the buffer editor. Scripts contained in the buffer editor may be loaded into an external editor for further work.

The first script you can enter is **select * from employees.** After pressing Enter, a 2 appears. This indicates that the first line was placed into the buffer, and SQL*PLUS is ready for you to enter the remainder of the script. Additional line numbers continue to appear until the script is completed. SQL command statements are completed by placing a semicolon (;) at the end. Upon seeing the semicolon, Oracle executes the statement. Listing 3.1 demonstrates these series of steps.

**Listing 3.1 L_03_01.TXT—Entering a Query into the SQL*PLUS Editor**

```
SQL> select * from employee
2  ;
PAYROLL_NUMBER LAST_NAME       FIRST_NAME       ABSENCES     WAGES STREET
-------------- --------------- --------------- --------- --------- -------------
CITY            ST PHONE         SOCIAL_SECU EMPLOYMEN BIRTH_DAT CURRENT_POSITIO
--------------- -- ------------- ----------- --------- --------- ---------------
➥FK_D GE
 ---- --
 25 COOLIDGE        CALVIN                  0       9500 12 MAPLE ROAD
PLYMOUTH        VT 435-897-3546  100-02-0500 07-AUG-21 01-JUL.-72 JANITOR
NIT
.
.
.
19 rows selected.
```

You have been entering your statement into the SQL*PLUS buffer. This statement is deleted when a new statement is entered or loaded into the buffer. You can view a buffer statement by entering the List Editor command. This consists of the letter **'L'** after the SQL> prompt. This causes the editor to list the current script in the buffer. Oracle has a number of buffer commands. Table 3.1 contains these commands.

**Table 3.1 SQL*PLUS Editor Commands**

| Command | Description |
|---|---|
| L*n* | Displays or (lists) linenumber n of the current SQL statement in the buffer. If n is omitted, L will list the entire buffer. |
| *linenumber 'text'* | Replaces existing line n with text. The text must be preceded by a line number, but does not have to be enclosed by any symbols. |
| C/old/new | Changes old to new on the current line. |
| C/old.../new/ | Changes from first occurrence of old through end of line to new. |
| A text | Appends text to the end of the current line. |
| DEL(ete) | Delete the current line. Entering "delete" will erase the entire buffer. Entering "del" will erase the current line. |
| I | Insert after the current line. |
| / or ®UN | Execute contents of the buffer. |
| SAVE *filename* | Save contents of the buffer in *filename.sql.* |
| GET *filename* | Load contents of *filename*.sql into the buffer. |
| START filename or @filename | Load *filename*.sql and execute. |

Listing 3.2 shows several of these commands in action. The first command lists the existing script. The next command changes the tablename from employee to department. The third command lists the buffer script again to show the changes.

**Listing 3.2 L_03_02.TXT—Editing Statements in the Buffer**

```
SQL> l
1* select * from employee
SQL> c/employee/department
1* select * from department
SQL> l
1* select * from department
```

Another method of entering and editing a script is to use an external editor such as Windows Notepad. Just enter **edit *filename*** at the SQL>. SQL*PLUS invokes the default editor, Windows Notepad. You can change the default editor by clicking Edit, Editor, Define. When the file name does not exist, an Alert box appears and asks whether you want to create a new file. After the script is finalized in the editor, save the file. Press Alt+Tab to invoke SQL*PLUS, and enter **start filename** or the **@filename** command**.** Either command loads the file into the buffer and executes it. Figure 3.4 shows an example of this procedure.



**FIG. 3.4**
Using the external editor.

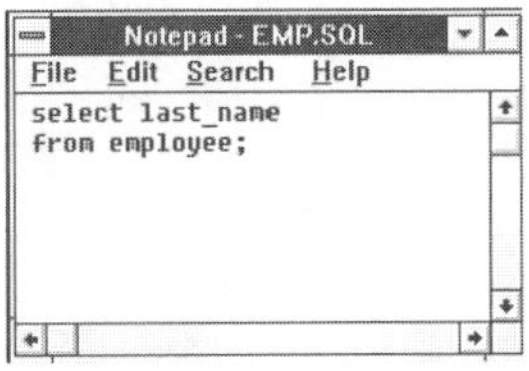


Oracle automatically places a default file extension of .SQL on any file saved from the SQL editor unless you specify a different extension. In addition, when loading or running a file from the editor, SQL*PLUS assumes this same default extension unless you specify a different extension in the command.

# Understanding the Select Command Format

SQL*PLUS commands are based on the SQL language. SQL stands for *structured query language.* The most basic command is Select**.** This command is used to retrieve and view data from the database. The *select* statement has six clauses: select, from, where, group by, having, and order by. Figure 3.5 shows the format of the statement.

**FIG. 3.5**
The select statement's clauses and syntax.

```
select columnname1, columnname2, columnname3          (Required)
from tablename1, tablename2                           (Required)
where condition_a = condition_b                       (Optional)
group by columnname1, columnname2                     (Optional)
having functionname(columnname1) > condition_b        (Optional)
order by columnname1, columnname2                     (Optional)
;                                                     (Required)
```

## The *Select* Clause

The first clause in the command statement is the `select`. This section is used to list the columns, literals, calculations, and functions (such as avg, sum, min, max) to be performed on columns. Each column is separated by a comma (,). Numeric columns may be added, subtracted, multiplied, or divided by placing an arithmetic operator between the column names. Oracle knows that the columns are part of one virtual column because a comma does not separate them. You can combine character columns by using the concatenation operator (||). *Literals* are numeric or character values placed in the clause. They appear in each row retrieved from the table.

## The *From* Clause

The `from` clause follows immediately behind the `select` clause. This section is used to list the Oracle tables that contain the columns listed in the `select` clause. Multiple tables may be listed in this section. A comma must separate each tablename.

## The *Where* Clause

The `where` clause is used to list conditions that limit the number of records retrieved by the statement. Without any conditions, the `select` statement retrieves and displays all the records in the listed tables. A condition consists of two table columns or one column and a value separated by an evaluation operator. Several of the evaluation operators are (=) equal to, (!=) not equal to, or (>) greater than. There are no limits to the number of conditions that may be listed. For the record to be selected from the database, each condition in the `where` clause must be evaluated to true.

## The *Group By* Clause

The `group by` clause is used to indicate the set of records on which to perform the functions. Several of the functions that can be listed in the `select` clause are `avg`, `sum`, `min`, and `max`. A function can be performed on the entire set of retrieved records table or on subsets. When the computation is performed on subsets of the records, you must include the `group by` clause in the `select` statement. This is done so that SQL*PLUS knows the subsets on which to perform the functions.

## The *Having* Clause

The `having` clause is similar to the `where` clause. It is used to limit the number of records retrieved from the database. The difference is that sets of records are evaluated in this section. You can use the functions `sum`, `avg`, `min`, and `max` as conditional operators in the having section only. The `where` clause does not allow functions to be used.

## The *Order By* Clause

Records are not stored in any particular order in the database. They are retrieved and displayed in the same order in which they are stored unless the `order by` clause is included in the `select` statement. The `order by` clause contains the name(s) or number(s) of the column(s) that determine the order. The number is the numeric place of the column in the `select` clause. You can list multiple columns in this section.



## *Simple Select*

A `simple select` statement contains only the required portions of the statement. It has one or more columns defined in the `select` clause, one tablename in the `from` clause, and a semicolon at the end of the statement. The statement retrieves all the rows from the table and displays the columns listed in the `select` clause. Listing 3.3 shows an example of this type of statement:

**Listing 3.3 L_03_03.TXT—Selecting the Last Name and First Name of the Employees**

```
SQL> select last_name, first_name from employee;
LAST_NAME       FIRST_NAME
--------------- ----------------
COOLIDGE        CALVIN
JOHNSON         LYNDON
REAGAN          RONALD
BUSH            GEORGE
JOHNSON         ANDREW
.
19 rows selected.
```

**NOTE** Most of the listings contained in this book do not have all of the retrieved records displayed. I displayed only a sample of the records in order to save space. When records were removed from the listing, a period was placed in the listing. In the preceding listing, five records are displayed and 19 were selected. The period denotes 14 were removed. ■

This statement lists all the last_name and first_name records from the employee table. In some cases you may want to list all the columns in each record. You can do this by listing each column name in the `select` clause or by using the ALL symbol. This symbol is an asterisk (*). When the asterisk is listed in the `select` clause, all table columns appear (see Listing 3.1).

# Ordering Records

When the `order by` clause is placed in the statement, the records will be ordered. The `order by` clause accepts column names or the column position number. This number is the position of the column in the `select` statement. Listing 3.4 shows equivalent examples using each naming approach.

**Listing 3.4 L_03_04.txt —Ordering Records by Using the Column Name and Column Number**

```
SQL> select first_name, last_name from employee
2  order by last_name;
FIRST_NAME      LAST_NAME
--------------- --------------
SUSAN           ANTHONY
GEORGE          BUSH
JIMMY           CARTER
WILLIAM         CLINTON
CALVIN          COOLIDGE
DWIGHT          EISENHOWER
.
19 rows selected.
SQL> select first_name, last_name from employee
2  order by  2;
FIRST_NAME      LAST_NAME
--------------- --------------
SUSAN           ANTHONY
GEORGE          BUSH
JIMMY           CARTER
WILLIAM         CLINTON
CALVIN          COOLIDGE
DWIGHT          EISENHOWER
.
19 rows selected.
```

Only columns in the `select` clause can be placed in the `order by` clause. The default column order is ascending (A–Z). You can change the type of ordering to descending by placing the Desc command following an order column. You can include more than one column in the `order by` clause. Each of these columns may have its own order type. Listing 3.5 demonstrates the use of a multi-column ordered `select` clause.

**Listing 3.5 L_03_05.TXT—Example of Multiple Order Columns**

```
SQL> select last_name, first_name
2  from employee
3  order by last_name desc, first_name;
LAST_NAME       FIRST_NAME
--------------- --------------
WILSON          WOODROW
TRUMAN          HAROLD
```

```
TAFT            WILLIAM
ROOSEVELT       ELEANOR
ROOSEVELT       FRANKLIN
ROOSEVELT       THEODORE
REAGAN          RONALD
.
19 rows selected.
```

# Conditional *Select* Statements

A `simple select` statement, as demonstrated in Listing 3.5, displays all the records in a table because it does not contain any criteria to limit the selected records. Generally, a `select` statement or query needs to obtain a subset of a table's records. To accomplish this, the developer uses the `where` clause to list a set of conditions each record must match to be retrieved. A *condition* is a pair of columns or a column and a value separated by an operator such as an equal sign. To be selected, the conditions must evaluate to true. Listing 3.6 contains an example of a conditional statement.

Part I Ch 3

**Listing 3.6 L_03_06.TXT—Example of a Conditional Select Statement**

```
SQL> select last_name, first_name, payroll_number
2  from employee
3  where fk_department = 'POL';
LAST_NAME        FIRST_NAME       PAYROLL_NUMBER
---------------  ---------------  --------------
JOHNSON          LYNDON                       31
JOHNSON          ANDREW                       21
CLINTON          WILLIAM                      37
NIXON            RICHARD                      32
KENNEDY          JOHN                         30
ROOSEVELT        FRANKLIN                     27
WILSON           WOODROW                      24

7 rows selected.
```

This example selects only those records from the employee table that have a value in the department column of 'POL'. Because department is defined as a character field in the table, you must enclose the value in single quotes. Numeric values are not enclosed by quotes.

**NOTE** Oracle is case sensitive. This means that the value 'A' does not equal 'a.' The developer should be careful when using character columns in a condition and ensure they evaluate properly. ■

Unlike the `order by` clause, values in conditional statements do not have to be in the `select` clause. The reason is that the database manager or Oracle7 uses the values as it is reading records from the disk. The database manager reads a table record, evaluates the record's values, and places the record into memory if the values agree with the conditions in the `select` statement. The database manager knows the value of the columns because it has just read the values from the disk. When records are ordered, the database manager has retrieved the records from the disk and placed the identified columns in memory. If the `order by` columns are not in memory, the database cannot order the selected records.

Oracle has a number of logical operators that you can use in conditional statements. Table 3.2 displays a list of these.

**Table 3.2 Logical Operators**

| Operator | Description |
|---|---|
| = | Equal to |
| != OR <> | Not equal to |
| • | Greater than |
| >= | Greater than or equal to |
| < | Less than |
| <= | Less than or equal to |
| in | Equal to any members of a list |
| between | Between two values, inclusive |
| like | Similar to a character pattern |
| is null | Missing value |
| not | Reverses any of the preceding four Operators |

## Equal Sign (=)

The first logical operator in Table 3.2 is the equality operator. This operator tests one value against another value to determine whether the values are the same. When testing for equality, character values must be the same case to be equal, and a numeric values is never equal to a character value. Character values must be enclosed by single quotes. Numeric values are not enclosed by quotes. Starting with Listing 3.7, the following two examples show a conditional select using an equality operator:

**Listing 3.7 L_03_07.TXT—Example of Character and Numeric Conditional Expressions**

```
SQL> select last_name, first_name
2  from employee
3  where last_name = 'HOOVER';
LAST_NAME       FIRST_NAME
--------------- ---------------
```

```
HOOVER          HERBERT
SQL> select last_name, first_name
2  from employee
3  where wages = 13000;
LAST_NAME       FIRST_NAME
--------------- ---------------
CARTER          JIMMY
FORD            GERALD
```

The first query selects records where the value in the last_name column is equal to 'HOOVER'. Last_name is a character field and the values are all uppercase. This means the value must be enclosed by single quotes, and the value must be capitalized.

The second query selects records where the value in the wages column = 13000. Wages is defined numeric in the database. This means the value must be numeric and must not be enclosed by single quotes.



## Inequality Sign (<> or !=)

The inequality operator is the opposite of the equality operator. This operator means the first value in the clause does not equal the second value. Two symbols are used as the inequality operator. The first symbol is the left-pointing arrow followed by the right-pointing arrow (<>). The second is the exclamation mark followed by the equal sign (!=). You can use either symbol with the same effect. Listing 3.8's query performs the exact opposite of the equality query in the preceding example. This query selects the records that do not have a value in the last_name column equal to 'HOOVER'.

**Listing 3.8 L_03_08.TXT—Executing a Not Equal Conditional Select Statement**

```
SQL> select last_name, first_name
2  from employee
3  where last_name != 'HOOVER';
LAST_NAME       FIRST_NAME
--------------- ---------------
COOLIDGE        CALVIN
JOHNSON         LYNDON
REAGAN          RONALD
BUSH            GEORGE
JOHNSON         ANDREW
CLINTON         WILLIAM
CARTER          JIMMY
FORD            GERALD
NIXON           RICHARD
KENNEDY         JOHN
EISENHOWER      DWIGHT
TRUMAN          HAROLD
ROOSEVELT       FRANKLIN
WILSON          WOODROW
TAFT            WILLIAM
```

*continues*

**Listing 3.8 Continued**

```
ROOSEVELT       THEODORE
ANTHONY         SUSAN
ROOSEVELT       ELEANOR
18 rows selected.
```

## Greater Than (>) and Less Than (<)

The greater than and less than operators evaluate to true if the value on the open side of the arrow is greater than the value on the closed side of the arrow. The statement is read left to right. A > B reads A is greater than B, and A < B reads A is less than B. When evaluating character values, upper case characters (A) have a smaller value than lower case characters (a). Alpha characters (a or A) are greater than numeric characters. Listing 3.9 shows an example of greater than conditional select statement.

**Listing 3.9 L_03_09.TXT—Using the Greater Than Operator in a Conditional Select Statement**

```
SQL> select last_name, first_name
2  from employee
3  where last_name > 'HOOVER';
LAST_NAME       FIRST_NAME
--------------- ---------------
JOHNSON         LYNDON
REAGAN          RONALD
JOHNSON         ANDREW
NIXON           RICHARD
KENNEDY         JOHN
TRUMAN          HAROLD
ROOSEVELT       FRANKLIN
WILSON          WOODROW
TAFT            WILLIAM
ROOSEVELT       THEODORE
ROOSEVELT       ELEANOR
11 rows selected.
```

When the value on both sides of the greater than operator are equal, the condition does not evaluate to true. If you would like to also select records that equal the evaluation condition, place an equal sign after the operator (>= , <=). This changes the operator to greater than or equal and less than or equal operators. Listing 3.10 shows an example of this type of operator:

**Listing 3.10 L_03_10.TXT—Example of a Greater Than or Equal Conditional Statement**

```
SQL> select last_name, first_name
2  from employee
3  where last_name >= 'HOOVER';
```

```
LAST_NAME       FIRST_NAME
--------------- ---------------
JOHNSON         LYNDON
REAGAN          RONALD
JOHNSON         ANDREW
NIXON           RICHARD
KENNEDY         JOHN
TRUMAN          HAROLD
ROOSEVELT       FRANKLIN
HOOVER          HERBERT
WILSON          WOODROW
TAFT            WILLIAM
ROOSEVELT       THEODORE
ROOSEVELT       ELEANOR
12 rows selected.
```



## Using the IN Operator

The IN operator enables you to evaluate one argument against a set of other arguments. The syntax of the statement requires the set of values to be enclosed by parentheses (()), and you must separate each value by a comma (,). There is no limit to the number of values that you can include in the set. This operator is useful because it reduces the number of condition statements needed to obtain the data. To obtain the data without the operator, you must list a statement for each value in the IN set. Listing 3.11 shows an example of an `IN` conditional statement:

**Listing 3.11 L_03_11.TXT—Example of an IN Operator**

```
SQL> select last_name, first_name
2  from employee
3  where last_name in ('HOOVER', 'ROOSEVELT');
LAST_NAME       FIRST_NAME
--------------- ---------------
ROOSEVELT       FRANKLIN
HOOVER          HERBERT
ROOSEVELT       THEODORE
ROOSEVELT       ELEANOR

4 rows selected.
```

## Using the BETWEEN Operator

This operator is also used to simplify the conditional statement in the `where` clauses. It enables the developer to select records that fall between two values. Records that equal the arguments are also selected. You can use this operator to compare numeric and character values. Listing 3.12 shows an example of a `BETWEEN` conditional statement:

**Listing 3.12 L_03_12.TXT—Example of the BETWEEN Operator**

```
SQL> select last_name, first_name, wages
2  from employee
3  where wages between 13000 and 15000;
LAST_NAME       FIRST_NAME          WAGES
--------------- ---------------- --------
REAGAN          RONALD              13500
BUSH            GEORGE              14000
CLINTON         WILLIAM             15000
CARTER          JIMMY               13000
FORD            GERALD              13000
5 rows selected.
```

## Using the LIKE Operator

The LIKE operator enables the user to select rows based on a specific set of characters in a character string. You cannot use this operator on numeric values. It compares the character-defined column against the identified pattern. Rows that contain a column value that match are selected.

Two symbols are used to record the sequence: the percent sign (%), and the underscore symbol (_). The % symbol designates the sequence of the character. For instance, 'a%' means the column must begin with a small letter 'a.' The % symbol tells Oracle to ignore any following characters. The string 'a%q%' means that the column must begin with a small letter 'a' and the string must also contain a small letter 'q.' This example does not care what character falls between the 'a' and 'q' or what character falls after it. The string 'a%q' is similar except that the string must end with a small letter 'q.'

The '_' symbol is used to indicate the position of the character. For example, '_a%' means the column value must contain a value of 'a' in the second position. It does care about any other characters. The string '%q_a' means that the column must have a letter 'q' with a letter 'a' following it two positions later. The 'a' must also be the last character in the string because it is not followed by the '%' symbol.

Listing 3.13 demonstrates a `LIKE` conditional statement. The statement selects records that begin with a letter 'R' in the last_name column and have a value of 'HE' in the second and third positions of the first_name column.

**Listing 3.13 L_03_13.TXT—Example of LIKE Operators Using Both Symbols**

```
SQL> select last_name, first_name
2  from employee
3  where last_name like 'R%'
4    and first_name like '_HE%';
LAST_NAME       FIRST_NAME
--------------- ---------------
ROOSEVELT       THEODORE

1 row selected.
```

## Using the NOT Operator

The NOT operator is used to negate any of the operators. The symbol for not is an exclamation mark (!) or the word *not*. Listing 3.14 shows an example of the NOT operator:

**Listing 3.14 L_03_14.TXT—Example of the NOT Operator**

```
SQL> select last_name, first_name
2  from employee
3  where last_name not like 'ROOS%';
LAST_NAME       FIRST_NAME
--------------- ---------------
COOLIDGE        CALVIN
JOHNSON         LYNDON
REAGAN          RONALD
BUSH            GEORGE
JOHNSON         ANDREW
CLINTON         WILLIAM
CARTER          JIMMY
FORD            GERALD
NIXON           RICHARD
KENNEDY         JOHN
EISENHOWER      DWIGHT
TRUMAN          HAROLD
HOOVER          HERBERT
WILSON          WOODROW
TAFT            WILLIAM
ANTHONY         SUSAN
16 rows selected.
```

This query selects all rows from the employee table where the last_name column does not begin with the letters 'ROOS.'



## Understanding Multiple Conditions

The examples portrayed thus far have contained at most two conditional statements. Generally, when obtaining records from the database, many conditional statements are required. Fortunately there are no limits to the number of conditions that you can include. Multiple statements are combined through the use of the 'and' and 'or' words. The 'and' word means both the statement preceding it and following it must be true. The 'or' word means either the statement preceding it or following it must be true. In the Listing 3.15, for example, both the conditions must be met for the record to be selected.

**Listing 3.15 L_03_15.TXT—Example of Multiple Conditions**

```
SQL> select last_name, first_name
2  from employee
3  where last_name = 'TAFT'
4    and first_name = 'WILLIAM';
LAST_NAME       FIRST_NAME
--------------- ---------------
```

*continues*

**Listing 3.15 Continued**

```
TAFT             WILLIAM

1 record selected.
```

In this next example, only one of the three conditions must be met for the set of conditions to be evaluated as true and the record selected (see Listing 3.16).

**Listing 3.16 L_03_16.TXT—Example of the Use of 'Or' in the *Where* Clause**

```
SQL> select last_name, first_name, wages
2  from employee
3  where last_name = 'TRUMAN'
4      or first_name = 'WILLIAM'
5      or wages = 13000;
LAST_NAME        FIRST_NAME           WAGES
---------------- ---------------- ---------
CLINTON          WILLIAM              15000
CARTER           JIMMY                13000
FORD             GERALD               13000
TRUMAN           HAROLD               11000
TAFT             WILLIAM               8500

5 records selected.
```

Problems sometimes occur when the two symbols 'and' and 'or' are both used in the same set of conditional statements. When conditions are linked using these words, sometimes it is necessary to group sets of statements together using parentheses (()). These enable the developer to change the logic of the condition. Listing 3.17 demonstrates the use of and, or, and () to document the selection criteria.

**Listing 3.17 L_03_17.TXT—Example of Using the 'and' and 'or' in the *Where* Clause Using Parentheses**

```
SQL> select last_name, first_name, fk_department
2  from employee
3  where last_name = 'ROOSEVELT'
4    and (fk_department = 'WEL'
5         or fk_department = 'POL');
LAST_NAME        FIRST_NAME       FK_D
---------------- ---------------- ----
ROOSEVELT        FRANKLIN         POL
ROOSEVELT        ELEAOR           WEL

2 records selected.
```

This query returns records of employees that have a last_name value of ROOSEVELT and are in department 'WEL' or 'POL.' If the parentheses are removed, as in Listing 3.18, the condition logic is changed.

**Listing 3.18 L_03_18.TXT—Example of How Removing Parentheses in the Where Clause Changes the Selection Logic**

```
SQL> select last_name, first_name, fk_department
2  from employee
3  where last_name = 'ROOSEVELT'
4    and fk_department = 'WEL'
5     or fk_department = 'POL';
LAST_NAME        FIRST_NAME       FK_D
---------------- ---------------- ----
JOHNSON          LYNDON           POL
JOHNSON          ANDREW           POL
CLINTON          WILLIAM          POL
NIXON            RICHARD          POL
KENNEDY          JOHN             POL
ROOSEVELT        FRANKLIN         POL
WILSON           WOODROW          POL
ROOSEVELT        ELEAOR           WEL
8 rows selected.
```



This query returns the employees that have a last_name value of ROOSEVELT and are in department 'WEL.' The change in the query causes all employees in the 'POL' department to be selected even though their last_name does not equal ROOSEVELT.

# Using Variables

Sometimes it is convenient to have variables in the `select` statement. *Variables* can cause SQL*PLUS to prompt the user for a value when the script is executed or can contain values that will be used in titles or footnotes. Prompting the user for a value is a useful device because you can design one query that can produce multiple different reports based on the user input. You may, for example, develop a query that produces a list of employees for a department. If you make the department number expression a variable, you can use one select script for multiple departments.

Listing 3.19 illustrates the use of an ampersand (&) character to prompt the user to enter a value when the script is executed. Whenever SQL*PLUS sees the &, it stops execution of the script and prompts for a value. To make the prompt more user-friendly, the example includes an `accept` statement that prints some boilerplate text describing for the user the information needed. Without the `accept` statement, SQL*PLUS shows only the name of the variable.

**Listing 3.19 L_03_19.TXT—Using a Variable and an Ampersand to Input Values into a Script**

```
SQL> select last_name, first_name, wages
2  from employee
3  where fk_department = '&dpt';
Enter value for dpt: POL
old   3: where fk_department = '&dpt'
new   3: where fk_department = 'POL'
```

*continues*

**Listing 3.19 Continued**

```
LAST_NAME       FIRST_NAME           WAGES
--------------- --------------- ---------
JOHNSON         LYNDON               12000
JOHNSON         ANDREW                7500
CLINTON         WILLIAM              15000
NIXON           RICHARD              12500
KENNEDY         JOHN                 11500
ROOSEVELT       FRANKLIN             10400
WILSON          WOODROW               9000
7 rows selected.
```

# Performing Column Arithmetic and Combination

Sometimes it's advantageous to perform mathematical functions on columns in a `select` clause. SQL*PLUS enables you to place common arithmetic operators between numeric columns or arguments. The calculation is known as an *expression.*

*Expressions* contain several column names and are separated from other columns by a comma (,). SQL*PLUS treats expressions or the columns and operators between commas in the select clause as one virtual column. You can use the addition (+), subtraction (-), multiplication (*), and division (/) operators. Listing 3.20 shows an example of a numeric expression that computes the weekly wages for each employee.

**Listing 3.20 L_03_20.TXT—Example of Column Arithmetic**

```
SQL> select last_name, first_name, wages, wages/52
2  from employee;
LAST_NAME       FIRST_NAME           WAGES  WAGES/52
--------------- --------------- ---------  --------
COOLIDGE        CALVIN                9500 182.69231
JOHNSON         LYNDON               12000 230.76923
REAGAN          RONALD               13500 259.61538
BUSH            GEORGE               14000 269.23077
JOHNSON         ANDREW                7500 144.23077
CLINTON         WILLIAM              15000 288.46154
CARTER          JIMMY                13000       250

.

19 records selected.
```

Character columns can be combined by using the concatenation (||) operator. This operator is used to combine table columns and literals. *Literals* are string characters listed in the `select` clause that are repeated on every row. The example shown in Listing 3.21 concatenates the literal ", " between the columns last_name and first_name.

**Listing 3.21 L_03_21.TXT—Example of Column Concatenation**

```
SQL> select last_name¦¦','¦¦first_name
2  from employee;
LAST_NAME¦¦','¦¦FIRST_NAME
COOLIDGE,CALVIN
JOHNSON,LYNDON
REAGAN,RONALD
BUSH,GEORGE
JOHNSON,ANDREW
CLINTON,WILLIAM
CARTER,JIMMY

.

19 records selected
```



When SQL*PLUS creates a virtual column using an expression, it places the entire expression in the default column heading. The reason for this is the expression becomes the de facto column name. It is the name used in `order by` and `group by` clauses as well as in column headings. Using a column alias can change this. The *alias* is a character string placed immediately behind any column or expression. Aliases that are one word may be entered without any single quotes. Aliases that are two or more words or that contain upper case characters are enclosed by double quotes (see Listing 3.22).

**Listing 3.22 L_03_22.TXT—Example of Column Aliases**

```
SQL> select last_name¦¦','¦¦first_name name,
2         wages "ANNUAL WAGES"
3  from employee;
NAME                            ANNUAL WAGES
------------------------------- ------------
COOLIDGE,CALVIN                         9500
JOHNSON,LYNDON                         12000
REAGAN,RONALD                          13500
BUSH,GEORGE                            14000
JOHNSON,ANDREW                          7500

.

19 records selected.
```

Finally, as Listing 3.23 shows, expressions may also be used in `where` clauses:

**Listing 3.23 L_03_23.TXT—Example of Using an Expression in the *Where* Clause**

```
SQL> select last_name, first_name, wages
2  from employee
```

*continues*

**Listing 3.23 Continued**

```
3  where wages - 200 < 12000;
LAST_NAME        FIRST_NAME             WAGES
---------------  ---------------     --------
COOLIDGE         CALVIN                  9500
JOHNSON          LYNDON                 12000
JOHNSON          ANDREW                  7500
KENNEDY          JOHN                   11500
EISENHOWER       DWIGHT                     0

5 records selected.
```

# Understanding Null Values and Expressions

*Null* means the value is unknown or blank. It does not mean the value equals zero or contains white space. This feature can cause many problems because Oracle does not perform calculations when one of the values is null. In Oracle, the result of a calculation with a null value is always unknown or null. Listing 3.24 illustrates a query that contains null values in the wages column. Notice the Eisenhower and the last Roosevelt records. The calculations were not made in these records. The reason is because the two records have a null value in their wages column. The result of a calculation with a null value is a null value. To correct this problem, you can use the NVL function discussed later in this chapter in its own section.

**Listing 3.24 L_03_25.TXT—Example of a Column Calculation when Null Values Exist**

```
SQL> select last_name, wages, wages+500
2  from employee;
LAST_NAME            WAGES WAGES+500
--------------- --------- ---------
NIXON                12500     13000
KENNEDY              11500     12000
EISENHOWER
TRUMAN               11000     11500
ROOSEVELT            10400     10900
ROOSEVELT             8000      8500
ANTHONY               7000      7500
ROOSEVELT

.

19 records selected
```

# Date Arithmetic

Date is a valid data format in SQL*PLUS. This means that the Oracle database actually stores the date as a numeric value. It is interpreted into a date that a user will understand when displayed. Because the date is stored as a numeric value, calculations can be performed on the column. Values can be added or subtracted from the date to produce another date, or two dates may be subtracted to determine the number of days between them. Listing 3.25 demonstrates several examples of the calculations that can occur.

**Listing 3.25 L_03_25.TXT—Examples of Various Date Calculations**

```
SQL> select last_name, employment_date, birth_date,
2    (employment_date-birth_date)/365 "age at hire",
3    employment_date+100 "100 days", birth_date + (365*65) retirement
4  from employee;
LAST_NAME       EMPLOYMEN BIRTH_DAT age at hire 100 days  RETIREMEN
--------------- --------- --------- ----------- --------  ---------
COOLIDGE        07-AUG-21 01-JUL-72    50.93425 15-NOV-21  15-JUN-37
JOHNSON         23-NOV-63 27-AUG-08   55.276712 02-MAR-64 11-AUG-73
REAGAN          03-MAR-80 01-OCT-24   55.457534 11-JUN-80 15-SEP-89
BUSH            05-JAN-88 06-FEB-11   76.964384 14-APR-88 21-JAN-76
JOHNSON         13-APR-65 29-DEC-08   56.326027 22-JUL-65 13-DEC-73
CLINTON         01-JAN-92 03-APR-40   51.780822 10-APR-92 18-MAR-05
CARTER          10-JUL-76 14-JUL-13   63.032877 18-OCT-76 28-JUN-78

.

19 records selected
```



You might notice that the default date picture for a date is '01-JAN-97'. You can change this picture by using a date picture. Date pictures are discussed in the next chapter.

The time of day is also stored in the date value. One hour is equal to 1/24 of the day, and a minute is equal to 1/1440 of a date. To add 10 minutes to the time, just add 10/1440 to the date. The default time of day is midnight. The date value does not contain a fraction. The select statement in Listing 3.26 adds 6 hours and 20 minutes to the hire_date.

**Listing 3.26 L_03_26.TXT—Example of Adding Hours and Minutes to the Date**

```
SQL> column a format a25
SQL> column b format a25
SQL> select last_name, to_char(employment_date, 'Month dd YYYY HH:MI') a,
2     to_char(employment_date + 6/24 + 20/1440, 'Month dd YYYY HH:MI') b
3  from employee;
LAST_NAME       A                         B
--------------- ------------------------- -------------------------
COOLIDGE        August    07 1921 12:00   August    07 1921 06:20
JOHNSON         November  23 1963 12:00   November  23 1963 06:20
REAGAN          March     03 1980 12:00   March     03 1980 06:20
BUSH            January   05 1988 12:00   January   05 1988 06:20
JOHNSON         April     13 1965 12:00   April     13 1965 06:20
```

*continues*

**Listing 3.26 Continued**

```
CLINTON        January   01 1992 12:00   January   01 1992 06:20

.

19 records selected
```

# Using Character Functions

SQL*PLUS provides the developer with a wealth of functions that he or she can use to manipulate character and date values, perform multi-row calculations (such as sums or averages), and convert column formats. These functions are used in the `select` and `where` clauses of the statement. Table 3.3 contains a description of the character functions.

**Table 3.3 Character Functions**

| Function | Format | Description |
|---|---|---|
| `¦¦` | `'string'¦¦'string'` | Combines two strings. |
| `ASCII` | `ASCII`(string) | Returns the ASCII value of the first character of the string. |
| `CHR` | `CHR`(integer) | Returns the character equivalent to the ASCII value of the integer. |
| `INITCAP` | `INITCAP`(string) | Changes the first letter of the string to uppercase. |
| `INSTR` | `INSTR`(string, set [, start [ , occurrence ] ]) | Finds the location of the beginning set of characters in the string. |
| `LENGTH` | `LENGTH`(string) | Returns the length of the string. |
| `LOWER` | `LOWER`(string) | Converts the entire string to lowercase. |
| `LPAD` | `LPAD`(string, length, [, 'set']) | Makes a string a specific length by adding a specific set of characters to the left of the string. |
| `LTRIM` | `LTRIM`(string [, 'set']) | Trims the occurrences of any one of a set of characters off the left side of a string. |
| `RPAD` | `RPAD`(string, length, [, 'set']) | Makes a string a specific length by adding a specified set of characters to the right. |
| `RTRIM` | `RTRIM`(string [, 'set']) | Trims the occurrences of any one of a set of characters off the right side of a string. |

| Function | Format | Description |
|---|---|---|
| SOUNDEX | SOUNDEX(string) | Converts a name to a code value. It is then used to compare names that might have small differences in spelling but sound alike. |
| SUBSTR | SUBSTR(string, start [, count]) | Extracts a piece of a string beginning at start position and counting for count characters from start. |
| TRANSLATE | TRANSLATE(string, if, then) | Changes a string, character by character, based on a positional matching of characters in the `if` string with characters in the `then` string. |
| UPPER | UPPER(string) | Converts every letter in a string into uppercase. |



**NOTE** In the following subsections, I discuss the major functions you are likely to use. You should gain an understanding of how to use all functions by these examples. Some of the functions such as `chr` and `ascii` are seldom used. These functions operate similar to any of the other functions. I don't feel it is necessary to illustrate these functions. ■

# The *Length* Function

The `length` function is used to determine the actual length of a character string. This length is not the defined length of the column, but the part of the column filled with characters. In Listing 3.27, the column last_name is defined as `char`(15). Notice the values computed by the length command.

**Listing 3.27 L_03_27.TXT—Example of Using the *Length* Function**

```
SQL> select first_name, length(first_name) from employee;
FIRST_NAME      LENGTH(FIRST_NAME)
--------------- ------------------
CALVIN                           6
LYNDON                           6
RONALD                           6
GEORGE                           6
ANDREW                           6

.

19 records selected.
```

## The Lpad Function

This function is used to pad the left side of a string with characters. These characters may also include white space (space bar). It produces a string of the length specified in the argument. Listing 3.28 shows an example of the `Lpad` function.

**Listing 3.28 L_03_28.TXT—Example of the Use of the *LPAD* Function**

```
SQL> select first_name, lpad(first_name, 15, ' ')
2  from employee;
FIRST_NAME      LPAD(FIRST_NAME
--------------- ---------------
CALVIN                   CALVIN
LYNDON                   LYNDON
RONALD                   RONALD
GEORGE                   GEORGE
ANDREW                   ANDREW

.

19 records selected
```

Notice that the values in the second column now have white space and the string is shifted to the right. The displayed column fills the entire 15 characters.

## The *Ltrim* Function

The `ltrim` function trims occurrences of unwanted characters from the left side of the character string. In Listing 3.29, the 'ROO' is trimmed from all the selected columns. The function removes characters from the left of the string until it reaches the first character not in the set. In Listing 3.2, the third character "O" in the name Roosevelt was also removed even though only two characters were specified in the `SELECT` statement. When Oracle7 performs the `ltrim` function, it looks at the first character in the function character list and trims all leading characters until the function encounters a different character in the string. The function then begins trimming the next specified character. It stops trimming when it reaches the end of the trim list and the leading character in the string does not match the specification. The second "O" in the string was trimmed because it matched the second character in the trim list.

**Listing 3.29 L_03_29.TXT—Example of the *Ltrim* Function**

```
SQL> select last_name, ltrim(last_name, 'RO')
2  from employee
3  where last_name = 'ROOSEVELT';
LAST_NAME       LTRIM(LAST_NAME
--------------- ---------------
ROOSEVELT       SEVELT
ROOSEVELT       SEVELT
ROOSEVELT       SEVELT

3 rows selected.
```

## The *Rpad* Function

`Rpad` is used to add characters to the right side of a string up to the specified length of the field. In Listing 3.30, dashes (-) are placed on the right side of the last_name field.

**Listing 3.30 L_03_30.TXT—Example of the *Rpad* Function**

```
SQL> select first_name, rpad(first_name, 15, '-')
2  from employee;
FIRST_NAME      RPAD(FIRST_NAME
--------------- ---------------
CALVIN          CALVIN---------
LYNDON          LYNDON---------
RONALD          RONALD---------
GEORGE          GEORGE---------
ANDREW          ANDREW---------
WILLIAM         WILLIAM-------

.

19 records selected.
```



## The *Rtrim* Function

This function is used to trim unwanted characters from the right side of a string. Columns that have null characters will not compare to columns with white space. The reason is that white space and null characters are actually two distinct characters. Another use for the `rtrim` function is to get rid of unwanted characters when concatenating columns(see Listing 3.31).

**NOTE** I often use this function when I need to compare columns from two tables, and I am concerned that one of the columns contains white space.

**Listing 3.31 L_03_31.TXT—Example of the *Rtrim* Functions**

```
SQL> select last_name¦¦','¦¦first_name,
2      rtrim(last_name, ' ')¦¦','¦¦first_name
3  from employee;
LAST_NAME¦¦','¦¦FIRST_NAME      RTRIM(LAST_NAME,'')¦¦','¦¦FIRST
------------------------------- -------------------------------
COOLIDGE       ,CALVIN          COOLIDGE,CALVIN
JOHNSON        ,LYNDON          JOHNSON,LYNDON
REAGAN         ,RONALD          REAGAN,RONALD
BUSH           ,GEORGE          BUSH,GEORGE
JOHNSON        ,ANDREW          JOHNSON,ANDREW

.

19 records selected.
```

## The *Substr* Function

The `substr` function selects a set of characters from a column character string. The function has three parameters: column name, beginning position, and number of characters to select or extract from the returned string. Oracle7 will only return the characters that match the defined parameter. The other characters in the column string will be discarded. This is a very common function to use. It is also very common for a SQL statement to use this function in the `where` clause to limit the number of records selected. Listing 3.32 shows an example of this.

**Listing 3.32 L_03_32.TXT—Example of the *Substr* Function**

```
SQL> select last_name, first_name,
2    birth_date, substr(to_char(birth_date), 4,3)
3  from employee
4  where substr(to_char(birth_date), 4,3) = 'JAN';
LAST_NAME       FIRST_NAME      BIRTH_DAT SUB
--------------- --------------- --------- ---
FORD            GERALD          09-JAN-13 JAN
ROOSEVELT       FRANKLIN        30-JAN-82 JAN

2 records selected.
```

The preceding statement produces a listing of employees that were born in January. It uses the `substr` function to extract the month from the birthdate column because the database does not have a column for month. The function extracts three characters from the date string, beginning at position four. You might notice that the example has one function nested within another. It is permissible to nest functions. To_char is a numeric function that converts numbers to characters. Because birth_date is defined as a date that is really a specially formatted number, it was necessary to convert the column to a character value.

# Using the *Decode* Function

`Decode` is a function that you can use on both numeric and column values. It is placed in the `select` clause and used to translate column values to another value. Databases often have columns that contain coded values that need to be translated for the user. The reason for the codes are to eliminate the amount of typing a user must perform to enter the data. The example tables use codes to denote the department name. 'POL,' for example, represents 'Political Science' and 'WEL' represents 'Welfare.' The `decode` function enables you to replace these codes with the more descriptive values. The syntax is: `decode`(column name, old_value_n1, new_value_n1). Listing 3.33 shows an example of how to use the `decode` function.

**Listing 3.33 L_03_33.TXT—Example of the *Decode* Function**

```
SQL> select last_name, first_name, fk_department,
2    decode(fk_department, 'INT ', 'INTERIOR', 'POL ',
3    'POLITICAL SCIENCE', 'WEL ', 'WELFARE', 'UNKNOWN')
4  from employee
```

```
5  order by 3;
LAST_NAME       FIRST_NAME      FK_D DECODE(FK_DEPARTM
--------------- --------------- ---- ----------------
COOLIDGE        CALVIN          INT  INTERIOR
BUSH            GEORGE          INT  INTERIOR
FORD            GERALD          INT  INTERIOR
TRUMAN          HAROLD          INT  INTERIOR
EISENHOWER      DWIGHT          INT  INTERIOR
ROOSEVELT       THEODORE        INT  INTERIOR
JOHNSON         LYNDON          POL  POLITICAL SCIENCE
CLINTON         WILLIAM         POL  POLITICAL SCIENCE

.

19 rows selected.
```



This statement changes the values in the department column. You might notice that the last value in the function does not contain a code. This tells SQL*PLUS to place the value of 'UNKNOWN' in the listing if the column value it encounters is missing or is not contained in the list. The `order by` clause uses a column number rather the than column. The reason is the column name changes to the entire decode expression unless an alias is recorded. An alias was not specified, so it was easier to enter a column number than the decode expression.

# Using Number Functions

SQL*PLUS contains a variety of numeric functions that enable the developer to perform computations as necessary. Table 3.4 contains a listing of these functions:

**Table 3.4 Numeric Functions**

| Function Name | Syntax | Description |
|---|---|---|
| + | value1 + value2 | Addition |
| – | value2 – value4 | Subtraction |
| * | value5 * value6 | Multiplication |
| / | *value7/value8* | Division |
| ABS | ABS(*value*) | Absolute value |
| CEIL | CEIL(*value*) | Smallest integer greater than or equal to the value |
| COS | COS(*value*) | Cosine |
| COSH | COSH(*value*) | Hyperbolic cosine of the value |
| EXP | EXP(*value*) | *e* Raised to the *value*th power |

*continues*

**Table 3.4 Continued**

| Function Name | Syntax | Description |
|---|---|---|
| FLOOR | FLOOR(*value*) | Largest integer less than or equal to the value |
| LN | LN(*value*) | Natural (base e) logarithm of the value |
| LOG | LOG(*base, value*) | Base *base* logarithm of the value |
| MOD | MOD(*value, divisor*) | Modulus (remainder) |
| NVL | NVL(*value, substitute*) | Substitutes a value for a null value |
| POWER | POWER(*value, exponent*) | Value raised to an exponent |
| ROUND | ROUND(*value, precision*) | Rounds a value to the specified precision |
| SIGN | SIGN(*value*) | Displays a minus one if the value is negative and a positive one if the value is positive. |
| SIN | SIN(*value*) | Sine of the value |
| SINH | SINH(*value*) | Hyperbolic sine of the value |
| SQRT | SQRT(*value*) | Square root of the value |
| TAN | TAN(*value*) | Tangent of the value |
| TANH | TANH(*value*) | Hyperbolic tangent of the value |
| TRUNC | TRUNC(*value, precision*) | Truncates the value to the specified precision |

**NOTE** The following subsections demonstrate the more common functions. You will be able to use any of the other functions by studying these sections.

# The *Nvl* Function

The `nvl` function is used to correct problems that occur when one of the values in the computation is null. When a null value exists in an argument, a null value results. This can cause a problem because it affects the value of computations. Assume that you have 20 records that total to 200, for example, and 10 of these records are null. Computing the average by using the `avg` function would result in a value of 20. The reason is the null records are not included into the denominator. If the `nvl` function were employed and the null value changed to 0, the value would be 10, which is the expected result. Listing 3.34 shows an example of averaging columns by using the `nvl` function:

**Listing 3.34 L_03_34.TXT—Example of the *Nvl* Function**

```
SQL> select avg(wages), avg(nvl(wages,0))
2  from employee;
AVG(WAGES) AVG(NVL(WAGES,0))
---------- -----------------
10905.882          9757.8947

.

1 record selected.
```

## The *Round* Function

The `round` function changes the value to the next higher unit if the value is 50 percent of that unit. It reduces the value to the lower unit if it is less than 50 percent. Listing 3.35 shows an example of rounding:



**Listing 3.35 L_03_35.TXT—Example of the *Round* Function**

```
SQL> select last_name, wages,
2          round(wages+1.05, 1), round(wages+1.04,1)
3  from employee;
LAST_NAME            WAGES ROUND(WAGES+1.05,1) ROUND(WAGES+1.04,1)
--------------- --------- ------------------- -------------------
COOLIDGE              9500              9501.1                9501
JOHNSON              12000             12001.1               12001
REAGAN               13500             13501.1               13501
BUSH                 14000             14001.1               14001
JOHNSON               7500              7501.1                7501

.

19 records selected.
```

## The *Trunc* Function

The `trunc` function eliminates the portion of a number outside the defined precision. Precision means the number of decimal positions. Unlike the `round` function, `trunc` does not change the value. Listing 3.36 provides an example of using the `trunc` function:

**Listing 3.36 L_03_36.TXT—Example of the *Trunc* Function**

```
SQL> select last_name, wages/52,
2          trunc(wages/52, 2)
3  from employee;
LAST_NAME         WAGES/52 TRUNC(WAGES/52,2)
--------------- --------- -----------------
COOLIDGE        182.69231            182.69
```

*continues*

**Listing 3.36 Continued**

```
JOHNSON          230.76923              230.76
REAGAN           259.61538              259.61
BUSH             269.23077              269.23
JOHNSON          144.23077              144.23

.

19 records selected.
```

# Understanding Date Functions

An array of functions exist for dates. Dates are, in reality, a number. They are stored in the database as a numeric value and displayed in a date format. The majority of these functions perform calculations such as the number of months between two dates. Table 3.5 lists the date functions.

**Table 3.5 Date Functions**

| Function Name | Syntax | Description |
|---|---|---|
| ADD_MONTHS | ADD_MONTHS(*date, count*) | Adds the specified number of months to the date |
| GREATEST | GREATEST(*date1, date2,...*) | Picks the most recent date from a list of dates |
| LAST_DAY | LAST_DAY(*day*) | Returns the last day of the month that the date is in |
| MONTHS_BETWEEN | MONTH_BETWEEN(*date2, date1*) | Calculates the number of months between the two dates. |
| NEXT_DAY | NEXT_DAY(*date, 'day'*) | Returns the date of the specified next day of the week |
| TO_CHAR | TO_CHAR(*date, 'format'*) | Reformats the date according to the format picture |
| TO_DATE | TO_DATE(*string, 'format'*) | Converts a string in a given format to a date. |

**NOTE** The following subsections demonstrate the more common functions. You will be able to use any of the other functions by studying these sections.

## The *Add_Months* Function

This function is used to add a number of months to a date. The example shown in Listing 3.37 computes the retirement date of each employee.

**Listing 3.37 L_03_37.TXT—Example of the *Add_Months* Function**

```
SQL> select last_name, first_name, birth_date,
2    add_months(birth_date, (12*65)) age
3  from employee;
LAST_NAME        FIRST_NAME       BIRTH_DAT AGE
---------------  ---------------  --------- ---------
COOLIDGE         CALVIN           01-JUL-72 01-JUL-37
JOHNSON          LYNDON           27-AUG-08 27-AUG-73
REAGAN           RONALD           01-OCT-24 01-OCT-89
BUSH             GEORGE           06-FEB-11 06-FEB-76
JOHNSON          ANDREW           29-DEC-08 29-DEC-73
CLINTON          WILLIAM          03-APR-40 03-APR-05
CARTER           JIMMY           14-JUL-13 14-JUL-78

.

19 records selected.
```



## The *Months_Between* Function

This function determines the number of months between two dates. Listing 3.38 uses this function to calculate the age of each employee when hired by dividing the number of months between the birthdate and hire date by 12.

**Listing 3.38 L_03_38.TXT—Example of the *Months_Between* Function**

```
SQL> select last_name, first_name,
2    employment_date, birth_date,
3    months_between(employment_date, birth_date)/12 age
4  from employee;
LAST_NAME        FIRST_NAME       EMPLOYMEN BIRTH_DAT       AGE
---------------  ---------------  --------- --------- ---------
COOLIDGE         CALVIN           07-AUG-21 01-JUL-72 50.90054
JOHNSON          LYNDON           23-NOV-63 27-AUG-08 55.239247
REAGAN           RONALD           03-MAR-80 01-OCT-24 55.422043
BUSH             GEORGE           05-JAN-88 06-FEB-11 76.913978
JOHNSON          ANDREW           13-APR-65 29-DEC-08 56.290323
CLINTON          WILLIAM          01-JAN-92 03-APR-40 51.744624
CARTER           JIMMY            10-JUL-76 14-JUL-13 62.989247

.

19 records selected.
```

## The *Next_Day* Function

This function calculates the next day of the week (such as Sunday) following a specified base date. Listing 3.39 determines the date of the first Friday following the employee's retirement date:

**Listing 3.39 L_03_39.TXT—Example of the *Next_Day* Function**

```
SQL> select last_name, first_name, birth_date,
2    next_day(add_months(birth_date, (12*65)), 'FRIDAY') party
3  from employee;
LAST_NAME       FIRST_NAME      BIRTH_DAT PARTY
--------------- --------------- --------- ---------
COOLIDGE        CALVIN          01-JUL-72 03-JUL-37
JOHNSON         LYNDON          27-AUG-08 31-AUG-73
REAGAN          RONALD          01-OCT-24 06-OCT-89
BUSH            GEORGE          06-FEB-11 13-FEB-76
JOHNSON         ANDREW          29-DEC-08 04-JAN-74
CLINTON         WILLIAM         03-APR-40 08-APR-05
CARTER          JIMMY           14-JUL-13 21-JUL-78

.

19 records selected.
```

# Using Date Pictures

A date picture is the format of a date. The default Oracle date picture or date format is 'dd-mon-yy'. This is a military date with the date followed by the month and year. SQL*PLUS offers a number of formats that enable the developer to change this picture. Table 3.6 contains a listing of various formats that you can use:

**Table 3.6 Date Formats**

| Format | Meaning |
|---|---|
| P.M. | Displays P.M. |
| D | Numeric day of the week |
| DAY | Day of the week is fully spelled out (MONDAY) |
| Day | Same as DAY, but only the initial letter is capitalized (Monday) |
| day | Same as DAY, letters are lower case (monday) |
| DD | Numeric day of the month (for example, Feb 23 = 23) |
| DDD | Numeric day of the year. (for example, Feb. 2 = 33) |
| DY | Three letter abbreviation of the day (FRI) |

| Format | Meaning |
|---|---|
| Dy | Same as DY, but only the initial letter is capitalized (Fri) |
| dy | Same as DY, but all the letters are lower case. (fri) |
| J | Julian day of the year (1997004) |
| WW | Number of the week of the year |
| W | Number of the week of the month |
| IW | Number of the week of the ISO standard |
| MM | Number of the month (12) |
| MON | Three-letter abbreviationof month (APR) |
| Mon | Same as MON, but only the initial letter is capitalized (Apr) |
| mon | Same as MON, but all letters are lower case (apr) |
| MONTH | Month fully spelled out (APRIL) |
| Month | Same as MONTH, but only the initial letter is capitalized (April) |
| month | Same as MONTH, but all letters are lowercase (april) |
| RM | Roman numeral month (XII) |
| I | Last digit of the ISO year |
| IY | Last two digits of the ISO year |
| IYY | Last three digits of the ISO year |
| IYYY | ISO four-digit standard year |
| RR | Last two digits of the year. |
| SYYYY | Signed year (1500 bc = -1500) |
| Y | Last digit of the year (7) |
| YY | Last two digits of the year (97) |
| YYY | Last three digits of the year (997) |
| YYYY | Four digit year (1997) |
| YEAR | The year spelled out (NINETEEN-NINETY-SEVEN) |
| Year | The year spelled out with initial capitals |
| year | The year spelled in all lower case letters |
| Q | Number of the quarter |
| CC or SCC | Century |

*continues*

**Table 3.6 Continued**

| Format | Meaning |
|---|---|
| BC or AD | Displays BC or AD |
| B.C. or A.D. | Displays B.C. or A.D. |
| bc or ad | Displays bc or ad |
| b.c. or a.d. | Displays b.c. or a.d. |
| AM or PM | Meridian indicator |
| A.M. or P.M. | Meridian indicator with periods |
| am or pm | Meridian indicator with all lowercase letters |
| HH | Hour of the day |
| HH12 | Same as HH |
| HH24 | Hour of the day in military format |
| MI | Minute of the hour. |
| SS | Second of the minute |
| SSSS | Seconds since midnight, the number is always between 0 - 86399 |

Date pictures must be used with the to_char function. This function is a date function. It can be used to change any numeric data into a string. It is used most often with date pictures. The picture is placed in the format section of the function (see Listing 3.40).

**Listing 3.40 L_03_40.TXT—Example of Various Date Pictures**

```
SQL> column date1 format a40
SQL> column date2 format a33
SQL> select last_name, birth_date,
  2    to_char(birth_date, 'DAY MONTH YEAR') DATE1,
  3    to_char(birth_date, 'dd-mm-yyyy hh mi ss') DATE2
4  from employee;
LAST_NAME       BIRTH_DAT DATE1                                    DATE2
--------------- --------- ---------------------------------------- -------------
--------------------
COOLIDGE        01-JUL-72 SATURDAY  JULY      Eighteen SEVENTY-TWO 01-07-1972 12
➥00 00
JOHNSON         27-AUG-08 THURSDAY  AUGUST    ONE THOUSAND NINE HU 27-08-1908 12
➥00 00
.
19 records selected.
```

**NOTE** In the preceding example, date 2 does not display the full year for the second record. The reason is because the column was not formatted to the proper size. This can be done by changing the column format settings. This command will be discussed in greater detail in the next chapter.

You can also add suffixes to values in the picture to enhance readability. These suffixes are sp, th, and spth. sp causes SQL*PLUS to spell the value (ten), th places 'th' after the value ($10^{th}$), and spth spells the value out and places a 'th' at the end. In addition to these suffixes, you can also include text in the picture by enclosing it with double quotes. Listing 3.41 shows an example of special formatting:

**Listing 3.41 L_03_41.TXT—Example of Using Literals in the Date Picture**

```
SQL> set linesize 130
SQL> column date1 format a90
SQL> select last_name, to_char(birth_date,
2    '"THE" ddth "of" MONTH "IN THE YEAR OF OUR LORD" YEAR') date1
3  from employee;
LAST_NAME       DATE1
--------------- --------------------------------------------------------------
-------------------------
COOLIDGE        THE 01 of JULY      IN THE YEAR OF OUR LORD EIGHTEEN SEVENTY-TWO
JOHNSON         THE 27 of AUGUST    IN THE YEAR OF OUR LORD ONE THOUSAND NINE
                                    ➥HUNDRED
REAGAN          THE 01 of OCTOBER   IN THE YEAR OF OUR LORD NINETEEN TWENTY-FOUR
BUSH            THE 06 of FEBRUARY  IN THE YEAR OF OUR LORD NINETEEN ELEVEN

.

19 records selected.
```

Notice that the date picture must be enclosed by single quotes. Within the single quotes, the special date characters may be placed along with any literal text. The literal text such as "THE YEAR OF OUR LORD" must be enclosed by double quotes.

# Understanding Group Functions

One last set of functions that you can use in the select clause is the group functions. These functions are performed on sets of data that range from one record to the entire table. They evaluate the records in the set and return a value. Table 3.7 contains a listing of group functions.

**Table 3.7 Group Functions**

| Function Name | Syntax | Description |
|---|---|---|
| avg | avg(*value*) | Computes the average of the set |
| count | count(*value*) | Counts the number of rows in the set |
| max | max(*value*) | Determines the greatest value of the set |
| min | min(*value*) | Determines the smallest value of the set |
| stddev | stddev(*value*) | Computes the standard deviation of the set |
| sum | sum(*value*) | Computes the sum or total of the set |
| variance | variance(*value*) | Computes the variance of the total |

## The *Average* Function

The `average` function is used to compute the average or mean of a group of data. Listing 3.42 shows an example that computes the average wage per employee in the table.

**Listing 3.42 L_03_42.TXT—Example of the *AVG* Function**

```
SQL> select avg(wages) from employee;
AVG(WAGES)
10905.882
```

Null valued records are not included in the calculation. When you think some records have nulls, be certain to use the `nvl` function (see Listing 3.43).

**Listing 3.43 L_03_43.TXT—Example of the *AVG* Function Using a Nested NVL Function**

```
SQL> select avg(nvl(wages, 0)) from employee;
AVG(NVL(WAGES,0))
9757.8947
```

The difference in the values returned for the two statements can be attributed to the fact that the `avg` function, and in fact all group functions, do not consider null valued records a part of the set of records for the calculation. This means the denominator used in Listing 3.42 is greater that the denominator in Listing 3.42. In both queries, the numerator is the same. This is why the result in Listing 3.42 is larger than Listing 3.43.

## The *COUNT* Function

The `count` function calculates the number of values in a set or group. When a column name is placed within the function, only those records that do not have a null value in the column are included in the computation. When an asterisk (*) is placed within the function, all the records are counted. Listing 3.44 shows what happens when the * is used.

**Listing 3.44 L_03_44.TXT—Example of the *Count* Function**

```
SQL> select count(*), count(wages) from employee;
COUNT(*) COUNT(WAGES)
-------- --------------------
19      17
```

The first column in the `select` statement counts each row selected. The second column counts only those records that contain a value in the wages column. When the word *distinct* is placed within the function, the function counts records of the same value only once. It computes the number of different values in the set. In the example employee table, three employees are named 'ROOSEVELT'. Listing 3.45 uses the *distinct* word; notice how many times this value was counted.



**Listing 3.45 L_03_45.TXT—Example of Using the *Count* and *Distinct* Functions**

```
SQL> select count(distinct last_name)
2  from employee
3  where last_name = 'ROOSEVELT';
COUNT(DISTINCTLAST_NAME)
1
```

## Multiple Group Functions

It is possible to use more than one group function in the same `select` clause. Listing 3.46 computes the last names with the minimum value and maximum value, the number of records in the table, and the number of distinct last names.

**Listing 3.46 L_03_46.TXT—Example of Multiple Group Functions**

```
SQL> select min(last_name), max(last_name),
2    count(*), count(last_name)
3  from employee;
MIN(LAST_NAME)  MAX(LAST_NAME)   COUNT(*) COUNT(LAST_NAME)
--------------  --------------   -------- ----------------
ANTHONY         WILSON                 19               19
```

# Understanding *GROUP BY* Functions

The group functions discussed so far have been performed on sets of data that consist of the entire table. It is possible to perform computations on multiple subsets of data. Listing the subset column names in the `group by` clause causes Oracle7 to group the selected records in subsets. The `group by` function is them performed against the subset. Listing 3.47 includes an example that performs computations on subsets of the entire data set. This example computes the total amount of wages per last_name.

**Listing 3.47 L_03_47.TXT—Example of the *Group By* Clause**

```
SQL> select fk_department, sum(wages)
2  from employee
3  group by fk_department;
FK_D SUM(WAGES)
---- ----------
INT       55500
POL       77900
WEL       52000
```

You do not have to list the columns listed in the `group by` clause in the select clause. Of course when they are not listed, it is difficult to determine what set of columns the function has computed a value for.

The columns do not have to be in any particular order in the `select` clause (see Listing 3.48). The order that the columns and functions are listed in the `select` clause should be determined by the desired presentation style.

If you list a column in the `select` clause and do not list it in the `group by` clause, however, an error occurs. The error is the result of the statement having ambiguity. Oracle7 does not know the columns that determine the subsets of data. The example shown in Listing 3.48 contains an additional column not included in the `group by` clause.

**Listing 3.48 L_03_48.TXT—Example of Column Ambiguity Error**

```
SQL> select last_name, first_name, sum(wages)
2  from employee;
select last_name, first_name, sum(wages)
       *
ERROR at line 1:
ORA-00937: not a single-group group function
```

This statement resulted in an error because the `select` clause had a group function preceded by two columns, and the statement did not have a `group by` clause. Oracle7 doesn't know how to calculate the function. When a `group by` clause is included in the `SELECT` statement, the error is eliminated (see Listing 3.49).

**Listing 3.49 L_03_49.TXT—Example of Mixing Function and Group Columns**

```
SQL> select sum(wages), last_name, first_name
2  from employee
3  group by last_name, first_name;
```

```
SUM(WAGES) LAST_NAME       FIRST_NAME
---------- --------------- ---------------
      7000 ANTHONY         SUSANNE
     14000 BUSH            GEORGE
     13000 CARTER          JIMMY
     15000 CLINTON         WILLIAM
      9500 COOLIDGE        CALVIN
         0 EISENHOWER      DWIGHT
     13000 FORD            GERALD
     10000 HOOVER          HERBERT
      7500 JOHNSON         ANDREW
```

## Understanding the *HAVING* Clause



You cannot include group functions in the `where` clause even though it is desirable to limit the number of records based on the value of the function. Assume, for example, that you want to produce a listing that contains only departments that have total wages greater $20,000. The statement computing this listing needs the group function sum in the `where` clause to limit the records. You cannot place this function in that clause, but you can place it in the `having` clause. This clause is used to limit the number of records selected (see Listing 3.50) through the use of a group function.

**Listing 3.50 L_03_50.TXT—Example of the *Having* Clause**

```
SQL> select fk_department, sum(wages)
2  from employee
3  group by fk_department
4  having sum(wages) > 20000;
FK_D SUM(WAGES)
---- ----------
INT       55500
POL       77900
WEL       52000

3 records selected.
```

The preceding example selects the departments that have total wages greater than $20,000. The `having` clause follows the `group by` clause in the `select` statement.

## Understanding Subselects or Subqueries

*Subqueries* are used in the `where` clause to create a virtual list of one or more values used in the conditional statement for evaluations. The subquery is performed before the main query because it is nested. After the subquery is completed and the values are determined, the main query is executed.

The benefit of the subquery is that values are determined at the time the select is performed. This means that values do not have to be hard coded. Hard-coded values may become obsolete over time. The subquery reduces the need to rewrite the query. A second benefit is that the subquery avoids the necessity of running one query, obtaining the result, and hard coding this value in the `where` clause of the second query. Listing 3.51 shows this benefit. The example query determines the name of the oldest employee in the employee database. Without the subquery, you must perform two queries. The first determines the oldest birthdate in the table. The second determines the name of the employee with that birthdate. The use of the subquery reduces this to one query.

**Listing 3.51 L_03_51.TXT—Example of the Use of a Subquery**

```
SQL> select last_name, first_name, birth_date
2  from employee
3  where birth_date = (select min(birth_date) from employee);
LAST_NAME        FIRST_NAME       BIRTH_DAT
---------------- ---------------- ---------
ANTHONY          SUSAN          15-FEB-20

1 record selected.
```

The preceding  example produces one value in the subquery. If the subquery produces multiple values, the `IN` function should be used. A `where` clause can contain the amount of subqueries as needed. Listing 3.52 shows an example of a multiple subselect query.

**Listing 3.52 L_03_52.TXT—Example of Multiple Subqueries**

```
SQL> select last_name, first_name, fk_department
2  from employee
3  where fk_department = (select fk_department from employee
  4                          where last_name = 'ROOSEVELT'
  5                            and first_name = 'FRANKLIN')
  6    and employment_date > (select employment_date from employee
  7                          where last_name = 'ROOSEVELT'
  8                           and first_name = 'FRANKLIN');
LAST_NAME        FIRST_NAME       FK_D
---------------- ---------------- ----
JOHNSON          LYNDON           POL
CLINTON          WILLIAM          POL
NIXON            RICHARD          POL
KENNEDY          JOHN             POL

4 records selected.
```

This query performs multiple subqueries to determine FRANKLIN ROOSEVELT's department and hire date. It then selects employees in the department that were hired before him.

# Understanding Pseudo Columns, Dual Table, Describe, and Tab Table

SQL*PLUS contains several pseudo columns that provide additional information for a report or listing. You can list these columns in the `select`, `where`, `order by`, or `group by` clauses. The following contains these columns.

| Column | Description |
|---|---|
| `null` | Null value |
| `sysdate` | The current system date |
| `rownum` | Sequential number indicating the order of retrieval |

The `null` places a null value into the column. Alternatively, you can use it in a `where` condition to evaluate another argument as null. `Sysdate` is the current date. `Rownum` is the sequential number of the row, indicating the order in which it was retrieved.



The `dual` table is used when a value must be introduced and an existing table does not contain that value. This could occur when a date is needed in a report, or possibly in a SQL*FORM. The example shown in Listing 3.53 uses the dual table to select and display the current date.

**Listing 3.53 L_03_53.TXT—Example of a Pseudo Column and the Dual Table**

```
31-SQL>  select sysdate from dual;
SYSDATE
MAY-97
```

The Describe or Desc command is used to list the contents of a table. It is an extremely useful command when you are not certain of a table's column names or the format of a column. Listing 3.54 includes an example of a Describe command in use.

**Listing 3.54 L_03_54.TXT—Example of the Describe Command**

```
SQL> describe employee
Name                                Null?    Type
 ------------------------------------ ----
 PAYROLL_NUMBER                      NOT NULL NUMBER(4)
 LAST_NAME                                    VARCHAR2(15)
 FIRST_NAME                                   VARCHAR2(15)
 ABSENCES                                     NUMBER(2)
 WAGES                                        NUMBER(8,2)
 STREET                                       VARCHAR2(20)
 CITY                                         VARCHAR2(15)
 STATE                                        CHAR(2)
 PHONE                                        CHAR(13)
 SOCIAL_SECURITY_NUMBER                       CHAR(11)
 EMPLOYMENT_DATE                              DATE
```

*continues*

**Listing 3.54 Continued**

```
BIRTH_DATE                                       DATE
CURRENT_POSITION                                 VARCHAR2(15)
FK_DEPARTMENT                                    CHAR(4)
GENDER                                           CHAR(2)
```

The Tab table contains the names of the tables to which you have access to on your Oracle id. The table is a view of the data dictionary and contains several fields about the table that may be of interest. When you need to know the name of a table, this view may be of interest. Listing 3.55 shows the results of a `select` statement using this table.

**Listing 3.55 L_03_55.TXT—Example of the Tab Table**

```
SQL> select * from tab;
TNAME                          TABTYPE CLUSTERID
------------------------------ ------- ---------
BONUS                          TABLE
CUSTOMER                       TABLE
DEPARTMENT                     TABLE
DEPT                           TABLE
DEPTCOST                       VIEW
DUMMY                          TABLE
EMP                            TABLE
EMPLOYEE                       TABLE
EMP_DEPT                       TABLE
EMP_GLASSES                    TABLE
EMP_HIST                       TABLE
EMP_TOOLS                      TABLE
GLASSES                        TABLE
ITEM                           TABLE
LOADTAB                        TABLE
ORD                            TABLE
PRICE                          TABLE
PRODUCT                        TABLE
SALES                          VIEW
SALGRADE                       TABLE
SECTAB                         TABLE
TNAME                          TABTYPE CLUSTERID
------------------------------ ------- ---------
TESTLOAD                       TABLE
TOOLCOST                       VIEW
TOOLS                          TABLE
WGE_MAINT                      TABLE
25 rows selected.
```

## Summary

This chapter introduced you to the SQL language. The first SQL command is `select`, which acquires data from the Oracle7 database. `Select` is used in all the Oracle products. The command has five clauses. The `from` clause identifies the database tables that contain the data. The `where` clause identifies the selected records. The `group by` clause determines the set of records to perform `group by` functions on. The `having` clause identifies selected records. This functionality is similar to the `where` clause, except it uses group by functions to identify records. The `order by` clause sorts the records for display in the specified manner.

The `select` command has a large array of functions. The date functions enable you to perform arithmetic on two dates. The character functions enable you to combine, extract, and modify character expressions. You can use the number functions to format numbers. The `decode` function enables you to substitute one value for one that is selected. Finally, you have pseudo columns such as `sysdate` and `rownum` that return special values.



## From Here...

You should now be comfortable with extracting data by using the select command. The next chapter shows you how to create formatted reports in SQL*PLUS. The Developer 2000 tool set has Oracle Reports 2.5, which is a more powerful tool. If you do not have access to Oracle Reports 2.5, you will find SQL*PLUS a good report writing tool.

## Review Questions

1. Find out the column names for the employee and department tables.
2. Select all the columns and records from the department table.
3. Use the SQL*PLUS editor Change command to change the tablename in the buffered query to the employee table.
4. List the employees by last name descending and first name ascending.
5. List the employees by gender. Be certain to translate the values in gender to 'MALE,' 'FEMALE,' and 'UNKNOWN.'
6. List all the male employees.
7. List all the male employees born in July.
8. Compute the average wages for all the employees.
9. Compute the average wages per department for all employees.
10. Compute the weekly net pay for the employees in the interior department. Assume that 10 percent of the gross pay is taken out for taxes and $150 is deducted annually for charity.

11. List the employees in the Political Science department with the greatest seniority.
12. Determine the employee in the Political Science department with the most seniority.
13. List the employees in the Interior department and Political Science department whose wages are greater than Truman's.
14. List the employees that have a 'W' in the second position of their first name.
15. List the employees whose last name contains a 'V' and a 'T'.
16. Compute the total wages for all departments except the Welfare department.
17. List the male employees from the employee table. Use the following example as a model for formatting the employee names: 'Mr. John Palinski'.
18. List all the tables to which you have access.

PART II

# Using SQL*PLUS to Access the Database

CHAPTER 4

# Formatting Reports in SQL*PLUS

- **Creating report titles**

  This section describes how you can create customized report titles in SQL*PLUS.

- **Creating report footers**

  This section describes how you can create customized report footers in SQL*PLUS.

- **Formatting report columns**

  This section describes how you can create customized report columns in SQL*PLUS.

- **Formatting numbers**

  This section explains how to format numbers. These formats are also used in Oracle Forms and Oracle Reports.

- **Defining page breaks**

  This section describes page breaks and how to create them in SQL*PLUS. Page breaks are also used in Oracle Reports.

- **Defining computes**

  This section describes the compute functions. You use these to perform page break calculations such as subtotal and average.

- **Setting Up the SQL*PLUS operating environment**

  This section describes the Set command. You use it to change environmental settings that control the SQL*PLUS environment.

As shown thus far, SQL*PLUS has the capability to query and acquire data. It also has powerful report writing features. In fact, SQL*PLUS is Oracle's first report writer. Even though it has been superseded by SQL*REPORTS, it is still an excellent tool for creating reports.

This chapter covers the format statements that enable the developer to create titles and footers, customize column headings, perform subtotals, and set environmental variables.

This chapter uses the same database used in Chapter 3. Installation instructions for the database are contained in Appendix D, "Practice Database Installation Instructions."

To format reports or queries, you enter special settings or commands prior to the select statement. You may enter these settings directly into the editor, or you may enter them in a command file. To then run the command file, use the `start` or `@` symbol. The command file proves advantageous because your report is saved where it can be run repeatedly. Obtaining an acceptable format often takes many tries. Having the settings in a command file eases the development task. ■

# Creating Report Titles

To place a title format into the buffer, use the ttitle command. The entered setting displays at the top of each page of the report. After the command is entered, it remains in the buffer until a new ttitle command or the ttitle off command is entered. The latter command clears the title format from the buffer. It is important to clear the buffer because queries will continue to use the title setting even though it may not have been intended for the query.

You can enter this command directly into the buffer, or you can place it in a file containing all the other format commands. Ttitle is the first word of the command, telling Oracle that the developer is entering a title format statement. Table 4.1 contains some special formatting words you can use in the ttitle statement.

**Table 4.1 Ttitle Settings**

| Name | Description |
|---|---|
| - (dash) | This character indicates that the command will continue on the following line. |
| ' ' (single quotes) | Literal text that will be included in the title is enclosed with single quotes. |
| center | Places the item following the keyword in the center of the line. |
| col n | Places text following it at the specified column. The column number is represented by the small n. |
| left | Places the item following it on the left side of the line. This is called left justification. |
| off | Suppresses display defaults. |
| skip n | Causes SQL*PLUS to skip the specified number of lines and print the remainder of the title. The letter n represent the number of lines to skip. |
| sql.pno | Displays or prints the current page number. |

Listing 4.1 illustrates some of the ttitle settings. It uses the left keyword to place the current date, which is placed in the command as a literal on the left side of the first line. The center keyword is used to justify the first line of the title in the center of the line. The skip 1 keyword tells SQL*PLUS to print the next part of the title on the next line. Because the entire command cannot be placed on one line, a dash (-) is placed at the end of the line. This tells the editor that you have not finished entering the complete command, and it is continued on the subsequent line. Notice that SQL*PLUS does not put a line number or the SQL> at the head of the line. It puts the > symbol, which means that SQL*PLUS considers instructions entered on this line a continuation of the previous line.

**Listing 4.1 L_04_01.TXT—Using the Ttitle Command to Create a Report Title**

```
SQL> ttitle left '17-AUG-97' center 'LAST NAMES' skip 1 -
> left sql.pno center 'AND FIRST NAMES' skip 1-
> col 45 'CONFIDENTIAL'
SQL> select last_name, first_name
  2  from employee;
17-AUG-97                                 LAST NAMES
        1                              AND FIRST NAMES
                                        CONFIDENTIAL

LAST_NAME       FIRST_NAME
--------------- ---------------
TAFT            WILLIAM
ROOSEVELT       THEODORE
ANTHONY         SUSAN
ROOSEVELT       ELEANOR
COOLIDGE        CALVIN
JOHNSON         LYNDON
REAGAN          RONALD
BUSH            GEORGE
JOHNSON         ANDREW
CLINTON         WILLIAM
CARTER          JIMMY
FORD            GERALD
NIXON           RICHARD
KENNEDY         JOHN
EISENHOWER      DWIGHT
TRUMAN          HAROLD
ROOSEVELT       FRANKLIN
HOOVER          HERBERT
sysdate                                 LAST NAMES
        2                              AND FIRST NAMES
                                        CONFIDENTIAL

LAST_NAME       FIRST_NAME
--------------- ---------------
WILSON          WOODROW

19 records selected.
```

The first setting placed on the continuation line in the preceding listing uses the left format keyword to left-justify the page number that will be printed as the result of placing sql.pno in the title. The second line of the title will be centered, and the literal "CONFIDENTIAL" will be printed on the following line beginning on column 45. By pressing Enter, you place the statement in the buffer because the second line does not contain a dash (-) character.

# Creating Report Footers

The btitle command works the same as ttitle except that it formats the bottom of each report, known as the footer. The entered settings display at the bottom of each page of the report. This command uses the same format words and characters contained in Listing 4.1. You can enter this command directly into the buffer or place the command in a command file. The setting must be placed before the select statement. The command remains in memory until you use the btitle off command or a new btitle command supersedes it. Listing 4.2 demonstrates entering a btitle command into the buffer.

**Listing 4.2 L_04_02.TXT—Using the Btitle Command to Create a Report Footer**

```
SQL> btitle left 'SEND TO Mr. Palinski'
SQL> select last_name, first_name
  2  from employee;
17-AUG-97                                       LAST NAMES
        1                                   AND FIRST NAMES
                                             CONFIDENTIAL

LAST_NAME       FIRST_NAME
--------------- --------------
TAFT            WILLIAM
ROOSEVELT       THEODORE
ANTHONY         SUSAN
ROOSEVELT       ELEANOR
COOLIDGE        CALVIN
JOHNSON         LYNDON
REAGAN          RONALD
BUSH            GEORGE
JOHNSON         ANDREW
CLINTON         WILLIAM
CARTER          JIMMY
FORD            GERALD
NIXON           RICHARD
KENNEDY         JOHN
EISENHOWER      DWIGHT
TRUMAN          HAROLD
ROOSEVELT       FRANKLIN
SEND TO Mr. Palinski
17-AUG-97                                       LAST NAMES
        2                                   AND FIRST NAMES
                                             CONFIDENTIAL
LAST_NAME       FIRST_NAME
--------------- --------------
HOOVER          HERBERT
WILSON          WOODROW
SEND TO Mr. Palinski

19 records selected.
```

# Formatting Report Columns

As shown in Chapter 3, placing a column alias immediately following the column or expression in the select clause will change the default column heading. If the alias is lowercase and consists of one word, it is not enclosed by single quotation marks. If it is uppercase, mixed case, or consists of two or more words, the alias must be enclosed by double quotation marks. The alias enables the developer to easily format a heading, but it has some limitations that the column command corrects.

This command is used to change column headings. The benefits of the column command is increased formatting functionality. Table 4.2 contains some examples and descriptions of the various and available column format settings.

**Table 4.2 Column Format Settings**

| Example | Description |
|---|---|
| column fk_department heading 'department' | Changes the column heading to department. |
| column first_name heading 'First \|Name' | Changes the column heading to First Name and stacks the two words on top of each other. The pipe (\|) symbol indicates when to begin the next row of the stack. |
| column last_name justify left | Positions the heading on the left side. Other options include center and right. |
| column last_name format a25 | Changes the format of the column to alphanumeric with a length of 25. This is a useful command when your column heading is larger than the column. It eliminates the heading truncation that will occur. |
| column wages format $99,999 | Changes the format to a numeric format. In this example, the values will begin with a dollar sign ($) and use a comma to designate thousands. |
| column taxes_owed like wages | Formats the taxes_owed column the same as the wages column. |
| column employment_date off | Turns off the column options without affecting the data. |
| column fk_department alias dept | Creates a column alias called dept for the fk_department column. |
| column birth_date newline | Starts a new line before printing the column value. |
| column fk_department new_val dpt | Creates a variable called dpt to hold the fk_department column's value for use in a ttitle command. |
| column fk_department null 'UNKNOWN' | Specifies the text or value to be displayed if the column has a null value. |

*continues*

**Table 4.2 Continued**

| Example | Description |
|---|---|
| column fk_department old_val odpt | Creates a variable called odpt to hold the fk_department column's value for use in a btitle command. |
| column payroll_number noprint | Turns the column's display off. |
| column payroll_number print | Turns the column's display on. |
| column address trunc | Truncates the value to the width of the column's definition. |
| column classification wrapped | Stacks the values of a column on multiple lines if it does not fit the defined width of the column. This option stacks at a letter, breaking apart a word. |
| column classification word_wrapped | Stacks or places the values in a column on multiple lines if it does not fit the defined width of the column. This option stacks at the end of a word. It will try not to break apart a word. |
| column clear | Eliminates the column definitions. |

You can enter the column command into the buffer directly from the editor or from a command file. After the command has been entered, it remains until you issue the column clear command or a new column command for the column. The clear columns command eliminates all the column formats simultaneously. Whereas the column clear command only clears the specified column.

**TIP** I always use this statement at the end of my command files to set the SQL*PLUS environment back to the default. This way I don't get any unexpected formats on subsequent queries.

The keyword *column* starts the command, and the name of the column to be formatted follows. Next comes the format settings. The command accepts as many of the settings as necessary. If you don't have enough room on the row to type all the settings, be certain to continue to the next line by placing the dash (-) symbol at the end of the row. You must place all the settings in one continuous command because subsequent *column* commands for the same column supersede each other.

Listing 4.3 demonstrates the use of several *column* commands. It gives custom headings to several columns: left justifies and stacks the last_name heading; right justifies the first_name heading; and center justifies, formats with a $, and prints the wages column on the next line.

**Listing 4.3 L_04_03.TXT—Using the Column Command to Format Column Headings**

```
SQL> ttitle off
SQL> btitle off
SQL> column last_name heading 'LAST¦NAME' justify left
SQL> column first_name justify right heading 'FIRST NAME'
SQL> column wages heading 'ANNUAL WAGES' justify center -
> format $99,999.99 newline
SQL> select last_name, first_name, wages
  2  from employee;
LAST
NAME                     FIRST NAME
-------------- --------------
ANNUAL WAGES
------------
TAFT            WILLIAM
   $8,500.00

ROOSEVELT       THEODORE
   $8,000.00

ANTHONY         SUSAN
   $7,000.00

ROOSEVELT       ELEANOR
        $.00
.

19 records selected.
```



The *new_val* and *old_val* settings are interesting. The *new_val* setting creates a local variable and causes SQL*PLUS to populate this variable with the column value for each row selected. You can use this functionality to place column values into the report title. When the report starts a new page, this value is placed in the title. Placing a column value in the title makes a report look nice, especially when used with the page break command. The *old_val* has the same functionality except the variable is used in the report footing. Listing 4.4 illustrates the use of these settings by placing the first_name value in the title and the last_name in the footing.

**Listing 4.4 L_04_04.TXT—Using the New_Val and Old_Val Settings**

```
SQL> ttitle off
SQL> btitle off
SQL> column last_name old_val ln
SQL> column first_name new_val fn
SQL> ttitle left fn center 'EXAMPLE REPORT -
> DISPLAYING A NEW_VAL SETTING'
SQL> btitle left ln center 'EXAMPLE REPORT -
> DISPLAYING AN OLD_VAL SETTING'
```

*continues*

**Listing 4.4 Continued**

```
SQL> select last_name, first_name
  2  from employee
  3  where payroll_number = 29;

DWIGHT                       EXAMPLE REPORT  DISPLAYING A NEW_VAL SETTING
LAST
NAME                  FIRST NAME
--------------- ---------------
EISENHOWER      DWIGHT
EISENHOWER                   EXAMPLE REPORT  DISPLAYING AN OLD_VAL SETTING
```

# Formatting Numbers

You can use special format settings to define numeric columns. The formats are placed in a *column* command. These format values are used in Oracle Forms and Reports in addition to SQL*PLUS. Table 4.3 lists these settings. The first column in the table is the format setting. The setting is placed in the *column* command. The second table column contains an example of a formatted value. The third column describes that format setting.

**Table 4.3 Number Formats**

| Format | Display | Description |
|---|---|---|
| 999990 | 123521 | The count of the nines and zeros determines the maximum length that can be displayed by the column. |
| 90 | 12 or 0 | A zero displays if the value is zero. |
| 99,999.99 | 12,345.34 | Places a comma to designate thousands, and has a two-digit decimal. |
| 09999 | 01234 | Displays the number with leading zeros. |
| $999 | $123 | Places a dollar sign at the beginning of the number. |
| B9999 | 1234 or blank | If zero, displays appear blank. |
| 99999MI | 12345- or 12345 | Places a minus sign after a negative number. |
| 99999S | 12345- or 12345 | Same as 99999MI. |
| S99999 | -12345 or 12345 | Places a minus sign before a negative number. |
| RM | LX | Displays the number as a Roman numeral. |
| 9999PR | <1234> | Displays negative numbers surrounded by arrows. |
| 9.99EEEE | 8.7656 19 | Displays the number in scientific notation (must be exactly four Es). |

# Defining Page Breaks

When a listing or report is created, some columns may have the same value repeated row after row. This often occurs when records from a base table are combined with records from a related table. The base table and the related table generally have a one-to-many relationship. When the records from the tables are combined, the primary key value from the base table is repeated for each of the matching records in the related table. Listing 4.5 illustrates a query of the employees in the 'POL' department. The value 'POL' repeats in each row.

**Listing 4.5 L_04_05.TXT—Example of Repeating Values**

```
SQL> ttitle off
SQL> btitle off
SQL> select fk_department, last_name, first_name
  2  from employee
  3  where fk_department = 'POL';
     LAST
FK_D NAME                    FIRST NAME
---- ---------------- ----------------
POL  JOHNSON          LYNDON
POL  JOHNSON          ANDREW
POL  CLINTON          WILLIAM
POL  NIXON            RICHARD
POL  KENNEDY          JOHN
POL  ROOSEVELT        FRANKLIN
POL  WILSON           WOODROW
7 rows selected.
```



To increase the readability of the report, these repeating values are often suppressed—and printed only when the value changes. This is called a *break*. SQL*PLUS performs this function by using the *break* command. Listing 4.6 displays an example of this command.

**Listing 4.6 L_04_06.TXT—Using the Break Command**

```
SQL>  break on fk_department
SQL>  select fk_department, last_name, first_name
  2   from employee
  3   where fk_department = 'POL';
     LAST
FK_D NAME                    FIRST NAME
---- ---------------- ----------------
POL  JOHNSON          LYNDON
     JOHNSON          ANDREW
     CLINTON          WILLIAM
     NIXON            RICHARD
     KENNEDY          JOHN
     ROOSEVELT        FRANKLIN
     WILSON           WOODROW

7 records selected.
```

A report may need multiple break columns for the preferred format. The *break* command accommodates this. The name of multiple columns can be placed in the *break* command. This will cause the value for each of the specified columns to be printed when they change. Each break colum name should be preceded by the keyword `on`. Multiple breaks allow each column to break independently of each other. Listing 4.7 demonstrates a multiple break command.

**Listing 4.7 L_04_07.TXT—Perform a Multiple Break Formatting Procedure**

```
SQL> break on fk_department on last_name
SQL> select fk_department, last_name, first_name
  2  from employee
  3  order by fk_department, last_name;
FK_D LAST_NAME       FIRST_NAME
---- --------------- --------------
INT  BUSH            GEORGE
     COOLIDGE        CALVIN
     EISENHOWER      DWIGHT
     FORD            GERALD
     ROOSEVELT       THEODORE
     TRUMAN          HAROLD
POL  CLINTON         WILLIAM
     JOHNSON         LYNDON
                     ANDREW
     KENNEDY         JOHN
     NIXON           RICHARD
     ROOSEVELT       FRANKLIN
     WILSON          WOODROW
WEL  ANTHONY         SUSAN
     CARTER          JIMMY
     HOOVER          HERBERT
     REAGAN          RONALD
     ROOSEVELT       ELEANOR
     TAFT            WILLIAM

19 records selected.
```

As with the other format commands, the *break* command remains in the buffer and is used on all subsequent queries until you issue a new *break* command or until you clear the command by using the *clear breaks* command. Break points also prove useful at times to perform special format procedures. Table 4.4 lists these commands.

**Table 4.4 Break Settings**

| Setting | Description |
|---|---|
| `Nodup`[licates] | Suppresses the printing of the values for every row except the first one after the break. |
| `Dup`[licates] | Causes the value to be printed on each row. |
| `On Report` | Causes the report to break at the end of the report. |

| Setting | Description |
|---|---|
| `On Row` | Causes the report to break on each row. |
| `Page` | Causes the query to print the next row after the break on a new page. |
| `Skip [n]` | Causes the report to skip [*n*] lines after the break. |

The `break` command can contain as many settings as needed. You can place settings after each break column. These setting work when that particular column breaks. The *break* command must be one continuous statement. By using the dash (-), you can continue it on a new line. Typing the command *break* with no settings causes the editor to display the current break settings. It is also important to order the columns with the *order by* clause in the same pattern as the break setting. A *break* command does not order data, and causes haphazard breaking without a matching *order by* clause. Listing 4.8 shows a *break* command that skips two lines at the secondary break and pages at the major break.

**Listing 4.8 L_04_08.TXT—Example of a Multiple Column Break Command**

```
SQL> clear columns
columns cleared
SQL> btitle off
SQL> title off
unknown command "title off" - rest of line ignored.
SQL> break on fk_department page on last_name skip 2
SQL> select fk_department, last_name, first_name, wages
  2  from employee
  3  order by 1,2;

FK_D LAST_NAME       FIRST_NAME         WAGES
---- --------------- --------------- --------
INT  BUSH            GEORGE             14000


     COOLIDGE        CALVIN              9500


     EISENHOWER      DWIGHT                 0


     FORD            GERALD             13000


     ROOSEVELT       THEODORE            8000


     TRUMAN          HAROLD             11000



FK_D LAST_NAME       FIRST_NAME         WAGES
---- --------------- -------------- ---------
```

*continues*

Part II Ch 4

**Listing 4.8 Continued**

```
POL  CLINTON         WILLIAM              15000


     JOHNSON         LYNDON               12000
                     ANDREW                7500


     KENNEDY         JOHN                 11500


     NIXON           RICHARD              12500


     ROOSEVELT       FRANKLIN             10400


     WILSON          WOODROW               9000



FK_D LAST_NAME       FIRST_NAME           WAGES
---- --------------- --------------- ---------
WEL  ANTHONY         SUSAN                 7000


     CARTER          JIMMY                13000


     HOOVER          HERBERT              10000


     REAGAN          RONALD               13500


     ROOSEVELT       ELEANOR                  0


     TAFT            WILLIAM               8500



19 rows selected.
```

# Defining Computes

It is useful to print subtotals or other calculations at the break points. To perform this functionality, use the compute command in conjunction with the command. The syntax of the command is: *compute {functions} of {column names} on {break column names}*. The various functions follow the word *compute*, the expressions or columns on which to perform the computations follow the *of*, and the columns that determine when to make the calculations follow the word *on*. Table 4.5 contains functions that can be performed using *compute*.

**Table 4.5 Compute Functions**

| Function | Description |
|---|---|
| Avg | Calculates the average of the not null values in the set |
| Count | Calculates the number of not null observations in the set |
| Maximum | Calculates the maximum value in the set |
| Minimum | Calculates the minimum value in the set |
| Number | Calculates the number of returned records, including nulls |
| Std | Calculates the standard deviation of the not null values in the set |
| Sum | Calculates the total of the not null values in the set |
| Variance | Calculates the variance of the not null values in the set |



Listing 4.9 illustrates a `compute` command. It computes the average and total wages per department. The command file causes the subtotals to print at the break point. A row of stars appears on the left side of the row indicating subtotals. Below the stars, the function names are listed on subsequent rows. One final word on the `compute` command: It remains in the buffer until you enter the `clear computes` command or another `compute` supersedes it.

**Listing 4.9 L_04_09.TXT—Using the Compute Command**

```
SQL> ttitle off
SQL> btitle off
SQL> clear breaks
breaks cleared
SQL> clear columns
columns cleared
SQL> clear computes
computes cleared
SQL> break on fk_department skip 2
SQL> compute avg sum of wages on fk_department
SQL> select fk_department, last_name, wages
  2  from employee
  3  order by 1,2;

FK_D LAST_NAME            WAGES
---- --------------- ---------
INT  BUSH                14000
     COOLIDGE             9500
     EISENHOWER              0
     FORD                13000
```

**Listing 4.9 Continued**

```
     ROOSEVELT             8000
     TRUMAN               11000
****                   --------
avg                        9250
sum                       55500


POL  CLINTON              15000
     JOHNSON              12000
     JOHNSON               7500
     KENNEDY              11500
     NIXON                12500
     ROOSEVELT            10400
     WILSON                9000
****                   --------
avg                   11128.571
sum                       77900

FK_D LAST_NAME            WAGES
---- --------------- ---------


WEL  ANTHONY               7000
     CARTER               13000
     HOOVER               10000
     REAGAN               13500
     ROOSEVELT                0
     TAFT                  8500
****                  ---------
avg                   8666.6667
sum                       52000


19 rows selected.
```

# Setting Up the Environment

To modify the SQL*PLUS operating environment and other parameters that can affect your report, use the set command. It enables you to change settings that control items such as screen output, page width, line size, margin width, or word wrap. You can place these settings in the command file before the select clause or enter them directly in the buffer from the editor. They remain until you enter a new setting or the SQL*PLUS session is ended. Table 4.6 contains a listing of these settings.

**Table 4.6 Set Command Modes and Values**

| Setting Name | Description |
|---|---|
| array *n* | This setting determines the number of rows SQL*PLUS fetches at one time. The n value represents the number of rows. The default is 20, and the range is 1 to 5000. The larger the size the greater the efficiency of the query; however, more memory will be needed. |
| auto or autocommit | This setting affects when SQL*PLUS commits changes to the database. It has three settings: off, on, and imm (or immediate). A setting of *on* or *imm* causes the commit to occur immediately after the execution of SQL commands. The default is *off.* |
| buf or buffer *setting* | The setting is used to change current buffers from the default SQL buffer to another or back to the default. |
| concat *symbol* | Changes the symbol used to concatenate string values. |
| copycommit *n* | This setting commits rows to the destination database on a cycle of *n* batches of rows. Values range from 0 to 5000. |
| def or define | Defines the character used in indicate a substitution variable. The default is an '&'. The setting may also be changed to *on* or *off.* These settings determine whether SQL*PLUS will scan for a substitution variable. |
| doc or document *setting* | A setting of *on* allows the *Document* command to work. This command tells SQL*PLUS a block of documentation is beginning. The default is *off.* |
| echo *setting* | The *on* setting causes the sql commands to display to the screen as they are executed from a command file. The default is *off.* |
| embedded *setting* | The *on* setting allows a new report in a series of reports to begin anywhere on a page. The *off* setting forces the new report to start at the top of a new page. |
| escape *symbol* | The escape symbol may be changed from the default '\' with this setting. In addition, changing this setting to *off* disables this setting. |
| Feed or feedback *setting* | This setting determines when the "records selected" value displays. If the amount of records selected is greater than or equal to the specified value, the amount of records selected by the query displays. The default setting is *'6'* records. To turn off the display, use the *off* setting. flush *setting*. The *off* setting is used when a command file can be run without needing any display or interaction until it has completed. It enables the operating system to avoid sending output to the display. |

*continues*

**Table 4.6 Continued**

| Setting Name | Description |
|---|---|
| hea or heading setting | The *off* setting shuts off column headings. The default is *on*. |
| heads *symbol* | This setting is used to change the default heading separator '\|' to another *symbol*. The setting can be turned *off* and *on*. |
| lin or linesize *n* | This setting specifies the length of a line of output. Output longer than this line will wrap to the next line. The default is *80* characters. |
| long *n* | This setting determines the maximum width for displaying or copying long values. The value may be set from 1 to 32767. |
| maxd or maxdata *n* | This setting determines the maximum total row width that SQL*PLUS can process. The default and maximum value vary with the operating sytem. |
| newp or newpage *n* | This setting *(n)* specifies the number of blank lines to be printed between the bottom of one page and the top title of the next. A value of zero (0) sends a form feed at the top of each page. |
| null *text* | This setting enables you to substitute *text* for a null value when they are discovered. |
| numf or numformat format[ormat] | This setting enables you to specify the default number format. See Table 4.3 for a listing of formats. |
| num *n* | This setting changes the default width for number displays. The original default is 10 digits. |
| Pages or pagesize *n* | This setting determines the number of lines per page. The default is *14*. |
| pau or pause *setting* | The *on* setting causes SQL*PLUS to wait for you to press enter before displaying the next page. The default is *on*. The setting may also be used to specify text that will be displayed during a pause. |
| recsep *setting* | This setting defines when a line of characters is printed. The *each* setting will print the characters after each line. The *wrapped* setting prints after the wrapped line. The *off* setting suppresses the printing. |
| recsepchar *symbol* | Sets the character used for the recsep setting. |
| scan *setting* | This setting suppresses substitution variables that may be defined in the command file. The settings consist of *on* and *off*. |

| Setting Name | Description |
|---|---|
| show | This settings causes SQL*PLUS to display the current and old value of the named set command. A setting of *off* suppresses this display. A settin of *on* will display the values. |
| spa or space *n* | This setting determines the number of spaces between columns in a row of the output. |
| sqlc or sqlcase setting | Converts all text in SQL commands or PL/SQL blocks before it is executed. You can use *mixed, upper,* or *lower* settings may be used to change the case. |
| sqlco or sqlcontinue *setting* | Changes the character(s) used in the editor for the continue line prompt. The default prompt is '>'. |
| sqln or sqlnumber *setting* | When this setting is *on,* each line of an SQL command will have a line number. When the setting is *off,* subsequent lines of the command will not have line numbers. The default is *on.* |
| sqlpre or sqlprefix *symbol* | Changes the SQL*PLUS prefix character. |
| sqlp or sqlprompt *text* | Change the SQL*PLUS prompt from the default 'SQL> to a new text string. |
| Sqlt or sqlterminator *symbol* | Changes the symbol that terminates a sql statement from ';' to a new value. The terminator can be turned off with the *off setting.* The *on* setting returns it to a semi-colon. |
| suffix *text*} | Changes the default file name extension the editor uses. The default is 'sql'. |
| tab *setting* | The *off* setting causes SQL to use spaces in formatting columns and text on reports. The default setting is system dependent. The show tab command displays the setting. The *on* setting tells SQL*PLUS to use tabs rather than spaces. |
| term or termout setting | Setting this value to *off* suppresses the display of SQL*PLUS output on-screen. The default setting of *on* causes the output to display. |
| ti or time[me] {off \| on} | A value of *on* causes the current time to display before each prompt command. The default value is *off.* |
| timi or timing[ng] setting | A setting of *on* shows timing statistics for each SQL command run. The default value *off* suppresses this display. |
| trim or trimout setting | A value of *on* trims blanks at the end of each displayed line rather than displaying them. The *set tab on* setting must be in effect. |
| und or underline *setting* | This setting turns the underlining *off* and *on.* |
| ver or verify setting | A value of *on* causes SQL*PLUS to show the old and new values of a variable before executing the SQL in which they have been embedded. |

You can use these settings from the editor, or you can change them at the beginning of a sql command file. To determine the current setting and the old value if it has been changed, use the *show* command.

To direct the output of your sql to a file for review or printing, use the *spool* command. To begin spooling, enter the command along with the name of the file directly into the editor or as a command in the command file. Be certain to put the full directory location (c:\user\test.txt) down for the file name. It never fails that I have several students that spooled their first report to a file and can't find the file because SQL*PLUS placed it in Oracle's default directory.

The output continues to be directed to the file until the *spool off* command is issued. At this time, you can view the file by using Notepad or some other text-editing product. You must also use these products to print the report because SQL*PLUS does not have print features.

SQL*PLUS has one additional way to open a spool file: clicking the File/Spool/Spool File menu option. An open file dialog box appears. Select the directory you want the file to exist in, and then enter the file name. Press OK. The output is directed to this file. To shut off the spooling, click the File/Spool Off option on the menu.

# Summary

SQL*PLUS has the functionality to create highly formatted reports. Titles and footers can be placed on the report by using the *ttitle* and *btitle* commands. A large variety of formats are available for the columns. Oracle7 also provides many different number formats that you can use in all the Oracle products. The *break* command page breaks the report at specified places on the report. The *compute* command calculates and returns subtotals at the page breaks. You can modify the SQL*PLUS environment by using the *set* command settings.

# From Here...

Up to this point, you have been selecting data from one table. The next chapter describes combining columns from more than one table into a new virtual record. You do this with a technique called a join. You can add records from two or more tables by using set operators called *union, minus,* and *intersection*. These techniques are used to relate the records from a normalized database. These very powerful tools create information for users. They can lead to some misleading results when used improperly.

# Review Questions

1. Create a report listing of the employees by birth date. The report should have a title and footer. The title should have the current date and some text explaining the purpose of the report. The footer should contain the page number.

2. Re-create a report listing the employee's wages by gender, wages descending. Follow this format:

```
   16-FEB-97                    EMPLOYEE WAGES               Page:    1
                                      BY
                                 GENDER, WAGES
                     LAST
  GENDER          NAME              WAGES
    M                CARTER             13000
```

3. Modify the report in #2 so that it displays each employee's department as well as ordering the report by employee. Modify the headings appropriately. Be certain that department is only printed when the department number changes, and two spaces precede the printing of this value.
4. Modify the report in #3 so that each department's employees are listed on a new page. Do not print the department number on each row. It should be included in the title.
5. Modify the report in #4 so that the each department's average and total wages are computed for each department.
6. Spool the output of #5 to a file. Change the default settings so that the output does not display on-screen. Print the report. *Be certain to change the settings back to the default.*

CHAPTER 5

# Combining Tables and Rows

This chapter covers different ways of combining records and tables. The concepts are pertinent for relational databases because the user needs to assemble the records from multiple tables. Oracle7 is a straight relational database, and the concepts apply. Oracle8 is an object-relational database. If Oracle8 is used as a relational database these principles apply.

One of the benefits of object design is that the relationships are part of the upfront design. This means the user/developer will not have to apply many of the techniques in this chapter to combine the records. Of course, it will take some time for object databases to appear in the industry. This means the topics in this chapter will be very important for the user/developer. The last section of the chapter describes some of the object technology used by Oracle8. You will have a better grasp of their importance after reading this chapter. ■

**Joining tables**

Joining tables is an important relational database technique where the rows from two or more tables are combined to create a new virtual combined row. This chapter explains how to perform this technique.

**Qualifying tables**

Tables are identified in join statements through the use of qualifiers. They tell Oracle7 which table contains the column.

**Unexpected results and performance problems**

Joining tables improperly can cause strange and misleading results. This section explains some of the problems that can occur.

**Combining tables**

Union, Minus, and Intersect are set operators that tell Oracle7 how to assemble the records from several tables into a virtual table. This section explores how to use these tools.

# Combining Data in Relational versus Object Database

In a relational database, the data resides in a number of "related" tables. Tables are related through the use of common columns. The common columns are usually the primary and foreign key columns. To produce information from the database, you must combine these records and tables in different ways. This chapter discusses techniques to combine records from different tables. These techniques include the use of joins to make combined virtual records and combining tables by using the Intersect, Union, and Minus commands.

A *join* is a relational database technique that takes the record from one table and temporarily combines it with a record from another table. The records are united by virtue of having common values in a column in each table. Figure 5.1 contains two tables that have duplicate columns. The department table has a primary key column of department, and the employee table has a foreign key column of fk_department. These columns contain the same values and can be used to match records for the combined virtual table. A virtual record is an assembled record that exists temporarily in memory only.

A `select` statement tells the relational database management system (RDBMS) to create a table join. The *`from`* clause contains the names of the tables to be joined. A comma (,) separates the table names. The *`where`* clause contains one or more conditional statements that contain the name of the common columns that can be used to match records. The statement uses the *equal* operator (=) to evaluate whether the column value in one table equals the column value in the other table. When this condition is true, the rdbms creates a virtual record in memory of the columns specified in the `select` clause. You can treat this virtual record as any other record that may have come from one table.

Listing 5.1 demonstrates the use of a join to display each employee's department name. The department name comes from the department table and relates to the employee table through the common columns department and fk_department.

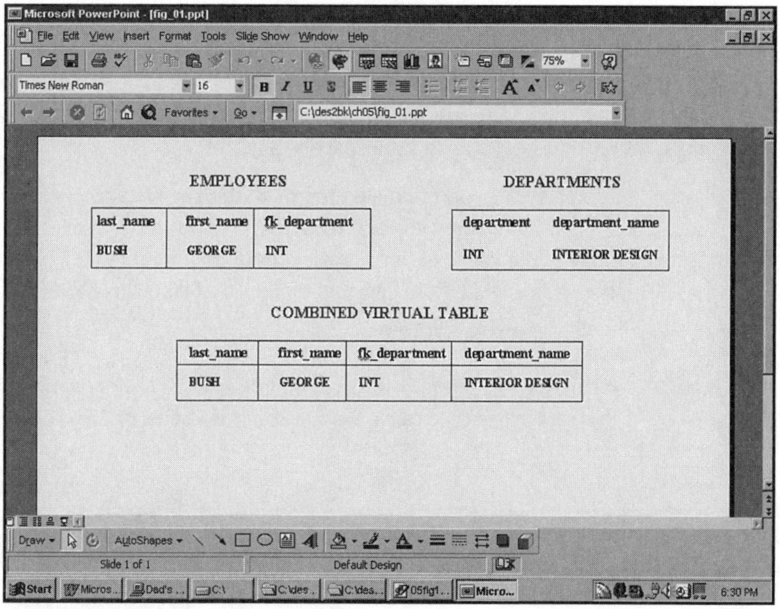


**FIG. 5.1**
Creating a combined virtual table.

### Listing 5.1 L_05_01.sql—Joining the Employee and Department Tables

```
SQL> select department_name, last_name, first_name
  2    from employee, department
  3    where department = fk_department;

DEPARTMENT_NAME     LAST_NAME       FIRST_NAME
---------------     --------------- ---------------
WELFARE BUREAU      TAFT            WILLIAM
INTERIOR DESIGN     ROOSEVELT       THEODORE
WELFARE BUREAU      ANTHONY         SUSAN
WELFARE BUREAU      ROOSEVELT       ELEANOR
INTERIOR DESIGN     COOLIDGE        CALVIN
POLITICAL SCIEN     JOHNSON         LYNDON
WELFARE BUREAU      REAGAN          RONALD
INTERIOR DESIGN     BUSH            GEORGE
POLITICAL SCIEN     JOHNSON         ANDREW
POLITICAL SCIEN     CLINTON         WILLIAM
WELFARE BUREAU      CARTER          JIMMY
INTERIOR DESIGN     FORD            GERALD
POLITICAL SCIEN     NIXON           RICHARD
POLITICAL SCIEN     KENNEDY         JOHN
INTERIOR DESIGN     EISENHOWER      DWIGHT
INTERIOR DESIGN     TRUMAN          HAROLD
POLITICAL SCIEN     ROOSEVELT       FRANKLIN
WELFARE BUREAU      HOOVER          HERBERT
POLITICAL SCIEN     WILSON          WOODROW

19 rows selected.
```

When the *join* is requested, Oracle scans the join columns in the two tables, identifying matching records, and retrieving them for the virtual record created by the join. The performance of this process is enhanced if the join columns have been indexed. This consists of defining the column in an index. The rdbms need only to read the index to identify the records to be combined rather than performing tablespace scans.

Forgetting to place the condition statements in the `select` statement will create a *Cartesian join*. This type of join combines each record in the first table to each record in the second table. As an example of the cause of performance degradation, if table 1 has 5000 records and table 2 has 3000, the rdbms will create a virtual table of 15,000,000 records. This causes a great deal of processing and memory usage.

**NOTE** A Cartesian join generally produces worthless data. It also is common for an experienced user such as myself to create this type of join inadvertently. So be careful when joining tables.

**TIP** One technique I use when joining tables is to be certain that I have at least one less join condition than tables to be joined. If I have fewer, I know I am missing a condition. This technique has saved me quite a bit of time in troubleshooting queries. As an example, you might return to Listing 5.1. The *from* clause contains two tables and the *where* clause one statement. If the statement had no condition statements, which would violate this tip, the result would be a Cartesian join.

# Qualifying the Columns

A column name problem often occurs when joining records. Because each table has a column with the same value, it more than likely is the same column and has the same column name. Duplicate column names that exist in the joined tables in a `select` clause cause the problem because the RDBMS does not know from which table to retrieve the data. Oracle aborts the query when this happens.

To solve this problem, the column names need to be preceded by a *qualifier*. It tells the RDBMS which table contains the data. The qualifier can be the name of the table or it can be a table alias. Wherever a duplicate column is used in the `select` statement, a period (.) separates the qualifier and the name of the column. Listing 5.2 contains an example of a qualifier that uses the name of the table.

The table alias is specified in the `from` clause of the `select` statement. By placing the alias immediately after the table name, you name it. The alias can then be used throughout the statement in place of the name of the table. They prove particularly useful when the table names are long, because a short alias eliminates keystrokes. Listing 5.2 illustrates the use of qualifiers and table aliases.

**Listing 5.2 L_05_02.sql—Joining Tables Using Qualifiers and Aliases**

```
SQL> select employee.fk_department, department_name,
  2  last_name
  3  from employee, department dept
  4  where dept.department = employee.fk_department;

FK_D    DEPARTMENT_NAME    LAST_NAME
----    ---------------    ---------------
INT     INTERIOR DESIGN    COOLIDGE
POL     POLITICAL SCIEN    JOHNSON
WEL     WELFARE BUREAU     REAGAN
INT     INTERIOR DESIGN    BUSH
POL     POLITICAL SCIEN    JOHNSON
POL     POLITICAL SCIEN    CLINTON
WEL     WELFARE BUREAU     CARTER
INT     INTERIOR DESIGN    FORD
POL     POLITICAL SCIEN    NIXON
POL     POLITICAL SCIEN    KENNEDY
INT     INTERIOR DESIGN    EISENHOWER
INT     INTERIOR DESIGN    TRUMAN
POL     POLITICAL SCIEN    ROOSEVELT
WEL     WELFARE BUREAU     HOOVER
POL     POLITICAL SCIEN    WILSON
WEL     WELFARE BUREAU     TAFT
INT     INTERIOR DESIGN    ROOSEVELT
WEL     WELFARE BUREAU     ANTHONY
WEL     WELFARE BUREAU     ROOSEVELT

19 rows selected.
```



In the preceding example, the employee table does not have an alias. Therefore, the table name is used as the qualifier for fk_department_number in the `where` and `select` clauses. The department table has an alias called dept. The department table qualifier is used in the `where` clause.

The example did not contain any duplicated column names, and did not actually need qualifiers. Both tables have a column that contains a department number, but the characters "fk" precede the column in the employee table. This is a common acronym used to denote that the column is a foreign key. Using this type of acronym reduces the need for qualifiers and aliases. This in turn reduces the amount of typing to produce a statement.

# Working with Multiple Joins

The number of tables that can be joined is not limited. In fact, you can include the same table in the `from` clause numerous times. This commonly occurs when you have description tables similar to the department table in a database. I have a system where I am employed that has a work order table with columns for five employee ids. The columns record the person performing a particular step in the approval process. I often have to produce a report that lists these employees by name. Since the names are not recorded on the work order table, I must join the four columns that contain payroll numbers to the employee table five times in order to acquire the employee's last name. Each join retrieves a different last name based on a column in the base table._When I do this, the duplicated table must have a unique qualifier. In this example I use T1, T2, T3, T4, and T5. Listing 5.3 illustrates this technique.

**Listing 5.3 L_05_03.TXT—Joining the Same Table Five Times**

```
select wo.work_order, t1.last_name, t2.last_name, t3.last_name,
  t4.last_name, t5.authorizer
from work order wo, employee t1, employee t2, employee t3,
     employee t4, employee t5
where wo.requestor = t1.payroll_number
    and wo.preparer = t2.payroll_number
    and wo.reviewer = t3.payroll_number
    and wo.approver = t4.payroll_number
   and wo.authorizer = t5.payroll_number;

This is an example only and cannot be produced from the practice database.  The
practice database does not have the data fields to support such a five table
join.
```

When joining multiple tables, it is easy to forget join conditions. Remember the rule discussed earlier: When tables are joined by one column only, the number of join conditions should be one less than the number of tables in the `from` clause.

# Unexpected Results with Joining Tables in a One-to-Many Relationship

When performing joins, sometimes the novice developer (and experienced developer) gets unexpected results. Duplicate records may appear, numeric calculations may be in error, and expected records may disappear. These problems result when join tables have a one-to-many relationship and related value(s) in one of the tables is optional. Suppose, for example, that you want to produce a listing of first and last names of the employees that have purchased tools. One method is to join the employee and tools tables. This results in a listing of the employees that have records in the tools table. Each record that matches the join criteria satisfies the criteria for the listing. Employees that have purchased multiple tools, however, are listed more than once because the rdbms creates a virtual record for each match. The developer may have expected to see one record for each employee with tools, but actually saw more than one. When tables in a one-to-many relationship are joined, the table on the many side determines the number of virtual records created. This can cause a problem if the developer is not careful.

**TIP** The use of the distinct keyword in the *select* clause will solve the preceding problem. Another method would be to avoid the join and use a subquery in the *where* clause. The primary query uses the employee table. The *where* clause contains an *in* evaluation operator. The operator uses a subquery that selects the payroll numbers from the tools table.

## Inaccurate Calculations Caused by a Table Join

In another example, if you want to calculate the number of departments that have employees purchasing tools, you can use a three table join. The tables will consist of employee, department, and tools. This join will produce a list of the departments. Listing 5.4. shows the result of this query.

**Listing 5.4 L_05_04.sql—Joining Three Tables and Getting the Wrong Number of Departments**

```
SQL> select count(department)
  2  from employee, department, tools
  3  where department = fk_department
  4    and payroll_number = fk_payroll_number;

COUNT(DEPARTMENT)
-----------------
               34
```

The answer to the preceding query is 34 departments, yet only 5 departments are in the department table. It cannot possibly be the correct answer. The reason for the miscalculation is that the query actually counts the number of records in the tool database, because the joins create a virtual record for each record in the tools database. Each tool record has a matching employee record, and each employee record has a department record.



**NOTE** If you would like to see the 34 virtual records, change the *select* clause in Listing 5.4 to select department, tool_name. ■

## Problems that Can Occur when the Value Exists in Only One of the Joined Tables

The next example illustrates a query where some records do not appear when expected. The query attempts to display the department names and the number of employees in the departments (see Listing 5.5).

One department, "CENSUS DEPT," does not appear. It was not listed because it does not have any employees and the join condition between the department and employee tables evaluates to false. This causes the record to not appear in the listing.

**Listing 5.5 L_05_05.sql—Joining Tables when the Value Is Contained in Only One of the Tables**

```
SQL> select department_name, count(*)
  2  from employee, department
  3  where fk_department = department
  4  group by department_name;

DEPARTMENT_NAME COUNT(*)
--------------- ---------
INTERIOR DESIGN         6
POLITICAL SCIEN         7
WELFARE BUREAU          6
```

**NOTE** This is a very common problem when joining tables. The base table has a value and the related table does not. Oracle has a number of tools that help you retrieve the data sets you actually want. One of these is the *outer join*, discussed in more detail in the next section. You can use the outer join to correct the problem of the missing department in Listing 5.5. The count (distinct department_number) also corrects the problem. I have made these mistakes countless times in my queries, so I'd like to caution you to always double check your results before giving them to others. This may save you some embarrassment.

## Performance Problems Caused by Nonmatching Data Formats

The last potential problem topic to discuss is performance. It is always more efficient to join columns that have been indexed. The RDBMS will use the indexes to match records instead of performing tablespace scans. A tablespace scan is a procedure where the rdbms reads every byte in a table. They should be avoided like the plague. An index scan will reduce the time needed to locate records. Sometimes I have had to use a `substr` function on a value in the join condition. When you alter the value, you also destroy the capability to use the item's index. This hurts performance. You cannot correct these problems by using SQL techniques. You must correct them when designing the database. When designing your tables, therefore, remember to look at the join columns to be certain that they are properly formatted for maximum performance.

**TIP** When designing tables, be sure that join columns have the same format and length. A partial value in varchar2(7) column will not match a char(7) format.

# Outer Joins

When joining tables, sometimes you want to retrieve records from one of the tables even though it does not have a matching record in the other table. You cannot accomplish this with a regular join because the join operator is an equal sign and the conditional statement must evaluate to true to be selected. If a record has a value that does not exist in the join column of the other table, Oracle assigns a null value to the missing column value. When the condition evaluation is done, the result is false and the record is not selected. In the practice database, if you join the department table to the employee table, you cannot see the Census department listed because it currently has no To select the Census department along with the other departments, you can use a technique called an *outer join*. An *outer join* is used by Oracle7 to select records that do not have a matching record in the related table. Oracle enables you to indicate an outer join by placing a plus sign (+) after the name of the column in the *where* clause that has the missing values. Only one of the columns in the conditional statement may have the symbol. You can use the symbol on multiple condition statements if necessary. The columns expected to be retrieved from the missing record will have null values. Listing 5.6 illustrates an outer join.

**Listing 5.6 L_05_06.sql—Joining Tables with an Outer Join**

```
SQL> select department_name, last_name, first_name
  2  from employee, department
  3  where department = fk_department(+)
  4  order by 1;

DEPARTMENT_NAME  LAST_NAME        FIRST_NAME
---------------  ---------------  ---------------
CENSUS DEPT
INTERIOR DESIGN  ROOSEVELT        THEODORE
INTERIOR DESIGN  COOLIDGE         CALVIN
INTERIOR DESIGN  FORD             GERALD
INTERIOR DESIGN  TRUMAN           HAROLD
INTERIOR DESIGN  EISENHOWER       DWIGHT
INTERIOR DESIGN  BUSH             GEORGE
POLITICAL SCIEN  JOHNSON          LYNDON
POLITICAL SCIEN  JOHNSON          ANDREW
POLITICAL SCIEN  CLINTON          WILLIAM
POLITICAL SCIEN  KENNEDY          JOHN
POLITICAL SCIEN  NIXON            RICHARD
POLITICAL SCIEN  WILSON           WOODROW
POLITICAL SCIEN  ROOSEVELT        FRANKLIN
TREASURY DEPAR
WELFARE BUREAU   TAFT             WILLIAM
WELFARE BUREAU   REAGAN           RONALD
WELFARE BUREAU   ANTHONY          SUSAN
WELFARE BUREAU   HOOVER           HERBERT
WELFARE BUREAU   CARTER           JIMMY

DEPARTMENT_NAME  LAST_NAME        FIRST_NAME
---------------  ---------------  ---------------
WELFARE BUREAU   ROOSEVELT        ELEANOR

21 rows selected.
```

**NOTE** My students often ask me how do you know which of the tables should have the outer join symbol? The answer is the table that contains the column as a foreign key. This table is the related table. In a relational database, the record in this table is generally optional, thus there is a chance that the base table may not have a matching value in the related table.

# Set Operators

Relational databases were founded on set theory. In *set theory*, combinations of observations in different sets are described through the use of *union* and *intersect* symbols. Oracle uses these same terms, providing three set operators used to acquire data or records from multiple sets.

The set operators are Union, Intersect, and Minus. The Union operator combines records returned from two *select* statements. The Intersect operator deducts records from the two sets that do not exist in both sets. The Minus operator returns the records that exist in the first set but do not exist in the second set. The following sections illustrate these operators.

## Unions

The *Union* operator combines data from the two *select* statements it separates. If the two sets have duplicate records or records with the same value, the duplicates are eliminated. The set operators are concerned only with the virtual records and columns returned by the *select* statements. When two records have the same values in the returned columns, one of the records is eliminated even if it has columns in the database table that are different. The *Union* operator does not display duplicate records, and you do not have to make certain that the two *select* statements have mutually exclusive `where` clauses.

**TIP** I find this operator extremely useful when I want to retrieve records from a table and I want to add different text literals to sets of the records. The union operator enables me to acquire multiple sets of records from the table, add different literals, and combine them into a virtual table for presentation. Listing 5.7 is an example of this procedure. The employee database has employees that were born in the nineteenth and twentieth centuries. The employees in the latter set will have the literal "Born Prior to 1900" added to the record. Records in the latter set will have the literal "Born After 1900."

**Listing 5.7 L_05_07.SQL—Combining Tables Using the Union OperatorSQL> Column Bday Format A15**

```
SQL> column birth_date noprint
SQL> select 'BORN PRIOR TO 1900' a, last_name,
       first_name, to_char(birth_date, 'DD-MON-YYYY') bday,
       birth_date
     from employee
     where birth_date < to_date('01-JAN-1900', 'DD-MON-YYYY')
     union
     select 'BORN AFTER 1900' b, last_name,
       first_name, to_char(birth_date, 'DD-MON-YYYY') bday,
```

```
  birth_date
from employee
where birth_date >= to_date('01-JAN-1900', 'DD-MON-YYYY')
order by 5 desc;

A                  LAST_NAME       FIRST_NAME      BDAY
------------------ --------------- --------------- ---------------
BORN AFTER 1900    CLINTON         WILLIAM         03-APR-1940
BORN AFTER 1900    REAGAN          RONALD          01-OCT-1924
BORN AFTER 1900    KENNEDY         JOHN            29-MAY-1917
BORN AFTER 1900    CARTER          JIMMY           14-JUL-1913
BORN AFTER 1900    FORD            GERALD          09-JAN-1913
BORN AFTER 1900    BUSH            GEORGE          06-FEB-1911
BORN AFTER 1900    JOHNSON         LYNDON          27-AUG-1908
BORN AFTER 1900    NIXON           RICHARD         27-AUG-1908
BORN PRIOR TO 1900 EISENHOWER      DWIGHT          14-OCT-1890
BORN PRIOR TO 1900 ROOSEVELT       ELEANOR         11-OCT-1884
BORN PRIOR TO 1900 TRUMAN          HAROLD          08-MAY-1884
BORN PRIOR TO 1900 ROOSEVELT       FRANKLIN        30-JAN-1882
BORN PRIOR TO 1900 HOOVER          HERBERT         10-AUG-1874
BORN PRIOR TO 1900 COOLIDGE        CALVIN          01-JUL-1872
BORN PRIOR TO 1900 ROOSEVELT       THEODORE        27-OCT-1858
BORN PRIOR TO 1900 TAFT            WILLIAM         15-SEP-1857
BORN PRIOR TO 1900 WILSON          WOODROW         28-DEC-1856
BORN PRIOR TO 1900 ANTHONY         SUSAN           15-FEB-1820
BORN PRIOR TO 1900 JOHNSON         ANDREW          29-DEC-1808

19 rows selected.
```



When the `select` statement in Listing 5.7 is performed, the RDBMS performs the first query, and then performs the second query. The results of the two are then compared, the duplicates are eliminated, and the RDBMS combines the records into one virtual table that can then be sorted and displayed. The first expression or column of the virtual table is named after the column or alias in the first column of the first select. The remaining columns take their name from the columns in the first select statement.

The syntax of the statement requires the two statements be separated by the Union operator. The statement can contain as many unioned queries as necessary. Each of the selects must have the same number of columns or expressions, and each of the columns must have the same format as the comparable column in subsequent statements. You cannot mix numeric columns with character columns. The columns do not need to have the same column names or aliases. Oracle uses the column names or aliases from the first select as the name of the columns and the default headings. Each select should have its own `group by` clause if necessary, but only the last statement can contain the `order` *by* clause. The `order by` at the end of statement orders all the records acquired. Finally, only the last `select` statement contains the semicolon. Placing this earlier in the statement causes Oracle to execute the statement at that point and to ignore subsequent statements.

**NOTE** If you would like to select all the rows from the two tables, including the duplicate records, changing the operator to *union all* causes the rdbms to leave these records in the retrieved set. ■

## Minus

You can use the Minus set operator to extract a set of records that exist in the first group but do not exist in the second group. Oracle performs the two selects and then compares the records. Those that exist in the first set and also exist in second set are eliminated along with the records that exist in the second set only.

This technique proves useful for testing one table to determine whether the value exists in the other. In Listing 5.8, the statement produces a list of departments that do not have any employees.

**Listing 5.8 L_05_08.SQL—Using the Minus Operator to Discard Common Values**

```
SQL> select department, department_name
  2    from department
  3  minus
  4  select fk_department, department_name
  5  from employee, department
  6  where fk_department = department;

DEPA DEPARTMENT_NAME
---- ---------------
CEN  CENSUS DEPT
TRF  TREASURY DEPAR
```

In this example, you needed to do a join in the second query to produce the same number of columns and values. The same syntax and rules apply to the Minus operator as apply to the Union operator. When you requested the department_name column in the first query, you also had to have the department_name appear in the second query. This means that you had to do a join between the employee and department table to produce the proper number of columns and values that can be evaluated.

**TIP** The Minus operator is equivalent to the *not in* conditional operator. You may find that the Minus operator increases your performance because it does not have to scan the virtual table created by the *not in* operator for every row of the major select.

## Intersect

The `intersect` operator retrieves records that two select statements have in common. It deletes the records in memory unique to each set. The `Intersect` operator requires the same syntax and rules as used for the *Minus* and *Union* operators. Listing 5.9 illustrates a `select` statement that retrieves records for employees that have purchased both glasses and tools. This requires the `select` statement to check the existence of employee records in both the glasses and tools tables. It uses the *Intersect* operator in a subquery to perform this check.

**Listing 5.9 L_05_09.SQL—Using the Intersect Operator to Select Common Records**

```
SQL> select last_name, first_name
  2  from employee
  3  where payroll_number in
  4    (select payroll_number from glasses
  5      intersect
  6     select payroll_number from tools);

LAST_NAME       FIRST_NAME
--------------- ---------------
COOLIDGE        CALVIN
JOHNSON         LYNDON
REAGAN          RONALD
BUSH            GEORGE
JOHNSON         ANDREW
CLINTON         WILLIAM
CARTER          JIMMY
FORD            GERALD
NIXON           RICHARD
KENNEDY         JOHN
EISENHOWER      DWIGHT
TRUMAN          HAROLD
ROOSEVELT       FRANKLIN
HOOVER          HERBERT
WILSON          WOODROW
TAFT            WILLIAM
ROOSEVELT       THEODORE
ANTHONY         SUSAN
ROOSEVELT       ELEANOR

19 rows selected.
```



# Combining Data with Oracle8

Oracle8 has features that allow the developer to define how data will combined. This eases the burden of combining and retrieving the data later. For instance, if you wanted to produce a report listing the employees names and the eyeglass purchases, a select statement joining the employee and glasses table must be written.

This join can be eliminated using Oracle8. The attributes or fields in the employee and glasses table can be defined into one object. The `select` statement can be executed against the object. The name of the object is treated as a tablename. Because the object knows how the data within the object is related, the developer does not need to worry about join conditions. Of course, if the query is combining the data from two or more objects, the same join techniques outlined in this chapter may be used to combine attributes from the objects.

The new Oracle8 object technology has the ability to reduce the complexity of many queries, but as long as the world is comprised of different objects, the developer will still need to use the techniques outlined in this chapter to combine data into information.

# Summary

This chapter covered combining rows from different tables through the use of a join. Multiple tables are included in the `from` clause, and the join condition is recorded in the `where` clause. When the tables contain columns with the same name, you must qualify the columns with the name of the table. Performance problems and unexpected results can occur when using joins. You can use the outer join symbol (+) to select a record that does not have a matching value in the other table. You place the outer join symbol after the column name in the where clause that does not contain the value.

The set operators *Union*, *Minus* and *Intersect*, are used to combine records from multiple tables. *Union* combines records from the tables discarding any duplicated records. The *Minus* operator selects records from the first table that do not exist in the second. The Intersect operator selects records that exist in both tables.

# From Here...

The next chapter discusses how to set up the database. The chapter covers the methods of creating, altering, and dropping the various objects. It also covers the attributes and settings of the various objects. It discusses database constraints used to maintain database integrity. In the following chapter, you will learn how to set up the user account, tablespace, tables, and indexes.

# Review Questions

1. Produce a listing of the employees who have purchased tools. The report should also list the tools these employees purchased.
2. Develop a report that you can pass out to each of the employees. The report should list the tools that were purchased. Be certain to include the employee's department name in the heading of the report.
3. Produce a listing of departments and the amount of money spent by each department to purchase glasses for its employees. The listing should be in descending order with the highest department at the top of the list.
4. Develop a query that lists the employees and the most recent date they purchased a tool and the most recent date they purchased a pair of glasses.

5. Develop a report similar to #2, except include the employee's glasses on the report.
6. Produce a list of employees that have purchased tools but not glasses.
7. Produce a list of employees by department that have purchased glasses but not tools.
8. Produce a list of employees by department that have purchased both glasses and tools.

CHAPTER 6

# Defining the Database Objects

**Managing the database table**

This section covers the tasks needed to manage a table. This consists of the definition of the items contained in a table. The section also covers the create, alter, and drop table commands.

**Creating and dropping indexes, views, synonyms, and creating database links**

This section covers the create and drop index commands. Indexes are used to increase database performance and ensure primary key uniqueness.

**Creating tablespaces, user accounts and granting database privileges**

This section covers the create and drop tablespace and user commands. Tablespaces identify the area and size of the hard disk used by the database. User accounts are used to designate the owner of the database objects. This section will also covers the grant and revoke privilege commands. These commands enable users to perform functions within the database.

**Creating the tablespace**

This section covers the create and drop tablespace commands. Tablespaces identify the area and size of the hard disk used by the database.

This chapter switches the emphasis from selecting data from the database to defining the tables and objects in the database. More specifically, this chapter covers techniques for creating, altering, and deleting tables, indexes, synonyms, and views. This is done in SQL*PLUS by using Data Definition Language (DDL) commands. This chapter also discusses table constraints, which are important devices for maintaining the integrity of the database. Finally, this chapter covers the commands to create user ids and tablespaces. After reading the chapter, you should have an understanding of the commands needed to create a database. The installment at the end of the chapter will give you an opportunity to create an actual database. ■

# Defining the Table Items

Oracle tables consist of one or more columns or fields. A column is a named cell within a record that contains a value. The columns are defined with a format or characteristic that allows for their most efficient use. Columns generally have character or numeric formats. The initial definition occurs in the *create table* command. This command consists of a series of column or field names and their data format. It is important to define these columns with the proper format. The format of the items determines their ease of use. It is very difficult, for instance, to sort records based on a column defined as character but populated with numeric characters. A character value of '9' has a higher sort value than a character value of '11.' This means that as you sort the column, the '11' appears before the '9' because character columns are sorted by position. Changing the '9' to '09' will change the sort order. This new value will have a lower sort order since a '0' is less than a '1.' If the developer wants the values to sort properly without having to enter the '0,' a numeric format should be used. Figure 6.1 illustrates the differences in sorting numeric and character values.

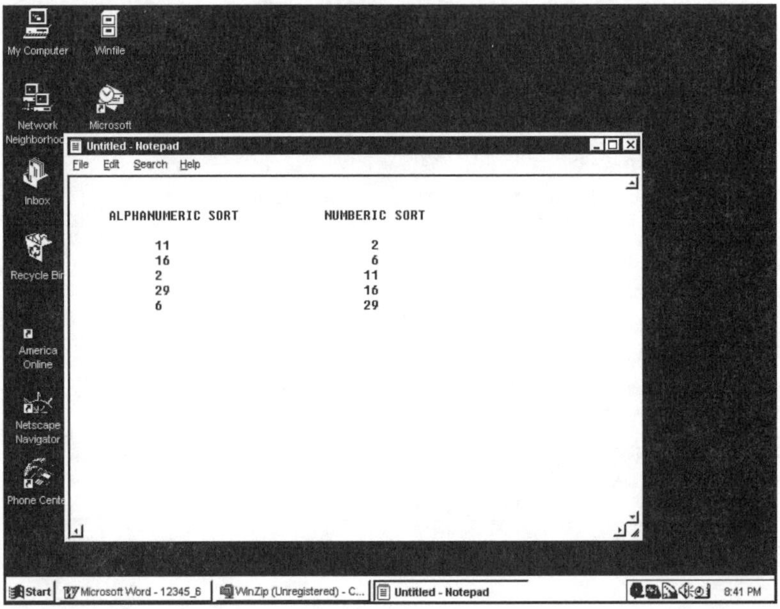


**FIG. 6.1**
Sorting alphanumeric versus numeric columns.

Columns defined numerically are evaluated in their entirety. The preceding sorting problem does not occur. With numeric columns, your concern is the size of the value and its precision. *Precision* is the number of decimal positions. Columns defined with one decimal position cannot contain a value with three positions. Columns that contain dates should be defined as a *date*. *DATE* is a special numeric format that stores the value as a number but displays the value in an alphanumeric format. The default format is 'DD-MON-YY' as in '08-APR-51.'

It is important to try to define the column formats correctly when the tables are created. If you need to change them, however, Oracle enables you to do it. Be aware, however, that special problems occur when the columns contain values and the format is changed to numeric or is made smaller. The section on the *alter table* command discusses this in more detail.

Table 6.1 contains the valid column formats.

**Table 6.1 Valid Data Types**

| Data Type | Description |
|---|---|
| char(*n*) | Defines a fixed length alphanumeric column of length (*n*). The maximum size is 255 characters. The default is 1 byte. |
| date | Defines a date format. It accepts valid dates from January 1, 4712 BC to December 31, 4712 AD. |
| decimal | Same as the NUMBER data type. It does not accept size or decimal digits as an argument. |
| float | Same as the NUMBER data type. |
| integer | Same as the NUMBER data type. It defines the value as a whole number and does not accept decimal digits as an argument. |
| integer(*size*) | Specifies an integer data type of the length specified in the *size* value. |
| long | Defines a character data type up to 65,535 characters. Only one LONG column may be defined per table. This type of column may not be used in subqueries, functions, expressions, where clauses, or indexes. |
| long raw | The same as LONG, except it contains raw binary data. |
| long varchar | The same data type as LONG. |
| mlslabel | Four-byte representation of a secure operating system label. |
| number | Defines a numeric data type with space for 40 digits, and a space for a sign and a decimal point. The numbers may be expressed in two manners: with numbers from 0 to 9, the signs + and -, and a decimal point; and in scientific notation (1.951E4 as 19510). |
| number(*size*) | Defines a number column that contains the number of digits equal to the value in *size*. The maximum number of digits is 105. |
| number(*size, d*) | Defines a number column that contains the number of digits equal to the value in *size* and contains the number of decimal position specified in *d*. A format specification of number(3,2) cannot contain a number greater than 9.99. |
| number(*) | The same data type as number. |
| smallint | The same data type as number. |

*continues*

**Table 6.1 Continued**

| Data Type | Description |
|---|---|
| raw(*size*) | Defines the column to contain raw binary data with a length specified in the value in *size*. |
| raw mlslabel | Defines the column as a binary format for secure operating system label. |
| varchar2(*size*) | Defines a variable length character string having a maximum length of the value specified in *size*. |

The *varchar2* and *char* data types are used to define the format of character or alphanumeric columns. They are not the same types of format. The *varchar2* format is variable length. This means that the amount of bytes the item actually uses equals the actual characters in the field. The unused spaces in the item contain null spaces. The column defined as *char* uses all the spaces in its definition. Spaces not occupied by a character contain "white space." White space is an invisible character similar to the space produced by pressing the space bar. A column defined as *varchar2(5)* that contains the characters 'ABC,' for example, is 3 bytes. On the other hand, a column defined as *char(5)* that contains the same characters has a size of 5 bytes. The values in the two columns are also not equal because the *varchar2* column has null values in position 4 and 5, while the *char* columns contains white space in these positions. It is very difficult to join *varchar2* columns to *char* columns because of this white space / nulls difference.

**TIP** The varchar2 definition is generally used for character fields not used for searching purposes or that do not have a long length. I always define columns that contain text or notes as varchar2(2000). This enables the user to enter a maximum of 2,000 characters into the item, but only takes up the actual disk space for the number of characters contained in the field. I use the char definition for fields such as zip code, phone number, or social security number because they are fixed length fields.

# Creating, Altering, and Dropping Tables

You can use the *create table* command to construct relational tables. You execute the command from SQL*PLUS. Listing 6.1 illustrates the *create table* command. This command defines a table similar to the employee table used throughout this book.

**Listing 6.1 Creating a Table**

```
SQL> create table ex_employee
  2    (payroll_number                 number(4),
  3     last_name                      varchar2(15),
  4     first_name                     varchar2(15),
  5     absences                       number(2),
  6     wages                          number(8,2),
```

```
  7      street                         varchar2(20),
  8      city                           varchar2(15),
  9      state                          char(2),
 10      phone                          char(13),
 11      social_security_number         char(11),
 12      employment_date                date,
 13      birth_date                     date,
 14      current_position               varchar2(15),
 15      fk_department                  char(4));
Table created.
```

**N O T E**  To execute any database commands including logging on to Oracle, the developer must have a user id and must be granted appropriate privileges. A user id with database administrator authority is needed to create the user id and grant the privileges. If you are using a trial copy of Personnel Oracle7, the system/manager id has the database administrator authority. The system/manager user id has the authority to create most of the database items in this chapter. For more discussion on user ids and granting privileges, see those sections within this chapter. ■

The command starts with the keywords *create table*, followed by the name of the table. The name must start with a letter of the alphabet, but it can contain letters, numbers, and underscores in one continuous string. The length of the name may be 1 to 30 characters. The names of the columns appear next. They have the same restrictions as the table names. The column names are enclosed by parentheses and separated by a comma. Each column name must be unique to the table. They do not have to be unique to the database. You cannot use Oracle-reserved words such as *resource* as a column name. Following the column name, the data type is defined. The column definition may also contain a constraint such as *not null*. This means that the item must always contain a value. Following the column definitions, an optional tablespace statement may be included. Inclusion of this statement causes the table to be created in a tablespace other than the default. Finally, a semi-colon completes the statement.

To erase or eliminate the table, use the *drop table* command.   Listing 6.2 provides an example of the *drop table* command. This command eliminates the table created in Listing 6.1. It will no longer be needed. The *drop* command does not contain any parameters. The command is used when the table is no longer needed or when a column is eliminated from the table. Columns cannot be eliminated from a table after it is created. In order to eliminate a column, the table must be dropped, the create command redefined without the column, and the table recreated. The data can then be reloaded into the table. The following section will further describe how to do this.

Part

II

Ch

6

### Listing 6.2   L_06_02.sql—Dropping the ex_employee Table

```
SQL> drop table ex_employee;
Table dropped.
```

# Altering the Table

After you create the table, you may need to add or modify columns. To accomplish this, use the *alter table* command and the *add* and *modify* options. The former option is used to add columns or constraints to the table. The latter is used to modify the existing columns. Columns that contain data may not be changed from character to numeric or decreased in size. They may only be increased in size. Listing 6.3 contains examples of various alter table commands.

**Listing 6.3 L_06_03.SQL—Modifying the Employee Table by Using the Alter Command**

```
SQL> alter table employee add hair_color char(1);

Table altered.

SQL> alter table employee modify hair_color char(2);
Table altered.
```

You can add and modify multiple columns by using the same alter table command. You cannot, however, delete columns with the alter table command. To delete columns, you must drop the table and redefine it. Of course, dropping the table causes the data it contains to be destroyed. You can copy the data to another table temporarily by using the *create table* command in conjunction with a *Select* statement. The data is reloaded into the redefined and recreated table by using an *insert* command. This command will be discussed in the next chapter. Listing 6.4 illustrates the copy technique.

**Listing 6.4 L_06_04.sql—Using the Create Table and Select Statements to Copy a Table**

```
SQL> create table temp_employee
  2    as select * from employee;

Table created.

SQL> select * from temp_employee;

PAYROLL_NUMBER LAST_NAME       FIRST_NAME       ABSENCES      WAGES STREET
-------------- --------------- ---------------- -------- ---------- -------------------
CITY            ST PHONE          SOCIAL_SECU EMPLOYMEN BIRTH_DAT CURRENT_POSITIO FK_D GE
--------------- -- ------------ ----------- --------- --------- --------------- ---- --
            23 TAFT            WILLIAM                 2       8500 1234 RIVERFRONT RD
CINCINNATI      OH 234-632-7806  340-90-9856 01-JUN-08 15-SEP-57 VICE PRESIDENT  WEL

.
.
```

```
19 rows selected.
SQL> drop table temp_employee;
Table dropped.
```

# Defining Table Constraints

Oracle enables the developer to set constraints on tables by using the create table statement. Constraints are important devices that enable you to maintain a strong database. You can use them to ensure that the primary key column(s) are unique to the table and always contain a value. Constraints are also used to maintain referential integrity. This means that the values in a foreign key column must exist as a value in a primary key column of another table. The constraint commands even cause dependant child records to be deleted when the parent record is deleted. Primary and foreign keys are discussed in Chapter 2.

**TIP** An imporatant database concept is that it is *always* better to let the database keep itself clean of bad data than having the applications perform this task. Programming errors are easy to make. The potential always exists that holes in the program logic will allow bad data into the database. Constraints make it much more difficult for this to occur. It is easier to define table constraints than to write and test the code that totally prevents corrupt data.

As an example, suppose you developed an application that allowed the operator to delete a record from a base table that has children's records in a related table. This will cause the related table to have orphan records. This can be prevented by placing logic in the application that prevents the base records from being deleted when children's records exist. This code can be complex. Placing a table constraint in the table definition is easier to write and is much more fool-proof.

Table 6.2 contains valid table constraints that you can use with the *create table* command.

**Table 6.2 Table Constraints**

| Constraint | Description |
|---|---|
| check | Ensures the values meet a specific range. |
| default | Places a default value into the column. |
| foreign key | Ensures the value(s) exists as a value in the primary key column of another table. When used with the *on delete cascade* setting, this constraint causes the record to be deleted when the parent record is deleted. |
| not null | Ensures the value always contains a value. |
| primary key | Ensures the value(s) is not null and unique to the table. |
| unique | Ensures the value is unique to the table. |

## The Check Constraint

The *check* constraint causes Oracle to evaluate new values that will be recorded in the table against a set of conditions. To define conditions, use the same operators as used in the *where* clause of the *Select* statement. The *in* operator, for example, is commonly used to make certain that the column value matches a set of specified values. Listing 6.5 demonstrates several *check* constraints. The *where* clause and conditional operators are discussed in Chapter 4.

**Listing 6.5 L_06_05.sql—Defining Check Constraints as Column Constraints**

```
SQL> create table checkexample
  2     (payroll_number       varchar2(10),
  3     gender                char(1) check (gender in ('M', 'F')),
  4     next_review_date      date,
  5     pay                 number check (pay between 12000 and 16500));

Table created.

SQL> drop table checkexample;
Table dropped.
```

In this example, the value in the gender column must equal an upper-case 'M' or 'F.' The pay value must be between 12,000 and 16,500. If the database evaluates any of these *check* constraints as false, it stops processing the record and issues an error message.

## The Default option

The *default* option causes the rdbms to place a default value into an item when the record is first inserted into the table. As discussed earlier in this book, numeric columns that are null cause problems with column arithmetic unless you use the `nvl` function. The null value occurred because no value was ever put into the item. You can use the *Default* command to ensure that numeric items have a default value of 0, thereby eliminating the need for the `nvl` function. The syntax of the constraint requires the default value to be specified following the *default* word. Listing 6.6 illustrates the use of this command.

**Listing 6.6 L_06_06.TXT—Defining a Default Constraint**

```
SQL> create table defaultexamp
  2     (payroll_number    varchar2(10),
  3      wages             number default(0));

Table created.

SQL> drop table defaultexamp;
Table dropped.
```

## The Foreign Key Constraint

The *foreign key* constraint is extremely useful for maintaining the referential integrity of the database. This constraint ensures the value contained in the column exists as a unique value or primary key in a column of another table. When the foreign key consists of one item, you can define it as a column constraint or as a table constraint. Defining it as a column constrain just require that the keyword *references* follows the column format. When the column it validates against is a primary key, the table name follows this word. Listing 6.7 illustrates this syntax. When the column validated against is not the primary key, the name of this validated against column must follow the name of the table and be enclosed by parentheses.

**Listing 6.7 L_06_07.TXT—Defining a Foreign Key Constraint as a Column Constraint**

```
SQL> create table example
  2    (fk_payroll_number number references employee,
  3     tool_name           varchar2(20));

Table created.

SQL> drop table example;

Table dropped.
```

**The Foreign Key Table Constraint** When the foreign key consists of multiple columns, you must define it as a table constant. Table constraints are placed after the last column definition. The definition begins with the words *foreign key* followed by the name(s) of the column(s) that will be constrained. These names are enclosed by parentheses. This is followed by the word *references* followed by the table name. As in column definitions, the name of the column validated against is only necessary if it is not the primary key. Listing 6.8 illustrates the definition of a foreign key table constraint clause.

**Listing 6.8 L_06_08.TXT—Defining a Foreign Key Constraint as a Table Constraint**

```
SQL> create table foreignkeyexamp
  2    (fk_payroll_number   number,
  3     tool_name            varchar2(20),
  4     foreign key (fk_payroll_number)
  5     references employee (payroll_number));

Table created.

SQL> drop table foreignkeyexamp;
Table dropped.
```

**The On Delete Cascade Option** Another component of the *foreign key* constraint is the *on delete cascade* option. When it is specified, the record is deleted from the table when the row it depends on is deleted in the parent table. This is an important option because it keep orphans from existing in the database. It also relieves the developer from having to write code that deletes records from dependant tables. You should be glad that you can avoid this complex task. Listing 6.9 illustrates the *on delete cascade* column. This option causes records to be deleted from the ondelete table when the record has a value that does not exist in the employee table.

**Listing 6.9 L_06_09.TXT—Defining the On Delete Cascade Option in a Foreign Key Table Constraint**

```
SQL> create table ondelete
  2    (fk_payroll_number       number,
  3     tool_name               varchar2(20),
  4     foreign key (fk_payroll_number)
  5     references employee (payroll_number)
  6     on delete cascade);

Table created.

SQL> drop table ondelete;
Table dropped.
```

**NOTE** One final word on the *foreign key* constraint concerns the order of creating tables. When the *foreign key* constraint is placed in the *create table* statement, Oracle checks to see whether the parent table exists. If it does not, Oracle will not create the table. You must always create the parent tables before the child tables that contain the constraint.

## The Not Null Constraint

The *not null* constraint ensures that the column always contains a value. Oracle will not allow a record to be inserted or updated if the constrained column contains a null value. Proper database design requires the primary key column(s) to always have this constraint. The syntax of this constraint consists of the words *not null* following the column's data type definition. Listing 6.10 illustrates the definition of a *not null* constraint.

**Listing 6.10 L_06_10.TXT—Defining a Not Null Column Constraint**

```
SQL> create table ondelete
  2    (fk_payroll_number       number,
  3     tool_name               varchar2(20) not null,
  4     foreign key (fk_payroll_number)
  5     references employee (payroll_number)
  6     on delete cascade);
```

```
Table created.

SQL> drop table ondelete;

Table dropped.
```

## The Unique Constraint

The *unique* constraint ensures that the value placed in the column row is unique to the table. Proper database design requires that the primary key column(s) always contain unique values. This constraint ensures this will happen. When this constraint is defined, Oracle creates an implicit unique index for the column. Implicit means Oracle7 creates and names the index. Before a record is inserted or updated, Oracle scans the index to determine whether the value exists. The syntax of this constraint is the same as *not null*; the keyword *unique* follows the column's data definition. You can specify both the *not null* and *unique* constraints in the same column definition. Listing 6.11 demonstrates the definition of the *unique* constraint. You can also use the constraint on multiple columns. Composite keys are composed of multiple columns, which need to be unique in the combination of their columns when they are also the primary key. The *unique* constraint ensures this requirement. Be aware, however, of a sixteen-column limit to the number of columns that may be included in the unique constraint.

**Listing 6.11 L_06_11.sql—Defining a Unique Constraint as a Column Constraint**

```
SQL> create table ondelete
  2   (fk_payroll_number       number unique,
  3    tool_name               varchar2(20) not null,
  4    foreign key (fk_payroll_number)
  5    references employee (payroll_number)
  6    on delete cascade);

Table created.

SQL> drop table ondelete;

Table dropped.
```

Part II Ch 6

## The Primary Key Constraint

Primary key columns always contain unique and not null values. This means that they need to have both a *unique* and *not null* constraint. Oracle has a *primary key* constraint that defines both of these constraints for you. When the constraint is defined, Oracle creates an implicit unique index on the specified column(s) and defines them not null. When the primary key is one column as it normally is in a base table, you can define the *primary key* constraint as a column constraint. Listing 6.12 illustrates this. When placing the constraint on primary keys that are also composite keys, you must place the definition as a table constraint. The related or child tables usually have composite primary keys and one of the composite key fields is also a foreign key. Listing 6.13 provides an example of defining a *primary key* constraint as a table constraint.

**Listing 6.12 L_06_12.sql—Defining the Primary Key Constraint as a Column Constraint**

```
SQL> create table example
  2    (payroll_number     number primary key,
  3     wages              number default (0));

Table created.

SQL> drop table example;
Table dropped.
```

**Listing 6.13 L_06_13.TXT—Defining the Primary Key Constraint as a Table Constraint**

```
SQL> create table example
  2    (fk_payroll_number          number,
  3     tool_name                  varchar2(20),
  4     primary key (fk_payroll_number, tool_name),
  5     foreign key (fk_payroll_number)
  6     references employee (payroll_number)
  7     on delete cascade);
Table created.
```

# Disabling Constraints

You may need to disable or drop constraints after they have been defined. To accomplish this, use the *alter table* command and the *disable*, *enable*, and *drop* options. After the *disable* option is issued, the referenced constraint is no longer active, but the definition of the constraint remains. You can reactivate it with the *enable* option. If the *drop* option is issued, the definition is eliminated from the database. You can add the constraint to the column, but the *alter table* command will need the full column constraint definition. Listing 6.14 contains examples of several of these options.

**Listing 6.14 L_06_14.TXT—Using the Alter Command to Enable, Disable, Add, and Drop Table Constraints**

```
SQL> alter table example disable primary key;

Table altered.

SQL> alter table example enable primary key;
```

```
Table altered.

SQL> alter table example drop primary key;

Table altered.

SQL> alter table example add primary key
  2   (fk_payroll_number, tool_name);

Table altered.

SQL> drop table example;

Table dropped.
```

# Defining the Index

*Indexes* are mini tables that contain a subset of one or more of a table's columns. You use the index to increase the performance of queries and to ensure uniqueness of values in the specified columns. Performance is enhanced when Oracle has the capability to scan an ordered index table rather than scan the data in the full table. Indexes ensure uniqueness. Oracle does this by scanning the index to determine whether the value exists prior to placing it in the table. Primary keys, foreign keys, and other columns frequently used to select records should be indexed columns.

You can use the *primary key* and *unique* constraints to create implicit indexes. You can implement explicit indexes by using the *create index* command. The syntax of the statement is the keywords *create index* followed by your name of the index, followed by the keyword *on*, the name of the table, and the names of the indexed columns enclosed in parentheses and separated by commas. Listing 6.15 illustrates the definition of an index on the fk_department column of the employee table.



**Listing 6.15 L_06_15.TXT—Creating a Table Index**

```
SQL> create index deptind on employee
  2   (fk_department);

Index created.

SQL> drop index deptind;

Index dropped.
```

You can define a unique index by placing the word *unique* between the words *create index*. Listing 6.16 demonstrates this command. It defines a unique index for the department column on the department table. Dropping the table that contains the indexed column or issuing the *drop* index command destroys indexes. The name of the index follows the command, and a semicolon terminates it.

**Listing 6.16 L_06_16.sql—Creating a Unique Index**

```
SQL> create unique index deptind2 on department
     (department_name);

Index created.

SQL> drop index deptind2;
Index dropped.
```

Remember these rules about indexes: You may index up to 16 columns of a table in a single index; and the name of the index must be unique and follow the same naming convention as used for tables.

# Creating and Dropping Views

*Views* are predefined queries that produce virtual tables or sets of data when executed. The *view* name is used in a *select* statement in place of a table. When Oracle encounters the *view* in the *from* clause, it executes the query to produce the virtual table. You can use *views* to simplify the acquisition of data for the users, to limit access to data, and to compile information that cannot be developed without the use of *views*. Listing 6.17 illustrates the creation of a view that compiles the total cost of each employee's tool purchases.

To define a view, use the *create view* command. The view name, the keyword *as*, and the *select* clause that will be used to produce the data follow the keywords. You do not use the *order by* clause in the view's *select* statement.

Listing 6.17 illustrates the creation of a view that joins the employee table and the tools table. The fourth expression *'sum(cost)'* will have a virtual column name of 'cost.' You use this name when the view is used as a table in a *Select* statement.

**Listing 6.17 L_06_17.sql—Creating a View Called Toolcost**

```
SQL> create view toolcost as
     select payroll_number, last_name,
      first_name, fk_department, sum(tool_cost) cost
     from employee, tools
     where payroll_number = fk_payroll_number(+)
     group by payroll_number, last_name, first_name,
     fk_department;
View created.
```

Listing 6.17 is an example of a view that simplifies the acquisition of data for the user. A user of this view would not have to worry about the joining of the two tables, the sum function, or the group by clause. A simple *select* statement using the view name in the *from* clause produces the results. Finally, this view accesses four columns from the two tables. Granting users access to this view, but not to the employee or department tables, effectively limits their access to data.

Listing 6.18 creates a view that sums the cost of each department's tools. The toolcost view and the deptcost view in Listing 6.19 will produce a virtual table of the employees, the cost of the employee's tools, the total tool cost of the employee's department, and the percentage that the tool cost is of the department's total. This query would be difficult or impossible to produce without the use of views. The reason for the difficulty is that each of the views compute different summary totals. To put these totals on the same row and use them in an arithmetic expression, you need to create the views and join the results.

**Listing 6.18 L_06_18.sql—Creating a View Called Deptcost**

```
SQL> create view deptcost as
  2    select department, sum(tool_cost) deptcost
  3    from department, employee, tools
  4    where payroll_number = fk_payroll_number(+)
  5      and department = fk_department
  6    group by department;
View created.
```

**Listing 6.19 L_06_19.sql—Using the Toolcost and Deptcost View to Produce a Listing**

```
SQL> select department, last_name, first_name,
  2   cost, deptcost, (cost/deptcost)*100 percent
  3   from toolcost, deptcost
  4  where department = fk_department;

DEPA LAST_NAME        FIRST_NAME            COST  DEPTCOST   PERCENT
---- ---------------- --------------- --------- --------- ---------
INT  ROOSEVELT        THEODORE               324     792.2 40.898763
INT  COOLIDGE         CALVIN                  35     792.2 4.4180762
INT  TRUMAN           HAROLD                         792.2
INT  EISENHOWER       DWIGHT                 375     792.2 47.336531
INT  FORD             GERALD                  12     792.2  1.514769
INT  BUSH             GEORGE                46.2     792.2 5.8318606
POL  JOHNSON          ANDREW                16.7    172.15 9.7008423
POL  ROOSEVELT        FRANKLIN                20    172.15 11.617775
POL  KENNEDY          JOHN                          172.15
POL  NIXON            RICHARD               18.5    172.15 10.746442
POL  CLINTON          WILLIAM                       172.15
POL  JOHNSON          LYNDON                        172.15
POL  WILSON           WOODROW             116.95    172.15  67.93494
WEL  ROOSEVELT        ELEANOR              61.95     226.5 27.350993
WEL  CARTER           JIMMY                          226.5
WEL  REAGAN           RONALD                28.7     226.5 12.671082
WEL  TAFT             WILLIAM                 23     226.5 10.154525
WEL  HOOVER           HERBERT                 24     226.5 10.596026
WEL  ANTHONY          SUSAN                88.85     226.5 39.227373
```

19 rows selected.

You cannot alter *views*; you can, however, drop them. To accomplish this, use the *Drop View* command followed by the view name. *Views* are data definitions and do not have any effect on performance because they are only activated when used in a *select* statement. This means that there are no performance reasons for them to be eliminated. You can use the *select name from Tab* command to list the views that you have created.

# Creating Synonyms

A *synonym* is another name for a table or view. You can use it to make a database more user friendly. At the company that I work for, the data administrators and database administrators believe in making the name of tables descriptive. I use a table called the 'T_and_D_Cable_Terminal_Poles,' for example. This name is very cumbersome and time consuming to use. I had the database administrator create a *synonym* for this table called 'CTPS.' This made the use of the table much more user friendly because the slang for the items in the table is 'CTPS,' and I only had to type 4 characters rather than 28 when I used the table. The syntax of the command is *create [public] synonym [user] synonym name for object name.*

Listing 6.20 illustrates the syntax of the command to create a synonym. The word *public* makes the synonym available to all users. When the table or view exists on another Oracle id, the '*user.*' qualifier needs to be used. This tells Oracle where the object exists. Synonyms can also tell Oracle on which server the table is located. This is done by incorporating the datalink into the synonym. The following section discusses the database link further. You use the link in a *Select* statement following the table name. To avoid the cumbersome process of putting a database link in the *from* clause, you can create synonyms that have the database link incorporated. This means that the user does not have to worry about incorporating the link in his *Select* statements. To delete the synonym, use the *Drop Synonym* command. Only DBAs can drop public synonyms or the synonyms of other users.

**Listing 6.20 L_06_20.TXT—Creating a Public Synonym Called CTPS**

```
SQL> create table t_and_d_cable_terminal_poles (ctpnum number);

Table created.

SQL> create public synonym ctps for t_and_d_cable_terminal_poles;

Synonym created.

SQL> drop public synonym ctps;

Synonym dropped.

SQL> drop table t_and_d_cable_terminal_poles;

Table dropped.
```

# Creating Database Links

A *database link* is an object stored in a local database that tells Oracle the name of the remote database that can be accessed through Oracle's SQL*NET. The remote database is the server that contains the table or data. You can access the remote database just like you access local tables, except that you must use the suffix @linkname after the table name. The syntax of this command is contained in Figure 6.2.

**FIG. 6.2**
The syntax of the command to access the remote database.

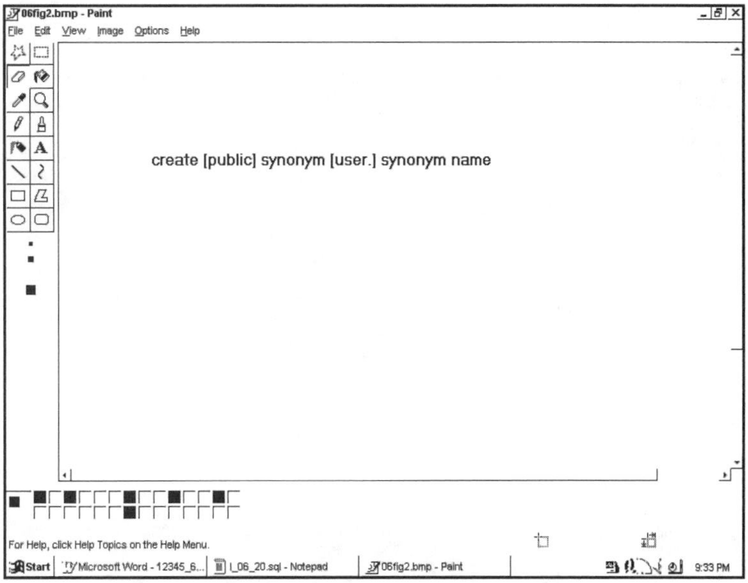


Database administrators are the only ones that have the ability to create *public* links. After public links are created, they are available to all users. Links created without this feature are available to the creator only.

To delete the *database link*, use the *drop database link* command followed by the name of the link. If the link is *public*, you must use the word *public*. Only a database administrator can drop a *public* database link.



# Creating User Accounts

When Oracle is first installed, before you can begin using the product for work, you need to *create* user accounts and *grant* privileges to the user. The user account enables the user to log on to Oracle. The privileges enable the user to create tablespaces, begin defining objects such as tables, indexes, and views, and populate the tables with data.

The database administrator creates user accounts by using the *create* command. Figure 6.3 illustrates the syntax and an example of a *Create* command used to create student I.D.'s for an Oracle class. When the password is supplied, users must supply the password each time they log on. Specifying the *externally* option, the access is verified through the operating system security. The *default tablespace* is the place the user creates objects such as tables, unless specified in the *create table* command. *Temporary tablespace* is where temporary objects are created. The *quota* option enables you to limit the amount of space that a user can allocate. Oracle assigns the default profile to the user unless the *profile* option lists a named profile.

**FIG. 6.3**
Creating a User Account command syntax and example.

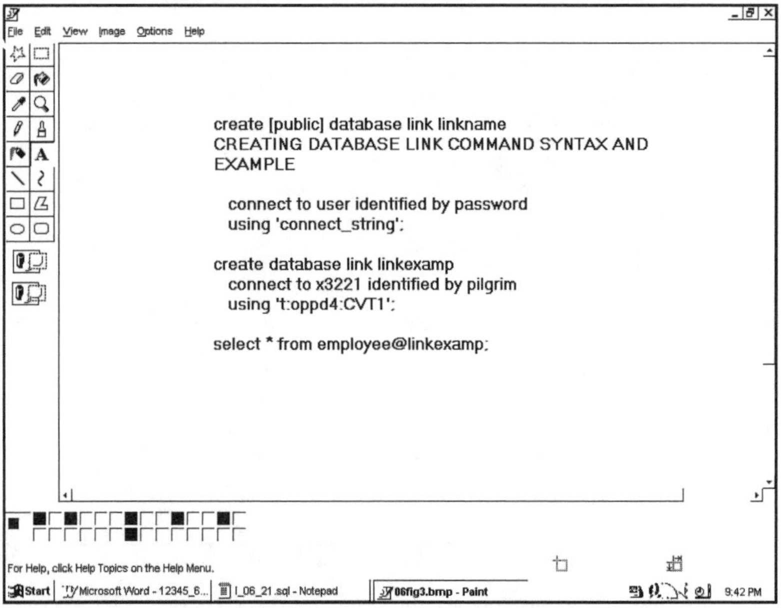


In the example, a user account called ostu6 was created. It requires a password of redskins, uses the tablespace oracle_class as the default, and enables the user to allocate 2M or 20,002,048 bytes.

# Creating Database Privileges

After creating the user account, you must *grant* the account *privileges*. Privileges are permissions to perform various functions. One of these privileges is *create session*. This privilege enables the user to log on to the database. Without granting this privilege, the user account cannot perform any functions.

Two types of privileges exist: system privileges and object privileges. The *system privileges* enable you to perform data definitions commands such as *create table* or *drop index*. You use the *object privileges* to perform data manipulation commands such as *insert*, *update*, and *delete*.

Figure 6.4 displays the two forms of the *grant* command used to give privileges. The two differ in that the command granting object privileges has the *on* clause specifying the object. The command can define several privileges at one time to multiple users. The optional *with admin option* enables the user to grant system privileges to other users.

**FIG. 6.4**
Granting privileges syntax and example.

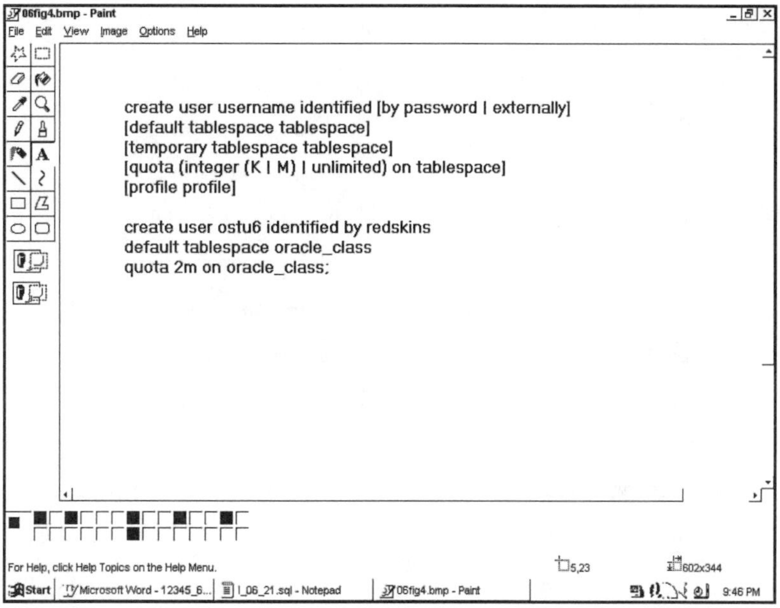


The final statement illustrates a *grant* command that used to grant privileges to students. It gives the user id *ostu1* the ability to perform a number of common functions. Table 6.3 contains privileges available for the users.

**Table 6.3 System Privileges**

| Privilege | Description |
|---|---|
| Alter any cluster | The ability to modify a cluster on any user id |
| Alter any index | The ability to modify an index on any user id |
| Alter any procedure | The ability to modify a procedure on any user id |
| Alter any role | The ability to modify a role on any user i.d. |
| Alter any sequence | The ability to modify a sequence on any user id |
| Alter any snapshot | The ability to modify a snapshot on any user id |
| Alter any table | The ability to modify a table on any user id |
| Alter any trigger | The ability to modify a trigger on any user id |

*continues*

**Table 6.3 Continued**

| Privilege | Description |
|---|---|
| Alter database | The ability to modify the user's database. |
| Alter profile | The ability to modify the user's profile. |
| Alter resource cost | The ability to modify session costs. |
| Alter rollback segment | The ability to modify a rollback segment. |
| Alter session | The ability to modify a session. |
| Alter system | The ability to modify a system. |
| Alter tablespace | The ability to modify a tablespace. |
| Alter user | The ability to modify a user id |
| Analyze any | The ability to analyze. |
| Audit any | The ability to audit. |
| Audit system | The ability to audit. |
| Become user | The ability to import objects from any user id |
| Backup any table | The ability to export objects from any user id |
| Comment any table | The ability to record comment on a table on any user id |
| Create any cluster | The ability to create a cluster on any user id |
| Create any index | The ability to create an index on any user id |
| Create any procedure | The ability to create a procedure on any user id |
| Create any sequence | The ability to create a sequence on any user id |
| Create any snapshot | The ability to create a snapshot on any user id |
| Create any synonym | The ability to create a synonym on any user id |
| Create any table | The ability to create a table on any user id |
| Create any trigger | The ability to create a trigger on any user id |
| Create any view | The ability to create a trigger on any user id |
| Create cluster | The ability to create a cluster on a user id |
| Create database link | The ability to create a database link for a user id |
| Create procedure | The ability to create a procedure on a user id |
| Create profile | The ability to create a profile on a user id |
| Create public database link | The ability to create a database link available for all user id's. |

| Privilege | Description |
|---|---|
| Create public synonym | The ability to create a synonym available for all user id's. |
| Create role | The ability to create a role. |
| Create rollback segment | The ability to create a rollback segment. |
| Create session | The ability to create a session for a user id |
| Create sequence | The ability to create a sequence for a user id |
| Create snapshot | The ability to create a snapshot for a user id |
| Create synonym | The ability to create a synonym for a user id |
| Create table | The ability to create a table on a user id |
| Create tablespace | The ability to create a tablespace. |
| Create trigger | The ability to create a trigger on a user id |
| Create user | The ability to create a user id |
| Create view | The ability to create a view on a user id |
| Delete any table | The ability to delete a table on any user id |
| Drop any cluster | The ability to drop a cluster from any user id |
| Drop any index | The ability to drop an index from any user id |
| Drop any procedure | The ability to drop a procedure from any user id |
| Drop any role | The ability to drop a role from any user id |
| Drop any sequence | The ability to drop a sequence from any user id |
| Drop any snapshot | The ability to drop a snapshot from any user id |
| Drop any synonym | The ability to drop a synonym from any user id |
| Drop any table | The ability to drop a table from any user id |
| Drop any trigger | The ability to drop a trigger from any user id |
| Drop any view | The ability to drop a view from any user id |
| Drop profile | The ability to drop a profile. |
| Drop public database link | The ability to drop a public database link. |
| Drop public synonym | The ability to drop a public synonym. |
| Drop rollback segment | The ability to drop a rollback segment. |
| Drop tablespace | The ability to drop a tablespace. |
| Drop user | The ability to drop a user id |
| Execute any procedure | The ability to run a procedure from any user id |

*continues*

**Table 6.3 Continued**

| Privilege | Description |
|---|---|
| Force any transaction | The ability to force a commit or rollback for a pending transaction. |
| Force transaction | The ability to force a commit or rollback on a user id |
| Grant any privilege | The ability to grant a database privilege. |
| Grant any role | The ability to grant a role to any user id |
| Insert any table | The ability to insert records into a table on any user id |
| Lock any table | The ability to lock any table. |
| Manage tablespace | The ability to manage any table. |
| Readup | The ability to query data with a higher access class than the current session normally allows. |
| Restricted session | The ability to logon during the restricted access mode by SQL*DBA. |
| Select any sequence | The ability to select a sequence on any user id |
| Select any table | The ability to select records from a table on any user id |
| Unlimited tablespace | The ability to surpass the assigned limits. |
| Writedown | The ability to create, alter, drop, insert, update, or delete database objects with access ratings lower than the current session. |
| *Writeup* | The ability to *create, alter, drop, insert, update,* or *delete* database objects with access ratings higher than the current session. |

The privileges that contain the word *any,* such as *Select any table,* enable the user to perform the function on all objects. When the privilege does not contain this word, the user can only perform the function on the database object he owns or has created.

You can use the *Revoke* command to take away privileges. Figure 6.5 illustrates the syntax and an example of the command. You can revoke privileges or in one group by using the option *all.* After you revoke privileges from a user, they are also revoked from any user granted a privilege from the revokee.

# Granting Access to Your Tables

The tables you create are initially available only to users of the Oracle ID or account that originally created them. You might, however, want other users to have access to the table. Other users can gain access to the tables with their Oracle ID'S through the use of the *Grant* command. There are several object privileges that can be granted. Listing 6.21 illustrates several *Grant* common grant commands.

**FIG. 6.5**
Revoke privilege system and example.

```
revoke (privilege [, privilege] ... I all [privileges])
REVOKE PRIVILEGE COMMAND SYNTAX AND EXAMPLE
 on [user.] object
 from (public I user [, user]

revoke create public synonym
from ostu1;
```

**Listing 6.21 L_06_21.sql—Granting and Revoking Privileges**

```
SQL> grant select on employee to ostu1;

Grant  I succeeded.

SQL> grant insert, update, select, delete
  2    on employee
  3    to ostu2, ostu3;

Grant succeeded.

SQL> grant insert, update, select, delete
  2    on employee
  3    to public;

Grant succeeded.

SQL> revoke insert, update, select, delete
  2    on employee
  3    from public;

Revoke succeeded.

SQL> revoke insert, update, select, delete
  2    on employee
  3    from ostu2, ostu3;

Revoke succeeded.

SQL> revoke select on employee from ostu1;

Revoke succeeded.
```

The *Grant* command has three components: the privilege granted, the name of the table, and user i.d.(s) gaining the privilege. You can extend four privileges: *select*, *insert*, *update*, and *delete*. The *select* privilege enables the user to perform *select* statements against the table. The *insert* option enables the user to add new records. *Update* enables the user to modify values in an existing record, and *delete* enables the user to remove records from the table.

You can set multiple privileges at one time to multiple users. Each user id can have different privileges if needed. In addition, all ids can be given the privilege when the word *public* is used. To take the privileges away, use the *revoke* command. That command has the same syntax as the *Grant* command.

You also use the *Grant* command to extend a variety of privileges. This chapter discusses these privileges in more detail in later sections.

# Creating the Tablespace

The *tablespace* is an area of the disk comprised of one or more files. The tablespace is where Oracle keeps the tables, indexes, and clusters that have been defined. The tablespace has a fixed size and can become filled. When this occurs, you can expand it by creating a new disk file and adding it to the tablespace. Oracle then begins using this file along with the existing ones for the objects it holds. The database administrator creates *tablespaces*. Listing 6.22 illustrates the syntax of the *create tablespace* command. *EMPLOYEE* is the name of the tablespace. The tablespace will initially contain one file '*emp.tab*' with a maximum space of 1000K or 1,024,000 bytes. The K symbol means 1,024 bytes, and the M symbol means 1,048,576 bytes. The default storage is used as the initial table storage size when it is not defined in the *create table* command.

**Listing 6.22 L_06_22.sql—Creating Tablespace Employee**

```
SQL> create tablespace employee datafile 'emp.tab' size 1000 k
  2    default storage (initial 25 k next 10 k
  3    minextents 10 maxextents 100);

Tablespace created.

SQL> drop tablespace employee;
Tablespace dropped.
```

When a table is first created, an area of disk space (*extent*) is set aside in the tablespace. This area is called the *initial extent*. In the example, this extent is defined as 25K and the *next extent* is defined at 10K. Additional extents are created automatically when the existing extents are filled up until the entire tablespace is full. The *minextents* option enables you to set aside a number of additional extents at the time the table is created. The *maxextents* setting is the limit to the number of extents the table can use. The *pct increase* option is a growth factor for extents. In the example, it is set at 25. This means that each additional extent will be 25 percent larger than the one before it.

Figure 6.6 illustrates the syntax of the *altertablespace* command and settings. The *add datafile* option enables you to increase the tablespace size by adding one or more files described according to the file_definition to the tablespace. The format of the file definition is: '*filename*' [size *integer* [K | M]] [reuse]. The name of the file is followed by the size of the file and the *reuse* option. This option without the *size* option means destroy the contents of any existing file with this name and give the file to this database. When both options are specified, the file is created if it does not exist, and changes the size if it does exist. Specifying the *size* option alone causes the file to be created if it doesn't exist and an error message to occur if it does.

**FIG. 6.6**
Creating tablespace command syntax.

```
alter tablespace employee
CREATING TABLESPACE SYNTAX

[add datafile file_difinition [, file_definition] |
rename datafile file [, file] to file [,file] |
default storage storage |
online | offline [normal | immediate] |
(begin | end ) backup )
```

The *rename* option enables you to change the name of one or more of the existing files in the tablespace. This option does not actually change the names of the files. It just associates the new name with the file. To actually change the name, issue the *alter tablespace offline* command, and then rename the files in the operating system. You can then rename the file(s) by using the *Alter Tablespace* command. The *Alter Tablespace online* command is then issued.

The *offline* option takes the tablespace out of production. If the *immediate* option is used, it performs the task even if users are logged on. Using the *normal* option causes Oracle to wait until the users have stopped using the tablespace. The *online* restores the tablespace to its normal mode.

You can drop the tablespace by using the *Drop Tablespace* command followed by the name of the tablespace. The command has an option called *including contents*. When this option is specified, the tablespace and all of its contents will be eliminated. Without the option, the tablespace must be empty before it can be dropped.

# Defining a Sequence

A *sequence* is an Oracle device used to generate a unique sequential number. This is a very good tool to use for generating sequential payroll numbers, work order numbers, or artificial primary keys. I use artificial primary keys in a transformer database I developed. This database does not have a unique value in any of the fields. Several manufacturers can use the serial number, which is the most logical key. This necessitates the use of the artificial key added to each record as they are added to the table. I use the sequence to give me the unique number.



Listing 6.23 illustrates the creation of a *sequence*. In this example, the name of the *sequence* is *pay_num_seq*. It is used as a qualifier for the *NextVal* and *CurrVal* values. The former value generates the next unique number. The number is guaranteed to be unique. The latter value returns the last number generated by the *sequence*. The Listing's second statement demonstrates the use of this command to populate a new record with an artificial key generated by the *sequence*.

**Listing 6.23 L_06_23.SQL—Creating and Using a Sequence**

```
SQL> create sequence pay_num_seq
  2   increment by 1 start with 100;

Sequence created.

SQL> insert into employee (payroll_number)
  2  values (pay_num_seq.nextval);

1 row created.

SQL> drop sequence pay_num_seq;

Sequence dropped.
```

# Defining Database Triggers

A *database trigger* is a useful tool used to automatically populate columns of a database. The trigger is a stored procedure written in PL/SQL that is associated with a table and executed when a specified operation occurs to the table.

**TIP** I have used database triggers to populate an artificial key with a new sequential number when a record was inserted. Because I defined the procedure as a database trigger, I did not have to populate the column with a value through the code in my application.

You can also use triggers to perform other complex functions—if you want to print a letter to a customer welcoming him after he opens an account, for example. You can accomplish such a procedure by creating a database trigger that fires when you insert a customer record into the customer file. The trigger contains the PL/SQL command necessary to produce the letter.

Users granted the *create trigger* or *create any trigger* privileges can create triggers. The event options that can cause the trigger to fire are the insert, update, or delete table operations. Another option will cause the trigger to fire before or after the above table operations. The trigger I created to populate the artificial key fired before the insert operation. If it did not, the not null constraint for the artificial primary key column would have prevented the record from being populated. The trigger to create the report fired after the record was inserted. Specifying an *of* clause on an update trigger causes the trigger to fire only when specific columns are updated. Figure 6.7 illustrates the syntax of the *create trigger* command.

Listing 6.24 also illustrates the syntax of the *Create Trigger* command. The words *old* and *new* are default qualifiers that you can use in the block to contain values before and after the procedure. The command enables you to change these qualifier names, *old* and *new*, to different names. The *for each row* option causes the trigger to be fired for each row affected by the operation. The *when* clause allows the trigger to be executed when specific conditions are met. You can disable the trigger by using the *Alter Trigger* and *Alter Table* commands. You can drop the trigger by using the *Drop Trigger* command.

**FIG. 6.7**
Create trigger syntax.

```
create trigger [user.]triggername
CREATING SEQUENCE COMMAND SYNTAX AND EXAMPLE
  (before I after)
  (delete I insert I update [of columna, columnb])
  on [user.]tablename
  [referencing (old as oldname) I (new as newname)]
  [for each row]
  [when (condition)]
  block
```

**Listing 6.24 L_06_24.SQL—Creating a Database Trigger Called payroll_numb**

```
SQL> create or replace trigger seq_trg
      before insert on employee
      referencing new as new
      for each row
      declare
        seq number;
      begin
       select pay_num_seq.nextval into seq from dual;
       :new.payroll_number := seq;
     end;
    /
Trigger created.
```

# Oracle8 Database Objects

The new Oracle8 database has several features that should be mentioned. The first is the ability to partition tables and indexes. This allows you to break the database tables into smaller pieces. You have the ability to break a large table into separate partitions that are located in separate tablespaces. These partitions can be located on different disk drives and at different locations.

Partitioning has advantages. It spreads the I/O across more drives. For instance, if the table is contained on four disk drives, each drive would have one-fourth the I/O as compared to having the data on one drive. This reduces contension and increases response time for active databases. Another advantage involves data recovery and backup. Since each partition is independent of the other, partitions can be backed up and recovered independently. In our example of four partitions, three partitions can be active while the fourth is being backed up or recovered. It also reduces the losses due to corruption. If a drive goes bad or some other problem occurs, the problem is confined to the partition.

To partition a table, you must tell Oracle8 how the data is partitioned and where to place the data. This is initially done using a partition statement at the end of the create statement. This statement has parameters that divide a table's data into partitions. Listing 6.25 contains a reference only create statement that is not meant for execution.

**Listing 6.25 L_06_25.SQL—Creating a Partitioned Table in Oracle8**

```
 create table ex_employee
    (payroll_number             number(4),
     last_name                  varchar2(15),
     first_name                 varchar2(15),
     .
     .
     fk_department              char(4))
partition by range (payroll_number)
     (partition t1 values less than (250) tablespace sp1,
      partition t2 values less than (500) tablespace sp2,
      partition t3 values less than (750) tablespace sp3,
      partition t4 values less than (maxvalue) tablespace sp4);
```

The partition clause follows the Create statement. The first part of the statement specifies the variable(s) that control where the data will reside. In the case of Listing 6.25, this variable is payroll_number. Employees with a payroll_number values less than 250 are placed in the first partition located in tablespace sp1. The next partition contains the payroll_number values greater than 250 and less than 500. The last partition uses an upper bound called maxvalue. This represents the greatest value in the table. If you do not use this bound, Oracle8 will not allow a payroll_number value greater than the specified bound. The maxvalue ensures that all records can be added to the database.

## Altering the Partitions

After the table has been created, the partitions can be managed through the use of the alter table command. This command is used in conjunction with the drop, add, modify, rename, and truncate options. Listing 6.26 illustrates several reference only versions of the alter table command.

**Listing 6.26 L_06_26.SQL—Using the Alter Command to Manage Partitions**

```
Alter table ex_employee add partition t5 values less than (900) tablespace sp5;
Alter table ex_employee drop partition t5;
Alter table ex_employee rename partition t5 to t10;
Alter table ex_employee truncate partition t10 drop storage;
```

## Partitioned Indexes

Oracle8 also gives you the ability to partition indexes. A partitioned index is an index that exists on multiple partitions. The declaration of a partitioned index is similar to that of a table. The partition clause follows the Create Index clause. Listing 6.27 illustrates an example of this. This listing is for reference, and not for execution.

**Listing 6.27 L_06_27.SQL—Creating a Partitioned Table in Oracle8**

```
 create index empindex
   on ex_employee (payroll_number)
partition by range (payroll_number)
     (partition t1 values less than (250) tablespace sp1,
      partition t2 values less than (500) tablespace sp2,
      partition t3 values less than (750) tablespace sp3,
      partition t4 values less than (maxvalue) tablespace sp4);
```

The command in Listing 6.27 partitioned the index on the payroll_number column. This type of index is called a local index. In this example, the index is partitioned and placed in the same tablespaces as the partitioned table. However, it is not necessary for the index partition to be the same as the table.

The normal Create Index command can still be used in Oracle8. The normal index command creates a global index. This means the index contains the keys for all of the table partitions.

## Creating Types

Oracle8 has a Create Type command that allows you to create additional data types and use them within another object. These data types consist of one or more variables. For instance, Listing 6.28 contains a reference only command to create a data type called features that contain variables for height, weight, and eye color.

**Listing 6.28 L_06_28.SQL—Creating a Data Type for Features**

```
create type features
    (height                         number(2),
     weight                         number(3),
     eye_color                      varchar2(2));
```

This data type exists independent of any table. It can be used with any number of other objects. For instance, Listing 6.29, a reference only example, uses the features data type as an attribute in a table.



**Listing 6.29 L_06_29.SQL—Using the Features Data Type in the ex_employee Table**

```
create table ex_employee
    (payroll_number                 number(4),
     last_name                      varchar2(15),
     first_name                     varchar2(15),
     employee_features              features,
     .
     fk_department                  char(4))
```

The beauty of these defined data types is that they are objects that can be used within many other objects. For instance, the features data type can be used with customers, vendors, or any other table or entity that tracks human features. It brings the power of object-oriented components to the database.

The objects contained in a type are not limited to variables. A type can also contain functions. This allows you to bind code and the data together. This is an important object-oriented concept called encapsulation. Data and code are bound together and can be used freely by other objects that need the data and functions.

## Using Varray

A new data type in Oracle8 is Varray. This type is an ordered list or array of elements. The array can be included as a type in a table. When specifying the varray you must declare the maximum number of values. Listing 6.30 contains two reference only commands. The first creates a varry of phone numbers. The second command uses the varray in a table. The effect is that the ex_employee table has the ability to retain multiple telephone numbers for an employee. Since this is a variable array, only the space contained by values will be used.

**Listing 6.30 L_06_30.SQL—Creating a Varray and Using It in a Table**

```
Create type numbers as varray(3) of varchar2(10);

 create table ex_employee
    (payroll_number                 number(4),
     last_name                      varchar2(15),
     first_name                     varchar2(15),
     employee_features              features,
     telephone                      numbers,
     .
     fk_department                  char(4))
```

# Summary

Databases are comprised on a number of objects. The *Create*, *Alter*, and *Drop* commands are used to make, modify, and eliminate the objects. Tables are objects that contain the data. They are comprised of *items* or *fields* that have alphanumeric or numeric properties. The table definitions often contain *constraints* used to maintain the integrity of the database.

Database performance is enhanced through the use of indexes. *Indexes* are mini-tables that reduce the amount of disk Oracle7 must read to acquire data. Indexes are also used to ensure uniqueness of the primary key. A *view* is a database object that creates a virtual table when executed. Views may be used as a table name in a Select command.

If the data you need is on a remote database, you can create a *database link* that tells Oracle7 where the data is located. A user account owns database objects. Before the user account can access your database, you must *grant* it the select privilege to the table. You can grant a large number of privileges to the user. In fact, there are no default privileges. To perform any function, including logging on the database, privileges must be granted.

Some other objects in the database are tablespaces. These objects contain the tables and other database objects. A *sequence* is an object that generates unique sequential numbers. A *database* trigger is a block of PL/SQL code executed when specific database events occur.

# From Here...

You have now seen how to create the various database objects. The second installment of the employee project appears at the end of this chapter. You can now create the tables and the database objects for the project. Future installments will use these tables.

The next chapter covers data manipulation language (dml) commands. These commands consist of the *insert*, *update*, and *delete* commands. These commands add, modify, or remove records from the database. You also use these commands in Oracle Forms to maintain the database.

# Review Exercises

1. Your company needs to begin recording information about its existing transformers. Your boss has asked you to create an Oracle table to retain this information. The information you are to keep in the file consists of the following:

| | | |
|---|---|---|
| serial number | alphanumeric | length of 10 |
| location | alphanumeric | length of 30 |
| purchase date | alphanumeric | length of 8 |
| cost | numeric | length of 8 |
| manufacturer | alphanumeric | length of 15 |

   What DDL do you use to create the table?



2. After you have created the table, your boss realized that the serial number field is actually 15 characters long and the table needs to keep track of the gallons of oil. This is a numeric field with a length of 4. In addition, the serial number item has been identified as the primary key to the table. The primary key constraints need to be placed on the table. To make these changes, what ddl do you need?
3. After subsequent discussions with the users, you determine that the table will be very large, and the users will identify transformers based on their addresses. You decide to index this column to increase the performance of their searches. To create the index, what ddl do you use?
4. Your boss has decided to keep track of each of the transformer's tests. Because each transformer can be tested multiple times, this tracking requires another table. The table should have the following fields:

| | | |
|---|---|---|
| serial number | alphanumeric | length of 15 |
| test date | alphanumeric | length of 8 |
| voltage | number | length of 3 |
| amps | number | length of 3 |
| overhauled | alphanumeric | length of 1 |

The value in the overhauled item is either y or n. Create the ddl for this table. Be certain to include a primary key, foreign key, and check constraint. The on delete cascade option should also be included.

5. A user called you and asked whether you could change the name of the transformer table to "trf." You decide to create a synonym for this table. What is the DDL for the synonym?
6. A user called and said he runs a report from the employee database listing each employee's eyeglass cost as a percentage of the department's. It is a rather complex query, so you decide to create several views to accomplish this report. What are the statements to create the views and select the data?
7. Drop all the items you created in 1–6.

## EMPLOYEE DATABASE PROJECT INSTALLMENT 2

Now that you have learned to define database objects, it is time to create them. At the end of Part II, you normalized the tables and created a table relationship diagram. These are the tables that you need to create. You need the following steps to create the database. Appendix C, Part II, lists the DDL you need to perform these tasks.

1. Create a tablespace called *emp*. The size of the tablespace should be approximately 3 million bytes.
2. Create a user id.
3. Grant the user id the following privileges:

   create session, alter session, create table, alter any table, drop any table, create view, drop any view, create synonym, drop any synonym, create any index, alter any index, drop any index, create public synonym, drop public synonym
4. Create the tables identified in the table relationship diagrams developed in Part II. Be certain that each table has a primary key constraint, foreign key constraint (where applicable), and check constraints (where applicable).
5. Create a sequence that will be used to generate payroll numbers. The sequence begins with the number 1.

CHAPTER 7

# Modifying Your Tables with DML Commands

To add records to a relational table, you use the `insert` SQL command. The command has three parts. It begins with the word `insert`. This is followed by a list of the table's columns that will be populated by the statement. The column name is separated by commas and enclosed by parentheses. The third section contains the list of values that will populate the columns listed in the previous section. The values are enclosed by parentheses and separated by commas. The statement must have the same number of values as columns to be populated. The statement need not contain all the table's columns. It must, however, contain all columns that have the not null constraint. String values must be enclosed by a single quotation mark and numeric values do not contain single quotation marks. ■

**Adding records to your tables**

This section covers the `insert` command. You use `insert` to add records to a table.

**Updating items in your table**

This section covers the `update` command. You use `update` to modify the values of items in your tables.

**Deleting records from your tables**

This section covers the `delete` and `truncate` commands. `Delete` removes records from your table with the option of restoring them. `Truncate` removes the records without this option.

**Saving your changes**

This section covers the `commit` and `rollback` commands. `Commit` causes Oracle to make the changes permanent. `Rollback` restores the tables to the state of the last `commit`.The Oracle7 database uses Data Manipulation Language (DML) command statements to modify records. These statements add records to your tables, update values, and delete the records. You can issue the commands in the SQL*PLUS product or in Oracle Forms 4.5. This chapter illustrates these commands.

# Adding Records to Your Tables

Listing 7.1 illustrates the `insert` command. You might notice that the value section has a character string that will be placed into the birth_date column. The statement performs the `to_date` function, automatically converting the character string into a numeric date value. This occurs so long as the character string is in the default date format of 'dd-mon-yy'. If the string value has a different format than the default, the last expression in the *values* clause must be enclosed by the `to_char` function. The function must have the proper date picture.

The following example populates the record with the wrong birth date. Because the default picture or format does not contain the century, Oracle populates the century in the column with the current century. If the record was inserted before the year 2000, the birth date would be '02-FEB-1909'. If it is populated in the twenty-first century, the birth date will be '02-FEB-2009'. Because Abraham Lincoln was born in the nineteenth century, the statement must use the *to_char* function with a date format of 'dd-mon-yyyy'. You must also change the string value to '02-FEB-1809'.

**Listing 7.1 L_07_01.sql—Inserting a Record into the Employee Table**

```
SQL> insert into employee (payroll_number, last_name,
  2  first_name, fk_department, birth_date)
  3  values (16, 'LINCOLN', 'ABRAHAM', 'POL',
  4  to_date('02-FEB-1809', 'DD-MON-YYYY'));

1 row created.
```

Listing 7.1's `insert` statement adds one row or record to the table. Sometimes you want to add a number of rows to the table. If the rows are contained in another Oracle table, you can replace the values clause with a `select` statement. An `insert` statement that contains a `select` statement adds a row to the table for each row fetched or obtained by the `select` statement.

Listing 7.2 illustrates the `insert` command using a `select` statement. Each employee in the Welfare Department was given a personal organizer. The department manager wanted to record the cost as a tool. The statement identifies the employees from the employee file and adds a record into the tool table for each selected employee. The `select` clause enables you to modify data that will be inserted into the table.

**NOTE** You can use all the functions identified in Chapter 4, "Formatting Reports in SQL*PLUS," to modify data in the row. I use this command whenever I convert data from an old system into a new one. One problem that always seems to hit me is converting alphanumeric data into numbers. The original data always has an alpha character in it or is longer than the field it will be moved into. So be certain to check out the data before inserting it into the new table.

**Listing 7.2 L_07_02.sql—Adding Multiple Records to a Table by Using a *Select* Statement in Place of a *Values* Clause**

```
SQL> insert into tools (fk_payroll_number, tool_name,
  2     purchase_date, payroll_deduct, tool_cost)
  3  select payroll_number, 'ORGANIZER',
  4     sysdate, 'N', 89.95
  5  from employee
  6  where fk_department = 'WEL';

6 rows created.

SQL> select fk_payroll_number, tool_name, purchase_date
  2  from tools where tool_name = 'ORGANIZER';

FK_PAYROLL_NUMBER TOOL_NAME       PURCHASE_
----------------- --------------- ---------
               35 ORGANIZER       23-AUG-97
               34 ORGANIZER       23-AUG-97
               26 ORGANIZER       23-AUG-97
               23 ORGANIZER       23-AUG-97
               20 ORGANIZER       23-AUG-97
               19 ORGANIZER       23-AUG-97

6 rows selected.
```

# Updating Items in Your Tables

You can modify values contained in items or columns of a table by using the `update` command. This statement also has three parts. The first part contains the name of the table that contains the records; the second is the name of the columns to be updated along with the value(s) to place in the column; and the third is an optional conditional statement that identifies the subset of records to update.

Listing 7.3 illustrates a simple update statement that changes the values in the last_name column of the employee table. The statement causes the first character to be uppercase and the remainder lowercase. Because this statement does not have the optional conditional clause, all records in the table are updated.

**Listing 7.3 L_07_03.sql—Update All the *last_name* Values in the Employee Table**

```
SQL> update employee
  2    set last_name = initcap(last_name);

19 rows updated.
```

Part II Ch 7

*continues*

**Listing 7.3 Continued**

```
SQL> select last_name from employee;

LAST_NAME
---------------
Taft
Roosevelt
Anthony
Roosevelt
Coolidge
Johnson
Reagan
Bush
Johnson
Clinton
Carter
Ford
Nixon
Kennedy
Eisenhower
Truman
Roosevelt
Hoover
Wilson

19 rows selected.
```

The conditional clause of the statement is the same as the `where` clause used in `select` statements. The `select` statement was discussed in Chapter 4. The clause follows the same rules, uses the same operators, and produces the same subset of records. Listing 7.4 illustrates the use of the `where` clause to update a set of subset of records. The statement changes the value in the first_name column to lower case when the last_name equals 'ROOSEVELT.' Notice that SQL*PLUS returns a value indicating the number of updated records. This is a useful indicator, telling you whether the `update` statement actually worked.

**Listing 7.4 L_07_04.SQL—Updating Specific Records Through the Use of a *Where* Clause**

```
SQL> update employee
  2    set first_name = initcap(first_name)
  3    where last_name = 'Roosevelt';

3 rows updated.

SQL> select first_name, last_name from employee
  2    where last_name = 'Roosevelt';

FIRST_NAME      LAST_NAME
--------------- ---------------
```

```
Theodore        Roosevelt
Eleanor          Roosevelt
Franklin        Roosevelt
```

You can also use `select` statements in the `update` statement. Listing 7.5 contains a statement that changes the first_name and last_name columns to upper case if the employee has not purchased glasses. This example also demonstrates that you can modify several columns with the same `update` statement. When updating multiple columns, you must place a comma after each assignment expression. If the new value is a string, you must enclose it in single quotation marks.

**Listing 7.5 L_07_05.SQL—Using a *Select* Statement in the *Where* Clause of an *Update* Statement to Identify Records to Update**

```
SQL> update employee
  2    set first_name = upper(first_name),
  3    last_name = upper(last_name)
  4    where payroll_number not in (
  5       select fk_payroll_number from glasses);

4 rows updated.

SQL> select first_name, last_name from employee;

FIRST_NAME      LAST_NAME
--------------- ---------------
WILLIAM         Taft
Theodore        Roosevelt
SUSAN             Anthony
Eleanor          Roosevelt
CALVIN          Coolidge
LYNDON          Johnson
RONALD          Reagan
GEORGE          BUSH
ANDREW          Johnson
WILLIAM         CLINTON
JIMMY            Carter
GERALD          Ford
RICHARD         Nixon
JOHN            KENNEDY
DWIGHT          Eisenhower
HAROLD          Truman
Franklin        Roosevelt
HERBERT         HOOVER
WOODROW         Wilson

19 rows selected.
```

The `values` clause can also contain a `select` statement because the result of a `select` statement is a value. The statement must only return one record. SQL*PLUS does not enable you to update one column with multiple values. Listing 7.6 contains an example of an `update` statement that uses a `select` statement to populate the multiple columns listed in the `values` clause. The statement selects the values for the street column for Franklin Roosevelt and updates the same column in Eleanor Roosevelt's record.

**Listing 7.6 L_07_06.SQL—Using a *Select* Statement as a Value in an *Update* Statement**

```
SQL> select last_name, first_name, street from employee
  2    where last_name = 'Roosevelt';

LAST_NAME       FIRST_NAME      STREET
--------------- --------------- --------------------
Roosevelt       Theodore        12 BROADWAY
Roosevelt       Eleanor         123 W 57 TH
Roosevelt       Franklin        12 CHERRY LANE

SQL> update employee
  2    set street = (select street from employee
  3                  where last_name = 'Roosevelt'
  4                    and first_name = 'Franklin')
  5  where last_name = 'Roosevelt'
  6    and first_name = 'Eleanor';

1 row updated.

SQL> select last_name, first_name, street from employee
  2    where last_name = 'Roosevelt';

LAST_NAME       FIRST_NAME      STREET
--------------- --------------- --------------------
Roosevelt       Theodore        12 BROADWAY
Roosevelt       Eleanor          12 CHERRY LANE
Roosevelt       Franklin        12 CHERRY LANE
```

# Deleting Records from Your Table

To *delete* records from tables, use the `delete` command. The statement contains two parts: the name of the table, and the optional `where` clause that limits or identifies the records to be deleted. When the `where` clause is not contained in the `delete` statement, all the records in the table will be deleted. Listing 7.7 illustrates a simple command that deletes all the records from the glasses table. Notice, SQL*PLUS displays the number of records that were deleted following execution of the command. If the number of records does not match what you expect, you can restore them by using the `rollback` procedure. The `rollback` command that restores the deleted records. You can see that the first `select` in the listing produces no records. It is performed immediately after the `delete` command was performed. After the `rollback` command is isssued, the `select` statement produces this original set of records. The reason the records were not permanently removed will be discussed in the next section.

**Listing 7.7 L_07_07.SQL—Deleting All the Records from the Employee, and Restoring Them with the *Rollback* Command**

```
SQL> delete from employee;

19 rows deleted.

SQL> select last_name from employee;

no rows selected

SQL> rollback;

Rollback complete.

SQL> select last_name from employee;

LAST_NAME
---------------
TAFT
ROOSEVELT
ANTHONY
ROOSEVELT
COOLIDGE
JOHNSON
REAGAN
BUSH
JOHNSON
CLINTON
CARTER
FORD
NIXON
KENNEDY
EISENHOWER
TRUMAN
ROOSEVELT
HOOVER
WILSON

19 rows selected.
```

Listing 7.8 illustrates a `delete` command containing a `where` clause.

**Listing 7.8 L_07_08.SQL—Deleting Specific Records from the Employee Table by Using the *Where* Clause**

```
SQL> delete from glasses where
  2    fk_payroll_number > 21;

14 rows deleted.

SQL> rollback;

Rollback complete.
```

When records are deleted, the database manager places a copy of each record into the database redo file. This is done because you have the option of having Oracle restore the deleted records if you made a mistake. This is a good feature except for two problems: When a large amount of records is being deleted, it takes a long time to write these records into another table on the disk; in addition, these records may fill up the temporary storage and cause the command to abort.

**NOTE** The only time I use the `delete` command in SQL*PLUS is when I am converting data from an old system to a new one. The reason is most users and developers do not have the privileges to use the `delete` command against production data. Having this privilege would `allow` users to accidently delete the records in a database. It is much safer to manage records through the applications.

When I am converting data, I spend a lot of time running my load programs and testing the results. When I find an error, I fix the problem and rerun it. I generally make a lot of errors before the programs run properly. This means that I may spend a lot of time waiting for Oracle to write the records to the archive file. I use the `delete` command when there are a few records in the table or if I want to delete a subset of the table's records. Deleting the records in a large table is a very time consuming practice. Rather than watch the cursor blink while records are placed in the redo file, I often use the `truncate` command.

The command removes all the rows from a table. It is much faster than the `delete` command because it does not write the records to the redo file. `Truncate` is a very useful command to use when developing conversion programs (see Figure 7.2). The one drawback is that you cannot undo this command. Listing 7.9 illustrates this command. The `drop` option releases the space from the deleted rows. If you specify the `reuse` option, the space remains allocated for new rows in the table.

**FIG. 7.1**
Truncate table syntax.

```
truncate (tablename | clustername)
  (drop | reuse ) storage
```

**Listing 7.9 L_07_09.SQL—Truncating a Table**

```
SQL> truncate table wge_maint;

Table truncated
```

# Saving the Changes to Your Tables

The DML commands do not permanently change database table records until the `commit` command is issued. `Commit` causes the database manager to make the changes permanent. Previous to the `commit`, the records are marked and the changes wait in temporary storage for the commit to occur. The reason the changes are not made permanent is because Oracle7 gives you the opportunity to undo or eliminate the changes using the `rollback` command. All changes caused by the DMS commands are temporary between database `commits`.

**NOTE** I once was modifying records in a table. I was working on a UNIX platform and had two different sessions going at the same time. I modified a table on one of the sessions. When I ran a `select` command on the other session against the modified table, I didn't see any of the changes. My first thought was that the `update` statement did not work. I checked the statement and executed it again. When I ran the `select` again on the second session, there were no changes. This really had me scratching my head. After a while, I ran the `select` on the session on which I had performed the `update` statement. The `select` statement listing showed the records were all modified.

I was dumbfounded at this turn of events until I remembered I am never issued a `commit` to save the records permanently. The point is that when you execute DML commands against a table and do not commit the changes, it may appear to you that the table has changed, but it will the changes will not appear to other sessions that may be looking at the table. In addition, if your session is abnormally terminated (such as shutting off your machine before logging off of Oracle7) the changes will not be permanently retained.

To make changes permanent, issue the `commit` command. Listing 7.10 illustrates the command. It consists of the word *commit* followed by a semicolon. This causes all records modified by your session since the last `commit` issued to be permanently recorded. The second way to permanently save the changes is to log off the session. You can autocommit the changes by two more means: issue a `create` or `drop` command.

**Listing 7.10 L_07_10.SQL—Saving Changes Permanently by Using the *Commit* Command**

```
SQL> commit;

Commit complete.
```

You can undo the changes by using the `rollback` command. This command reverses all changes that have occurred since the last `commit`. The command consists of the word rollback followed by a semicolon. If the `commit` procedure is inconvenient, you can use the `autocommit set` command to permanently record the changes every time the DML commands are issued. The normal setting is off. Changing the setting to on makes the changes permanent without having to use the commit.

# Summary

Records are added to tables by using the `insert` command. The command consists of a `columns` clause and a `values` clause. You can add multiple records to the table by using a `select` statement in the `values` clause. You use the `update` command to modify records. The command has two parts. The first part is the items to be updated and the new values. The second section is a `where` clause that identifies the records to be updated. The `delete` and `truncate` commands delete records. `Delete` removes the records from the table and stores a copy in temporary storage for restoration purposes. It also has an `optional where` clause that identifies the records to be deleted. `Truncate` removes all the records in the table. You cannot restore these records. Changes to the database are temporary until you issue the `commit` command or you log off the database. To restore the database, use the `rollback` command. `Rollback` restores records since the last `commit` was issued.

# From Here...

This concludes part II of the book. The next section covers Oracle's procedure language called PL/SQL and Oracle's table loader called SQL*LOADER. PL/SQL is an excellent tool used in all the Oracle products to perform special functions. It is used extensively in Oracle Forms to fine-tune the form mechanics. It is also used for data conversion purposes. The SQL*LOADER product loads Oracle tables with records from flat text files. It is used when converting data from an older system into the new Oracle database If you are anxious to get into learning Oracle Forms, you could skip this next section and start with part IV. You need to return to this section, however, at some point. Without an understanding of PL/SQL, you do not fully understand the power of Oracle Forms.

# Review Exercises

1. Insert a record into the employee table for AL Gore. He was born on April 1, 1948. His payroll number is 40, and he makes $18,567 a year in the POL department. His address is 444 S. Main St, Nashville, Tennessee. His employment date is '20-JAN-92'. His social security number is '508-34-8912'. His phone number is 894-123-8765, and his position is 'BILL COLLECTOR'.
2. Insert a record into the employee table for Dan Quayle. He was born Dec. 4, 1947. His payroll number is 41, and he makes $20,456 a year in the POL department. His address is 1600 Pennsylvania Ave, Washington, DC. His employment date is '20-JAN-2000'. His social security number is '405-39-1212'. His phone number is 101-100-0001, and his position is 'Chief Executive'.
3. Create a temporary table with the same columns as the employee table. Insert records for the employees from the Welfare Department in employee table into this temporary table.
4. Update the wages in the temporary table. Each employee gets a 15 percent raise. Be certain to commit the changes.5.Update the wages in the temporary table again. Give each employee that has never purchased glasses another one percent.
5. Delete Al Gore's record from the employee table. Check to see whether the record deleted. Perform the rollback command. Check to see whether the record is still deleted. If it hasn't been deleted, delete it again and be certain to commit the change. Perform the rollback. Has the Al Gore's record been deleted?
6. Update the wages in the employee table with the values contained in the temporary table.
7. Truncate the temporary table created in problem 2. Perform a rollback. Are there any records in the table?
8. Drop the temporary table.

PART III

# PL/SQL Oracle's Procedure Language

CHAPTER

# 8

# Creating Your First PL/SQL Program

This chapter introduces the PL/SQL language. It starts with a look at the basic PL/SQL block. The complexity of the topics increases with the coverage of variables, cursors, loops, and error handling. ■

**Understanding PL/SQL**

This section introduces you to Oracle's procedure language PL/SQL. The language is used in many Oracle products such as Oracle Forms and Oracle Report Writer. The section also introduces you to the PL/SQL block,the basic form for PL/SQL program scripts.

**Using *if-then-else* logic**

This section covers the `if-then-else` conditional statement. The statement provides decision-making logic and control to your PL/SQL.

**Using loops and exits**

This section covers simple loops. Loops are a device in PL/SQL that allow your program to repeat a section of code multiple times.

**Understand PL/SQL cursors**

This section introduces you to a cursor. This powerful device enables you to process set of records one record at a time.

**Controlling your cursors with cursor commands**

This section covers the `Open`, `Fetch`, and `Close` commands. Each of these commands performs a special cursor function.

# Understanding PL/SQL

PL/SQL is Oracle's procedure language or programming language. It is very similar to other programming languages such as BASIC, FORTRAN, C, or COBOL. PL/SQL enables you to define local variables, acquire data from the database, process the data, and return it to the database. You can record specific instructions in PL/SQL that tell your applications how to act. PL/SQL has a wealth of tools that greatly enhance the processing of records. PL/SQL has looping statements that enable you to perform the same function a number of times. It has condition logic that enables you to process records when certain conditions are met. It has cursors that enable you to move sets of records into memory and process them one at a time. It has techniques that enable you to easily assign values to local variables. You can use SQL commands illustrated in Chapters 3–7 to acquire records and modify the database. PL/SQL is a powerful tool for performing complex processing tasks.

PL/SQL is the programming language used in most of the Oracle products. It is a very effective tool for converting data from an old database to a new database. The procedures can be written in Windows Notepad and executed from SQL*PLUS. The programs read records from the Oracle database by using a cursor. The values in the records are placed in the local variables. The variables are processed using condition statements. The data is then placed into the new tables.

You can also use PL/SQL in Oracle Forms to customize the behavior of the form. In addition to data manipulation statements, PL/SQL can contain built-in subprograms. They perform special functions in a form such as navigating to the next record. PL/SQL can be tied to events that can occur on the form. When the event, such as inserting a record occurs, the PL/SQL commands associated to the event are executed.

**NOTE** Built-in subprogram is a special procedure developed by Oracle to perform a special function on a form. An example of a built-in subprogram is `next_item`, which moves the cursor to the next field on a form.

Most Oracle products use PL/SQL to some degree. They are used to perform calculations, format items, or to customize the application. Without a strong knowledge of the PL/SQL language, you limit your abilities to customize your form applications.

## Understanding the PL/SQL Blocks

PL/SQL statements are generally contained in code blocks. The code block consists of four sections:

- Header—Defines the type of block. The options are procedure, function, or anonymous.
- Declare—Defines local variables and cursors. The section begins with the word *Declare*.
- Executable—Contains the execution statements. It is where the commands are recorded. This section starts with the word *Begin*.
- Exception—Contains exception handling logic. An exception is an error or event that occurs during the execution of the commands in the executable section. When this

happens, the processor immediately moves to this section. It then looks for an exception handler associated the error. If it finds one, it performs the actions specified.

**NOTE** Exception handler is a statement included in the Exception section of the PL/SQL block. It begins with the word *when* followed by the name of the exception it is to handle. An example of an exception name is `no_data_found`. If the exception occurs, the processor performs the commands in the handler.

There are three types of PL/SQL blocks (see Figure 8.1). The first is an anonymous block that cannot be called by another application. This type of block does not have a header section. The other two types of blocks, procedures and functions, must have a header section because they may be called by another application. The difference between the two is that functions return a value and procedures do not. This chapter covers anonymous blocks. The next chapter covers procedures and functions. Procedures and functions have additional rules and functionality that do not apply to anonymous blocks. PL/SQL block statements must end with a semi-colon. The keywords *Declare*, *Begin*, and *Exception* identify the beginning of a block section. Semi-colons do not follow these words because they are not a statement or command. In an anonymous block, the first word is *Declare*. It denotes the beginning of the section where local variable and cursors are declared. When the program does not contain these items, the section does not have to be included in the block. The *Executable* section starts with the word *Begin*. All blocks must have an Executable section or they have no purpose. The *Exception* section begins with the keyword *Exception*. It is placed after the instructions in the *Executable* section. It is optional and does not have to be in the block. The word *end* completes the block.

**FIG. 8.1**
Format of the PL/SQL block.

| BLOCK FORMAT | DESCRIPTION |
|---|---|
| Declare | The declare section is used to define local variables and cursors used in the program. |
| Begin | The executable section starts with the word begin. Statements in this section cause Oracle to perform work. |
| Exception | The exception section is used to handle processing irregularities such as no data found. This is an optional section. The application will terminate if an exception occurs and there is not a handler in this section |
| End; | The PL/SQL block is terminated by the word end. A semi-colon must follow it. |
| / | The slash tells SQL*PLUS to execute the block |

You can execute PL/SQL programs from SQL*PLUS.Oracle does not run the program until it encounters the slash (/) symbol. You normally place this symbol in the script file after the keyword end. You can also enter the slash symbol at the SQL*PLUS prompt.

## Nested Blocks and Block Labels

Blocks can have nested blocks within them. The nested block can have all the sections of any other PL/SQL block. The nested block is contained in the executable section of the outer block. As the processor moves through the executable section, it begins processing the code in the nested block when it is reached. Variables declared in the nested block can only be used in that block.You can identify blocks with ***block labels***. You can use these undeclared identifiers as a qualifier for a block's local variables. The label name enclosed by greater than and less than symbols (<< >>) denotes the beginning of the ***block label***. The label must appear at the beginning of the block. The label name preceded by the word ***end*** denotes the completion of the marked code. Labels prove useful in marking sections of code. When the label is used as a qualifier, it tells Oracle in which block the variable was defined.

> **TIP** Block labels prove very useful when you name your local variables the same name as your table columns. It easy to get the rdBms and yourself mixed up as to which is a table column or local variable. The block label can be used as a qualifier for the local variables. This reduces confusion as to what the variable represents.

PL/SQL has a `Goto` command used in conjunction with a *label*. A label is an undeclared identifier enclosed by double brackets. It differs from the block label in that you can place it anywhere in the block and it does not have an *end* keyword. The label is the destination for the `Goto` command. It is used to redirect the flow of the program.

Listing 8.1 illustrates an anonymous block that contains only the executable section. It has a block label called "ONE". It also contains labels and a `Goto` command. The program prints the word "Hello," and then is redirected to label "Two" to print the words "What did you say." The `Goto` command causes the program to skip the line that would print "Goodbye."

**Listing 8.1 L_08_01.sql—Using the *GOTO* and Label Commands to Change the Program Flow**

```
SQL> set serveroutput on;
SQL> <<one>>
begin
  dbms_output.put_line ('Hello');
  goto two;
  dbms_output.put_line ('Good Bye');
  <<two>>
  dbms_output.put_line ('What did you say?');
end one;
/
Hello
```

```
What did you say?

PL/SQL procedure successfully completed.
```

**NOTE** I do not find the `Goto` command very useful. I believe it is a throwback to early programming techniques. It is hard for me to follow the logic of the program when the `Goto` commands are included. I recommend that you use `Goto` commands with special care. In the next several chapters, I use the dbms output package to display values. This is a package available for displaying information while running the program. PL/SQL normally has no output except the words `PL/SQL procedure successfully completed`. These statements help you follow the logic and execution of the programs. To see the output of these commands, the `set serveroutput` *on* setting must be used.

## Defining Your PL/SQL Variables

Variables are the mechanism PL/SQL uses to hold data for the purpose of evaluation and modification. If you want to read records from the database; evaluate them; modify them when the conditions are correct; and return the modified values back to the database, you need local variables. The reason is Oracle cannot act on the values unless they are placed in memory. The `Select` command acquires the record and values from the database table for the PL/SQL program, but the `select` clause does not put it into memory. This is done with the `into` clause or by a Fetch command. They are the devices that assign values to local variables. The local variables are holders of values in memory. Thus the PL/SQL program can now use the values for its purposes.

You name variables in the `Declare` section of the PL/SQL block. The definition of variables reserves a place in memory for the variable. The variables use the same data types that Table 6.1 illustrated. These types can be alphanumeric or numeric. The alphanumeric variables can be fixed length (`char`) or variable length (`varchar2`). The numeric fields can be an integer or have a specified precision. An example of a variable declaration is: `payment number(6,2)`. This declaration defines a numeric value that contains six spaces with two decimal positions.

You can define two additional types of variables in the Declare section. The first is a *Boolean* variable. This data type contains an evaluation value of true, false, or null (unknown). It is used when a function returns an evaluation rather than a specific value. The value is true if all conditions have been met. It is false if some of the conditions have not been met, and null if the results of the evaluation are unknown.The second variable type is *exception*. This data type is used to set up the variable for a user-defined exception that will be used in the Exception section of the program. This chapter discusses this in greater detail in following sections.

The data type, size specification, and a semicolon follow the name of the variable. The variable name must start with a letter, but can have any alphanumeric character up to 30 characters. It cannot be an Oracle reserved word and must be continuous. Figure 8.2 illustrates methods of defining variables. The most common data types are *char*, *varchar2*, and *number*. In the Figure, the definition of "pi" uses the word *constant*. This means that the value cannot be changed at any time during the program. You must assign it a value at the time it is created. If the program inadvertently tries to reassign this type of variable a value, Oracle issues an error message and stops execution of the program.

**FIG. 8.2**
Defining variables.

```
last_name          varchar2(15);
payroll_number     char(2);
pi                 constant number(9,8) := 3.14159265;
age                number(3);
dept               employee.fk_department%type;
emp_row            employee%rowtype;
bday               emp_row.birth_date%type;
is_true_or_not     boolean;
bad_error          exception;
first_name         varchar2(10) not null := 'JOHN';
```

The "first_name" definition has a not null constraint placed on it. This means that the variable must always have a value in it. If you inadvertently place a null value into the variable, an error occurs and the program terminates. Not null variables must always have a value assigned to them as part of the declaration. Because "first_name" is a not null variable, you must assign it a value during the definition.

## Using the *%Type* and *%Rowtype*

The `%type` definition is an important device for ensuring the local variable has the same data type as the database column that supplies it the value. In Figure 8.2, for example, the "`employee.fk_department%type`" expression is used to define the "dept" variable the same format type and size as the fk_department field in the Employee table. The `%type` definition causes this to happen. The syntax requires the table name and field name to precede the `%type`. A period (.) separates the table name (employee) and the field name (fk_department).

The `%rowtype` definition performs a similar function. It sets up an array of local variables in memory for each field in the referenced table. In the Figure, the "`emp_row`" definition creates an array of variables based on the Employee table. The syntax of the definition requires the name of the table to precede the `%rowtype`. When the variable is used in the PL/SQL program, the variable has the same name as the column in the Employee table, and it must have "`emp_row`" as a qualifier. An example of the syntax is "`emp_row.last_name`". It represents the `last_name` variable in the array defined as `emp_row`.

**TIP** The `%type` and especially `%rowtype` definitions are excellent devices for defining variables accurately. One of the most common mistakes I make in writing PL/SQL is defining local variables with a different format or length than the column in the corresponding database table. This causes problems when comparing values in my programs. Varchar2 data types do not compare well with char data types. When mistakes occur on evaluations, the program does not operate as designed. Another error consists of moving larger values into the smaller variables. This error causes the application to stop. The `%type` and `%rowtype` eliminate this problem because you do not have to investigate and possibly mistype in the definitions. In addition, the `%rowtype` saves considerable typing of definitions.

## Assigning Values to the Variables

To assign values to variables, use the `Equal to` (:=) operator or a `Select` command. Figure 8.2 shows the use of the `Equal to` operator. The "pi" and "first_name" variables were assigned a value by using this operator.

**CAUTION**

Users sometimes mix up the `Equals (=)` and `Equal to` (:=) operators. Such a mix-up causes the PL/SQL program to abort. The `Equals` (=) operator is used in evaluations such as *a = b, true or false.* The `Equal to` operator is used in variable assignments such as *a := b. A is now equal to b.*

You can use the `select` statement to assign values. It has an additional clause not yet discussed called `into`. The `into` clause follows the `select` clause and contains the names of variables that will be assigned values. Listing 8.2 shows two examples of assigning variables by using the `select` statement. The top example assigns two specific table fields into two variables contained in the `into` clause. The variables in the `into` clause are the local variables defined with `%rowtype`, obvious because of the "`emp_row`" qualifier.

**Listing 8.2 L_08-02.sql—Assigning Values to Variables by Using the *SELECT* Statement**

```
SQL> set serveroutput on;
SQL> declare
     emprow        employee%rowtype;
     holder        varchar2(100);
     begin
       select max(first_name), min(last_name)
       into emprow.first_name, emprow.last_name
       from employee;
       holder := ('1st select '||emprow.first_name||' '||emprow.last_name);
       dbms_output.put_line (holder);
       select * into emprow from employee where last_name = 'WILSON';
       holder := ('2nd select '||emprow.first_name||' '||emprow.last_name);
       dbms_output.put_line (holder);
     end;
     /
```

*continues*

**Listing 8.2 Continued**

```
1st select WOODROW ANTHONY
2nd select WOODROW WILSON

PL/SQL procedure successfully completed.
```

The second select illustrates assigning values to each field in the "`emp_row`" array. The names of the fields do not need to be contained in the statement. Oracle knows that all the fields from the Employee record have been selected because of the *all* (*) symbol. It also knows that the array "`emp_row`" has all the fields as the Employee table. Oracle ensures that the proper variable gets the right value.When using the `select` statement to assign values, the `select` clause must have the same number of variables as the `into` clause. You must assign the value in the first variable in the `select` clause to the first variable in the `into` clause. Likewise, you must assign the second variable to the second one in the `into` clause and so forth.

**TIP** The `select` statement is the only method in PL/SQL to assign multiple variables a value at the same time.

# Using *If-Then-Else* Logic

One of the excellent features of PL/SQL is the conditional control that you can exercise by using `if-then-else` constructs. The `if` portion of the construct performs the evaluation. When the evaluation is true, the actions following `then` are performed. Sometimes the statement contains the word `else`. This part of the construct is optional. When the evaluation is false and an `else` section exists, the commands following it are performed. The construct is terminated by the words "`end if;`". Figure 8.3 illustrates the syntax components of an `if-then-else` statement.

The `if` clause contains the evaluation expressions. The clause can contain more than one expression. The expressions are separated by either the `and` predicate or the `or` predicates. The expressions are evaluated exactly as the conditional statements contained in the `where` clause of a `select` statement.

When the initial evaluation is true, the commands following `then` are executed. This section can contain one or more commands. A semi-colon completes each command in the section. When the evaluation is false, the commands in this section are not executed. The commands following the `else` are executed. The `else` section is optional. When it is missing, the program leaves the `if-then-else` construct any `executes` and statement following the construct..

Listing 8.3 illustrates a simple PL/SQL block and how it uses an `If-then-else` statement to determine the current month. The `declare` section is used to name a variable called "month." In the first line of the `begin` section the `substr` function is used to assign "month" with the characters that represent the current month from the `sysdate` function.

**FIG. 8.3**
Basic `if-then-else` statement.

```
select first_name, last_name, fk_department
   into emp_row.first_name, emp_row.last_name, emp_row.fk_department
from employee;



select *
  into emp_row
from employee;
```

### Listing 8.3 L_08-03.txt—Using an *If-Then-Else* Statement in a PL/SQL Block

```
SQL> set serveroutput on;
SQL> declare
  month  char(3);
 begin
  month := upper(substr(to_char(sysdate), 4, 3));
  dbms_output.put_line (sysdate);
  if (month = 'JAN' or month = 'FEB' or month = 'MAR'
    or month = 'APR' or month = 'MAY' or month = 'JUN') then
    dbms_output.put_line ('I say hello. Hello !');
  else
     dbms_output.put_line ('I say goodbye. Goodbye !');
   end if;
 end;
 /
23-APR-97
I say hello. Hello !

PL/SQL procedure successfully completed.
```

The initial evaluation in the construct compares the value of "month" with values that represent the first six months of the year. The evaluation clause uses the `or` predicate to link the various condition expressions. If one of the expressions is true, the commands following the `then` are executed. If none of the expressions are true, the commands following the `else` are executed.

The script was executed in April, therefore the expressions evaluated as true, as the commands following the `then` were executed.

Several rules apply to the `if-then-else` construct.

- An `If` can only contain one `else`.
- `Else` is not followed by a semicolon.
- `If` condition expressions are always followed by a `then`.
- `End if` terminates the `If-Then-Else` construct.

## Using Nested *If* Statements

`If-then-else` constructs can contain nested `If-Then-Else` constructs , the `then` or `else` sections can contain one or more `If-then-else` constructs. These `If` statements can also contain nested `If` statements. This capability to nest `If-then-else` constructs enables developers to outline complex algorithms for their programs. This is a very important tool for use in your data conversion and Form programs.

Listing 8.4 contains an `If-then-else` construct with a nested `If-then-else` constructs. The PL/SQL block determines whether the date is in February and what the date of the last day of the month is. The program has '01-FEB-97' assigned to the `sample_date` variable. The first line of the program extracts the month from the original date. The first `If` statement determines whether the month is February. If it is, the year is divided by four. The *MOD* function calculates the remainder. If there is no remainder, the last day of the month is the "29$^{th}$." The date in the PL/SQL program is not in a leap year. The program prints "The Last Day of the Month is the 28$^{th}$."

**Listing 8.4 L_08_04.sql—Using Nested *If* Statements in a PL/SQL Block**

```
SQL> declare
     sample_date     char(9) := '01-FEB-97';
     remainder       number;
     month           char(3);
     last_day        char(2);
   begin
     month := substr(sample_date, 4, 3);
     if (month = 'FEB') then
       remainder := mod(to_number(substr(sample_date, 8,2)),4);
       if (remainder = 0) then
           last_day := '29';
           dbms_output.put_line ('This is a Leap Year');
           dbms_output.put_line ('The Last Day of the Month Is The
'||last_day||'th');
       else
           last_day := '28';
           dbms_output.put_line ('This is not a Leap Year');
           dbms_output.put_line ('The Last Day of the Month Is The
'||last_day||'th');
```

```
      end if;
    else
         dbms_output.put_line ('The Month is Not February');
    end if;
 end;
 /
This is not a Leap Year
The Last Day of the Month Is The 28th

PL/SQL procedure successfully completed.
```

This program has a number of conditions to evaluate. The first evaluation is whether the month is February. When it is, it needs to determine whether the year is a leap year or not. This is the nested `if-then-else` construct. Without the ability to nest the constructs, you could not document complex logic needed for your programs.

## Using *Elseif* in Your *If* Construct

Instead of using a nested `if-then-else` construct in the `else` section, you can use the `elseif` word. This word sets up a structure similar to an `if-then-else` construct except that it does not have its own `else if`. Because it is in the `else` portion of the structure, it uses the `end if` of the structure to denote its completion. You can use this construct as many times as needed in the section. Listing 8.5 illustrates the use of the `elseif` construct. The intent of the PL/SQL block is to determine the current month of the year and output a holiday that occurs during that month. The `if-then-else` construct has a series of conditions used to determine the month of the year. The first condition following the `If` checks to see whether the month is January. The remaining conditions follow each `elseif` and check for the months from February to June. Each of the conditions is mutually exclusive. If any of the conditions are met, the commands following are performed and the program exits the structure.

**Listing 8.5 L_08_05.sqk—Using the *Elseif* Construct to Display the Correct Monthly Events**

```
SQL> set serveroutput on;
SQL> declare
  month  char(3);
 begin
  month := substr(to_char(sysdate, 'DD-MON-YY'), 4,3);
  if (month = 'JAN') then
   dbms_output.put_line ('January has Martin Luther King's Birthday');
   elsif (month = 'FEB') then
    dbms_output.put_line ('February has Valentines Day');
   elsif (month = 'MAR') then
     dbms_output.put_line ('March has Spring Training');
    elsif (month = 'APR') then
     dbms_output.put_line ('April has My Birthday');
    elsif (month = 'MAY') then
     dbms_output.put_line ('May has Mothers Day');
    elsif (month = 'JUN') then
```

*continues*

**Listing 8.5 Continued**

```
    dbms_output.put_line ('June has My Wedding Anniversary');
   else
    dbms_output.put_line ('I Ran Out Of Room In The Example');
  end if;
 end;
 /
April has My Birthday
PL/SQL procedure successfully completed.
```

Following the final `elsif` in Listing 8.5 is an `else` section. It is used as a catch-all for any instances that do not match the conditions in the `If` statements. In the case of the preceding example, the months July to December do not match any the conditions contained in the `if-elseif` statements. Thus, if the current month is between July and December, none of the commands that followed these statements will be executed. The command following the `else` keyword is executed.

**TIP** The `Elseif` structure is a good tool to use when a large number of options need to be evaluated in the `if-then-else` structure. It ensures that each path through the structure is mutually exclusive of the others. This is not true with a series of nested `If` statements.

# Using Loops and Exits

PL/SQL has several structures that allow your programs to execute the same procedure repeatedly. These structures are very powerful devices that enable you to process multiple records using the same set of PL/SQL statements The first structure considered here is called a *loop*.

The Loop structure has three parts: the `Loop` command, an `Exit` command, and an `End loop` command. The following bulleted list illustrates these commands. The keyword *loop* denotes the beginning of the structure. It tells Oracle to execute the commands within the structure until the `Exit` command is encountered. The `End loop` command tells Oracle that it has reached the end of the Loop structure. Oracle then begins to re-execute the commands from the beginning of the structure, continuing until the `Exit` command is executed. The components of a loop structure are:

- `Loop`—The loop structure begins with the `loop` command. The commands that follow it are executed repeatedly until the loop procedure is terminated by an `exit` command. The `loop` command is not followed by a semicolon.
- `Exit`—The `exit` command terminates the loop. It is usually a command in an `If` statement. When the condition is true the `exit` command is executed and the loop terminated.
- `End loop`—The loop structure ends with the `end loop` keywords. Then these keywords are reached, the control moves back to the beginning of the loop structure. The `end loop` command is followed by a semicolon.

Listing 8.5 is a PL/SQL program that outputs each number from 1 to 50. To do this, the loop must be executed 50 times. The program has a counter variable that increases by a value of one with each iteration of the loop. An `If` statement is contained in the program. When the value of the counter reaches 50, the `Exit` command is issued and the loop terminates.

**Listing 8.6 L_08_06.sql—Using a *Loop Structure* to Output a Series of Numbers**

```
SQL> set serveroutput on;
SQL> declare
 2  counter  number := 1;
 3 begin
 4  dbms_output.put_line ('This is the beginning of the series of numbers');
 5  loop
 6   dbms_output.put_line (counter);
 7   counter := counter + 1;
 8   if (counter > 50) then
 9     exit;
 10   end if;
 11  end loop;
 12  dbms_output.put_line ('This is the end of the numbers');
 13 end;
 14 /
This is the beginning of the series of numbers
1
2
.
.
49
50
This is the end of the numbers
PL/SQL procedure successfully completed.
```

You can also terminate the loop by using a `When` operator rather than an `If` statement. It has a slightly different syntax. The `Exit` command is followed by the word `when` and an evaluation expression. You can use the `When` operator when you are testing for conditions not related to counters. An example of this type of condition is `no_data_found`. This condition can exist when the `Select` command was issued and no records were found. In the next chapter, you are introduced to a number of conditions that can be used as evaluation conditions to terminate the loop. Listing 8.6 illustrates the use of the `When` operator. It replaces the `If` statement from the program executed in Listing 8.5.

**Listing 8.7 L_08_07.sql—Using the *When* Operator to Terminate the Loop**

```
SQL> set serveroutput on;
SQL> declare
 2  counter  number := 1;
 3 begin
 4  dbms_output.put_line ('This is the beginning of the series of numbers');
```

*continues*

**Listing 8.7 Continued**

```
loop
 dbms_output.put_line (counter);
 counter := counter + 1;
 exit when counter > 50;
end loop;
 dbms_output.put_line ('This is the end of the numbers');
end;
/
This is the beginning of the series of numbers
1
2
.
.
48
49
50
This is the end of the numbers

PL/SQL procedure successfully completed.
```

You can use two other types of repeating structures in PL/SQL. They are the `while` loop and the `for` loop. The `while` loop does not need an `Exit` command. The `for` loop performs specialized functions by using cursors. The next chapter covers these two structures in more detail.

> **CAUTION**
>
> When using any loop statement, be certain to check whether a condition always exists that terminates the loop. I have written many programs where I didn't have a condition to terminate a loop. This causes a condition called an *infinite loop*. When this happens, I spend a great deal of time watching the cursor on my machine blink.
>
> To break an infinite loop, the *control+c* keys may be pressed. This will generally break the processing. It is an abnormal break, so none of the changes that may have been performed will be saved. Oracle will rollback the changes. If there are not pending changes, Oracle will respond immediately to the sequence. If a large number of changes are pending, Oracle must rollback the changes before responding. This may take a period of time.

# Understanding PL/SQL Cursors

A database *cursor* is a device in PL/SQL that acquires a set of records and places them in memory for individual processing. It is not the same thing as a screen cursor which designates a position on a screen Cursors can be compared to a bookmark placed inside the pages of the book. Each page is a record in the set or records acquired by the database manager per the cursor's instructions. When the book is first opened, you are on the first page or record. The bookmark is also on the first page. As you read one page after the other, you move the bookmark to identify the current page. A cursor operates in much the same way. When the cursor is initiated with an `Open cursor` command, Oracle places the set of records in memory and places the cursor on the first record. As you retrieve records to your program by using the `Fetch` command, the cursor moves to the next record. This is the same as you did with your bookmark when you moved to the next page. When you are done looking at the records, you close cursor and remove the records by using the `Close` command.

## Controlling Your Cursors with Cursor Commands

Several commands and steps are used in relation to cursors. Figure 8.4 illustrates these commands. The first task is to define the cursor. This occurs in the Declare section of the PL/SQL block. The definition consists of the words "`cursor cursor_name is`" followed by a `Select` statement. The `Select` statement is used to retrieve the desired records and values for the cursor. A semicolon completes this cursor definition.

**FIG. 8.4**
Cursor definition and cursor commands.

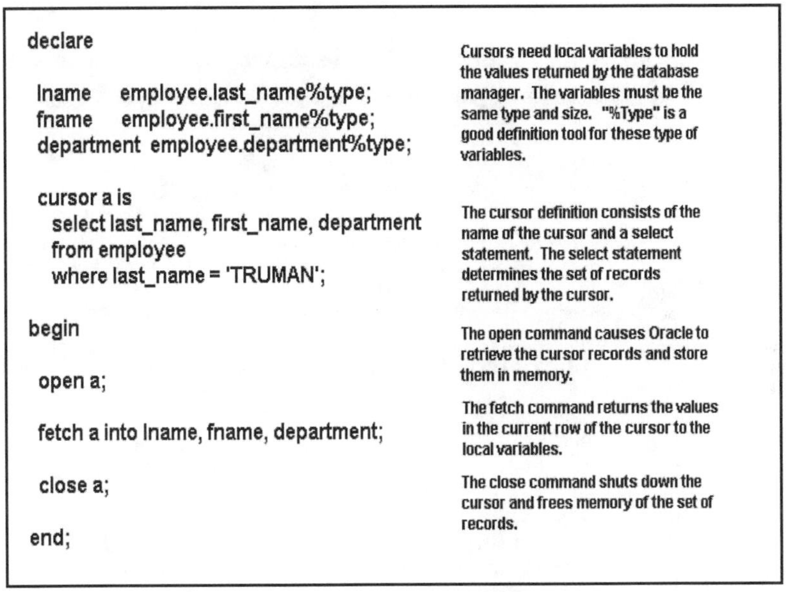
declare
lname employee.last_name%type;
fname employee.first_name%type;
department employee.department%type;
cursor a is
select last_name, first_name, department
from employee
where last_name = 'TRUMAN';
begin
open a;
fetch a into lname, fname, department;
close a;
end;
Cursors need local variables to hold the values returned by the database manager. The variables must be the same type and size. "%Type" is a good definition tool for these type of variables.
The cursor definition consists of the name of the cursor and a select statement. The select statement determines the set of records returned by the cursor.
The open command causes Oracle to retrieve the cursor records and store them in memory.
The fetch command returns the values in the current row of the cursor to the local variables.
The close command shuts down the cursor and frees memory of the set of records.

Cursors retrieve values from the database. They need local variables to place the retrieved values into. As you have seen in the section of this chapter about defining variables, these variables are defined in the `Declare` section. There must be one local variable for each column named in the cursor. The variables must be the same data type and must be at least as large as the column.

The cursor is activated when the "`open cursor name`" command is issued in the `Executable` portion of the PL/SQL block. Issuing the command causes the database manager to retrieve the records identified in the `Select` statement and to place the records in memory. A semicolon terminates the command.

The `Fetch` command assigns the values of the current cursor record to the local variables. The syntax of this statement is the keyword *fetch* followed by the name of the cursor. This is followed by the local variables that will contain the values from the cursor columns. The value for the first column in the `Select` statement will go in the first variable listed in the Fetch command. The command must contain the same number of variables as the `select` statement. A semicolon terminates this command. The cursor is ended with the "`close cursor name`" command. This command frees memory of the records the `Select` command placed in it. A semicolon terminates this command also.

Listing 8.8 is a PL/SQL block that examines the birthdays of the employees and determines the most common day of the week for birthdays. The program employs a number of the features discussed thus far in this chapter. The `Declare` block defines a number of variables and initializes them during the declaration. The *`bday`* variable is used to hold the birthday values returned by the cursor "birthday". It is defined with the `%type` declaration to ensure it has the same data type as the cursor column.

**Listing 8.8 L_08_08.TXT—Executing a Cursor in a Loop to Determine the Most Common Day of the Week that Our Employees Were Born**

```
SQL> set serveroutput on;
SQL> declare
      bday        date;  day_of_week  varchar2(10); sunday     number := 0;
      monday      number := 0; tuesday     number := 0; wednesday  number := 0;
      thursday    number := 0; friday      number := 0; saturday   number := 0;
      cursor birth_days is select birth_date from employee;
    begin
      open birth_days;
      loop
        fetch birth_days into bday;
        if (birth_days%notfound) then
              exit;
        end if;
        day_of_week := rtrim(to_char(bday, 'DAY'), ' ');
        if (day_of_week = 'SUNDAY') then
          sunday := sunday + 1;
          elsif (day_of_week = 'MONDAY') then
            monday := monday + 1;
          elsif (day_of_week = 'TUESDAY') then
            tuesday := tuesday + 1;
          elsif (day_of_week = 'WEDNESDAY') then
            wednesday := wednesday + 1;
          elsif (day_of_week = 'THURSDAY') then
            thursday := thursday + 1;
          elsif (day_of_week = 'FRIDAY') then
            friday := friday + 1;
          elsif (day_of_week = 'SATURDAY') then
            saturday := saturday + 1;
        end if;
       end loop;
       close birth_days;
```

```
    dbms_output.put_line ('There were '||sunday||' births on Sunday');
    dbms_output.put_line ('There were '||monday||' births on Monday');
    dbms_output.put_line ('There were '||tuesday||' births on Tuesday');
    dbms_output.put_line ('There were '||wednesday||' births on Wednesday');
    dbms_output.put_line ('There were '||thursday||' births on Thursday');
    dbms_output.put_line ('There were '||friday||' births on Friday');
    dbms_output.put_line ('There were '||saturday||' births on Saturday');
end;
/
There were 1 births on Sunday
There were 5 births on Monday
There were 4 births on Tuesday
There were 3 births on Wednesday
There were 5 births on Thursday
There were 0 births on Friday
There were 1 births on Saturday

PL/SQL procedure successfully completed.
```

You open the cursor in the first line of the `Executable` section. The program then initiates a loop. It is needed to evaluate each of the records in the employee table using the same code. The loop's first task is to fetch the first record from the cursor into the program for evaluation. Because birthday is a date data type, it is converted to a character string. It uses the *day* picture to format the date properly for evaluation. The day_of_week variable is then evaluated in a series of mutually exclusive `elsif` condition expressions in an `if-then-else` structure to determine the birth day-of-the-week counts. When the program reaches the end loop statement, it returns to the top of the loop and fetches the next record. When it reaches the end of the records, the `no_data_found` exception occurs and the loop terminates. The cursor is then closed, and the count of employee birthdays is the output. Some things you might want to remember about cursors include the following:

- Issuing an `open` command when the cursor is still open causes an exception error.
- Issuing a `close` command when the cursor is not open causes an exception error.
- Fetching a record when the cursor has not been opened causes an exception error.
- Fetching a record when you have reached the end of the records in memory does *not* cause an exception error to occur. The database manager continues to return the values in the last record in the set with each fetch.
- Continuing to open cursors without closing them eventually eliminates the memory needed to run the program. Termination of the PL/SQL program closes the cursors.

# Identifying Exceptions

*Exceptions* are problems, errors, or abnormal conditions that occur when your PL/SQL program is operating. Some of these exceptions have already been discussed. In the previous section, you learned that opening a cursor already open or closing a cursor that is not open causes an exception. When an exception occurs, the program switches control from the Executable section to the Exception section of the PL/SQL block. If an *exception handler* exists for the exception, the program follows the instructions in the handler. If an exception handler does not exist, the program terminates with an error message.

```
operating as if the error did not occur.
```

A variety of exceptions can occur. To create an exception handler, you must identify the exception with the name of the handler. In addition to system exceptions, you can define and name user named exceptions. The next section, "Logging and Displaying Your Errors," discusses these. Table 8.1 contains the names and descriptions of many of the possible exceptions.

**Table 8.1—Predefined PL/SQL Exceptions**

| Name | Description |
|---|---|
| Cursor_already_open | Occurs when the application tries to open a cursor currently open. (ORA-6511 SQLCODE = -6511) |
| Dup_val_on_index | Occurs when Oracle tries to perform an insert or update operation and attempts to put a non-unique value in a field defined with a unique constraint. (ORA-00001 SQLCODE = -1) |
| Invalid_cursor | Occurs when the application references an undefined cursor in program. (ORA-01001 SQLCODE –1001) |
| Invalid_number | Occurs when the application tries to put an incorrect value in a local variable or database column. Examples of incorrect values are alphanumeric values being placed in a numeric field, a value either numeric or alphanumeric larger than the field it is to be assigned to, or a date that is invalid or is not in the defined format. (ORA-01722 SQLCODE = -1722) |
| Login_denied | Occurs when a database login is attempted by using either an invalid user name or password. (ORA-01017 SQLCODE = -1017) |
| No_data_found | Occurs when a select statement is executed against a table and no values are returned. (ORA-01403 SQLCODE = +100) |
| Not_logged_on | Occurs when a call to the database happens and the application is not connected. (ORA-01012 SQLCODE = -1012) |
| Program_error | Occurs when and internal PL/SQL error happens. (ORA-06501 SQLCODE = -6501) |
| Storage_error | Occurs when memory is used up. (ORA-06500 SQLCODE = -6500) |
| Timeout_on_resource | Occurs when the database manager decides to stop waiting for a resource to become available. This often happens when a table is locked by another user. (ORA-00051 SQLCODE = -5100) |
| Too_many_rows | Occurs when a select statement returns more than one row |

| Name | Description |
|---|---|
| | and the application is expecting one row. (ORA-01422 SQLCODE = -1422) |
| Transaction_backed_out | Occurs when part of a database transaction has been rolled back. (ORA-00061 SQLCODE = -61) |
| Value_error | Occurs when PL/SQL cannot convert character data to numbers. It also occurs when errors related to constraints and truncation happen. (ORA-06502 SQLCODE = -6502) |
| Zero_divide (-1476) | Occurs when a number is divided by zero. (ORA-01476 SQLCODE = -1476) |
| Others | A catch-all exception used to handle any undefined or unnamed exceptions. |

The error numbers following the preceding descriptions are the Oracle error number and the value returned to SQLCODE. *SQLCODE* is a built-in function that returns the status of the last executed database command. When there are no errors, the value is 0.

# Logging and Displaying Your Errors

The exceptions identified in the preceding section cause the execution of statements in the Executable section to stop. The focus of the program shifts to the Exception section of the PL/SQL block. The processor reviews this section for an exception handler that contains the name of the exception. After it finds the handler, it performs the commands that follow it. If it does not find a handler, it terminates the program abnormally. Terminating the program abnormally can cause some problems. Unless a commit was issued in the program, all insert, update, or delete actions performed by the program are rolled back. In addition, when the PL/SQL program is terminated, an Oracle predefined error message issues. The message may be vague and meaningless to an operator. This proves especially troublesome to operators of an Oracle Form. More descriptive error messages would certainly increase the user-friendliness of the application.

The purpose of the exception section of the block is to eliminate these problems. Listing 8.9 illustrates a `no_data_found` exception. The `Select` statement attempts to find an employee with the name of "Buchanan". This employee does not exist in the Employee database, and the `no_data_found` exception will be raised. The first block does not contain an exception section. Notice the error message displayed.

**Listing 8.9 L_08_09.sql—Raising a *No_Data_Found* Exception with and Without an Exception Handler**

```
SQL> set serveroutput on;
SQL> declare
  2  lname    employee.last_name%type;
  3  fname    employee.first_name%type;
  4 begin
  5  select last_name, first_name
  6   into lname, fname
  7  from employee
  8  where last_name = 'BUCHANAN';
  9 end;
 10 /
declare
 *
ERROR at line 1:
ORA-01403: no data found
ORA-06512: at line 5


SQL>
SQL> set serveroutput on;
SQL> declare
  2  lname    employee.last_name%type;
  3  fname    employee.first_name%type;
  4 begin
  5  select last_name, first_name
  6   into lname, fname
  7  from employee
  8  where last_name = 'BUCHANAN';
  9 exception
 10  when no_data_found then
 11   dbms_output.put_line ('EMPLOYEE NOT FOUND');
 12 end;
 13 /
EMPLOYEE NOT FOUND

PL/SQL procedure successfully completed.
SQL>
```

The second block contains an exception section and an exception handler for the `no_data_found` exception. This block displays the message `No Employee Found` when the exception occurs. This is a much more preferable message to display when users execute the program.

## Renaming Standard Errors with Your Own Names

Custom-named exceptions can make your programs easier to interpret. To name the exception, you must first declare an exception in the `Declare` section of the program. Next, you identify the named exception with an exception number. Table 8.1 lists standard exceptions. Each of the exceptions has a particular number. In fact, all Oracle errors have a number. The named exception is associated with this exception number. To identify the named exception with an exception number, use the `pragma exception_init` declaration. Pragma tells Oracle that the remainder of the statement is a directive to the compiler. *Pragmas* are special instructions to the compiler. The special instruction is the association of the new exception name with the Oracle error. Listing 8.10 illustrates a named exception called "`way_too_many_rows`". This exception will be associated to the –1422 error. This is the "`way_too_many_rows`" error.

**Listing 8.10 L_08_10.sqlTXT—Defining a User-Named Exception**

```
SQL> set serveroutput on;
SQL> declare
 2  lname   employee.last_name%type;
 3  way_too_many_rows exception;
 4  pragma exception_init (way_too_many_rows, -1422);
 5 begin
 6  select last_name
 7   into lname
 8  from employee;
 9 exception
 10  when way_too_many_rows then
 11   dbms_output.put_line ('Too Many Records For The Value');
 12 end;
 13 /
Too Many Records For The Value

PL/SQL procedure successfully completed.
```

In the third line, the exception "Way too many rows" is declared. This exception is associated to the ORA-01422 exception by using "`pragma exception_init`." The `Select` statement in the executable section attempts to place all the last name values from the Employee table into the local variable lname. This caused the ORA-01422 exception to occur. The application then moves to the exception section and performs the "`way_too_many_rows`" exception. The result of the exception is the message `"Too Many Records For The Value."`

## Using the *Exception* Section for Your Own Exceptions

You can use the `Exception` section for your own types of exceptions. You might have a program that is evaluating a set of records, for example. When an invalid condition exists in a record, you raise the exception through the use of an `If` statement. The exception handler causes the application to display a message telling the user an incorrect value exists. You can create an exception of this type by declaring and naming an exception in the `Declare` program. You do not have to create a *pragma* because this exception is not going to replace a standard exception. To use the exception, you place the exception name in the `Executable` section following the raise keyword. If a certain condition causes the exception to occur, you can place that condition in an `If` statement. When the exception name is encountered, the focus of the program shifts to the `Exception` section of the program. The exception handler is then executed. Listing 8.11 contains a program that looks at the first names of the employees. It attempts to find a misspelled first name. After the mistake is found, the exception "Incorrect First Name" is raised.

---

### Listing 8.11 L_08_11.SQL—Raising An *Incorrect First Name* Custom Exception

```
SQL> set serveroutput on;
SQL> declare
  2  incorrect_first_name  exception;
  3  fname           employee.first_name%type;
  4  lname           employee.last_name%type;
  5  cursor a is select last_name, first_name from employee;
  6 begin
  7  open a;
  8  loop
  9   fetch a into lname, fname;
 10   dbms_output.put_line(fname);
 11   if (a%notfound) then exit;
 12     end if;
 13   if (fname = 'ELEANOR') then raise incorrect_first_name;
 14     end if;
 15  end loop;
 16 exception
 17  when incorrect_first_name then
 18    dbms_output.put_line (fname¦¦' '¦¦lname¦¦' has an incorrect spelling');
 19 end;
 20 /
CALVIN
LYNDON
.
.
.
SUSAN
ELEANOR
ELEANOR ROOSEVELT    has an incorrect spelling
PL/SQL procedure successfully completed.
```

---

In the Listing, the incorrect_first_name exception is named in the Declare section. An exception handler using this name is placed in the Exception section. The Executable section contains a cursor and a loop. This allows the program to look at each record in the Employee table until it finds a record with a first name value of 'ELEANOR'. If this occurs before the cursor runs out of records, the custom exception Incorrect_First_Name is raised and the exception handler statements executed.

**N O T E** I write three types of PL/SQL programs. The first type consists of programs that I run from the SQL*PLUS prompt to convert data. I never put exceptions in this code because the program is used by me alone. The program will be thrown away when done and I know how to interpret the messages. Speed of writing these programs is more important than good error messages. The second type of program is one run in batch at night. There isn't anyone to see the messages at night, so I don't usually put messages in these. Those programs embedded in my Oracle Forms comprise the third type of PL/SQL program I write. These programs are executed by the users I support. I always put exception handlers and custom messages in these applications. It greatly increases the user-friendliness of the applications. The exception handlers I use cover the common database and Form errors the user may encounter. I can't, however, place a handler for all exceptions. I always use an "others" handler, which is a catch-all for any unnamed exception. I highly recommend that you include exception handlers, including the "others" exceptions, in all your Forms applications. Your users will appreciate your efforts.

# Summary

PL/SQL is a Oracle's programming language. PL/SQL has three types of structures or blocks: anonymous blocks, procedures, and functions. Anonymous blocks are not callable by another object. Procedures are callable. Functions are also callable, but return a value that procedures and anonymous blocks do not. A PL/SQL block contains several sections: the `Header` section, which contains the name of the procedure and parameters; the `Declaration` section, which is used to name the local variables, exceptions, and cursors used in the application; the `Executable` section, which contains the statements performed; and the `Exception` section, which is used to handle errors. PL/SQL programs have several types of looping procedures that allow them to perform the same section of code repeatedly. The simplest looping procedure begins with the word *loop* and is completed by the phrase *end loop*. Between the two, SQL statements perform functions and an exit command terminates the looping procedure. Cursors are an important component of PL/SQL. They are used to retrieve a set of records one at a time for processing. The `Cursor` is command declares the specifications of the cursor. The `Open` command executes the cursor. The `Fetch` command retrieves values from the cursor to local variables in the program. The `Close` command eliminates the cursor and frees memory. Oracle has defined a number of standard errors. These errors are handled in the `Exception` section of the program. You can rename these exceptions if you choose. You also cancreate your own exceptions. Whenever either of these types of exceptions is encountered in the `Executable` section, it causes the processor to skip to the `Exception` section of the program and perform the statements in its handler.

# From Here...

The next chapter builds on what you learned in this chapter. It introduces you to the `while` loop and `for` loop. The `for` loop is an especially powerful loop that automatically performs many of the functions of a cursor. The next chapter also discusses the creation and use of named procedures and functions. It also covers methods of storing your procedures in the database.

# Review Exercises

1. Create a PL/SQL anonymous block that displays the words "I am a PL/SQL guru".
2. Create a PL/SQL anonymous block that computes and displays the average starting age of all employees.

3. Create a PL/SQL anonymous block that displays the full name of each employee. Please use this format: “Palinski, John”.
4. Create a PL/SQL anonymous block that displays the employees born in a leap year.
5. Create a PL/SQL anonymous block that causes a `no_data_found` exception. Display a custom message when this occurs.
6. Rename the exception in #4 to “No_Record_Found”. Display an error message when this exception occurs.
7. Create your own custom exception that displays an exception message when the program encounters an employee whose first name is “Franklin”.

CHAPTER 9

# Increasing the Power of Your PL/SQL Blocks

This chapter offers you a more complex and sophisticated view of PL/SQL, and introduces you to two additional looping procedures that offer more power. This chapter also explains how procedures and functions are named and executed. The chapter also discusses Oracle's package concept. This is a very object-oriented concept that enables the developer to group procedures, functions, and cursors together. ■

**Using cursor attributes**

This section illustrates the use of cursor attributes to control your cursors. Cursor attributes enable you to know the status of the last Fetch command, whether the cursor is open, or how many records have been fetched from the database.

**Using the *While* loop**

This section covers the `While` loop. This is the second looping procedure that you can use to execute a PL/SQL statement repeatedly.

**Using the *For* loop**

This section covers the `For` loop. The `For` loop consists of two different looping procedures that begin with the keyword *For*. The first is the numeric `For` loop, and the second is the `Cursor For` loop. The latter is an especially powerful looping procedure that performs cursor commands automatically.

**Using the *For Update Of* and *Current Of* options**

This section covers the use of the `For Update Of` cursor option. It causes Oracle7 to lock the records selected by the cursor. The section also covers the `Where Current Of` option. It is a clause in an `update` or `delete` statement that causes the command to modify the last record feteched by the customer.code are callable by other applications and procedures.

# Using Cursor Attributes

In the preceding chapter, several examples used the `%notfound` cursor attribute in `If` statements. The attribute was used in a condition expression to determine whether the looping procedure should be terminated. Without the `%notfound` attribute, it would have been very difficult to stop the loop at the desired time. Cursor attributes are devices that determine the status of the cursor. Determining this status is important for knowing when to terminate loops or perform other procedures. The syntax of the cursor attribute is the name of the cursor followed by the cursor attribute. The name is needed to identify the particular cursor in which the application is interested. It is common to have multiple cursors open at a given time.

Table 9.1 lists PL/SQL's four different cursor attributes.

**Table 9.1 Cursor Attributes**

| Name | Description |
|---|---|
| `%found` | This attribute is true when the last fetch returned a record from the cursor. When it did not, the attribute is false. |
| `%notfound` | This attribute is false when the last fetch returned a record from the cursor. It is true when the fetch did not retrieve a record. |
| `%rowcount` | This attribute returns the number of records fetched from the cursor up to that point. |
| `%isopen` | This attribute is true when the named cursor is currently open. It is false when it is closed. |

## Using the *%found* Attribute

The `%found` attribute returns a value of true when the last fetch returned a record from the cursor. This attribute and its exact opposite, `%notfound`, are useful evaluation devices in a condition statement. In the preceding chapter, several examples use the `%notfound` in `if` or `when` statements as a test to execute the Exit loop command. These are arguably the best tools to determine the proper time to close a looping procedure.

**NOTE** Many of the applications I develop contain nested cursors in nested `while` loops. The nested cursors are used to retrieve records from a related table for each record selected from the base table. The cursor attributes are a good tool to help the applications control the opening and closing of the cursors.

Listing 9.1 demonstrates the use of the `%found` and `%notfound` cursor attributes. The listing displays the number of tools and eyeglasses purchased by the employees in the company.

**Listing 9.1 L_09_01.SQL—Using the *%found* and *%notfound* Cursor Attributes to Terminate Looping Procedures**

```
SQL> set serveroutput on;
SQL> declare
 2  cnt number := 0;
 3  tool_record  tools%rowtype;
 4  glasses_record glasses%rowtype;
 5  cursor tool is select fk_payroll_number from tools;
 6  cursor glass is select fk_payroll_number from glasses;
 7 begin
 8  open tool;
 9  loop
 10    fetch tool into tool_record.fk_payroll_number;
 11    exit when tool%notfound;
 12    cnt := cnt + 1;
 13  end loop;
 14  dbms_output.put_line (cnt¦¦' Tools were purchased');
 15  cnt := 0;
 16  close tool;
 17  open glass;
 18  loop
 19    fetch glass into glasses_record.fk_payroll_number;
 20    exit when not glass%found;
 21    cnt := cnt + 1;
 22  end loop;
 23  close glass;
 24  dbms_output.put_line (cnt¦¦' Eyeglasses were purchased');
 25 end;
 26 /
34 Tools were purchased
18 Eyeglasses were purchased

PL/SQL procedure successfully completed.
```

In this listing, two looping procedures are established. The first procedure counts the number of tool purchased by employees. It uses the `%notfound` attribute to determine when to stop the loop. The loop should be terminated when the last record from the cursor has been counted. The condition is contained in line 11. When the `%notfound` attribute is true, the exit statement can be performed. This attribute is true when the last record from the cursor has been fetched. You might notice that the count variable (`cnt`) on line 21 is incremented after the condition is evaluated. If it was incremented before the exit condition, it would have counted an additional record. It would have counted the iteration when the fetch was negative.

The second looping procedure uses the `%found` attribute as the condition in the exit. Because this attribute is true when a record is fetched, and you do not want the loop terminated when the value is true, you must use the `not` keyword to change the termination logic. When the `%found` attribute is not true, the loop is terminated. Of course, not true means the value is false. These two attributes give you a lot of control when performing loops that contain cursors.

**NOTE** My personal favorite attribute is the `%found`. I find this logic easier for me to understand. I use it in as the loop continuation determinate in my `while` loops.

## Using the *%rowcount* Attribute

The `%rowcount` attribute returns the current number of records that have been fetched. When the cursor is opened, this number equals 0. When the first fetch is executed, the attribute equals 1. This attribute helps to limit the number of records fetched from the cursor. You can also use it to number each fetched from the cursor. Listing 9.2 illustrates these uses.

**Listing 9.2 L_09_02.SQL—Using the *%rowcount* Attribute to Limit the Records Fetched from a Cursor and to Number Each Fetched Row**

```
SQL> set serveroutput on;
SQL> declare
 2   emp_record    employee%rowtype;
 3   cursor employee_list is
 4    select last_name, first_name from employee order by 1;
 5 begin
 6   open employee_list;
 7   loop
 8    fetch employee_list into emp_record.last_name, emp_record.first_name;
 9    exit when employee_list%rowcount = 5;
 10    dbms_output.put_line (employee_list%rowcount¦¦' '¦¦emp_record.last_name);
 11   end loop;
 12 end;
 13 /
1 ANTHONY
2 BUSH
3 CARTER
4 CLINTON

PL/SQL procedure successfully completed.
```

The listing uses the `%rowcount` attribute in the `exit` statement to terminate the loop after fetching the fifth record from the cursor. The attribute is also used in the `dbms_output` statement to number the various records displayed. Notice the `%rowcount` attribute is incremented before the `exit` statement is evaluated. Because this evaluation occurs before the record is output, only four records display. To display five records, move line 10 to line 9.

```
0
1 ANTHONY
2 BUSH
3 CARTER
4 CLINTON
```

## Using the *%isopen* Attribute

The last cursor attribute is `%isopen`. It is used to determine whether the cursor is currently open. This is a potentially important attribute to know because issuing a `Fetch` or `Close` command when the cursor is not open causes an exception. A closed cursor also causes an exception when the `%found`, `%notfound`, and `%rowcount` cursor attributes are evaluated. When you have a complex program and you want to avoid these exceptions, this command could save some problems. Listing 9.3 uses the `%isopen` to check the status of the cursor before opening it. The `cursor for` the script opens only if the cursor attribute `%isopen` is false. This evaluation occurs in line 6 and 7 of the Listing.



**Listing 9.3 L_09_03.SQL—Using the *%Isopen* Attribute to Check Whether a Cursor Is Open Before Issuing the *Open* Command**

```
SQL> set serveroutput on;
SQL> declare
 2  emp_record    employee%rowtype;
 3  cursor employee_list is
 4   select last_name, first_name from employee order by 1;
 5 begin
 6  if not employee_list%isopen then
 7   open employee_list;
 8  end if;
 9  loop
 10   fetch employee_list into emp_record.last_name, emp_record.first_name;
 11   exit when employee_list%rowcount = 5;
 12   dbms_output.put_line (employee_list%rowcount¦¦' '¦¦emp_record.last_name);
 13  end loop;
 14 end;
 15 /
1 ANTHONY
2 BUSH
3 CARTER
4 CLINTON

PL/SQL procedure successfully completed.
```

## Using Explicit and Implicit Cursors

In the preceding examples, the name of the cursor preceded all the cursor attributes. Cursors that have specific names are called *explicit cursors*. All the cursors discussed thus far are explicit cursors.

There are a number of other cursors called *implicit cursors*. Oracle creates implicit cursors when `Select`, `Insert`, `Update`, or `Delete` commands have been issued. Sometimes it is important to your PL/SQL program to know the state of these cursors. Fortunately, you can use the same cursor attributes described in the preceding sections for explicit cursors with *implicit cursors*. The difference is the implicit cursor attributes begin with the word *SQL* rather than the name of the cursor. When they are used, they return the value of the most recent executed

SQL command. The following are the implicit cursor attributes: `sql%found`, `sql%notfound`, `sql%rowcount`, and `sql%isopen`.

The `While` loop is the second looping procedure of three PL/SQL loops available. It consists of two components. The first is the condition statement placed at the beginning of the loop. The second is the keywords *end loop*, which denote the completion of the looping procedure. Because the `While` loop has its continuation evaluation done at the beginning of the loop, the condition must be true initially for the loop to ever be performed. This differs from the simple loop you learned about in the preceding chapter. The continuation evaluation occurs somewhere in the body of the loop. This means the condition evaluation does not have to be true to enter the looping procedure.

Listing 9.4 shows a simple `While` loop that displays the last names of the employees. The cursor attributes discussed earlier in this chapter are excellent devices to use with a `While` loop. This example uses the `%found` attribute to decide whether to enter and continue the loop. For the condition to be true, the last fetch from the cursor has to be true. This means the block has to have a successful fetch performed prior to the beginning of the loop. Without this statement, the loop would never be executed. The loop also has another fetch before the end. This is needed to bring a fresh record into the loop. It also is placed as the last step in the loop because the application needs a fresh `%found` attribute when the program returns to the beginning of the loop. If the attribute is false because the last record was fetched, the loop terminates.

**Listing 9.4 L_09_04.sql—Executing a *While* Loop**

```
SQL> set serveroutput on;
SQL> declare
   e_rec    employee%rowtype;
   cursor a is select * from employee order by last_name;
  begin
   open a;
   fetch a into e_rec;
   while a%found loop
    dbms_output.put_line (e_rec.last_name);
    fetch a into e_rec;
    end loop;
    close a;
   end;
  /
ANTHONY
BUSH
.
.
TRUMAN
WILSON

PL/SQL procedure successfully completed.
```

**TIP** When using a `%found` cursor attribute with a `While` loop, the first `Fetch` command is placed outside the loop usually preceding the first line. If a succesful fetch occurs, the `while` loop can be performed. If a successful fetch does not occur, the `%found` attribute contained in the `while` evaluation will prevent the loop from being performed. A second fetch is placed before the end of the loop. This retrieves a fresh record to be processed as the loop is repeated. If the fetch is unsuccessful, the loop will be terminated as it returns to the `while` evaluation.

When using the `%notfound` cursor attribute, there is only one fetch and it is usually the first line of the loop statements. This allows the application to enter the loop. The `%notfound` attribute is true since a record was not successfully fetched. The `fetch` command is placed at the top of the loop in order to retrieve a fresh record for the statements.



`While` loops can contain nested `While` loops. This technique is often used when converting data. In a recent re-engineering project of an existing Substation Transformer system, for example. The existing system used the transformer serial number for the primary and foreign keys. It was determined that the serial number is not always unique because several manufacturers use the same numbering. In addition, the serial number can change when the transformer is remanufactured. This is not a good condition for relational databases.

It was decided that each transformer would have an artificial (or unseen) key called rec_id that would never change or be duplicated. The old system had a related table of tests that used the serial number for its foreign key. The nested `While` loop procedure was used to generate a unique rec_id value for each transformer and test record. In addition, the program populates each test record with the foreign key rec_id of its parent transformer. This maintains the referential integrity of the tables.

Figure 9.1 shows a representation of the conversion program used to create the new primary keys and to load new transformer and transformer tests tables. The block contains two *cursors* and two `While` loops. The outer loop uses the trf_main cursor to retrieve each of the transformers. On each iteration of this loop, a new record number is computed and assigned to the transformer during the insert into the new transformer table.

Inside the outer loop is an inner `While` loop. For each of the transformer records fetched by the trf_main cursor, the inner loop fetches the test records for the transformer from the old table. Each of these test records is assigned the transformer's rec_id as a foreign key value. Each test record is also assigned a sequential artificial key. The modified test record is then inserted into the new test table. The inner loop is completed when the last test record for the transformer is inserted into the table. The cursor is closed and the statements in the outer `While` loop are executed.

This procedure continues until the last transformer record is inserted into the table. The outer `While` loop is ended, the associated cursor is closed, and the program is terminated. The program results in two transformer tables, each table having a unique primary key , and the tests table having a foreign key relating the record to the new primary key in the transformer table.

**FIG. 9.1**
Using nested `While` loops in a conversion routine to create two tables.

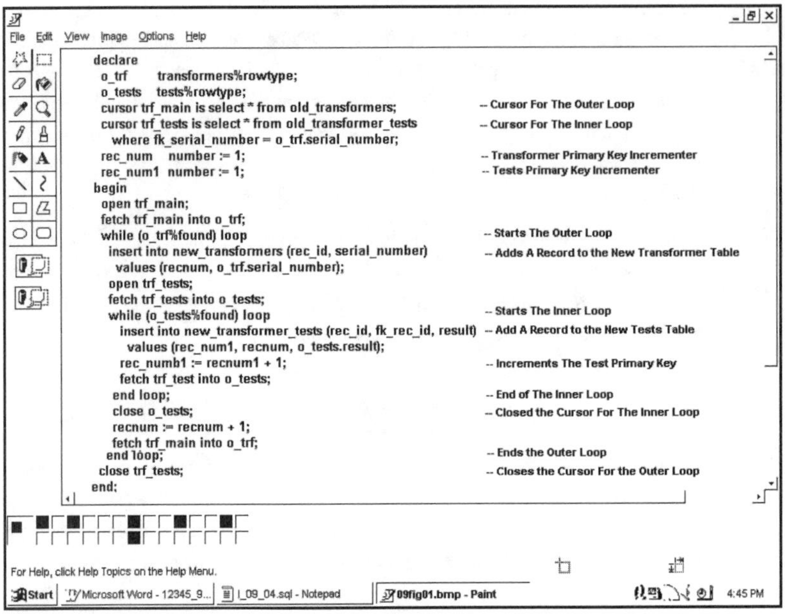


# Using the *For* Loop

The numeric `For` loop is used to process records a predetermined number of times. This loop has a variable that counts each iteration of the loop and compares it to two variables that represent the high and low iteration ranges. A second type of `For` loop is called a `Cursor For` loop. This cursor is associated with an explicit cursor. It is an extremely powerful loop because of the integration of cursor commands into the procedure.

The following sections describe how to create and use the numeric `For` and the `Cursor For` loops.

## Creating and Using the *Numeric For* Loop

This type of cursor executes the loop a predetermined number of times. The cursor has two settings, an upper number and lower number. It also has a count variable that contains the number of iterations for the current loop. As long as this variable is between the high and low settings, the loop continues. When the value falls outside the range of these values, the loop terminates. Figure 9.2 illustrates the components and layout of the loop.

The first line contains the parameters of the loop. The line begins with the keyword *For,* followed by the name of the counting variable, the keyword *In*, the lowest iteration number, and the highest iteration number. The counting variable is initially assigned the value of the lowest iteration number. This increases by one with each iteration. Using the *reverse* option causes the counting variable to initially be assigned the highest iteration number. This number decreases by one with each iteration. The high and low iteration number values can be assigned during the execution of the program. You can list variables in the declaration line. This enables the developer the opportunity to assign values on-the-fly. The parameter line is followed by the keyword *loop*, the loop executable statements, and the *end loop* keyword.

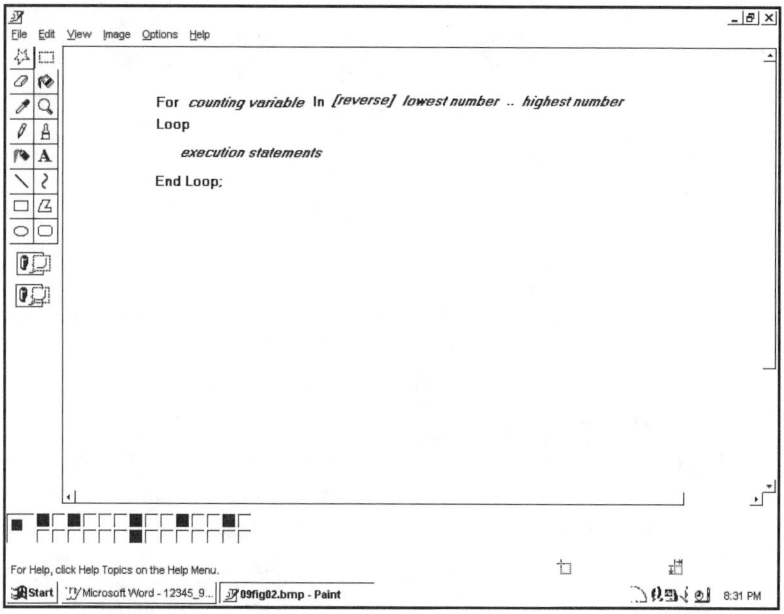


**FIG. 9.2**
Components and layout of the `Numeric For` loop.

Listing 9.5 contains a simple block that has a `Numeric For` loop. The statements in the loop cause the output of the last name of the employee. The counting variable (cnt_var) has a value of 1 on the first iteration. It increments by one on each pass through the loop. Because the high increment parameter is set to 5, there are five passes through the loop.

### Listing 9.5 L_09_05.sql—Defining a Simple *Numeric For* Loop

```
SQL> set serveroutput on;
SQL> declare
   e_rec   employee%rowtype;
   cursor a is select * from employee;
  begin
   open a;
   for cnt_var in 1..5
    loop
     fetch a into e_rec;
     dbms_output.put_line (e_rec.last_name);
     end loop;
    close a;
   end;
   /
COOLIDGE
```

*continues*

**Listing 9.5 Continued**

```
JOHNSON
REAGAN
BUSH
JOHNSON
PL/SQL procedure successfully completed.

TAFT
ROOSEVELT
ANTHONY
ROOSEVELT
COOLIDGE
```

The following rules apply to these type of loops:

- The counting variable is not declared in the `Declare` section. PL/SQL creates it dynamically, and it cannot be used outside the loop.
- Do not use an `Exit` command in the loop. Use the elements within the loop to control its behavior.
- Use the *reverse* option to decrement the counting variable.
- PL/SQL looks at the high and low values before initiating the loop. Changing the values of these variables within the loop has no effect.

The `Numeric For` loop works well when you know the number of iterations in advance. When you don't know the number, you need to perform extra statements such as a `Count(*)`, which was covered in Chapter 3, "Acquiring Data by Using the `SELECT` Statement," using the cursor select conditions to calculate this number in advance. If your high iteration parameter is greater than the number of records retrieved by the cursor, the cursor will not terminate after the last record has been reached. The last fetched record will display repeatedly until the high parameter is met. This problem does not exist with the `Simple` loop or `While` loop because you have the cursor attributes to control the exit of the loop.

The `cursor for` loop enables you to use the for loop structure without having to know the iterations in advance. The next section discusses this loop.

## Creating and Using the *Cursor For* Loop

The `Cursor For` loop is a sophisticated looping procedure that integrates many of the cursor commands into the looping procedure. This loop does not have lowest or highest iteration parameters. It just evaluates or processes each of the records in a cursor until the last record in the cursor has been fetched. Although you can use the `Numeric For` loop for procedures that do not involve cursors, you can only use this loop with cursors. Figure 9.3 illustrates the basic structure of the loop.

The first line in this example contains the loop's parameters. It begins with the keyword *For* followed by the count variable, the keyword *In*, and the name of the cursor. The loop executable statements begin with the keyword *loop* and are completed by the keywords *end loop*. You can open the cursor before the first line of the `cursor for` structure or between the `For` declaration line and the keyword *Loop*.

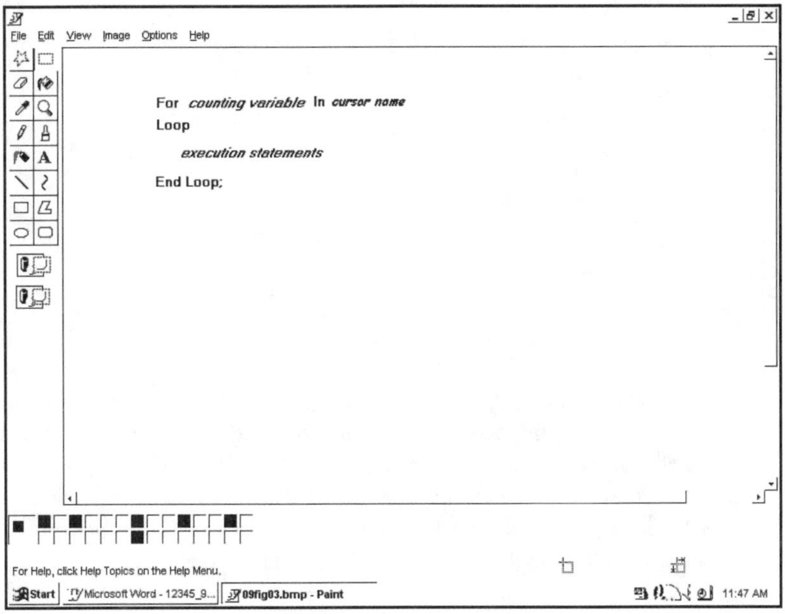


**FIG. 9.3**
The basic structure of the Cursor For loop.



Listing 9.6 illustrates a simple `cursor for` loop. The procedure displays the last name of the employees.

**Listing 9.6 L_09_06.sql—Executing a *Cursor For* Loop to List the Last Names of the Employees**

```
SQL> set serveroutput on;
SQL> declare
 e_rec   employee%rowtype;
 cursor a is select * from employee;
begin
 for cnt_var in a
  loop
   fetch a into e_rec;
   dbms_output.put_line (cnt_var.last_name);
  end loop;
 end;
 /
COOLIDGE
REAGAN
.
.
```

*continues*

**Listing 9.6 Continued**

```
ROOSEVELT
ROOSEVELT

PL/SQL procedure successfully completed.

TAFT
ANTHONY
COOLIDGE
REAGAN
JOHNSON
CARTER
NIXON
EISENHOWER
ROOSEVELT
WILSON
```

The `Cursor For` loop enables you to omit the cursor commands and attributes that you used with other looping procedures. The first statement that you can eliminate is the e_rec local variable array. The `cursor for` loop automatically sets up local variables for each of the items in the cursor. Because the `Cursor For` loop is used for cursors only and is terminated when the `%notfound` attribute is true, the structure does not need the `Open`, `Fetch`, and `Close Cursor` commands. Listing 9.7 illustrates this concept.

**Listing 9.7 L_09_07.sql—Using the *Cursor For* Loop Without Declaring Local Variables**

```
SQL> set serveroutput on;
SQL> declare
  2    cursor a is select * from employee;
  3   begin
  4    for cnt_var in a
  5    loop
  6     dbms_output.put_line (cnt_var.last_name);
  7    end loop;
  8  end;
  9  /
COOLIDGE
JOHNSON
.
.
ANTHONY
ROOSEVELT

PL/SQL procedure successfully completed.

f

TAFT
ROOSEVELT
ANTHONY
ROOSEVELT
```

```
COOLIDGE
JOHNSON
REAGAN
BUSH
JOHNSON
CLINTON
CARTER
FORD
NIXON
KENNEDY
EISENHOWER
TRUMAN
ROOSEVELT
HOOVER
WILSON
```



Notice that the `Declare` section contains only the cursor definition. It does not have any local variable definitions. The `Executable` section no longer contains any cursor commands. PL/SQL moves the cursor values into local variables qualified by the name of the cursor counting variable. The dbms_output command on line 6 illustrates this variable naming scheme. The `Cursor For` loop also opens the cursor, fetches each record into the loop, determines when the last record was fetched, and closes the cursor. Each of these commands is implicit to the `Cursor For` loop.

The `Cursor For` loop also enables the developer to define the cursor inside the loop, as shown in Listing 9.8. The program in this listing defines the cursor's `select` statement in the `For` declaration line. Because there is not a cursor name, the name of the `Cursor For` loop qualifies the local variables used in the loop.

**Listing 9.8 L_09_08.SQL—Defining the Cursor Inside the *Cursor For* Loop**

```
SQL> set serveroutput on;
SQL> begin
  2  for cnt_var in (select * from employee)
  3    loop
  4      dbms_output.put_line (cnt_var.last_name);
  5    end loop;
  6  end;
  7  /
COOLIDGE
JOHNSON
.
.
ANTHONY
ROOSEVELT
PL/SQL procedure successfully completed.
```

Listing 9.8 embodies these built-in functions. You can see the beauty and sophistication of the `Cursor For` loop. It leaves all the work to Oracle to process the records in the cursor, enabling the developer to concentrate on the processing statements.

# Using the *For Update Of*

When you issue a `select` statement, Oracle does not lock the records in the table. Locking consists of marking a table record so that other users cannot modify the record. This is done for concurrency reasons. A user would not want another user to modify a record that he was in the process of modifying. Locking procedures prevent this from occuring. The `update` and `delete` commands lock the record. Normally, a `select` statement does not.

Sometimes the developer wants to lock the records selected for the cursor, preventing other users from updating the records until they have been released. A `Rollback` or `Commit` command releases locked records. The cursor `For Update` option enables you to lock the records selected by the cursor. Listing 9.9 illustrates an example of the `For Update` option. In this example, cursor "a" has a `For Update` option specified.

**Listing 9.9 L_09_09.sql—Locking Cursor Records with the *For Update* Option**

```
SQL> set serveroutput on;
SQL> declare
 2  old_lname    employee.last_name%type;
 3  pay#      employee.payroll_number%type;
 4  cursor a is
 5   select payroll_number, last_name from employee
 6    for update;
 7 begin
 8  open a;
 9  fetch a into pay#, old_lname;
 10  while (a%found) loop
 11   update employee set last_name = upper(last_name)
 12    where payroll_number = pay#;
 13   fetch a into pay#, old_lname;
 14  end loop;
 15  close a;
 16  commit;
 17 end;
 18 /

PL/SQL procedure successfully completed.
```

Because the select statement on line 5 does not have a `where` clause, all the records in the employee table will be selected for the cursor. The `For Update` option causes all the records in the table to be locked from update or delete. The record locking occurs when the cursor is opened. The `While` loop executes an update statement for each row of the table. The `update` statement has a `where` clause. It uses the payroll number of each employee to determine the record to be updated. Upon execution of the `Commit` command, the locks are released.

**CAUTION**

You should not issue `Commit` commands until all the records in the cursor have been processed. Issuing a commit while a `For Update` cursor is open closes the cursor. The application will not be capable of fetching any records from the cursor. This does not cause your application to issue an exception statement, and it continues to execute any statements not needing the cursor. You may be deceived into thinking your application processed all the records when in reality only a partial set were processed.



You can follow the `For Update` clause with the keyword *Of* and some table column names. This option provides as an easy mechanism to identify the columns you intend to modify with the cursor. If the `For Update Of` clause does not have a column contained in the set of fields contained in the cursor's `select` clause, the cursor rows will not be locked. In order to lock the fetched row, one of the columns must be contained in the `For Update Of` column list. If the select list and the `For Update Of` columns do not have to match. The cursor operates correctly, but the records will not be locked.

# Using the *Where Current Of* Option

The `Where Current Of` option is used with the `Update` and `Delete` DML commands that were described in Chapter 7, "Modifying Your Tables with DML Commands." The option enables you to avoid having to define a `where` clause for the statements. The `where` clause is used with these statements to identify the records to update or delete. The `Where Current Of` option tells Oracle that the record to be modified is the current record in the cursor.

In Listing 9.9 (refer to the preceding section), the `update` statement contained in the `While` loop has a `where` clause specified. It needs this clause to identify the record from the employee table to update. Provisions need to be designed in the application to identify the primary key of the record to be updated. To cause the update statement to modify the correct record, you must also move this value to the `where` clause of the `update` statement.

The `Where Current Of` cursor name option simplifies this process. When this option is specified, Oracle updates or deletes the last record fetched by the cursor, eliminating the need to include `where` clauses in the `Update` or `Delete` commands. Listing 9.10 illustrates the use of this option.

**Listing 9.10 L_09_10.SQL—Using the *Where Current Of* Option to Update Records**

```
SQL> set serveroutput on;
SQL> declare
  old_lname    employee.last_name%type;
  cursor a is
   select last_name from employee
    for update;
 begin
  open a;
```

*continues*

**Listing 9.10 Continued**

```
fetch a into old_lname;
while (a%found) loop
  update employee set last_name = upper(last_name)
   where current of a;
  fetch a into old_lname;
 end loop;
 close a;
 commit;
end;
/

PL/SQL procedure successfully completed.
```

This PL/SQL block in this listing is a modified version of the one in Listing 9.9. The PL/SQL block in this listing does not have a need for the pay# local variable used for the primary key of the record. This variable was eliminated from the block along with the `where` clause of the `update` statement.

The `Where Current Of` clause has another advantage besides making your code simpler. It increases the speed of your record processing. Because it uses the last record fetched from the database, Oracle knows the record's exact location. Oracle does not have to perform any searches such as an index or tablespace scan to find the record. This increases the performance of the application. It especially enhances performance if the tables are large or the `update` statement `where` clause must perform tablespace scans to identify the row to be updated.

# Creating and Using Named Procedures

Up to this point, the PL/SQL blocks discussed have been anonymous blocks. This means they did not have a Header section containing a name. Another block cannot call or execute them because they are nameless. This section, however, covers *procedures*. They are named PL/SQL blocks that are callable by other objects.

The Header section of the procedure block determines the way the block must be called. The block's name and a parameter list comprise the header's components. You include the parameter list when values are to be passed to or from the procedure. The procedure also has a Declare section, an Executable section, and an Exception section. Besides having the Header section, the procedure block is the same as an anonymous block. Figure 9.4 shows the structure of a procedure.

The procedure name listed in the *header* section is used to call the block. The parameters are used to bring values into and out of the procedure. The *Declare* section is placed after the keyword *Is*. Procedures do not have to contain the keyword *Declare*. If the procedure has a nested block, this block can have a *Declare* section using the *Declare* keyword. Listing 9.11 illustrates the creation and execution of a procedure that lists the employees in a particular department. The department number is passed into the procedure through the parameters listed in the header.

**FIG. 9.4**
Procedure structure.

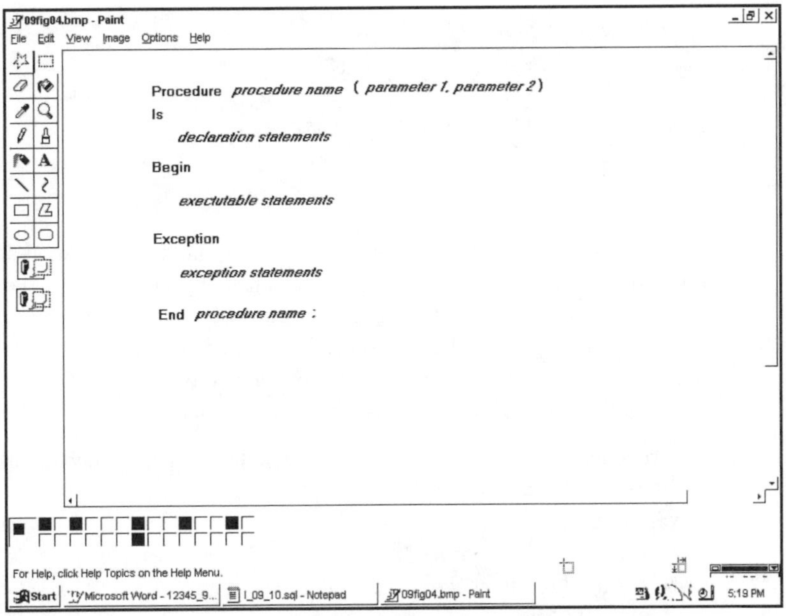




### Listing 9.11 L_09_11.SQL—Using a Named Procedure to List Employees

```
SQL> set serveroutput on;
SQL> create procedure dept_employees (dept in char)
  2  is
  3    cursor a is select last_name from employee
  4      where fk_department = dept
  5      order by 1;
  6  begin
  7    for deptlist in a
  8       loop
  9       dbms_output.put_line (deptlist.last_name);
 10       end loop;
 11  end dept_employees;
 12  /

Procedure created.

SQL>
SQL> begin
  2    dept_employees ('WEL');
  3  end;
  4  /
ANTHONY
CARTER
HOOVER
REAGAN
ROOSEVELT
TAFT
```

*continues*

**Listing 9.11 Continued**

```
PL/SQL procedure successfully completed.

SQL> drop procedure dept_employees;

Procedure dropped.
```

Procedures are not like anonymous blocks. They cannot be executed directly; they must be called from another application. Procedures must also be defined in the database using the *Create Procedure* command before they can be called. The first block of the preceding Listing illustrates the creation of the procedure called "dept_employees". The second PL/SQL block illustrates calling the stored procedure from an anonymous block. The purpose of the procedure is to list the employees of a particular department.

The procedure is passed the name of the department using the variable in the Header section. This section has a variable called "dept". It is followed by the keyword *In* and the data type of the variable. The *In* keyword means the variable is used as an input variable. It cannot be used to pass values out of the procedure. To pass values out, the *Out* parameter is used. When the variable is used for input and output, the *In Out* parameter is used. When defining the variable data type, you do not have to specify its size.

The procedure contains a cursor that is used in a `Cursor For` loop to display the employee last names. The `cursor select` statement uses the input variable "dept" in its `where` clause to select only the employees of the "WEL" or Welfare department.

The second block is an anonymous PL/SQL block that calls the "dept_employees" procedure. It calls the procedure by listing the name of the procedure as if it were a statement. In fact, the name of a procedure is a statement and should be treated as one. Because this procedure is expecting an input variable, the calling statement must supply it. This is accomplished by the literal "WEL" that follows the procedure name. "WEL" is the code for the Welfare department. It is used in the `cursor where` clause. The procedure is then executed.

You can eliminate procedures by using the `Drop Procedure` command.

**NOTE** Procedures are a good technique to modularize your code. I have managed projects that developed multiple applications that perform the same calculation. It is surprising that the same calculation in different applications sometimes produces different results. A single stored procedure that is callable from the various applications would solve this problem.

## Creating and Using Functions

A function is a block of PL/SQL code called from another application. A function differs from a procedure in that a function always returns a value. It also differs in that it cannot be called as its own statement. It must always be called as part of an executable statement. In fact, a function is used as an expression in a statement because the function returns a value and the value is used in the expression.

Figure 9.5 illustrates the structure of a function. It begins with the keyword *Function* followed by the pass into and out of parameters. The second line is used to define the `Return data type` parameter. The remainder of the block contains the Declaration, Executable, and Exception sections. Like a procedure, the function must be stored in the database for it to be called by another application.



**FIG. 9.5**
The structure of a function.

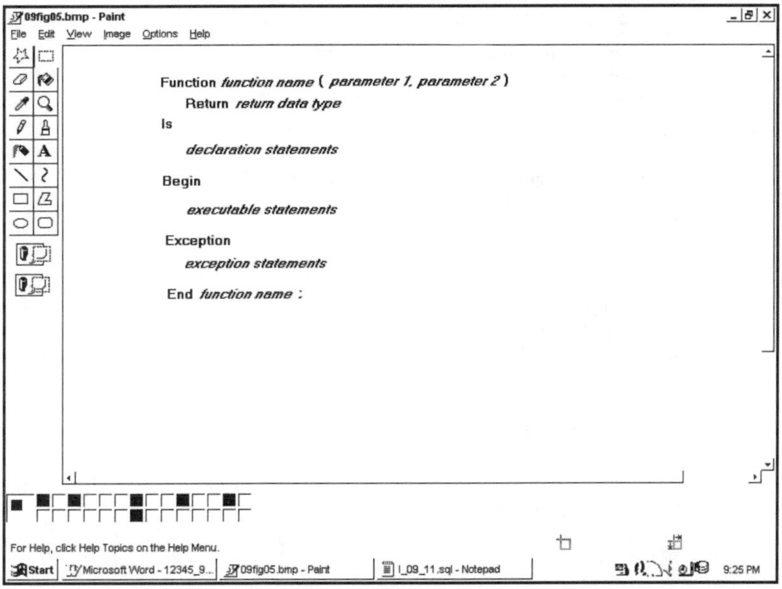


`Return data type` is used to define the value that will be supplied to the calling expression. It can be any of the approved types such as number or varchar2. It cannot be an exception data type or a cursor name. The data type of the return parameter must agree with the data type the expression is expecting. In the expression a = 3, for example, if you replace the value 3 with a function, the return type of the function must be number. Specifying a different data type causes an error.

In Listing 9.12, a PL/SQL block calculates the average age of the employees hired for each department. This value is used in a calling expression to compare the hiring age of each employee to the department average. The application computes the difference in the employee's age at hire and the average for his or her department.

**Listing 9.12 L_09_12.sql—Using a Function to Calculate the Average Hiring Age of Employees per Department**

```
.
SQL> create function a_age (dept in employee.fk_department%type)
      return number
     is
      avg_age      number;
     begin
      select avg((employment_date-birth_date)/365)
      into avg_age
      from employee
      where fk_department = dept;
      return avg_age;
     end;
     /

Function created.

SQL>
SQL> set serveroutput on;
SQL> declare
       age       number;
       age_dif   number;
       lname     varchar2(15);
       fname     varchar2(15);
       dept      varchar2(4);
       cursor a is
        select last_name, first_name, fk_department,
          (employment_date - birth_date)/365
        from employee;
     begin
     open a;
     fetch a into lname, fname, dept, age;
     while (a%found) loop
       age_dif := age - a_age(dept);
       dbms_output.put_line (lname¦¦' '¦¦fname¦¦' '¦¦'Age Diff '¦¦a_age(dept));
       fetch a into lname, fname, dept, age;
     end loop;
     end;
     /
COOLIDGE CALVIN Age Diff 59.005936073059360730593607305936073059 33
JOHNSON LYNDON Age Diff 53.46536203522504892367906066536203522514
REAGAN RONALD Age Diff 48.421004566210045662100456621004566 21
BUSH GEORGE Age Diff 59.00593607305936073059360730593607305933
JOHNSON ANDREW Age Diff 53.46536203522504892367906066536203522514
CLINTON WILLIAM Age Diff 53.46536203522504892367906066536203522514
CARTER JIMMY Age Diff 48.421004566210045662100456621004566 21
FORD GERALD Age Diff 59.00593607305936073059360730593607305933
NIXON RICHARD Age Diff 53.46536203522504892367906066536203522514
KENNEDY JOHN Age Diff 53.46536203522504892367906066536203522514
EISENHOWER DWIGHT Age Diff 59.00593607305936073059360730593607305933
TRUMAN HAROLD Age Diff 59.00593607305936073059360730593607305933
ROOSEVELT FRANKLIN Age Diff 53.46536203522504892367906066536203522514
HOOVER HERBERT Age Diff 48.421004566210045662100456621004566 21
```

```
WILSON WOODROW Age Diff 53.465362035225048923679060665362035225l4
TAFT WILLIAM Age Diff 48.421004566210045662100456621004566 21
ROOSEVELT THEODORE Age Diff 59.005936073059360730593607305936073 05933
ANTHONY SUSAN Age Diff 48.421004566210045662100456621004566 21
ROOSEVELT ELEANOR Age Diff 48.421004566210045662100456621004566 21

PL/SQL procedure successfully completed.
```

This listing is produced by executing l_09_12a.sql to create the function, and l_09_12b.sql to use the function.



The first block in the listing creates the function. You must store it in the database before an application can call it. To declare or place the function in the database, use the `Create Function` command. The Header section follows this command. It contains the name of the function (a_age) , an input parameter named dept, and a return data type of number.

The parameter (dept) uses the *in* mode operator to designate that it is an input variable only. "Dept" is defined with the same data type as the fk_department column in the employee table. To do this, use the `%type` declaration. The declaration section of the function begins after the keyword *is*. The avg_age variable is used to hold the value returned to the calling expression. It is declared with a data type of number. The Executable section of the function contains a `select` statement. It calculates the average hire date of employees in a department. The `where` clause uses the "Dept" input variable to determine for which department to calculate the average.

The `Select` statement returns one value. This value is assigned to the avg_age variable. This value is returned to the calling application by the *return* statement in line 10.

The second section of the listing contains the PL/SQL block that calls the function. It is an anonymous block that contains several local variables and a cursor that calculates the hiring age for the employee. In the Executable section, a `While` loop processes each record in the Employee table. The first step of the loop is to calculate and assign the age difference to the variable age_dif. This value is calculated by using the `a_age` function. This function returns the second value in the age_dif computation. When Oracle encounters this function, it calls the function and passes it the value of the "Dept" variable. You specify this variable is specified following the name of the function. The function is then executed and returns a value to be used in the expression. This value is used to complete the age_dif calculation. The output of the calculation displays at the end of the loop.

Functions enable the developer to use the same calculations in multiple applications. A benefit of having the function in your program is that you do not have to test the code in each application in which the calculation is used. If you test the code when you create the function, it will work correctly in all applications in which it is used.

To discard the function from the database, use the `Drop Function` command.

# Creating and Using Packages

A *package* is a structure that brings an element of object-oriented design to PL/SQL. *Packages* are a collection of PL/SQL objects such as *cursors, variables, constants, exception* names, *procedures,* and *functions.* In object-oriented design, the developer identifies an object or entity such as an employee. The object is set up as a class and its properties are defined and functions programmed. These properties and functions are linked to the object. When the developer wants to manipulate an object, he just looks at the object to determine whether the *function* exists. He can use any of the predefined functions in the object.

You do not have to tie *packages* to a specific object. Object-oriented concepts can be used, however. If the developer has an object such as an employee, the developer can place all the *functions, procedures, constants,* and *cursors* into one package. The objects in this *package* can then be used in other applications that are developed. This is the height of reusable code. It reduces coding time because the developer has reusable code, ensures that calculations and properties are the same across applications, and frees the developer from having to test the *functions* used from the *package.*

By incorporating *packages* into your application design, some other benefits accrue, including the following:

- Object-oriented capabilities—This enables the developer to group functions into a logical group. Its easy to define procedures and functions in the database. Its also easier to forget their names or existence. Defining objects into a package(s) for an entity enables the developer to maintain better control over the objects.
- Performance—When an object in a package is called, all the objects in the function are placed in the system global area of memory. The objects remain throughout the session. This decreases the time needed to execute other objects from the package because they are already in memory.
- Top-down design—You can initially define packages with just the high-level objects. You can develop the detailed sections of the code later. This enables the developer to begin at the top and identify major components before developing the detail.
- Global data—Objects declared in a package act as global data for other applications that have the privilege to execute the package. You may access the package with one application, modify data within the package, and access the modified data with another application. If an application opens a cursor in a package, it remains open for another application.

## Package Structure

Packages consist of two parts: the package specification and the package body. The package specification contains the names of the objects other applications can access. These are called *public* objects. This section does not contain any of the code that actually performs work.

The body section contains the actual statements that perform work. It also contains objects not available to other applications. These are called *private* objects. These objects can only be referenced by components of the package body. Figure 9.6 illustrates the basic structure of two package components.

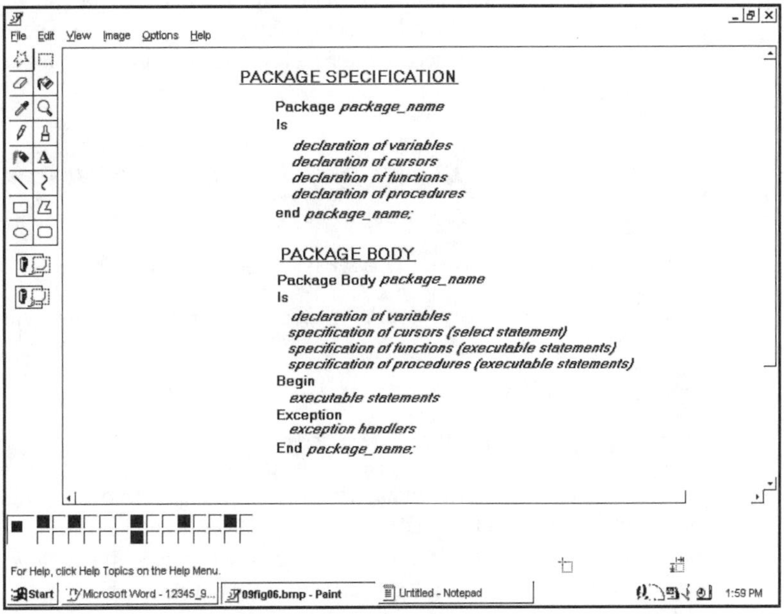


**FIG. 9.6**
Structure of a package specification and a package body.



The *package specification* begins with the keyword *package* followed by the name of the package. The specification or *Declaration* section begins with the keyword *is.* This section contains the definition of the *procedures, functions, variables,* and *cursors* that will be accessible from applications. These are the *public* elements. The definitions should also include the procedure or function parameters. This part of the package does not contain executable statements or exception handlers. The *package specification* contains all the information a developer needs to call objects in the package. The developer should never have to see the code behind the objects. The *package specification* is completed by the keyword *end* followed by the name of the package.

The *package body* begins with the keywords *package body* followed by the name of the package. The package name needs to be the same as in the package specification. The specifications begin following the keyword *is.*

The *package body* can also contain its own executable section. This section starts with the keyword *begin.* It can have an exception section and is completed by the keyword *end.* The purpose of the package body *Executable* section is to initialize variables or execute some statements when the package is initiated. The *package body* is terminated by the keyword *end* followed by the name of the package.

## Creating a Package Specification

Listing 9.13 illustrates the creation of a package that contains many of the objects that have been developed as examples in this chapter. It contains a cursor similar to Listing 9.3, a procedure similar to Listing 9.11, and a function similar to Listing 9.12. These examples have one thing in common: They all access the Employee table. It enables you to exercise object-oriented design by centralizing Employee objects into one package.

**Listing 9.13 L_09_13.sql—Creating an Employee Package**

```
SQL> create package employee_objects
     is
       cursor employee_list     return employee%rowtype;
       procedure dpt_employees (dept in char);
       function avg_age (dept in employee.fk_department%type) return number;
     end employee_objects;
     /

Package created.
```

To create the *package specification*, use the `Create Package` command. You must create the *package specification* before the *package body*. This means that the actual executable statements contained in the *package body* do not have to exist to create the *package body*. If the objects are called and code does not exist, the package does not produce any results. It is possible to have packages that do not contain a body. These are called *bodiless packages*. They may contain objects that do not need code such as exception handler definitions.

The specification in Listing 9.13 defines three objects. The first is a `cursor` called employee_list. This `cursor` returns the first and last names of each employee. The second object is a *procedure* that lists the employees for a particular department. The final object is a *function* that computes the average hiring age for employee in a particular department.

The *cursor* definition begins with the keyword *cursor* followed by the cursor name. Cursor package specifications need a *return data type*. This specifies the variable that will contain the cursor object. In the case of this cursor, the data definition consists of creating a variable array called a table record. To accomplish this, use the `%rowtype` declaration preceded by the table name Employee. When the cursor contains multiple values in the `select` statement, you must use a virtual record in the return variable specification. This can be a *cursor record* or a table record. To create a *cursor record*, placing the name of the cursor before the `%rowtype`. Placing the name of the table creates a table record.

The *procedure* definition begins with the keyword *procedure* followed by the procedure name. This procedure is similar to the one contained in Listing 9.11. Because this procedure needs to have the department number value supplied to it, an input variable (dept) is defined. This specification uses the keyword *in* to denote dept is an input variable. You might notice that the data type size did not need to be specified. In fact, when the size is specified, the package will not compile.

The final object defined is the *function* avg_age. The *function* definition begins with the keyword *function* followed by the name of the object. This *function* is similar to the one illustrated in Listing 9.12. The procedure computes the average employee hiring age for a department. The *function* needs the department value supplied to it. It also has a return data type because it returns a value to the calling application.

## Creating a Package Body



Listing 9.14 illustrates the definition of the *package body* for the employee_objects package. This script contains the executable statements for the *cursor*, *procedure*, and *functions* in the employee_objects specification.

**Listing 9.14 L_09_14.sql—Creating a Package Body for the Employee_objects**

```
SQL> create package body employee_objects is
  cursor employee_list return employee%rowtype
  is
   select *
    from employee
   order by 1;
  procedure dpt_employees (dept in char)
  is
   e_rec    employee%rowtype;
   cursor a is select last_name from employee
     where fk_department = dept
     order by 1;
 begin
   for deptlist in a
      loop
      dbms_output.put_line (deptlist.last_name);
      end loop;
 end;
 function avg_age (dept in employee.fk_department%type) return number
  is
  avgage     number;
  begin
  select avg((employment_date-birth_date)/365)
  into avgage
  from employee
  where fk_department = dept;
  return avgage;
 end;

 end employee_objects;
 /

Package body created.
```

The first package body definition is for the *cursor* employee_list. The *procedure* performs the same function as the cursor definition in Listing 9.3. The cursor selects all the records from the Employee table. The package definition is similar to a regular cursor except it has a *return* keyword followed by a data type. This specifies the variables and data types that hold the cursor rows. Because the cursor selects all the rows from the employee table, this Listing necessarily defines a device that holds those rows. In this case, the definition used the `%rowtype` declaration to set up an array of variables that match the Employee table's row.

The second definition consists of a *procedure* called dpt_employees. It is very similar in functionality to the procedure defined in Listing 9.11. The procedure displays the last names of employees of a specified department. The department number is fed into the *procedure* by using the "dept" variable. This variable is then used in a cursor internal to the *procedure* to limit the records to those of the specified department. When declaring the *procedure* in a *package*, you do not have to include the name of the *procedure* following the *end* keyword.

The third definition is a *function*. It is based on the *function* created in Listing 9.12. The *function* computes and returns the average hiring age for the employees in the specified departmentto the calling application.

You should be careful about several things concerning the creation of packages, including the following:

- A *package specification* can exist and be used without a corresponding *package body*. You can use a *bodiless package*, for example, to hold all your custom-designed *exception handlers*. A *package body*, however, cannot exist without a *package specification*.
- A *package body* can have *procedures*, *functions*, and *cursors* that are used internal to the *package body*. You do not need to declare these items in the package specification. You cannot, however, create a *package body* unless you include all the *procedures*, *functions*, and *cursors* declared in the *package specification* in the *package body*.
- The variables and data types declared in the *package specification* must be the same as those in the *package body*.

**CAUTION**

I find it somewhat difficult to build packages in the SQL*PLUS environment. The problems occur when your statement are not correct. SQL*PLUS does not give you good error messages. You simply get a warning such as: "Warning: Package Body created with compilation errors." When you see this warning, the object you created will not work. You must then find the problem and correct it.

## Calling Package Objects from Your Applications

The package objects are called by other applications using the name of the package and the name of the object. The names are separated by dot notation. This is the same notation discussed in Chapter 5 to qualify table columns in a *join select* statement. Listing 9.15 illustrates the use of the cursor "Employee_list" that was defined in the previous section. You do not have to declare the cursor in the application. The definition occurred in the package. To use the cursor, you must just use the full cursor name "employee_objects.employee_list." The first part of the expression uses the package name "employee_objects." The second part, following the dot, is the name of the cursor.



**Listing 9.15 L_09_15.sql—Calling a Package Cursor from an Application**

```
SQL> set serveroutput on;
SQL> declare
    e_rec    employee%rowtype;
   begin
    open employee_objects.employee_list;
    fetch employee_objects.employee_list into e_rec;
    while (employee_objects.employee_list%found) loop
      dbms_output.put_line(e_rec.last_name);
      fetch employee_objects.employee_list into e_rec;
    end loop;
    close employee_objects.employee_list;
   end;
   /
ROOSEVELT
ANTHONY
JOHNSON
ROOSEVELT
TAFT
WILSON
COOLIDGE
HOOVER
ROOSEVELT
TRUMAN
EISENHOWER
KENNEDY
JOHNSON
NIXON
FORD
CARTER
REAGAN
BUSH
CLINTON

PL/SQL procedure successfully completed.
```

Listing 9.16 illustrates the use of the package procedure object "dpt_employees." The procedure is called using dot notation. The package name followed by the procedure name calls the object. The calling of this object is virtually identical to the way this procedure would be called if it were a stored procedure. You might check Listing 9.11 to see the similarities.

**Listing 9.16 L_09_16.sql—Calling a Package Procedure**

```
SQL> set serveroutput on;
SQL> begin
  2    employee_objects.dpt_employees ('WEL');
  3  end;
  4  /
ANTHONY
CARTER
HOOVER
REAGAN
ROOSEVELT
TAFT

PL/SQL procedure successfully completed.
```

Calling a function package object is the same as calling the function when it is a stored function. Listing 9.17 illustrates the use of a package function. This program is identical to the function called in Listing 9.12 except for the name of the function in line 15. The name of the package precedes the function in this block.

**Listing 9.17 L_09_17.sql—Calling a Package Function**

```
SQL> set serveroutput on;
SQL> declare
  2    age      number;
  3    age_dif  number;
  4    lname    varchar2(15);
  5    fname    varchar2(15);
  6    dept     varchar2(4);
  7    cursor a is
  8     select last_name, first_name, fk_department,
  9       (employment_date - birth_date)/365
 10     from employee;
 11  begin
 12  open a;
 13  fetch a into lname, fname, dept, age;
 14  while (a%found) loop
 15    age_dif := age - employee_objects.avg_age(dept);
 16    dbms_output.put_line (lname¦¦' '¦¦fname¦¦' '¦¦'Age Diff '¦¦age_dif);
 17    fetch a into lname, fname, dept, age;
 18  end loop;
 19  end;
 20  /
COOLIDGE CALVIN Age Diff -9.874429223744292237442922374429223744 26
JOHNSON LYNDON Age Diff 1.811350293542074363992172211350293541 98
REAGAN RONALD Age Diff 7.036529680365296803652968036529680365 34
BUSH GEORGE Age Diff 17.958447488584474885844748858447488584 51
JOHNSON ANDREW Age Diff 2.860665362035225048923679060665362035 13
CLINTON WILLIAM Age Diff -1.684540117416829745596868884540117416 92
CARTER JIMMY Age Diff 14.611872146118721461187214611872146118 77
FORD GERALD Age Diff 1.394063926940639269406392694063926940 67
```

```
NIXON RICHARD Age Diff 6.87710371819960861056751467710371819952
KENNEDY JOHN Age Diff -9.84070450097847358121330724070450097856
EISENHOWER DWIGHT Age Diff 3.46529680365296803652968036529680365 3
TRUMAN HAROLD Age Diff 1.96940639269406392694063926940639269409
ROOSEVELT FRANKLIN Age Diff -2.28180039138943248532289628180039138952
HOOVER HERBERT Age Diff 5.26940639269406392694063926940639269411
WILSON WOODROW Age Diff 2.25792563600782778864970645792563600774
TAFT WILLIAM Age Diff 2.32146118721461187214611872146118721466
ROOSEVELT THEODORE Age Diff -14.91278538812785388127853881278538812782
ANTHONY SUSANNE Age Diff -28.28675799086757990867579908675799086753
ROOSEVELT ELEANOR Age Diff -.95251141552511415525114155251141552507

PL/SQL procedure successfully completed.
```



These preceding three examples show that it is easy to call objects from a procedure. You call them in the same manner as any other object, except you preface them with the name of the package.

# Summary

You can use several cursor attributes to control cursors. The `%found` attribute is true when the last fetch returned a value. The `%notfound` attribute is true when the last fetch did not return a value. The `%isopen` attribute is true when the specified cursor is currently open. Finally, the `%rowcount` cursor attribute returns the number of records fetched by the cursor.

The `While` loop is another type of loop available. This loop evaluates the exit condition at the beginning of the loop. This means the condition must be true before the application can even enter the loop. `While` loops can be nested, enabling you to use nested cursors within your applications.

There are two types of `For` loops. The first type is the `Numeric For` loop. It has a counting variable evaluated with each iteration of the loop. When the counting variable is within the high and low parameters, the loop is performed. When the counting variable falls outside these parameters, the loop terminates. The `Cursor For` loop is an especially powerful procedure that performs many of the cursor functions for you. This cursor operates as long as the `%found` cursor attribute is true. The loop performs all the Cursor commands for you. It also enables you to define the `select` statement as part of the `For` loop.

The `For Update` cursor option locks the records retrieved into the cursor. This prohibits other users from updating the records while the cursor is open. The `where current of` clause is used with `update` and `delete` statements. It allows these DML statements to identify the record to perform their operation on by using the cursor position rather than a `where` clause. This avoids having to perform index or table scans.

Procedures are named blocks of code defined and stored in the database. The name of the procedure is contained in the Header section of the PL/SQL block. Because the blocks are named, other applications can call them. They enable the developer to create code that is usable in multiple applications. Procedures can have parameters that allow values to be passed to and from it. The mode of transfer is specified in the parameter declaration by using the *in*, *out*, and *in out* keywords. You can use the name of the procedure as the statement that calls the procedure.

Functions are also named PL/SQL blocks similar to procedures. The difference is that functions return a value and are part of a PL/SQL expression. They cannot exist by themselves in a block of code like a procedure can. Both functions and procedures are devices used to define reusable code.

Packages are PL/SQL devices that enable the developer to group cursors, procedures, and functions into logical groupings. A package has two parts. The first is the package specification that contains a declaration of the public objects. These objects are the ones that other applications can use. The second part of the package is the package body. This part contains the actual PL/SQL statements for the package objects. It also contains private objects that only objects in the package can use. Objects in a package are referenced by other applications using the name of the object preceded by the package name.

## From Here...

This chapter concludes the discussion of PL/SQL. The next chapter covers Oracle's SQL *LOADER product. You use SQL *LOADER to load Oracle tables with data from flat files. This is a very common procedure to perform when moving data from one system to another. At the end of the next chapter, you will be presented with installment III of the Employee project. This installment requests you to load the tables created at the end of part II with data. You must use SQL *LOADER to accomplish this.

## Review Exercises

1. Create a `While` looping procedure that displays the name of each employee and the number of tools purchased by the employee. This application should use the `%found` attribute to terminate the `While` loop.
2. Change the `%found` attribute in the answer to #1 to `%notfound`.
3. In the middle of the `While` loop you created in #2, place an `Open Cursor` command. Run the application. Use the `%isopen` cursor attribute to avoid the exception that has occurred.
4. Change the application developed in #3 to terminate after five iterations. Use the `%rowcount` attribute to control the iterations.
5. Create an application the displays the three oldest employees. Use a numeric cursor in the application.
6. Create an application that lists the employees of the 'INT' department. You should calculate the date of retirement for each employee. Use a `Cursor For` looping procedure

in this application. Define all the cursor functions with the `For` Looping structure.

7. Modify the application in #6 to display the tools and glasses each employee purchased. This requires two nested looping procedures in the `cursor for` loop.
8. Create a function that calculates the total wages per department.
9. Create a procedure that displays the employees of a given department. This procedure should call the function created in #8. The function should be used to determine the percentage that each employee's wages are of the department total. The procedure should list the results.
10. Create an anonymous block that calls the procedure in #9.
11. Create a package that contains a cursor that selects the employees from the Employee table, the function in #8, and the procedure in #9. The procedure should use the package cursor. Create anonymous blocks that call these objects.

CHAPTER 10

# Using SQL*LOADER

This chapter teaches you about the PL/SQL language used in applications discussed in the next several parts of the book. You'll also learn about SQL *LOADER, which is used to load data into the Oracle tables. ■

**Using SQL*LOADER**

This section provides an overview of SQL*LOADER. It is an Oracle product used to load data into Oracle tables. The section also explains how to start SQL*LOADER, and the major load settings and commands.

**Defining a control file**

This section covers the control file, which contains the information needed by SQL*LOADER to load the table. This section also discusses the various load or data files that can be used for the source data.

**Using conditional logic in your control files**

This section covers the use of conditional logic in your control files. The section also discusses methods of creating multiple logical records from one physical record.

**Other control file keywords and clauses**

This section covers the control file clauses in greater depth. Some of the clauses are the *fields*, *concatenation*, and *continueif*.

**Executing SQL*LOADER from the command line**

This section explains how to use SQL*LOADER from the command line. You use this method when the Windows version of SQL*LOADER is not available.

**NOTE** Many of the figures in this chapter depict files that can be executed. However, they are not intended for practice execution. It can be a complex task to load tables that currently contain data and have table constraints. I felt it was best to place the load files in figures rather than in executable files to prevent using them for practice. I feel it would be best to read the entire chapter before practicing the various concepts.

In most cases, the control files in the figures can be executed if a replace load style option is added. However, this may disrupt your database. The exercises at the end of the chapter were intended to be used for your practice. An answer file that works is also included in the book. In addition, the Chapter also has an installment to load the Employee Information system tables. The purpose of this installment is to offer the reader additional practice using SQL*LOADER. Working files for this task are also contained in the book.

If you would like to execute the files contained in the figures, remember the database can be restored to its original shape using the original database load instructions or by following the steps in the review exercises.

# Understanding SQL*LOADER

SQL*LOADER is Oracle's product for reading text files and placing the data into Oracle tables. SQL*LOADER has the ability to read data that is formatted in a variety of methods. You can use the product to load fixed position or comma separated value files. The product offers the developer the ability to load multiple Oracle tables during the loading procedure. SQL*LOADER also enables you to use logic to control the records that can be loaded into the table. The condition expressions are based on the same type of conditional logic used in a *where* clause.

SQL*LOADER is Oracle's product for reading text files and placing the data into Oracle tables. SQL*LOADER can read data that is formatted in a variety of ways.

You can use SQL*LOADER to load fixed-position and variable-formatted records. SQL*LOADER can load multiple Oracle tables during the loading procedure.

SQL*LOADER enables you to use document logic that controls which records can be loaded into a table. The condition expressions are based on the same type of conditional logic used in a *where* clause.

SQL*LOADER offers the developer the ability to manipulate data fields before the data is added to the table. The product has the ability to combine several physical records into a logical record. SQL*LOADER can treat physical records as multiple logical records.

You also have the ability to manipulate data fields before the data is added to the table. SQL*LOADER can has the ability to combine several physical records into a logical record. It also can treat a physical record as multiple logical records and allows you to load multiple tables from the same load procedure.

SQL*LOADER is the product to use when converting data from a non-relational database to an Oracle database.

SQL*LOADER is the product to use when you're converting data from a nonrelational database to an Oracle database. I use it for two purposes. For example, you can use it when you're converting a PC-based system to a new Oracle Forms system that you've developed. This is part of my conversion work.

SQL*LOADER is the product to use when converting data from a non-relational database to an Oracle database. For example, you can use it when you're converting a PC based system to a new Oracle Forms system. Or you can use SQL*LOADER to read external data into an existing system.



**NOTE** I have developed a transformer at my place of employment. Each transformer manufacturer sends test results for our newly purchased transformers. Each month a clerk uses SQL*LOADER to read the results from a text file into an Oracle table. When you have a data source comprised of many different file types, it's easiest to turn the data into a text file and load it into the Oracle table by using SQL*LOADER. The manufacturer supplies test results with each shipment of their transformers. The results arrive in a variety of formats and file types. ■

When you have so many different file types of files, we have found it's easiest to turn the data into a text file and load it into the Oracle table by using SQL*LOADER. It has worked well for the tasks for which we've used it.

# How Do You Start Executing SQL*LOADER?

You can start executing SQL*LOADER two ways. The first method is to execute the statements from the operating system command line. This is the method that was used before the product was moved into Windows. It is still used with non-Windows operating systems in non-Windows environments such as UNIX. (More on this method will be described at the end of the chapter.)

The second method is to double-click the SQLLOAD icon or launch the SQL*LOADER executable file in the Oracle icon grouping. This icon is shown in Figure 10.1. It is shaped like a funnel with letters of the alphabet on top. It is displayed with a number of other icons for Oracle products.

If you cannot locate the icon, a search of the \orawin\bin directory on your PC or server can be performed to locate the executable that will start SQL*LOADER. The name of the executable is different depending upon the version of the database. The executable for Oracle7 is SQLLDR72.EXE or SQLLDR73.EXE. The executable for Oracle8 is SQLLDR80.EXE. Each version of the product operates the same.

Double-clicking the icon or executing the SQL*LOADER utility brings up will bring up the SQL*LOADER dialog box, as shown in Figure 10.2.

The dialog box contains two sets of fields. The top fields must be filled in. The bottom fields contained in the Optional frame do not have to be filled in. SQL*LOADER will provide the values for these fields if left empty. The dialog box has a number of boxes that require information. The following is a description of the boxes:

**FIG. 10.1**
The SQL*LOADER icon.

SQL*LOADER icon

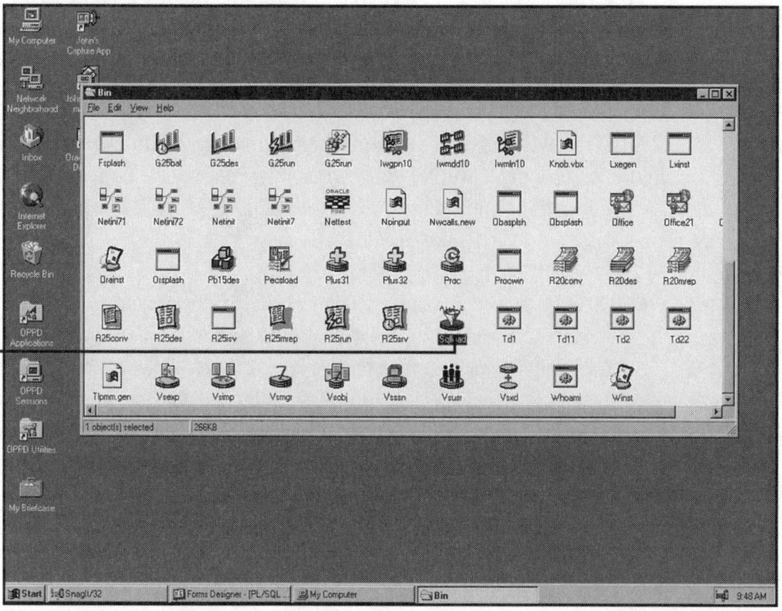

**FIG. 10.2**
The SQL*LOADER dialog box.

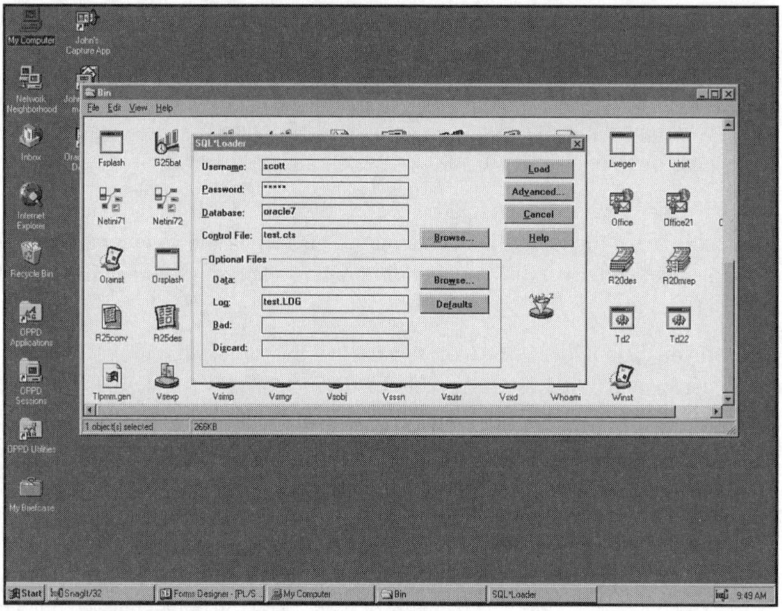

- **Username**—This field is for the name of the user account that has access to the Oracle tables. This user name id must have insert authority to add records and delete authority to use the *replace* option.
- **Password**—This field is for the password for the value of the user account password.
- **Database**—This value identifies the database that contains the Oracle tables. This value will also contain the location of the database when it's remote. This field is often called the *connect string* or *host string*.
- **Control File**—This field is for the name and location of the file that holds the loading instructions. The default file extension is *.CTL*.
- **Data**—This is an optional field that contains the name of the file that holds the load data. This file name may also be contained in the control file.
- **Log**—This is an optional field that contains the name of the file that will hold the results of the loading process. This file will defaults to the name of the control file with a file extension of *.LOG* when no value is supplied.
- **Bad**—This is an optional field that contains the name of the file that will contain any records that can't be loaded into the tables. This file will default to the name of the control file with a file extension of *.BAD* when no value is supplied.
- **Discard**—This is an optional field that contains the name of the file that will hold any records discarded by Oracle during the loading procedure. Discarded records are those that don't meet the load criteria specified in the condition logic in the load file. This file will default to the name of the control file with a file extension of *.DSC* when no value is supplied.



The SQL*LOADER dialog box also has a number of buttons. The *Browse* button adjacent to the *Control File* and *Data* fields will open a file-search dialog box you can use to find the desired file you want. When the file is found, the search dialog box will return the full file address to the field.

The *Defaults* button will populate the optional files with default file names that match the name of the control file. The *Cancel* button closes the dialog box without any action occurring. The Help button displays the Oracle SQL*LOADER help. It is part of the Database Tools Users' Guide facility.

The *Load* button starts the execution of the load program. However, before you can start the load program, the Loader Options must be reviewed and set. This is accomplished by clicking the *Advanced* button, which brings up the Advanced SQL*LOADER Options dialog box, as shown in Figure 10.3.

Following are the fields in the Advanced SQL*LOADER Options dialog box. The dialog box contains a number of values. Descriptions of these values are as follows:

- **Records to Skip**—This field tells Oracle how many records to skip before adding records to the tables. This is a useful tool when you've performed only a partial table load. For instance, assume you're loading 500,000 rows into a table. The load program is terminated at 150,000 rows because of table space constraints.

After the constraints are removed, you can begin loading data beginning at record 150,001. This will save you the time that was spent on the initial loading procedure. The default is 0. The load procedure will load all rows into the table.

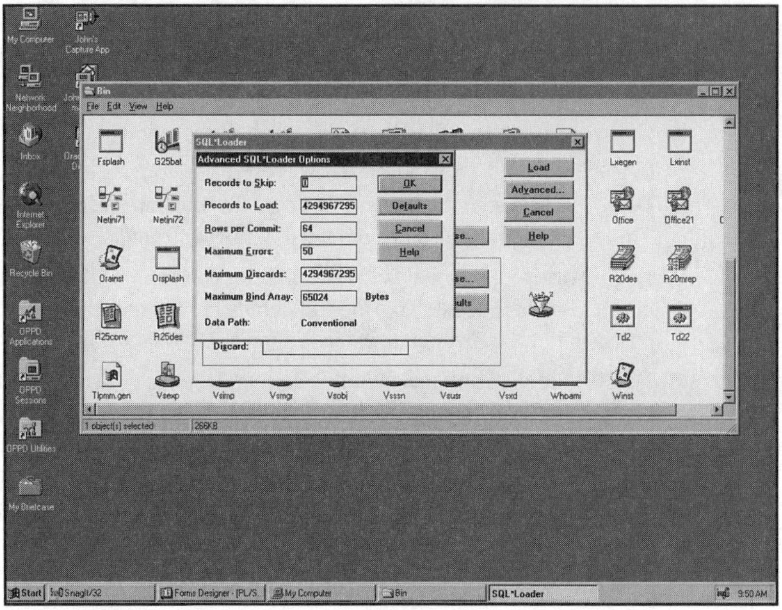


**FIG. 10.3**
The Advanced SQL*LOADER Options dialog box.

**NOTE** Table constraints were discussed in Chapter 6, "Defining the Database Objects." ■

- **Records to Load**—This field tells Oracle to terminate the loading procedure when the value in this field is reached. It's often useful to load several records with the first execution of the procedure. This allows you the opportunity to check the table to be sure the loading procedure worked correctly without waiting for the full load to occur.

  You can also use this option to stop the loading at a predefined point—for instance, if you're concerned with space in your table. This option allows you to terminate the load at a given point, check the table space, and continue loading. The default setting will allow the procedure to load 429,496,729 records to be loaded before terminating.
- **Rows per Commit**—This field tells Oracle when to commit the load records. The default setting is 64. This means Oracle will commit the inserted records at the end of each set of 64 inserted records.
- **Maximum Errors**—This field tells Oracle when to terminate the loading procedure based on errors. The default is 50. This means Oracle will terminate the procedure when the 50th error has been encountered.
- **Maximum Discards**—This field tells Oracle to terminate the loading procedure when the specified number of discarded records is reached. The default value is 429,496,729

records before terminating. Consider setting this at a low value. It's better to find out sooner than later in the long loading process that your condition logic is in error and is discarding good records early.

- **Maximum Bind Array**—This field is used to specify the maximum size of the bind array.

When you've reviewed these settings, press OK. This will return you to the SQL*LOADER dialog box. Press Load to start the loading procedure. When the load program is initiated, this brings up the SQL*LOADER Status dialog box. This screen will display error, commit, or status messages.

The loading is complete when no more messages are displayed. Press Close to close the dialog box. Figure 10.4 shows the Status dialog box.



**FIG. 10.4**
The SQL*LOADER Status screen.

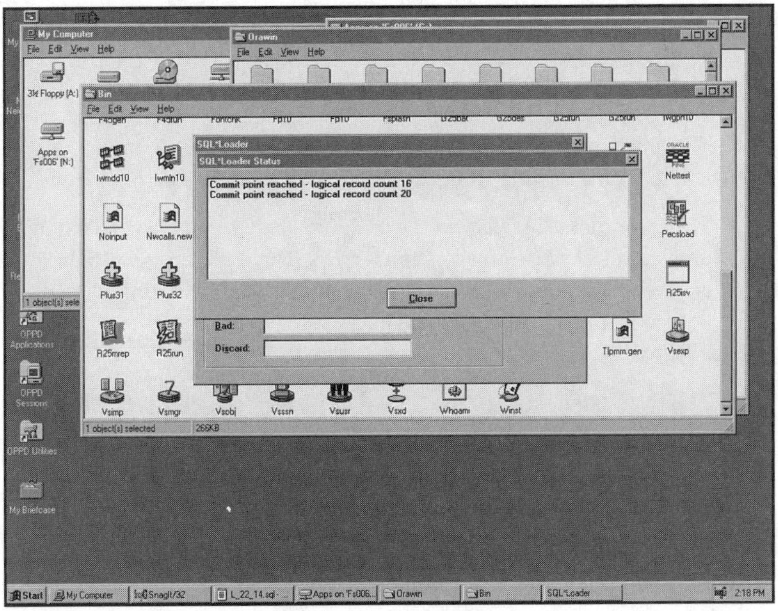


# Using the Various Load Files

The previous section discussed five files used in the loading procedure: *control, data, log, bad,* and *discard.*

The *control* file holds the loading instructions and will be discussed at length in the next section. The *data* file holds the data that will be loaded into the Oracle tables. It will be discussed under "Defining Control Files in the next section." Next you learn about the remaining three files: *log, bad,* and *discard.*

# Using the Log File

The most important of the three output files is the *log* file, which contains the results of the load procedure. You should always review this file after executing a load procedure. Listing 10.1 contains an example of a typical *log* file.

The file informs the developer whether the load procedure was successful. The *log* file has several parts. The first part contains the names of the various files used in the procedure: *control*, *data*, *discard*, and *bad*.

The second part lists the values of the various *load* options. It tells you if the procedure is to load all the records from the *data* file. It lists the number of records the program was to skip, and how many errors the procedure can encounter before it terminates. Finally, the section lists the bind array value, and the load path.

The next part lists the load style option. This is discussed at length in the next section on control files. Following this option is a listing of all the table data fields that were to be populated. Also listed are the expected data type and format of the load data. (Additional information is also contained in the Defining a control file section.)

The fourth section is important because it displays an error message for any record that could not be loaded. Listing 10.1 is an example of a log file that has error messages.

The error message tells you the problem: the section tells you that eight records failed the load procedures because of formatting errors. The error message tells you the problem. The associated record number tells you the row number of the record in the data file. It helps the developer to identify the record to be fixed.

**Listing 10.1 L_10_01.TXT—The Log File Holds the Run Statistics for the Load Procedure Run Statistics; These Tell You the Results of the Procedure**

```
SQL*LOADER: Release 7.1.4.0.2 - Production on Thu May 15 21:44:24 1997
Copyright  Oracle Corporation 1979, 1994.  All rights reserved.
Control File:   C:\BOOK\INSTALL\TOOL1.DAT
Data File:      C:\BOOK\INSTALL\TOOL1.DAT
  Bad File:     C:\BOOK\INSTALL\TOOL1.BAD
  Discard File: C:\BOOK\INSTALL\TOOL1.DSC
 (Allow all discards)
Number to load: ALL
Number to skip: 0
Errors allowed: 50
Bind array:     64 rows, maximum of 65024 bytes
Continuation:    none specified
Path used:      Conventional
Table TOOLS, loaded from every logical record.
Insert option in effect for this table: INSERT
   Column Name                  Position   Len  Term Encl Datatype
------------------------------------------------------------------------
FK_PAYROLL_NUMBER                   FIRST     *    ,  O(") CHARACTER
PURCHASE_DATE                        NEXT     *    ,  O(") DATE dd-mon-yy
PAYROLL_DEDUCT                       NEXT     *    ,  O(") CHARACTER
```

```
TOOL_NAME                              NEXT     *   ,  O(") CHARACTER
TOOL_COST                              NEXT     *   ,  O(") CHARACTER
PAYMENT_AMOUNT                         NEXT     *   ,  O(") CHARACTER
LAST_PAYMENT_AMOUNT                    NEXT     *   ,  O(") CHARACTER
FIRST_PAYMENT_DATE                     NEXT     *   ,  O(") DATE dd-mon-yy
LAST_PAYMENT_DATE                      NEXT     *   ,  O(") DATE dd-mon-yy
Record 1: Rejected - Error on table TOOLS, column PURCHASE_DATE.
Column not found before end of logical record (use TRAILING NULLCOLS)
Record 2: Rejected - Error on table TOOLS, column PURCHASE_DATE.
Column not found before end of logical record (use TRAILING NULLCOLS)
Record 3: Rejected - Error on table TOOLS, column PURCHASE_DATE.
Column not found before end of logical record (use TRAILING NULLCOLS)
Record 4: Rejected - Error on table TOOLS, column PURCHASE_DATE.
No terminator found after TERMINATED and ENCLOSED field
Record 5: Rejected - Error on table TOOLS, column TOOL_NAME.
Column not found before end of logical record (use TRAILING NULLCOLS)
Record 6: Rejected - Error on table TOOLS, column LAST_PAYMENT_AMOUNT.
Column not found before end of logical record (use TRAILING NULLCOLS)
Record 7: Rejected - Error on table TOOLS, column PAYROLL_DEDUCT.
Column not found before end of logical record (use TRAILING NULLCOLS)
Record 8: Rejected - Error on table TOOLS, column PURCHASE_DATE.
Column not found before end of logical record (use TRAILING NULLCOLS)
Table TOOLS:
  34 Rows successfully loaded.
  8 Rows not loaded due to data errors.
  0 Rows not loaded because all WHEN clauses were failed.
  0 Rows not loaded because all fields were null.

Space allocated for bind array:                 63180 bytes(27 rows)
Space allocated for memory besides bind array:  107167 bytes
Total logical records skipped:          0
Total logical records read:            42
Total logical records rejected:         8
Total logical records discarded:        0
Run began on Thu May 15 21:44:24 1997
Run ended on Thu May 15 21:44:33 1997
Elapsed time was:     00:00:08.68
CPU time was:         00:00:00.00     (May not include ORACLE CPU time)
```

Following the error part is the run part. I always look at this part when I run a load procedure. This part, along with the error part, tells you the results of the procedure and identifies any problems that occurred.

These statistics tell you how many rows were loaded into the table, how many were rejected because of a format or database error, how many were discarded due to control file logic, and how many were not loaded because all of the fields in the logical record were null.

This section along with the error section tells you the results of the procedure and identifies any problems that occurred.

The remaining parts offer statistics on the number of logical records that were read, the number of records skipped, the number discarded, and the number rejected by the database. They also show the time the procedure was executed and the time it was completed.

**NOTE** I mentioned earlier in this section that I always review the log file after I load data. I do this because the status screen doesn't list errors unless the procedure is terminated. The log file holds all errors even if the application is not terminated.

As you saw in Listing 10.1, there were errors for eight records. They were rejected and placed in the bad file. Yet, the status screen doesn't give you a clue that errors occurred. This is why it shows the importance of viewing the log file.

## Using the Bad File

The records rejected by Oracle during the load procedure are placed in a file with an extension of *.BAD*. The records that exist in this file will have the same format as the records Oracle found in the load data file. You can look at this file to determine where to correct the records.

Following are some of the common errors you may encounter when loading data that causes records to be rejected.

- **Dates in an Incorrect Format**—Records that don't match the date picture format specified in the control file will be rejected. For example, records that have incorrect dates such as 31-APR-97 will be rejected.
- **Numeric Columns with Alpha Characters**—Oracle will reject any records that contain a value that can't be converted to a number. These are values that contain alpha characters or numeric values that contain spaces within the digits.
- **Values that Don't Match Database Constraints**—Oracle will reject any records that do not have valid values. Trying to place a null value in a field that isn't null-defined, or placing a value that does not match a check constraint will cause the record to be rejected. Another common error is to insert the same primary key values into multiple records.

The *bad* file is a good useful tool to identify problems with the data. After you view the error message in the *log* file, you may have to view the record to find and fix the error. The easiest way to do this is to look at the record in the *bad* file to view the incorrect data.

There's less data to look through in the *bad* file than in the *data* file. In addition, each record in the bad file has an error. Listing 10.2 shows the *bad* file for the tools load procedure. Notice that we have been discussing. You might notice that the *bad* file looks the same as the data file except that it has fewer records.

**Listing 10.2 L_10_02.TXT—The Contents of the Bad File for Tools Loading Procedure Bad File**

```
25,01-OCT-22,Y,Pliers,"25",10,"5",01-SEP-22,"01-OCT-22"
25,01-FEB-23,N,Vice Grips,"10",10,,,
35,04-JUN-80,Y,3/4" Wrench,"4",2,"2",01-JUL-80,"15-JUL-80"
35,06-NOV-82,Y,Tool Chest,"16.75",6,"4.75",01-DEC-80,"01-JAN-81"
35,24-APR-81,N,Knife,"7.95",7.95,,,
```

**TIP** You will find it much easier to fix errors in the *bad* file rather than in the data file in cases where the load procedure is completed. You can fix the errors in the *bad* file, change your control file to read the *bad* file instead of the original data file, and change the load option to *append*. (Load styles are discussed in the Defining the Load Style Section.)

Performing these steps will allow you to avoid deleting the rows you have added to the table. You'll also save the time it takes to reload all of the records in the data file into the table.

## Using the Discard File

The *discard* file is identical in format to the *bad* file except that it holds the records rejected by the load program because of the user-defined conditional logic contained in the control file program. The *discard* file has an extension of DSC.

As you'll see in the next section, the control file can contain logic used to evaluate records to be loaded into the table. Records that don't agree with the logic are discarded.

The beauty of the discard file is that it lets you look at the records to see if the logic in the control file was right to reject the records. If you find records that should not have been discarded, you can use the procedure outlined in the tip in the previous section to add the records to the table.

Listing 10.3 illustrates a *discard* file, which has an identical format. It looks identical to a *bad* file.



**Listing 10.3 L_10_03.TXT—A Typical Discard File**

```
25,01-OCT-22,Y,Pliers,"25",10,"5",01-SEP-22,"01-OCT-22"
25,01-FEB-23,N,Vice Grips,"10",10,,,
35,04-JUN-80,Y,3/4" Wrench,"4",2,"2",01-JUL-80,"15-JUL-80"
35,06-NOV-82,Y,Tool Chest,"16.75",6,"4.75",01-DEC-80,"01-JAN-81"
35,24-APR-81,N,Knife,"7.95",7.95,,,
```

# Defining Control Files

A *control* file contains the instructions for SQL*LOADER. These instructions consist of the name and location of the data file. The file also contains the loading option that tells Oracle what to do with the records. It contains the names(s) of the tables that will receive the records. It contains a listing of the table columns that are to be populated. The file contains formatting instructions that tell Oracle how to format the physical load record and where to find the values to place into the Oracle table columns. Finally, in some cases the *control* file can even contain the data that is to be loaded.

The following sections discuss these *control* file instructions.

## Defining a Simple Control File

A control file consists of a series of expressions that instruct Oracle how to load the data. The first part of the file script begins with the keywords *load data*, which means that the procedure lets Oracle know this application is to load data into a table.

The next second part of the file begins with the keyword *infile,* which tells Oracle the name and location of the data file. This definition begins with the keyword infile. The file name (enclosed in single quotation marks) and file location follows this keyword. When the control file holds the data, an asterisk (*) is placed after the *infile* keyword.

The next part of the script contains the name of the Oracle table that will receive the data. This name is prefaced by the keywords *into table.* The final part (enclosed in parentheses) tells Oracle the names of the table columns that will be populated. It also tells Oracle where to find the data in the physical record row, and what type of data it can expect to be received.

A *fixed-position* control file is shown in Figure 10.5. Fixed-position means a column's values begin and end in the same location in the control file.

**FIG. 10.5**
A simple fixed-position control file.

```
load data
infile 'c:\book\install\dept.dat'
into table department
(
department      position(01:04) char(4),
department_name position(06:20) char(15)
)
```

```
                   1111111111222222
Column #  1234567890123456789012345
          POL  POLITICAL SCIEN
          INT  INTERIOR DESIGN
          WEL  WELFARE BUREAU
          TRF  TRESURY DEPAR
          CEN  CENSUS DEPT
```

The control file in Figure 10.5 is a fixed-position file. It is this type of file because of the way the data is defined. Each field name is followed by the keyword *position,* and two numbers separated by a colon and enclosed by parentheses. These values represent the start and end position of the data.

The control file shown in the Figure 10.5 contains the data that is to be loaded by the procedure. Notice that above the data is a series of numbers that represent the column numbers. These numbers are not part of the control file but are shown in this example for the purpose of discussion.

Using the column numbers, the value begins in row 1 and ends in row 4. The first value (1) is the start position parameter for the department column. The second value (4) is the end position parameter. These are the values included in the department definition. They tell SQL*LOADER where the data for the department column is located.

The department name column begins at column 6 and ends at column 20. These values are also placed in the position parameters for the department name column definition. A final parameter consists of the data type and size of each of the load fields.

When SQL*LOADER executes the preceding control file in this example, it will place the characters in positions 1–4 into the department field of the Tools table and the characters in position 6–20 in the department_name name field.

The *char* data type specification tells SQL*LOADER that the characters should be treated as character data. If you specify some type of numeric data type, SQL*LOADER will try to convert the characters to a number. If it can't do this because of alpha characters, it will reject the record and place it into the *bad* file.

The reason this type of file is called *fixed* is because the values in each row are in the exact same position. This differs from variable formats such as *comma-* and *quotation-delimited* physical records.



Comma-delimited records have a comma that denotes the completion of the value. Quotation-delimited records are enclosed by quotation marks.

## Defining the Load Style

The control file allows you to use four different loading styles. The loading style option precedes the keyword *into.* The loading styles are as follows:

- **Insert**—This is the default load style. It tells SQL*LOADER to add the records into the table. The table must be empty in order to use this loading style. Trying to load records into a populated table will cause the procedure to terminate.
- **Append**—This load style is used to add records to a table that already contains records. This style adds records to the end of the table. You use this style to load records from the bad or discard files.
- **Replace**—This load style deletes records in the table before adding the records from the load procedure. This style causes a delete command to be issued against the table before the new data is loaded. The deleted records are placed in the rollback log and can be restored if necessary.
- **Truncate**—This load style truncates the table before loading the records.

  Truncating causes the records to be deleted without the overhead of writing them in the rollback log. You can't restore records after using this load style.

Figure 10.6 shows the *replace* load style. The load procedure causes the records in the Department table to be deleted before the new records are loaded into the table.

**NOTE** Figure 10.6 is not intended as a practice example. It is included for discussion only. If you try to use the control file to populate the department table, you will get the following error message:

*continues*

*continued*

```
SQL*LOADER SQL*LOADER-926: Oci error while executing deleting (due to REPLACE
keyword) from table for table DEPARTMENT
ORA-02292: integrity constraint (SCOTT.SYS_C00388) violated - child record found
```

This error message resulted in the attempt to delete the existing department records while the database is populated and constraints exist. Records cannot be deleted from the department table until the records are deleted from the employee table. A foreign key constraint exists on the fk_department column of the employee table.

**FIG. 10.6**
A control file that uses the replace load style to delete the table records before loading new ones.

```
load data
infile 'c:\book\install\dept.dat'
replace into table department
(
department      position(01:04) char(4),
department_name position(06:20) char(15)
)
```

# Defining the Data Format

You may encounter many types of data formats, but three are the most common and are discussed in this section. The first is the fixed-position format (discussed earlier in this chapter). Second is a comma-delimited format, and third is quotation-delimited. Most software packages can output data in one of these delimited formats.

In the *comma-delimited* format, each field on the load row is separated from the other fields by a comma. This is a common data format for when converting data. You will often see files that contain this type of data format. Files using this format have an extension of *.CSV*.

In the *quotation-delimited* format, each field is enclosed by quotation marks. Most software packages have the ability to output their data in delimited formats. I find these format the easiest to define in a control file.

The load data format and table columns definitions follow the *into* clause. The definition of a fixed-position row consists of the field that will receive the data, followed by the data type and location on the physical record.

Delimited data formats don't need to have the positions recorded in the column definition. When using either of the delimited formats SQL*LOADER knows (by the mark) where to start and stop each field. This means you don't have to count columns to determine the start and stop position of fields.

When you're using the fixed-position data format, it's easy to make a mistake determining where the field starts and stops. It is especially easy to make errors if some records have null values because you can't visually identify the fields.

The delimited records allow you to avoid this problem because they don't use column position. This means that you can document the column names in the same order that the values appear in the load row.

Finally, when specifying data fields, a date picture format is usually listed in the control file data specification. This lets Oracle know how the data is formatted.

# Defining Condition Logic in Your Control Files

SQL*LOADER control files can have record-selection logic placed in them. This allows the developer to have the procedure evaluate each record in the data file and decide whether to allow the record to be added to the table. This is useful when the load table contains records with bad data.



You can use the control file to reject these records, correct them in the discard file, and add them to the table by using the *append* loading style. This is useful when you want to load several tables during one load procedure. You can use mutually exclusive conditions so the procedure loads only one table in a set of tables.

You write the logic by using a *when* conditional clause, which must evaluate the record as true for the record to be loaded. If the record is evaluated as false, the record is placed in the discard file.

Figure 10.7 shows a load program that will load records into the Tool file only for employee number 25.

**FIG. 10.7**
Using a when clause to limit the records entered into the Tools file.

```
load data
infile *
into table tools
when fk_payroll_number = "25"
fields terminated by "," optionally enclosed by '"'
(fk_payroll_number, purchase_date date "dd-mon-yy",
 payroll_deduct, tool_name, tool_cost, payment_amount, last_payment_amount,
 first_payment_date date "dd-mon-yy", last_payment_date date "dd-mon-yy")
begindata
25,01-OCT-22,Y,Pliers,"25",10,"5",01-SEP-22,"01-OCT-22"
25,01-FEB-23,N,Vice Grips,"10",10,,,
35,04-JUN-80,Y,3/4" Wrench,"4",2,"2",01-JUL-80,"15-JUL-80"
35,06-NOV-82,Y,Tool Chest,"16.75",6,"4.75",01-DEC-80,"01-JAN-81"
```

The *when* clause follows immediately after the *into* clause. The program illustrated in Figure 10.7 is slightly different from the ones you saw earlier in this chapter. In this example, the data is in the control file and the data is comma-delimited.

The *when* clause may also be used with fixed-position formatted data. Any of the SQL evaluation operators discussed earlier in this chapter may be used in this expression.

You can use multiple conditions in the *when* clause. The expressions should be separated by the *and* operator.

Note that the *or* operator isn't used between expressions in the *when* clause. This means that each of the expressions in the clause must be true.

Figure 10.8 shows a control file that contains a *when* clause that contains multiple expressions.

**FIG. 10.8**
Using multiple expressions in the when clause to limit the number of records loaded into the table.

```
load data
infile *
into table tools
when fk_payroll_number = "25" and tool_name = "Pliers"
fields terminated by "," optionally enclosed by '"'
(fk_payroll_number, purchase_date date "dd-mon-yy",
 payroll_deduct, tool_name, tool_cost, payment_amount, last_payment_amount,
 first_payment_date date "dd-mon-yy", last_payment_date date "dd-mon-yy")
begindata
25,01-OCT-22,Y,Pliers,"25",10,"5",01-SEP-22,"01-OCT-22"
25,01-FEB-23,N,Vice Grips,"10",10,,,
35,04-JUN-80,Y,3/4" Wrench,"4",2,"2",01-JUL-80,"15-JUL-80"
35,06-NOV-82,Y,Tool Chest,"16.75",6,"4.75",01-DEC-80,"01-JAN-81"
```

# Loading Multiple Tables Using the Same Load Procedure

You can load several tables simultaneously by using the same physical record. This is done by using multiple *into* clauses in the control file. This is a handy feature when you load records that come from a de-normalized database.

Tables designed by inexperienced users often have multiple fields defined to hold repeating values. This is done because the developer found it easier to work with one table rather than several related tables.

An example is an employee record with four sets of fields to record eyeglass purchases. The multiple-table loading features of SQL*LOADER allow you to reorganize the data from the de-normalized physical record file into normalized logical records.

SQL*LOADER Oracle knows to load multiple tables because of the *into* clauses. Each of these clauses contains a data format description. These descriptions tell Oracle where the data begins.

In Figure 10.9, you can see a control file with a physical record that contains both an eyeglass purchase record and a tool purchase record. The file has two *into* clauses. The first clause is used to load a record into the Glasses table and the second clause loads records into the Tools table.

**FIG. 10.9**
Loading two tables using the same control file.

```
load data
infile *
into table glasses
fields terminated by ","
trailing nullcols
(fk_payroll_number, purchase_date date "dd-mon-yy",
 optician, cost, check_number)
into table tools
fields terminated by "," optionally enclosed by '"'
(purchase_date date,
 payroll_deduct, tool_name, tool_cost, payment_amount, last_payment_amount,
 first_payment_date date "dd-mon-yy", last_payment_date date "dd-mon-yy",
 fk_payroll_number position(1))
begindata
34,12-AUG-97,Greenberg Optical,175,N8754,01-OCT-97,Y,Pliers,"25",10,"5",01-SEP-22,"01-OCT-22"
25,15-NOV-97,Greenberg Optical,175,A12356, 06-NOV-97,Y,Tool Chest,"16.75",6,"4.75",01-DEC-80,"01-
31,31-JAN-97,Peralman Optical,170,B9054, 10-MAR-97,Y,RIFLE,"290",70,"10",15-MAR-05,"15-MAY-05"
```

As SQL*LOADER scans each comma-delimited data row, it places each value into the corresponding field in the data definition. When it reaches the end of the data definition, SQL*LOADER loads the record into the Glasses table.

SQL*LOADER then reaches the second *into* clause and begins scanning the logical record from the point where it left off. SQL*LOADER places each value into the corresponding field. When the end of the definition is reached, SQL*LOADER loads the record into the Tools table.

**NOTE** Both the Glasses table and Tools table need a value for the fk_payroll_number fields. The logical record has only one value for the payroll number. In order to populate the fk_payroll_number field in the second *into* clause, the control file uses the *position* keyword to begin scanning from the indicated position. ■



The fixed-position data format gives you more flexibility to create multiple records and add them to multiple tables or even to the same table. This is because you don't have to rely on sequentially scanning the logical record as you do when using delimited file formats.

SQL*LOADER expects the next value to follow the last one scanned. The values for fixed-position logical records allows you to specify the exact location of the data. You can use the same data values repeatedly or jump around the physical record to select the values you needed.

Figure 10.10 shows a control file that creates two eyeglass purchase records for each logical record read into the procedure.

**FIG. 10.10**
Using the fixed-position data format definition to create multiple records for the same table.

```
load data
infile *
into table glasses
fields terminated by ","
trailing nullcols
(fk_payroll_number position(1:2), purchase_date position(4:13) date "dd-mon-yy",
 optician position(14:30), cost position(32:34), check_number position(36:41))
into table glasses
fields terminated by "," optionally enclosed by '"'
(purchase_date position(43:51) date "dd-mon-yy", fk_payroll_number position(1:2),
 cost position(71:73), check_number position(75:79), optician position(53:68))
begindata
34 12-AUG-97 Greenberg Optical 175 N8754  31-JAN-96 Peralman Optical  170 U9054
25 15-NOV-97 Greenberg Optical 175 A12356 27-FEB-97 Westgate Optical  130 XX890
31 31-JAN-97 Peralman Optical  170 B9054  08-APR-97 Ralston EyeGlass  189 Y6549
```

In this example, the data definition for the second *into* clause shows that you can skip around the physical record, picking up values as needed. The fk_payroll_number field is listed third and is read from the beginning of the record.

This field was read once before in the previous *into* clause. In addition, the cost and check_number values are scanned before the optician value.

The functionality discussed in this section, coupled with the *when* clause, gives you a high degree of flexibility to rearrange data during the loading procedures. The alternative to using SQL*LOADER to rearrange the data is to load the physical record into a table and using PL/SQL to load the various tables.

Using PL/SQL is a typical method for converting data. This method requires disk space to hold the temporary file and it requires the data to be read twice. You may find that using SQL*LOADER to rearrange your conversion data is preferable.

# Other Control File Keywords and Clauses

A control file can have these parts:

- The *options* clause
- The *unrecoverable/recoverable* clause
- The *load data* clause
- The *infile* clause
- The load style contained in the *into table* clause
- The *concatenation* clause
- The *into table* clause

The *load data* clause is the first clause needed in the control file. It indicates that the purpose of the procedure is to load data and that additional settings will follow the keywords. The *infile* clause holds the name of the data file with the logical records to be loaded.

When the data file is part of the control file, the keyword *infile* is followed by an asterisk (*). (The load style options were covered earlier in this chapter.) The remaining clauses are discussed in the following sections.

# The Options and Recoverable/Unrecoverable Clauses

The *options* clause is another part of a control file. When it's used in a control file, the *options* clause is usually the first statement. It specifies runtime settings that affect the loading of data.

Table 10.1 shows the settings available.

**Table 10.1 Load Options**

| Option | Description |
|---|---|
| Bindsize = n | Number of bytes in the bind array. |
| Direct = | This option specifies the load path method. The options are true or false. True causes a direct load path method. The *direct path method* disables all database triggers and some of the table constraints during the loading process. The other method is the *conventional path*. This method applies all integrity constraints and insert triggers. |

| Option | Description |
|---|---|
| Errors = n | The number of errors allowed before the procedure is terminated. |
| Load = n | The number of records to load before the procedure is terminated. |
| Parallel = | Tells SQL*LOADER Oracle to run multiple loading sessions. The values are true or false. |
| Rows = n | The number of rows in the bind array used when doing a conventional load. The number of rows between saves during a direct load procedure. |
| Silent = | Suppresses messages. Message options are header, feedback, discards, and all. |
| Skip = n | Number of records to skip before loading the table. |



You can set most of these options in the SQL*LOADER dialog box shown in Figure 10.3. You can't set the parallel option in this dialog box—you have to by using the *options* clause. This option allows you to load multiple input files concurrently into tablespace files.

The *unrecoverable/recoverable* clauses are used in *direct* load path method. When you specify the *recoverable* mode, the loaded data is written to the redo log. This means the data in the table can be restored.

## The Into Table Clause

The *into table* clause is a necessary part component of the control file. It can contain a number of items, including the name of the table receiving data, the load style option, a *when* clause (discussed in the previous "Defining Condition Logic in your control file" section), a *fields* clause, a *trailing nullcols* clause, an *index* option, a *fields* condition expression, and a data-specification section.

**The Fields Clause** The *fields* clause is used to load variable-format data records such as comma-delimited records. The *fields* clause indicates the characters that identify the field boundaries.

Since the values don't have a fixed position, you have to specify how to identify the values. The *fields* clause uses two different sets of keywords. The first is *terminated by* and the second is *enclosed by.*

The *terminated by* keywords indicate the character that denotes the end of the value. In the case of comma-delimited records, the comma terminates the field.

The *enclosed by* keywords indicate the characters that denote the beginning and end of the value.

Figure 10.11 shows several versions of the *fields* clause.

The first example in the figure is used for comma-delimited records. The *fields* clause indicates that the value is completed by a comma so SQL*LOADER knows where the field values begin and end, based on the comma.

The termination character can be other character types, including white space (space bar). The second fields example shows that white space terminates the field value.

**FIG. 10.11**
Examples of the *Fields* Control File clause.

```
fields terminated by ","

        Dickey, Tayla, 03-May-79, Clerk

fields terminated by whitespace

        Dickey  Tayla  03-May-79  Clerk

fields enclosed by '"'

        "Dickey" "Tayla" "03-May-79" "Clerk"

fields terminated by "," optionally enclosed by '|'

        Dickey, Tayla, |03-May-79|, Clerk
```

Whenever SQL*LOADER encounters white space, it knows to begin placing the next characters scanned into the next field in the data definition.

The third example uses the *enclosed by* keywords. This is used for physical records that are enclosed by a character.

In this example, the data record values are enclosed by double quotation marks. The *fields* clause has to specify the double quotes as the character that denotes the start and stop of the value.

The fourth example uses both the *terminated by* and *enclosed by* keywords. In this example, the fields can be terminated by a comma and enclosed by the pipe symbol (|). When SQL*LOADER encounters the pipe symbol, it knows that all the characters scanned until the next pipe symbol are part of the current value.

If SQL*LOADER encounters a comma before it reaches the concluding pipe symbol, it considers the comma a part of the value and not a field-termination character.

**NOTE** Optionally enclosing a value is handy when some of the fields can't use the same delimiting device as the rest of the fields. For instance, values that contain multiple words such as an address (9814 Adams Road) are hard to load using a white-space as a termination character unless it can be enclosed.

**The Trailing Nullcols Clause, Index Options, and Field Condition Expressions** Some of the figures shown in this chapter use the keywords called *trailing nullcols*. These keywords indicate that when it encounters a physical record that doesn't have as many values as fields in the data definition, SQL*LOADER should treat the missing fields as null columns. Without this clause, SQL*LOADER Oracle will consider the record as erroneous and put it in the *bad* file.

The *Index* option is used when the load data is sorted. This is specified by using the *sorted indexes* keywords. The table indexes are built directly from the incoming data; sorting routines are used on the index.

This reduces the loading time since sorting records is time-consuming. But if you use this option and the data is not sorted properly, the index will be invalid and you'll have to drop it and recreate it.

The *fields condition* clause is used with the *nullif* and *defaultif* keywords. This clause is used to change the values of certain fields under certain conditions.

The *nullif* keyword changes the value to null when the condition is met. The *defaultif* keyword changes the value to blank or zero when evaluated as true.

In Figure 10.12, the *nullif* keyword is used to change the cost value to nulls when the cost = 175. The *defaultif* keyword is used to change the value of check_number to null when the check_ number = 'N8754'. These changes occur in the first two records.



**FIG. 10.12**
Using the *fields* clause to change the value of a field.

```
load data
infile *
replace into table glasses
fields terminated by ","
(fk_payroll_number, purchase_date date "dd-mon-yy",
 optician, cost nullif (cost = '175'),
 check_number char defaultif (check_number = 'N8754'))
begindata
34,12-AUG-79,Greenberg Optical,175,N8754
25,15-NOV-23,Greenberg Optical,175,A12356
31,31-JAN-64,Peralman Optical,170,B9054
35,23-OCT-83,Greenberg Optical,165,X6789
21,31-MAY-67,Greenberg Optical,165,B7865


SQL> select * from glasses;

FK_PAYROLL_NUMBER PURCHASE_ OPTICIAN                   COST CHECK_NUMB
----------------- --------- -------------------- --------- ----------
               34 12-AUG-79 Greenberg Optical
               25 15-NOV-23 Greenberg Optical                A12356
               31 31-JAN-64 Peralman Optical            170 B9054
               35 23-OCT-83 Greenberg Optical           165 X6789
               21 31-MAY-67 Greenberg Optical           165 B7865
```

When the logical record you're loading contains white space in the position you specify, this white space is loaded into the field. It may be advantageous to make the field null because SQL*LOADER doesn't consider white space the same as nulls.

You can ensure that your fields contain nulls rather than white space by using the BLANKS keyword. Specifying *nullif fieldname* = BLANKS causes the field to be null.

# The Concatenation and Continueif Clauses

The *concatenation* and *continueif* clauses are used to combine several physical records into a logical record by combining the various records together.

The *concatenation* clause is the simplest. You use it when SQL*LOADER always has the same number of physical records to combine. The syntax is "Concatenate *n*." *n* represents the number of consecutive physical records to combine.

Figure 10.13 shows the use of the *concatenation* clause. The load program combines two consecutive physical records into one logical record. The *concatenate* keyword follows the *replace* keyword in the *into* clause.

**FIG. 10.13**
Using the *concatenate* clause to combine physical records into one logical record.

```
load data
infile *
replace
concatenate 2
into table glasses
fields terminated by ","
(fk_payroll_number, purchase_date date "dd-mon-yy",
 optician, cost,
 check_number)
begindata
34,12-AUG-79,
Greenberg Optical,175,N8754
25,15-NOV-23,
Greenberg Optical,175,A12356
31,31-JAN-64,
Peralman Optical,170,B9054
35,23-OCT-83,
Greenberg Optical,165,X6789
```

In Figure 10.13, the data has the same number of physical records for each logical record created by the load procedure. Sometimes you don't have the same number of physical records. When this condition happens, you can use the *continueif* clause to combine the physical records.

The *continueif* keyword indicates whether the data continues on the next row. You use the keyword with the *this*, *next*, and *last* keywords. These keywords indicate that the current record, next record, or previous record determines whether the next record should be used as the beginning of the logical record.

Figure 10.14 shows the use of the *continueif* clause. The *continueif* keyword is placed after the *replace* keyword. It's followed by the keyword *this* keyword, indicating that a value on the current row determines whether the next row should be included in the logical record. The remaining value is an asterisk (*) in position 1 of the row.

**FIG. 10.14**
Using the *continueif* clause to combine physical records.

```
load data
infile *
replace
continueif this (1) = '*'
into table glasses
fields terminated by ","
(fk_payroll_number, purchase_date date "dd-mon-yy",
 optician, cost,
 check_number)
begindata
* 34,12-AUG-79,
 Greenberg Optical,175,N8754
* 25,15-NOV-23,
 Peralman Optical,170,B9054
* 35,23-OCT-83,
 Greenberg Optical,165,X6789
 21,31-MAY-67,Greenberg Optical,165,B7865
* 34,08-SEP-77,
 Pearlman Optical,164,B9087
* 33,01-FEB-74,
 Downtown Optical,145,B9876
 32,23-JUN-70,Downtown Optical,123,B897
```

Since in this example the *continueif* character is in position 1, this position can't be used for the load data. SQL*LOADER will looks at this position on each row for instructions about combining the records.

# Executing SQL*LOADER from the Command Line

Earlier in this chapter, you saw that SQL*LOADER can be executed directly from Windows by using the SQL*LOADER icon and associated dialog boxes. SQL*LOADER can also be executed from the command line when you're using a non-Windows operating system such as UNIX.

The basic syntax of the command is shown in Figure 10.15.

**FIG. 10.15**
The SQL*LOADER command line initiation syntax.

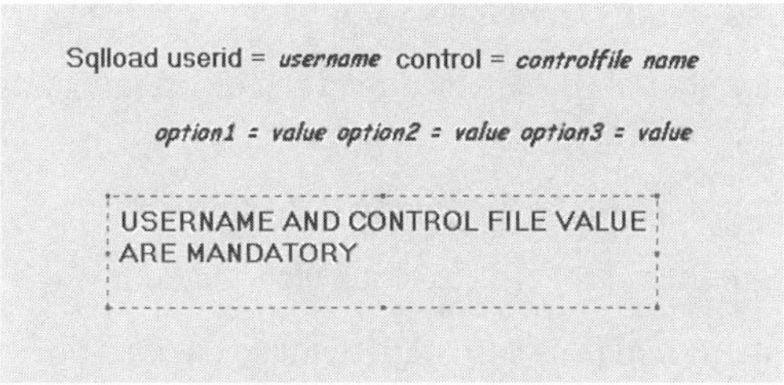




The SQLLOAD keyword is used to initiate SQL*LOADER. The command must contain the Oracle database user ID and the name of the control file. The bad file, discard file, and log file default to the name of the control file if no options are set.

In addition, the same default load set as discussed earlier in the chapter. You can change any of the default settings by entering the option and corresponding value on the command line.

The command line options are listed in Table 10.2.

**Table 10.2 Command Line Load Options**

| Option | Description |
|---|---|
| Bad | The name of the bad file. |
| Bindsize | The size of the conventional path bind array. |
| Control | The name of the control file. |
| Data | The name of the data file. |
| Direct | Use the direct path load method. |
| Discard | The name of the discard file. |
| Discardmax | The maximum number of discarded records allowed before termination of the procedure. |
| Errors | The maximum number of rejected records allowed before termination of the procedure. |
| File | The name of the file from which to allocate extents. |

*continues*

**Table 10.2 Continued**

| Option | Description |
|---|---|
| Load | The number of logical records to load with this procedure. |
| Log | The name of the log file. |
| Parallel | Perform a parallel loading procedure. |
| Parfile | The name of the parameter file that can be used in place of entering the options on the command line. |
| Rows | The number of rows to load between direct path data saves or in a conventional path bind array. |
| Silent | Suppress messages during the procedure. |
| Skip | The number of records to skip before loading. |
| Userid | The name and password of the Oracle database. |

# Summary

SQL*LOADER is Oracle's product for loading text-based data files into Oracle database tables. The procedure can be initiated from Windows using the SQL*LOADER icon in the Oracle icon group. You must have insert authority on the database to use the product.

Several files are important to the SQL*LOADER process. The control file holds the loading instructions and, optionally, the load data. The data file holds the load data.

The log file holds statistics about the success or failure of the loading process. The bad file holds the records rejected during the procedure. The discard file holds the records rejected due to logic in the control file.

The control file contains a number of parts. The *Load data* keyword initiates the procedure. The *infile* clause indicates where the load data is located.

The *into* clause contains the name of the table receiving the logical record. The clause also contains a variety of other values.

A portion of the clause tells indicates where to append the records to the table, replace the existing records in the table to allow for rollback, truncate the current table and insert the records, and insert the records into an empty table.

The *into* clause indicates whether the data is terminated or enclosed by a specific character. It also contains instructions for where the values are located in the physical record.

The control file can also contain logic that prevents the loading of some records. This logic is contained in a *when* clause. When records are prevented from loading due because of this logic, they are placed in the discard file.

SQL*LOADER can create multiple logical records from a physical record and load multiple tables in a procedure. This is done using multiple *into* clauses in the control file.

SQL*LOADER can also create a single logical record from multiple physical records using the *concatenate* and *continueif* clauses.

SQL*LOADER can also be initiated from the command line by using the SQLLOAD keyword. This option is used with an operating system other than Windows.

# From Here...

This chapter completes Part III. You have now learned about the PL/SQL language used in applications discussed in the next several parts of the book. You have also learned about SQL*LOADER, which is used to load data into the Oracle tables.

The next chapter is about Oracle Forms 4.5, the product used to create the graphical user interface (GUI) applications that manage and display the data contained in the Oracle tables.

The next chapter introduces you to an Oracle form and tells you how to use it. Oracle forms have a sophisticated searching capability, as you'll learn in the next chapter.



# Review Exercises

1. Delete the records in the Glasses, Tools, Employee, and Department tables.
2. Load the data in the DEPT.DAT file into the Department table. Use a fixed-position data format.
3. Load the data in the EMP.DAT file into the Employee table. Put the data in the control file. This is an enclosed data file.
4. Load the data in the GLASSES.DAT file into the Glasses table. This is a comma-delimited file.
5. Load the data in the TOOLS.DAT file into the Tools table. This is a combination command and enclosed file.

EMPLOYEE DATABASE PROJECT INSTALLMENT 3

The task of this installment is to populate the tables created in installment 2 with data from the original Employee database that is to be replaced by this project. The data from the original system is in the "RAWDATA.CSV" file. The data is in a comma-delimited format.

The fields in the logical record are:

```
last_name,first_name, absences, wages, street, city, state,
phone, social_security_number, employment_date, birth_date,
current_position, position_date, department, department_name,
department_1, historic_position_1, position_date_1, wages_1,
comments_1, department_2, historic_position_2, position_date_2,
wages_2, comments_2, department_3, historic_position_3,
position_date_3, wages_3, comments_3, department_4,
```

```
historic_position_4, position_date_4, wages_4, comments_4,
department_5, historic_position_5, position_date_5, wages_5,
comments_5, department_6, historic_position_6,
position_date_6, wages_6, comments_6, purchase_date_1, optician_1,
cost_1, check_number_1, purchase_date_2, optician_2, cost_2,
check_number_2, purchase_date_3, optician_3, cost_3, check_number_3,
tool_purchase_date_1, payroll_deduct_1, tool_name_1, tool_cost_1,
payment_amount_1, last_payment_amount_1, first_payment_date_1,
last_payment_date_1, tool_purchase_date_2,
payroll_deduct_2, tool_name_2, tool_cost_2, payment_amount_2,
last_payment_amount_2, first_payment_date_2, last_payment_date_2,
tool_purchase_date_3, payroll_deduct_3, tool_name_3,
tool_cost_3, payment_amount_3, last_payment_amount_3,
first_payment_date_3, last_payment_date_3
```

Create a temporary Oracle table to hold the values in the "RAWDATA.CSV" file. Write an SQL*LOADER procedure to populate the temporary table. Write a PL/SQL conversion program to populate the emp_dept, emp, emp_tools, and emp_glasses tables from the data in the temporary table.

Note that the employees in the original Employee database did not have a payroll number and that all employees in the new database will have a payroll number as the primary key. Your conversion program has to generate the payroll number for each employee, and populate the primary and foreign key fields in the tables.

PART IV

# Oracle's User Interface (Oracle Forms 4.5)

CHAPTER 11

# Using an Oracle Form

This chapter begins Part IV of the book, which covers Oracle's user interface, the Oracle Forms 4.5 rapid application development software, a component of the Oracle Developer 2000 package. This chapter introduces you to a form and form terminology. The main goal of the chapter is to show you how to operate a form. Subsequent chapters cover all facets of the product. When you have finished this part of the book you should be able to develop the applications for the prototype system. In fact, the installment at the end of this chapter is designed to develop the on-line application for the Employee system. ■

**What is a form?**

This section provides an overview of Oracle's SQL Forms 4.5 product. The section also describes the purpose of a form and covers the various form terms.

**Developer 2000 forms applications and files**

This section discusses the various Oracle Forms 4.5 applications that are available. It also describes the various files or modules used by Forms Designer.

**Launching and operating a form by using forms runtime**

This section covers the execution of a form. Forms are executed by using Oracle's Forms Runtime. The section also covers the various form operating modes.

**Function keys**

This section covers form function keys. They provide a large variety of functionality to the form, ranging from duplicating values to displaying the on-line help.

**Querying a record**

This section covers techniques used in a form to retrieve records.

**NOTE** You can use the EMPLOYEE.FMX form to practice the techniques discussed in this chapter. It is available on the CD.

# What Is a Form?

A *form* is a graphical user interface (GUI) application that allows the user to add, modify, delete, and view database records. There are many products on the market that are used to develop forms. Some of the non-Oracle products available that you can use to develop forms are Visual Basic and Borland's C++. These products offer powerful tools for developing Windows-type forms, but in my opinion cannot hold a candle to developing applications by using Oracle Forms.

Oracle Forms is a preferred software development package because Oracle has tied the Oracle7 database directly to the application development software. When the developer first places fields on the form, the ties to the database are created. The developer does not have to develop application code to add, update, delete, or retrieve records. As part of the basic form, Oracle has built-in the DDL commands that other software products require the developers to define. In addition, when the form items are linked to the database, the database constraints are automatically added to the form as edits. It is literally possible to develop a fully functional application by using Oracle Forms in minutes. I don't know of other packages that give the developer this power.

A screen or form developed by using Oracle Forms can have many features that allow developers to fully exercise their creativity. Developers can place push buttons, radio buttons, pick lists, lists of values, and check boxes on their forms. The product has a screen painter that allows the developer to move and reshape items. The developer can choose from an array of colors and fonts. Oracle's screen painting environment is a very powerful tool for the creative developer.

Some applications require sophisticated programming logic. PL/SQL can be embedded into the form by using triggers to execute the code. This offers the developer an excellent tool to control the behavior of the application. Oracle Forms also has a menu module that allows the developer to create menus. These menus have pull-down lists and can be used to tie applications together.

# A Form Example

Figure 11.1 illustrates the form discussed in the next several chapters. This form contains information from the sample Employee database. The form displays an employee's principal attributes as well as eyeglass and tool purchases. The application is a *master-detail* form, which means the form contains a master record and associated detailed records about the employee listed in the master record. In this example form, the master record is the employee and the detail records are the eyeglass and tool purchases. *Master-detail* forms exist when there are too many relationships between tables (discussed in Chapter 2). A nice feature of Oracle Forms, it develops the code that keeps the sets of records in sync on a form. Users do not have to develop it as they do in other products.

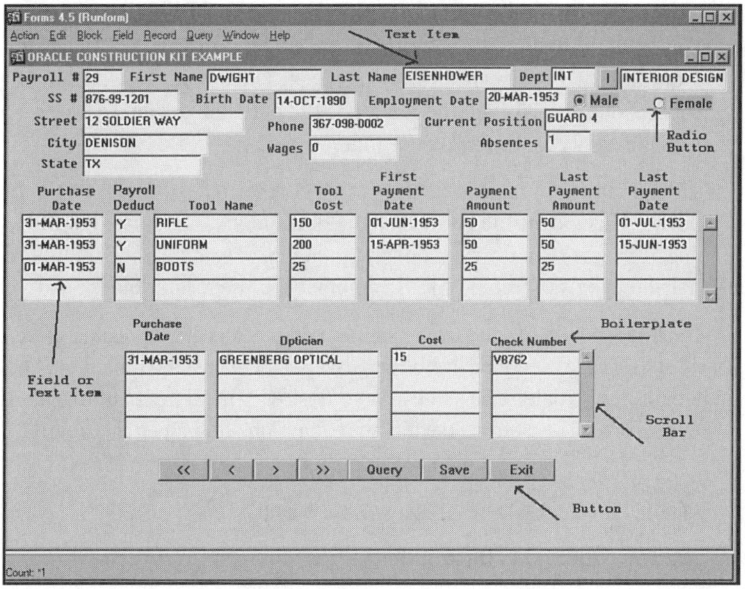


**FIG. 11.1**
A Master-Detail form containing employee database records.

The sample form in this chapter has a number of features that increases its user friendliness. It contains a button that displays a list-of-values (LOV) for the department name. The LOV can be launched by pressing the button to the left of the department field. Pressing this button causes a dialog box to appear, which displays the values from the department table. The form also has radio buttons that are pushed to denote the correct gender value. At the bottom of the screen are push buttons that allow the user to scroll forward and backward, query a record, save changes, and quit the application.



# Form Terminology

The form in Figure 11.1 has a number of components worth mentioning. To begin with, Oracle calls the application or form a *module*. The area of the screen that contains fields, buttons, or boilerplate is called a *canvas*. The canvas may be larger or smaller than the screen. A *window* overlays the canvas. If the canvas is larger than the window, vertical and horizontal scrollbars appear. They allow the user to scroll and display previously hidden parts of the canvas. At the top of the screen is a menu tool bar. The one in Figure 11.1 is the default menu. At the very bottom of the screen is a status line that contains pertinent messages.

The rectangular boxes on the screen contain data values, which are called *items*. An example of an *item* is the box that contains the last name "EISENHOWER." The items of the form are preceded by text or *boilerplate*. Boilerplate is textual information on the canvas, used to describe *items*. The words "Last Name" are the boilerplate for the last name item.

The *items* are generally linked to an Oracle table and are grouped into *records*. The top-third of the screen contains a number of items that comprise one employee record. The form in the figure has three sections. Form sections are called *blocks*. The first section is the *master block*.

This block is the top section and displays one record from the employee table. The second and third sections below the *master block* are called *detail blocks*. The middle block is linked to the Tools table and is displaying three records. The bottom block is linked to the Glasses table and displays one record even though it has the potential to display four records at a time. Blocks have the ability to display one or more *records*.

The top block is a master block because it determines the records in the associated detail blocks. This means the records in the detail blocks are related to the record in the master block in a one-to-many relationship. In the form example, the middle and bottom blocks display tool and eyeglass records for the employee in the master block.

The final portion of the form is an optional button palette located at the bottom of the screen. It consists of a series of push buttons that perform specific functions. Oracle Forms create a default button palette if the developer desires. The default buttons are the first six from the left on the form. The buttons perform the functions described in Table 11.1.

**Table 11.1 Default Button Functions**

| Button Label | Description |
|---|---|
| << | Causes the form to display a previously displayed set of records when the input focus is in a multiple record block. |
| < | Causes the form to display the previously displayed record for the block that contains the input focus. |
| > | Causes the form to display the next record from a set of retrieved records for the block that contains the input focus. |
| >> | Causes the form to display the next set of retrieve records for the block that contains the input focus. |
| Query | Causes the form to clear the form of values and place it in the query mode when the form is in the input or query mode. It executes a query or retrieves the specified records when the form is in the query mode. |
| Save | Causes the form to permanently save any changes that occurred on the form. |

# Developer 2000 Oracle Forms Applications

Three Oracle Forms 4.5 applications are of interest in the Developer 2000 folder. These are as follows:

- Forms Designer — This is the Forms Development application software. It is used to create and maintain the Forms source code. It also has the ability to create the compiled or executable Forms code.
- Forms Generate — This software is used to generate or create the Forms executable code from the Forms source code.

- Forms Runtime — This software is used to launch or execute the Forms executable code.

Figure 11.2 illustrates the Developer 2000 Group Icons. The icons used to launch the three Forms products are contained in this group.

**FIG. 11.2**
The Developer 2000 Icons used to launch the various products.

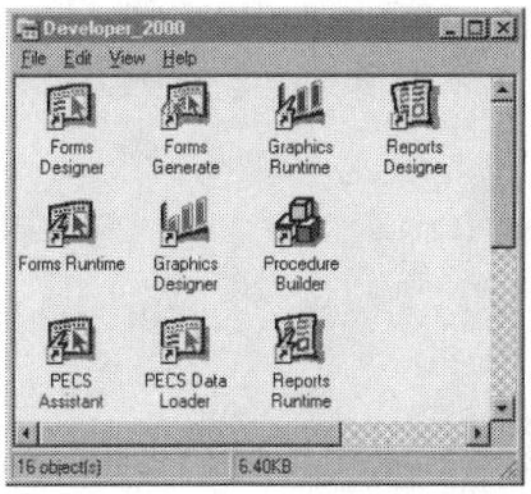


Oracle Forms Designer is the main Forms development product, used to create the source or readable code. Source code cannot be executed. It is the code that the developer can read. It must be turned into machine or executable code. Executable or machine code is not readable by developers. Executable code is created by generating or compiling the source code. Although the source code may be generated by using the Oracle Forms Designer product or the Forms Generate product, it is usually done within Forms Designer. A Forms application is executed by using the Forms Runtime product. This is the only product that understands the Forms executable file. The Forms Runtime application can also be launched from Forms Designer.



Oracle Forms uses three types of modules or files: form, menu, and library. The form file contains the code for a GUI application such as that in Figure 11.1. The menu module contains the code for the menu. A library file is a collection of subprograms. These include procedures, functions, and packages. Table 11.2 describes the file extensions for the various form, menu, and library modules.

**Table 11.2 Oracle Forms File Type Extensions**

| Extension | Description |
|---|---|
| .FMB | This is a binary file that contains the Form source code. It is the only type of form file that Forms designer can read. |
| .FMT | This type of file is a version of an .FMB file that can be read and modified by using an editor other than Forms Designer. |
| .FMX | This type of file contains the Form executable code. Generating the Form .FMB file creates this type of file. It is the only type of file that may be used by Forms Runtime. |
| .MMB | This is a binary file that contains the Menu source code. It is the only type of menu file that Forms designer can read. |

*continues*

**Table 11.2 Continued**

| Extension | Description |
|---|---|
| .MMT | This type of file is a version of an .MMB file that can be read and modified by using an editor other than Forms Designer. |
| .MMX | This type of file contains the Menu executable code. Generating the menu .MMB file creates this type of file. It is the only type of file that may be used by Forms Runtime. |
| .PLL | This is a binary file that contains the Library source code. |
| .PLD | This type of file is a version of a .PLL file that can be read and modified by using an editor other than Forms Designer. |
| .PLX | This type of file contains the Library executable code. Generating the library .PLL file creates this type of file. |

# Launching a Form by Using Forms Runtime

Forms Runtime can be launched by double-clicking the Forms Runtime icon in the Developer 2000 icon group. When this is performed, the Forms Runform Options dialog box appears, as shown in Figure 11.3. The top box contains the name of the executable (.FMX) file that is to be executed. The browse button adjacent to the field opens a File Open dialog box that can be used to identify the name of the file to be placed in the field.

**FIG. 11.3**
The Forms Runform Option dialog box used to launch a form.

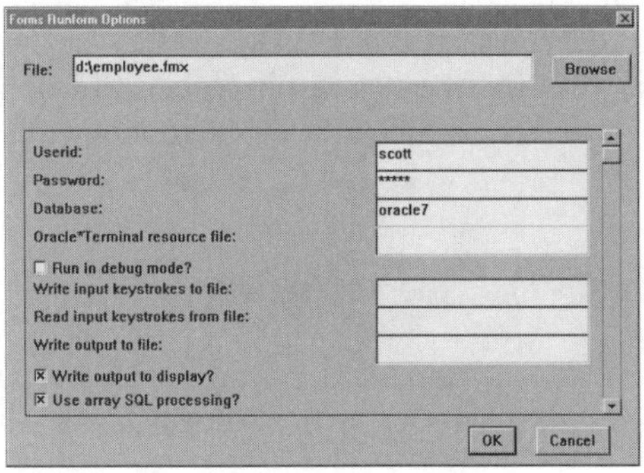


Other important fields in the dialog box are as follows:

- Userid — The name of the User Account I.D. that can access the Oracle7 or Oracle8 database.
- Password — The password for the Oracle User Account ID
- Database — The name and location of the database. This is sometimes called a connect or host string.

- Oracle*Terminal Resource File — The name of the Oracle File that contains the terminal settings.
- Run in Debug Mode — Checking this box causes the form to be run in debug mode. This mode causes messages to occur when certain events occur.
- Write Input Keystroke to File — This field contains the name of the file that will hold the input keystrokes. This file is only populated when the application is run in debug mode.
- Read Input Keystrokes From File — This field contains the name of the file that holds the keystrokes to be used as input to testing while in the debug mode.

**NOTE** At this point, you may want to use Oracle Forms Runtime to execute the EMPLOYEE.FMX form.

Forms can also be launched by using a command line expression. This is the more common way of launching the applications when they are in production. The launch command is tied to an icon. Double-clicking the icon causes the Forms Runtime to be launched along with the application. Figure 11.4 illustrates the command line syntax and an example of a command expression that executes the Employee form from the DOS prompt. When the userid and password are included in the command line expression, the Runtime Options Dialog will not be displayed when the application is launched.



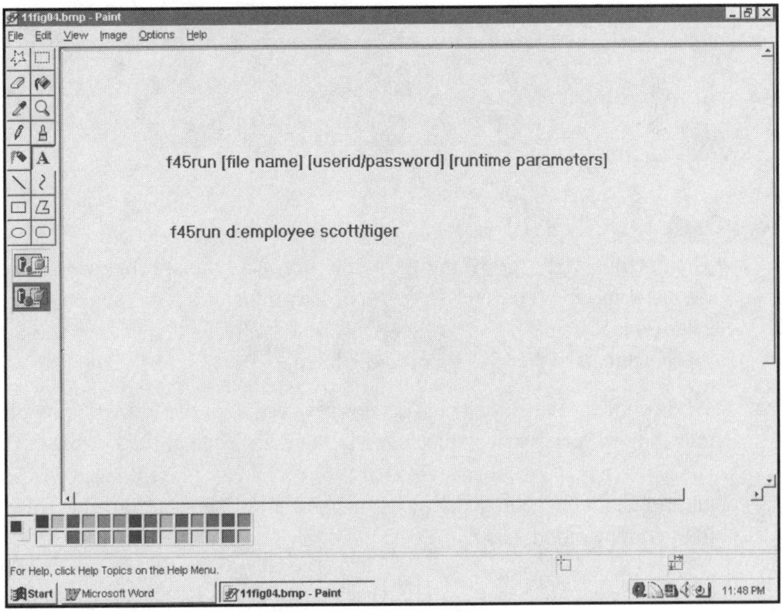


**FIG. 11.4**
Command Line expression to launch a form.

# Form Operating Modes

When a form file is executed by using Forms Runtime, three operating modes are available. These are: *input, change,* and *query.* It is very important to understand the differences between the modes and how to identify the differences. One of the first problems users unfamiliar with Oracle Forms encounter is entering data in the wrong mode and losing the data.

## The Form Input Mode

The form *input* mode is used when the user is creating a new record. It is the default mode when the form is initially launched. The form is entirely blank at the time and there isn't a message on the bottom of the screen prompting the user to enter query data. Values entered into this screen will be inserted into the database as a new record. Figure 11.5 illustrates the Employee form as it would appear in the *input* mode.

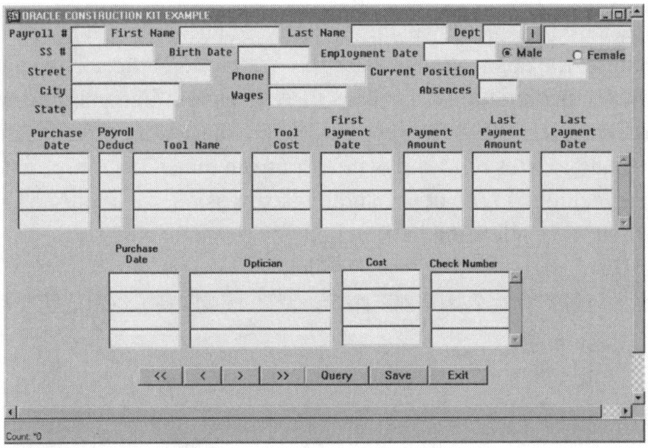


**FIG. 11.5**
The Employee Form in the Input mode.

## The Form Query Mode

The Form is in the *query* mode when it prompts the user for record selection information. Before a specific record or set of records can be presented on the screen, the user must enter a value(s) into a field(s) on the screen. The form will attempt to match database records with these values and retrieve them to the form.

When your form is initially in the *query* mode, all of the fields will be blank. In addition, the following message will be displayed in the status line at the bottom of the screen: `Enter a query; press F8 to execute, Ctrl+q to cancel`. This message is prompting the user to enter data and execute a query by pressing the F8 key. Figure 11.6 displays the Employee form in the query mode.

**NOTE** The form in Figure 11.5 and the form in Figure 11.6 are very similar looking. The only difference is the message displayed during the query mode (Figure 11.6). This is the cause of many errors. Users often think the screen is in the input mode when it is in the query mode. They enter data into the form and press the Save button. Oracle will not save the data since it is in the query mode. The user has just entered a screen full of data that is lost.

**FIG. 11.6**
The Employee Form in the Query mode displaying the "Enter Query" message.

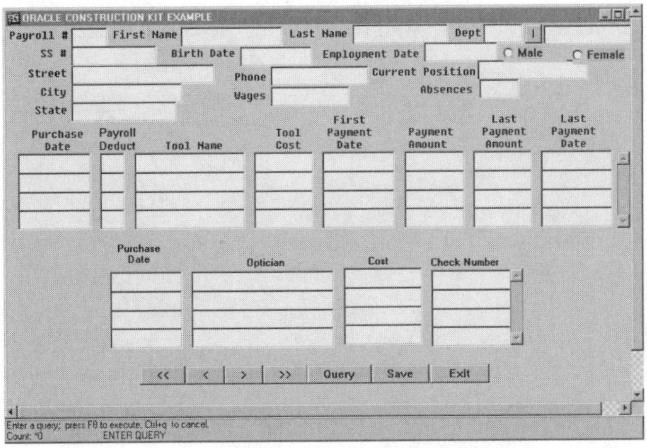


# The Form Change Mode



When the F8 key is pressed, the form will dynamically create a select statement and retrieve the specified record(s). The form is in the *change* mode when it is displaying records. Values that are contained on the form can be changed. This mode is differentiated by the other modes in that the form contains values. The forms are blank in the other modes. Figure 11.7 illustrates the Employee form in the *Change* mode.

**FIG. 11.7**
The Employee Form in the Change mode.

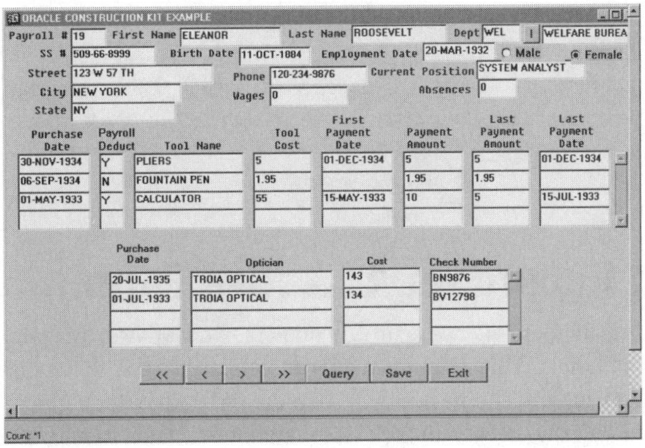


It is possible for a form to be in multiple modes at the same time. In Figure 11.7, the middle and bottom sections are in both the *change* and *input* modes. The records with values are in the *change* mode and the blank records below them are in the *input* mode.

## Using Function Keys with an Active Form

Oracle has provided a form with a large variety of functions that are executed by pressing a keyboard key. These keys are called *function keys* (see Figure 11.8). A dialog box listing the various function keys can be viewed by pressing the Ctrl + F1 key combination.

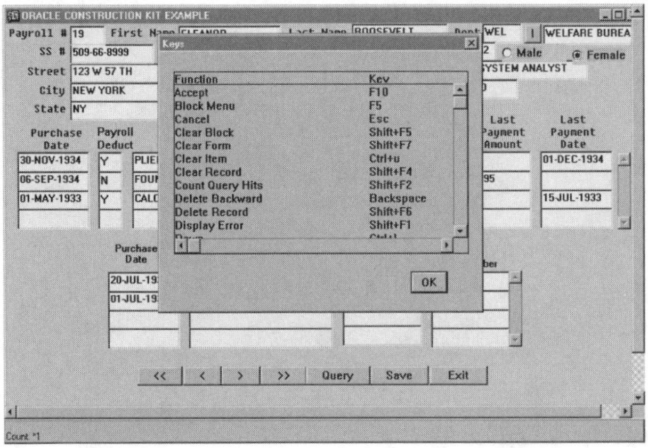


**FIG. 11.8**
Function Keys dialog box displaying the various function keys.

These keys perform a number of important functions. For instance, the F7 key places the form in the query mode, and F8 completes or executes the query. Each function key listed in the dialog box is actually a subprogram developed by Oracle. The function key name is the same as the name of the subprogram the key launches. Appendix A, "Built-In Subprograms," may be used to obtain a better description of the function keys.

> **CAUTION**
>
> The function key designations used in this book are the default keys. It is possible to change these by using the Oracle*Terminal product. The function keys may not match this key designation if your company has elected to change the defaults.

# Querying a Record on an Active Form

Oracle Forms' ability to query records is one of its most powerful features. Each field on the form is a search field. This means a value can be placed into the item and the form will return records that match the entered value. When the form executes a query against the database, the form dynamically creates an SQL select statement. Each item that contains a value is placed in the where clause of the statement.

Performing a query on the form consists of retrieving the records from the database and placing them on the form. To perform a query, place the form into the query mode, enter a value(s) into an item(s), and finally execute the query.

The form can be placed into the query mode in three ways: clicking the Query button, pressing the F7 function key, and selecting the Query/Enter option from the menu. The query can be executed in three ways: clicking the Query button when the form is in the Query mode, pressing the F8 function key, and selecting the Query/Execute option from the menu located at the top of the form.

**Query Values** The same types of values or expressions used in the where clause of a select statement (discussed in Chapter 3) can be placed into the item. This consists of entering a number in a numeric field or a character string in an alphanumeric item. Oracle Forms return values that match the entered value. You may also use the *like* symbols '%' and '_'. For instance, placing the characters 'WOOD%' in the first name field and executing the query will return the records for 'WOODROW WILSON.'

**NOTE** Alphanumeric or character values do not need to be enclosed by single quotes. When creating the form, each item has a defined data format. When you enter a value into the item Oracle makes the entered value the same as the defined data format. Thus, entering a value of 1 in a character defined item makes the value a character value of 1. This eliminates the need for single quotations, since Oracle knows what the data type is.

Relational operators can also be placed in the fields. Table 11.3 illustrates examples of various expressions that contain relational operators.



**Table 11.3 Examples of Various Operators that Can Be Used in Item Values**

| Operator | Example | Description |
|---|---|---|
| = | =WILSON | Equal to Wilson |
| <> != | <>WILSON or !=WILSON | Not equal to Wilson |
| >= | >= WILSON | Greater than or equal to Wilson |
| <= | <=WILSON | Less than or equal to Wilson |
| < | <WILSON | Less than Wilson |
| > | >WILSON | Greater than Wilson |
| # | #BETWEEN 1 and 3 | Between 1 and 3 |

The # operator is used when the queried value consists of an evaluation function. The between and in evaluation functions are examples this type of function. The # operator must precede the expression.

In Figure 11.9, the query is to retrieve records from the Employee table where the value in the Wages field is null. This requires the keywords '#is null' to be placed in the Wages item.

**FIG. 11.9**
Querying a record that contains a null value in the wages column.

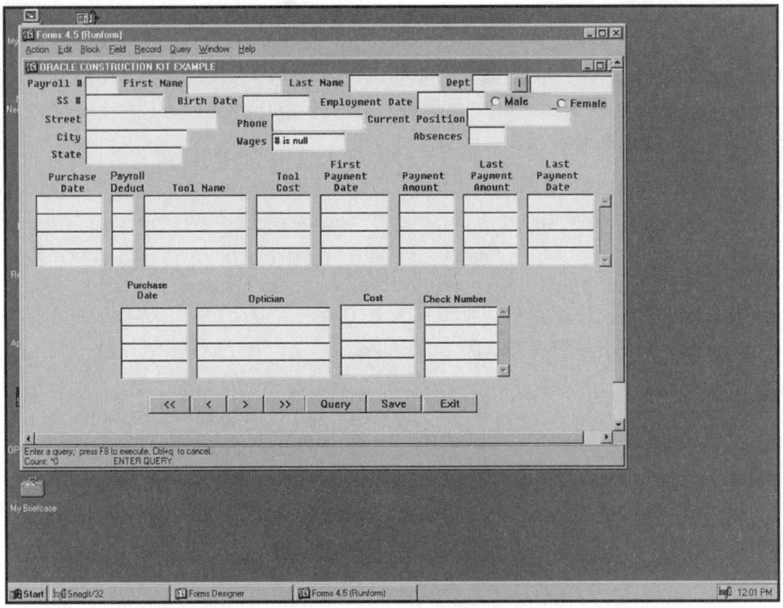


**TIP** When an item is first defined, it defaults to the length of the corresponding table field. This may be a shorter length than the amount needed for an expression using the # key symbol. Each field has a query length property that will be discussed later in Chapter 14. This property can be set to a larger value enabling the item to hold a larger expression.

## Retrieving Multiple Records with a Query

When you perform a query, sometimes more than one record is retrieved by Oracle. In fact, if you press the F8 or Execute function key, Oracle returns all of the rows of the table as the results of the query. When you are looking at a one-record form or block, it may not seem like multiple records were retrieved because the form can show only one record at a time. You can navigate to other records in the set by pressing the next record button or pressing the down-arrow on the keyboard. You can return to the previously displayed records by pressing the previous record button or the up-arrow. When you have navigated past the last record in the set, the form will change to the input mode (all fields are blank) and a message will appear on the status line indicating the last record was displayed. When navigating to the previous record, the form will issue a message that you are at the first record when you try to navigate past it.

You might try this procedure using the EMPLOYEE.FMX form file contained on the CD. Use a value of "WEL" as the value in the department item. This value should retrieve a set of five records.

# Other Form Procedures

A number of common procedures are executed on a form. You have already seen how to query the database and navigate through the records. Other common procedures consist of placing the form in the input mode, canceling a query, saving the changes, and displaying errors.

## Placing the Form in the Input Mode

The form can be placed in the input or create record mode in several ways. The first method is to navigate past the last record in the set of queried records. A second method is to press the insert record function key. This causes the record that contains the input focus to clear of existing value, placing the record in the input mode. A third method is to cancel the query mode.

When a master block is placed in the input mode, special code exists to place the related detail block in the input mode as well. When the input focus is in a detail block, only the record that contains the input focus will be placed in the input mode. Figure 11.10 illustrates placing a detail block record in the input mode. Notice row three of the Tools block is blank. This was caused by pressing the insert record or F6 function key while the input focus was on row two.



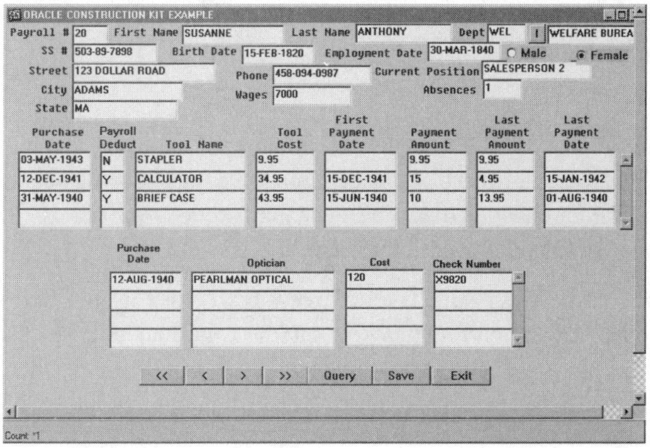


**FIG. 11.10**
The Create Record function key is used to place a Tools Detail Block Record in the Input mode.

**Cancelling a Query** Queries are cancelled by attempting to exit from the form. This may be done in several ways. The first is to press the exit or Ctrl + Q function key. The second is to press the application close button located at the top left of the window. A third is to press the Action/Exit menu option. When the user cancels the query, the `Enter a query;...`. message disappears, a `FRM-40353: Query cancelled` message appears, and the block is placed in the input mode. Figure 11.11 illustrates the Employee Form after the query has been cancelled.

When the query does not return any records, a message appears stating `FRM-40301: Query caused no records to be retrieved. Re-enter.` The query values will remain on the screen. The form is still in the query mode. New values may be entered and the query re-executed.

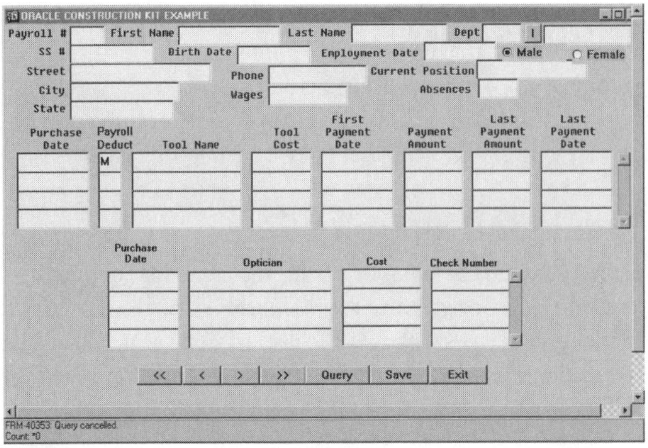

**FIG. 11.11**
The Employee Form after the query has been cancelled.

> **CAUTION**
>
> A common error users make with Oracle Forms occurs when the query does not return records. The users see that the majority of the fields are blank. They believe the form is in the input mode and enter values into the form. When they try to save the record, an error message occurs. In addition, the values they have entered will be lost.

## Saving Changes

Records added to the form are not placed into the database until a commit command is issued. This is also true for changes made in the change mode or for record deletions. The database modifications are temporary until the commit is issued.

The commit command is issued one of three ways: press the Save button on the button palette, or press the F10 or commit function key, or select the Action/Save option from the menu. When the changes have been saved, the form displays a message saying `FRM-40400:Transaction Complete`... A successful save procedure is illustrated in Figure 11.12.

## Displaying Errors

At times database errors occur when operating a Form. This occurs often when the PL/SQL code does not have adequate exception handling. A common error is trying to add a record that has the same primary key as an existing record. It is important to see what the error is in order to correct the problem. Oracle Forms provides a special database error dialog box that can be displayed. It is displayed by pressing the shift-F1 function key or selecting the Help/Display Error menu option. Figure 11.13 illustrates the `Database Error` dialog box. The box displays an error message for a unique duplicate primary key error.

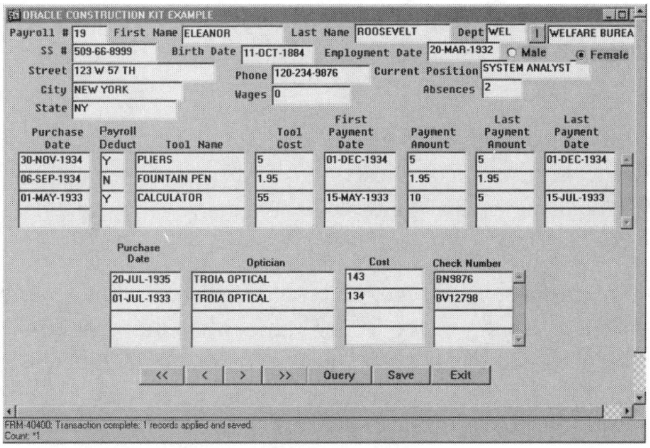


**FIG. 11.12**
A successful Form Save procedure.

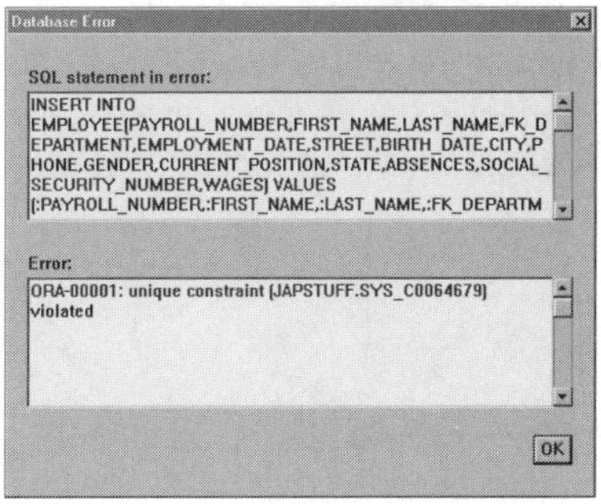


**FIG. 11.13**
Using the Database Error dialog box to identify a database error.

# Summary

A form is a graphical user interface application used to maintain a database. Oracle Forms 4.5 is Oracle's product for developing a form. A form has a number of components, generally consisting of a number of sections or blocks linked to a specific table. The block resides on a canvas and has a number of fields or items. When multiple blocks reside on a canvas, one of the blocks is the master block and the others are detail blocks. The master block generally contains information unique to the entity. The detail blocks contain records from the related tables.

Oracle Forms uses three types of files or modules. They are the form, menu, and library modules. The form source code resides in file with a file extension of .FMB. The executable code file has an extension of .FMX. The menu source and executable code reside in .MMB and .MMX type files. Finally, the library module uses .PLL and .PLX.

Forms have three products. Forms Designer is used to build and maintain the application. Forms Generate is used to create an .FMX executable file. Forms Runtime is used to launch and execute a form.

A form has three operating modes. The input mode is used to add records to the database. The change mode is used to update records. The query mode is used to retrieve records for update or display.

When querying a record, all fields on the form can be search fields. Pressing the execute query function key causes the application to create a dynamic or runtime select statement. Each item that contains a value will be contained in the where clause of the statement. The fields also support wildcard searches using '%' and "_'.

Queries may be canceled by pressing the exit-form function key. Queries are executed by pressing the F8 function key or the Query button when the form is in Query mode. Screen changes are saved permanently when the Save button or F10 function key is pressed. The form can be place in the input mode by canceling a query or pressing the create record function key.

# From Here...

The next chapter introduces you to Oracle Forms Designer. This is the product used to develop the forms that we learned to operate in this chapter. You see how easy it is to create a simple form. The chapter also discusses how to use the object navigator and the Designer menu options.

# Review Exercises

1. Launch the EMPLOYEE.FMX form by using Forms Runtime.
2. Place the form in the Query mode. Select the employees from the "WEL" department. Use the *next* and *previous* buttons to navigate through the records.
3. Place the form into the Query mode. Cancel the query. Enter a new record into the employee database. Be sure to save the record.
4. Press the *next* record button. The form should be in the input mode. Press the duplicate record function key. Save the record. What error message does the display error function key display? Change the value of the employee number. Save the record.
5. Use the form to identify employees that have a null value in their wages field or have wages greater than $15,000.

CHAPTER 12

# Using the Object Navigator to Create Your First Oracle Form

This chapter covers SQL*Forms Designer screens, the Object Navigator, and various menu options. After you're acquainted with the basic product, you learn how to develop a simple form.

**Launching Forms Designer**

This section introduces you to Forms Designer, including how to launch the application and a brief overview of Forms Designer's major components.

**Using the Object Navigator**

This section covers the Object Navigator and the objects that reside on it. The Object Navigator is the central screen in Forms Designer. It allows you to quickly access the various objects of a form.

**Designer menu options**

This section covers the default menu options on the Forms Designer. These are on the File menu, Edit menu, Tools menu, and Navigator menu.

**Creating your first form**

This section covers the steps to create your first single-block form.

# Launching Forms Designer

Forms Designer 4.5 is Oracle's software product for developing the forms you learned to run using Forms Runtime in Chapter 11, "Using an Oracle Form." Forms Designer is launched by double-clicking the Forms Designer icon in the Developer 2000 icon group.

Figure 12.1 shows the Designer 2000 group and the Forms Designer icon.

**FIG. 12.1**
The Oracle Developer 2000 icon group and Forms Designer icon.

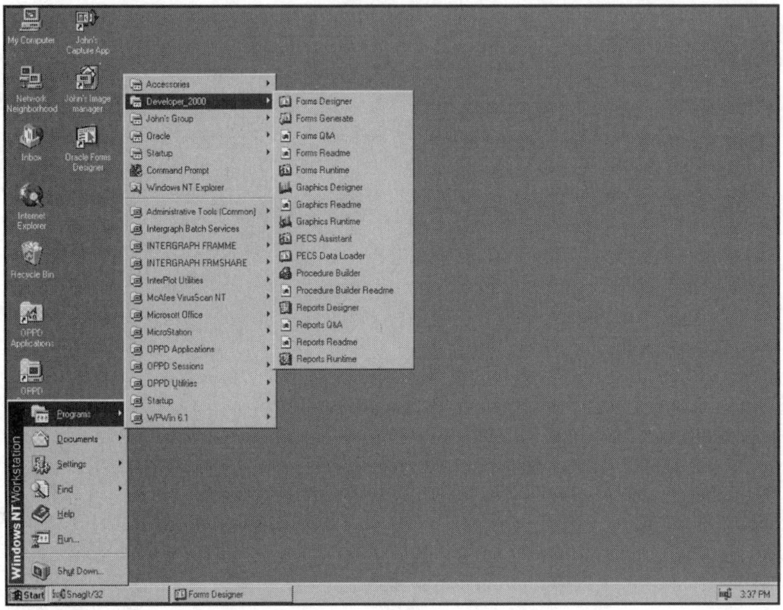


## Forms Designer's Initial Screen

When you double-click the Forms Designer icon, the Forms Designer default screen is displayed. The Object Navigator is displayed first.

This screen contains a default form file ready to be used to create a form. The Object Navigator displays a list of various high-level objects in the objects window. These objects are the components of the form.

The Designer default window has four parts. These are as follows:

- Menu Bar The menu bar at the top of the screen offers a variety of options, from opening files to changing the order in which the objects are displayed. Additional submenus are displayed, depending on the current editor.
- Tool Palette The tool palette on the left side of the Object Navigator screen consists of a series of icons that perform many of the same functions as the menu. The tool palette is more commonly used than the menu bar. The tool palette icons change as different editors are displayed.

- Object Navigator  The Object Navigator dialog box on the left side of the Designer screen displays all the open modules or files.
- Status Bar  At the bottom of the screen is the status bar. It displays information appropriate to your application. On the left side of the line is the name of the current form module and file.

Figure 12.2 shows the Forms Designer screens immediately after you've launched Forms Designer.

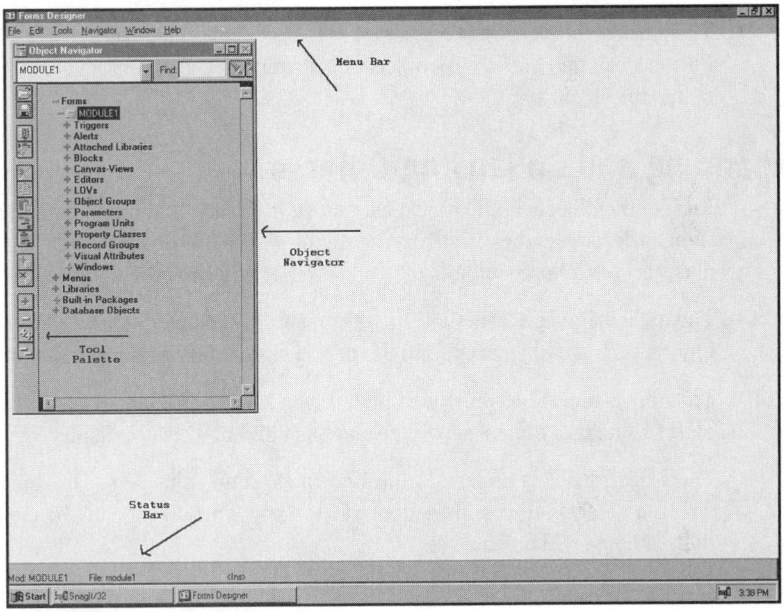


**FIG. 12.2**
The first forms designer screen, containing the Object Navigator.



# Using the Object Navigator

The Object Navigator is a dialog list box containing Designer objects. The Object Navigator is laid out like a tree branch.

On the left side of the branch or list are the high-level objects. Each of the high-level objects is similar to a stalk of the branch. As you move down from the stalk, additional branches occur. The branches are the child-objects of the high-level object. As you move down this next level of branches, other branches or objects can appear. That is how the object navigator works. The objects you see on the first object navigator are the high-level object. Under each of these objects, child objects can be created. In many cases, the child object can have child objects. The object navigator is used to create and trace these various objects.

In Figure 12.2, you can see three levels of objects. At the highest or parent level, objects in the default Object Navigator are Forms, Menus, Libraries, Built-In Packages, and Database Objects. Each of these objects can have multiple child objects.

The Forms object in Figure 12.2 has one type of child object: the form module or application. In this example, there's one module called MODULE1.

This is the default name of a blank form that's created when you launch Forms Designer or create a new form module. Each module or file object has children.

The module child objects are indented below and to the right of MODULE1. They include the Triggers, Alerts, Attached Libraries, Blocks, Canvas-Views, Editors, LOV's, Object Groups, Parameters, Program Units, Property Classes, Record Groups, Visual Attributes, and Windows.

The purpose of the Object Navigator is to quickly find and access any object created or used in Forms Designer. You access objects by starting at the parent level and following the branches to the object you want.

## Expanding and Collapsing Objects

Each of the objects in the object list shown in Figure 12.2 has a symbol at the left. You can see three different symbols: a turquoise minus sign (-), a turquoise plus sign (+), and a darkened plus sign (+). These symbols tell you whether you can create or see additional child objects.

The minus sign indicates that the object is fully expanded, showing all of its child objects. In Figure 12.2, two objects contain the minus sign: the Forms object and the MODULE1 objects.

The Forms object has only one child object, MODULE1, and it is displayed. The Module1 object contains a minus sign since all of its child objects are displayed.

The Triggers object under Module1 has a darkened plus sign. This means the object can have children objects but currently doesn't have any. This object can't be expanded further since there are no child objects yet.

The Windows object has a turquoise plus sign preceding it, which means that it has existing child objects. You can see the child objects by expanding the Windows object.

You can expand objects in several ways. The easiest is to place the cursor on the plus sign and click the mouse button. This causes all children objects to be displayed.

When you expand multiple objects, the Object Navigator gets cluttered. You can remove the clutter by collapsing objects. The easiest way to collapse an object is to place the cursor on the minus sign and click the mouse button.

Figure 12.3 shows the default Object Navigator after the Forms object is collapsed and the Built-in Packages object is expanded.

## Defining Form Objects on the Object Navigator

The Object Navigator offers a variety of objects that are used in forms. These are shown in Table 12.1, with a brief description of each. (The objects are discussed in more detail in the next four chapters.)

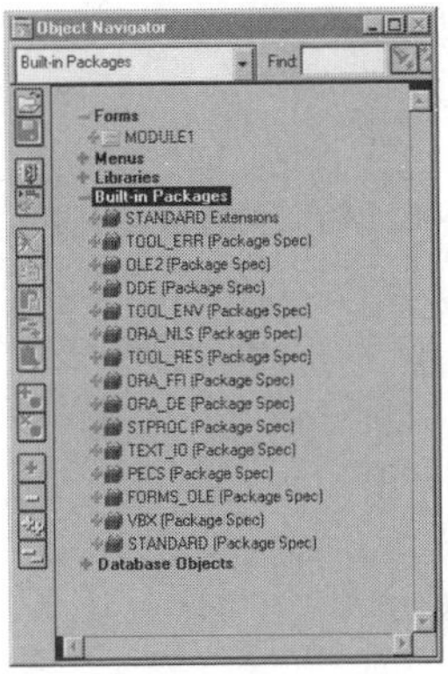


**FIG. 12.3**
Collapsing the Forms object and expanding the Built-In Packages.

Some of these objects such as triggers can be children under several different types of parent objects. For instance, a trigger can be under a form, a block, or an item. It's the same object but with different parents.

**Table 12.1 Object Navigator Objects**

| Object Name | Description |
|---|---|
| Attached Libraries | Objects containing the names of PL/SQ libraries that are attached to the form. |
| Blocks | Form module child objects that identify a section of a form usually related to a table or view. |
| Built-In Packages | Objects containing the name of packages or programs developed by Oracle. |
| Canvas-Views | Form child objects. A canvas is an area that contains objects such as fields and boilerplate. A view is a rectangle positioned on the canvas. This is the area of the canvas visible to the user. |
| Database Objects | Objects containing the name of database objects such as database triggers. |
| Editors | Names of the external editors that can be used by the form. |
| Forms | Objects consisting of form source code modules or files. |
| Libraries | Objects containing the names of available libraries. Libraries are collections of procedures, subprograms, functions, and packages. |
| LOV's | Names of the various list-of-value (LOV) objects used by the form. |
| Menus | Objects consisting of menu source code modules or files. |
| Modules | Objects containing form or menu source code. |

*continues*

**Table 12.1 Continued**

| Object Name | Description |
|---|---|
| Object Groups | Containers consisting of a group of objects. Objects such as a canvas, trigger, or block can be packaged and used in other files. |
| Object Group Children | Objects listing the names of the objects in the Object Group. |
| Parameters | Objects consisting of parameter lists that are used to pass values from one form to another. |
| Program Units | Objects containing the names of any procedures, functions, package specifications, or package bodies that can be called by the form. |
| Property Classes | Objects consisting of sets of properties that can be inherited by other form objects. |
| Record Groups | Objects containing named select statements that are used to retrieve records for objects such as LOVs. |
| Visual Attributes | Objects containing predefined sets of format property values that are assigned to common objects. |
| Triggers | Objects containing PL/SQL code. The code is executed when a specific event occurs. |
| Windows | Objects containing the name of the window used by the form to view the canvases. |

## The Object Navigator Tool Palette

The Object Navigator tool palette on the left side of the object Navigator consists of 15 icons arranged in a vertical row. To learn each icon's function, place your cursor on the icon. You'll see a message called a tooltip over the icon describing what the icon does.

Figure 12.4 shows the tool palette with the cursor over the third icon. This is the Start icon, which starts the current application in Forms Runtime.

The tool palette has two parts. The upper part contains two icons, the first one of which pictures a folder. When you click this icon, the folder-browsing dialog will appear. You can use this dialog box to find a file and bring it into the Object Navigator.

The second icon, picturing a disk, is the Save icon. You use it to save the currently selected file in the Object Navigator.

The lower part of the palette contains two icons.

The first icon pictures a green light. This icon launches Forms Runtime and the current application.

**FIG. 12.4**
The Object Navigator tool palette.

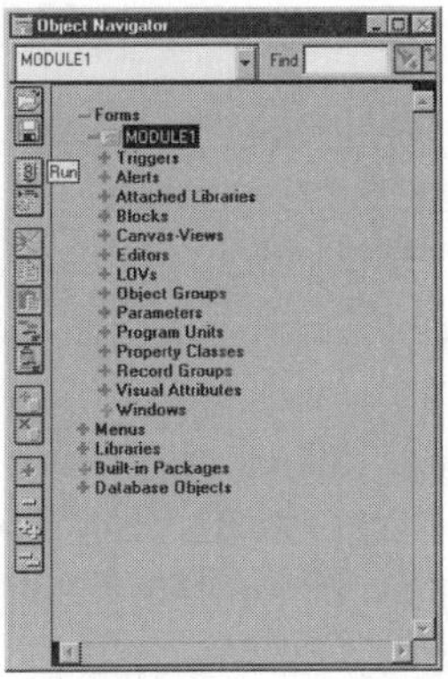


The second icon pictures the figure of a bug. This icon causes Forms Runtime to operate in the debug mode.

The middle part of the palette contains the cut, copy, and paste icons.

The first icon pictures a pair of scissors. You use this icon to cut marked items and place them in the Clipboard.

This is followed by the copy icon. You use this icon to place a copy of the selected item into the clipboard.

The next icon is the paste icon. You use this icon to paste items from the Clipboard to the marked spot.

You use the icon with the black and blue bars to copy properties from a property sheet onto the Clipboard.

You use the bottom icon to paste copied properties into a property sheet.

You use the icons in the second part from the bottom to create and delete objects.

When you click the top icon (picturing a green plus sign), it creates a new object. The new object is the same type as the one you marked in the Object Navigator.

The icon with the red negative "X" deletes any object you've marked in the Object Navigator. Clicking on this icon brings up an alert dialog box asking if you are sure you want to delete the object.

The bottom part contains expand and collapse icons. Like the turquoise icon, the icon with the plus sign expands marked objects.

The icon with the plus sign expands the marked object.

The icon with the negative sign collapses the marked object.

The icon with the double plus signs expands the marked object and all of its child objects.

The icon with the double minus signs collapses the marked object and all of its child objects.

**TIP** The Expand-All icon saves you time when you're trying to identify an object. It's tedious to open each object in the Object Navigator one at a time.

When you're searching a form for an object, you can mark the form module or file in the navigator. Then you can click the Expand-All icon to display all the objects in the file.

You can scroll through the list and, when you're done, collapse the form using the Collapse-All icon. This returns the Object Navigator to its original condition.

# Designer Menu Options

At the top of the Forms Designer window is the menu bar. This menu bar offers a variety of options that are used throughout the design process. The default menu bar has six pull-down menus: File, Edit, Tools, Navigator, Window, and Help.

Displaying other Designer screens causes additional pull-down menus to be placed on the menu bar. These menus, along with their associated Forms Designer screen, are discussed next.

## File Menu Options

The File menu, shown in Figure 12.5, offers administrative types of options.

To the right of some of the menu options are *hot key* symbols. You can save time by using these hot keys to select the option without having to open the menu to select it.

For instance, Ctrl-Y is listed next to the Form option. When you press Ctrl and Y simultaneously, Designer creates a new form file and places it in the Object Navigator.

**The New, Open, Close, and Save Options** The New option creates a new default file in the Object Navigator.

When you select this option either by tabbing to the option and pressing Enter or by clicking it with the mouse, another menu is displayed to the right (see Figure 12.5).

The menu prompts you to select one of the three types of files: form, menu, or library. When you select the file type, the menu collapses and the new file is placed in the Object Navigator.

The Open option launches the standard Windows Open File dialog box, an easy way to find and open the file you want. The Close option closes the selected file and removes it from the Object Navigator.

If unsaved changes are pending, you're prompted to save the changes before closing the file.

The Save option saves the selected file. If you haven't named the file, the standard Windows Save As dialog box prompts you to name the file. The Saved As option also displays the Save As dialog box.

**The Revert Option** You can use the Revert option when you've changed the file and you want to discard the changes. Revert removes all changes since the last time you saved the file.

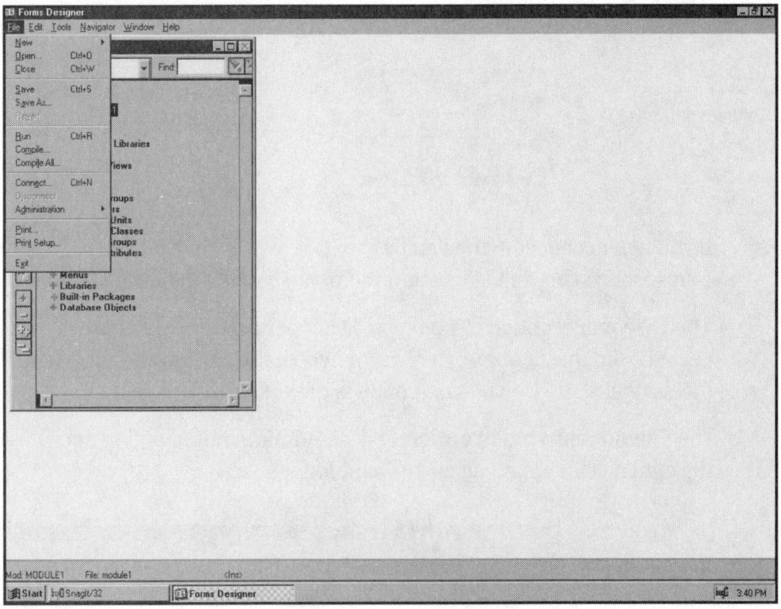


**FIG. 12.5**
File menu options.

You'll see the alert, `Do you really want to revert module?` before the file is deleted. This is a safety feature provided by Oracle.

Figure 12.6 shows the Revert alert.

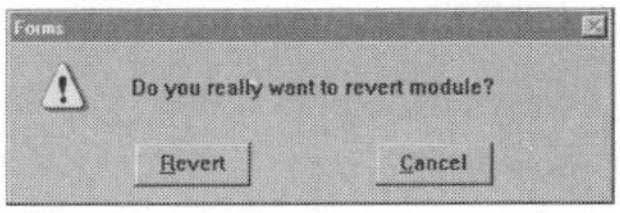


**FIG. 12.6**
The Revert alert message box.

**The Run Option** The Run option launches Forms Runtime and executes the selected file. The Compile option compiles the PL/SQL code for the selected object. The Compile All option compiles the PL/SQL code for all of the selected file's objects that contain PL/SQL code.

If there are errors in the PL/SQL code, an error dialog box appears that lists the error and the object that contains the error. You'll seldom use these two options since the PL/SQL editor has a compile button.

It's much easier to compile and test your code from the PL/SQL editor. In addition, all the PL/SQL code is compiled when the file is generated.

**The Connect and Disconnect Options** The Connect option is used to connect Designer to the Oracle database. You must do this before you can use many of the database functions in Designer.

When you select the Connect option, a Connect dialog box appears. It prompts you for the Oracle database user ID, password, and connect string.

Figure 12.7 shows the Connect dialog box.

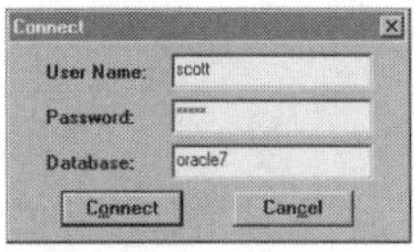


**FIG. 12.7**
The Connect database dialog box.

If you don't connect to the database before you try a database procedure, Designer automatically displays this dialog box and prompts you for a database ID.

The Disconnect option disconnects Designer from the database. When Designer is disconnected from the database, the Disconnect option is grayed out. When Designer is connected to the database, the Connection option is grayed out.

**The File Administration options** The Administration option opens a submenu to the right of the option. This submenu is shown in Figure 12.8.

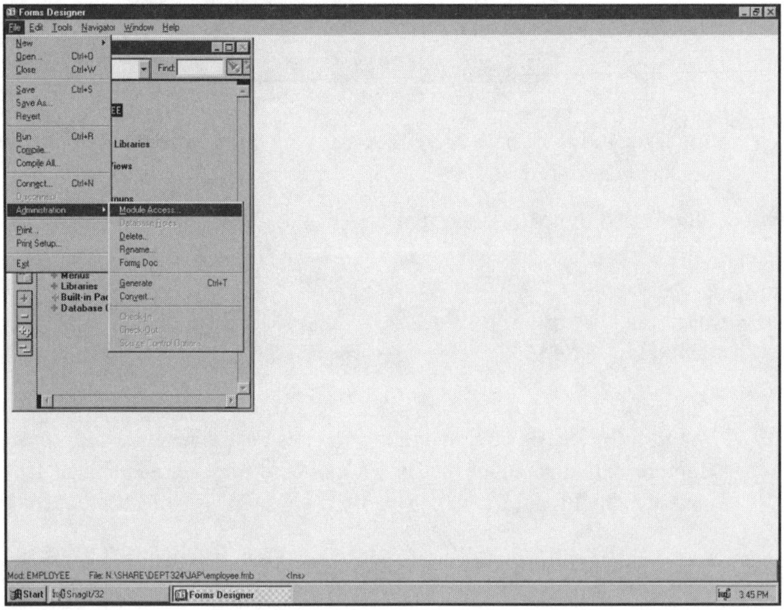


**FIG. 12.8**
The Administration menu options.

***The Module Access option*** The first option is Module Access. This option brings up the Grant Module dialog box, which allows you to grant or revoke other developers access to a form.

Figure 12.9 shows the Grant Module dialog box. You can view any modules saved to the database by pressing the Retrieve List button.

**FIG. 12.9**
The Grant Module dialog box is used to grant or revoke access to Forms modules.

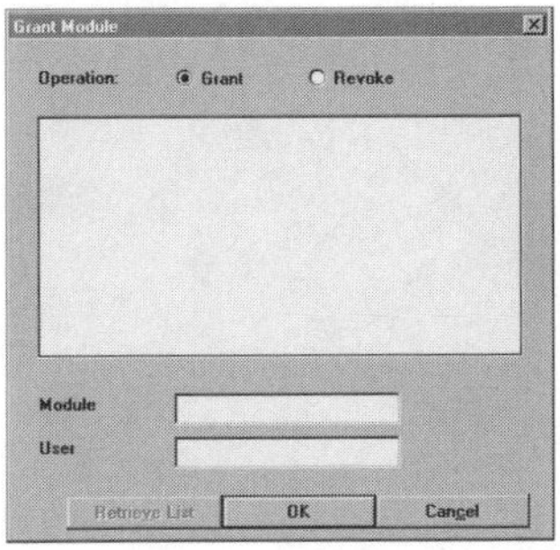


***The Database Roles option*** The Database Roles option opens the Role List dialog box. Roles are a set of privileges that enable holders of the role to perform database functions. These sets of privileges are granted to individual users. The dialog box allows you to create, change, or delete roles in the database. You must have the authority to update roles to use this option.

The dialog box lists the roles for the current user. Figure 12.10 shows the Role List dialog box.

**FIG. 12.10**
The Role List dialog box lists the roles available to you.

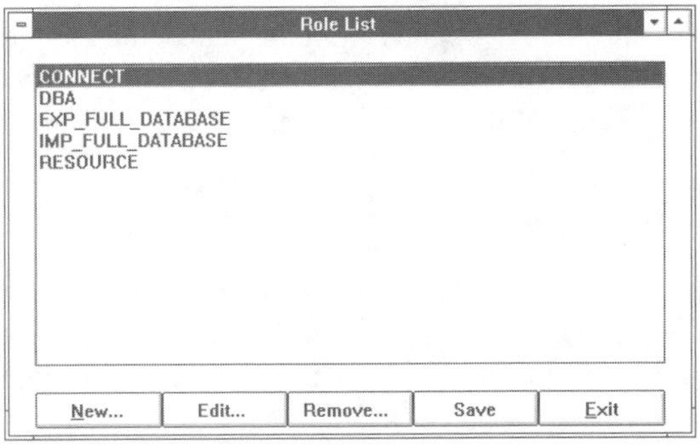




***The Delete option*** The Delete option invokes the Delete From Database dialog box, which allows you to delete modules saved to the database.

Figure 12.11 shows the Delete From Database dialog box.

**FIG. 12.11**
The Delete From Database dialog box is used to delete database objects.

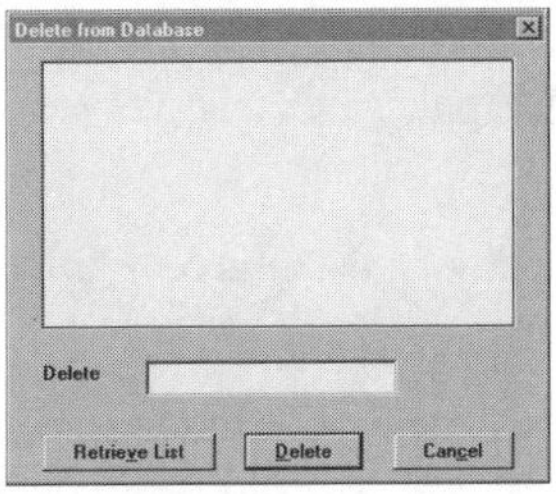


***The Rename option*** The Rename option is used to change the name of Designer files saved to the database. Selecting this option brings up the Rename in Database dialog box.

Figure 12.12 shows the Rename in Database dialog box.

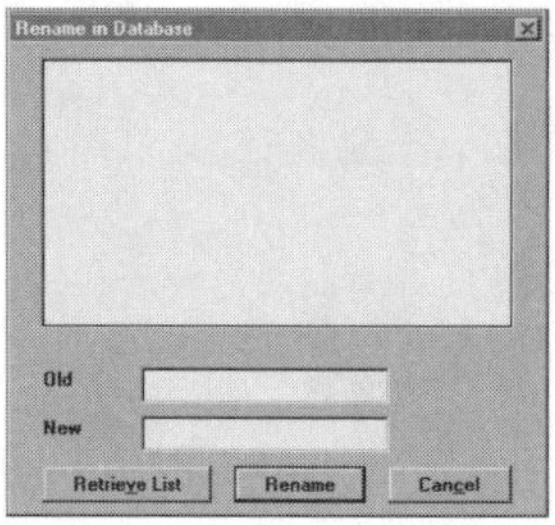


**FIG. 12.12**
The Rename in Database dialog box is used to rename files saved to the database.

***The Forms Doc option*** The Forms Doc option is used to create an ASCII file listing all the objects in the select module. This file has an extension of .TXT and can be printed.

***The Generate option*** The commonly used Generate option compiles all objects in the module and creates the executable form of the file. The file types executable by Forms Runtime are .FMX, .MMX, or .PLX.

***The Convert option*** The Convert option is used to change the module source code file from a binary file to an ASCII text file or vice versa. The ASCII text file is in a readable format and has file extension types of .FMT, MMT, or .PLD.

Selecting the Convert option brings up the Convert dialog shown in Figure 12.13. The three fields to be populated are as follows.

Type, a pick list, allows you to select the file type from form, menu, or library file. File holds the name and location of the file to be converted. Direction allows you to choose a conversion from binary-to-text or vice versa. You press the Convert button to initiate the procedure.

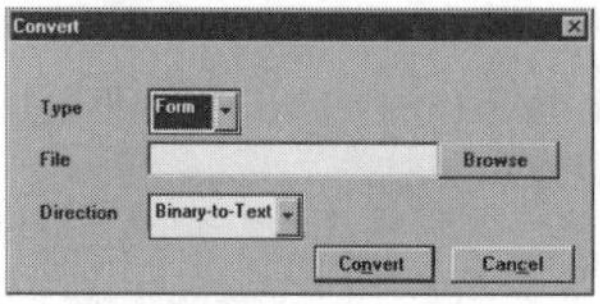


**FIG. 12.13**
The Convert dialog box is used to convert forms files from binary to ASCII.

***The Check-In, Check-Out, and Source Control options*** The Check-In, Check-Out, and Source Control options are available when Intersolv's Polytron Version Control System, used to control software, is installed.

The Check-In option allows you to place a module in the source archive. The Check-Out option allows you to take files from the source archive.

***The Print Option*** The Print option launches a standard Windows Print dialog box, which allows you to capture and print the current screen. The Print Setup option displays a Windows Print Setup dialog box.

Several print options, such as page orientation, paper size, source, and the type of printer, are available. The Exit option closes Forms Designer.

## Edit Menu Options

The Edit menu offers a variety of options to change items in the Object Navigator. Figure 12.14 shows the Edit menu options.

When an option is grayed out, you can't use that option. Notice in Figure 12.14 that the Cut option is grayed out. It can't be used because no text has been highlighted.

**FIG. 12.14**
The Edit menu options.

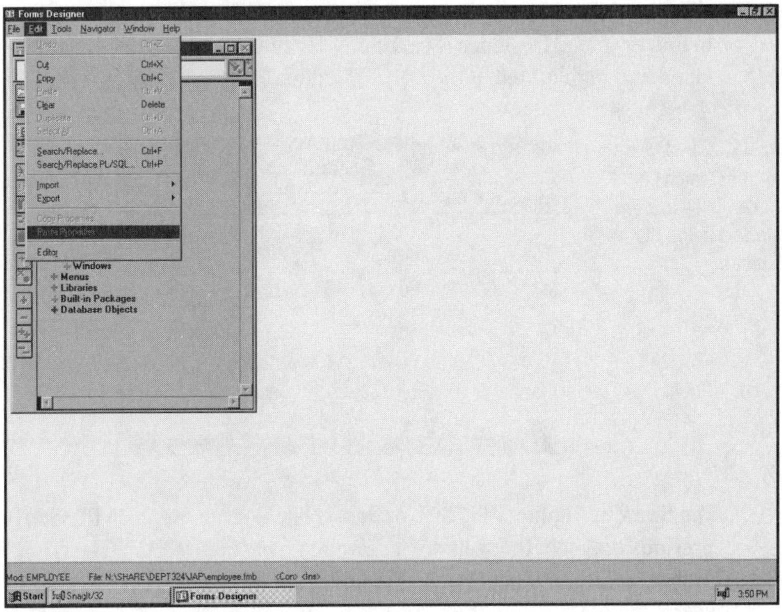




**The Undo option** Undo is one option you should remember. Undo returns the form to the state it was in before the last change. Undo doesn't eliminate all changes but primarily changes to the layout of the form, which are made in the screen painter or Layout Editor.

This is important because some of the Layout Editor functions can substantially change the layout of the form and these changes may not be what you envisioned.

The Undo option can save you rework time. When you press Undo, it changes to Redo. This allows you to reverse the undo procedure and return the form to its original state before you pressed Undo.

**The Cut, Copy, Paste, and Clear options** The Cut, Copy, Paste, and Clear options are similar to the standard Windows options with these names. You use them in the Forms PL/SQL editor and the Layout Editor.

The Cut option removes the selected object from the editor and puts it on the Clipboard for later use. The Copy option puts a copy of the selected object on the Clipboard.

The Paste option puts the object from the Clipboard into the editor. The Clear option removes the object from the editor and doesn't put it on the Clipboard.

**The Duplicate and Select All options** The Duplicate option puts a copy of the selected object on the editor it was selected from. The Select All option selects all objects in the current editor.

**The Search/Replace option** The Search/Replace option is used to locate and replace text in an opened PL/SQL editor. Selecting this option brings up the Search/Replace dialog box shown in Figure 12.15.

In this example, Designer is searching for the word "failure" in the search field. The word was found and highlighted in the PL/SQL editor.

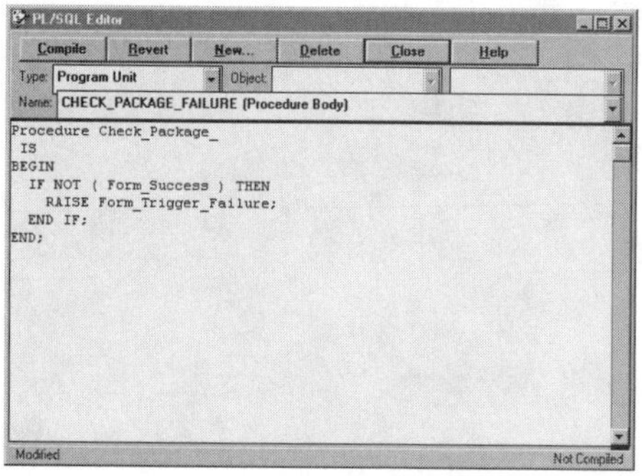


**FIG. 12.15**
Using the Search/Replace dialog box to locate text in the PL/SQL editor.

**The Search/Replace/Pl/SQL option** The Search/Replace PL/SQL option differs from the previous option in that you don't search in a particular PL/SQL script. When you select this search option, Designer opens the first PL/SQL object after the selected object and continues searching objects until the phrase is found.

When the phrase is found, pressing the Search, Replace, or Replace All buttons causes Designer to continue scanning scripts for the next occurrence of the phrase.

**TIP** The Search/Replace PL/SQL option is an excellent tool for finding and changing variable names. When you need to change variable names in your code, you can use this tool to find all occurrences of the old variable name in the code.

**The Import option** The Import option is used to bring external objects into the form. These objects can be a drawing, image, color palette, or text. Figure 12.16 shows the menu and import object selection.

The drawings and images are placed inside an image object on the Layout Editor. You can also import a color palette into the Layout Editor to bring different colors into the editor.

You can import text into the PL/SQL editor. Importing images is discussed in the next chapter in the context of the Layout Editor.

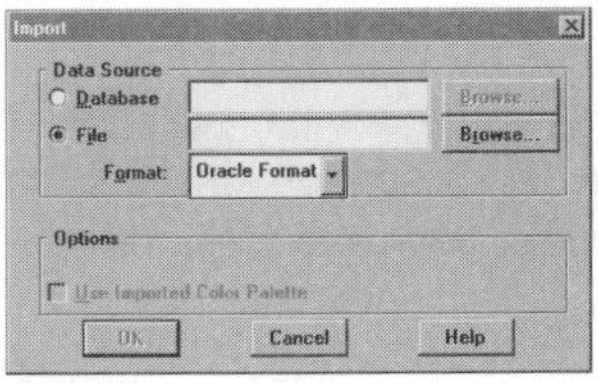


**FIG. 12.16**
The Import object edit options.

**The Export option** The Export option opens a submenu that allows you to move drawings, images, color palettes, and text to external files. The options on the menu are: Drawing, Image, Color Palette, and Text.

***The Export|Image option*** When you select the Export/Image option, the Export Image dialog box is displayed, as shown in Figure 12.17.

You can save the image to a file or to the database. A variety of formats are available for the image. Click on the Format pick list to see a list of the formats.

You can save the file using a variety of data types and compression types via the picklists in the Export/Image dialog box.

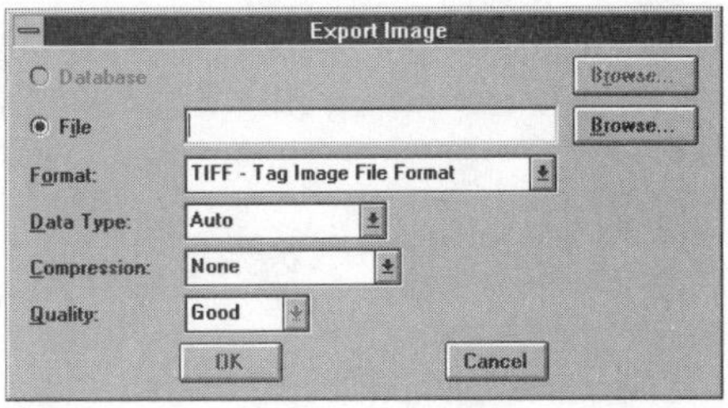


**FIG. 12.17**
The Export/Image dialog box.



***The Export|Drawing option*** The Export/Drawing option displays the Export dialog box, shown in Figure 12.18. It is used to move line drawings from the Layout Editor. You can also save the drawing in the database or in a file, and in the Oracle format or in CGM format. If the drawing is exported in CGM, only the the object will be exported without the object definition. A variety of compression types are available.

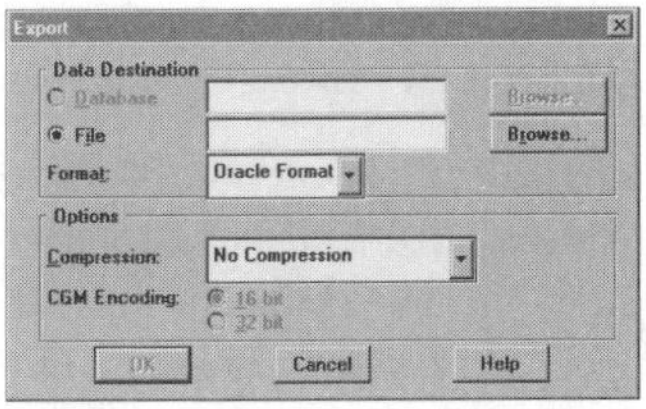


**FIG. 12.18**
The Export dialog box is used to export drawings and color palettes.

***The Export|Color Palette option*** The Export/Color Palette option is used to export color palettes from the Layout Editor. When you select this option, the Export dialog box shown in Figure 12.18 is displayed. The Compression box is removed from the dialog since it's not needed.

***The Export|Text option*** The Export/Text option is used to save selected text from the PL/SQL editor to an external file. When you select this option, the standard Windows Save As dialog box is opened. You can type the name of the saved file in this dialog box.

## The Tools Menu Options

The Tools menu is used to open the various editors available in Designer. You can also use the Tools menu to create a new form block, place Forms Runtime in the debug mode, or create a select statement. Figure 12.19 shows the Tools menu options.

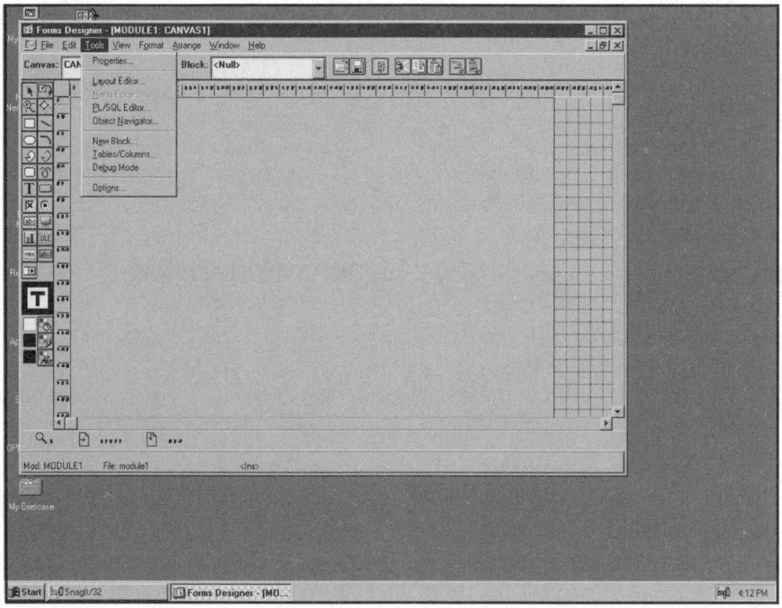


**FIG. 12.19**
The Tools menu options.

**The Properties option** The Properties option is used to open a property window or sheet for the selected object. You can select the object in the Object Navigator or in the Layout Editor.

As we can see from our discussion of the Object navigator, a form has a variety of objects. Most of the objects in a form have a set of properties that control a feature of the object.

For instance, some of the properties of a block are the number of records displayed, whether the items on the block can be updated, or whether the block has a scroll bar. These properties are contained in the property sheet for the item. The Properties menu option allows you to open the property sheet for a selected object to view or change and of the object's properties. The next several chapters have much discussion on the various properties.

Figure 12.20 shows a block property sheet.

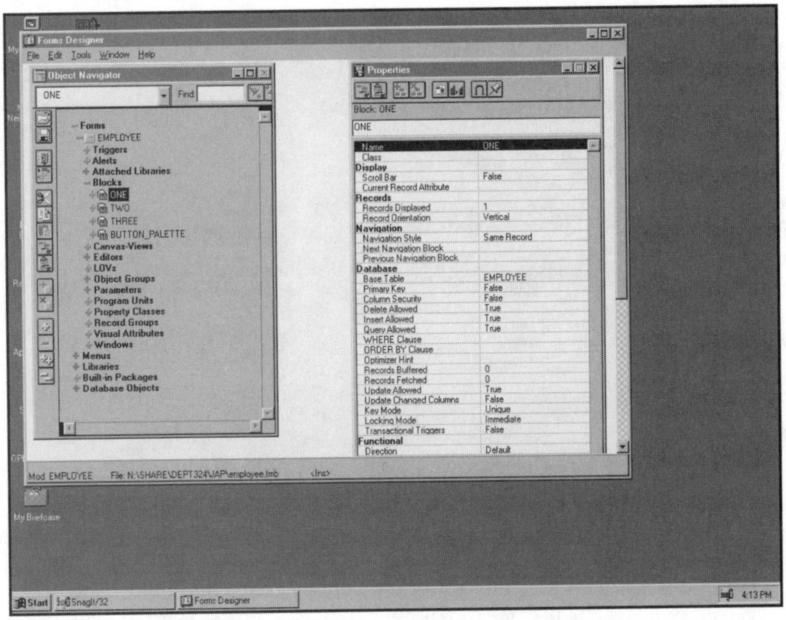


**FIG. 12.20**
A block property sheet.

**The Layout Editor option** The next option on the Tools menu is Layout Editor. When you select this option, the Layout Editor appears. This is the Forms tool used to format the canvas or screen. (The Layout Editor is discussed in Chapter 13, "Formatting Your Form.")

**The Menu Editor option** The Menu Editor option is used to initiate or display the Menu Editor. This option is only available when the selected object is a menu object. A menu object will only be available when a menu module has been opened. The Menu Editor, a special screen used to construct pull-down menus, is discussed in Chapter 16, "Calling Other Forms and Using Menus."

**The PL/SQL Editor option** The PL/SQL Editor option displays the PL/SQL Editor. This editor, used to write the PL/SQL code in triggers and procedures, is discussed in Chapter 15, "Using Triggers and Modifying Classes."

**The Object Navigator option** The Object/Navigator option is used to display the Object Navigator. When you're developing Designer applications, it's common to move between the Object Navigator, PL/SQL Editor, Layout Editor, and property sheets. This option allows you to easily navigate among these tools.

**The New Block option** The New Block option opens a dialog box used to create new form blocks. This is the same as selecting a block object on the Object Navigator and clicking the Create icon. At the end of this chapter, you'll learn about creating new blocks using this option.

**The Tables/Columns option** The Tables/Columns option opens the Tables/Columns dialog box. This dialog box is used to create SQL statements. Figure 12.21 shows a select command that was built using this option.

In this example, there are two dialog boxes. The top is the Tables/Columns dialog box opened when you select the option. The bottom dialog box is the PL/SQL Editor that will receive the select statement.

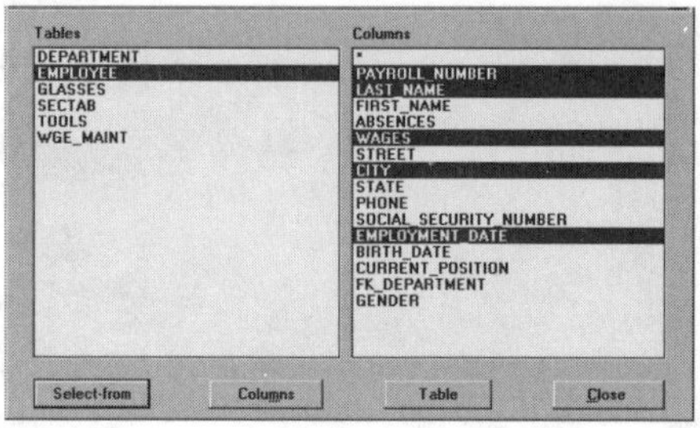


**FIG. 12.21**
The Tables/Columns dialog box is used to create the SQL statement in the PL/SQL Editor.

When the Table/Columns dialog box is first displayed, the right window, Columns, does not contain values. The left window lists the tables and views you have access to.

Selecting a table in the left window will cause it to highlight. This will populate the right window with the fields from that table, as shown in Figure 12.21. The Employee table is selected and the right window has the Employee table's fields listed.

Several of these fields have been selected. Pressing the Select-From button populates the PL/SQL Editor with the select statement. This statement holds the selected table and fields.

When the select statement contains multiple tables, the Select-From button doesn't construct the full statement because it can't highlight multiple tables. But you can construct the statement using the dialog box.

You can use the Columns button to select columns. Place your cursor in the PL/SQL Editor where you want the column. Go to the Tables/Columns dialog box, select the column you want to transfer, then press the Columns button.

The values you select are placed in the PL/SQL Editor where you put your cursor. Enter the select and from statements manually. This same procedure works for table names using the Table button.

**TIP** When selecting multiple items from a list, remember that the Ctrl and Shift keys allow you to select additional items without deselecting others. In Figure 12.21, the columns are not contiguous. The Ctrl key was held down as the items were selected.

This keeps the initial selection from being deselected. If you hold down the Shift key, all the items between the two selections are selected. You can use these two keys in the Object Navigator and in the Layout Editor. They'll save you a considerable amount of time.

**The Debug Mode option** The Debug Mode is used to place Forms Runtime in the debug mode. This invokes break processing if the Break built-in is used in any trigger. This will cause the form to stop processing at the given break points. When you initiate the Debug Mode, a check mark is placed to the left of this option.

**Designer Options** Selecting Options on the Tools menu opens the Designer Options dialog box. This dialog box consists of two tabbed sheets. The default tab is the Designer Options. The Options dialog box is shown in Figure 12.22.

**FIG. 12.22**
The Designer Options dialog box.

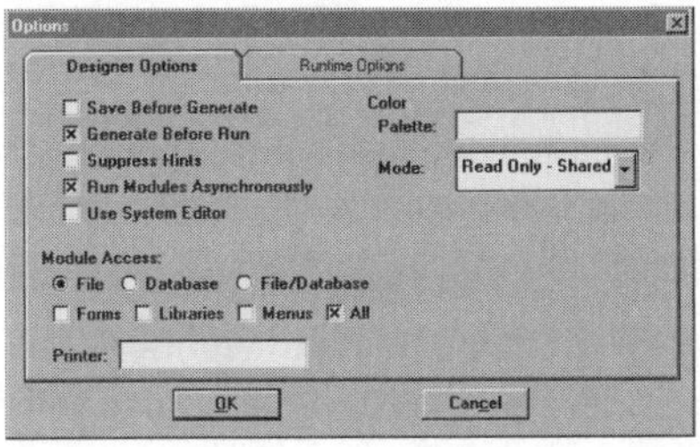


- Save Before Generate—This option saves the file automatically before the file is generated. The default is unchecked, meaning do not save the file.
- Generate Before Run—This option compiles and generates the form file before it is run. The default is checked, meaning the form file will be generated before runtime.

**NOTE** You don't need to change the Save Before Generate or Generate Before Run options. Generating the form causes Designer to check PL/SQL syntax.

When errors occur and you have trouble finding a new error, you'll be glad you haven't saved a bad version of the application. You can always use the Revert option to get a good copy of the application if you don't like to save applications that have errors.

You may want to generate the form before you run it to make sure you'll be looking at the latest version. If you don't generate the form before running it, you'll run the version of the application that was generated last. This can really confuse you if you forgot to generate the form manually.

- Suppress Hints—This option suppresses hints from the message line. The default, unchecked, means hints aren't suppressed.
- Runs Modules Asynchronously—This option allows you to run the form and Designer at the same time. You can move between Designer and the form.

  When this option is unchecked, you must close the form before returning to Designer. The default, checked, causes Forms to run modules asynchronously.
- Use System Editor—This option substitutes an external editor for the Oracle default editor. This means you can use Notepad or another external editor in Designer in places where multiline editing is needed.

  One of these places is the Order by Block property. The default, unchecked, means Forms won't use the default system editor.

- Color Palette—This option is used to change the default color palette used in the Layout Editor. Designer loads the file named in this box as the default. If you leave this option blank, the default Designer color palette is used.
- Mode or Color Mode—This option is a pick list with three values: Editable, Read Only—Shared, and Read Only—Private. This option determines how a color palette is loaded. The Editable value is used when you want to change the color palette. The Read Only—Shared options is the default. The Read Only—Private is not relevant for Forms.
- Module Access—This option is used to determine where the modules or files are saved. They may be saved in the file system, the database or both. The File, Database, and File/Database radio buttons represent the save options.

  When you press the File radio button, the files are saved in the file system. When you press the Database radio button, Designer saves the file in the database.

  When you press the File/Database radio button, files can be loaded and saved from either the file system or the database.

  The Forms, Menus, and Libraries check boxes determine whether Forms displays only forms, menus, library or all of the database modules in the Database dialog box.
- Printer—This option is used to define the default printer.

**The Runtime Options** Pressing the Runtime Options tab displays the Runtime Options check boxes. Figure 12.23 shows the Runtime Options tab sheet of the Options dialog box. These checkbox options control how Forms Runtime operates.

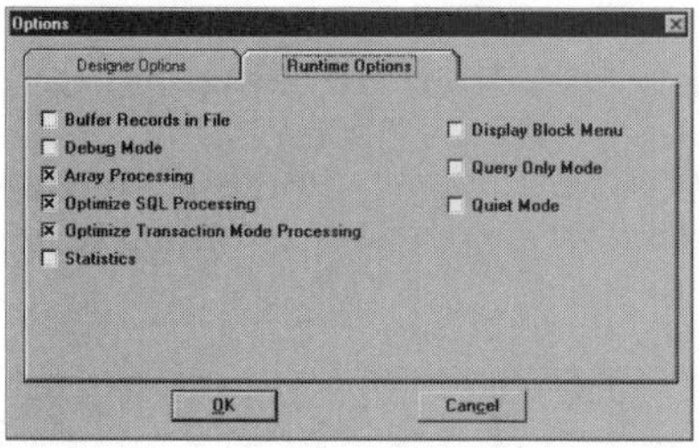


**FIG. 12.23**
The Runtime Options tab sheetab.

Following are descriptions of the various Runtime options contained on the tab sheet:

- Buffer Records in File—This sets the buffered records in memory equal to the minimum allowable number of rows plus 3. Additional records are buffered in a temporary file on disk.

  The option saves Runform memory but increases disk I/O. The default, unchecked, means records aren't buffered in a file.
- Debug Mode—This check box is used to place Forms Runtime in the debug mode. This invokes break processing if the Break built-in is used in any trigger. The default, unchecked, means Forms Runtime doesn't run the form in Debug Mode.

- Array Processing—This check box is used to enable array processing. When the check box is unchecked, the database returns only a single row of a query at a time.

  This causes the first record to be returned more quickly than normal but increases the overall processing time. The default, checked, allows Forms Runtime to do array processing.
- Optimize SQL Processing—This check box tells Forms Runtime to optimize SQL statement processing in Version 2 triggers by sharing database cursors. The default for this option, checked, means Forms Runtime does optimizing.
- Optimize Transaction Mode Processing—This check box tells Forms Runtime to assign a separate cursor for each SQL statement. When the box is unchecked, Forms only assigns a separate cursor for each select statement.

  This saves memory but slows processing. The default, checked, means transaction processing is optimized.
- Statistics—This check box displays a message at the end of the session indicating the maximum number of simultaneous cursors used. The default, unchecked, suppresses the statistic message display.
- Display Block Menu—This check box automatically displays the block menu rather than the form as the first screen. The default, unchecked, means the block menu is not displayed.
- Query Only Mode—This check box displays the called form first in the query mode. The default mode for a new form is the input mode. The default for this option, unchecked, means that the called form is not first displayed in the query mode.
- Quiet Mode—This checkbox suppresses audible sounds made by messages. The default, unchecked, means that audible sounds are not suppressed.



## The Navigator Menu Options

The Navigator menu is displayed when the Object Navigator is the current screen. This menu is seldom used. Figure 12.24 shows the options on this menu.

**The Ownership View and Visual View options** The first two options on the Navigator menu control how the objects are arranged in the Object Navigator. Ownership View is the default. In this arrangement, all the form objects are displayed and the items are listed according to the hierarchy.

A form contains blocks and blocks contain items. When you select an object, you can see the child objects by expanding the object. This is the default view and is recommended.

Pressing the adjacent radio button enables the Visual View. This view changes the arrangement of the objects in the Object Navigator. In this view, only windows, canvases, and items are displayed.

This corresponds to the hierarchy of items in a window. In this view, canvases are assigned to windows and items are assigned to canvases. Figure 12.25 shows the Employee form in the Visual View.

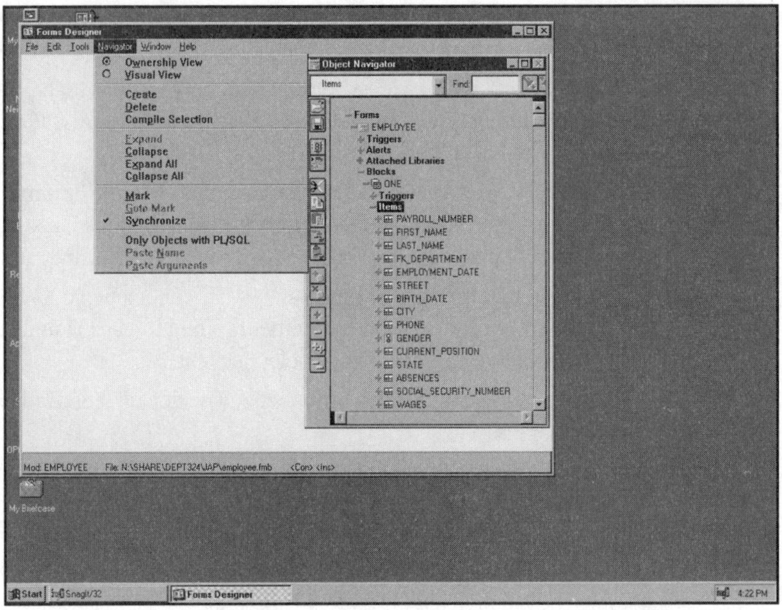


**FIG. 12.24**
The Navigator menu options.

**NOTE** You can try this yourself by loading the EMPLOYEE.FMB file located on the CD into the Object Navigator. Select the File | Open menu option to launch the Open dialog box. Locate and select the EMPLOYEE.FMB file on the CD. Press the OK button. You should the various components of the file displayed in the Object Navigator.

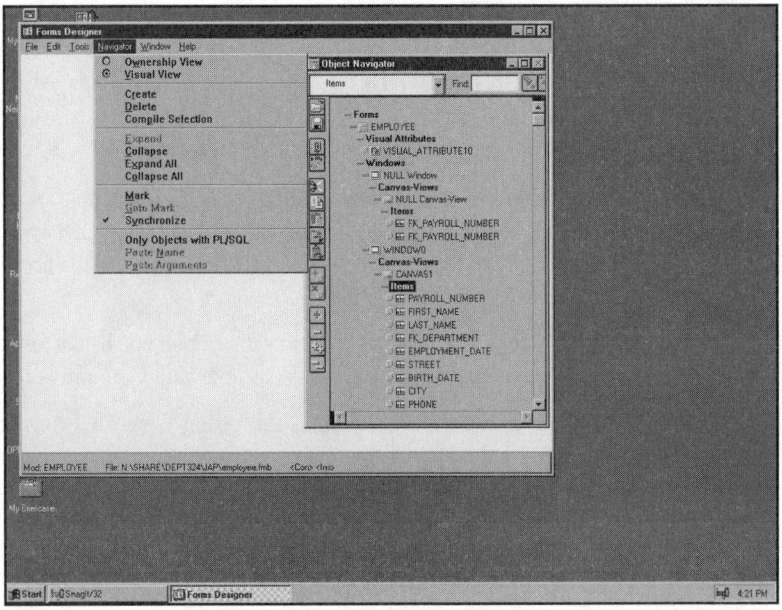


**FIG. 12.25**
The Employee form in the Visual View.

**The Create, Delete, and Compile Selection options** The Create option is the same as the green plus sign button on the Tool Palette. This option creates a new object like the item currently selected in the Object Navigator.

The Delete option is the same as the red "X" button on the tool palette. This option deletes the selected object. The Compile Selection option compiles any object that's currently selected.

**NOTE** After you use Forms Designer for a while, you'll find that there are a number of different ways to do the same thing. For instance, you can delete an item using the delete option on the menu, using the delete option on the tool palette, pressing the delete key on the keyboard, using the cut option, or using the clear option.

If you don't want to select the item in the Object Navigator, you can select it in the Layout Editor and do the same functions.

**The Expand, Collapse, Expand All, and Collapse All options** The next part of the Navigator pull-down menu offers options to expand, collapse, expand all, or collapse all objects. These options are identical to the icons on the tool palette.

**The Mark, Goto Mark, and Synchronize options** The Mark option is used to label a spot in the Object Navigator for quick return using the Goto Mark option. This is a useful way to return to an object when the form contains a large number of objects.

The Synchronize option turns the procedure that maintains synchronization between the Object Navigator and the Layout Editor on and off. When this option is turned on, an object that is selected in the Object Navigator is also selected in the Layout Editor.

The default is turned on, indicated by check mark to the left of the option.

**The Only Objects with PL/SQL option** The Only Objects with PL/SQL options eliminates any object from the Object Navigator that does not contain PL/SQL code. This is handy when you're searching a form for PL/SQL scripts.

The default for this option is turned off. The option is turned on when there's a check mark to the left of the option. Figure 12.26 shows the Object Navigator when this option is turned on.



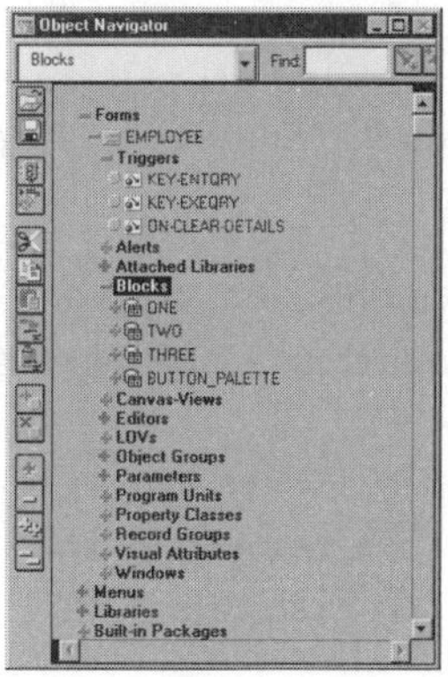


**FIG. 12.26**
The Object Navigator when the Only Objects with PL/SQL option is turned on.

# Creating Your First Form

Now that you've seen the components of the Object Navigator, you can create a form file and a default block. When you've done this, you'll have a fully functional form that you can use to add records to the database, retrieve records based on search criteria, change records, delete records, and save the changes in the database.

The next section gives you a list of steps to create the form. After that is a section that shows you how a form is created.

## Steps for Creating a Simple One-Block Form

The following steps show you how to create a simple one-block form. These steps are handy for creating any new form blocks.

1. Create a new form module in the Object Navigator.
2. Create a new default block.

    Select the block object on the form.

    Press the Create (green plus sign) button on the Object Navigator tool palette.

    Update the values on the General tab sheet of the New Block Option dialog. Enter the name of a table or view in the Base Table field. Change the values of the other fields as needed.

    Press the Items tab. Press the Select Columns button to populate the Items window. Deselect items as desired. Items that are highlighted or have an "X" in the Include checkbox are selected. Change the item labels as needed.

    Press the Layout tab. Populate the fields on this dialog as needed. Click OK.
3. Change the name of the module on the Object Navigator.
4. Save the file.
5. Run the file by pressing the Run button on the Tool palette.

## Creating the Form

The following sections contain the settings used to create the first part of a form used in the next several chapters. You may use the settings contained in the figures to create your own form. The finished form will be similar to form EMPCH13.FMB that will be used in Chapter 13 to practice techniques.

1. Creating the Form module of file

    The first step in creating a form is to initiate a new blank module or file. This can be done in several ways. The first is to launch Forms Designer, which contains a blank form module when it first appears.

    Another way is to select and highlight the Forms keyword or object in the Object Navigator, as shown in Figure 12.27, and then click the Create icon. This causes Designer to create a new module.

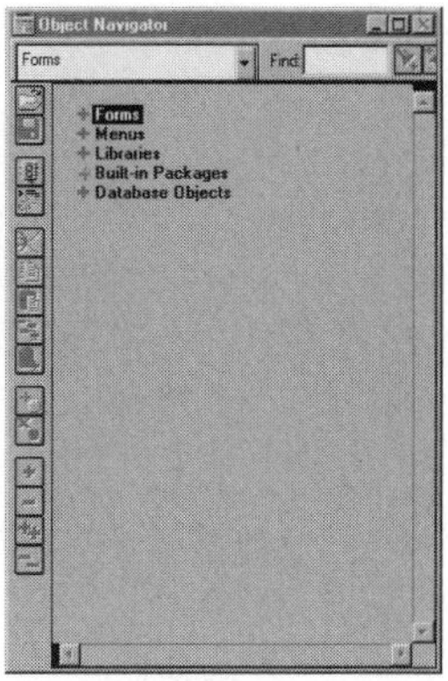


**FIG. 12.27**
Creating a default form module.

2. Launching the New Block Options dialog box

   The next step is to create a block in the form. This can also be done in several ways. The first is to select the Tools/New Block option on the Tools menu.

   The second is to select and highlight the Blocks keyword on the Object Navigator, as shown in Figure 12.28, then click the Create icon on the tool palette to open the New Block Options dialog box.

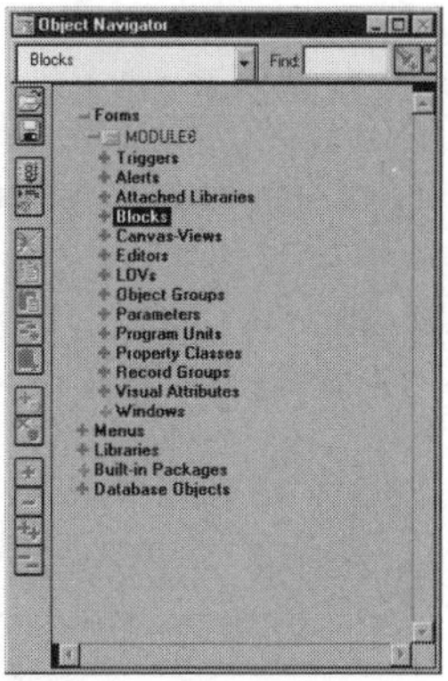


**FIG. 12.28**
The Object Navigator after creating a new blank form. The Blocks object is highlighted and the Create icon is about to be clicked.

   The New Block Options dialog box consists of four tabbed sheets. The sheets contain settings for the new block.

   The tabbed sheets are: General, Items, Layout, and Master/Detail. The dialog box with the General tab is shown in Figure 12.29.

3. Filling out the General Tab sheet

   The Base Table item contains the name of the table or view that supplies the block with records. If you're not sure of the table name, you can use the Select button to identify the table. This opens a dialog box with the tables you can access.

The Block Name field contains the name of the block. As you tab from the Base Table field, this field is populated with the same name as the Base table. You can change this name.

The Canvas field contains the name of the canvas. If the form is new, Designer puts a new default canvas name in this field and creates this canvas at the same time as the block. If the form has existing blocks, Designer uses the canvas that was last selected.

If you want to change the name of the canvas and you don't know the name, you can use the Select button to the right of the field to open a dialog box with the various canvases.

The Sequence ID field contains the order of block navigation. You use it only when you're creating multiple blocks on the form.

Figure 12.29 contains a filled out General tab sheet.

**FIG. 12.29**
The New Block Options dialog box showing the form settings for the General Tab sheet.

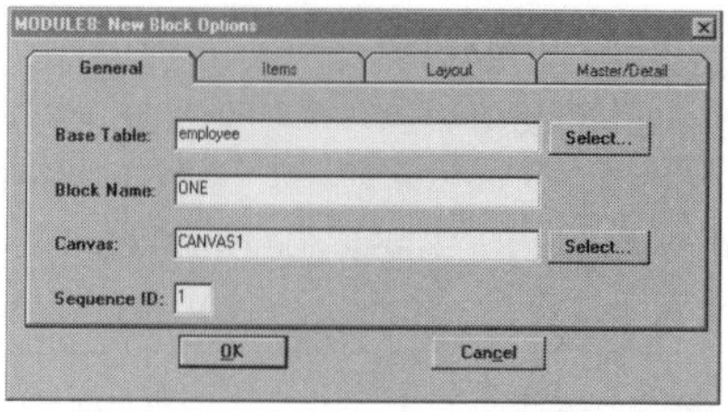


4. Filling out the Items tab sheet

   The next step is to press the Items tab to open the Items tab sheet, shown in Figure 12.30. Press the Select Columns button to populate the item window on the left side of the dialog box with the items from the table named in the previous tab.

   Then decide which of these fields will appear on the block. By default, all the fields are selected. This is indicated by the plus sign in front of the field or a check mark in the Include checkbox.

   In Figure 12.30, the highlighted field, SOCIAL_SECURITY_NUMBER, is displayed but the EMPLOYMENT_DATE field is not. You can select or deselect a field by entering or removing the check mark in the Include checkbox or double-clicking the item in the window.

**FIG. 12.30**
The New Block Options dialog box displaying the Items Tab sheet.

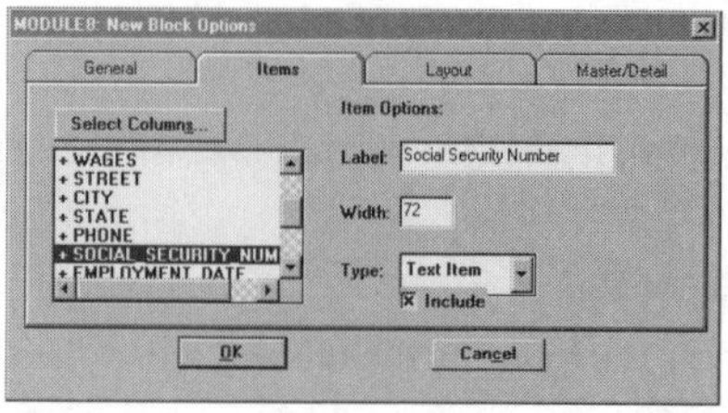


The Label field contains the default boilerplate or text that will be placed in front of the item. You can change this value. The Width field contains the display width of the field on the block. This width is not the size of the database item, but the size of the text item that will display the database item.

The initial value is based on the length of the field in the table. The value of the SOCIAL_SECURITY_NUMBER field in Figure 12.30 is 72.

This means the value is 72 points, not 72 characters. The value in this field conforms to the current metric set in the form properties. One of these properties is the Coordinate system. The Form Coordinate system is currently set to real. The form size metric for real is pixels, centimeters, inches, or points. The Coordinate system can also be changed to character. This will be discussed in Chapter 13, "Formatting Your Form."

The Type field indicates the type of item to be created. Item types are explained in Chapter 14, "Creating and Modifying Master/Detail Forms."

**NOTE** All of the items on the employee table should be selected and labeled to suit.

5. Filling out the Layout tab sheet

   You can press the Layout Tab, shown in Figure 12.30, when you're done with the items. The Style pick list contains two values: Tabular and Form.

   The tabular style places each column in a single row with each field adjacent to the other. This style is appropriate for detail blocks that contain multiple records.

   The Tools block and Glasses block of the Employee form used in Chapter 11 are examples of a tabular block. The top block containing unique information about the employee is an example of a form style. This style is generally used for master blocks. Figure 12.31 shows a filled out Layout tab sheet you can use for your practice form.



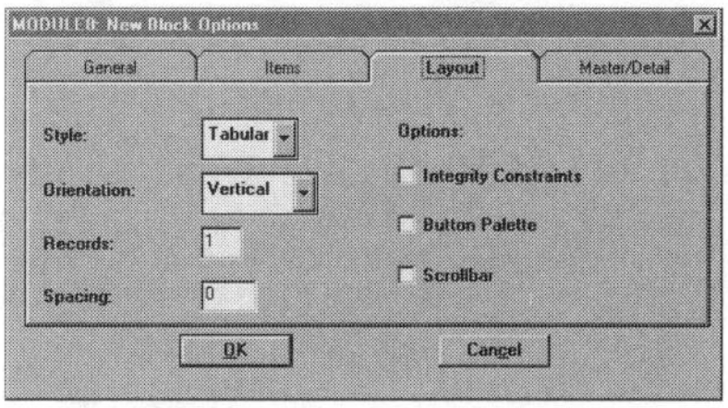


**FIG. 12.31**
The New Block Options Layout Tab settings

The Orientation pick list determines the direction the records are laid out in when multiple records are shown on the block. The vertical setting places each additional row below the previous one.

The horizontal setting places each additional record to the right of the previous record. Generally, the vertical setting is used.

The Records item determines the number of records the block displays. The Spacing field controls the amount of space between each item. The values in this field are in character cells.

The Integrity Constraints field tells Designer whether to enforce table and column constraints in the table. This changes block and item properties to match those in the table.

The Button Palette check box places a default button palette at the bottom of the form. The palette contains buttons to navigate up or down, scroll up, scroll down, query a record, and save the changes.

The Scrollbar check box is used to place a scrollbar on the block. It's generally used when the block contains multiple records.

The Master/Detail tab is used to create master-detail blocks, which are two related blocks. It also creates some special triggers that coordinate the two blocks. This tab is discussed in Chapter 14, "Creating and Modifying Master-Detail Forms."

Everything is now filled in and you can create the block. Press the OK button.

The dialog box disappears and the Object Navigator contains some new objects. These objects consist of the block called "One" and the selected items from the Items tab.

Figure 12.32 shows the new objects in the Object Navigator.

**FIG. 12.32**
The Object Navigator after the new block "One" is created.

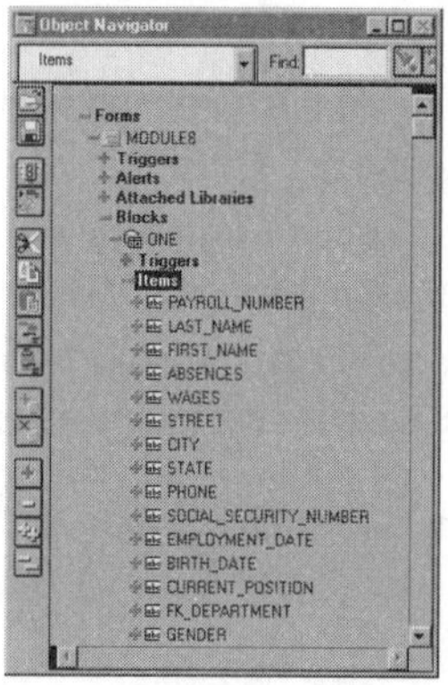


**CAUTION**

Each of the four tab sheets on the New Block options dialog box has an OK button. Pressing this button causes the block to be created, even if you've never viewed some of the tab sheets.

When this happens, the block has missing objects such as fields, scrollbar, or button palette. You can add these items but it takes time. It's usually easier to delete the block objects and start over.

Be *sure* to completely fill in each of the tab sheets before pressing the OK button!

6. Naming your form

   The next step is to name the file. Since this is a new file, it has a default name beginning with "module." You can change the name of the form in the Object Navigator.

   Double-click the form name. This highlights the name. Press the Backspace key. This deletes the name. Now type in the new name.

Figure 12.33 shows the Object Navigator after this sequence. You can use this procedure to update any object name.

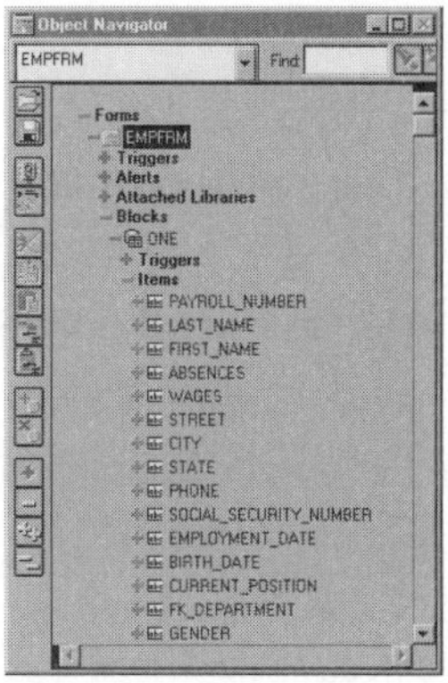


**FIG. 12.33**
The Object Navigator after the form name is highlighted and changed.

7. Saving your form

   The last step is to save the file. You can do this by pressing the Save button on the tool palette or by selecting the file/save option on the menu bar.

---

**TIP** A number of techniques are useful and time saving when you create a form. You can use the names "one," "two," "three," "four," and "five" for your block names rather than the default names.

There are two reasons for doing this. The first is that the names are short and easy to spell. The block name is often used as a qualifier in PL/SQL scripts in the forms. So this prevents typing errors and having to type lengthy names.

The second reason for using these names is standardization. Generally, there's only one master block on a form. If you always name the master block "one," you always know the name of the master block. You may find this standardization preferable to using table names as block names.

Another technique is to always edit the item labels on the Items tab. It's much easier and quicker to change them in this dialog box rather than after they are created on the Layout Editor. It'll save you time to do the job properly here.

A third technique is to put the button palette on the form when you create the last block. If you create the button palette after the first block, Designer places subsequent blocks beneath the palette.

If you usually place the button palette at the bottom of the screen, you have to move all the items above the palette. It saves formatting time to create the button palette when you create the last block.

---



# Summary

Forms Designer is used to develop the form applications. When Forms is launched, the first screen is the Object Navigator, the main Forms Designer screen. It contains all the objects that can be changed, and offers an easy mechanism to reach all form, menu, and library objects.

The Object Navigator has several parts. The top of the screen contains menu options, the left side of the screen contains a tool palette, the bottom of the screen displays messages, and the center of the screen displays the objects.

The objects are arranged in levels. The highest-level objects can be expanded to expose the child objects. The objects can also be collapsed to make the Object Navigator easier to read.

The File menu options offer a variety of options. There are options to open, save, close, and generate the files.

The Edit menu options allow you to cut, copy, paste, clear, and duplicate items.

The Tools menu options are used to display an item's property sheets, Layout Editor, Object Navigator, Menu Editor, PL/SQL Editor, and the Object Navigator. This menu is used to create new blocks and to call a special dialog box that creates select statements.

The Object Navigator menu has options to change the arrangement of the objects in the Object Navigator. It also has options to add and delete objects, as well as to expand and collapse them.

You can create a form by highlighting the forms object in the Object Navigator and clicking the Create icon. Then you add a block to the form. You do this by selecting the blocks object and pressing the Create icon.

A dialog box is displayed with a variety of settings that determine the type of form created. After you mark these settings, Designer creates the form. You can then save and run the form.

# From Here...

The next chapter covers the Layout Editor, a screen painter that is used to format a form. The chapter discusses the formatting options available, including arranging and coloring items, adding text, placing images, changing fonts, viewing options, and formatting the form created in this chapter.

# Review Exercises

1. Create a one-block form using the Department table as the base table. The form uses the tabular style, display 12 records, and has a button palette.
2. Create a one-block form using the Employee table as the base table. The form uses the form style and display 1 record. Do not add a default button palette.

Be sure to save the forms. You'll use them in the exercises for Chapter 13.

CHAPTER 13

# Formatting Your Form

This chapter covers the Layout Editor, a screen painter used to format a form. The chapter also discusses the formatting options available, including arranging and coloring items, adding text, placing images, changing fonts, viewing options, and formatting the form created in Chapter 12. ■

**The Layout Editor menu**

This screen formats the form canvas, which contains the objects that interface with the user.

**Using the Layout Editor menu**

The Layout Editor has three special pull-down menus that perform many functions, such as arranging fields, changing the grid, and changing text fonts.

**Using the Layout Editor tool palette**

The tool palette lets you add boilerplate text, text items, images, and a host of other objects to the canvas.

**Defining canvas properties**

This part discusses the canvas-view properties.

**Defining window properties**

This section discusses the window properties.

**Formatting the Employee form**

This section teaches you how to format the master block of the Employee Update form created in Chapter 12.

**NOTE** The figures in this chapter use several different files. The last section about Formatting the Employee form uses file EMPCH13.FMB. It contains the block created in Chapter 12. This file is used in many of the figures that require a form. Figures 13.13 to 13.15 use the SHOWVIEW.FMB file. Figure 13.31 uses the MOVE.FMB. These files are all contained on the CD. The remainder of the figures used a blank form that was not saved.

# The Layout Editor

The Layout Editor is the Forms screen that allows the developer to customize the canvas used in the form. A canvas may contain a variety of objects, such as boilerplate text that describes an object, text items that contain database values, images, pushbuttons, radio buttons, check boxes, and other graphic features. You can size, shape, color, and move each of these items around the screen by using the tools on the Layout Editor.

You can start the Layout Editor by following either of these steps.

1. Open the Object Navigator, expand the canvas object, and double-click the button to the left of the canvas name. The selected canvas appears in the Layout Editor.
2. Select Layout Editor from the Tools menu. The canvas for the currently selected object appears in the Layout Editor.

Figure 13.1 illustrates the Layout Editor. The figure contains the default canvas for the Employee Update form created at the end of Chapter 12.

**NOTE** You may view the canvas displayed in Figure 13.1 by opening the sample form you created in Chapter 12 or by using the EMPCH13.FMB form on the CD. The figures in this chapter were taken by using the EMPCH13.FMB form file.

**FIG. 13.1**
The Layout Editor containing the Employee Update form.

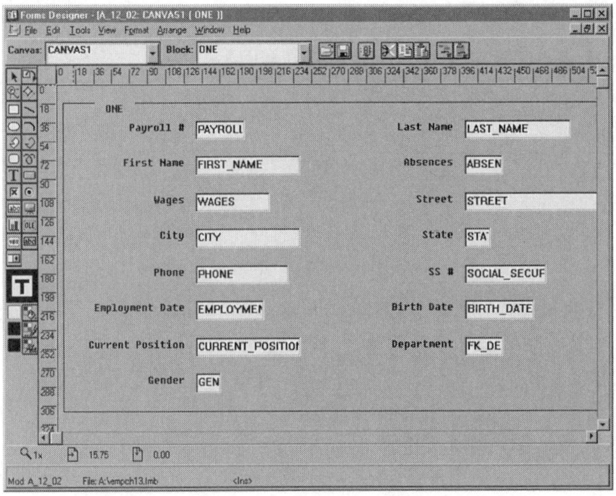

The Layout Editor has the following four components:

| | |
|---|---|
| Menu Bar | The menu bar has two types of pull-down menus. The first is the default options used for file management and editing. These options are available at all times on the menu. The second is available only when the Layout Editor is the active screen. The Layout Editor menu bar has three of these menus: View, Format, and Arrange. |
| Top Tool Bar | This toolbar is similar to the Object Navigator toolbar. It contains a variety of buttons, such as Save file, Run the file, and Copy properties. |
| Tool Palette | Located on the left-hand side of the Layout Editor, the tool palette contains an array of formatting tools Layout Editor uses to create boilerplate text, form items, color form objects, and create images. |
| Layout | The layout area is the central part of the Layout Editor and is used to format the canvas. The functions contained on the tool palette and menu bar are applied to objects in this area. |

# The Layout Edit Menu Bar

The Layout Editor Menu bar has three pull-down menus available only when the Layout Editor is the active screen. The first menu is *View,* and is used to change the way the layout area looks to the developer. The second is *Format,* which contains options that allow the developer to change the way an object looks. The third is *Arrange,* which is used to position objects on the canvas. Each menu is discussed in more detail in the following sections.

## The View Pull-Down Menu

The View pull-down menu has a number of options used to rearrange the way the layout area is viewed. Changing the view can aid the developer in formatting the canvas. Figure 13.2 illustrates the View pull-down menu.

**FIG. 13.2**
The View pull-down menu.

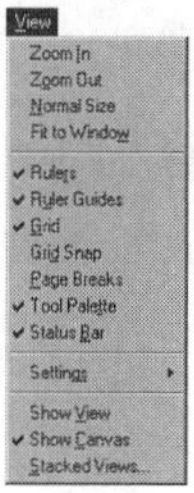




**The Zoom In Option** The first section of the menu controls the amount of the viewing area the developer can see at a given time. At times it is advantageous to see smaller or larger areas of the canvas. The first option on the menu is *Zoom In*. This option makes objects look larger by causing forms to show less area in the layout area. Figure 13.3 shows the example screen used in Figures 13.1 and 13.2 after pressing the Zoom In option once.

**FIG. 13.3**
The Layout Editor after performing a Zoom In.

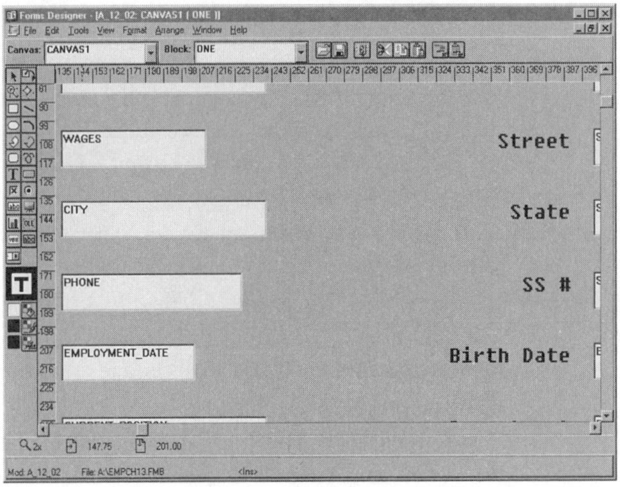


**The Zoom Out Option** The *Zoom Out* option does the exact opposite of Zoom In—it makes the objects look smaller by displaying more of the layout area. Figure 13.4 shows the Layout Editor after pressing the Zoom Out option twice.

**FIG. 13.4**
The Layout Editor after Zooming Out twice.

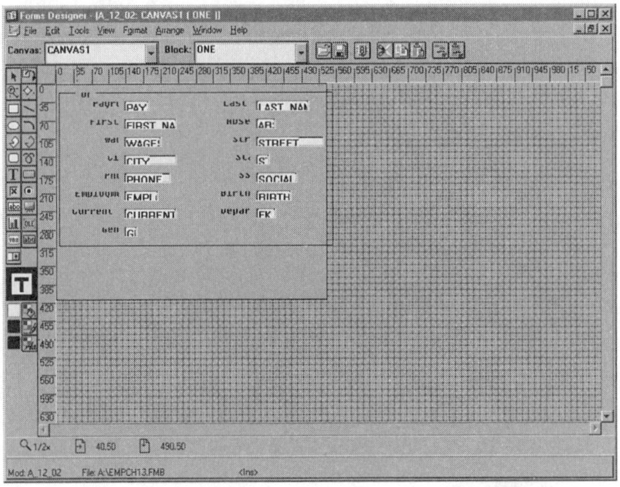


**The Normal Size Option** The next option is the *Normal Size* option. It does as its name suggests—returns the layout to the default size. Figure 13.5 illustrates the example form after selecting the Normal Size option.

**The Fit to Window Option** The last option in the first section of the *View* menu is *Fit to Window.* This option reduces the size of the layout area so that the entire work area can be seen at one time. Figure 13.6 illustrates the layout when you select this option.

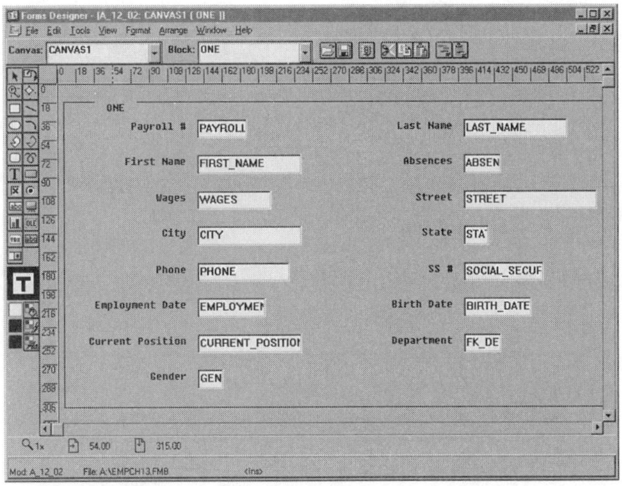


**FIG. 13.5**
The Layout Editor after pressing the Normal Size option.

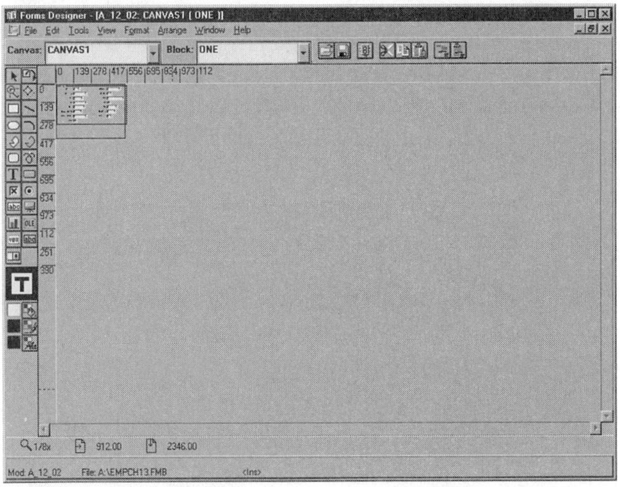


**FIG. 13.6**
The Layout Editor after pressing the Fit to Window option.



**The Rulers Option** Along the top and left borders of the layout area in Figure 13.6 are a series of numbers and hash marks. These borders are called *vertical* and *horizontal rulers*, and are used to identify the relative position of objects. Each object that appears on the canvas has two properties: an x position coordinate and a y position coordinate. These coordinates refer to the top-left corner of the object. When manually setting these coordinates, or determining the size of the canvas or window, the ruler is a useful tool. The ruler scale in Figure 13.6 is in points. It can be changed to other metrics by using the Setting option on this menu. When the Ruler option is checked, the ruler is displayed as shown in Figure 13.6. When the option is unchecked, the ruler does not appear. This gives the developer slightly more room for the canvas in the layout area. Figure 13.7 displays the Layout Editor without the ruler guides.

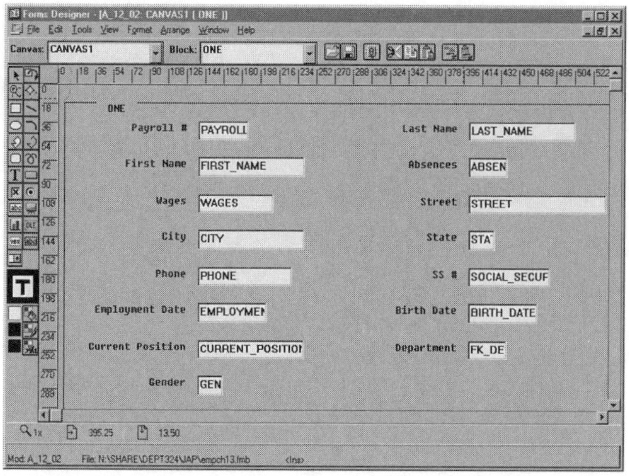


**FIG. 13.7**
The Layout Editor without the horizontal and vertical rulers.

**The Ruler Guides Option** The *Ruler Guides* option places custom vertical and horizontal guide marks on the layout. To place a ruler guide, touch the ruler with the mouse pointer. Hold down the left mouse button, and drag the guide to the desired location. The top ruler creates horizontal guides and the left ruler creates vertical guides. Figure 13.8 illustrates a layout that contains several ruler guides. The vertical guides are located on x coordinates 22 and 181. The horizontal guides are located on y coordinates 89 and 203.

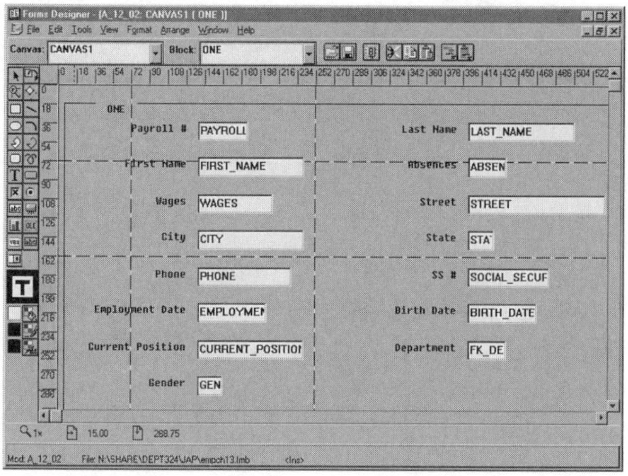


**FIG. 13.8**
The Layout Editor after ruler guides are placed.

Clicking the Ruler Guides option shuts off the ruler guides function. The check mark next to the option also disappears. The ruler guides and the check mark reappear when the option is turned on. The ruler guides can be removed permanently by clicking on the guide, holding the left mouse button down, and dragging the guide to the ruler.

**NOTE** Sometimes it is extremely difficult to place ruler guides. You may have to repeatedly touch the edge of the ruler with the mouse pointer. It happens to experienced Forms designers also.

**The Grid Option** The *Grid* option places grid lines in the layout area. The default setting is "checked," which means that the grid lines show. When the canvas appears in the layout area, it covers the grid lines. If you are going to use the *grid* to align your canvas objects, it is best not to display the canvas. For example, if you look at Figure 13.8, you do not see any grid lines. Figure 13.9 was captured with the *Show Canvas* option turned off. As you can see, the grid is a series of parallel horizontal and vertical lines, used to align objects.

**FIG. 13.9**
Using Grid lines with the Show Canvas option turned off.

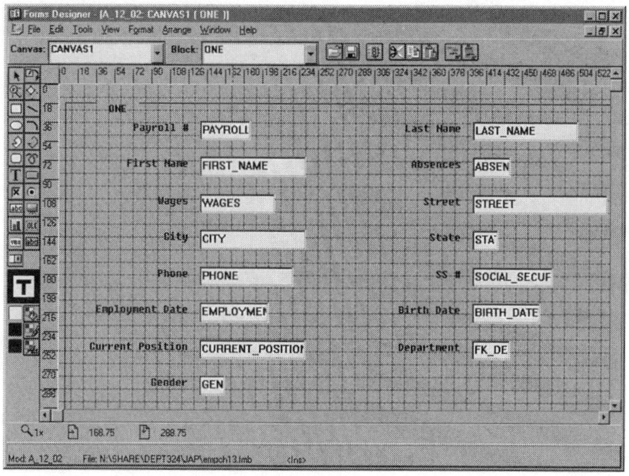


**The Grid Snap Option** The *Grid Snap* option is an excellent tool to use when arranging objects by using the grid. The option causes objects to automatically jump or "snap" to the nearest grid line, which makes it easy to align objects. One problem with this technique is that the spot the developer may want the object to appear on may not be a grid line. The object may not be placed at the desired position when grid snap is turned on. It is possible to change the snap points to alleviate this problem. This can be done by using the Settings/Ruler options discussed later in this part.

The object can be placed without snapping when the option is turned off. However it is sometimes difficult to align objects. Grid Snap can make the alignment of objects easier.

**The Page Breaks Option** The *Page Breaks* option places a black line border in the layout area, designating the areas that will be printed on a page if the print command were issued. The default setting is "unchecked," which does not display the page breaks.

**The Tool Palette and Status Bar Options** The *Tool Palette* option closes the Layout Editor tool palette located on the left side of the screen. This increases the layout area workspace. The *Status Bar* option removes the status bar at the bottom of the screen, which also adds more space to the layout area. The default is for the tool palette and status bar to be displayed.

The options will have a check mark to the left when they are displayed. Figure 13.10 shows the Layout Editor without the tool palette and status bar.

**FIG. 13.10**
The Layout Editor after the Tool Palette and Status Bar are removed.

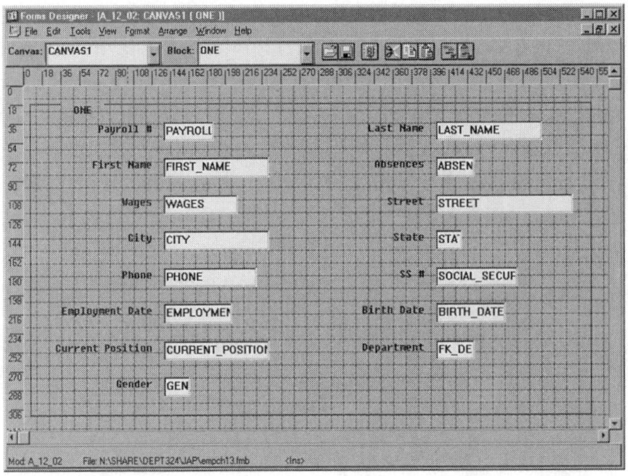

**The Settings Option** When you select the *Settings* option, a submenu opens and displays two setting options: the Layout option at the top, and the Ruler option at the bottom. Select the layout option and the Layout Settings dialog box appears, as shown in Figure 13.11. This box is used to control the size of the layout area and the direction pages will be printed. The two bottom radiobuttons determine the printing direction. If the left button is pressed, Designer will print layout pages from left to right. If the other button is pressed, Designer will print layout pages from top to button.

**FIG. 13.11**
The Layout Settings dialog box.

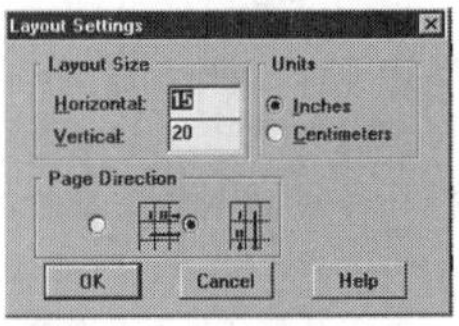

The two settings on the top left of the box determine the size of the layout area. In Figure 13.11, the horizontal setting, or work area, width is set at 8.5 inches. The vertical setting, or height, is set at 20 inches. The radio button on the top-right of the dialog box determines the unit of measure, which means that the work area or the maximum size of the canvas is 8.5 inches by 20 inches. This is larger than the size of the screen. Forms allow the developer the ability to create a canvas larger than the screen.

**NOTE** I do not like to create canvases greater than the size of the maximized window on my PC screen. I find it a great inconvenience to have to use a vertical or horizontal scroll bar to see parts of the form. There are some cases for making the canvas bigger than the window, but I try to avoid them.

Designer usually creates a default canvas that is not the size of a normal maximized window. It also has a layout area larger than the window, which makes it difficult for the developer to know if the objects are properly placed. Sometimes they are placed out of the window view where you need a scroll bar to see them.

In order to place the fields properly, I change the layout settings to 8.5 inches wide and 5.5 inches high. I then change the height and width properties for both the canvas and window objects so that they cover the layout area. I now have a work area exactly the size of the window of my user. This helps me to properly place items without having to run the form to see how the fields are displayed.

Not all PC monitors have the same resolution. The settings change depending on the resolution. You should use trial and error to come up with the property size values you desire, and place them into the form when you first create it.

**The Show View Option** Turning on the *Show View* option places a frame around the current view. The view is the area of the form that can be seen at a given time when the form is executed in Forms Runtime. Selecting the view by clicking it causes drag handles to appear. This allows you to change the size of the selected view. You can move the view drag handles to change the width and height. The view of the EMPCH13.FMB form was reduced horizontally and vertically. The form was then executed by using the Run menu option. Figure 13.12 shows the executed form. Notice the effect of changing the size of the view. A blank border appears between the edge of the view and the window.

This option is turned on when a check mark exists to the left of the option on the menu. It is turned off when the check mark is missing.

**The Show Canvas Option** The *Show Canvas* option shows or hides the canvas. The main purpose for removing the canvas is to show the underlying grid lines, demonstrated earlier in this section. When the canvas is removed, the objects that lay on the canvas, such as boilerplate text and fields, remain.

**The Show Stacked Views Option** The *Show Stacked Views* option displays *stacked* views. A form can simultaneously display multiple views and canvases. There are four types of canvas-views in forms: *content*, *stacked*, *horizontal toolbar*, and *vertical toolbar*. The Canvas Type property determines how the canvas will be viewed. The *content* canvas-view is the default type. It is the base of the form and covers the entire window.



Multiple canvases can be assigned to a window and displayed at the same time. When this is done, one canvas is a content canvas and the remainder must be *stacked* canvas-views. A stacked canvas can overlay a content canvas. The Show Stacked Views option enables the developer to design the display of multiple canvases. It brings additional views to the layout area in order to coordinate their placement.

The SHOWVIEW.FMB file was created to demonstrate this concept. This file is available on the CD. The file contains three canvas-views: canvas1, canvas2, and canvas3. The first is a content canvas-view and the remaining two are stacked canvas-views. Figure 13.13 shows canvas1 after the Stacked Views option has been selected. Selecting this option brings up the Stacked Canvas-Views dialog box. Canvas2 has been selected, as shown by the highlighted item. If you press the OK button, canvas2 appears and overlays canvas1.

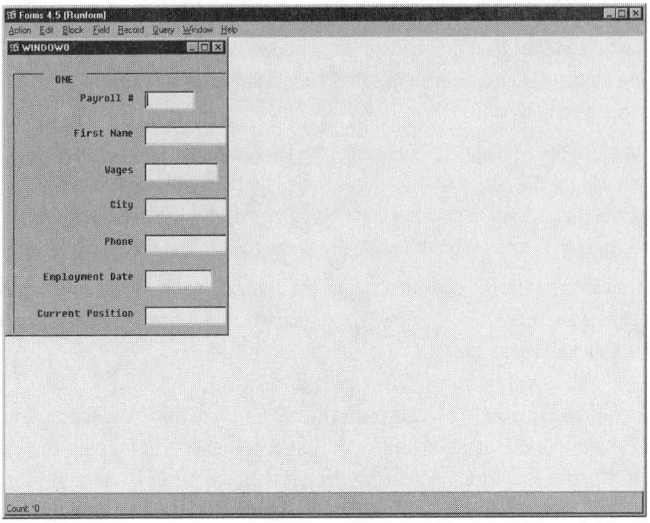


**FIG. 13.12**
Using the Show View option to shrink the area of the form that can be seen.

**NOTE** The Stacked Canvas-Views dialog box is used to overlay stacked canvases over the content canvas. The canvases that are highlighted will appear. The canvases that are not highlighted will not appear. If you want all of the stacked canvases to appear, you must select all of the canvases.

When there are multiple stacked canvases, as in our example, selecting one canvas will deselect the other. To select both canvases, select the first canvas by clicking it. To select a subsequent canvas without deselecting the original selection, press the control key while clicking the canvas. This procedure should also be followed when de-selecting canvases. Use the control key to enable you to deselect the last canvas. ■

When you first display stacked canvases, they cover a part of the content canvas depending upon their size and position. However, the size can be modified and the canvas position changed. Views are resized by selecting the stacked canvas and using the drag handles to resize them. Figure 13.14 shows canvas2 after it has been resized and is being dragged to the right of canvas1. Notice the drag handles around canvas2.

The showview form has a third canvas. This canvas-view can be displayed by opening the Stacked Canvas-Views dialog. Select canvas3 while pressing the control key. Press the OK button. The results of this are shown in Figure 13.15. All three canvas-views are shown. Canvas1 is at the top-left, canvas2 at the top-right, and canvas3 at the bottom-middle.

**NOTE** A stacked canvas can be displayed without having to overlay it on the content canvas. You can open any canvas by selecting the canvas on the Object Navigator and double clicking the item. ■

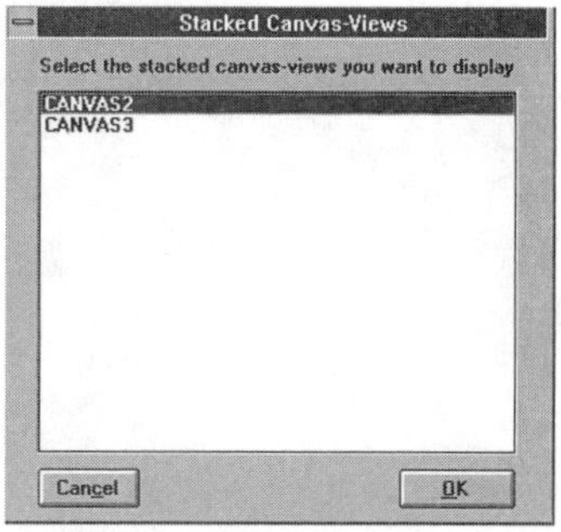


**FIG. 13.13**
Using the Stacked Views option to overlay canvas1 with canvas2.

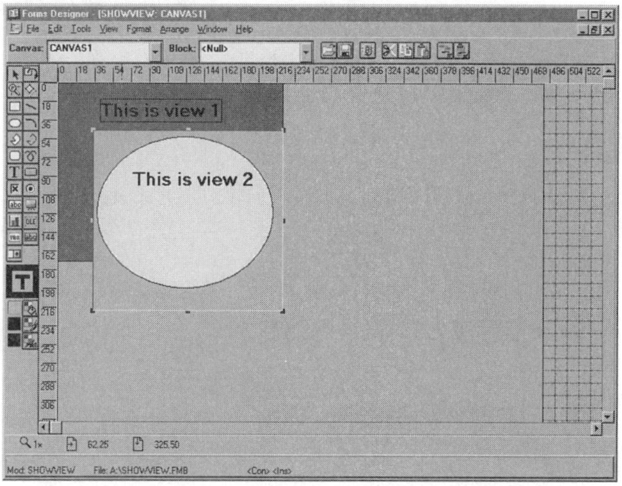


**FIG. 13.14**
Resizing and moving the stacked view.

# Using the Format Pull-Down Menu

The Layout Editor Format pull-down menu contains options used to format items on the canvas. To format an item, select the item(s) by clicking it. The next step is to select an option from the Format pull-down menu. Figure 13.16 illustrates the pull-down menu and the formatting options.

**The Font Option** The *Font* option is at the top of the menu. Pressing this option produces the Font dialog box, as shown in Figure 13.17. It contains four sets of settings: *Font*, *Font Style*, *Size*, and *Effects*.

The Font is set by using a list box located at the top-left of the dialog box. The list box contains the font types available to the developer, who can view any font by clicking on its name. A sample of the formatted text appears in the sample window on the bottom-right. In Figure 13.17, the text in the sample window is in the MS Sans Serif font.

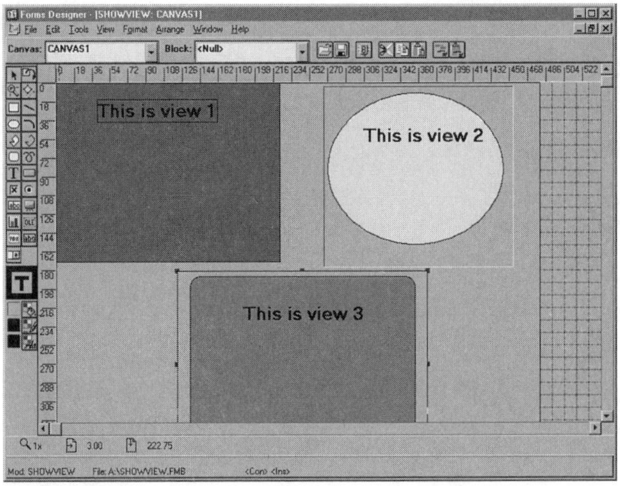


**FIG. 13.15**
The Layout Editor displays canvas1, canvas2, and canvas3 at the same time.

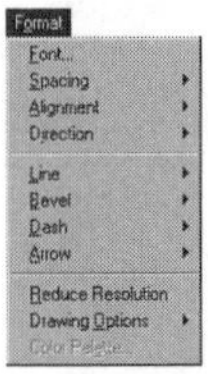


**FIG. 13.16**
The Layout Editor Format pull-down menu.

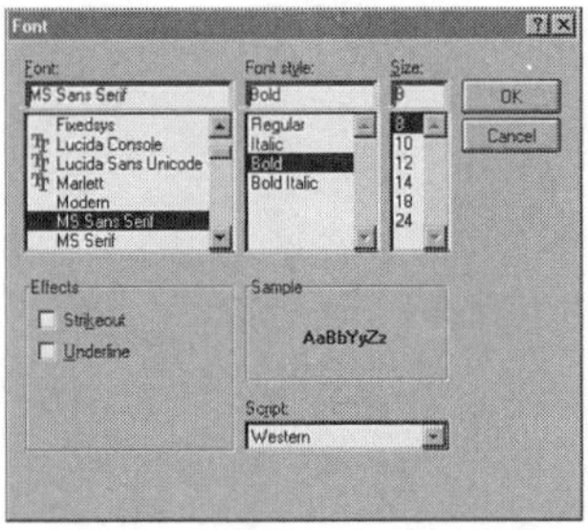


**FIG. 13.17**
Reformatting the Gender item by using the Font dialog box.

Selecting a font changes the range of values in the Size list box. This list box contains the available text sizes. Each font has a different range of sizes. The larger the number, the larger the size of the text. The text in the figure is size 18.

The third setting is Font Style. The available Font Style settings can also change with the type of font selected. The settings are generally regular, Italic, bold, or bold Italic. The sample text is in the figure is formatted in bold Italic.

The final setting type in the dialog box is contained in the Effects frame. The frame consists of two check boxes located at the bottom-left of the dialog box. Checking the Strikeout check box places a line through the text. Checking the Underline check box underlines the text. The Sample Window shows the effect of checking these options.

**The Spacing Option** The *Spacing* option spaces multiple-line boilerplate text. Selecting the Spacing option displays a submenu with four options: *single, space and one-half, double-space,* and *custom*. Figure 13.18 illustrates the submenu and examples of the various spacing.

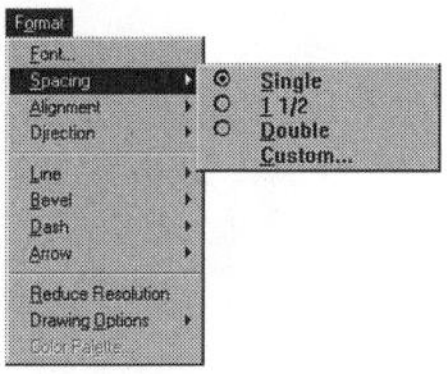


**FIG. 13.18** Examples of using the spacing and alignment options on boilerplate text.

**NOTE** The formatting techniques discussed in this section and some of the following sessions can be practiced on a blank canvas. Create a new form on the Object Navigator. Select the Tools, Layout Editor option. This will create a blank canvas that can be used to practice formatting techniques.

**The Spacing/Custom Option** When you select the *Spacing/Custom* option, a custom dialog box appears, which offers spacing settings in 6-, 12-, and 18-point sizes. In addition, the developer can specify any desired number of points.

**The Alignment option** The *Alignment* option sets text justification. Pressing this option causes a submenu to open to the right, which lists a number of text-alignment settings. Figure 13.19 shows this menu and examples of left, center, and right alignment. *Left* alignment places the first word of each text row on the left side of the text box, with the first letter of each row aligned. *Right* alignment places the last character of each row on the right side of the text box, with the last character of each row aligned. *Center* alignment places each row of the text in the middle of the text box. The first and last characters of the row are of equal distance from the edge of the text box.

**The Direction Option** The *Direction* option changes the layout direction of the text. Some languages read from left to right. The *Left-to-Right* setting supports the layout. The *Right-to-Left* setting supports right to left. The *Start* and *End* alignment settings are used when the direction is *Left-to-Right* or *Right-to-Left.* When the direction is Left-to-right and alignment is Start, alignment is Left alignment. Specifying End alignment causes Right alignment. When the direction is Right-to-Left and alignment is Start, the alignment is Right alignment. It changes to Left alignment when you specify End alignment.



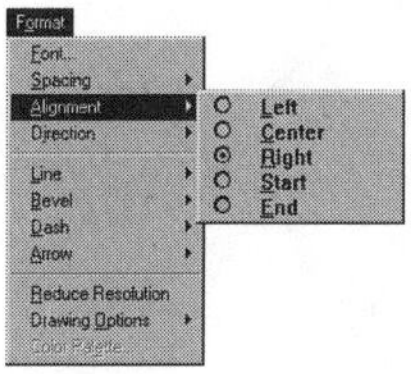


**FIG. 13.19** The Alignment options and examples.

**The Line Option** The *Line* option changes the width or weight of lines drawn on the canvas. These lines can be part of a text box or graphic image. Figure 13.20 illustrates the various settings. To change the line weight of an object, select the line to be changed, then select the desired setting.

**FIG. 13.20**
Various settings of the Line width options.

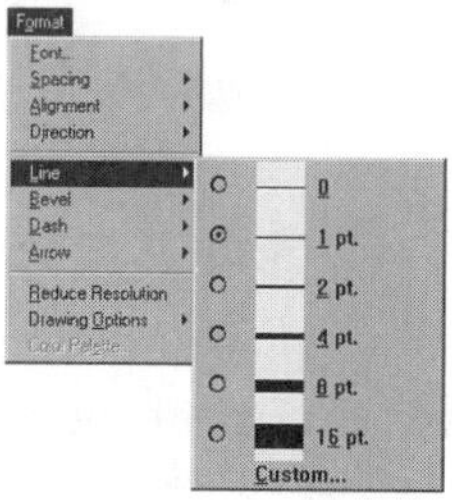


**The Bevel Option** The *Bevel* option modifies the appearance of an object border. This option is used for text items, chart items, custom items, and stacked items. Figure 13.21 illustrates the menu and the appearance of the various bevels. The Bevel option has five settings:

- *None*—No bevel used.
- *Inset*—Places a white line inside the normal border, making the border seem indented.
- *Outset*—Places the white line outside the border, making the border seem raised.
- *Raised*—Places a white border on the top and left, and a darker border on the bottom and right of the object, giving an illusion of raising the object above the canvas.
- *Lowered*—Reverses the light and dark borders, making the object appear indented into the canvas.

**FIG. 13.21**
The Bevel format settings and examples.

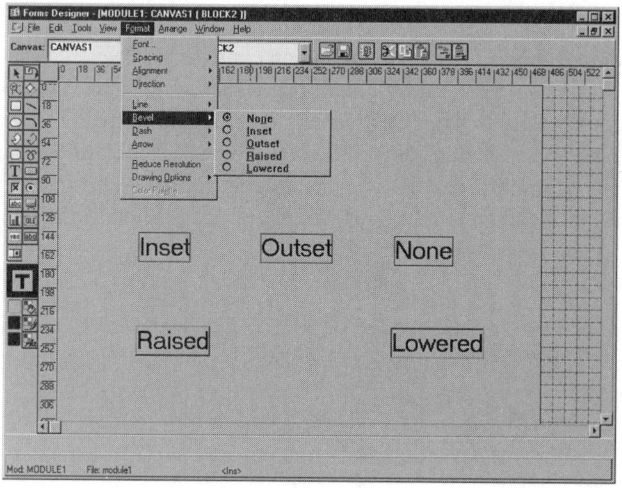

**The Dash Setting** The *Dash* setting changes the lines or borders from a solid line to a dashed line. Figure 13.22 illustrates the menus and examples of the settings.

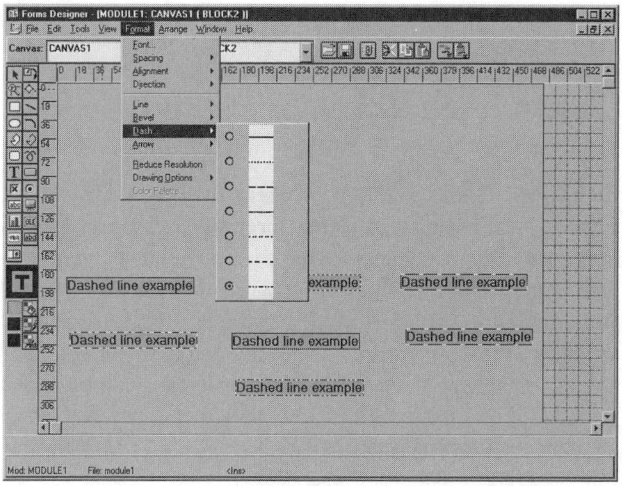


**FIG. 13.22**
The Dash menu options and examples.

**The Arrow Setting** The *Arrow* places an arrowhead at the end of a line. Figure 13.23 displays the Arrow submenu and options.

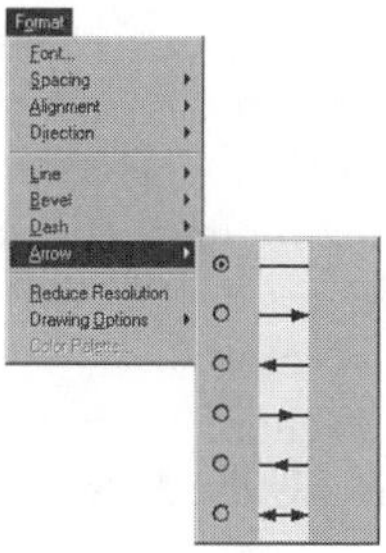


**FIG. 13.23**
The Arrow line options.



**The Reduce Resolution Option** The *Reduce Resolution* option works on images by reducing the quality of the selected image. When reducing the image size, forms tries to maintain the original resolution. The smaller image may not need the higher resolution. Lowering the resolution may save memory as well as disk storage.

**The Drawing Options** The *Drawing Options* selection has a submenu with four options: general, arc, rounded rectangle, and image, as shown in Figure 13.24.

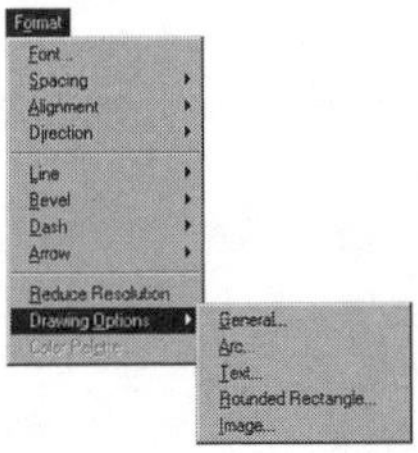


**FIG. 13.24**
The Drawing Options submenu.

**The General Option** The *General* option opens the General Drawing Options dialog box, shown in Figure 13.25. The dialog box has three sets of settings: *Cap Style, Join Style,* and *Object Creation. Cap Style* specifies whether the end points of lines should be *butt, round,* or *projected. Join Style* specifies whether the corners of rectangles are rendered *bevel, miter,* or *round. Object Creation* settings determine how the objects are created. *Draw from corner* is the default manner, and the image is created or enlarged in the direction the mouse is dragged. *Draw from center* enlarges the object in the opposite direction the mouse is dragged.

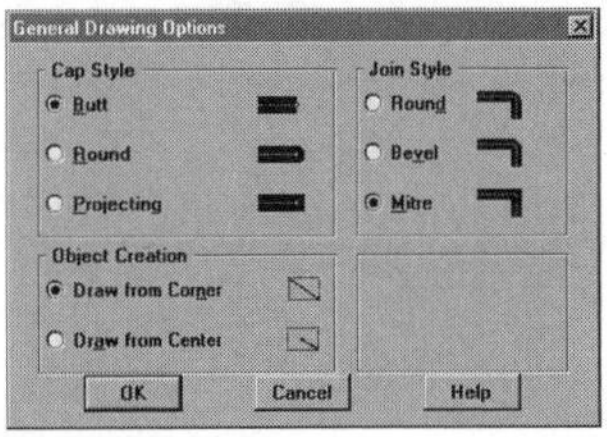


**FIG. 13.25**
The General Drawing Options dialog box.

**The Arc Option** The *Arc* drawing option opens the Arc Drawing Options dialog box. as shown in Figure 13.26. The box contains two sets of check box settings. The first is Arc Fill. The *Pie* setting renders the fill from the center-point of the circle. *Chord* renders the fill with a line segment between the arc's two end points. The second set of check boxes control Arc Closure. The *Closed* setting renders the border of the arc on the entire perimeter of the arc objects fill region. *Open* is used to have the border circumscribe only the arc itself.

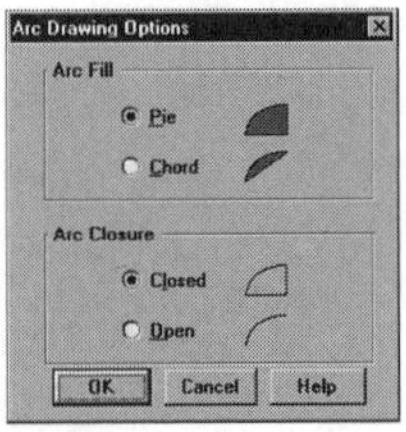


**FIG. 13.26**
The Arc Drawing Options dialog box.

**The Text Option** The *Text* option launches the Text Drawing Options dialog box. The dialog box contains three sets of settings: *Horizontal Origin*, *Vertical Origin*, and *General Options*, as shown in Figure 13.27, and in the following bulleted items:

- *Horizontal Origin* and *Vertical Origin*—Control how boilerplate text objects are aligned.
- *Scalable Fonts*—Determine whether the boilerplate text objects are scaled proportionately when the object is resized.
- *Invisible Text*—Determines whether the boilerplate text object is hidden or shown.
- *Fixed Bounding Box*—Determines whether the boilerplate bounding box is resized automatically when the text is resized.
- The *Wraparound*—Determines where text in a boilerplate text object wraps to the next line to fit the bounding box.
- The *Scalable Bounding Box*—Determines whether the bounding box of the boilerplate text can be resized. The settings that you select will remain as the defaults for any subsequent boilerplate created.

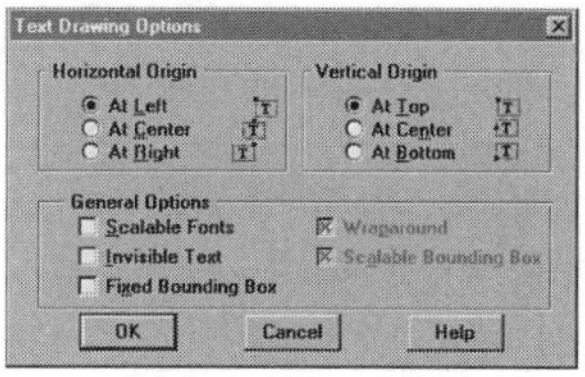


**FIG. 13.27**
The Text Drawing Options dialog box.

***The Rounded Rectangle Option*** The *Rounded Rectangle* option, as shown in Figure 13.28, launches the Rounded Rectangle Drawing Options dialog box. The box contains settings that determine the *Corner Radius* and *Units*. The *Corner Radius* specifies the amount of rounding that Forms applies when drawing the corners of a boilerplate-rounded rectangle object. The *Units* setting specifies the unit of measure. The units can be in inches, centimeters, and points.

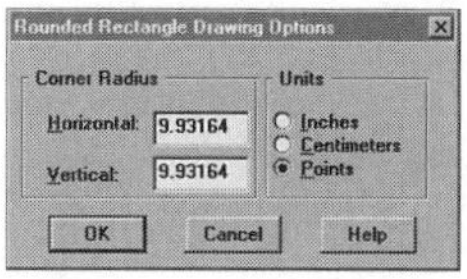


**FIG. 13.28**
The Rounded Rectangle Drawing Options dialog box.



***The Image Option*** The *Image* option launches the Image Drawing Options dialog box. This dialog box controls the *Image Quality* and *Image Dither*. *Image Quality* controls the quality of the image. The higher the quality, the better the screen looks. It also takes longer for the screen to redraw. *Image Dither* is a process by which Forms simulates colors that appear in the image but are not available in the color palette. If the image is not dithered, Forms substitutes colors. Dithered images look better, but the form has slower response. It will take longer to appear or refresh. Figure 13.29 illustrates the Image Drawing Option dialog box.

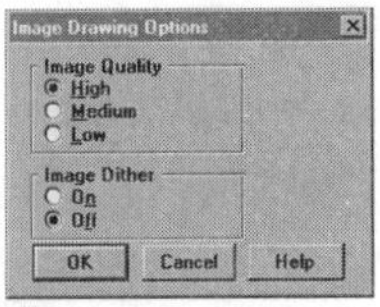


**FIG. 13.29**
The Image Drawing Options dialog box.

## Using the Arrange Pull-Down Menu

The Arrange Pull-Down menu has a variety of options to arrange objects on the canvas. The menu, displayed in Figure 13.30, has three sections. The top section rearranges objects or figures that overlay each other, the middle section aligns objects vertically or horizontally, and the bottom section contains options to group sets of objects.

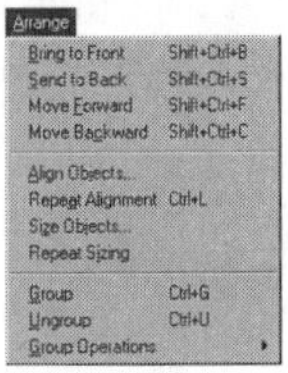


**FIG. 13.30**
The Arrange options menu.

**Moving Objects Forward and Backward** The top section of the Arrange menu contains four options, which arrange objects that overlay each other, as shown in Figure 13.31. On the left side of the canvas are three overlapping objects. The text object, "SAMPLE TEXT," is at the base. The rectangle overlays the text object and is under the oval. These objects are the object piles before the move options are applied. The figures on the right are the object piles after the option is applied.

The *Bring to Front* option brings the selected object to the top of the object pile. In Figure 13.31, the top example places the selected text object on top of the rectangle and oval. The *Send to Back* option places the selected object on the bottom of the pile. In the Figure 13.31, in the second row, the oval was selected. The *Send to Back* option placed the oval beneath the rectangle and text.

In the third row, the *Move Forward* option brings the text object forward one layer. After selecting the text item and the object, the text item is moved above the rectangle. This function differs from the *Bring to Front* option in that it moves the selected object forward one layer or object at a time. The *Move Backward* option also differs from the *Send to Back* option in that it moves the selected object one layer at a time. In the bottom example, the oval is moved back one layer, overlays the text, and is under the rectangle.

**NOTE** The canvas in figure 13.31 was created by using a file called MOVE.FMB. This file is on the CD. You can use this file to practice moving objects by using the menu options. ■

**FIG. 13.31**
Examples of moving overlaid objects by using menu options.

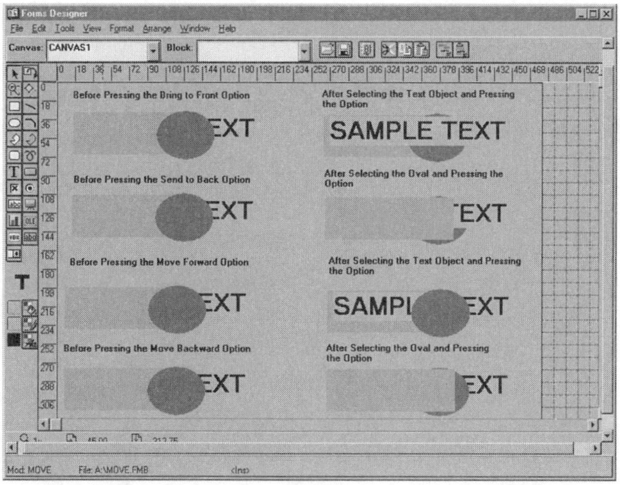


**The Align Objects option** The Align Objects menu option, the formatting tool I use the most, aligns objects vertically and horizontally and also stacks and distributes objects. Pressing Align Objects brings up the Align Objects dialog box, shown in Figure 13.32.

**FIG. 13.32**
The Align Objects dialog box.

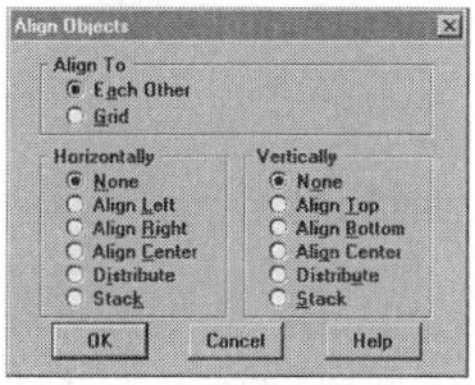


This dialog box has three sets of radio buttons: Align To, Horizontally, and Vertically. The base alignment object is determined by the Align To set of buttons. The options are to align the objects to *each other* or to the closest *grid* line. Selecting the *each other* option does not necessarily place the select objects adjacent to each other. It means the farthest edge of an object in the selected set is the base alignment object. For instance, if a set has two rectangles, the left edge of the farthest rectangle is the base alignment object for a left alignment. The right edge of the farthest to the right rectangle is the base alignment object for a right alignment.



The Horizontally radio buttons determine the horizontal alignment through the following options:

- *None*—The default and will cause no alignment.
- *Alignment Left*—Aligns the left edge of the selected objects.
- *Align Right*—Aligns the right edge of the selected object.
- *Align Center*—Aligns the center of each object.
- *Distribute*—Moves the selected objects an equal distance without moving the left-most and right-most objects.

- *Stack*—Places the selected objects so that their sides touch each other and there is no space between the objects.

Figure 13.33 contains examples of the various Horizontally settings. The alignments are based on the *each other* setting.

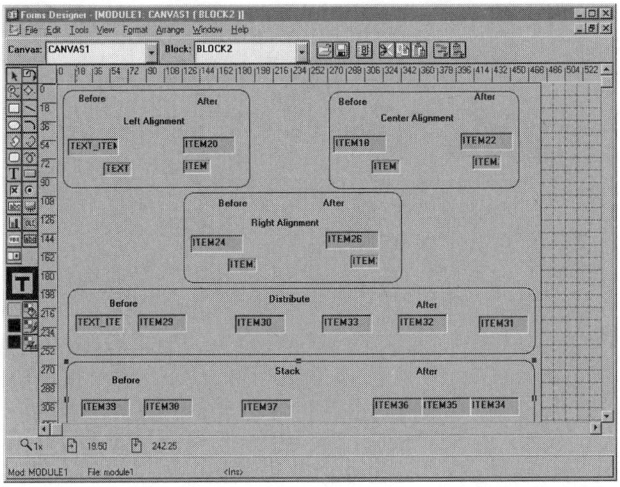


**FIG. 13.33**
Examples of Horizontally alignment options.

The Vertically radio buttons determine the vertical alignment of objects through the following options:

- *None*—The default and causes no alignment.
- *Alignment Top*—Aligns the top of each object in the set.
- *Alignment Bottom*—Aligns the bottoms of the selected objects.
- *Alignment Center*—Aligns the vertical center of each object.
- *Distribute*—Moves the selected objects an equal distance without moving the top-most and bottom-most objects.
- *Stack*—Places the objects so that the top or bottom edges abut.

Figure 13.34 illustrates the various Vertical settings.

**NOTE** When I design a screen, I use Arrange options extensively. I first position the fields and boilerplate by eyeballing them. At this point, I am interested only in relative positions. When the objects are roughly in place, I select the items and objects on the first row. I then align the remainder of the objects, using this row as the base.

The *Repeat Alignment* option is a short-cut option for when the same alignment is repeated on another set of objects. It performs the same alignment performed the last time the Alignment dialog box was used, and saves one step over the normal *Align Objects* option.

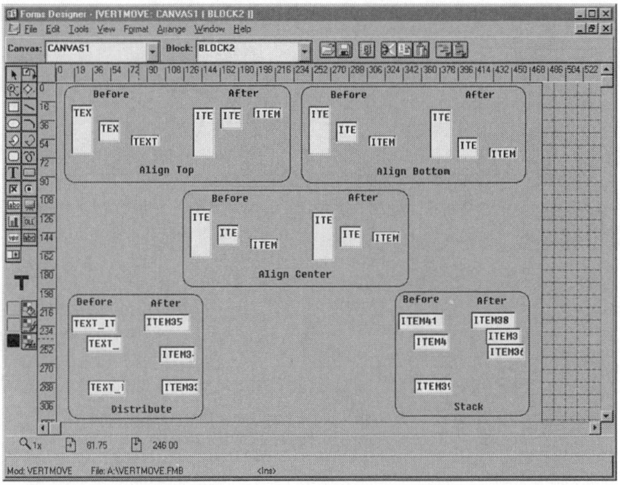


**FIG. 13.34**
Examples of Vertically alignment options.

**Resizing Objects** The *Size Objects* option makes the vertical or horizontal size of a set of selected objects the same. Pressing the option brings up the Size Object dialog box, as shown in Figure 13.35. This dialog box contains three sets of settings: *width*, *height*, and *units*.

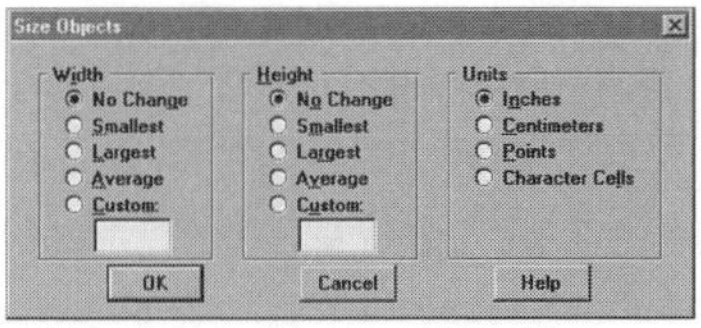


**FIG. 13.35**
The Size Objects dialog box.

The Width radio buttons set the width of the selected items, and the Height radio buttons control the height of the selected items. The two sets of buttons have the following five settings:

- *No Change*—Default settings, and do not cause resizing.
- *Smallest*—Changes the size of all the selected items equal to the size of the smallest item.
- *Largest*—Changes the size of all the selected items equal to the size of the largest item.
- *Average*—Computes the average size for the selected objects, and applies this value to all the objects in the set.
- *Custom*—Puts in a specific value and is used with the *Units* radio buttons. The value in the *Custom* setting can represent inches, centimeters, points, or character cells.

Figure 13.36 displays examples of the various settings.

The *Repeat Sizing* option resizes additional sets of objects and applies the last settings selected in the Sizing Objects dialog box.

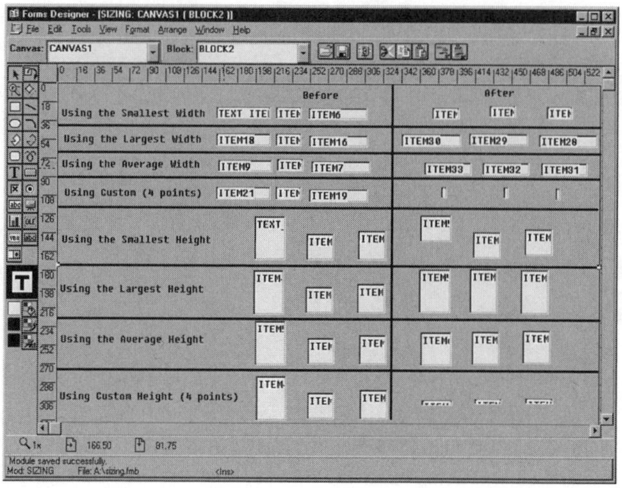


**FIG. 13.36**
Examples of Resizing Objects.

**Using Object Groups** When you are formatting the canvas, groups of objects often have the similar properties or are positioned closely together. It is convenient to format common sets of objects at the same time. Designer gives you the ability to format multiple items in one formatting operation. Selection is done by clicking each object while holding down the shift key. When the developer selects an item from a different set, all of the items in the previous set are deselected. If you want to perform another procedure on the original set, you must select each item again. This can be a time-consuming process if you select the same object sets repeatedly.

**The Group and Ungroup Options** The *Group* option allows the developer to avoid having to reselect set of objects. Selecting this option places all currently selected objects into a group. When another object is selected, the group items are deselected. However, when one item in the group is reselected, all of the items in the group are re-selected. This saves the developer the time spent reselecting each of the objects. Selecting the group and choosing the *Ungroup* option eliminates the grouping.

**The Group Operations Options** At the bottom of the Arrange submenu is the *Group Operations* option. This option opens the submenu displayed in Figure 13.37 and modifies groups by using the following options:

- *Select Parent*—Selects the parent group of the selected object.
- *Select Children*—Selects all of the children of the current group.
- *Add to Group*—Makes the selected object a child of a group.
- *Remove from Group*—Removes the currently selected object from a group without destroying the group.

# Using the Layout Editor Tool Palette

The Layout Editor Tool Palette is located on the left side of the Layout Editor. It contains a variety of options that allow the developer to place graphic objects, data objects, and pushbuttons on a canvas. It also has options to color the objects on the canvas. The function of the button is displayed when the cursor is placed over the button.

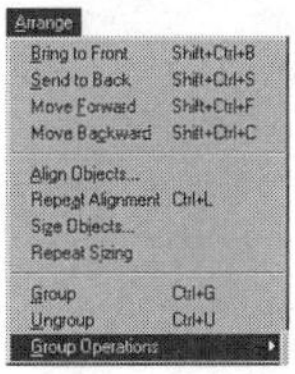


**FIG. 13.37**
The Group Operations options.

## The Select Tool

The *Select* tool is located on the first row and first column of the palette, and has a picture of an arrow on it. Select is the default tool and allows the cursor to be used as a selection device. Whenever the developer wants to perform an action, the item(s) must be selected by clicking it with the cursor. This button may be clicked when another tool has been selected and the developer no longer wants to use the tool.

## The Rotate Tool

The button on the first row, second column, is the *Rotate* function, which rotates objects. In order to rotate the object, you must select the object, grab a handle, and pull the object. As the object is moved, a status line appears showing the current angle of rotation. If you double-click the button, you can make the Rotate tool the default. This allows you to select and rotate objects without switching tools. Figure 13.38 illustrates a rotating graphic object.

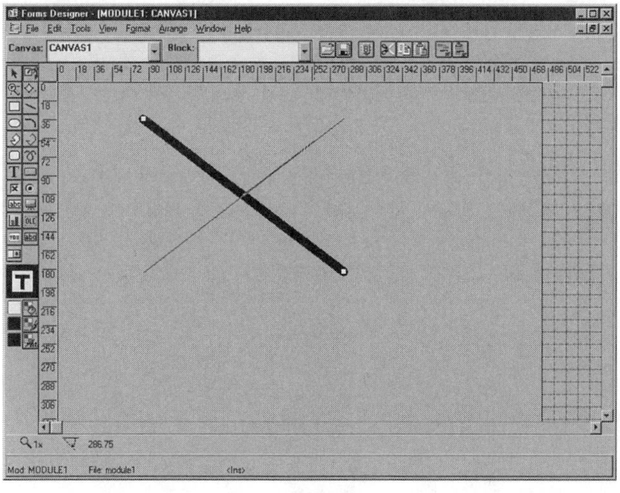


**FIG. 13.38**
Rotating a graphic object.

***The Magnify Tool*** The *Magnify* tool on the second row, first column, has a picture of a magnifying glass on it. This tool is the same as the Zoom In function on the View options menu. Magnify causes objects in the Layout Editor to appear as if they had increased in size.

The objects will remain the same size during the zooming operation. When using this function, the center of the newly displayed area is the spot where you clicked the cursor. This gives the developer more control over the area to enlarge than the Zoom In menu function.

## The Reshape Tool

The *Reshape* tool changes the shape of an object. The tool allows the developer to change the sweep angle of an arc to the desired angle. The default angle of the arc is 90 degrees. The use of this tool is necessary to change it to another value. When performing freehand graphics, the tool causes special drag handles to appear on the object. These handles can be used to reshape the object. The Reshape tool allows the developer to move any vertex (corner) of a rectangle or rounded rectangle that has been rotated to another position.

## Graphic Shape Tools

The Layout Editor Tool Palette uses eight tools to create graphic shapes.

**The Rectangle Tool** The tool in the third row, first column, is the *Rectangle* tool. It has a square rectangle as a button symbol. You can create a rectangle by placing the cursor at the position where you want a corner to exist. Then click and drag the frame to obtain the desired size. If you want to ensure that the object is a square, hold the shift key while dragging the object.

**The Line Tool** The tool on the third row, second column, is the *Line* tool. Draw a line by clicking where you want the original endpoint to be, and then drag the line to the other endpoint. Holding the shift key down while dragging the line ensures that it is vertical, horizontal, or diagonal.

**The Ellipse Tool** The *Ellipse* tool is located on the fourth row, first column. This tool is used to draw circles or ellipses. To draw a symbol, place the cursor at the intersection of the top and left most edge axis'. Hold the button down and the shape the box that will appear. The box is a temporary device showing where the edges of the ellipse will appear. The ellipse will fit inside the box. If the box is square, a circle will be drawn.

**The Arc Tool** The *Arc* tool is used to draw an arc. To draw an arc, position the cursor where you want the first tip of the arc to begin. Press and hold the mouse button while dragging the arc. The end point of the arc will be the position of the mouse insertion point when the mouse button is released.

**The Polygon TTool** The *Polygon* tool, on the fifth row, first column, creates polygons. Do this by selecting the tool, clicking once at each vertex, and double-clicking on the last vertex. The editor completes the polygon frame by drawing a line from the last vertex to the beginning of the frame. Holding down the shift key causes the line segment to be vertical, horizontal, or diagonal.

The *Polyline* tool creates a shape similar to a polygon, except that the last vertex is not automatically joined to the first vertex when double-clicked.

**The Rounded Rectangle Tool** The *Rounded Rectangle* tool beneath the Polygon tool operates the same as the Rectangle tool except that the object has rounded edges.

**The Freehand Tool** The last of the graphic tools, *Freehand* tool, is next to the Rounded Rectangle button on the sixth row, second column. It creates freehand objects. Use the click-and-drag method to draw the objects.

Figure 13.39 contains examples of each type of graphic. The area inside several of the objects is white, and is called *fill*. It can be made a specific color. Coloring the fill is discussed later in the chapter.

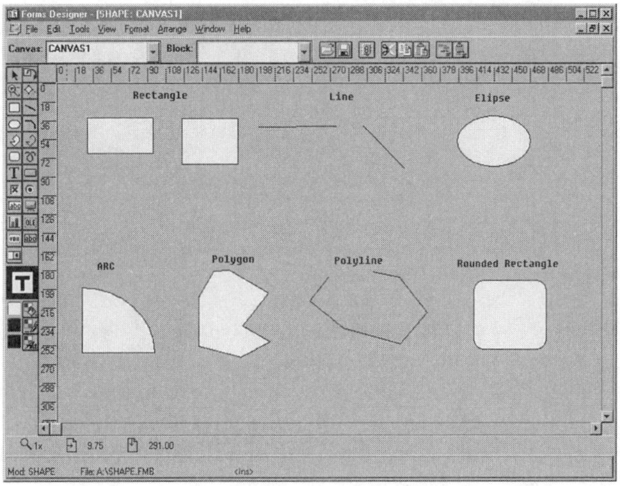


**FIG. 13.39**
Examples of the Graphic Objects created by the Tool Palette.

# Item Tools

The Tool Palette also contains 11 buttons used to place item objects on the canvas. These items consist of a variety of objects used to display text, represent data in a graphic manner, or display data.

The following sections describe the tools used to create the various control items.

**The Text Tool** The *Text* tool on the seventh row, first column, creates and modifies boilerplate text, which is static text that appears on the form. Text explains objects and procedures to the user. The preceding chapter discussed field labels that may be edited on the Items tab of the Default block dialog. When the block is created, the labels become text—the same type of item created by the Text tool. Text or boilerplate can only be modified by using this tool.

When you click the Text tool and make it active, the cursor changes to a crosshair. Clicking the cursor button causes an empty text frame to appear at the spot of the crosshair, and you can begin entering text into the frame. If the cursor is moved over the text frame, it changes to a white "I." Positioning the cursor over a letter and clicking the mouse places the input focus at that position. Text may be entered or deleted at that point. Figure 13.40 shows a text item, and the active cursor is the cross-beam." The input focus is a vertical line following the word "is."

You can select and move text frames by using the regular selection tool. The Text tool is used only for entering and removing text for the frame.

**FIG. 13.40**
The text item with the input focus after the word *is*, and the cursor over the word *sample*.

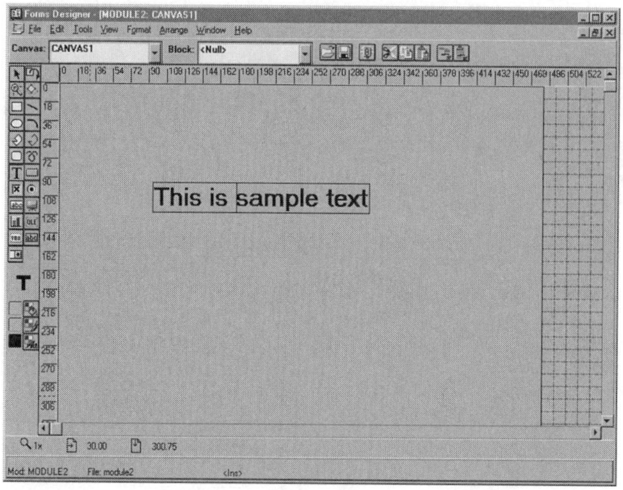


**The Button Tool** The *Button* tool (with an image of a button), next to the Text item, creates buttons. Use buttons to initiate a PL/SQL script. The Employee form used in Chapter 11 has a number of buttons that were used to scroll, query, and save records. You make this tool active by clicking it. After you click it, a default button appears on the canvas at the position where the cursor is clicked. You can resize the button by using the normal tools. Tying the button to the PL/SQL trigger is discussed in a later chapter.

**The Check Box Item** The Check Box item is a graphic item that represents two distinct data values. If the data item equals one value, the check box contains a check mark. If the data item does not equal the value, it remains unchecked. The item is created by first making the Check Box tool active, and then clicking on the spot where it is to be placed. You can resize and reposition it by using the normal selection techniques.

**The Radio Button Tool** Two concentric circles represent the *Radio Button* item. This item represents a data item that has a defined set of data values. Each radio button represents a distinct value in the set of values. When you select the value, the inner circle of the button is black. This circle is white when the value is not selected. Radio buttons come in sets, and only one of the values may be selected at a given time.

**The Text Item Tool** A *Text* item holds database or editable values. When you create a default block, the selected values are placed in text items. The button that activates the Text item tool has an "abc" enclosed by a box symbol. You can resize and move this item by using the normal selection techniques.

**The Image Tool** The *Image* tool on row nine, column two, shows a colored image of a country scene on the button and holds images imported into the form. To create an image item, select the tool and click the spot for the image. You can resize and move the image. Image items are displayed with an "X."

**The Chart Tool** The *Chart* tool creates an object that displays a chart created by Oracle Graphics. This item will also have an "X" displayed within the object box. You can resize and move the object by using the normal tools.

**The OLE Tool** The *Ole* tool, denoted by the word "OLE," creates an OLE container. OLE containers bring objects created by other products into the form.

**The VBX Tool** The *VBX* tool creates an item that will hold a VBX control. A VBX control is a Visual Basic standard control developed outside Oracle Forms.

**The Display Item Tool** The *Display Item* tool creates display items similar to text items, except values cannot be entered or edited. Values are assigned to this item programmatically during runtime. The button for this tool contains a grayed out "abc," enclosed by a box.

**The List Item Tool** The final item tool, on row 12, column 2, is the *List Item* tool, which creates a list of values that can be displayed in the form of a pick list, combo box, or text list. The lists contain predefined sets of acceptable values. The user uses the lists to select a value for entry into the field.

## Object Coloring Tools

At the bottom of the Tool Palette are colored buttons adjacent to three display boxes. These buttons are the color tools. Most Oracle items, such as a text item, have three color components: *line*, *fill*, and *text*. When an item is created, Designer places a border, or line, around the object and colors the line. Designer also colors the second component which is the area within the border, or fill Finally, Designer colors the third component which is the text itself. The color buttons are used to change the color of each of these components. Figure 13.41 illustrates the three components by using a boilerplate text item.

**FIG. 13.41**
The three color-components: fill, line, and text.

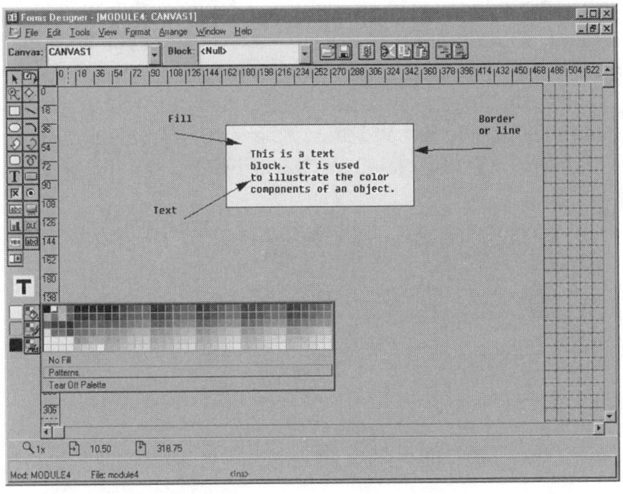

The color tools are used to color each of the three components. The top tool is the *Fill Color* tool and colors the item fill. The middle tool is the *Line Color* tool and colors the border or surrounding line. It may also be used to color any line drawn on the canvas. The bottom tool is the *Text Color* tool, which colors text. The three tools allow the developer to color components separate from each other.

**Using the Color Tools** You color items by first selecting the item on the canvas, and then selecting the appropriate color tool, which brings up a color palette. You then select the appropriate color by clicking the color button. This closes the palette and changes the color of the selected item. Figure 13.42 shows the Fill color palette. The cursor is shown as a white arrow. The color button on which the cursor is positioned to pick is raised. It lowers as the cursor is moved. As the cursor is dragged across the palette, other color buttons are raised. You click the color button to color the fill area with the selected color.

**NOTE** You may practice the coloring techniques on the SHAPE.FMB or the EMPCH13.FMB files contained on the CD. The EMPCH13 file can be executed. It will show you what colored text will look like when records are fetched into the form.

In Figure 13.41, you might notice the display windows to the left of the color tools. These are the selected color windows. As you drag the cursor across the palette, the color in the window changes. When the palette is closed, these windows show the color of each component for the selected item. In addition, above the tools is an area with a "T." This area also shows the component color. The "T" represents the color of the text. In the case of Figure 13.41, the text color is black. Two boxes surround the figure "T." The inner box represents the fill color. In the example, it is a red color or the color of the raised button on the palette. The outer box is the line or border color. The selected color is black.

***Using the Color Palette Options*** At the bottom of the three palettes are several options. The *Fill* tool has three, the *Line* tool two, the *Text* tool one. The *Tear Off Palette* option, available on each of the three palettes, is used when the developer wants the palette to remain open. The feature is useful when the developer wants to color a number of items. When the palette is in the normal mode, it closes after each selection. When the palette is in the *Tear Off* mode it remains open. You can select this option by clicking the *Tear Off Palette* button on the palette. This causes the button to disappear and the palette to turn into a dialog box with a title. The dialog box can then be selected and dragged to any location on the screen. Figure 13.42 shows the Fill Color palette after the option has been selected and dragged to another area.

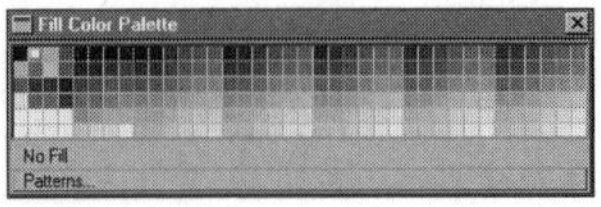


**FIG. 13.42**
The Fill Color Palette after you have selected the Tear Off Palette button.

The *No Fill* and *No Line* options are on the Fill palette and Line palette, respectively. When you select these options, the fill or line will be transparent.

**NOTE** I generally select these two options for any boilerplate text I place on a form. I make the line or border transparent. I think the text is more readable without an enclosing box. I also shut the fill off because it makes the text look like it was written directly on the canvas.

***Using the Fill Pattern Option*** The last option appears on the Fill palette (see Figure 13.43). It is the *Pattern* option, which places a pattern in the fill area of an item. Clicking this option brings up the Fill Pattern palette, which has three sections. These sections consist of the pattern, the foreground color, and the background color.

The top section contains the various patterns available. As the cursor moves over the pattern button, the button raises, indicating that this is the pattern that can be selected. The pattern is also displayed in the Fill boxes on the Tool palette. When you click a button, the selected object's fill area receives the pattern.

At the bottom of the Fill Pattern Palette are two arrows used to color the background and texture portions of the fill area. The left arrow, when selected, opens a color palette that colors the texture portion of the pattern. The right arrow opens a color palette that colors the background portion of the pattern.

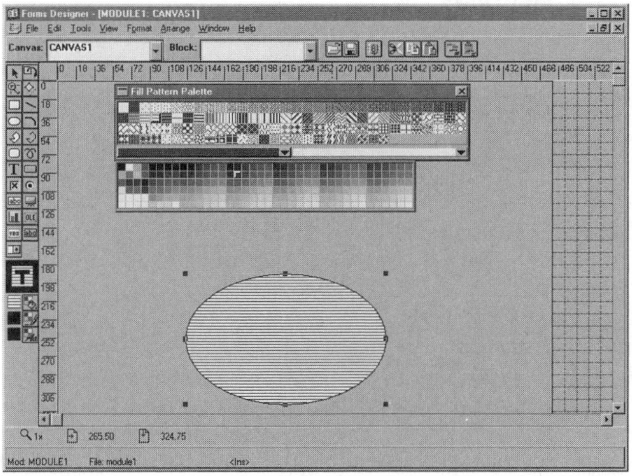


**FIG. 13.43**
The Fill Pattern Palette and the texture color palette.

# Canvas Properties

The canvas is the Forms object that holds the objects that interact with the user. It is where you place the text items, buttons, or other objects. Before you can begin formatting the objects placed on the canvas, however, some of the Canvas properties need to be reviewed and updated.

You read earlier that most of the objects in a Form have properties. A property is a value that controls an attribute of an object. For example , each form has a number of items. One of the properties of an item is *Item Type.* The valid values for this property are as follows:

- Check box
- Display item
- Image
- Button
- Radio group
- List item
- Text item
- VBX control
- OLE container
- User area

The Item Type property or attribute determines the item. Objects have a variety of properties that determine what the object is, the color of the object, or a host of other attributes. Because the canvas is an important Forms object, it has a set of properties that control it.

## Opening the Canvas Property Sheet

You can edit Object properties by opening the object's property sheet. Do this by using one of the methods in the following list:

- Double-click the object in the Layout Editor.
- Double-click the object in the Object Navigator.
- Select the object in the Layout Editor or Object Navigator and select the Properties option on the Tools menu.

**NOTE** You can open the property sheet for most objects by using any of the three methods. However, you can open the canvas property sheet by using only the third method.

## The Canvas Property Sheet

A property sheet contains several sections. At the top are series buttons, the first two of which copy and paste properties from one property sheet to another. The remainder of the buttons are discussed in Chapter 15 during a discussion of property classes. Below the buttons is the name of the object and an update window. The window changes property values and contains the value of the property currently selected. In Figure 13.44, the Font Style property is selected. The value in the update window pertains to this property. When one of a specific set of values can be selected, a pick list arrow appears to the right of the update window. This opens a pick list or list of values displaying the various settings. Below the update window are the properties.

Figure 13.44 contains a typical canvas property sheet.

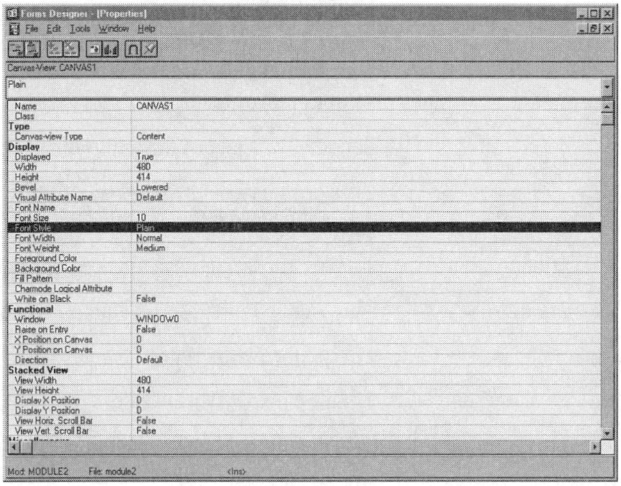


**FIG. 13.44**
A typical canvas property sheet.

Table 13.1 contains a description of the various canvas properties.

**Table 13.1 Canvas Properties**

| Property | Description |
|---|---|
| Background Color | The color of the canvas. |
| Bevel | Determines the appearance of the canvas edge. The *raised* setting makes the canvas appear that it is above the overlaying object. The *lowered* setting makes it appear it is lower. The *none* setting causes no bevel to appear. |
| Canvas-View Type | The type of canvas or view. The options are: *content, stacked, vertical toolbar,* and *horizontal toolbar*. Content is the default. It indicates that the canvas is a base canvas. The stacked setting indicates that the canvas can be displayed over a content canvas. A vertical toolbar is a vertical canvas that contains buttons or tools. A vertical toolbar is a horizontal canvas that contains buttons or tool. The toolbar canvases also overlay the content canvas. |
| Charmode Logical Attribute | Specifies the name of a character mode logical attribute defined in an Oracle Terminal resource file. |
| Class | The name of the property class supplying values to the canvas properties. |
| Comment | This property records pertinent information about the canvas. When you select this property, a special button |



*continues*

**Table 13.1 Continued**

| Property | Description |
|---|---|
| | appears on the right of the update window. Clicking this button opens the default text editor. This property is seldom if ever used. |
| Direction | Specifies the layout direction for bi-directional objects. |
| Displayed | This property determines whether the canvas is displayed. The values are true and false. |
| Display X Position | The X coordinate for a stacked canvas's top-left corner. |
| Display Y Position | The Y coordinate for a stacked canvas's top-left corner. |
| Fill Pattern | The pattern used on the canvas. |
| Font Name | The default font for all items placed on the canvas. |
| Font Size | The default font size for all items placed on the canvas. |
| Font Style | The default font style for all items placed on the canvas. |
| Font Weight | The default weight for all items placed on the canvas. |
| Font Width | The default font width for all items placed on the canvas. |
| Foreground Color | The color of the canvas foreground. |
| Height | The height of the canvas. |
| Name | The name of the canvas. |
| Raise on Entry | Determines how Forms displays the canvas when the operator navigates to an item on the canvas. It is used when a window displays multiple canvases. A value of *false* raises the view to the top only if the target item is behind another view. A value of *true* always raises the canvas to the top when navigating to an item. |
| View Height | Determines the height of the view. This property is used when the canvas-view type is stacked. |
| View Horizontal Scroll Bar | Determines whether the horizontal scroll bar will be visible. This property is used when the canvas-view type is stacked. |
| View Vertical Scroll Bar | Determines whether the vertical scroll bar will be visible. This property is used when the canvas-view type is stacked. |
| View Width | Determines the width of the view. This property is used when the canvas-view type is stacked. |
| White on Black | Specifies that the object is to appear on a monochrome bitmap display device as white text on a black background. |

| Property | Description |
|---|---|
| Width | The width of the canvas. |
| Window | The name of the form window that will display the canvas. |
| Visual Attribute Name | The name of the visual attribute supplying values for the font, background, and foreground properties. |
| X Position on Canvas | Determines the X coordinate of the top- left corner of the canvas. |
| Y Position on Canvas | Determines the Y coordinate of the top- left corner of the canvas. |

## Reviewing and Setting Canvas Properties

Several canvas-view settings should be reviewed on each form. The first is *Canvas-Type*. The developer needs to determine whether the canvas is a *content* type or *stacked*. *Content* type canvases are base canvases and completely replace underlying canvases. Only one content canvas can be shown at a time. *Stacked* canvases can be displayed over a *content* canvas. Stacked canvases can be displayed without entirely covering a content canvas.

The developer also needs to check the width and height settings. When the form window is fully maximized, the canvas may not completely cover the window. The resolution of the monitor controls the size of the displayed area. Higher resolution screens will show a canvas in a smaller area than lower resolution. The developer should always determine whether the content canvas is the proper size. If the canvas is stacked, the developer must also determine the desired size of the canvas.

The final setting on the canvas is the *Background Color*. Canvases can be colored to improve their presentation. Selecting the *Background Color* property causes a pick list button to appear on the right of the update window. When you select the pick list, it brings up the Colors dialog box as shown in Figure 13.45. The developer can scroll through the box until the desired color is identified. Selecting the color and clicking the OK button changes the color of the canvas.



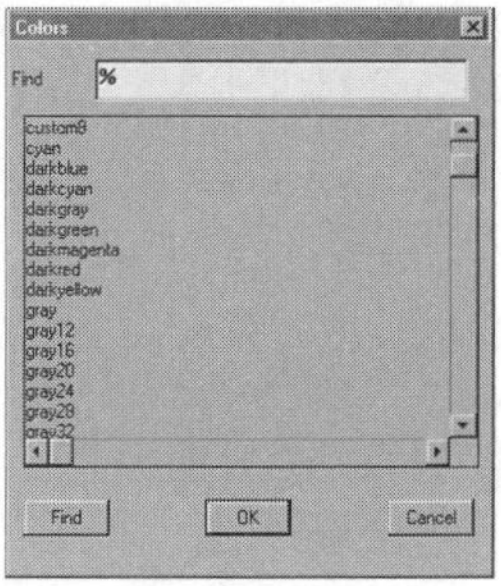


**FIG. 13.45**
The Color dialog box.

**TIP** When you attempt to change the color of the background, you get a Dialog box that identifies various colors with a value formatted similar to "r0g80b88." The number represents a blend of red, green, and blue. I find it extremely difficult to determine the color I want by using this number.

To identify the color I want and its number, I use the Layout Editor. To do so, I open the color palette and place the cursor over the desired color. Its number is visible on the bottom-left of the screen, as shown in Figure 13.46. Copy this number down, return to the property sheet, and select the number for the Color dialog box. This method will save you a lot of trial and error.

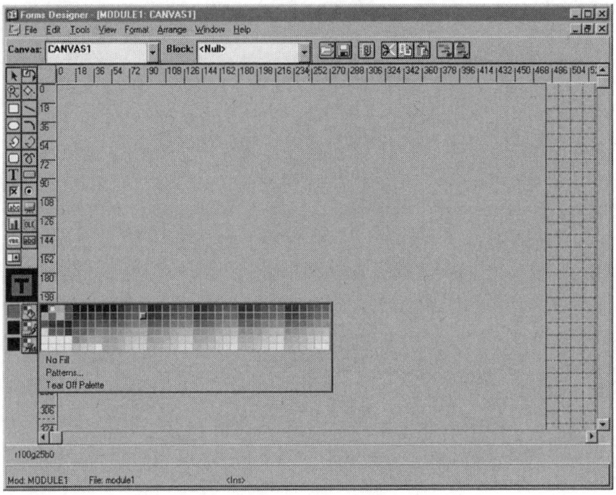


**FIG. 13.46**
Identifying the color number by using the color palette on the Layout Editor.

# Defining Window Properties

Another Form object that should be reviewed during the formatting procedure is the *Window*. A window is the shape or frame that appears over the canvas and controls the amount of canvas that you can see. When the canvas is wider than the window, a horizontal scroll bar appears. This allows the user to view hidden parts of the canvas. When the canvas is longer than the window, a vertical scroll bar appears. When the canvas and the window are the same size, no scroll bars appear.

Table 13.2 contains a list and description of the various window properties.

**Table 13.2 Window Properties**

| Property | Description |
|---|---|
| Background Color | The color of the background. |
| Bevel | Determines the appearance of the window edge. The *raised* setting makes the window appear as if it's above the |

| Property | Description |
|---|---|
| | overlaying object. The *lowered* setting makes it appear lower. The *none* setting causes no bevel to appear. |
| Charmode Logical Attribute | Specifies the name of a character mode logical attribute defined in an Oracle Terminal resource file. |
| Class | The name of the property class supplying values to the window properties. |
| Closeable | Specifies whether the Close command is enabled or disabled for a window. The Close command is available on the window's menu or by double-clicking the box on the top-left corner of the window. This option cannot be applied to a root window. |
| Comment | This property records pertinent information about the canvas. When this property is selected, a special button appears on the right of the update window. Clicking this button opens the default text editor. |
| Direction | This property specifies the layout direction for bi-directional objects. |
| Fill Pattern | The pattern used on the window. |
| Fixed Size | This property determines whether you can resize the window. This property does not apply to root windows. |
| Font Name | The default font for all items placed on the window. |
| Font Size | The default font size for all items placed on the canvas. |
| Font Style | The default font style for all items placed on the window. |
| Font Weight | The default weight for all items placed on the window. |
| Font Width | The default font width for all items placed on the window. |
| Foreground Color | The color of the window's foreground. |
| Height | The height of the window. |
| Horizontal Scroll Bar | This property determines whether secondary windows are displayed with a scroll bar. |
| Horizontal Toolbar | The name of the horizontal toolbar used by the window. |
| Iconifiable | This property determines whether you can turn the window into an icon. This option does not apply to root windows, which can always be iconified. |
| Icon Name | The name of the icon resource you want to represent the window. This property is valid when the iconifiable property is set to true. |

*continues*

**Table 13.2 Continued**

| Property | Description |
|---|---|
| Icon Title | The text screen that appears below an iconified window. |
| Inherit Window | Determines whether the window should display the current form menu. |
| Modal | This property determines whether the window is modal. *Modal windows* require the operator to respond before the window can be closed. |
| Moveable | This property determines whether the operator can move the window. The property does not apply to root windows. They are always moveable. |
| Name | The name of the window. |
| Remove on Exit | This property determines whether the window is automatically hidden when the operator navigates to another window. This setting applies to modeless windows. |
| Title | The expression that appears in the title bar of the window. |
| Vertical Scroll Bar | Determines whether a vertical scroll bar appears on the side of the window. |
| View | The name of the canvas-view that appears in the window. |
| White on Black | Specifies that the object is to appear on a monochrome bitmap display device as white text on a black background. |
| Width | The width of the window. |
| Window Style | This property determines whether the window is used as a *document* window or a *dialog* window. Document windows always remain open within the window frame. Dialog windows are free-floating and the operator can move them outside the application window. |
| Visual Attribute Name | The name of the visual attribute supplying values for the font, background, and foreground properties. |
| Vertical Toolbar | The name of the vertical toolbar used by the window. |
| X Position | Determines the X coordinate of the top- left corner of the window. |
| Y Position | Determines the Y coordinate of the top- left corner of the window. |
| Zoomable | Determines whether the operator can resize the window by using zooming capabilities. This property does not apply to root windows, which are always zoomable. |

**NOTE** When I develop a form, I generally review and modify three properties during the formatting process. I change the *width* and *height* properties to the same size as the canvas. I do not like applications that I have to scroll to see parts of the screen. I like to size the content canvas and root window so that scroll bars do not exist on the window. The third property is the *title*. I place the name of the application in this property. The name will then appear in the Title bar of the window. This saves canvas space for data items.

# Formatting the Employee Form

Chapter 12, "Using Object Navigator to Create Your First Oracle Form," illustrates the creation of the master block form of a master-detail form. This section of the chapter discusses formatting this application. You should find this file on the CD accompanying this book. The name of the file is EMPCH13.FMB. Open the file in Forms Designer.

## Setting the Canvas and Window Properties

The first task to perform is to ensure that the canvas and window cover the entire area of your screen when you maximize the window. You can determine this coverage by running the application and maximizing the window. If you have a vertical or horizontal scroll bar on the window, the canvas is larger than the screen. If you see a white gap on one side of the canvas, the canvas is too short. Figure 13.47 illustrates the EMPCH13.FMB application before the canvas size is changed. Notice the vertical scroll bar and the white space on the right side of the canvas. This indicates that the canvas is longer than the window, but not as wide.

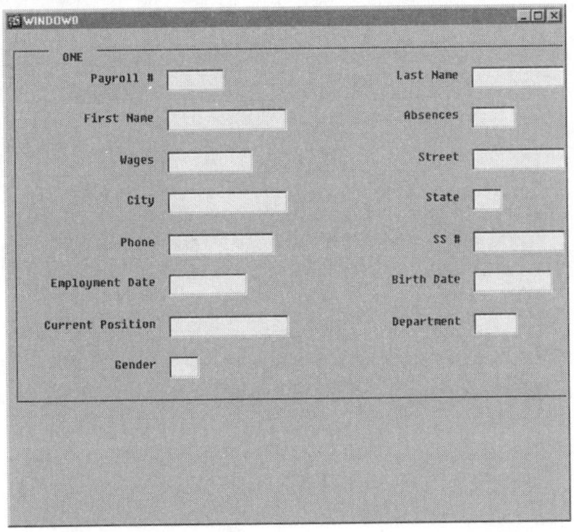


**FIG. 13.47** The initial run of the EMPCH13.FMB file showing that the canvas is longer than the window, but not as wide.

The canvas and window are resized by changing their width and height properties on their property sheets. The following are the tasks needed to modify the canvas property sheet:

1. Open the property sheet for canvas1 by highlighting the canvas on the Object Navigator and selecting the Tools, Properties menu option

Part IV Ch 13

2. Change the width property to 591 and the height property to 378. You may also change the size of the canvas by opening the Layout Editor, selecting the Show View menu option, and dragging the view edges to the proper location.
3. Change the background color to "cyan."

The next step is to modify the form's window properties. Perform the following:

1. Open the property sheet for window0 by highlighting this object and double-clicking the button to the left of the object.
2. Change the title to "EMPLOYEE UPDATE." This name reflects the function of the form.
3. Change the width property to 591 and the height property to 378.

You should now save and run the form. This can be done by pressing the Save button on the tool palette and then the Run button.

Figure 13.48 illustrates the executed form containing these changes.

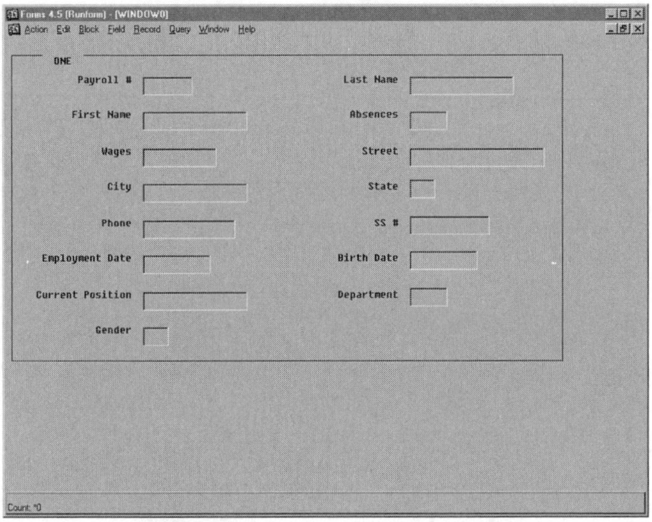


**FIG. 13.48**
The Employee Update form after resizing, adding a window title, and changing the canvas color.

**TIP** When you develop a form, remember to generate and run your form often. If you make a change you don't like, it is easier to identify the change if you haven't made a lot of changes since the last application run.

Looking at the executed form, notice that the fill color of the text items is "cyan." Make the Text item fill color white.

1. Open the Layout Editor.
2. Select each of the text items. Hold the shift key down to avoid deselecting items.
3. Open the Fill Color Palette. Click one of the white colors located on the bottom row of the palette.

**FIG. 13.49**
The Layout Editor after the text items have been selected.

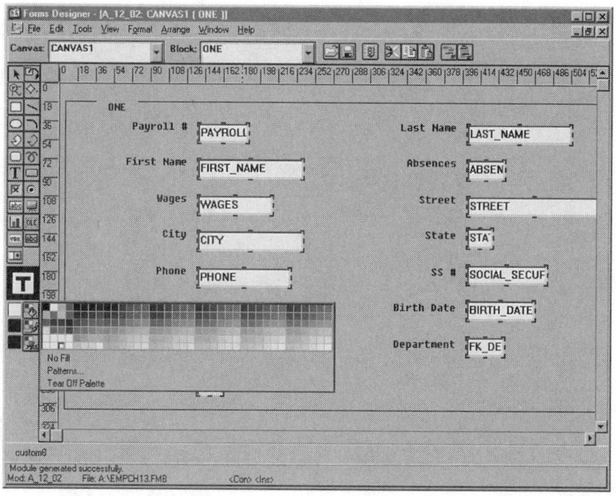


Because the text items are selected, change the font, by using these steps:

1. Select the Format, Font menu option to display the Font dialog box.
2. Select the "MS Sans Serif" font, the "bold" style, and size "8". Press the OK button to change the font format of the selected items.

**NOTE** I prefer to use the MS Sans Serif font, style bold, size 8 for regular use. I use one of the Small Fonts when I need a smaller font.

The next step is to eliminate the block border. When Forms creates a default block, it places a frame around the block. The name of the block is also displayed within the frame.

1. Open the Layout Editor.
2. Select each component of the frame. Press the delete key.

Figure 13.50 shows the executed form with the changes. You might compare this figure to Figure 13.51 to see the effect of the formatting procedures.

The finished Employee Update form is to be a master-detail form, with a block containing tool records and a block containing eyeglass records. The form will also have a button palette, which means that the items on the form need to be moved and arranged to give room for these blocks. In addition, Forms placed the text items when the default form was created. The placement of the items does not make sense to the user, which makes the rearrangement of the text items a mandatory task.

To rearrange the text items, do the following:

1. Select a text item and its associated boilerplate.
2. Drag the selected items to their new location. Eyeball the placement and alignment of the items. Do not worry about perfect placement.
3. Repeat steps 1 and 2 for each of the items on the Employee Update form.

**FIG. 13.50**
The executed Employee Update form after the fonts were changed and the block frame was deleted.

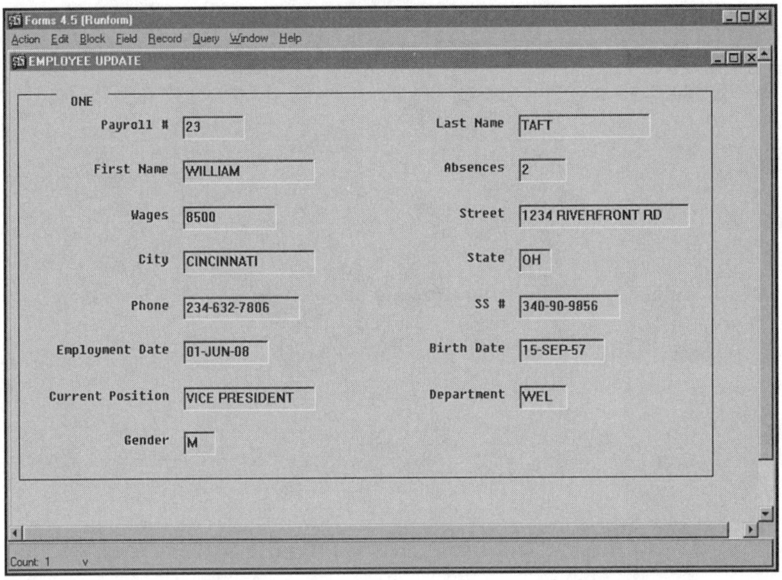


Figure 13.51 shows the Employee Update after the objects have been moved by using the "Eyeball" technique.

**FIG. 13.51**
The Employee Update after the objects have been moved to their approximate location.

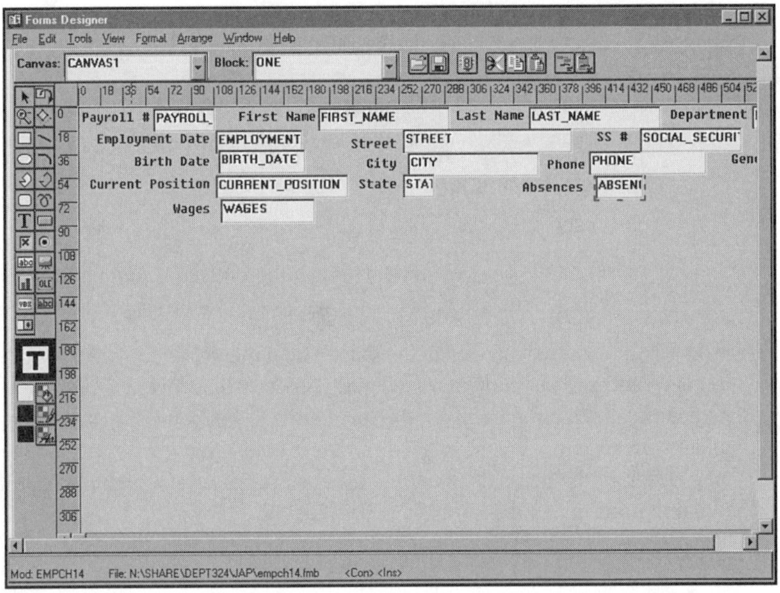

The next move is to place the objects by using the Arrange/Alignment menu option. To do so, perform the following:

1. Select each of the items on the top row.
2. Select the Align Top option from the Align Objects dialog box. This aligns all of the items in the first row.
3. The next step is to select the first-name, street, city, and state items.
4. Use the Vertically Stack option from the Align Objects dialog box. This spreads the items evenly.
5. Then align the items in each row with the street, city, and state items by selecting the items in each row and arranging them by using the Align Top option.

The final task is to perform the justification. Do so by performing the following:

1. Selecting the text items employment-date, birth-date, current-position, and wages and align them by using the Align Left option.
2. Then move the "Employment Date" boilerplate text to the desired position next to the text item.
3. Select the "Birth Date," Current Position," and "Wages" boilerplate and align them by using the Align Right option.

This completes the arrangement of the first data column. Perform the same procedure on the remainder of the data columns, which completes the formatting of the master block. Figure 13.52 illustrates the final format. The form EMPCH14.FMB located on the CD contains the Employee Update form and the modifications discussed in this chapter. This form will be used in subsequent chapters.

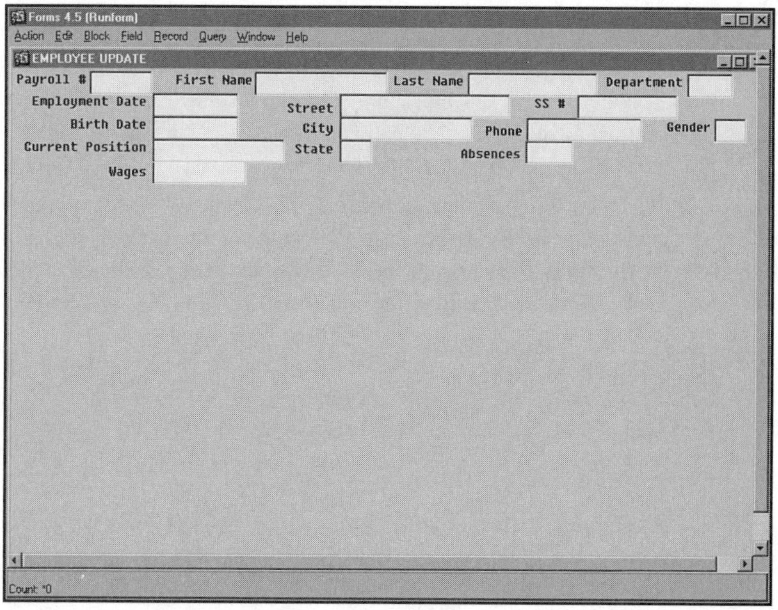


**FIG. 13.52**
The final format of the Employee Update master block.

# Summary

The Layout Editor formats the Form canvas and has several different sections. The Layout menu has three special pull-down menus: View, Format, and Arrange.

The View menu changes the amount of the layout area that can be seen at one time. Showing less area is called Zooming In and showing more area is Zooming Out. The menu also has options to turn on or off some of the design aids. Some of these aids are the rulers, ruler guides, grid, page break, tool palette, or status bar. Finally, this menu has options to let you view stacked views.

The Format menu contains options to change fonts, item spacing, and text alignment. It is also used to change the weight of a line. The line can be changed to a dashed line or an arrow pointer.

The Arrange menu has options to rearrange overlapping objects. It also has a dialog box used to align or resize objects. Objects can also be placed into groups by using this menu.

The canvas-view has a number of properties. Some of the more common ones are the height, width, and background color of the canvas. The window object also has three important properties: height, width, and title.

# From Here...

In the next chapter, you complete the Employee Update form first created in Chapter 11. The next chapter also covers form, block, and item properties, as well as the steps necessary to create a detail block.

# Review Exercises

1. Format the Employee form created in Chapter 12. This form will eventually contain a Tool block, Eyeglass block, and a button palette. The canvas-view for this form will be a content form. Be sure the name of the form is "Employee Update." You may use the form you created in Chapter 12, problem 1, or file A_12_01.FMB from the CD.
2. Format the Department form created in Chapter 12. This form will eventually be called an Overlay the Employee form. The name of the form will be "Department Update." The form canvas should be stacked. The canvas should be positioned so that the form covers only the center portion of the maximized window. You may use the form you created in Chapter 12, problem 2, or file A_12_02.FMB from the CD.

CHAPTER 14

# Creating and Modifying Master-Detail Forms

You can use the EMPCH14.FMB file on the CD to practice procedures discussed in this chapter. ■

**Adding blocks to the Employee form**

This section covers the creation of detail blocks. It shows the modification of the Employee Update form with detail blocks for the Tools and Glasses tables.

**Form properties**

This section covers the various `Form` properties. It also shows how to use the `Current Record Attribute` property and the `Coordinate Information` property. Finally, the section describes how to create and use a visual attribute.

**Block properties**

This section covers the various `Block` properties. The section highlights the use of the `where` and `order of` properties.

**Item properties**

This section covers the various Item properties.

**Item types**

This section covers the creation and use of some of the important item types. These consist of a check box, image, button, radio group, list item, and text item.

**List of values**

This section covers the use and creation of list of values (LOV).

# Adding Blocks to the Employee Update Form

In the previous chapters, the master block of the Employee Update form was created and formatted. The next step in the development of the form is to add detail blocks for the Tools table and the Glasses table. The Employee table used in the master block of the Employee Update form is related to the Tools and Glasses tables in a one-to-many relationship. Detail block tables are usually related to the master block tables in one-to-many relationships. Detail blocks usually contain many records for one record in the block.

Master blocks and detail blocks are joined together by using the primary key/foreign key. The primary key value in the master block is the value of the foreign key in the detail block. When creating the detail block, this relationship will be documented and become part of the form. Forms will create special form objects and triggers to programmatically retain this relationship. This is important functionality, because we want the records displayed in the detail block to pertain to the record in the master block.

## Creating the Tools Detail Block

Detail blocks are created by using the same New Block Options dialog box shown in Chapter 12, "Using Object Navigator to Create Your First Oracle Form". We begin by following the procedure outlined in Chapter 12 to create default blocks. Perform the following steps:

1. Select a block object and press the create button on the Object Navigator tool palette. The General tab of the New Block Options dialog box appears.
2. Enter **Tools** in the Base Table field and **TWO** in the block name. Figure 14.1 shows the dialog box and settings.

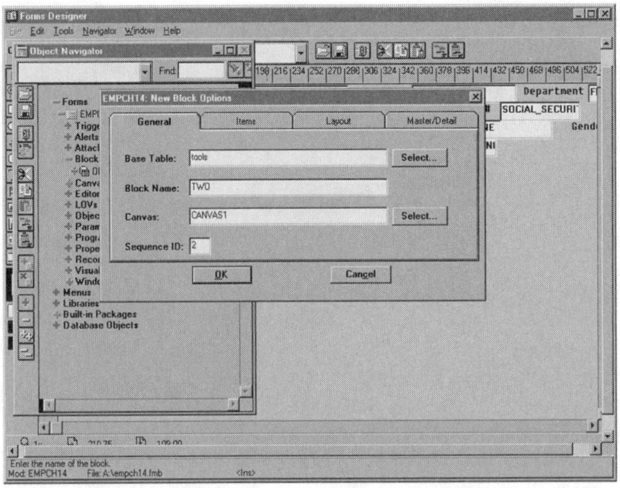


**FIG. 14.1**
Naming the Base Table and Block name of the Tools detail block.

3. Click the Items tab.

4. Click the Select Columns button to retrieve the Tools columns.
5. Select each of the listed fields and modify the their labels.
6. Click the Layout tab. This opens the Layout tab sheet. Figure 14.2 shows the Layout tab and the settings.

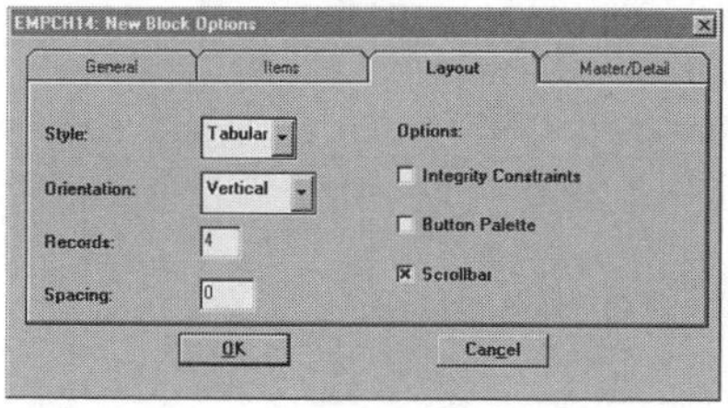


**FIG. 14.2**
Setting the number of Records for the Tools Block and adding a ScrollBar.

7. Change the number of records to 4 and click the scroll bar check box.

   If the block were a master block, you could click the OK button and create the block. However, this block is a detail block related to the Employee master block, which requires the Master/Detail tab sheet to be filled out. This sheet is shown in Figure 14.3. The sheet contains two items. The top item is the Master Block field, which contains the name of the master block. This is the block that will control the records that appear in the detail block.

8. Enter **ONE** as the name of the master block. This is the name of the block on the Employee Update form created for the Employee table.

   The current record from this table will control the records in the detail block you are creating.

   The Join Condition window documents the join condition, which is one or more conditional statements that join the tables from the two blocks. This statement uses the same syntax used in joining tables by using a Select statement. The outer join option is not needed because Forms will always display the master record even if a corresponding detail record does not exist. The join condition in Figure 14.3 joins the blocks by using the payroll_number fields. Payroll_number is the primary key in the Employee table and a foreign key in the Tools table. When entering the join condition, you do not need to use the where keyword. You simply place the names of the join fields and the evaluation operator.

9. Populate the Join Condition window with the following expression: "payroll_number = fk_payroll_number." Figure 14.3 shows the Master/Detail tab sheet and settings.
10. Click the OK button to create the detail block called TWO. The block will be placed on the canvas. Figure 14.4 shows block TWO.



## Block Coordination Objects and Settings

When a detail block is created, some special things occur. The first is that the join field(s) on the detail block are not displayed. In Figure 14.4, the fk_payroll_number field does not appear on block TWO because the field must always have the same value as the corresponding join value on the master block. Forms places the field on the block but sets the item's canvas property to null. This means the field can contain a value but does not appear on the form. Forms also places the name of the master block's join field in the detail block's `Copy From` property. This means the fk_payroll_number field on block TWO will copy its value from the payroll_number field on block ONE. This is an important feature in keeping the records in the two blocks in sync. Because the foreign key field (fk_payroll_number) on block TWO always has the value of the primary key on block ONE, block TWO will always display records that pertain to the record on block ONE. It cannot display records that apply to a different record.

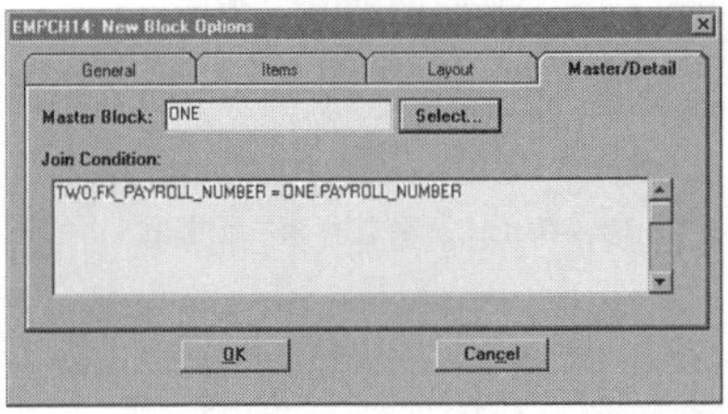


**FIG. 14.3**
The Master/Detail tab sheet and settings that contains the join condition to the master block called ONE.

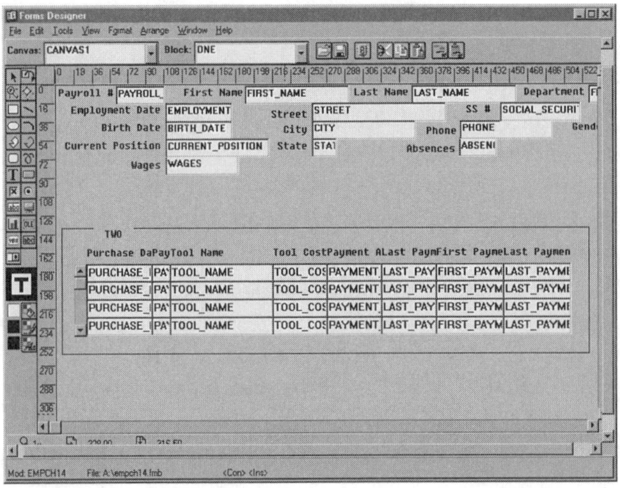


**FIG. 14.4**
The Employee Update form after the detail block TWO is created.

Forms creates several other `Form` objects that work to keep the blocks in sync. It creates a form-level trigger called `On-Clear-Details`. This trigger fires during coordination events and clears the records in the detail block. Forms also creates two block-level triggers on the master block. These are the `On-Check-Delete-Master` and `On-Populate Details` triggers. The former trigger fires during an attempt to delete a master record. This trigger determines whether children records exist for the record. If they do not exist, the record can be deleted. When they exist, an error message appears. The `On-Populate Details` trigger fires during the creation while the form is populating the block. It checks the status of the master record and the value of its primary key field. It then navigates to the detail block to issue the appropriate query.

A final object that Forms creates is a Relations. This object has a set of properties and contains the settings for the join conditions. It is possible to change the join conditions by modifying these properties.

**NOTE** I have listed the triggers and relations created for information purposes. These items are seldom if ever modified. Forms does an excellent job of developing the objects to keep blocks in sync. This is one of the truly nice things about Forms. The developer does not have to worry about developing the synchronization programming.

## Formatting the Tools Block

Formatting block TWO is easier than block ONE because it was created in tabular style. Tabular blocks are usually aligned on the top and stacked horizontally. Forms creates the initial block in this manner. The one problem may be that the items may not be placed in the correct order. This will require the developer to select and drag the items to the proper row location.

Figure 14.5 shows selecting and dragging an item. When the block displays multiple records, each item will consist of a set of item records. Selecting the item will cause the entire set of item records to be selected. Figure 14.5 shows the selected tool_name item being dragged to a new location.

**FIG. 14.5**
Dragging a multiple record item.

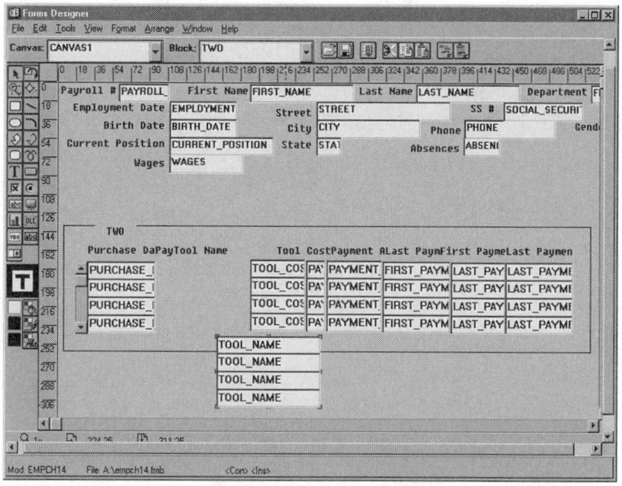


It is more common to reformat boilerplate text on tabular blocks because the text appears above the text item rather than to the left when using the form block style. There is generally not enough room available for the text. In tabular style blocks, the available space is usually equal to the length of the field. This lack of space requires the developer to change the text font size, wrap the text, abbreviate words, or perform a combination of each of the above. Figure 14.6 shows the form after the boilerplate text is reformatted. Try formatting block TWO that was created on form EMPCH14.FMB. Make it similar to Figure 14.6. The Employee Update form after the second block was added and reformatted.

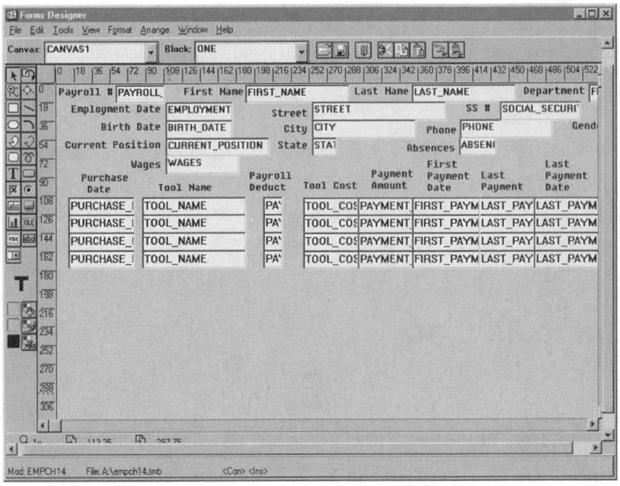


**FIG. 14.6**
The Employee Update form after the second block was added and reformatted.

# Creating the Glasses Block

You create the Glasses block by filling out each of the four tab sheets in the New Block Options dialog box. Use the steps outlined in the "Creating the Tools Block" section and the following setting and instructions to create the block. This block will be the last one added to the form. You can now enter a button palette to the form. While populating the Layout tab, be sure to check the Button Palette check box. Fill out the General, Items, and Layout tab sheets with the settings in Table 14.1. The next section will discuss auto-generating the join condition for the Join Condition tab.

**Table 14.1 Glasses Block Settings**

| Setting | Value |
|---|---|
| Base Table | Glasses |
| Block Name | THREE |
| Style | Tabular |
| Records | 4 |
| Button Palette | Checked |
| Scroll bar | Checked |

**Generating the Block Join Conditions** Instead of entering the join condition, let Forms create the join expression. Forms has the capability to create the join condition between the Glasses block and the Employee block. After a block has been used once as a master block, and the form saved and generated, the block is accessible as a master block by using the Select button on the Master/Detail tab sheet. Clicking this button will activate the Blocks dialog box displayed in Figure 14.7.

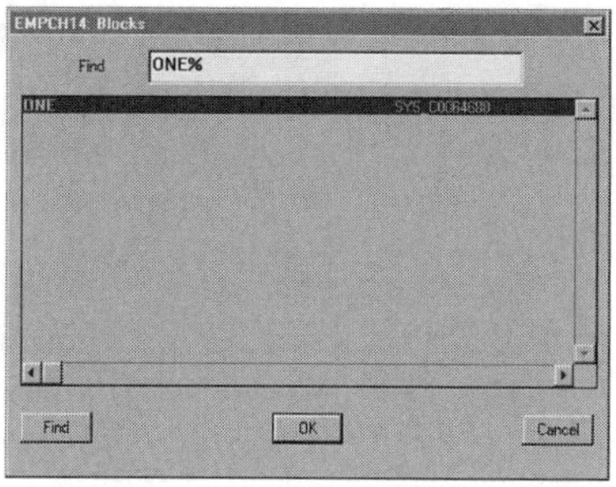


**FIG. 14.7**
The Blocks dialog box displaying master form blocks.

This dialog box will display any master blocks generated by the form. Select the appropriate master block and click the OK button. Forms will fill in the boxes on the Master/Detail tab sheet. Figure 14.8 displays the Master/Detail tab sheet for the Glasses block after selecting block "ONE" as the master block.

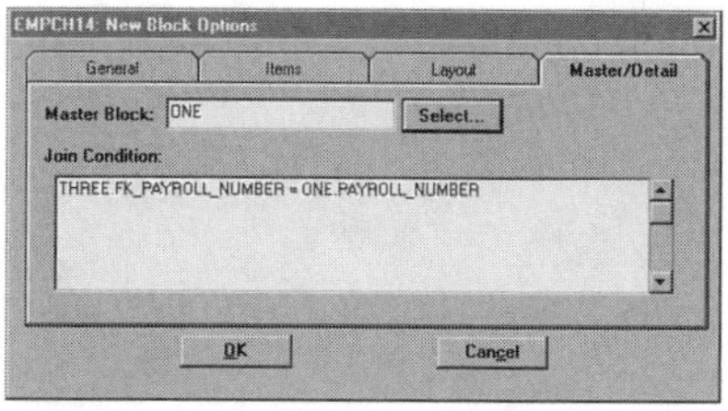


**FIG. 14.8**
The Master/Detail tab sheet after Forms fills in the settings.

**Creating the Glasses (THREE) Block** Clicking the OK button will create detail block THREE, which will contain the records from the Glasses table. Block THREE and the button palette need to be reformatted by using the techniques described earlier. Figure 14.9 shows the completed form, which is now a fully functional application that displays the records from three tables. It has the programming to keep the block records in sync. The user can query, add, update, or delete records from any of the tables. The fields are formatted in a pleasing manner. What is really neat is that this powerful application has been developed thus far without the developer writing a single line of code. There are still some minor modifications that need to be made to the form, which will be discussed in later chapters.

The form has properties that can be modified. The properties are used to change the way the form operates and looks. The next several sections discuss form, block, and item properties.

# Understanding Form Properties

Double-clicking the form button, the first object located on the Object Navigator, activates the form property sheet as shown in Figure 14.10. The various Form properties are described in Table 14.2.

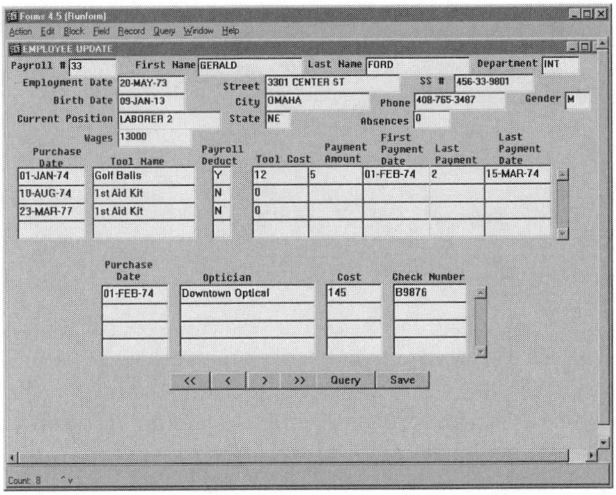


**FIG. 14.9**
The Employee Update Form after final formatting.

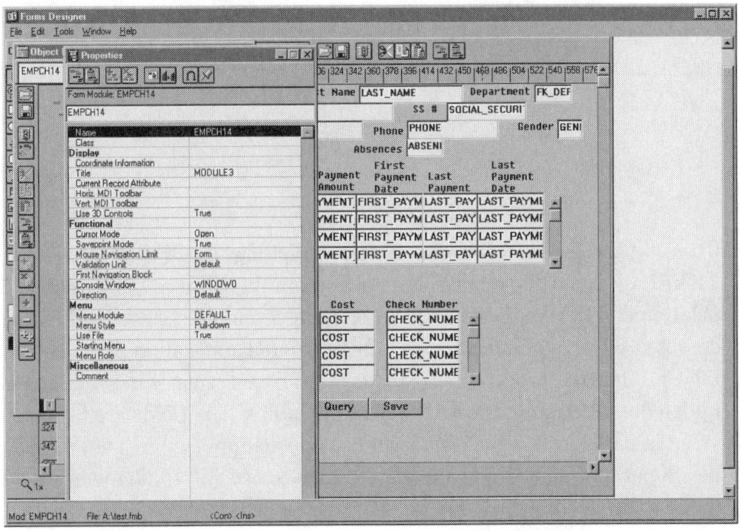


**FIG. 14.10**
The Employee Update form property sheet.

## Table 14.2 Form Properties

| Property Name | Description |
|---|---|
| Class | The name of the property class that supplies the values to the various form properties. Comment Miscellaneous text the developer recorded about the form. |
| Console Window | Determines the console window that will display the status line and message line. It will be displayed at the bottom of the screen. If you do not want a console window, set the property to null. |

| Property Name | Description |
|---|---|
| Coordinate Information | This property consists of a set of values that control the coordinates used in the form. |
| Current Record Attribute | This property contains the name of a visual attribute. The normal record attributes will be superseded by the attributes supplied by the visual attribute when a record is the current block record. |
| Cursor Mode | Determines whether database cursors will remain open across applications. The default is *open*. The cursor will remain open. The *close* setting will close cursors when a commit is issued. |
| Direction | Determines the layout direction of bidirectional objects. |
| First Navigation Block | Determines the initial active block when the form is launched. |
| Horiz.MDI Toolbar | The name of a horizontal toolbar displayed with the form. |
| Menu Module | Contains the name of the compiled menu file to be used with the form. When the property is null, Forms will run the form without a menu. |
| Menu Role | Determines the security role Forms uses to run the menu. This property is included for backward version compatibility. It is not recommended for current applications. |
| Menu Style | Determines the type of menu to be used with the form. Options are *pull-down*, *bar*, and *full-screen*. The default is *pull-down*. |
| Mouse Navigation Limit | Determines where the mouse can navigate. *Form* is the default. It allows the operator to navigate anywhere on the form with the mouse. The *Block* setting allows navigation only within the current block. The *Record* setting allows navigation within the current record. The *Item* setting prevents all mouse navigation. |
| Name | The name of the form. |
| Savepoint Mode | Determines whether savepoints are issued during a session. The default value is *true*, meaning Forms should issue a savepoint at startup or at the start of each Post and Commit process. The *false* setting will cause Forms to issue no savepoints, and that no rollbacks to savepoints are to be performed. |
| Starting Menu | Determines the individual menu in a menu module that should be used as the main menu. |
| Title | Contains the form title. |

*continues*

**Table 14.2 Continued**

| Property Name | Description |
|---|---|
| Use 3D Controls | Causes the form to display items with a 3-dimensional, beveled look. Setting the value to true will cause any canvas with a visual attribute name set to default to be displayed with background color gray. It will also cause the bevel for each item to be lowered. |
| Use File | Specifies the location of the .MMX runfile when you attach a custom menu to a form module. |
| Validation Unit | This property determines the amount of data that may be entered before Forms performs validation. The default is item. This means Forms will validate after the operator navigates from an item. |
| Vert. MDI Toolbar | The name of the vertical toolbar displayed with the form. |

## The Coordinate Information Property

Selecting the Coordinate Information property on the Form property sheet causes a button to appear at the top of the property sheet. Clicking this button causes the Coordinate Info dialog box to appear, as shown in Figure 14.11. This dialog box controls the unit of measure used for height, width, and object placement.

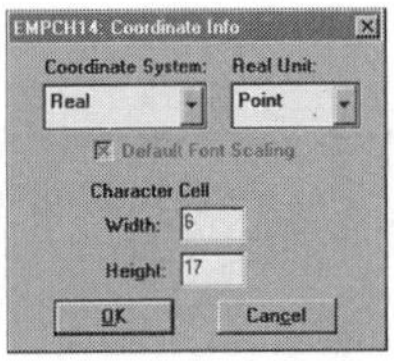


**FIG. 14.11**
The Coordinate Info dialog box displaying default settings.

The developer has the choice between two coordinate systems: *real* and *character*. Real is the default and uses pixels, centimeters, inches, and points as units of measure. Character uses each character as a single unit of measure.

In a Character Cell coordinate system the layout is subdivided vertically and horizontally into character cells. The actual size and position of objects depends on the size of a default character on the particular platform. When you use this type of system you cannot edit the Character Cell Width/Height values. Character systems can produce unexpected results in the layout editor, particularly when using the mouse to position items. This type of system produces a "snap-to-grid" effect. The item will always move to the nearest grid increment because each character or object on the form must fit within the predefined cell.

**NOTE** I recommend that you use the default coordinate settings. They allow you to drag and drop items precisely.

## Using *Current Record Attribute*

The `Current Record Attribute` form property is an extremely important property to use when the form is displaying multi-record tabular style records. The reason is the user does not know which record is the active block record on the tabular block when the cursor is located in another block. Normally, the user knows the active record by the blink of the cursor. When the cursor is outside the block, there isn't a blinking cursor within the block to show the user the active record. This is even more crucial when a tabular block is a master block to a multi-record tabular detail block. How does the user know which master record the detail records are related to?

Figure 14.12 uses form module CURATT.FMB located on the CD. The figure contains two multi-record tabular style blocks. The master block at the top displays the various Department records. As the user navigates from one department record to the next, the employees on the bottom block change. In the figure, the cursor is missing from the bottom block. Any user viewing this application would be hard pressed determining which person and department to look for.

**FIG. 14.12**
A multi-record tabular style form that does not use the current record attribute.

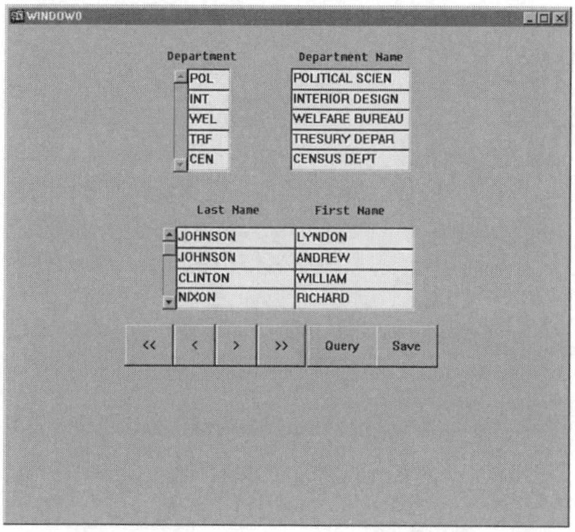


To solve this problem, the form was modified. A visual attribute was created and the `Current Record Attribute` form property was populated with the visual attribute. The visual attribute has a background color of red and a foreground color of white. This setting will cause the current record for any block to be red with white text. The noncurrent records will be white with black text. As Figure 14.13 shows, it is much easier to identify the person and the person's department by using the `Current Record Attribute` property with a visual attribute.

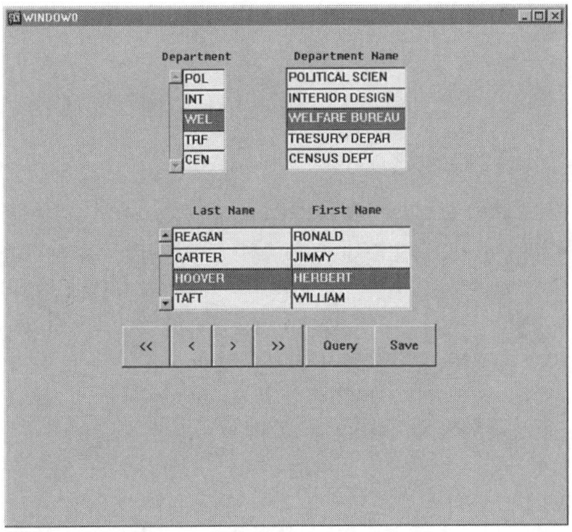


**FIG. 14.13**
A multi-record tabular style form using the current record attribute.

**NOTE** You can see the effects of a visual attribute by running the CURATT.FMB form located on the CD. Load the form into Forms Designer. Press the Run button to generate and run the file. To delete the visual attribute, open the form property sheet and blank out the visual attribute property value. Run the form to see the effect.

## Defining a Visual Attribute

Defining a visual attribute is a simple procedure. Select the Visual Attributes object on the Object Navigator, click the create button and Forms will create a new visual attribute. Click the button to the left of the visual attribute name. This will open a property sheet similar to the one displayed in Figure 14.14. The visual attribute has a number of display properties, which will supersede any object's properties when the visual attribute is used with that object.

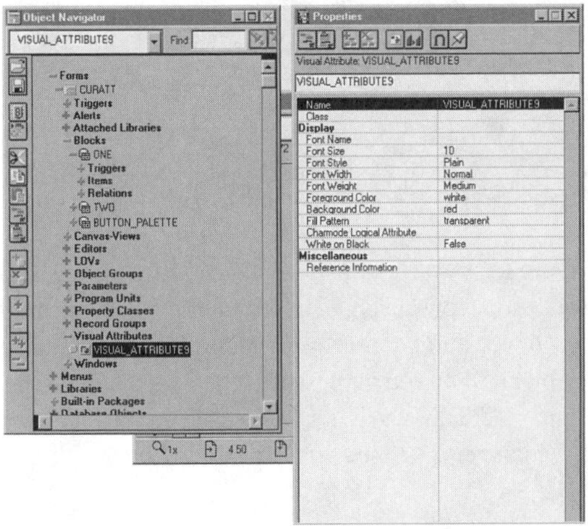


**FIG. 14.14**
The visual attribute property sheet used in the CURATT.FMB form.

**TIP** Defining and using visual attributes will save a great deal of time when formatting items. Placing one visual attribute into the object is easier than setting each individual setting. It also gives consistency to the form. I try to use the visual attributes on most objects I create.

# Understanding Block Properties

Forms are comprised of one or more blocks. The Form properties apply to all blocks and items on the form because a block is a child object of the form. A block has properties that control attributes only on the specified block. Each block on a form has its own set of properties. These properties control important form attributes such as navigation. Table 14.3 describes block properties.

**Table 14.3 Block Properties**

| Property Name | Description |
|---|---|
| Base Table | The name of the table or view that supplies the records to the block. |
| Block Description | The block label that will appear in the menu. |
| Class | The name of the property class that supplies the values to various block properties. |
| Column Security | Determines whether Forms should enforce column-by-column security. If an operator does not have privileges on a particular column, Forms will make the corresponding item non-updateable for the particular operator by dynamically changing the Update Allowed item property to false. |
| Comment | An area on the property sheet used to record comments. |
| Current Record Attribute | This property contains the name of a visual attribute. The normal record attributes will be superseded by the values of the visual attribute named in this property when a record is current. |
| Delete Allowed | Determines whether the block will allow records to be deleted. The values are *true* or *false*. |
| Direction | Specifies the layout direction for bidirectional objects. |
| In Menu | Determines whether the block should be listed in the block menu. |
| Insert Allowed | Determines whether the block will allow records to be inserted. The values are *true* or *false*. |
| Key Mode | Determines how Forms identifies rows in a database. This property is included for applications using non-Oracle |

*continues*

**Table 14.3 Continued**

| Property Name | Description |
|---|---|
| | databases. *Unique* is the default value and causes Forms to use ROWID constructs to identify unique rows in an Oracle database. *Updateable* causes Forms to use update statements that include the primary key values. *Non-Updateable* causes Forms to not include the primary key columns in any update statement. |
| Locking Mode | Tells Forms when to obtain database locks on rows that correspond to queried records in the form. The *Immediate* setting causes Forms to obtain the lock when the operator modifies the row. The *Delayed* setting causes Forms to wait for the lock until the transaction is about to be committed. |
| Name | The name of the block. |
| Navigation Style | Determines the navigation method. The property has three values: *Same Record*, *Change Record*, and *Change Block*. The *Same Record* property is the default. This setting will cause the form to return the cursor to the first item in the record after tabbing from the last item in the record. The *Change Record* setting causes the cursor to move to the next record in the block after tabbing from the last item on the current record. The *Change Block* setting causes the cursor to move to the first record in the next block after tabbing from the last item in the record. |
| Next Navigation Block | Determines the next block the form will navigate to when the Next Block function key is pressed or the navigation style is *Change Block*. |
| Optimizer Hint | Contains a hint string the form can pass to the Oracle database. It is used to construct queries and can improve performance. |
| Order By Clause | Contains an order by expression that will be used by the form to order the displayed records. |
| Prev. Navigation Block | Determines the block the form will navigate to when the Previous Block function key is pressed. |
| Primary Key | Forces the form to determine whether any inserted or updated records in the block have a unique primary key before committing the record. |
| Query Allowed | Determines whether the operator may perform a query on the block. |
| Record Orientation | Determines whether the records will be displayed in a *tabular* or *form* style. The tabular style places record items adjacent to |

| Property Name | Description |
|---|---|
| | each other. The form style spreads the items. Orientation generally applies only when multiple records are displayed. |
| Records Buffered | Determines the minimum amount of records buffered in memory during a query. Processing speed can be improved by increasing this value. |
| Records Fetched | Determines the number of records fetched from the database at one time. A smaller value will increase response time, but will increase overall processing time. |
| Records Displayed | Determines the number of records displayed by the block. |
| Scroll Bar | Determines whether the block will have a scroll bar. The values are *true* or *false*. |
| Transactions Triggers | Specifies that the block is a transactional control block. This is a nondatabase block that Forms should manage as a transactional block. |
| Update Allowed | Determines whether the records on the block may be modified. |
| Update Changed | A value of *true* will cause Forms to update only the columns that have been changed during an update transaction. A value of *false* will update all columns on the database. |
| Where Clause | Contains conditional statements that identify a specific subset of records to be returned by a query. |

## Using the Order By and Where Clause Block Properties

Two common block properties are the *order by* and *where clause*. The *order by* property orders a block's records. This is a very common procedure. Ordering presents the records in a more meaningful format than random display.

**NOTE** Many of the tabular blocks I create have a date as a key component of the record. I like to sort these records by descending date. This means the record with the most recent date appears as the first record in the block. In our Employee Update form, blocks TWO and THREE contain records that have dates. These records would be presented better if they were ordered.

You may want to reopen the EMPCH14.FMB file that contains blocks TWO and THREE to see the effect of changing the various block properties. Figure 14.15 shows the Employee update form after the `order by` property is populated in blocks TWO and THREE. The block TWO `order by` property receives the expression "purchase_date desc." The block THREE `order by` property also receives the expression "purchase_date desc." Populating these properties causes the records in the two blocks to be ordered by descending purchase_date.

**FIG. 14.15**
The Employee Update form after block TWO and THREE's `order by` properties are populated.

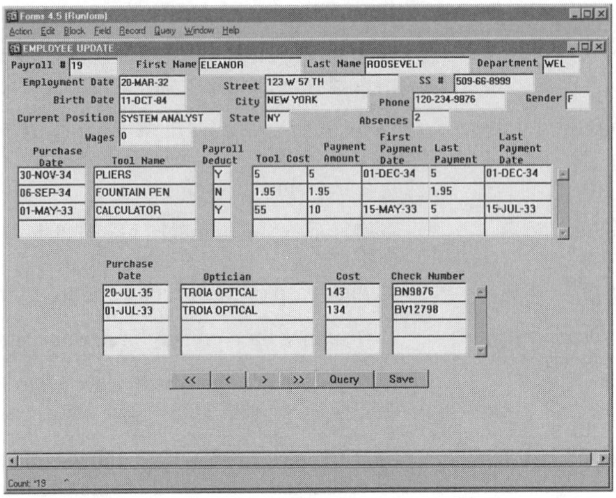


The `Where Clause` property limits the records displayed in a block. As an example, the `Where Clause` property in the Employee Update form is populated with the expression "tool_cost > 2." This causes the block to display only tool records that cost more than two dollars. Figure 14.16 shows the Employee Update form after this change has been made. Compare it to Figure 14.15 to see the effects of the `Where Clause`.

**FIG. 14.16**
The Employee Update form after the block TWO `Where Clause` property is populated to exclude tool records that cost more than two dollars.

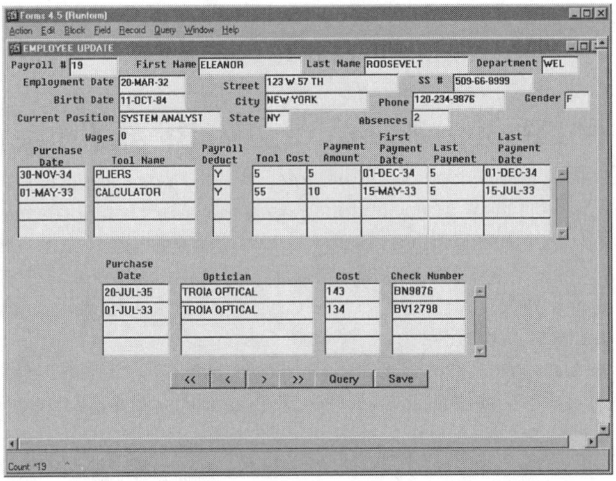


## Changing the Navigation Style

The `Navigation Style` property determines where the cursor moves to after reaching the last item in the record. The *same record* setting places the cursor on the first item of the record. The *change record* setting places the cursor on the first item of the next record. The *change block* setting places the cursor on the first item of the block specified in the `Next Navigation Block` property.

**NOTE** I generally change this property from the default, *same record*, to the *change block* settings. The users I support appear to prefer tabbing through all of the fields on a form rather than having to use the mouse or a function key to navigate to another block. For this reason, I generally set the navigation style property to this setting.

# Understanding Item Properties

A block is comprised of a number of objects. These consist of boilerplate text and a variety of items. Some of these items are text items, radio buttons, check boxes, and pick lists. Each of the items contains a set of properties. Some item properties are common to all of the item types, but some are dependent upon the type of item. Table 14.4 contains the various item properties and their descriptions. The Item Used For column identifies the type of item the property applies to. The item type codes are: B=button, C=check box, CT=chart item, D=display item, I=image, L=list item, O=OLE container, R=radio group, T=text item, U=user area, and V=VBX control.

**Table 14.4 Item Property Types**

| Property Name | Item Used For | Descriptions |
|---|---|---|
| Access Key | C, B, R, L | Determines the character used as the access key. The key allows the operator to select or execute an item (push a button) by pressing the key combination. |
| Alignment | D, T | Determines the text alignment. A value of *left* causes left justification. The *center* value centers the text. *Right* causes the text to be right justified. The *start* value aligns the text with the starting edge of the item bounding box. The *end* value aligns the text with the ending edge of the item bounding box. |
| Auto Hint | C, I, B, R, L, T, V, O, U | Determines when the hint text will be displayed. A value of true displays the hint whenever the input focus enters the item. When the property is *false,* the hint will only be displayed by pressing the Help command. |
| Auto Skip | T | Causes the cursor to move to the next item after entering the last digit of the item. |

*continues*

**Table 14.4 Continued**

| Property Name | Item Used For | Descriptions |
|---|---|---|
| Background Color | C, D, I, B, R, L, T, V, O, U, CT | The color of the item's background. Background may be considered the surface on which text resides. |
| Base Table Item | C, D, I, R, L, T, V, O, U | Determines whether the item will be linked to the block's table. |
| Bevel | D, I, T, V, O, U, CT | Determines whether the item border will appear *lowered* or *raised.* |
| Canvas | C, D, I, B, R, L, T, V, O, U, CT | The name of the canvas that displays the item. |
| Case Insensitive Query | T | Determines whether the form can perform a case insensitive query by using the item. *Case insensitive* means that upper, lower, and mixed case values can be used alike. |
| Case Restriction | T | Determines the case of the text. Valid values are *mixed*, *upper*, or *lower.* |
| Charmode Logical | C, D, I, B, R, L, T, V, O, U, CT | Specifies the name of a character mode. |
| Attribute | | Logical attribute defined in an Oracle Terminal resource file. |
| Check Box Other Values | C | Determines how any fetched value that does not match the "checked" or "unchecked" values should be interpreted. |
| Checked Value | C | The value of the check box item when it is checked. |
| Class | C, D, I, B, R, L, T, V, O, U, CT | The name of the property class that supplies the values to various block properties. |
| Comment | C, D, I, B, R, L, T, V, O, U, CT | This property records pertinent information about the item. |
| Compression | I | Determines whether an image being read into a form should be compressed when converting to the Oracle internal form. |
| Copy Value From Item | C, D, R, L, T, V, O, U | Identifies an item that will supply a value to the current item. |
| Curr. Record Attribute | C, D, I, L, T, V, O, U | This property contains the name of a record attribute. The normal record attributes can be superseded by the attributes in this property when a record is current. |

| Property Name | Item Used For | Descriptions |
|---|---|---|
| Data Type | C, D, R, T, V, U | Identifies the type of data the item contains. Valid data types vary with the type of item. |
| Default Button | B | Determines that the button should be identified as the default button. During runtime, Forms will invoke this button by pressing Select. |
| Default Value | C, D, R, L, T, V, O | The value of the item when it is initially created. |
| Direction | C, B, R, L | Specifies the layout direction for bidirectional objects. |
| Displayed | C, D, I, B, L, T, V, O, U, CT | Determines whether the item will be displayed. Values are *true* or *false*. |
| Editor | T | Contains the name of the external editor used for the item. |
| Editor X Position | T | Determines the horizontal position of the upper-left corner of the item editor. |
| Editor Y Position | T | Determines the vertical position of the upper-left corner of the item editor. |
| Enabled | C, I, B, L, T, V, O, U | Determines whether the item can use the mouse to manipulate the item. It is usually grayed out when the value is *false*. |
| Fill Pattern | C, D, I, B, R, L, T, V, O, U, CT | Determines the type of item fill. |
| Fixed Length | T | A value of *true* will cause forms to consider this item's value valid only when it fills the maximum number of characters allowed. |
| Font Name | C, D, I, B, R, L, T, V, O, U, CT | The name of the font used on the item's text. |
| Font Size | C, D, I, B, R, L, T, V, O, U, CT | The font size of the item's text. |
| Font Style | C, D, I, B, R, L, T, V, O, U, CT | The style of the item's text. |
| Font Weight | C, D, I, B, R, L, T, V, O, U, CT | The weight of the item's text. |
| Font Width | C, D, I, B, R, L, T, V, O, U, CT | The font width of the item's text. |

*continues*

**Table 14.4 Continued**

| Property Name | Item Used For | Descriptions |
|---|---|---|
| Foreground Color | C, D, I, B, R, L, T, V, O, U, CT | The color of the item's foreground. This usually consists of the item's text. |
| Format Mask | T | Determines the item's display format and correct input type. |
| Height | C, D, I, B, L, T, V, O, U, CT | The height of the item. |
| Hint | C, I, B, R, L, T, V, O, U | Contains the expression that forms will display as an item hint. |
| Horizontal Scroll Bar | I | Specifies whether the item has a horizontal scroll bar. |
| Iconic | B | Tells Forms the button is to be an iconic button. Tool bar items are iconic buttons. |
| Iconic Name | B | Identifies the name of the icon resource used to represent the button, menu item, or window. |
| Initial Keyboard State | D, L, T | Sets the keyboard to generate Local or Roman characters when the item receives the input focus. |
| Insert Allowed | C, I, R, T, V, O, U | Determines whether the values can be entered into the item during the input mode. |
| Items Displayed | C, D, I, B, R, T, V, O, U, CT | The number of items displayed. This property is used when the block displays multiple records and the developer would like to see fewer records for specific items. This property can be used to create a page break effect. |
| Item Type | C, D, I, B, R, L, T, V, O, U, CT | The type of item. Values are button, check box, display item, image, list item, OLE container, radio group, text item, user area, and VBX control. |
| Keep Position | T | Causes the cursor to return to the exact position within the item as when last exited. |
| Label | C, B | This property contains text or characters that appear in the item's boilerplate |
| List Elements | | Selecting this property will open the List Item Elements dialog box. This box is used to record items that appear on the list and their associated database value. |

| Property Name | Item Used For | Descriptions |
|---|---|---|
| List Style | L | Determines the display style of the item list. The values are *poplist*, *tlist*, or *combo box*. |
| Lock Record | T | Determines whether Forms should lock the associated database row whenever the item is updated. |
| LOV | T | Contains the name of the list-of-values to be used for the item. |
| LOV For Validation | T | Determines whether the associated LOV will be used to validate entries into the item. |
| LOV X Position | T | Determines the horizontal position of the upper-left corner of the LOV. |
| LOV Y Position | T | Determines the vertical position of the upper-left corner of the LOV. |
| Maximum Length | C, D, R, L, T, V, O, U | This property determines the maximum number of characters the item can have. |
| Mirror Item | C, D, I, R, L, T, V, O, U | Consists of the name of an item that gives the current item its value. Setting this property will ensure the two items are in sync. |
| Mouse Navigable | C, B, R, L, V, O, U | Determines whether the operator can navigate to the item by using a mouse. |
| Multi-Line | T | Determines whether the item can contain multiple lines. Setting this property to true causes the item to operate similar to a word processor. |
| Name | C, D, I, B, R, L, T, V, O, U, CT | The name of the item. |
| Navigable | C, I, B, R, L, T, V, O, U | Determines whether the input focus can be placed in the item during default navigation. |
| Next Navigation Item | C, D, I, B, R, L, T, V, O, U, O, U, CT | Determines the item Forms will move to after pressing the tab or next-item function key. |
| OLE-Activation Style | O | Determines the event that activates the OLE containing item. The valid events are: *double-clicking*, *focus-in*, and *manual*. |
| OLE Class | O | Specifies the class of OLE objects that reside in an OLE container. |
| OLE Do In Out | O | Tells Forms whether the OLE server of the embedded object allows inside-out support during in-place activation. |

*continues*

**Table 14.4 Continued**

| Property Name | Item Used For | Descriptions |
|---|---|---|
| OLE In-Place Activation | O | Edits embedded OLE objects. A value of *true* turns the function on. A value of *false* turns it off. |
| OLE Popup Menu Items | O | Activates the OLE menu used to select item to appear in the OLE popup menu. |
| OLE Resize Style | O | Tells Forms how to display an OLE object in an OLE container. The *clip* setting causes the object to be cropped to fit the container. The *scale* setting causes the object to be scaled to fit into an OLE container. The *initial* setting causes Forms to resize the OLE container to fit the OLE object at creation time. The *dynamic* setting causes Forms to resize the container to fit the object whenever the object size changes. |
| OLE Tenant Aspect | O | Specifies how an OLE object appears in an OLE container. The *content* value is the default. The content of the OLE object is displayed. The content depends upon the value of the OLE Resize Style property. The *icon* value cause an icon of the object to be displayed. The *thumbnail* values displays a smaller view of the object. |
| OLE Tenant Types | O | Determines the type of OLE objects that can be tenants of the OLE container. The valid values are: *Any, Embedded, Linked, None*, and *Static.* |
| Other Values | R, L | Determines how any fetched values that are not pre-defined values associated with the radio button or list element will be interpreted. |
| Previous Navigation Item | C, D, I, B, R, L, T, V, O, U, CT | Determines the item Forms will move to after pressing the previous-item function key. |
| Primary Key | C, D, R, T, V, U | Informs the application that the item is a primary key column. |
| Quality | I | Specifies the level of image quality used to display the image. The higher the quality the slower the response time. |
| Query Allowed | C, R, T, V, O, U | Determines whether the item may be entered and used during the query mode. |

| Property Name | Item Used For | Descriptions |
|---|---|---|
| Query Length | T | Determines the number of characters that can be entered into the item during the query mode. |
| Query Only | C, D, I, R, L, T, V, O, U | A value of true will cause the item to be usable only during the query mode. |
| Range Low Value | T | Determines the lowest value that can be entered into the item. |
| Range High Value | T | Determines the highest value that can be entered into the item. |
| Reading Order | D, T | Determines the reading order for groups of words in the same language within a single text item. |
| Rendered | D, T | Tells Forms to display the item as a rendered item when it does not have the focus. |
| Required | I, L, T, V, O, U | Tells Forms that the item must be populated before the cursor can leave the item and before it can be committed to the database. |
| Secure | T | This property causes the entered characters to be hidden. This property is useful for items that contain passwords. |
| Show OLE Popup Menu | O | Causes the right mouse button to display a popup menu of commands for interacting with the OLE object when set to *true*. |
| Show OLE Tenant | O | Tells forms to display a border defining the Type OLE object around the OLE container. |
| Sizing Style | I | Tells Forms the display style of the image when the image size does not match the size of the image item. |
| Space Between Records | C, D, I, B, L, T, V, O, U, CT | Determines the amount of space between records in a multi-record block. |
| Unchecked Value | C | The value of the check box item when it is unchecked. |
| Update Allowed | C, I, R, L, T, V, O, U | Determines whether the item may be entered during the update mode. |
| Update Only If Null | I, T | Tells Oracle that the item may only be updated if it contains a null value. |
| VBX Control File | V | Contains the name of the file for the VBX control. |

*continues*

**Table 14.4 Continued**

| Property Name | Item Used For | Descriptions |
|---|---|---|
| VBX Control Name | V | Contains the form name of the VBX control. |
| VBX Control Value Prop. | V | Determines the value property of a VBX control. |
| Vertical Scroll Bar | I, T | Tells Forms that the item is to have a vertical scroll bar. |
| Visual Attribute Name | C, D, I, B, R, L, T, V, O, U, CT | The name of the visual attribute that supplies the values for the various font and back ground properties. |
| White on Black | C, D, I, B, R, L, T, V, O, U, CT | Specifies that the object is to appear on a monochrome bitmap display device as white a black background. |
| Width | C, D, I, B, L, T, V, O, U, CT | The width of the item. |
| Wrap Style | T | Determines the type of word wrap multi-line items will use. Valid values are: *word, character,* or *none.* |
| X Position | C, D, I, B, L, T, V, O, U, CT | The horizontal position of the item's top-left corner. |
| Y Position | C, D, I, B, L, T, V, O, U, CT | The vertical position of the item's top-left corner. |

# Using the Multi-Line Property

The `multi-line item` property enables a text item to contain multiple lines of data. The text items we have seen thus far were single-line items. This means the characters were displayed in a single row within the item. Some data fields such as comments would be more favorably presented by displaying the data in a multi-line format. This can be accomplished by setting the multi-line property to *true*. This will allow the item to be used similar to a text editor. The item will accept tab character and carriage returns.

The `Wrap` property is also used in conjunction with the multi-line property. There are three wrap settings: word, character, and none. *Word* breaks the text following the last complete word, *character* breaks the text at the last visible character, and *none* causes Forms not to break the text. Figure 14.17 shows a single-line text item and several multi-line text items using various `Wrap` settings. In the middle and top-left examples the data expression is contained on one line. Parts of the expression cannot be seen. The user may view the unseen text by selecting the item and using the right arrow. The text items also behave differently. In the top example, even if a carriage return is issued, the data stays on one line. In the middle-left example, a carriage return character causes the next word to appear on the next line.

**FIG. 14.17**
Examples of multi-line text items and various wrap settings.

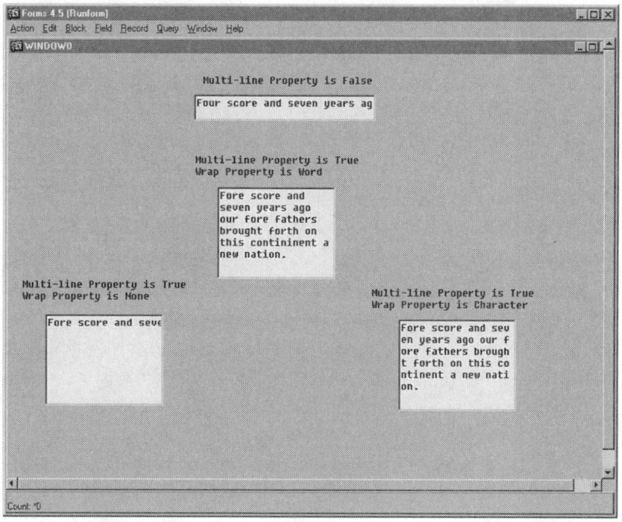


**TIP** I have developed many systems where the user requested an area to enter in free-format comments. In order to support this request, I often create a 2,000 length varchar2 column in each table. I then use the `Multi-Line` and `Wrap` property settings to populate the field. The 2,000 character size offers the user plenty of space to record information. The varchar2 data type ensures the item will use only the amount of space needed to save actual data. The `Multi-Line` and `Wrap` properties ensure that the text item behaves like a word processor.

This technique has proven to be very simple and produces a feature the users really like.

# A Word on Some of the Useful Text Item Properties

There are a number of text item properties that are useful to the developer.

**The *Range Low Value* and *Range High Value* Properties** Two of these item properties are the `Range Low Value` and `Range Low Value`, which act as edits. Forms will issue an error message and prevent the user from navigating from the field when the entered value is outside the ranges.

**The *Format Mask* Property** The `Format Mask` property ensures that the data in a text item is formatted in a particular manner. The property is excellent for dates, Social Security numbers, or phone numbers. Many companies are concerned about the year 2000 dates. The Oracle7 database is year-2000 compliant, but the default date format does not show the century. It is possible to enter a date with the wrong century. Some of these companies decided to change the format of all dates contained on Forms to show the century. In order to achieve this, the `Format Mask` property for each of the form dates was given a property of 'dd-mon-yyyy' or 'dd-mon-rrrr.' Figure 14.18 shows the use of the format mask. The purchase date of the middle block has had the format changed.

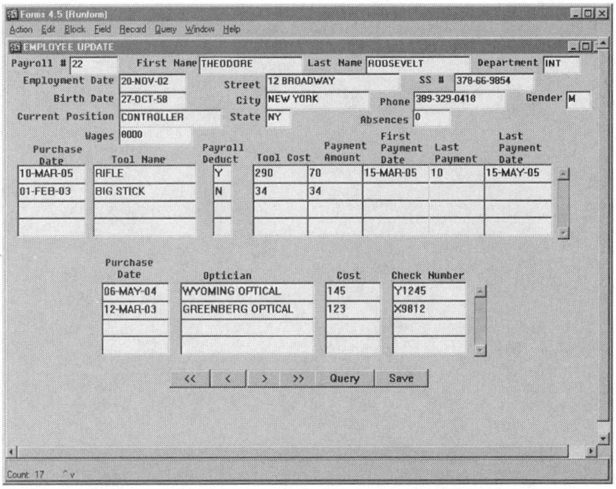


**FIG. 14.18**
The purchase date format changed to include the century using the Format Mask property.

**The *Case Restriction* Property** The `Case Restriction` property controls the case of the text. In Part II, you saw that Oracle is case sensitive, which means that a value of 'a' does not mean 'A.' For this reason, I have a rule that all text items in my forms have this property set to *upper*. This ensures that the data entered into the system is uppercase. Users of the data outside the form know they need to use uppercase expressions in their queries.

**The *Query Only* Property** The `Query Only` property determines whether the text item can be entered during the query mode. By default all form text items can be queried. In some cases it is not advisable to use the text item as a query field. For instance, the item may be an nonindexed column in a large table. Querying this item may cause unacceptable response time. In addition, some text items are almost never queried. I believe it increases user friendliness by allowing the user to avoid tabbing through these fields to reach another field.

**The *Insert Allowed* Property** The `Insert Allowed` property controls the form's ability to input a value into the item during the input mode. The `Update Allowed` property determines whether the user can update the item during the input mode. The `Navigable` property prevents the user from tabbing into the fields during the input or update mode. These properties are very important in controlling data input. There are times when the developer will not want values updated or inserted. Generally, it is bad practice to allow a user to change the primary key. It will destroy the relationships between tables and could possibly create orphan records in the related table. In another example, some forms have generated values that have meaning. A transformer number would be an example of this type of item. The developer would not want a user to enter a free format value into such an item. The value may not conform to the generated value.

**The *Case Insensitive Query* Property** Occasionally, I have had trouble with detail blocks joined to the master block by using character fields. In these situations, the detail block would not display the records for the corresponding master block. The problem occurs when one of the tables has uppercase characters and the other table does not. Setting the `Case Insensitive query` property to true will solve this problem. It makes the case irrelevant in database queries performed from the form. It also is a good property to use when your database has mixed character columns.

**The *Required* Property** When a block is created, any items in the block that are linked to table columns defined as not null will have their `Required` property marked true. This will prevent the user from navigating from the item when it is null. On the surface, it seems that this is a good feature. However, I have found that users seem to have a great deal of problems with required fields. For some reason users (including me) place their cursors into these required items by accident, and become frustrated when they can't leave the field. In order to avoid this problem, I always make the `Required` property on every form text item false.

# Understanding Item Types

As you have seen in the previous section, Forms gives the developer the ability to create a variety of item types. Use of these items can enhance the user friendliness of your forms. Some of the more commonly used items are check boxes, images, buttons, radio groups, list items, and text items. The type of item can be specified at the time the block is created by using the Items dialog box. The type can also be easily changed later by using the item's `Item Type` property. The following sections cover these items.

**NOTE** If you have trouble creating and operating any of the following items, a working example containing the items is available on the CD. This form is called EMPCH14X.FMB. You may compare your application to the settings in this form.

## Check Boxes

A *check box* is a graphical item that displays a box checked when the item contains one value, and unchecked when the item contains another value. This item type is used when the item contains no more than two mutually exclusive values. An example of a data item that can be used as a check box is gender. The values can only be male or female. The values are mutually exclusive.

To create a check box, perform the following steps:

1. Create an item by using the Layout Editor tool palette, or the New Block dialog box, or the create button on the Object Navigator. Be sure the item type is "Check Box."
2. Open the item's property sheet. Locate the Functional properties at the bottom of the sheet. Enter a label or description of the item in *label* property.
3. Populate the `Checked Value` property. This should be the value of the item when the box is checked.
4. Populate the `Unchecked Value` property. This should be the value of the item when the box is unchecked.
5. Select the value for the `Check Box Other Value`. This property determines what the check box will do when the item does not have a checked or unchecked value.

6. Enter the value used in the `Checked` or `Unchecked` properties into the `Default` property.
7. Format the item on the layout editor.

The following example, as shown in Figure 14.19, consists of changing the payroll_deduct item on the Employee Form from a text item to a check box. You may use the EMPCH14.FMB form that has been used throughout this chapter to practice the procedure.

1. Open the item's property sheet.
2. Change the item type to *check box*. The `Checked Value` property should be `Y` and the `Unchecked Value` should be `N`.
3. Change the `Label` property to `Pay Ded`.

**FIG. 14.19**
The payroll_deduct item property sheet displaying the check box properties.

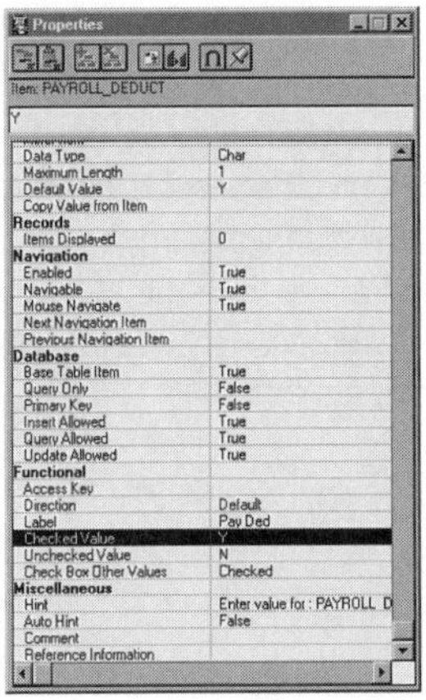


4. The next step is to open the Layout Editor. The check box items on the block must be rearranged and the size of the item changed.

Figure 14.20 shows the executed form. The first tool record has a checked value, which indicates that the item was purchased on payroll deduction. The second item is unchecked or was paid at the time of purchase.

## Radio Group Buttons

A *radio group* is a set of buttons that identify a value. A radio group is an appropriate graphic object when the item is comprised of two or more mutually exclusive values. Each value is assigned to a specific radio button in the radio group. When the button is depressed or blackened, the item equals the value assigned to the button.

To create a radio button group, perform the following:

1. Create an item by using the Layout Editor tool palette, the New Block dialog box, or the create button on the Object Navigator. Be sure the item type is Radio Group.
2. Select the radio group item on the Object Navigator. Expand the item.

3. Select the `Radio Buttons` object located under the radio group. Create a button object for each possible value in the group.
4. Open each button's property sheet by double-clicking the button next to the object. Enter a description of the button in the `Label` property. Assign a value to the button by using the *value* button.
5. Open the radio group's property sheet by double-clicking the button to its left. Enter a default value into the `default value` property.
6. Open the layout editor and format the various buttons.

**FIG. 14.20**
The Employee Update form showing the payroll _deduct check box.

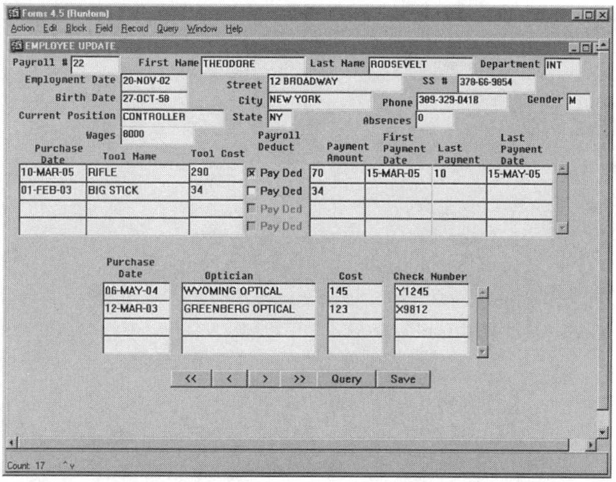


In the following example, the gender item on block ONE of the Employee Update form is to be changed to a radio group. Figure 14.21 displays the Object Navigator after the gender item type was changed to *radio group* and two radio buttons were added.

**FIG. 14.21**
The Object Navigator displaying the gender radio group and buttons.

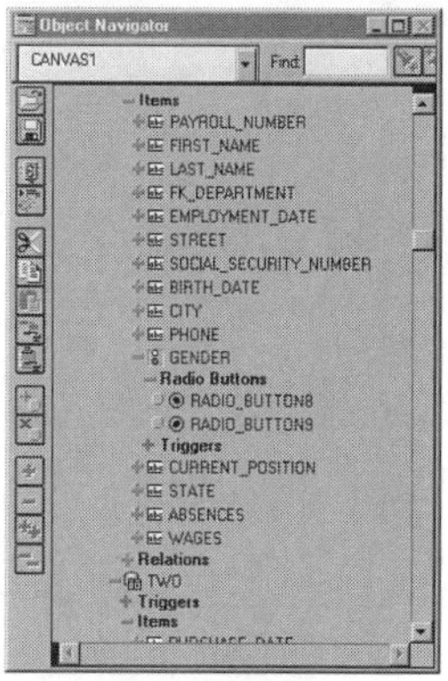

The next step is to add the name of the button and assign a value to the button. This is done on the button's property sheet. The filled-in sheet is displayed in Figure 14.22. The *label* contains a value of Male and the *value* property M. The properties are described in Table 14.4.

**FIG. 14.22**
The Male radio button property sheet.

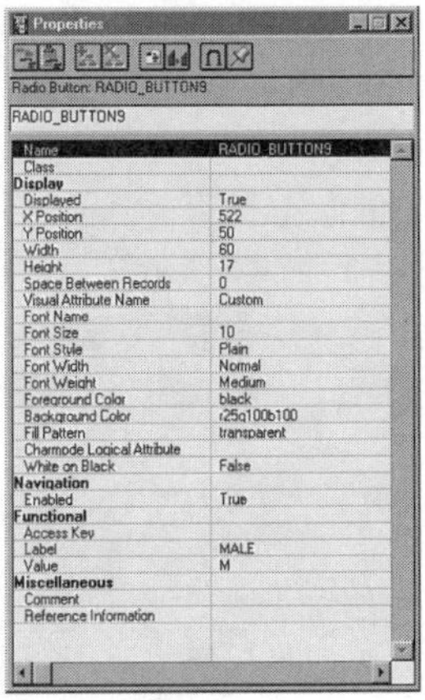


The final step is to open the Layout Editor and format the buttons. The background color can be changed and their position moved. Figure 14.23 shows the executed form displaying a female employee.

**FIG. 14.23**
The Employee Update form with gender radio buttons. The female button is depressed.

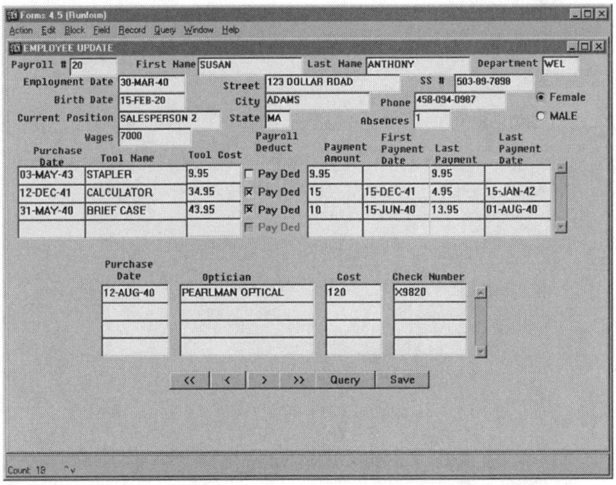


## List Items

Another very useful device is a *list item*. It is a graphical device that displays a fixed set of values for the user to select. A list item is used when the item contains a number of defined values not likely to change. I generally use this device when the item contains between 3 and 15 values. I use a radio group or check box for less than three values and a list-of-values when more than 15 values are needed or the list of values can change.

Three types of list items are available: Poplists, TLISTS, and Combo Boxes. Figure 14.24 shows the three types. Each of the three contains a down-arrow on the right side of the item. Pressing this button on the poplist will cause a drop-down list of values to appear. A Poplist item cannot be inputted or updated directly. Selecting a value from the list must populate it.

A Combo Box is a cross between a text item and a poplist. It contains an arrow on the right side that drops the predefined value list. The user can select a value from the list to populate the item. This is the same as a poplist. Unlike a poplist item, a combo box item is enterable. The user can enter a value directly into the item. This means the combo box item may contain values that do not match the predefined list.

The TLIST List contains an up- and down-arrow on the right side. This item does not show the entire value list. It only shows the currently selected value. Pressing the up-arrow will display the previous value, and pressing the down-arrow will display the next value from the list.

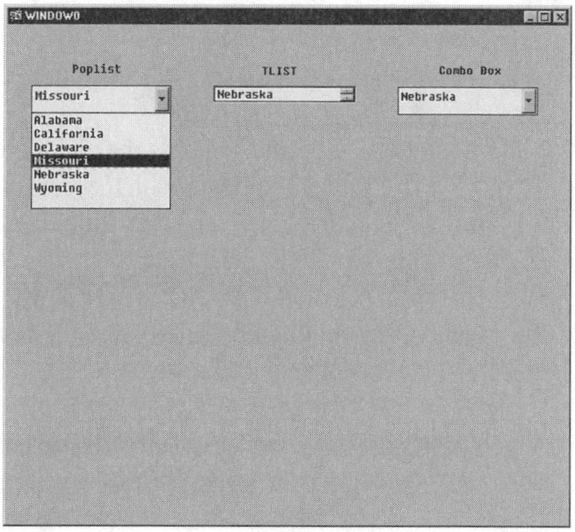


**FIG. 14.24**
Examples of a Poplist, TLIST, and Combo Box.

Perform the following steps to create an item list:

1. Create an item by using the Layout Editor tool palette, or the New Block dialog box, or the create button on the object navigator. Be sure the item type is List Item.
2. Open the item's property sheet. Locate the Functional properties located near the bottom of the property sheet. Select the type of list by using the `List Style` property.
3. Select the `List Elements` property. This will cause a button labeled More to appear at the top of the sheet. Click this button, and a List Item Elements dialog box appears.
4. This dialog box contains each of the list's values and a corresponding description. Enter the value descriptions in the top box labeled List Elements. Enter the actual value in the lower box labeled List Item Value. Click OK when done.
5. Open the Layout Editor. Position and format the list item to suit.

As an example, the state column on the Employee Update form will be changed to a poplist item. The first step is to open the property sheet, as shown in Figure 14.25. The `Item Type` property, which is not displayed, has been changed to list item. The figure displays the item's functional properties. The `List Style` property is poplist. The `List Elements` property is selected and the More button appears at the top of the property sheet.

**FIG. 14.25**
The functional properties on the `State Item` property sheet.

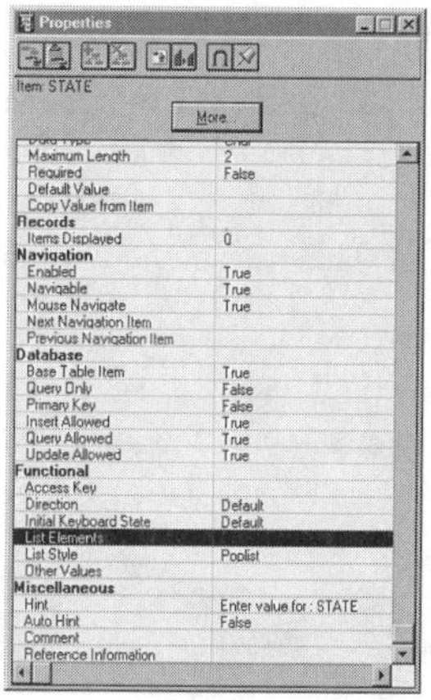

Clicking the More button brings up the List Item Elements dialog box to the right of the property sheet. This dialog box records the values that appear on the poplist and its associated actual value retained in the database. The top window contains the descriptions and the bottom window contains the actual value. The value in the List Item Value window corresponds to the element in the top box that is currently selected. Clicking the OK button will save the values. The default property on the property sheet must be filled in with a value from the list. You will get a compile warning when the default property is empty.

**TIP** On some of the list items, it's nice to have a null as the default value. In order to create a null on the list, select the element row immediately following the last description. Then remove the corresponding value in the bottom window. This procedure will validate the lack of a value in the item's default property.

The final step is to open the Layout Editor to position and format the item. Figure 14.26 displays the executed Employee Update form with the State list item.

## Using Images

The *image item type* displays an image that is read into the form during runtime. The image can be contained in the database or in an external file. The image is read into the form by firing a trigger. An image can be a useful device. For example, suppose that the user wants to view an image of each employee on the Employee Update form. This can be achieved by creating an image item and displaying the employee's scanned image file into the image item. The example later in this section will display the employee's image on the Employee Update form.

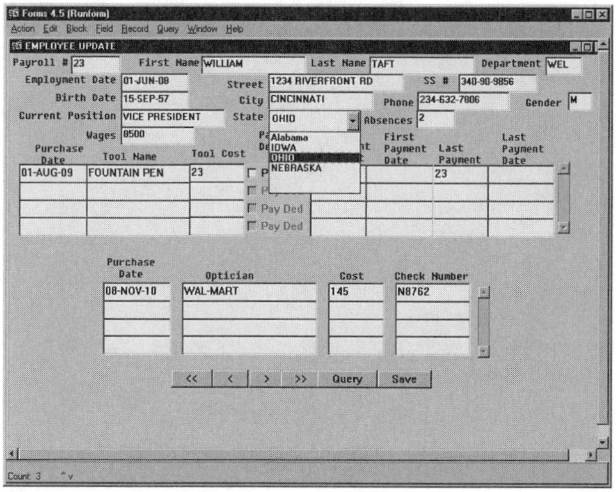


**FIG. 14.26**
The Employee Update form with an open poplist for the State item.

Perform the following to create an image:

1. Create an item by using the Layout Editor tool palette, or the New Block dialog box, or the create button on the object navigator. Be sure the item type is Image.
2. Open the property sheet and locate the Functional properties. Change the Sizing Style to adjust. If the image does not come from the database, be sure to change the Base Table Item to false.
3. Open the Layout Editor. Size and position the image item.
4. Create a trigger that will populate the image by using the *read_image_file* built-in function.

The images of each employee in our employee database were scanned into PCX files. They are contained on the CD. The name of each file begins with the employee's payroll number followed by the expression EMP.TIF. Concatenating the employee number to the front of the filename makes each file unique and allows the form to easily identify the corresponding file. For example, Ronald Reagan's employee number is 35 and the image file is 35EMP.PCX.The following are the steps to add an image item to the Employee Update form:

1. The first step is to create the image item. Start by clicking the image tool on the Layout Navigator. The image item should be on block "ONE."
2. Place and size the image by using the drag handles. Open the property sheet and change the Base Table Item to false and the *Sizing Style* to false.

Figure 14.27 displays the image property sheet after the properties have been modified.

The next step is to create a trigger that will load the image file into the form image. Triggers will be discussed triggers in greater depth in the next chapter. The trigger used in this example is a block-level post-query trigger. This means when Oracle displays a new record on the block, this trigger will be executed or fired. The trigger contains the PL/SQL commands that will populate the image item.

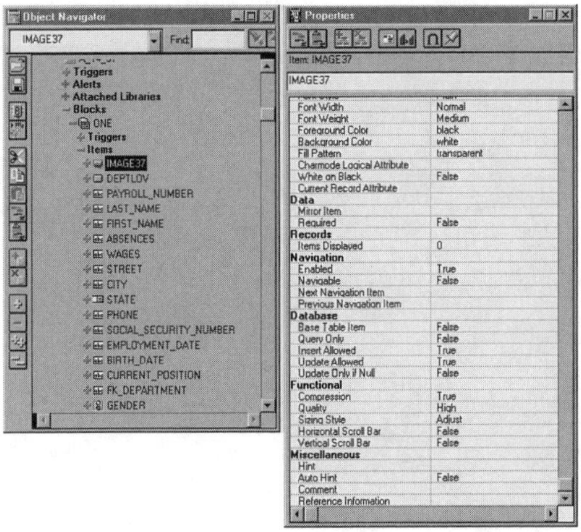

**FIG. 14.27**
The Employee Update form employee image property sheet and settings.

1. Select and expand the block ONE object on the Object Navigator.
2. Select the triggers object under block "ONE." Press the create button on the Tool Palette. The Triggers dialog box will appear.
3. Select post-query as the type of trigger from the dialog box. Press the OK button. The PL/SQL editor will appear.
4. Enter the PL/SQL script from Figure 14.27 into the PL/SQL editor for the trigger. The script assumes the image files will be on the CD (drive d). If you change the location, the directory path will change also. Press the compile button to syntax check the PL/SQL script.
5. Generate and run the application.

Figure 14.28 illustrates the PL/SQL block contained in the post-query trigger.

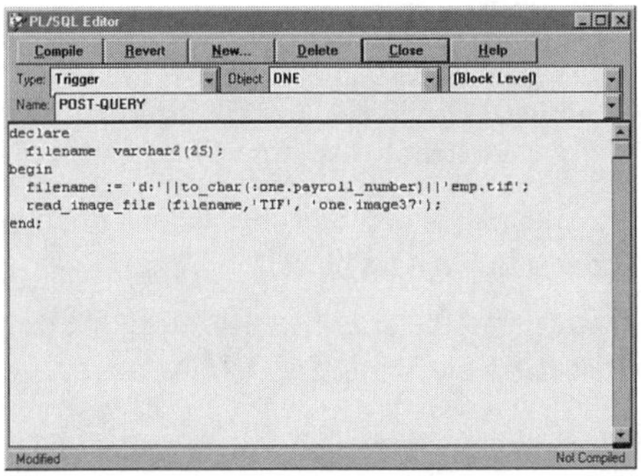


**FIG. 14.28**
The post-query trigger PL/SQL statements used to populate the image item.

This trigger constructs the filename by using the employee's payroll number from block ONE. The trigger is fired as each new record is displayed on screen. This will populate the image item with the contents of the image file. Figure 14.29 displays the executed Employee Update form showing the employee's photograph.

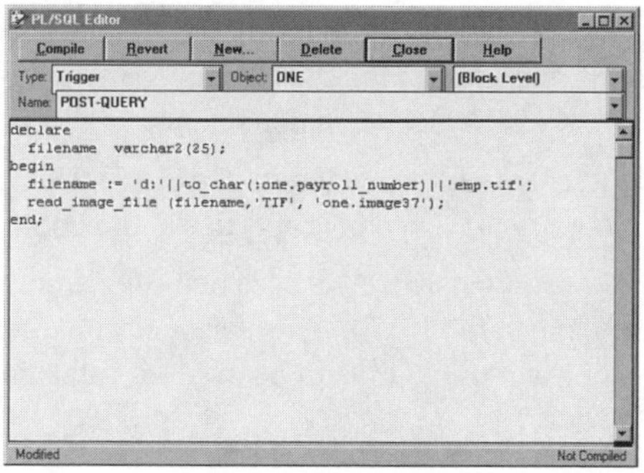


**FIG. 14.29**
Displaying the photo of the employee on the Employee Update form.

# Creating List of Values

A *list of values*, or *LOV*, is a modal dialog box that displays the results of a Select statement or record group. The results of the record search can place a value into an item or validate a value placed into the item. Items that are foreign keys are always a candidate for a list of values. The reason is the value contained in the foreign key must always exist in a related table. On the Employee Update form, the employee's department number is a foreign key. It is used to relate the Employee table to the Department table. It is a prime candidate for a list of values.

A LOV consists of two objects. The first is the data acquisition object called a *record group*. This object consists of a `SELECT` statement that will return the records needed by the LOV. The second object is an LOV dialog box. It displays the records returned by the record group. Normally the record group is created at the same time the LOV is created. However, it can be created separately and referenced by the LOV.

Perform the following to create a LOV and record group:

1. Open the Object Navigator, select the LOVS object, and click the create button. This will open the New LOV dialog box.
2. Enter a `SELECT` statement into the Query Text window of the dialog box. You may instead select an existing Record Group by clicking the Existing Record Group radio button. This will activate the Select button and display a list of existing record groups to select from. Press OK when done. Be sure to use an `order by` clause if you desire the list to be ordered.
3. The default names of the LOV and record group are generic. Change the names of each of these items to a more meaningful name. Double-click the button and modify the item's name property. It can also be changed directly on the Object Navigator.
4. Open the LOV property sheet. Modify the properties to suit. Be sure to give the LOV a name by updating the `Title` property.

5. Select the `Column Mapping` property. This will bring up the More button. Click this button. This will launch the LOV column mapping dialog box.
6. The top window contains the name of the LOV columns. If you want the value to be selected into an item, place the name of the form item including its block name as a prefix in the Return Item window. Change the `Column Title` property to suit. Perform this procedure for all items. Press OK when done.
7. Open the Object Navigator and select the item that will use the LOV. Open the item's property sheet. Locate the `Miscellaneous` properties at the end of the sheet.
8. Enter the name of the LOV in the `LOV` property. When selecting this property a pick list button will appear. The name of the LOV can be selected from the list. Change the `LOV For Validation` value to true if the LOV is to be used for validation. Update the `X` and `Y` coordinate properties to suit.

This example will illustrate the creation of a LOV for the department field on block ONE of the Employee Update form. The following are the steps to add the LOV.

1. The first step is to open the Object Navigator and create a `LOV` object.

   This will bring up the New LOV dialog box, as shown in Figure 14.30. The Select clause in the Query Text window will retrieve the department records for the LOV.

**FIG. 14.30**
The New LOV dialog box containing the `Select` statement for the LOV's record group.

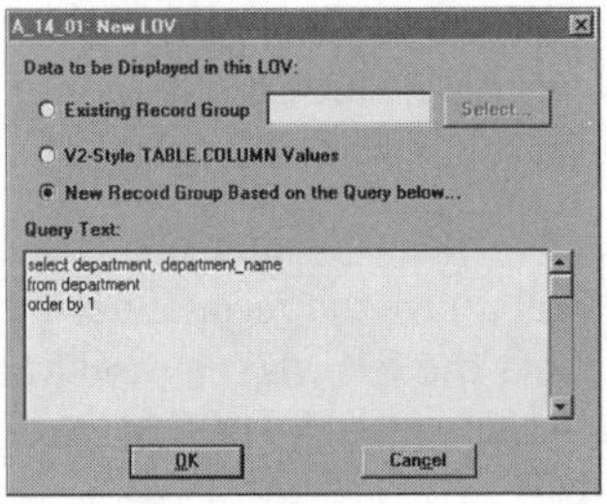


2. Enter the `select` clause contained in Figure 14.30 into the Query Text window.
3. Click the OK button on the dialog box to create the `LOV` object and a `record group` object.

Figure 14.31 displays the Object Navigator and the default names created by Forms.

4. Change the name of the `LOV` and `record` group to `DEPT`.
5. The next step is to open the `LOV`'s property sheet, which contains a number of format settings.
6. Change the settings in the property sheet to match those contained in Figure 14.32.

Figure 14.32 shows the completed property sheet for the Department LOV. The `X Position` and `Y Position` properties were changed in order to locate the LOV in the middle of the screen. The LOV was given a title by using the `Title` property.

A visual attribute was used to populate the properties on the LOV in Figure 14.32. It was used in order to maintain consistency in look between this LOV and any other LOV created on the form. The equal sign in front of the properties denotes that the value was supplied by the visual attribute.

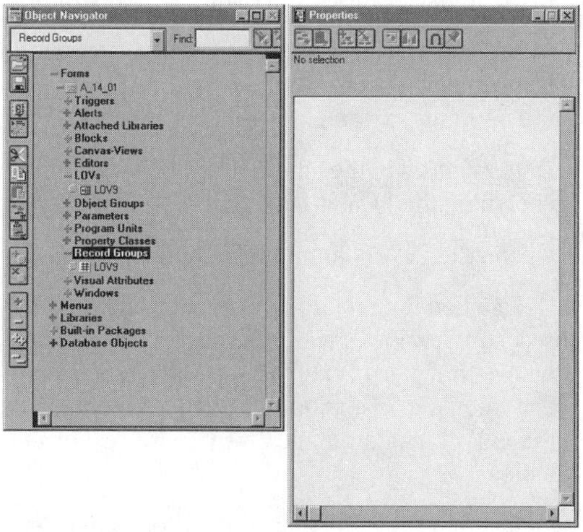


**FIG. 14.31**
The LOV and record group on the object navigator.

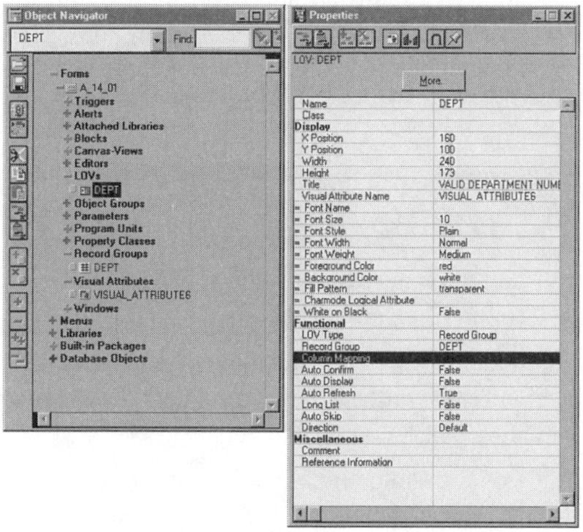


**FIG. 14.32**
The Dept LOV property sheet.

The Functional set of properties contains several properties that you would be interested in. These properties are described in Table 14.5.

**Table 14.5 LOV Properties**

| Property Name | Description |
|---|---|
| Auto Confirm | Determines what happens when the list is reduced to ONE item. A value of true will automatically dismiss the LOV and assign the value |

*continues*

**Table 14.2 Continued**

| Property Name | Description |
|---|---|
| | to the item. A value of *false* allows the operator to select the row or dismiss the LOV. |
| Auto Display | Determines whether the LOV will be displayed automatically when the operator navigates to the item to the LOV. |
| Auto Refresh | Determines whether the query will be performed to populate the LOV each time the LOV is launched. |
| Column Mapping | Opens the LOV column mapping dialog box. |
| Long List | Used when the results of the query will produce a large amount of records. A value of *true* will cause a Criteria Select box to appear before the query is performed. This box will allow the user to enter conditional information that reduces the number of records fetched to the LOV. It can dramatically increase response time against large tables. |
| LOV Type | Determines how the developer intends to reference the record group. Selecting the *record group* values indicates that the LOV will use an existing record group. The *query* setting indicates you intend to create a record group for the LOV. Selecting t the value will allow you to open a multi-line field to enter and apply your query. The V2-Style is used from backward compatibility. |

The Functional section properties retain their default values. The column mapping properties need to be modified.

7. Select this property and click the More button at the top of the property sheet. This will bring up the LOV Column Mapping dialog box, as shown in Figure 14.33.

   This dialog is used to identify the columns that will appear in the dialog, the column title of the column, the displayed width of the column, and the name of the form item to which the LOV returns a value.

   In this example, the department column will be used to return a value to the block-one item fk_department. If you are to use the LOV as a validation tool, you must specify the return item value on this dialog box.

8. Enter one.fk_department into the Return Item window for the department column.
9. Enter one.department_name into the Return Item Window for the department_name column. Press OK.

**TIP** I have had some LOVs that populate four or five fields. They are usually based on a record group that contains a join query. These values go into nondatabase reference text items on the form. An example of this type of field would be the department_name field on block ONE. It is not contained on the Employee table but would enhance the information on the block.

I don't like to see all of these reference fields on the LOV when I select a value, but I want to return the values to the form. I solve this problem by placing the values on the LOV column mapping dialog box, but making sure the LOV window width is small enough they cannot be seen by the operator.

---

**FIG. 14.33**
The LOV Column Mapping dialog box for the DEPT LOV.

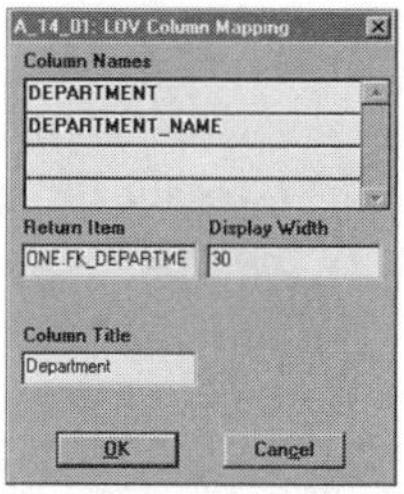


The next step is to link the LOV to an item on the fk_department item on block ONE of the Employee Update form. This is done on the item's property sheet, as shown in Figure 14.34. There are four relevant properties. The LOV property specifies then name of the linked LOV. The `LOV X Position` and `LOV Y Position` properties are used to position the LOV on the form. These do not need to be set if properties were set on the LOV property sheet. The final property is `LOV For Validation`. Setting this property to true will cause Forms to use the LOV record group query during the validation process. The form will not allow the operator to navigate from the item unless the entered value exists as a value in the set of records returned by the record group. If the value does not exist, Forms will automatically display the LOV. The operator can then choose the correct value.

**FIG. 14.34**
The Fk_department item's property sheet displaying the LOV properties

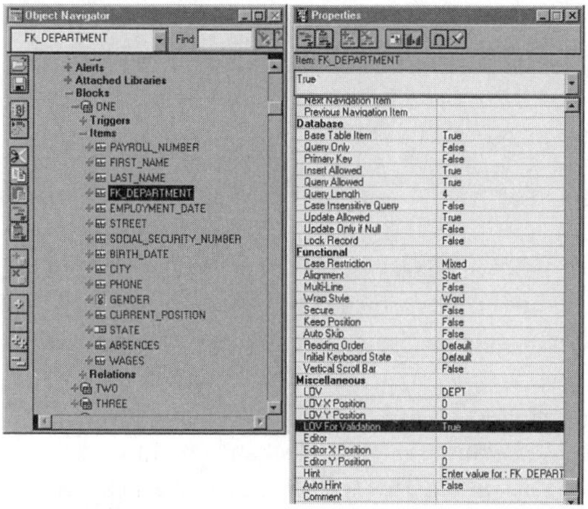


10. Modify the fk_department item's properties to match those contained in Figure 14.34.
11. Generate and Run the form.

# Calling the LOV

Forms has two manners of launching LOV's. The first method is to display it automatically when the operator navigates into the item. This happens when the `LOV Auto Display` property is set to true. The second method is to launch the LOV by navigating to the item and pressing the List of Values function key (F9).

The operator determines the item has a linked LOV by a message at the bottom of the screen. Figure 14.35 displays the Employee Update form with the message displayed. Whenever the operator navigates into an item that has an attached LOV, the expression `<List>` is displayed in the message line.

**FIG. 14.35**
The Employee Update Form displaying the <List> message.

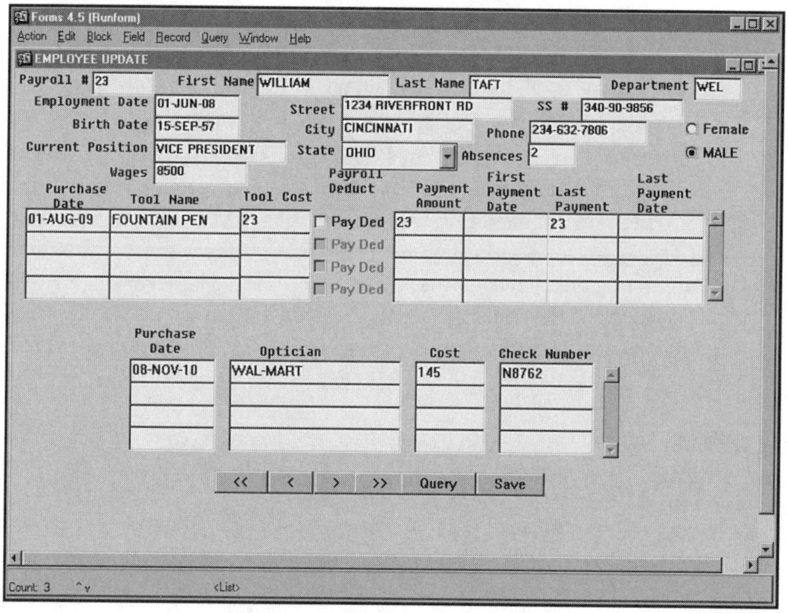


Clicking the F9 function key will display the DEPT LOV, as shown in Figure 14.36. The LOV displays by default all of the records returned by the query. The operator can scroll through the list by using the scroll bar. If the list is large, the operator can place some characters into the Find item at the top of the LOV. When the Find button is clicked, the query will be re-executed by using these characters in a conditional statement. The LOV will display only records that match the Find expression. To select an item into the form item, select the row on the list and press the OK button. This will shut down the LOV with the values returned to the form items.

# Displaying the LOV With a Button

The function key method is not a very user-friendly method. The users seldom remember the function key and usually don't notice the `<list>` message. To solve this problem, the developer can place a button item next to the text item. This button is reduced in size, and makes the item appear to be a pick list. The users like this feature because when they see the button, they know it will open a list of some sort by simply clicking the button.

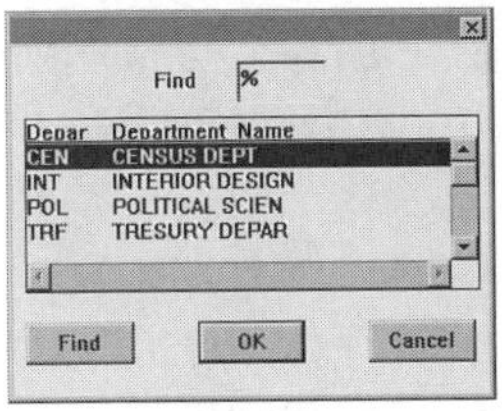


**FIG. 14.36**
The DEPT LOV used to return values to the fk_department item.

To create the button on the form, perform the following:

1. Open the Layout Editor.
2. Select the push button tool from the tool palette. This will change the cursor to a cross-hairs.
3. Select a spot and click the left cursor button. This will place a default button on the canvas.
4. Resize and position the button using the drag handles. Place it after the fk_department item.
5. Double-click the button to open its property sheet.
6. Change the *label* to a pipe symbol '¦'.

Figure 14.37 shows the button on the Layout Editor after these changes have been made.

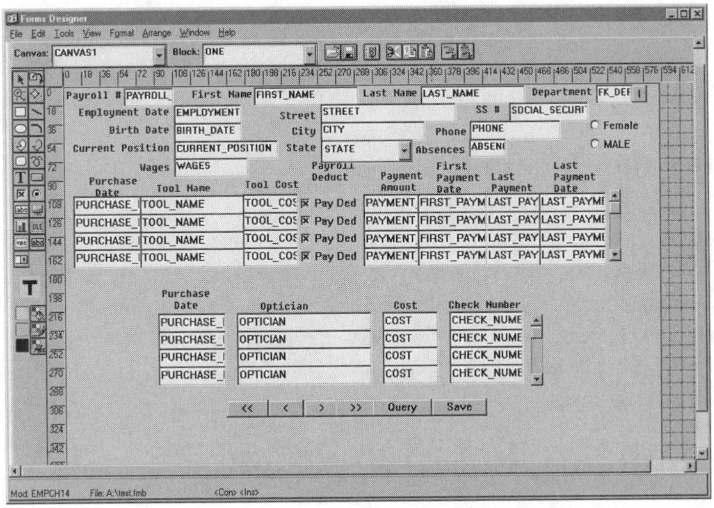


**FIG. 14.37**
The layout editor containing the reformatted LOV button.

The final step is to create a trigger that will be activated when the button is clicked. This will require a `When-button-pressed` trigger to be assigned to the button. We will discuss creating triggers in the next section. Figure 14.38 displays the text of the trigger.

1. Open the Object Navigator and locate the button. Make sure it is on block **ONE** and follows the fk_department field. This will ensure proper tabbing order. If you need to move the button, select the button and drag it to the proper location on the Object Navigator.
2. Expand the button object to expose its triggers child object.
3. Press the create button on the Tool Palette. The Triggers dialog box will appear.
4. Select the when-button-pressed trigger. Press OK. The PL/SQL editor will appear.
5. Enter the PL/SQL script contained in Figure 14.38. Press the compile button to ensure no errors exist.
6. Close the PL/SQL editor. Generate and run the application.

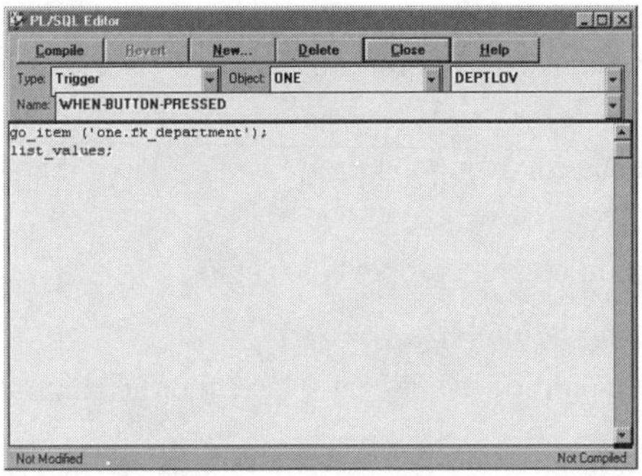


**FIG. 14.38**
The `When-Button-Pressed` PL/SQL statements that cause the display of the LOV.

The script causes the form to shift the input focus to the fk_department item on block ONE. After changing the focus, it displays the LOV linked to the fk_department item.

## Modifying the Record Group

Occasionally, it is necessary to modify the record group. This occurs when the developer wants to add another column to a LOV. Modifying the `Record Group Query` property changes the query. The record group property sheet is displayed in Figure 14.39. When the `Record Group Query` is selected, the property sheet will display a yellow button at the top of the sheet. Clicking this button opens an edit window that can be used to modify the query. Clicking the OK button will cause forms to compile and validate the query. It may then be used to modify or create a LOV.

# Understanding Relation Properties

When the developer creates a master/detail form, Forms creates an object called a *relation*, a child object of the master block. It contains the conditions that relate the two blocks. Generally it is not necessary to use this object. However, sometimes the join condition needs to be modified. Changes in the database tables or possibly an error by the developer may cause this. Rather than dropping the detail block it may be easier to modify the `Join Condition` property of the relationship. Figure 14.40 displays a relationship property sheet.

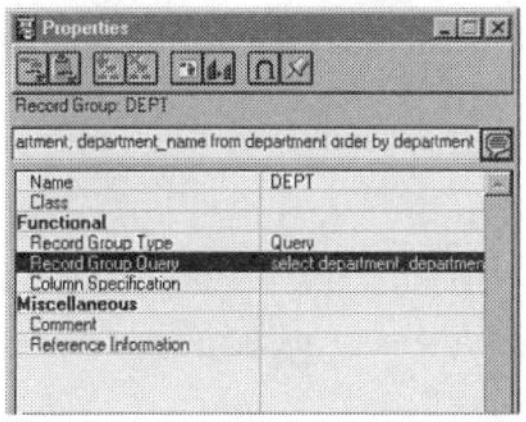


**FIG. 14.39**
The record group property sheet and the record group query edit window.

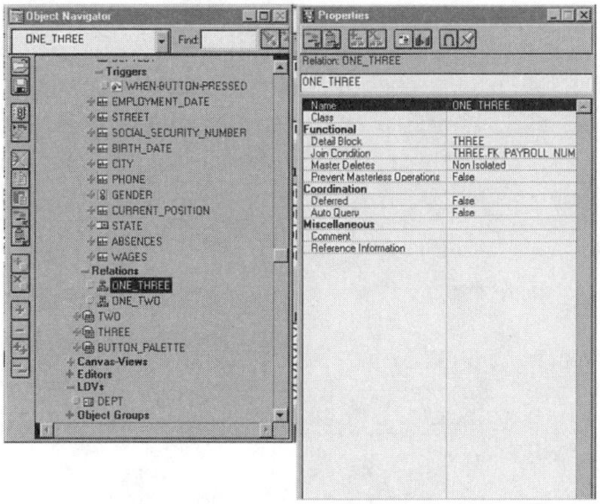


**FIG. 14.40**
The relationship property sheet for block ONE and block TWO of the Employee Update form.

# Summary

Forms often contain records from multiple tables. The records from the two tables are related in a master detail relationship. Forms enables the developer to add blocks related to existing blocks. Using the master-detail tab of the New Block dialog does this. The chapter discussed the creation of two detail blocks for the Employee Update form.

The form object has a number of properties or attributes. The coordinate information setting determines the coordinates used in the Forms designer to place objects. The current record attribute uses a visual attribute to change the look of the current block record. The menu property is used to identify the menu used by the form. The cursor mode determines the navigation range of the cursor.

The block object also has a number of properties. The base table property contains the name of the table or view. The delete allowed, insert allowed, and query allowed settings determine whether these functions can be performed on the block. The navigation style determines where the cursor navigates after tabbing from the last item. The `order by` and `where clause` properties order the records and limit the number selected. The records displayed property determines the number of record displayed by the form.

There are eleven types of items that can be displayed on the canvas: push button, check boxes, chart items, display items, images, list items, OLE containers, radio groups, text items, user areas, and VBX controls. The items contain a variety of properties. The `alignment` property control justification. The `Font` properties control the text format. The LOV property determines the LOV used for the item. The `required` property determines whether the item must have a value. The `Multi-Line` property is used to enable the user to enter text on multiple lines of the item.

A LOV is an item that can be used to display a dialog box that displays values for the item. The LOV can be used to validate values entered into the item. A relationship is an object that contains the conditions of the join between a master and detail block.

# From Here...

The next chapter covers triggers. Triggers are events that execute PL/SQL code. The chapter describes how to incorporate triggers into the form. It also covers the PL/SQL editor. It is the tool used to write the PL/SQL. The chapter also covers built-in subprograms, system variables, global variables, and alerts. The last part of the chapter describes a template security scheme that can control who updates a form.

# Review Exercises

Use the a_13_02.fmb to perform these exercises.

1. Add a tools and glasses block to the Employee Update form. Be sure to include a button palette. Format the blocks.
2. Create a visual attribute that has a red foreground color. Use this attribute to denote the current record in the tools and glasses block.
3. Create a LOV for the fk_department field in block ONE.
4. Create a button that displays the LOV.
5. Change the payroll_deduct item on the tools block to a check box.
6. Change the gender item on block ONE to a radio group.
7. Change the state field on block ONE to a poplist item.
8. Place a button on canvas that will call up the employee photo. The files are located on the CD and have the following filename format: *paryoll_number*||emp.pcx.

CHAPTER 15

# Using Triggers and Modifying Classes

You can use form file EMPCH15.FMB to practice any of the techniques in this chapter. Form file EMPCH15A.FMB is used in the Using Triggers to Change Form Canvases section, later in this book. This form is similar to the final form created in Chapter 14 (EMPCH14X.FMB). The difference is that the Post-query trigger that displays the employee images was removed. ■

**What is a trigger?**

This section introduces you to triggers. Triggers are events that execute PL/SQL scripts. The section discusses the purposes of triggers and how they are used in a form.

**The PL/SQL editor**

This section covers the PL/SQL editor, which is used to document PL/SQL statements used in triggers, procedures, and packages.

**Using built-in subprograms**

This section covers built-in subprograms. These are functions developed by Oracle that can perform a myriad of functions on a form.

**Using system and global variables**

This section covers system variables, which determine events that have occurred on the form. The section will also cover global variables. They place values in memory for use in multiple applications.

**Using triggers and program units to check user security**

This section shows a security trigger scheme that can be used in a form to protect against unauthorized database transactions.

# What Is a Trigger?

A trigger is an Oracle object that contains PL/SQL code and is fired or executed by a specific event. Triggers have a number of uses. They can be used to validate user entries, link and synchronize blocks of a form, redefine function keys, call other forms, define the action of a button, or perform a score of other functions. The techniques and functions that you learned in the PL/SQL chapters (Chapters 8 and 9) can be used in a trigger. This includes cursors, functions, procedures, packages, `WHILE` and `FOR` loops, and exception handling. In fact, it will be to your benefit to employ the full power of PL/SQL in your triggers.

When I first encountered triggers eight or nine years ago, the applications that I had been writing consisted of a single block of code in one file. The program began by reading the first line and continued executing statements until the last line of the file was read. I was able to follow the flow of the program following the logic from one line to the next. The programs had looping statements and goto keywords used to perform iterative procedures. These programs sometimes had stopping places where user input was requested. Essentially an application was a self-contained list of commands and all of the languages I knew such as BASIC, COBOL, or Focus worked in that manner.

Oracle Forms took the program listing out of my hands and replaced it with a series of event-driven triggers. The PL/SQL code is linked to a form object such as a block, item, or button and is executed by a specific action occurring. The developer no longer had the listing to follow. The developer needed to know what event occurred before the problem and what object was affected by the event. I found this an alien way to look at applications, but quickly found it a much easier way to develop and debug programs. I found it interesting that when I took my first look at Visual Basic, it looked a lot like Oracle Forms. Visual Basic ties the basic code to events and the events are linked to a form object. Microsoft had moved toward making its product look and operate like Oracle Forms.

## Trigger Events

Triggers are named for the event that causes them to fire. In Chapter 14, a trigger was created to place a picture of an employee on the form when the employee's records were displayed. The name of the trigger was "Post-query" and was attached to block one, which meant that the associated PL/SQL code executed after a query was performed on block one.

There are many events that can fire a trigger. Some of these are pressing a button or function key, committing a record, or navigating to another record. Appendix B, "Triggers," contains a listing of the triggers and a description of the event that executes them.

Understanding the events that fire a trigger gives the developer a lot of control over the behavior of the form. For some triggers, it is easy to understand the event that executes the trigger. A When-button-pressed trigger fires when the associated button is clicked. For some of the triggers it is more difficult to determine which of the possible events to use. For instance, when an item is validated, six events occur. Triggers exist for each of the events. The item validation events and their order of occurrence are as follows:

- Pre-text-item—Occurs when the cursor is moved into the item.
- Validation Window Specification—Consists of checking the range property values.
- Post-Change—Occurs when a value is changed in the item.
- When-Validate-Item—Occurs when the item is compared to the LOV specified for the item.
- Post-Text-Item—Occurs when the cursor is moved from the item.
- On-Validate-Record—Occurs when the entries are validated against the database specifications.

In looking at the preceding list there doesn't seem to be much difference between each of the events. Most of the time, the developer may choose any of the events and the trigger will produce the required results. Occasionally, the form requires the PL/SQL trigger to be executed at a specific time. For instance, the developer may want the trigger to format a value in an item. It might be more advantageous to format the item before the user tabs into the item rather than after the user tabs out. This gives the user the opportunity to change the formatting while the cursor is in the item rather than when it is in another item. This is why it is important to know that a variety of events can occur in sequence. The developer may choose or test a variety of events in the form to determine whether the desired results are attained.

## Trigger Names

The name of a trigger contains information about when the trigger will be fired and the type of trigger. The beginning of the trigger name contains a keyword expressing when the trigger will be fired in relation to the specified event that follows the keyword. The keywords consist of When, On, Pre, and Post.

Triggers that begin with the word When provide extra processing to what is already being performed by Oracle as a result of the event. The On triggers take the place of the default processing for the event. The Pre triggers execute before the specified event occurs. The Post triggers fire after the specified event.

## Trigger Failures

Triggers contain SQL statements. When a statement in the trigger fails, all processing stops and the form returns to the state before the event occurred. An error message appears on the message line at the bottom of the screen declaring a failure. If you do not want the processing to terminate, be sure to include exception handling in the PL/SQL. This will allow you to use more-descriptive error messages or save processing steps.

In some cases, the purpose of the trigger is to validate values. When the validation or edit process fails, the developer needs a way to terminate processing and return to the original state of the form. Triggers can be placed in the failure mode by executing the following command: raise form_trigger_failure. This command will terminate any trigger.

## Trigger Levels

Triggers can exist on three levels: form, block, and item. Form-level triggers execute when the event occurs anywhere on the form. Block-level triggers fire when the event happens on the block. Item-level triggers fire as a result of item events.

Some triggers are unique to the level, but many of the triggers can be placed on any of the levels. For instance, a Post-query trigger cannot be placed on an item; it is usually placed as a block-level trigger. The Key-exeqry trigger, which is fired when the execute-query function key is clicked, can be placed on all three levels. A lower-level trigger overrides triggers defined at a higher level. This can cause unexpected results when the same trigger is used on different levels. Triggers should always be created on the lowest possible level.

## Creating a Trigger

The following steps can be used to create a trigger:

1. Open the Object Navigator and select the form object linked to the trigger. Expand the object. Select the triggers object. Click the Create icon on the tool palette. This opens the Triggers dialog box.
2. Select the appropriate trigger from the Trigger dialog box. Click OK. This opens the PL/SQL editor.
3. Enter the PL/SQL statements in the editor. Click the Compile button to validate the statements. Click the Close button when done.

As an example of the preceding procedure, the following illustrates the creation of a When-validate-item trigger that allows only a future date to be entered for the last_payment_date on block two. When an invalid date is entered, the form processing is terminated and an error message placed on the message line.

1. The first step is to create a trigger object. Open the Object Navigator.
2. Select and expand block two.
3. Select and expand the items object.
4. Select and expand the last_payment_date item. The triggers object will be visible.

Figure 15.1 displays the Object Navigator after these steps have been performed.

To open the Triggers dialog box, select the trigger object and click the Create icon on the left side of the navigator.

This opens the Triggers dialog box, as shown in Figure 15.2. The dialog box is a list box that can be used to identify and select a trigger. The scroll bar on the right side of the window may be used to scroll through the triggers. At the top of the box is a window item to place characters that can be used in a search. The find button executes the search by using the characters. Figure 15.2 shows a search for triggers that begin with a "W" and have a "V" in the expression.

To open the PS/SQL editor, select the When-Validate-Item trigger and click the OK button.

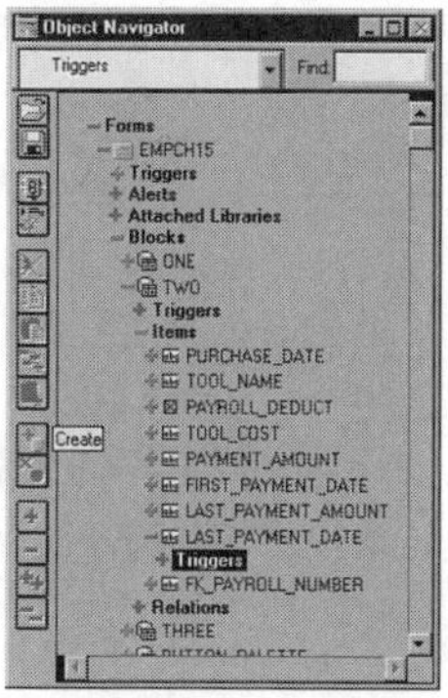

**FIG. 15.1**
The Object Navigator ready for the trigger to be created on the last_payment_date item.

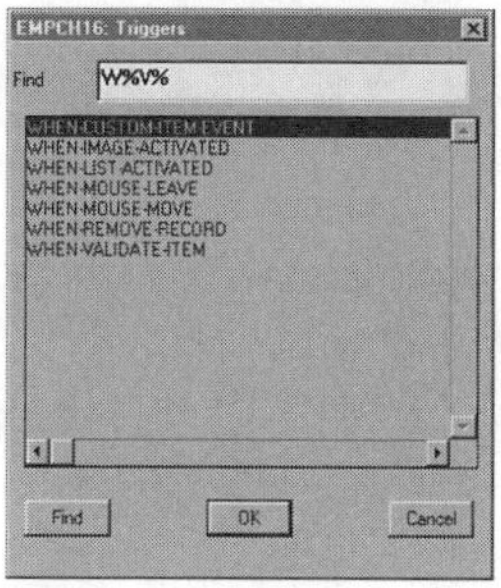

**FIG. 15.2**
The Triggers dialog box that displays the results of a character string search.

This opens the PL/SQL editor displayed in Figure 15.3. This editor records the PL/SQL code that will be executed by the trigger. The PL/SQL block in the figure consists of a typical PL/SQL block. It consists of an `if-then-else` statement. If the date in the last_payment_date item on block two is less than the current date, the trigger will display an error message and terminate processing. The "bell" keyword is a built-in subprogram that causes a sound alerting the user to the error condition. Processing is terminated by the "raise form_trigger_failure" command. Enter the PL/SQL script contained in Figure 15.3 into the When-Validate-Item trigger.

**NOTE** PL/SQL code used in a trigger must have a colon precede any non-database variable used by the code. In Figure 15.3, the variable `:two.last_payment_date` is a form item. It must have the colon precede the name. In addition, assignment operators must also use the colon. This last item is standard PL/SQL symbology, but an error I make consistently. ■

When done placing the code, click the Compile button to validate the script. The code in figure 15.3 is correct and will compile successfully. In Figure 15.4, the colon in front of the :two.last_payment_date item was removed. The figure illustrates the error message displayed when faulty PL/SQL code is compiled.

After the PL/SQL is validated, press the Close button. The trigger can now be used. Generate and run the form. Figure 15.5 displays the executed Employee Update form after the trigger detects an error during the validation process.

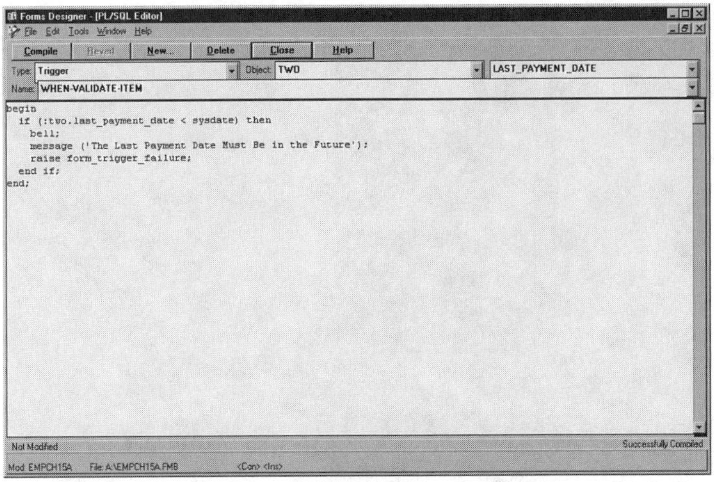


**FIG. 15.3**
The When-Validate-Item trigger PL/SQL code block.

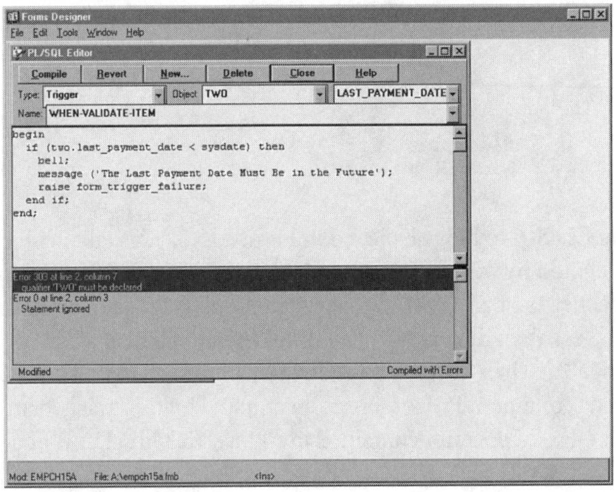


**FIG. 15.4**
The PL/SQL code containing an error in the syntax of the two.last_payment_date.

# Using the PL/SQL Editor

The PL/SQL editor records PL/SQL statements in the form. Selecting the Tools/PL/SQL menu option or double-clicking a PL/SQL item on the Object Navigator opens it. The editor has six buttons near the top of the box, as follows:

| Button | Description |
|---|---|
| Compile | The button on the far left. Itcompiles and syntax checks the PL/SQL statements currently in the editor. |
| Revert | The next button, which returns the statements in the editor to the contents of the editor when last saved. This button allows the developer to undo any problems the modifications may have caused. |

| Button | Description |
|---|---|
| New | Launches the Triggers dialog box, from which the developer can specify a type of trigger. Designer then clears the contents of the editor, allowing the developer to begin development of a new trigger. |
| Delete | Removes the PL/SQL object from the form. |
| Close | Closes the current window. |
| Help | Launches the Designer Help facility. |

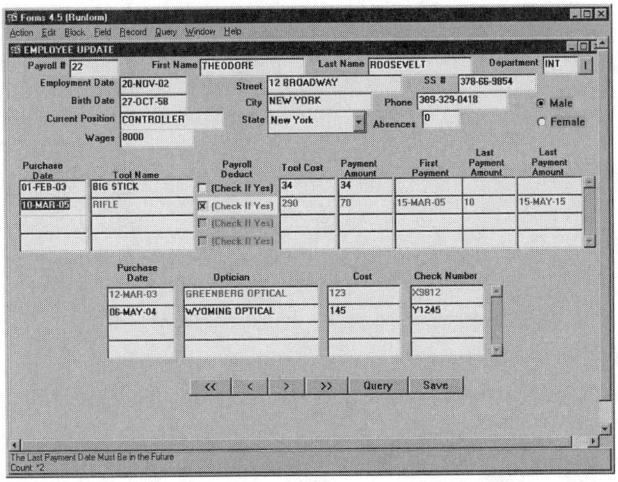


**FIG. 15.5**
The Employee Listing displaying the error message produced by the When-Validate-Item trigger.

Following the buttons are several picklists that locate PL/SQL objects. *Type* picklist contains two types of objects: program units and triggers. Selecting "program unit" causes the *Name* picklist to contain the name of the form's program units. The *Object* boxes are grayed out because they do not apply to program units.

Selecting the Triggers value in the *Type* picklist causes the *Name* picklist to display the triggers available on the form. The *Object* picklists are active for this type of object. The first *Object* picklist has a value called "(Form Level)" and lists values for each of the form's block. When this picklist contains a value of (Form Level), the *Name* picklist displays all of the form's triggers. When a particular block is selected, the *Name* picklist displays the triggers for that block. This activates the *Object Items* picklist, which contains the name of each of the block's items. It can be used to select an item and further limit the trigger contained on the *Name* picklist. Figure 15.6 displays the PL/SQL editor with the *Object Items* picklist displaying the items for block one.

# Using Built-In Subprograms

Oracle Forms has developed programs that control the behavior of a form. They provide a myriad of functions such as moving the cursor from one item to another, navigating from a block, executing a query, or displaying a message. Appendix A, "Built-In Subprograms," contains the names and descriptions of the subprograms available for use by the developer. Some of the subprograms can be considered a complete PL/SQL statement. *Execute_query* is an example of a subprogram that can be used as a complete statement. Other subprograms must be followed by an expression that supplies a value to the subprogram. The *go_block* subprogram is an example of this type. It must have the name of a block following the function name in order to know where to move the input focus. The subprogram name or subprogram name and expression must end with a semi-colon.

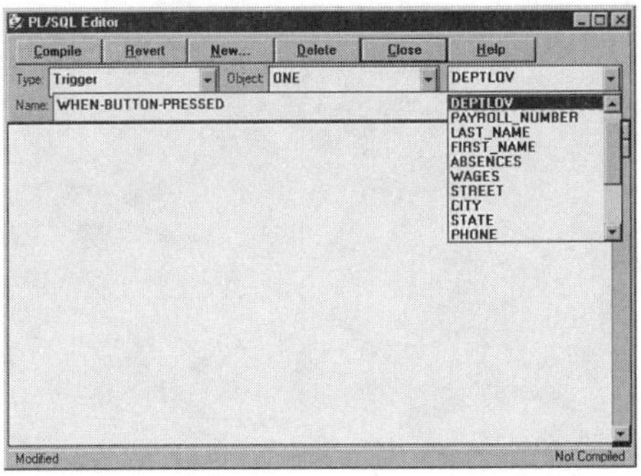


**FIG. 15.6**
The PL/SQL editor displaying the block one items.

In every master-detail form I create, I use two triggers that contain the go_block subprogram. These triggers are the Key-entqry and a When-button-pressed trigger. These triggers redefine the enter-query function key as well as the Query button. The triggers are defined so that the input focus moves to block one before placing the form into the query mode. Entering a query while the input focus is in a detail block causes the query to be performed in the detail block. I do not allow users to query detail blocks. If they did, they would simply get a subset of the block's records. I believe that when a user clicks the query button on a master-detail form they intend to query the master record the majority of the time. Placing the go_block subprogram in the triggers saves the form users from having to manually move the cursor to block one. Figure 15.7 displays the modified When-Button-Pressed trigger used for the Query button. Designer created the button's trigger and PL/SQL code at the time the button palette was created.

**NOTE** You should modify the When-button-pressed trigger for the Query button and add a Key-entqry trigger to the empch15.fmb form. This will allow you to see the effect of the triggers. Be sure to perform queries before making the changes.

Figure 15.8 shows the PL/SQL code for the form level Key-entqry trigger that also needs to be created. This trigger fires whenever the F7 function key is clicked . Because it is a form-level trigger, the location of the cursor does not determine whether it will be fired.

These examples were used to illustrate how the behavior of a form can be modified by the use of triggers that use subprograms. Be sure to look at Appendix A to see the various subprograms and restrictions on their usage.

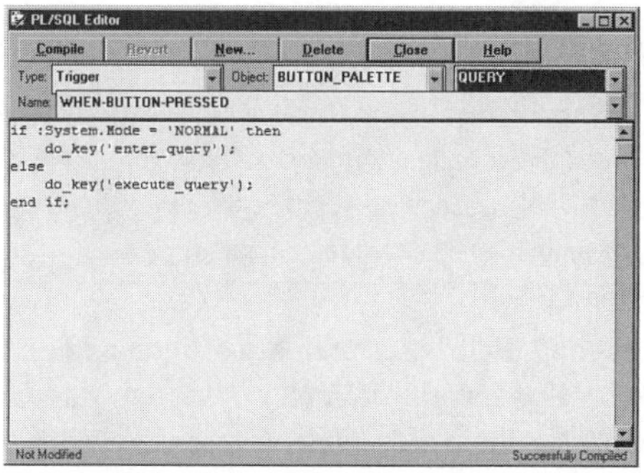


**FIG. 15.7** The When-Button-Pressed trigger for the Query button after a go_block subprogram was added.

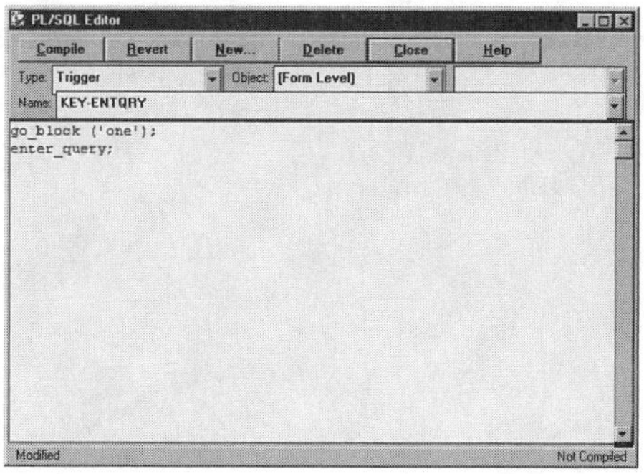


**FIG. 15.8** The form-level trigger Key-entqry used to always place block one in the query mode when the F7 function key is clicked.

# Using System and Global Variables

At times, it is important to control or monitor system parameters. This can be done by using system variables. In Figure 15.7, the `if` condition uses a system variable called *mode* to determine the current mode of the form. The trigger places the form in the query mode if the form is currently in the input or update mode. It executes the query if it is in the query mode. If the trigger had performed the enter_query subprogram when the form was in the query mode, an error would have occurred. In Figure 15.7, the system variable is used to prevent the error from occurring.

Another very useful system variable is *message_level*. All Oracle errors have a numeric severity rating. The lowest rating is 0 and the highest level is 25. The messages on the lower end of the scale are generally informational in nature. They do not usually affect the data or cause problems. It is convenient to occasionally shut these messages off so the user does not see them. Raising the value of the system's message level causes Forms Runtime to stop displaying certain error messages. Oracle does not display messages that have a rating lower than the value of the system message level.

**TIP** I have several applications that use PL/SQL fired from a trigger to create records. After the records are inserted into the database, I issue a commit to save the records permanently. A message appears

*continues*

*continued*

stating `No changes were pending on the form.` This message tells the user the form did not contain modifications and the commit did not affect form records. This is true, but it is useless information. I do not like users to see this message, so I change the message level to 20 before the commit command and return it to 0 immediately after the command.

The available system variables and their descriptions are contained in Appendix A, "Built-in Subprograms." Figure 15.9 contains several examples of system variables. The syntax requires the variable to be proceeded by the keyword *system*. A colon precedes the expression because it is a nondatabase field.

**FIG. 15.9**
Examples of system variable expressions.

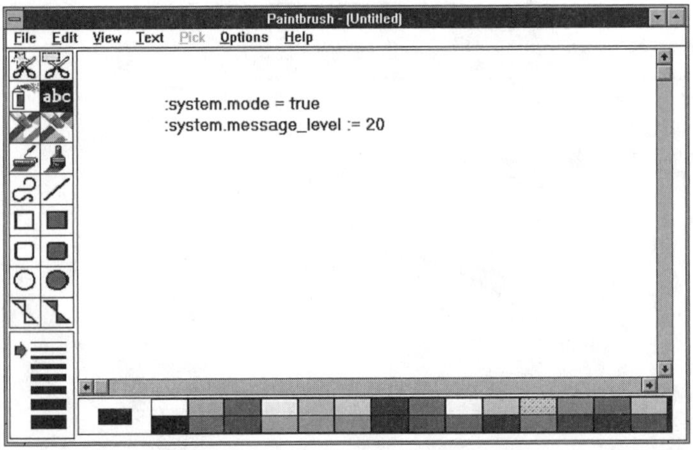


The local variables and items created for a form are only available as long as the form is active. As soon as the form is closed, the area of memory where the values are stored is purged. It is a very common need to keep values available after the application is closed. For instance, when you call another application, you may want to carry the primary key to the new application so the application will know what records to retrieve.

Values can be placed in memory for the life of the session through the use of global variables. Global variable expressions consist of the variable name preceded by the keyword *global*. The variable does not have to be assigned a character type. It will assume the character type of the value it is assigned. Later in this chapter, you'll see a security scheme that contains global variables. They are used to carry security values to the applications in a system.

**TIP** When you use global variables in a system that calls a number of forms, it is good practice to initialize all global variables in the start-up application. This initialization can consist of assigning a null value to the variable. If you reference the global variable in a trigger and it has never been referenced, Forms Runtime will issue an error message. This procedure will eliminate the possibility of the error.

# Using Triggers and Program Units to Check User Security

This section of the chapter illustrates a common security procedure I use on forms that I create. The technique consists of two security triggers. The first trigger authenticates a user by means of a password. The second trigger determines whether the user has the proper security to perform the transaction. The section also covers the use of program units to create common PL/SQL code blocks.

## Form Security Triggers

Most of the forms and systems that are developed require security features to be embedded. I have seen various types of security requests. Some forms allow all users to query the records but not to add, update, or delete the records. The same form allows other users to perform database modifications. In several systems, a security trigger is used to prevent some users from launching specific applications. This section presents a security scheme you can use to meet most security demands.

The heart of the system is a security options table called Sec_tab in the practice database. The table contains two columns: payroll_ number and security_option. Throughout a typical system, various transactions are identified and given a code if security is needed. For instance, the privilege to add, update, or delete records on a form will be represented by a security_option value of AUD. Users without this privilege will not have the authority to update the database through the use of the form. Each unique type of transaction that requires security in the system will be assigned a code.

Users will have a record in the security table for each type of transaction they are permitted to perform. In addition, each user that has a security privilege will have a record containing a password in the security option field. Listing 15.1 displays the contents of the Employee security table. Employees #25 and #35 have passwords of FUZZ and RON. Each of the employees also has the ability to add, update, and delete records. This privilege has not been extended to the remainder of the employees.

**Listing 15.1 L_15_01.TXT—Example Security Password and Option Records for the Employee Update Form**

```
SQL> select * from sectab order by 1;

FK_PAYROLL_NUMBER SECU
----------------- ----
               25 AUD
               25 FUZZ
               35 AUD
               35 RON
```

**NOTE** This is an example of what security options may look like. The sec_tab table does not have any values in it at this time.

Security monitoring is activated when the user launches the system's startup form. On the form are two text items. The user enters a payroll number into the first item, and the corresponding password into the second. Each of the form items has a post-change trigger. The payroll number trigger assigns the global variable payroll_number with the contents of the item. The password trigger performs a security check.

The password post-change trigger is shown in Figure 15.10. This trigger verifies the authenticity of the user. This trigger is executed when the user navigates from the item. It opens a cursor that counts the number of records in the security table that match the values entered by the user in the payroll_number and password fields. If the cursor finds a match, a message is issued stating the user has passed the initial security check. The global variable security_check receives a value of OK. This variable is passed to the various applications in the system.

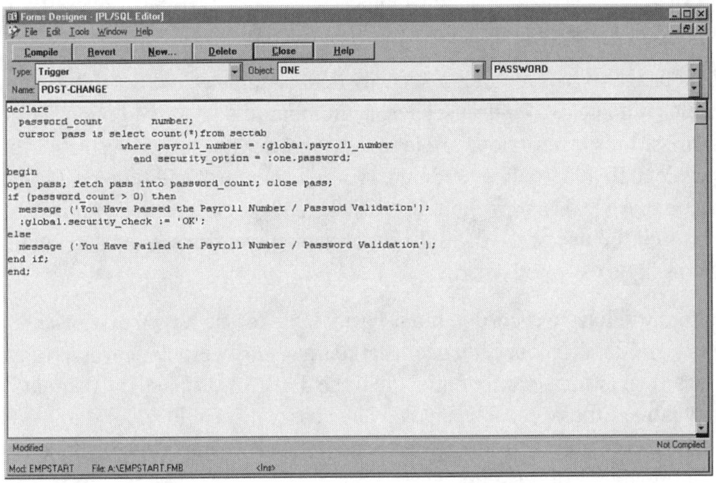
Forms Designer - [PL/SQL Editor]
File Edit Tools Window Help
Compile
Revert
New...
Delete
Close
Help
Type: Trigger
Object: ONE
PASSWORD
Name: POST-CHANGE
declare
password_count number;
cursor pass is select count(*)from sectab
where payroll_number = :global.payroll_number
and security_option = :one.password;
begin
open pass; fetch pass into password_count; close pass;
if (password_count > 0) then
message ('You Have Passed the Payroll Number / Passwod Validation');
:global.security_check := 'OK';
else
message ('You Have Failed the Payroll Number / Password Validation');
end if;
end;
Modified
Not Compiled
Mod: EMPSTART
File: A:\EMPSTART.FMB

**FIG. 15.10**
The password post-change trigger used to validate that the user has security options.

The second part of the security scheme consists of a trigger that fires before the controlled action is performed by the form. The controlled action consists of calling a form or performing a database transaction. When-button-pressed, Pre-insert, Pre-update, and Pre-delete triggers are used for the security checks. The When-button-pressed trigger is attached to a menu option that calls a form. It prevents the user from launching the form. The Pre-insert, Pre-update, and Pre-delete triggers prevent database transactions. Use of these triggers allows all users to call forms and query records. The security check fires when the database transactions are performed and only prevents database transactions.

Figure 15.11 shows a form-level Pre-insert trigger that performs the security check on the Employee Update form. This trigger has a cursor that counts the number of security records for the user. The selected records must have a security_option value of AUD, the security code for performing database transactions. Before the cursor is opened, the first `if` statement determines whether the user has passed the original security check. If the user has not passed the check, an error message appears and the insert transaction is terminated by the *raise form_trigger_failure* statement. If the user passes the security check procedure, the cursor executes. The second `if` statement evaluates the result of the cursor. If the user does not have a record with a value of AUD in the security_option column, an error message appears and the transaction terminates. The transaction occurs only when the user passes the password security procedure and has the proper security option record.

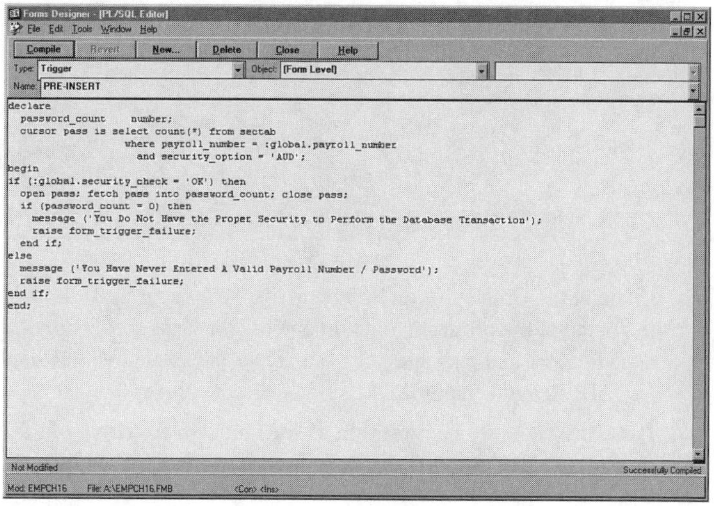
Forms Designer - [PL/SQL Editor]
File Edit Tools Window Help
Compile
Revert
New...
Delete
Close
Help
Type: Trigger
Object: [Form Level]
Name: PRE-INSERT
declare
  password_count    number;
  cursor pass is select count(*) from sectab
                  where payroll_number = :global.payroll_number
                   and security_option = 'AUD';
begin
if (:global.security_check = 'OK') then
  open pass; fetch pass into password_count; close pass;
  if (password_count = 0) then
    message ('You Do Not Have the Proper Security to Perform the Database Transaction');
    raise form_trigger_failure;
  end if;
else
  message ('You Have Never Entered A Valid Payroll Number / Password');
  raise form_trigger_failure;
end if;
end;
Not Modified
Successfully Compiled
Mod: EMPCH16
File: A:\EMPCH16.FMB
<Con> <Ins>

**FIG. 15.11**
A Pre-insert trigger prevents unauthorized users from adding records to the database.

You can use the same trigger PL/SQL code block in the Pre-delete and Pre-update triggers. In this example, the transaction triggers were created at the form-level. The security checks can be used to control block and even items. This is done by assigning the triggers to a block or item. I think you will find this scheme an efficient security mechanism.

## Using Form Procedures

The security scheme in the previous section used the same PL/SQL code block in the Pre-update, Pre-insert, and Pre-delete triggers. It is bad practice and time consuming to have the same code in multiple places. It is very easy to modify the code in one of the locations and forget to modify it in the remainder of the locations. Even if the developer remembers to change the code in all of the locations, it still takes more time than changing it in one location. Form procedures allow the developer to avoid this problem.

Form procedures are program units that are defined in the form. They have a name and can be called by other PL/SQL objects in the form. To create a program unit perform the following:

1. Open the Object Navigator.
2. Locate the program unit object and click the create icon.

   Figure 15.12 displays the Object Navigator and the program unit object.

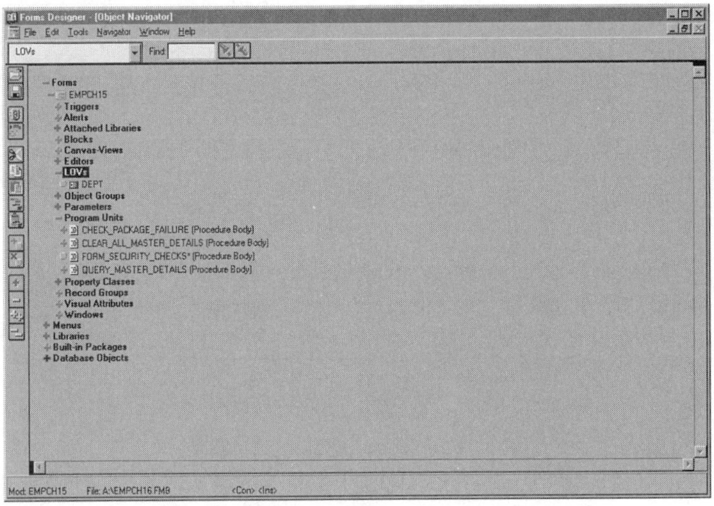


**FIG. 15.12**
The Object Navigator and the program units object.

Clicking the Create button brings up the New Program Unit dialog box, which records the name of the program unit and one of four types: procedure, function, package specification, and package body. The types are explained in Chapter 10, "Using SQL *LOADER, and Chapter 11, "Using an Oracle Form."

3. Populate the New Program Unit dialog box with the name of the program unit and the type of program unit. Press the OK button when done. Figure 15.13 shows the box.

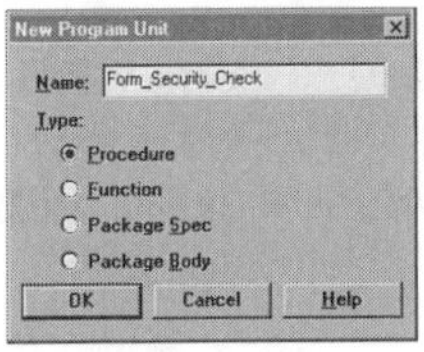


**FIG. 15.13**
The New Program Unit dialog box ready to create a procedure called Form_Security_Checks.

After the OK button is clicked , Designer opens the PL/SQL editor for the procedure. It will contain an empty PL/SQL structure.

1. Enter the PL/SQL for the trigger into the structure.
2. Perform a syntax check by pressing the Compile button.

Figure 15.14 shows the Form_Security_Checks procedure, which has the same PL/SQL statements used in the Pre-insert trigger defined earlier.

To use this procedure in any of the security triggers, place the name of the procedure in trigger code. Figure 15.15 shows the Pre-delete security trigger using the security procedure.

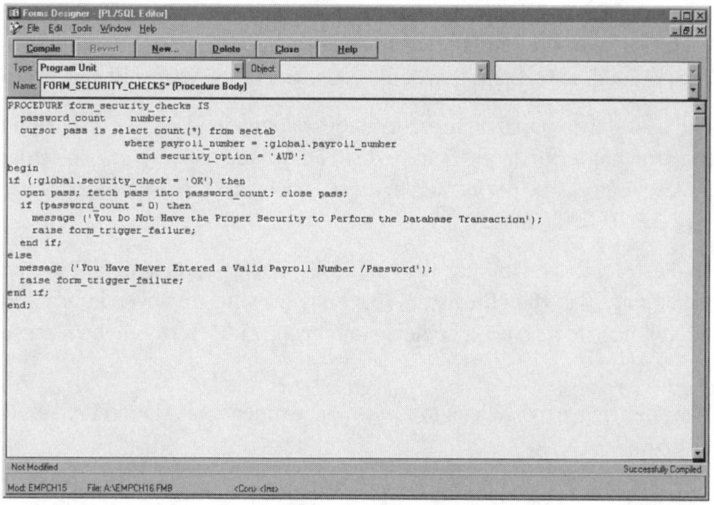
Forms Designer - [PL/SQL Editor]
File Edit Tools Window Help
Compile
Revert
New...
Delete
Close
Help
Type Program Unit
Object
Name FORM_SECURITY_CHECKS* (Procedure Body)
PROCEDURE form_security_checks IS
password_count number;
cursor pass is select count(*) from sectab
where payroll_number = :global.payroll_number
and security_option = 'AUD';
begin
if (:global.security_check = 'OK') then
open pass; fetch pass into password_count; close pass;
if (password_count = 0) then
message ('You Do Not Have the Proper Security to Perform the Database Transaction');
raise form_trigger_failure;
end if;
else
message ('You Have Never Entered a Valid Payroll Number /Password');
raise form_trigger_failure;
end if;
end;
Not Modified
Successfully Compiled
Mod: EMPCH15
File: A:\EMPCH16.FMB
<Con> <Ins>

**FIG. 15.14**
The Form_Security_Checks procedure.

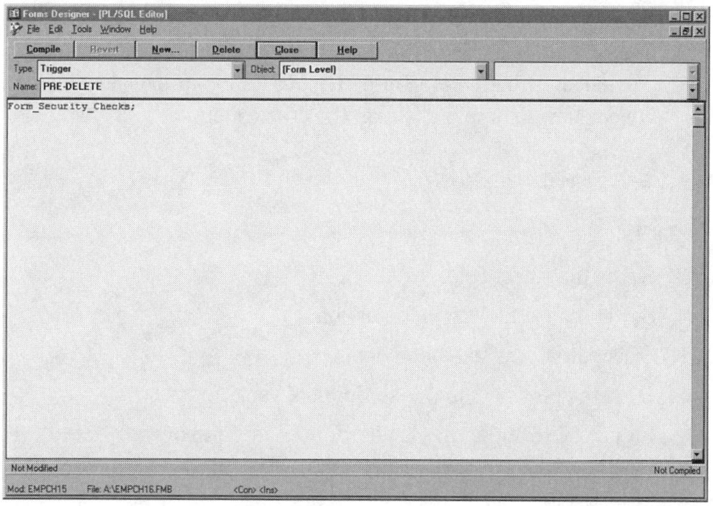
Forms Designer - [PL/SQL Editor]
File Edit Tools Window Help
Compile
Revert
New...
Delete
Close
Help
Type Trigger
Object (Form Level)
Name PRE-DELETE
Form_Security_Checks;
Not Modified
Not Compiled
Mod: EMPCH15
File: A:\EMPCH16.FMB
<Con> <Ins>

**FIG. 15.15**
The Pre-delete trigger using the Form_Security_Checks procedure.

# Adding and Populating Non-Base Table Text Items

Relational tables often contain foreign key columns that relate one table to another table. These related tables usually contain descriptive information about the entity. For example, the Department table contains the name of the department. The department name provides more description about the employee than the value of the fk_department column on the Employee table.

These descriptive fields enhance the presentation of a form. In order to get the fields on the form, it is possible to create a view joining the tables. The view is then used as the base table name for the block. The descriptive fields will be populated as the result of normal form operations. There are two problems with this technique. A form cannot perform insert, update, or delete operations against a view. The second problem is performance. Each time a query that contains a join is executed, Oracle creates a new virtual table. When the database contains a large amount of records, this could cause performance problems.

The best way to populate these form description fields is to fire Post-query or post-change triggers that populate the fields, which allows the block to use an actual table name. Database transactions can be performed and the Oracle will not have to process a table join when retrieving records to the form.

To illustrate this technique, the Employee Update form is modified and the employee's department name placed on the form. This enhances the employee information on the form. The user will not have to interpret the department value to determine the name of the employee's department.

The following are the steps to place a department description field on the Employee Update form.

1. The first step is to create a new text item on block one and place it on the form.

   The best spot for the department name is on the second row below the department, which means the social security number item must be moved.

2. Create a new text item by using the button tool on the Layout Editor, or by copying and pasting an existing item on the Layout Editor, or by selecting a text item object on the Object Navigator and clicking the create icon.

**NOTE** I prefer the copy/paste method.

3. Select the street field.
4. Select the Edit, Copy menu option.
5. Select the Edit, Past-menu option.
6. Drag the new item to the appropriate spot.

   Figure 15.16 shows the Layout Editor after the new text item (item12) has been positioned.

7. The next step is to change the item's properties. Double-click the item in the Layout Editor. Update the properties to the following:

| **Name** | **Department_name** |
|---|---|
| Base Table | False |
| Maximum Length | 30 |
| Navigable | False |
| Query Allowed | False |
| Insert Allowed | False |
| Update Allowed | False |

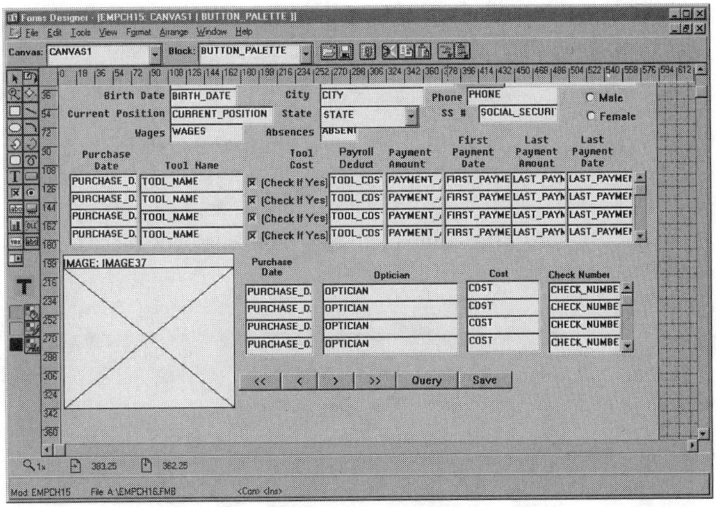

**FIG. 15.16**
The Employee Update form after a new text item that will contain the department name has been added.

Changing the base table property makes this field a nonbase-table text item. This means the item will not be populated through the normal Forms Runtime query process. The text item will be populated by using a block-level Post-query trigger.

The Post-query trigger executes a SELECT statement after the Employee record is fetched to the form. The `select` statement retrieves the department name from the Department table based upon the value contained in the fk_department field on block one. The trigger is shown in Figure 15.17. The upper and `rtrim` functions are used in the `where` clause to ensure that any case sensitivity problems are eliminated.

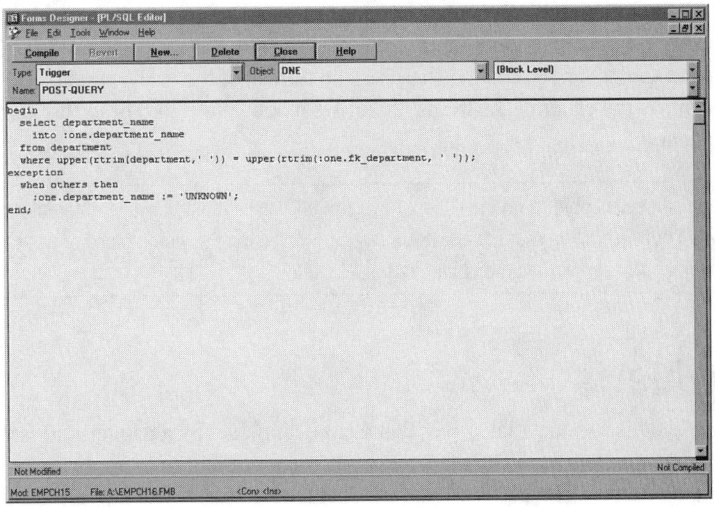


**FIG. 15.17**
The Post-query trigger that will populate the department name field.

**NOTE** When using a Post-query trigger, you must include an exception handler. I feel it looks professional to place a value in description fields when the search value is Null or does not exist in the queried table. More importantly, if the search value does not exist in the master table, a `no-record-found` error occurs. Forms Runtime issues the error message for each record returned by the main query. This will cause your users a great deal of trouble and probably get you some phone calls.

Figure 15.18 displays the completed form. The employee record now contains the department name.

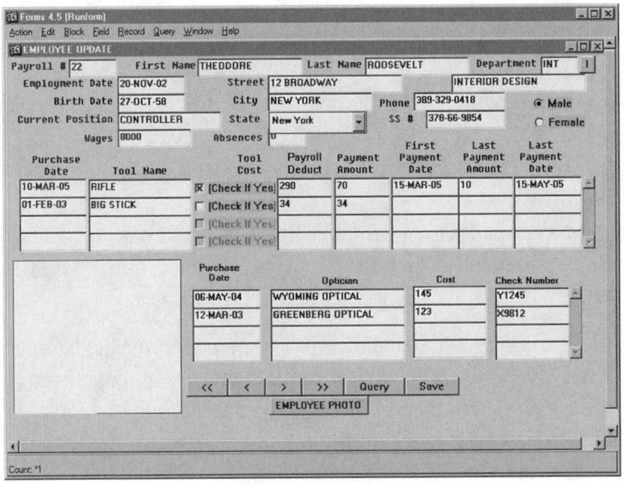


**FIG. 15.18** The Employee Update form displaying the department name in a non-base table item.

When placing new items on a form or rearranging the text items, the tab order of the items is generally disrupted, and the tab order of the items is changed on the Object Navigator. To reset the tab order, expand the block so that all of the items can be seen. The tab order of the items is the order of the items under the block. Select and drag the items to their proper sequence.

**TIP** You can select objects on the Object Navigator and move them between different blocks on a form and even between different modules. If you place an object on the wrong block or want to copy an object from another form, drag the object on the Navigator.

# Using Alerts

An alert is a modal dialog box that can be launched by a trigger and is used to get the operator's attention. Thus far, we have seen a number of triggers that issue passive messages. Passive messages are placed on the message or status line and are easy for the operator to miss. The alert is displayed within the window and requires a clicking action by the operator. Alerts are very difficult for an operator to miss or ignore.

**NOTE** I generally use alerts in security triggers or whenever the operator may be in danger of making a serious error.

I have a form that generates sequentially numbered records. The form has a field for the number of records to generate. It is right next to a payroll number field. One day I placed my payroll number into the Number of records to generate field. I successfully generated 3,221 sequentially numbered records. I had to ask the DBA to delete the records for me. This error caused me to create an alert for the application prompting the operator to approve the generation of any number of records greater than 10.

To illustrate an alert, the security trigger contained in the Pre-insert trigger in Figure 15.11 will be changed to display alerts rather than passive messages. The steps to create this alert are as follows:

1. Open the Object Navigator.
2. Create an alert object by selecting the alert object and click the create icon.

   Designer will create a sequentially numbered alert. Because the dialog box has two messages, two alerts are needed. The Object Navigator containing the two alerts is displayed in Figure 15.19. The alert object navigator icon is a red flag.

**FIG. 15.19**
The Object Navigator listing the two alerts and the alert property sheet.

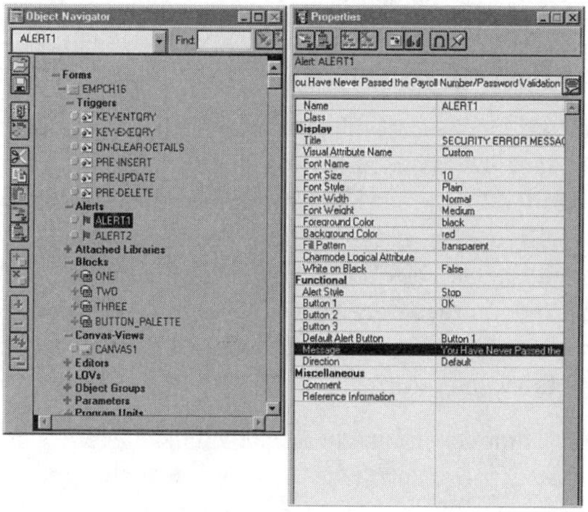


3. The next step is to modify the alert's properties.

   The alert property sheet is also contained in Figure 15.19. The Display Properties section controls the alert's title and color format, properties described in earlier chapters. The functional properties are peculiar to the alert. Table 15.1 contains a description of the various functional properties.

**Table 15.1 Alert Functional Properties**

| Property | Description |
|---|---|
| Alert Style | Determines the style of alert. Three styles are available: Stop, Caution, and Note. Stop contains the picture of a stop sign, and indicates the highest degree of danger. Caution contains an exclamation mark (!) surrounded by a white circle. Note uses a small letter I surrounded by black a circle. This symbol represents the lowest degree of danger. |
| Button 1 | Contains the label for the first button on the alert. |
| Button 2 | Contains the label for the second button on the alert. |
| Button 3 | Contains the label for the third button on the alert. |
| Default Alert Button | Identifies the default alert button. This button is normally formatted differently than the remainder of the buttons. |

The alert style for the security error messages is *stop*, which indicates the highest degree of danger. The alert can have more than one button, but this alert will have only one. Buttons 2 and 3 will not be displayed because their properties are Null. The *message* property contains the message that will be displayed in the alert. `Alert1` will contain the message about not validating the password, and `Alert2` will contain the second trigger error message.

Alerts are activated by the *show_alert* built-in subprogram. The subprogram is a function that returns a numeric constant. This constant is used to determine which of the three buttons was pressed. The value returned by the alert can be compared to the `alert_button1`, `alert_button2`, and `alert_button` variables. If the returned value is equal to the value of `button_alert1`, then button one was clicked . If the value equals `alert_button2` or `alert_button3` the clicked buttons were 2 or 3. The developer can assign a different set of procedures to each of the buttons clicked . This makes it possible to perform different procedures depending upon the value returned.

Because `show_alert` is a function it must be contained in an expression. Figure 15.20 displays the `Form_security_checks` procedure. This procedure was changed to use the `show_alert` function to display `Alert 1` and `Alert 2` rather than the messages. Your next steps are as follows:

1. Modify this procedure to display the alerts rather than the error messages.
2. Generate and run the form.

Figure 15.21 contains the Employee Update form with the Alert1 dialog box displayed. It was displayed as a result of trying to update the Employee table.

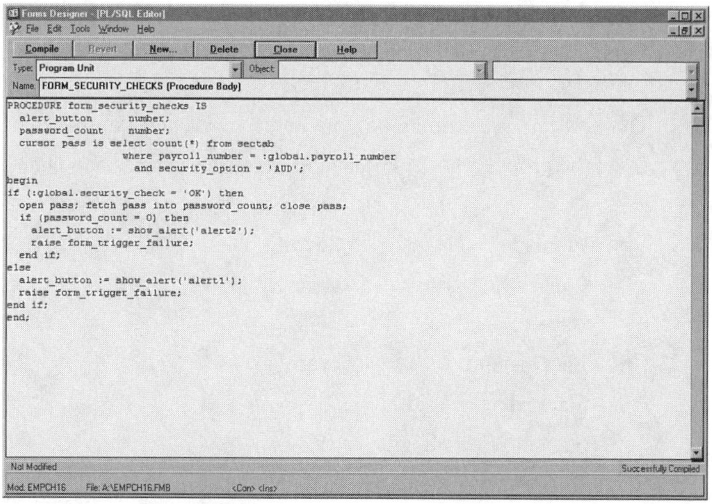
Forms Designer - [PL/SQL Editor]
File Edit Tools Window Help
Compile Revert New... Delete Close Help
Type: Program Unit
Object:
Name: FORM_SECURITY_CHECKS (Procedure Body)
PROCEDURE form_security_checks IS
alert_button number;
password_count number;
cursor pass is select count(*) from sectab
where payroll_number = :global.payroll_number
and security_option = 'AUD';
begin
if (:global.security_check = 'OK') then
open pass; fetch pass into password_count; close pass;
if (password_count = 0) then
alert_button := show_alert('alert2');
raise form_trigger_failure;
end if;
else
alert_button := show_alert('alert1');
raise form_trigger_failure;
end if;
end;
Not Modified
Successfully Compiled
Mod: EMPCH16 File: A:\EMPCH16.FMB <Con> <Ins>

**FIG. 15.20**
The Form_Security_Checks procedure after it was modified to include alerts.

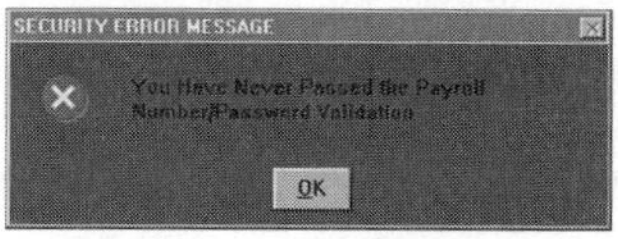
SECURITY ERROR MESSAGE
You Have Never Passed the Payroll Number/Password Validation
OK

**FIG. 15.21**
The Alert 1 dialog box displayed as a result of trying to update the Employee table.

# Using Triggers to Change Form Canvases

All forms and screens have one fundamental problem. The form has a defined height and width and the data viewed must fit within this space. To fit the space, you can lower the font sizes so additional data is displayed. Or you can place scroll bars on the windows so additional fields can be viewed by scrolling. I am not particularly fond of either method. There is a definite limit to the size a font can be reduced before the user can no longer read the screen. A technique that I have found and used extensively to solve this problem is to create a form with multiple canvases. The canvases can be displayed by clicking a button. This allows me to create a completely new view of the data.

To illustrate this concept, suppose the operator of the Employee Update screen wanted to see more than four Tools and four Glasses records at a given time but didn't need to see both sets of records at the same time. The Employee Update form cannot handle this request because there is not enough vertical height on the form to display increased amounts of Tools and Glasses records. To create additional space, the employee image and Glasses records can be placed on separate canvases, which would free up enough space to display 10 records.

The following steps can be used to create and display multiple canvases on the Employee Update form.

The first step to modify the Employee Update form is to create two additional canvases.

1. Open the Object Navigator.
2. Select the canvas object and click the Create icon twice. This creates two default canvases.
3. The new canvases should be renamed canvas2 and canvas3.
4. Open the property sheet for each of the new canvases and change the following properties:

| **Property** | **Setting** |
|---|---|
| Canvas-view type | stacked |
| Bevel | none |
| Background | cyan |
| Stacked View Width | 592 |
| Stacked View Height | 210 |
| Display Y Position | 90 |

The next step is to place the image item and the block-three items used for the Glasses records on the new canvases.

5. Open the Layout Editor and select each of the block-three items (Glasses records).

   Items will not be deselected if the shift key is held down while selecting additional items.
6. Double-click any of the selected items to open a multiple item property sheet.
7. Change the canvas property to canvas2. This causes the items to disappear from the Layout Editor.
8. Select all of the block-three boilerplate items.
9. Select the Edit, Cut menu options, which removes the boilerplate from the original canvas.
10. Open canvas2 and select the Edit, Paste menu option. The boilerplate appears on canvas two with its original spacing.
11. Format the canvas to your taste.
12. Open the block-three property sheet and change the `records displayed` property to 10.

    Figure 15.22 displays canvas2 after the changes have been made.
13. The image item, image37, is placed on canvas3 by changing the item's canvas property to canvas3.
14. Open the Layout Editor for canvas3 and reformat the position of the image item. Canvas1 now has sufficient space.
15. The block-two property, `records displayed`, should be changed to 10.

    The reformatted canvas is shown in Figure 23.

    A form displays a canvas when the input focus moves into an item contained on the canvas. This can occur by tabbing from one item to another or by navigating to another block. The Employee Update form uses buttons and the go_block subprogram to display the various canvases. The go_block subprogram is placed in a When-button-pressed trigger linked to a button. When the button is clicked, Forms Runtime navigates to the block specified in the subprogram and displays the canvas for the first item on the block. Figure 15.24 shows the trigger that calls canvas2 or the Glasses records.

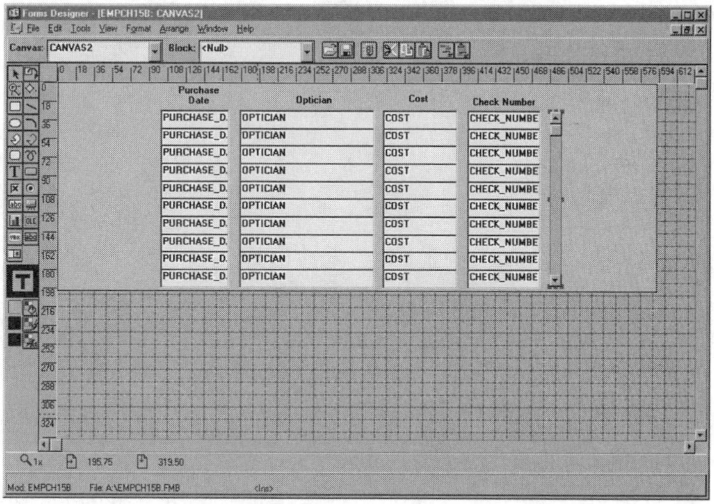

**FIG. 15.22** Canvas2 after the block-three items have been formatted.

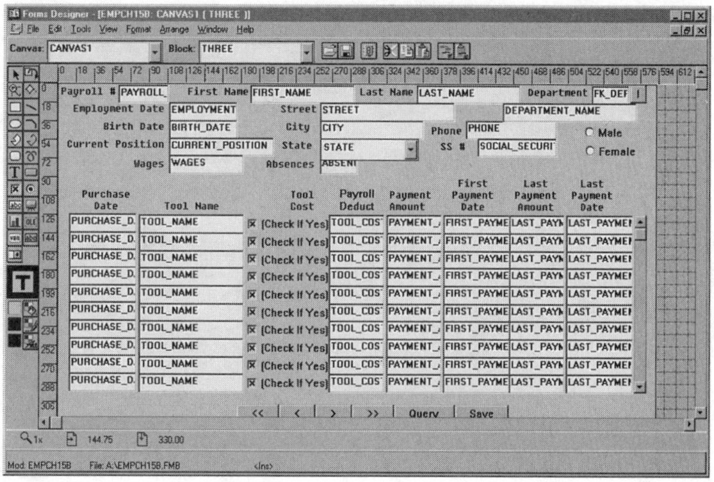

**FIG. 15.23** The reformatted canvas1 displaying 10 Tools records.

16. Create the button and trigger that will call canvas2 or the Glasses records.
17. Create a similar button that call canvas1 or the Tools records.

The default canvas in the Employee Update form is canvas1, containing the Tools record. The Glasses records are displayed by clicking the Glasses button. This causes block-three/canvas2 to appear. Because it is a stacked canvas, it overlays the Tools records on canvas1. Clicking the Tools button causes block-one/canvas1 to appear. Because it is a content canvas, it covers the entire screen. Figure 15.25 displays the Employee Update form after the Glasses button is clicked.

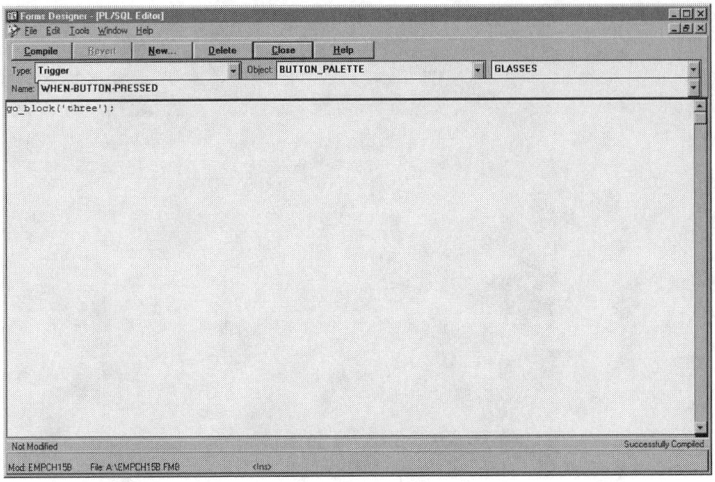


**FIG. 15.24**
The PL/SQL script for the Glasses button that causes the display of the canvas containing the Glasses records.

18. Generate and run the form. Try pressing the Glasses button.

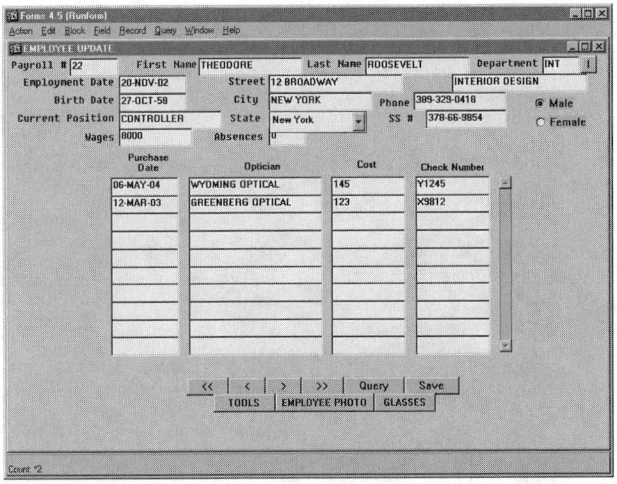


**FIG. 15.25**
The Employee Update for after he Glasses button is clicked.

The Employee photo is still displayed by the Employee Photo button. The When-button-pressed trigger for this button needed to be modified. This button requires the go_block subprogram but also requires a go_item subprogram. The reason for the go_item subprogram is that image37 is contained on block one but is not the first navigation item on the block. When the go_block ('one') subprogram is executed, the input focus is moved to the payroll_number field because it is the first item on the block. The canvas property for payroll_number is canvas1. Thus, the Tools block will appear. The go_item subprogram is necessary to move the input focus to the Image37 item after it is moved to block one. Image37 is located on canvas3 and navigation to the item displays canvas3. Figure 15.26 illustrates the trigger for calling this canvas.

19. Modify the trigger for the image button so that it displays the canvas3.

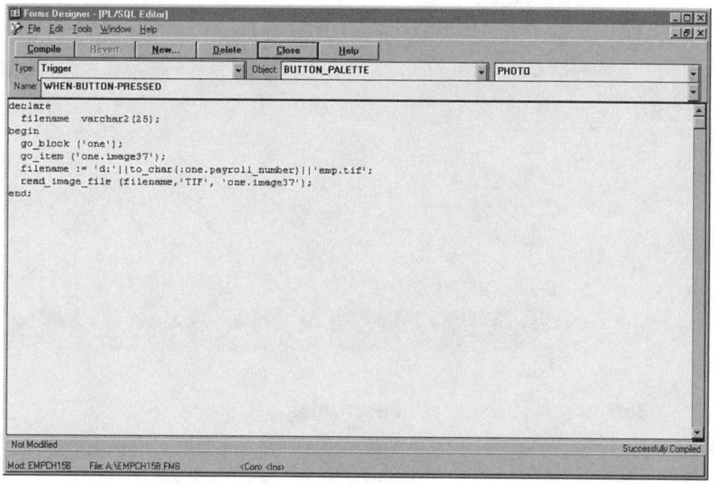


**FIG. 15.26**
The Employee Photo button trigger script that displays canvas3.

I find this technique very useful and preferable over scroll bars and small text. The users of the application seem to really appreciate the ease of obtaining different views of data.

**NOTE** Form module EMPCH15B.FMB, on the CD, contains the final application with the additional canvases. ■

# Using Property Classes

A `property class` is a set of properties that can pass its property values to other objects. Each object that has been reviewed in this part of the book contains a `property class` property. When this property is populated with the name of a property class, the values of the property class override those contained in the object. A property class is similar to a visual attribute in that it can supply property values to an object. It differs in that the visual attribute has a set number of properties. These properties only pertain to formatting attributes. A property class can have as few or as many properties as needed, and they can consist of properties other than formatting properties.

The next several subsections discuss some special tools that exist on the property sheet form. Several of these tools are used to create and modify a property class.

## Using the Property Sheet Tools

The property sheet dialog box contains eight icon buttons on a tool bar at the top-left of the box. From left to right, the buttons are as follows (see Figure 15.27):

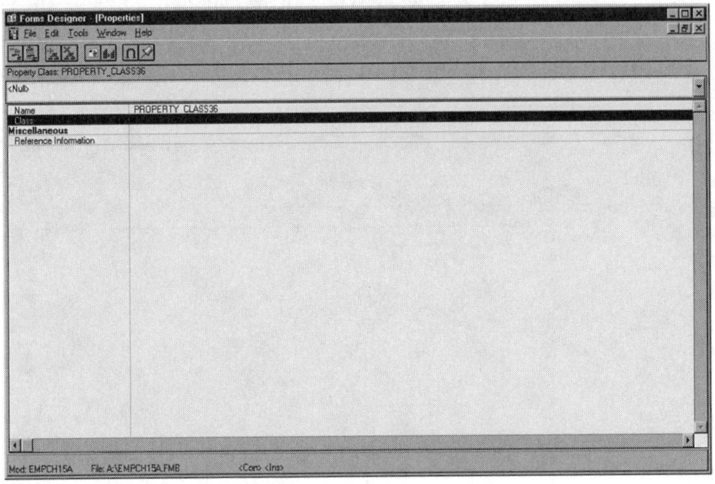

**FIG. 15.27**
The Property Sheet toolbar.

| **Button** | **Description** |
|---|---|
| Copy property | The tool on the far left, which copies an object's properties into the property clipboard. |
| *Paste property* | The properties in the clipboard can be transferred into the current object by clicking the tool. It is the second tool from the left. |
| Add property | Adds properties to a property class. |
| Delete property | The fourth button is the *tool*. It deletes properties from the property class. |
| Property class | The fifth button (with the white figure) is the tool. Clicking this button causes Designer to create a new property class. The new class contains the same properties as the original property sheet. |
| Inherit | The sixth button (with the red figure) is the tool. Clicking this button causes the properties on the property sheet to return to their original default value. |
| Intersection/Union | The tool with the intersection symbol is the tool, which changes the list of properties displayed in a multi-object property list. This button can be toggled, causing the property sheet to display either an *intersection* list or a *union* list. The *intersection* list displays the properties common to all of the |

| Button | Description |
|---|---|
| | selected items. The *union* list displays all of the properties from the selected items. |
| Freeze/unfreeze | The final tool (with the pin symbol) is the tool. It keeps a property sheet from being deselected. This is useful when the developer would like to view two property sheets at the same time. |

# Creating, Modifying, and Using Property Classes

Property classes can be created in one of two methods. The first method is to open a property sheet for an existing item. Clicking the *Property Class* icon creates a property class that contains the same properties and values as the selected item. The second method is to open the Object Navigator, select the property class object, and click the Create tool. This creates a property class with the same properties as shown on the property sheet in Figure 15.28.

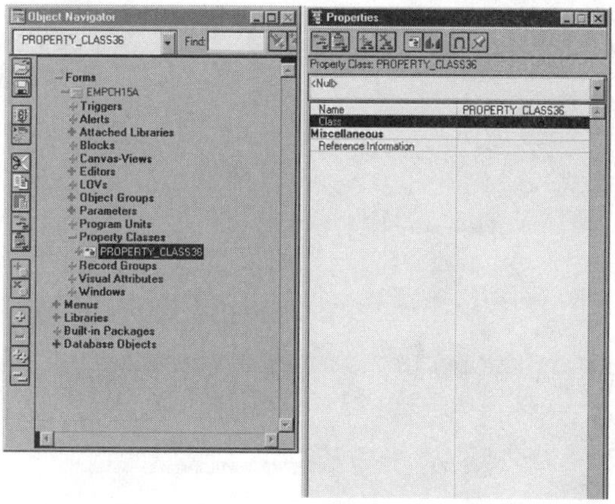


**FIG. 15.28**
A default property class created from the Object Navigator.

The default property class does not contain many properties. Properties can be added to the property class by using the *Add Property* tool. Clicking the tool launches the Properties dialog box displayed in Figure 15.29. This dialog box lists all of the available properties. The developer may scroll through the list and select properties to be added to the class.

Items can be removed from the class by using the *Delete Property* tool.

In the following example, a property class, Property_Class_35, was created, as shown in Figure 15.30. This class contains several properties. The most notable is the `Font Name` property with a value of "Old-English."

Property_Class_35 is then used as a property for the payroll_number item. The property sheet for this item is contained in Figure 15.31. Notice that the properties that receive their values from the property class have an equal sign in front of the property name.

**FIG. 15.29**
The Properties dialog box used to select properties for a property class.

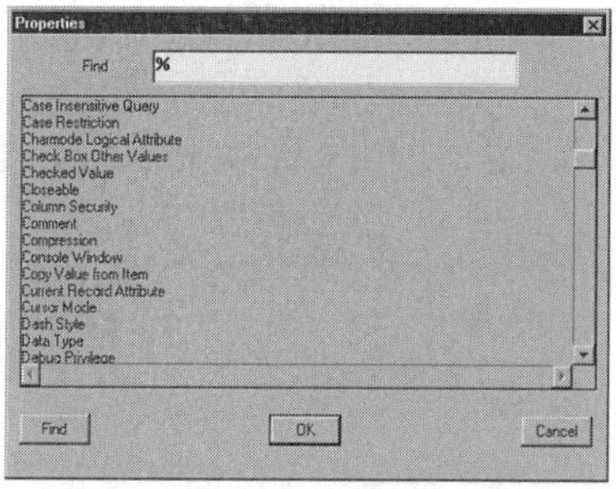


**FIG. 15.30**
Property_Class_35 property sheet.

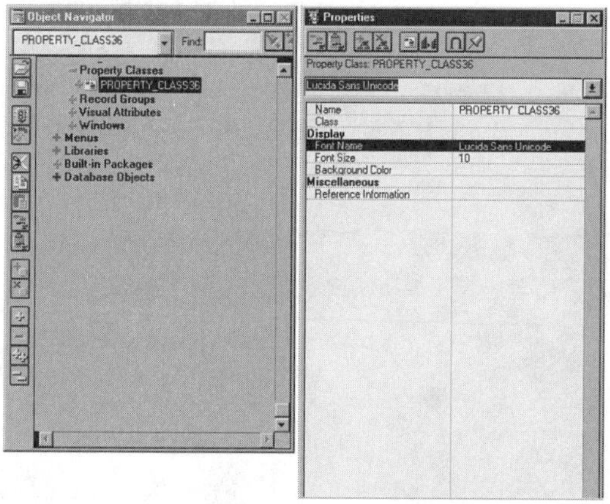


**FIG. 15.31**
The payroll_number item property sheet that is receiving values from a property class.

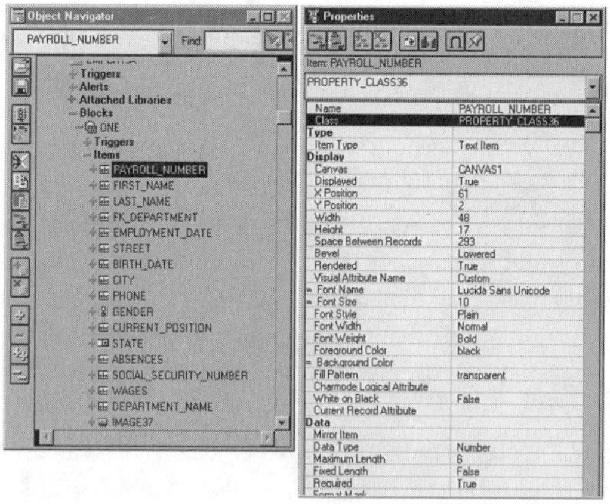


# Viewing Two Property Sheets at the Same Time

Two property sheets can be viewed at the same time by using the *Freeze/Unfreeze* tool. This tool has a yellow pin symbol. To display the two property sheets, follow these steps:

1. Open a property sheet. Click the Freeze/Unfreeze tool. The symbol on the tool changes shape when it is in freeze mode. It will not show the pin.
2. Identify the second object whose property sheet is to be compared. Hold down the shift key while double-clicking the icon to the left of the object.
3. A new property sheet is opened. Position the sheet for the best view in relation to the original property sheet.

The pinned or frozen property sheet remains until the sheet's freeze/unfreeze button is clicked or another property sheet is activated without holding down the shift button.

## Using the Intersection/Union Tool

The *Intersection/Union* tool on the property sheet is used when a multi-object property sheet is being viewed. When the intersection mode is selected by toggling the button, the properties common to all of the objects are seen. Toggling the tool activates the union mode, which shows all of the distinct properties in the set of selected objects. To show the effect of the button, a radio group item and a button were selected. Figure 15.32 shows the property sheet when the tool is in the *intersection* mode.

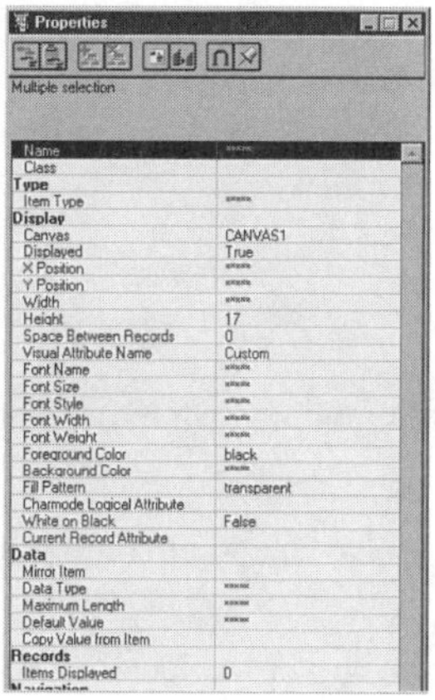


**FIG. 15.32**
A multi-object property sheet in the intersection mode. It displays only the properties common to all objects.

# Summary

A trigger is a PL/SQL object launched when a specific event occurs. Names of the triggers begin with the keywords when, on, pre, and post. The names describe when they fire in relation to the event. Triggers contain SQL statements that cause the trigger to stop processing when the statement produces an error. The trigger can be placed on objects at the form, block, or item level. Lower-level triggers override higher-level triggers of the same name.

The PL/SQL editor documents the PL/SQL code used in a trigger or other PL/SQL form object. Oracle has developed a large number of built-in programs, which perform form functions. They are used in PL/SQL objects.

System variables control system parameters. Global variables store values throughout the life of the session. Security procedures are often required in systems. Triggers can be used to control the access to applications and the ability to make database modifications. Form procedures can also be used in security triggers to reduce errors and increase programming efficiency.

Nonbase table text items are often placed on a form. They increase the information displayed on the form. The items are populated by post_query or post_change triggers.

Alerts are modal dialog boxes that catch a user's attention. Triggers launch the alert. Multiple canvases can be used on a form to increase the amount of information displayed. A stacked canvas can overlay a content canvas. They are displayed by using the go_block subprogram fired by a trigger.

A property class is an object that supplies values to other objects. The property sheet contains eight tools on the tool bar: copy property, paste property, add property, delete property, property class, inherit, intersection/union, and freeze/unfreeze.

## From Here...

The next chapter is the last one to cover SQL*FORMS. Chapter 16 covers the call_form command. It is used to call one form from another. It also discusses how to create a menu and use it to tie applications into a system. Finally, the chapter also describes how to create a directory. This is a special screen used to produce a list of records.

## Review Exercises

You may use form a_14_01.fmb, or the form you modified when performing the Chapter 14 exercises, to perform the following exercises.

1. Create a post-change trigger on block two/last_payment date. This trigger should ensure that the field contains only future dates.
2. Create a form lever trigger that moves the cursor to block one when the enter_query control key is clicked. Modify the Query button trigger to navigate to block one when entering a query.
3. Add a nonbase table text item to the employee form that contains the department name. Create a when-validate-item trigger to populate the item.
4. Add an alert to the trigger created in exercise 1.
5. Modify the employee form to display 10 records on block two and block three. Use a copy of a form for this exercise.

CHAPTER 16

# Calling Other Forms and Using Menus

Forms EMPCH16.FMB and DEPCH16.FMB can be used to practice chapter examples. Forms EMPCH16A.FMB, EMPCH16B.FMB, and EMPSTART.FMB contain final examples.

In this chapter, many of the examples call one form or object from another. When you call an object, you must specify the full file path of the executable file. Because it is impossible to know the filepath you may be using for the follow-along practice, all examples and source code supplied have the filepath of the CD (d:). If you are developing these forms in Designer, or running them from Designer, you may want to change the default filepaths to the filepath you are using. You should also move the called files from the CD to your work directory. Be sure to generate the files in the directory you are using.

Executable files that contain the final modifications have been provided. You may use these to see the effect of the modications. The executable files (.FMX) provided on the CD cannot be loaded into Forms Designer. They must be run from Forms Runtime. ■

**Calling forms**

This section covers the `call_form` and `new_form` subprograms, which are used to launch another form. The chapter also describes various ways of presenting the new forms.

**Creating and using a directory**

This section discusses how to create and use a directory. A directory is a special application used to identify records.

**Creating and using menus to combine applications into a system**

This section describes how to create a menu that ties various applications together into a system.

**Creating a toolbar**

This section discusses how to create a custom tool bar, which is a block object used to perform special functions.

# Calling Forms

A form or menu can call another form by using the call_form or the new_form built-in subprograms. The call_form subprogram takes the new application and overlays it on the original application. The original application is still available to the operator, but is not the current application. The new_form subprogram replaces the calling application with the called application. The calling application will no longer be available to the operator.

I generally use the call_form subprogram in systems that I develop. These systems have a startup application that is the central core of the system. The startup application is the first screen displayed in the system. Other applications are called from this screen. It is the place where the operator always returns when terminating the called applications.

My applications often have the capability to call another form. The reason is to view some additional information not available on the original form. I generally want to return to the calling form with all of its data intact to continue the work. The call_form subprogram enables the operator to return to the previous form with the data intact. Using the new_form subprogram the operator will have to call the previous form, enter the query data, and execute the query. This reduces the operator's productivity.

The one problem with the call_form subprogram is that users sometimes do not terminate the applications. They continue to call additional forms from the menu or from a form. These forms are still active and eventually the user will run out of memory on the PC. The operator usually learns to avoid this problem quickly.

## Using *call_form*

The call_form subprogram launches another form while keeping the original form active. Figure 16.1 shows the call_form syntax and options. The form_name option is the only mandatory option. It contains the name of the form. The name should include the full file path. The display_type option consists of two values: hide and no_hide. The hide option will cause the called form to completely cover the parent application. It will cover the application even if it has a smaller window than the parent does. The no_hide option will allow parts of the parent application not covered by the child application to appear. A following subsection, "Using the Call_form Subprogram with the Hide and No_hide Options Specified," will demonstrate this feature.

The switch_menu option uses two values: no_replace and do_replace. The no_replace option keeps the menu used by the parent application. The do_replace option replaces the menu with the one specified in the child form menu property. The query_mode properties determine whether the child form can be run in the normal mode or in the query mode. The No_query_value setting causes the form to be run in the normal mode. The operator will be able to perform queries, inserts, updates, and deletes. The query_only option disables the form's capability to insert, update, or delete records. Finally the parameter_list option contains the name of a parameter list that will provide values to the child application.

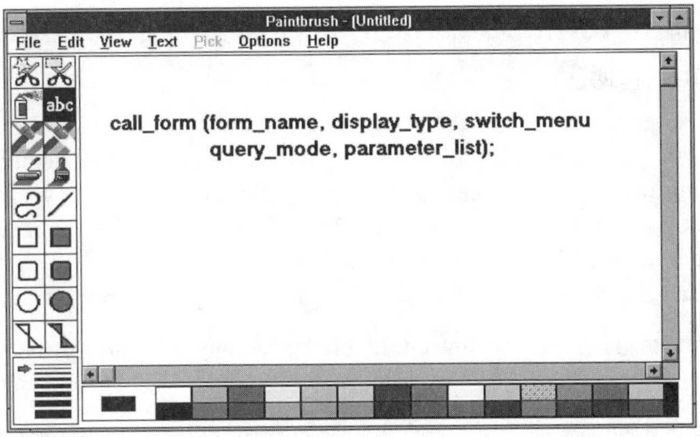


**FIG. 16.1**
Call_form syntax and options.



## Using *new_form*

The `new_form` subprogram activates a new application and terminates the original form. Figure 16.2 shows the syntax of the subprogram and its various options.

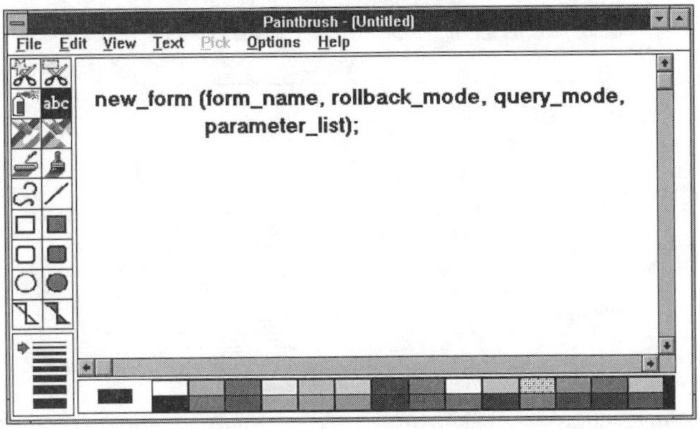


**FIG. 16.2**
`New_form` subprogram and its options.

The `form_name` option contains the name of the child form. This is the only option that is mandatory. The `rollback_mode` option consists of three values: `to_savepoint`, `no_rollback`, and `full_rollback`.

The `to_savepoint` option will roll back all uncommitted changes to the last time a commit was performed. The `no_rollback` option exits the parent form with rolling back to a savepoint. The `full_rollback` rolls back all uncommitted changes that were made during the current Runform session. The `query_mode` option and the `parameter_list` option are exactly the same as the `call_form` options explained in the previous section.

## Using the *call_form* Subprogram with the *hide* and *no_hide* Options Specified

To call another form from an existing form, you must create an item and a trigger. The item can consist of a menu selection, a button on the form, or a button/icon on a tool bar. I generally use a button on the button palette block as the device to call the new form. In the following example, the Employee Update form (EMPCH16.FMB) will be modified to call the Department Update form (DEPCH16.FMB) by using a button. The Department Update form is a smaller form that does not completely cover the Employee Update form.

The first step is to create a new button on the Employee Update form. To do so, follow these steps:

1. Open the Layout Editor and choose an existing button, and then select Edit, Copy. This will copy the button into the clipboard.
2. Select Edit, Paste to place a copy of the button on the canvas. Reposition the new button.
3. Open the button's `When-button-pressed` trigger and enter the trigger text shown in Figure 16.3.

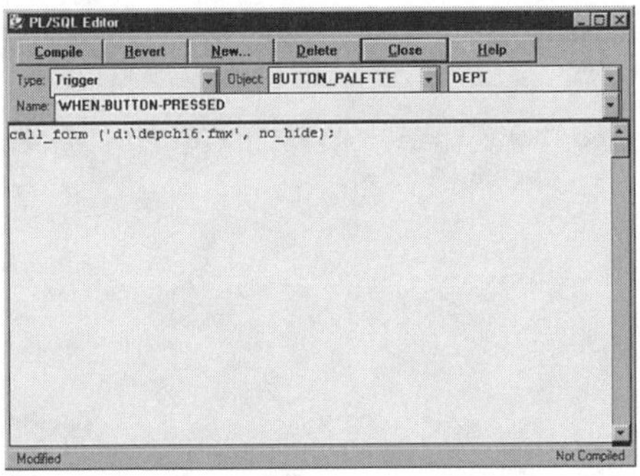


**FIG. 16.3**
The `When-button-pressed` trigger that calls the Department Update form.

The `call_form` subprogram calls the Department Update form. It does not have any options specified so it will hide the parent form. Figure 16.4 shows how the Department Update form will be displayed by using the subprogram in Figure 16.3.

Figure 16.5 contains the `When-button-pressed` trigger with the `no_hide` option specified. This will cause the Department Update form to partially cover the Employee Update form.

Figure 16.6 displays the Department Update form after it was called by using the `no_hide` option.

**TIP** In the preceding examples, the Department Update form was displayed with no records. It's sometimes convenient to have the records displayed for the operator when the form is presented. This is especially true for forms that will not contain a large amount of records. This can be accomplished by creating a `When-new-form-instance` trigger that contains the `execute-query` subprogram.

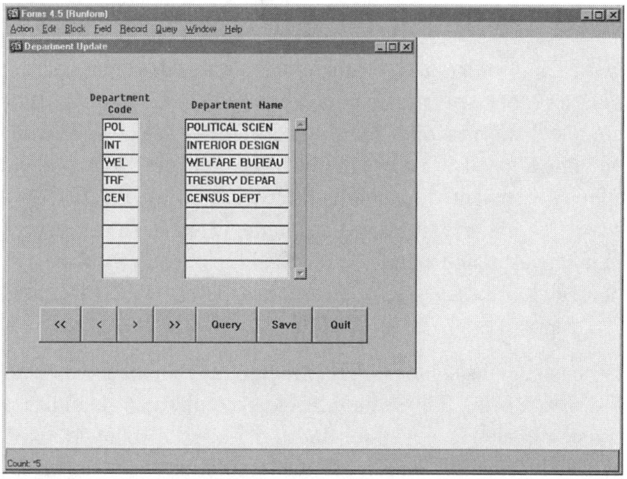


**FIG. 16.4**
The Department Update form as it would appear by using the `call_form` subprogram with no options specified.

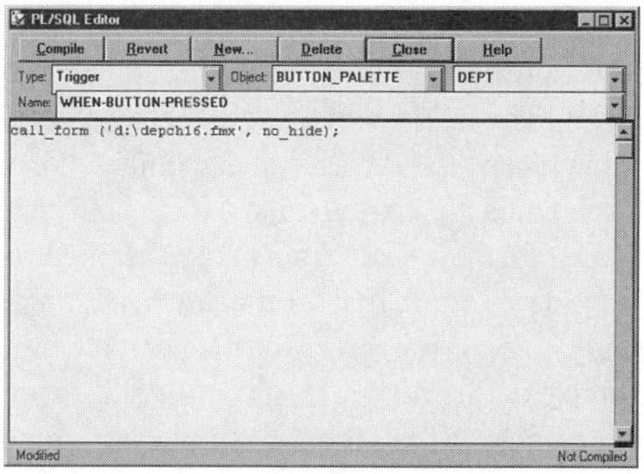


**FIG. 16.5**
The `When-button-pressed` trigger that calls the Department Update form. It contains the `no_hide` option.

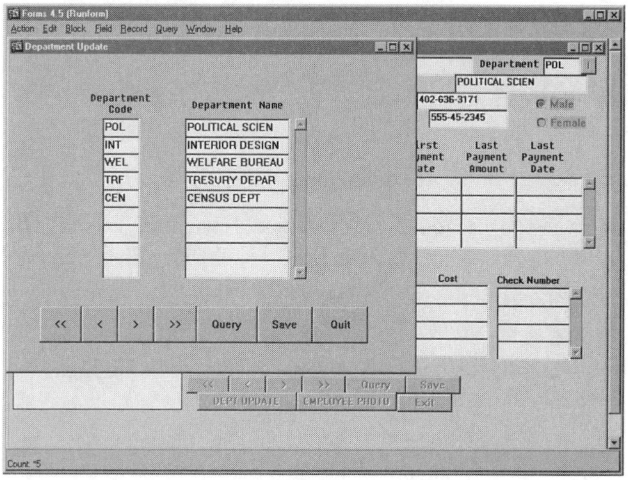


**FIG. 16.6**
The Department Update form as it would appear by using the `call_form` subprogram with the `no_hide` option specified.

# Creating and Using a Directory

A *directory* is an application used to help the operator identify records. It is a tabular style form that produces a set of records based upon entered search criteria. At times the operator does not have complete information about the record to be selected. The directory allows the operator to enter some information and compile a visible list to records to choose from. For instance, suppose the operator wanted to identify the record for the employee with the last name "Kwasniewski." This is an extremely hard name to spell. The operator can enter the following expression in the last name search field: "K%ski". This will produce a short list of employee records that match the expression. The operator likely will be able to identify the record from the list.

Directories consist of three blocks. The first block is a nonbase table form style block that contains the search fields. The second block is a multi-record tabular style block that displays the results of the query. The operator does not have the ability to enter search values into this block. The third block is the button palette. In addition to the normal buttons, it generally contains buttons that call related forms. These forms are used to view additional information about the selected instance.

This design offers some distinct advantages over the straight tabular style form that uses the display fields as the search fields. The fields contained in the search block do not have to be visible in the display block. This means the directory can contain more search fields than the typical tabular form. The search fields are contained in a form pattern and are not limited to the width of the screen as in a tabular form. A second advantage of the directory is that the search criteria remains after the query is executed. In a normal form, after a query is performed, the search criteria are cleared. The operator must reenter the search expressions before a query can be performed. In our example of directory use, if the "K%ski" expression produced a large record set, the operator might be able to limit the set by entering a department number or adding additional characters to the expression. The operator would not have to re-enter the original search criteria since it was still contained in the search text item. This will increase operator efficiency.

## Creating a Directory

The following are the basic steps needed to create a directory:

To create the search block, use the following steps:

1. Create a new form module on the Object Navigator. Select the blocks object and press the create button. This will open the Default Block dialog box.
2. Enter the name of the view or table that will be used in the Display block. The block name should be "one."
3. Select the search fields from the items displayed in the Items tab. Change the item labels to suit your desire.
4. On the Layout tab: the Style is Form, the Orientation is Vertical, and the Records equal one. Click OK to create the block.

5. Open the Layout Editor. Arrange the items and boilerplate. Select all of the text items. Open a multi-item property sheet by double-clicking one of the items. Change the base table property to false, and the case restriction property to upper.
6. Open the Object Navigator. Change the tab order of all the items by dragging and changing their positions. Open the block-one property sheet. Change the Base Table property to `<Null>`.



To create the display block, use the following steps:

1. Open the Object Navigator. Select the blocks object and click the create icon. This will open the Default Block dialog box.
2. Enter the name of the view or table in the base table item. The block name should be "two."
3. Click the Items tab. Select the fields that will be displayed on the block. The block-one search fields that are not displayed fields should also be selected. Change the item labels to suit. Delete the label text for the fields that will not be displayed.
4. Click the Layout tab. On this tab: the Style is "tabular," the Orientation is "Vertical," and the number of records equal to 10. The Button Palette and Scrollbar checkboxes should be checked. Click the OK button to create the block.
5. Open the Layout Editor. Select all of the items that will not be displayed. Open the multi-item property sheet by double-clicking one of the items. Change the Canvas property to "<Null>" and the Displayed property to "false."
6. Select all of the displayed items. Open the multi-item property sheet. Change the Insert Allowed property to "false" and the Update Allowed property to "false."
7. Rearrange and position the block-two items and the button palette buttons.
8. Open the Object Navigator. Select each of the items on block two that are search fields on block one. Open the property sheet of each item and enter the name of the corresponding block one item in the Copy Value From Item property. Be sure to preface the item name with the block name.
9. Create a form level `Key-entqry` and `Key-exeqry` trigger. The PL/SQL code block for these triggers is as follows:

   ```
   go_block go ('two');

   execute_query;
   ```
10. Open the `When-Button-Pressed` trigger for the Button Palette Query button. Delete the existing code block and replace it with the code from #9.
11. Open the Layout Editor. Select the Edit, Select all menu option. Open a multi-item property sheet. Change the Required property to "false."

The preceding steps can be used to create a basic directory. The developer may add LOVs and form calling buttons as needed. The following section demonstrates the creation of an Employee directory.

## Creating the Employee Directory

Take the following steps to create an Employee Directory:

1. The first step in creating the employee directory is to create a new form module.
2. Select the Blocks object and press the create icon. This will open the New Block Items dialog box.
3. Change the Base Table value to Employee and the Block Name value to one.
4. Click the Items tab.
5. Press the Select Columns button to display the items.
6. Select the following items: payroll_number, last_name, first_name, employment_date, birth_date, current_position, fk_department, and gender. Format the labels to suit your needs.
7. Click the Layout tab.
8. Change the Style property to "form." The orientation should remain "vertical" and Records equals 1.
9. Click the OK button to create the default block.
10. Open the Layout Editor and select the Edit, Select All menu option.
11. Double-click one of the text items to open a multi-item property sheet. Be sure the Union property sheet tool is activated. Change the Base Table property to "false" and the Case Restriction property to "Upper." Close the property sheet.
12. Place and format the block one items.
13. Open the Object Navigator. Open the block-one property sheet. Change the Base Table property to "false." Close the property sheet.
14. Change the tab order of the items by dragging them. The tab order is from left to right, top row to bottom row.

    Figure 16.7 shows block one of the Employee Directory.

    Create the display block.
15. Open the Object Navigator and select the Blocks object.
16. Click the Create tool. This will open the New Block options dialog box. The Base Table value is "employee" and the Block Name is "two."
17. Click the Items tab. Click the Select Columns button to display table columns. The columns that will be displayed and all search columns must be selected. Select the following fields: payroll_number, last_name, first_name, employment_date, birth_date, current_position, fk_department, gender, wages, and phone. Delete the labels for the birth_date and gender fields.
18. Click the Layout Tab. The Style setting will be "tabular." The Orientation is "vertical." The value for the Records setting is 10. The Button Palette and Scrollbar check boxes should be checked. Press the OK button to create the display block.

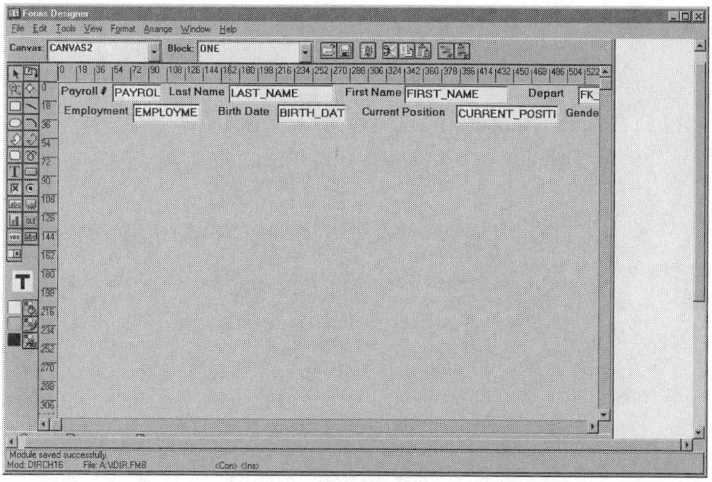

**FIG. 16.7**
Block one of the Employee Directory.

19. Open the canvas property sheet. Change the `Width` property to "592" and the `Background` to "r50g100b50."
20. Open the Windows object property sheet. Set the `Width` property to "592" and the `Title` property to "Employee Directory."
21. Open the Layout Editor and format the items on the canvas.

    Figure 16.8 shows the canvas at this point. The block two fields stretch beyond the edge of the canvas.

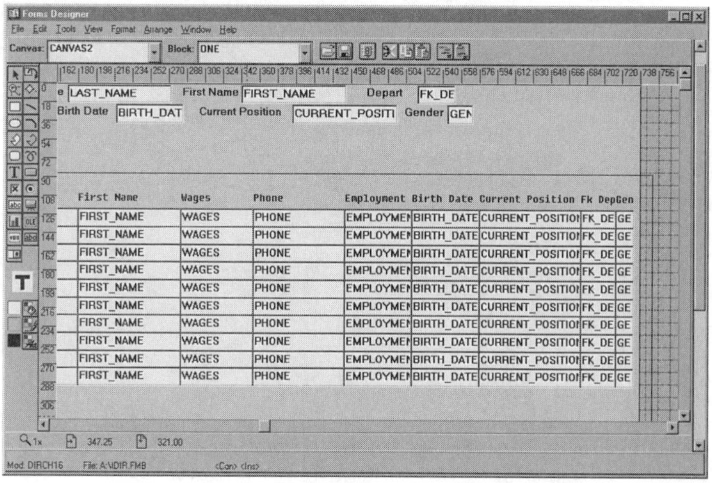

**FIG. 16.8**
The Block two fields before formatting.

22. Select Edit, Select All menu option. Change the font for all canvas objects to MS San Serif, Bold, 10.

23. Select the birthdate and gender items. Open the multi-item property sheet and change the Canvas property to Null and the Display property to "false." This will cause the items to disappear from the canvas.
24. Format the remainder of the items to suit.

    Figure 16.9 shows the canvas after it has been reformatted.

**FIG. 16.9**
The Employee Directory after formatting.

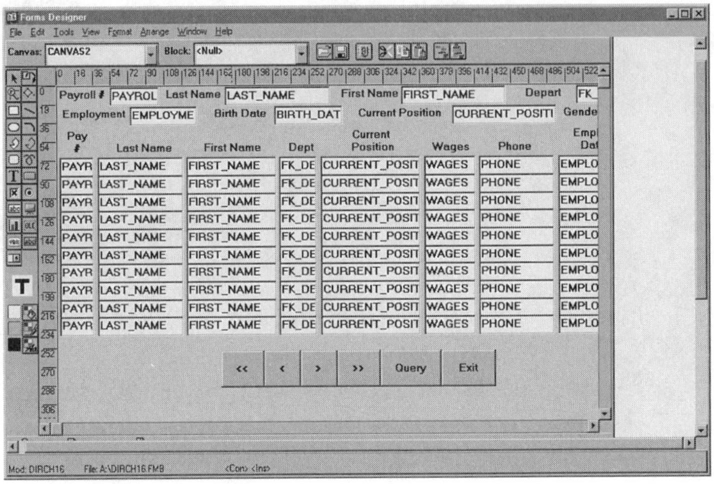

25. Select all of the display items on block two.
26. Double click any of the selected items to open a multi-item property sheet. Change the `Required` property to "false," the `Insert Allowed` property to "false," and the `Update Allowed` property to "false."

    Figure 16.10 displays the property sheet with the settings.

**FIG. 16.10**
The multi-item property sheet used to set the block two common properties.

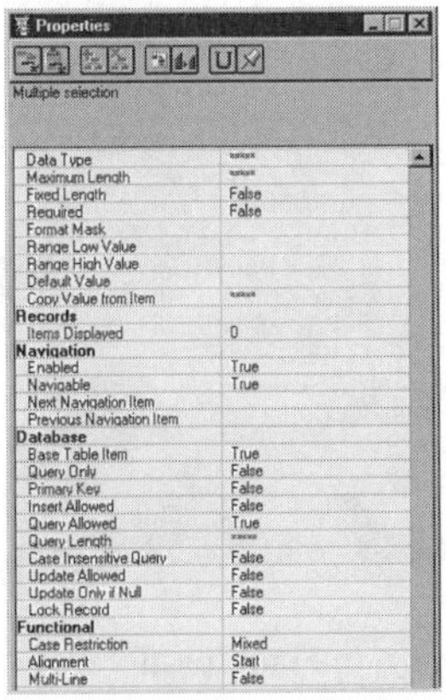

27. Select each of the items on block two that have a corresponding search field on block one. These items consist of payroll_number, last_name, first_name, fk_department, employment_date, birth_date, current_position, and gender. Place the name of the corresponding bloc-one search field into the `Copy Value from Item` property.

    Figure 16.11 shows the property sheet and `Copy Value from Item` property for the payroll_number item.

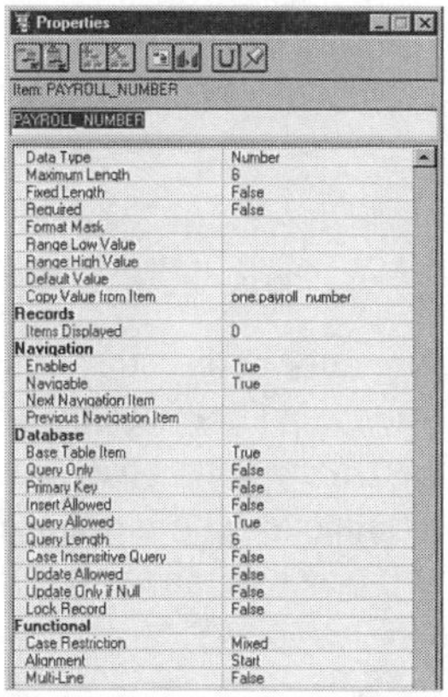


**FIG. 16.11**
The Payroll_number item property sheet and the value for the Copy Value from Item property.

The next step is to create a form-level `Key-entqry` and `Key-exeqry` trigger. These triggers will cause all queries to be performed on block two. Figure 16.12 shows the `Key-entqry` code block. This same code is in the `Key-exeqry` trigger and the `When-button-pressed` trigger for the Query button.

28. Create a `Key-entqry` form trigger that contains the trigger script contained in Figure 16.12.
29. Create a `Key-exeqry` from trigger that contains the trigger script containe in Figure 16.12.
30. Modify the `When-button-pressed` trigger for the Query button. Replace the trigger script with the script contained in Figure 16.12.

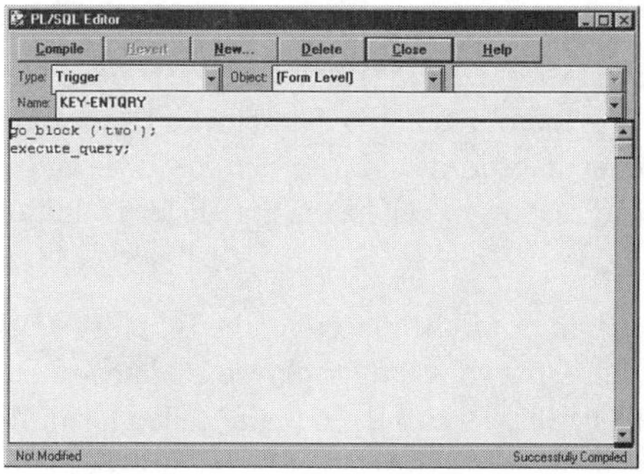


**FIG. 16.12**
The `Key-entqry` trigger code block used to perform queries on block two.

Although at this point the directory is operational, one additional task should be performed. Place an exit button on the form. Because this form does not need a Save button, this button can be changed to an Exit button. To do so:

31. Open the Layout Editor and double-click the Save button. This will open the button's property sheet.
32. Change the Name property to "Exit" and the Label to "Exit."
33. Open the button's `When-button-pressed` trigger and change the code block to "exit_form."

    The directory is now ready for operation.
34. Generate and run the directory.

## Operating the Employee Directory

Figure 16.13 shows the completed Employee Directory. A directory is simple to operate. The top block contains the search criteria. The operator can enter a value in any of the search fields. Pressing the F7 or F8 function keys or the Query button will cause a query to be executed on block two. Figure 16.13 displays the Employee Directory as it displays the results of a query based upon search criteria entered into the last_name field.

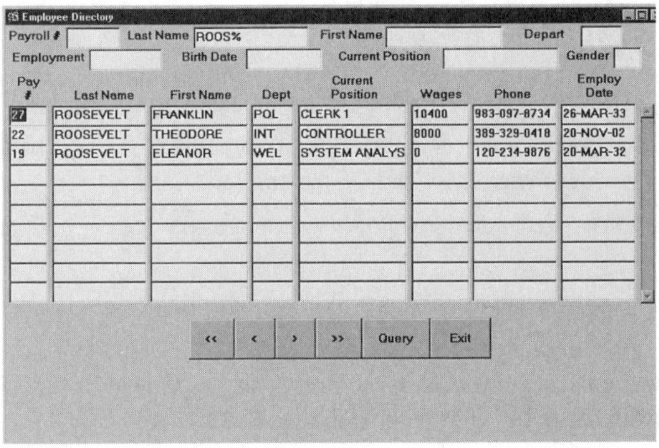


**FIG. 16.13** The Employee Directory displaying the results of a query.

## Calling Other Forms from the Employee Directory

The purpose of a directory is to identify records. Directories by their nature can display only a small amount of a record's data. In order to aid the operator in viewing additional information, buttons can be placed on the directory to call forms that display additional information about the entity.

To illustrate this technique, a button will be placed on the Employee Directory. Pressing this button will cause a trigger to fire that calls the Employee Update form. When the form is called, the employee's payroll number will be transferred to the called form. When this form is displayed, the employee's records will appear. The user will not have to enter search criteria to retrieve the employee's record.

The following are the tasks to create a new button on the Button Palette called "Main Rec," that will display the Employee Update form.

1. Open the directory's layout editor and select any of the existing buttons.
2. Place a copy of the button in the clipboard by selecting Edit, Copy, Menu option.
3. Place a copy of the button on the form by selecting Edit, Paste.
4. Drag the new button to the right side of the button palette.
5. Open the button's property sheet by double-clicking the button.
6. Change the Name property to "main" and the Label property to "Main Rec." Close the property sheet.
7. Open the PL/SQL editor for the button's `When-button-pressed trigger`. This is done by selecting the button and select the Tools, PL/SQL Editor menu option. Enter the code shown in Figure 16.14 into the trigger.

**FIG. 16.14**
The Main Rec button's `When-button-pressed` code block.

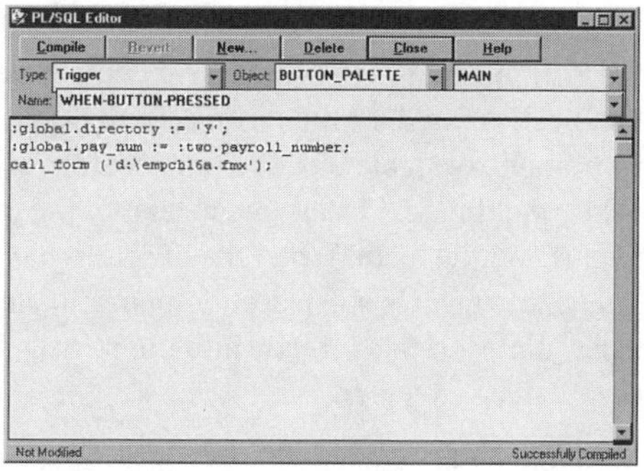


The purpose of the global.directory variable in the trigger is to let the Employee Update form know it was called from the directory. A `When-new-form-instance` trigger will evaluate this variable and execute a query if the value is Y. The trigger will place the form in the Query mode if the variable does not have a value of Y.

**TIP** I generally place a `When-new-form-instance` trigger on all non-directory forms that I create. I believe that the user goes to the form to query an existing record more often than to enter a new record. Thus the user will want to use the Query mode more often than the Input mode. Using the trigger to place the form in the query mode saves the operator the task of pressing the query button upon entry.

The next step is to place a form level `When-new-form-instance` trigger in the Employee Update form (EMPCH16.FMB on the CD). Figure 16.15 shows the code block used in the trigger. The major component of the code block consists of an `if-then-else` statement. If the form was called from the directory, the global.directory variable will be a Y. The global.pay_num variable is populated with the payroll number of the directory record currently selected. The value of this variable is transferred to a form variable and a query is executed. If the application was not called from the directory, the value of global.directory will not be a Y. The trigger will place the form in the Query mode.

**NOTE** You may place this trigger into the EMPCH16.fmb form in you are practicing the modifications. Be sure to generate this form when done.

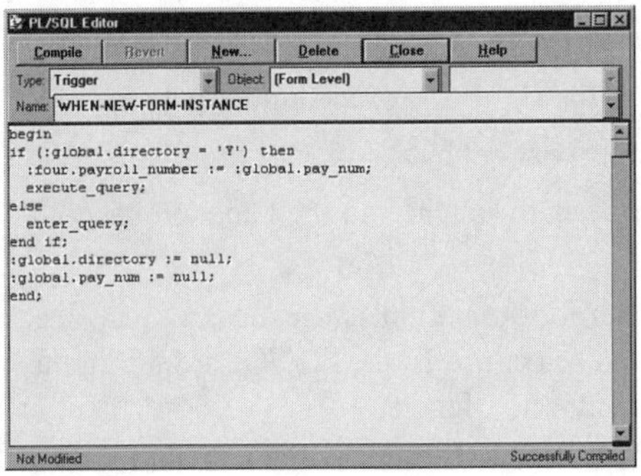


**FIG. 16.15**
The `When-new-form-instance` trigger that is fired when the Employee Update form is opened.

You may have noticed that the third line of the trigger referenced a variable on block four. This is the name of a nonbase table block created for the form. A form that automatically retrieves records when called must have a nonbase table block to hold search values. The reason is that forms are initially opened in the input mode. Placing the form into the query mode causes Forms Runtime to clear any values on the form. When the `execute_query` subprogram is issued to a block in the input mode, the form is still placed temporarily in the query mode. This precludes placing the global.pay_num variable directly into the payroll_number field. The value will be cleared before the query can be executed.

The value also cannot be placed into a block that contains a base table. Placing a value into this type of block will cause the form to think the block has been updated. The form will then try to commit the change before the form can be closed or a query performed. Therefore, any values supplied to a form from another form must be placed in a nonbase table block. This can be a special block such as block four or the button palette block.

One final problem exists in the technique. The value contained in the nonbase table block must be placed in the master block after the block is placed in the query mode and before the query is executed on the block. This is done by using the `Copy Value from Item` property. This property ensures that the value in the item is always the same as the item specified in the property. Thus, the `When-new-form-instance` trigger populates the payroll_number item on block four. The trigger then issues the `execute-query` subprogram. Forms Runtime then places block one in the query mode. The Copy Value from Item setting move the value from the payroll_number item on block four into the payroll_number field on block one. The query is then executed by retrieving the records into the form.

Before closing the Employee Update form, an Exit button should be placed on the form by using the same procedure described in the Employee Directory section. This button will close the form and return the operator to the directory.

Figure 16.16 displays the Employee Directory with the new Main Rec button. The directory is displaying the employee records. To select a record to display when navigating to the Employee Update screen, click on any of the items on a row. In Figure 16.16 the record for Truman is selected.

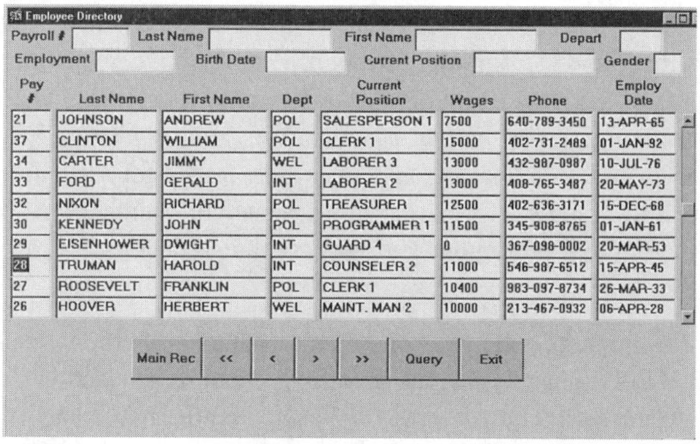

Employee Directory
Payroll #
Last Name
First Name
Depart
Employment
Birth Date
Current Position
Gender
Pay #
Last Name
First Name
Dept
Current Position
Wages
Phone
Employ Date
21 JOHNSON ANDREW POL SALESPERSON 1 7500 640-789-3450 13-APR-65
37 CLINTON WILLIAM POL CLERK 1 15000 402-731-2489 01-JAN-92
34 CARTER JIMMY WEL LABORER 3 13000 432-987-0987 10-JUL-76
33 FORD GERALD INT LABORER 2 13000 408-765-3487 20-MAY-73
32 NIXON RICHARD POL TREASURER 12500 402-636-3171 15-DEC-68
30 KENNEDY JOHN POL PROGRAMMER 1 11500 345-908-8765 01-JAN-61
29 EISENHOWER DWIGHT INT GUARD 4 0 367-098-0002 20-MAR-53
28 TRUMAN HAROLD INT COUNSELER 2 11000 546-987-6512 15-APR-45
27 ROOSEVELT FRANKLIN POL CLERK 1 10400 983-097-8734 26-MAR-33
26 HOOVER HERBERT WEL MAINT. MAN 2 10000 213-467-0932 06-APR-28
Main Rec
<<
<
>
>>
Query
Exit


**FIG. 16.16**
The Employee Directory with Truman's record selected.

Pressing the Main Rec will cause the Employee Update form to appear with Truman's records displayed. Figure 16.17 shows this form.

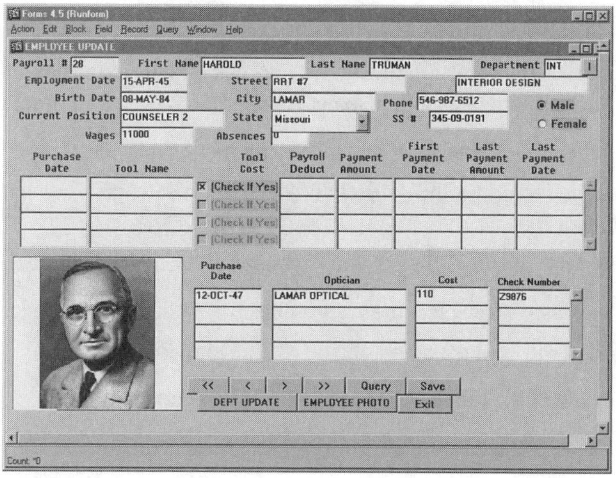


**FIG. 16.17**
The Employee Update form after it has been called from the Employee Directory.

Pressing the Exit button on the Employee Update form will return the operator to the Employee Directory.

**NOTE** You may try this by using your modified forms. If you have not created a form, you may launch the DIRCH16.FMX executable code file from Forms Runtime. The file is located on the CD.

# Creating and Using Menus to Combine Applications into a System

Most applications are part of a group of applications called a *system*. One of the bigger systems I have seen is the T and D Equipment System. This system contains numerous forms and reports. It contains information on distribution transformers, cable terminal poles, padmount switches, substation transformers, breakers, relays, and regulators. Each of these equipment entities has between five and 25 forms. Some of the forms generate numbers. Some of the forms are directories and some of the forms are used to maintain the records. The forms and reports have one thing in common: They are combined in a system through the use of a common menu.

The T and D Equipment System has one menu located at the top of the screen. This menu is used by each of the applications in the system. It contains a selection for each of the applications in the system. Each equipment entity is listed on the menu bar. The entity has a pull-down menu list that displays each of the applications that pertain to the entity. This gives the operator the ability to move from a breaker form to a cable terminal pole form by selecting a new menu option. More important, it gives the operator one common, simple access method to over one hundred applications.

## Creating a Menu

A menu is an Oracle Forms module with a source code file extension of .MMB. Menus are created in Forms Designer on the Object Navigator. To create a menu, follow these steps.

1. Open the Object Navigator and locate the menus module object.
2. Select the menus module object and click the create icon. Forms will create a new menu module or file.

   Figure 16.18 displays the Object Navigator after the menu module has been created.

3. The next step is to select the *menus* object and click the create icon.

   This step will create a menu object, as shown in Figure 16.19.

   To the left of the menu object is a pull-down menu icon.

4. Double-click this button to open the Menu Editor dialog box, as shown in Figure 16.20.

The box is a screen painter used to lay out the menu.

At the top of the menu editor are a series of buttons and a picklist. The picklist is used to select or change menu objects.

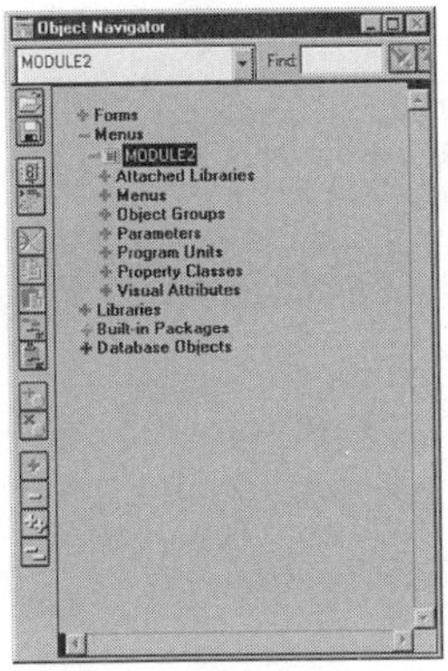


**FIG. 16.18**
A new menu module on the object navigator.



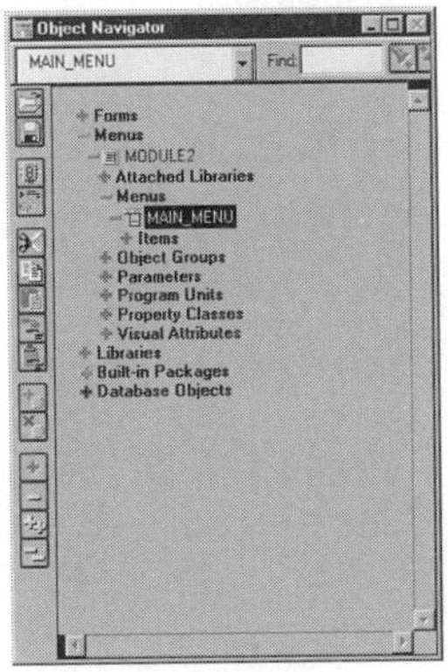


**FIG. 16.19**
A newly created menu object.

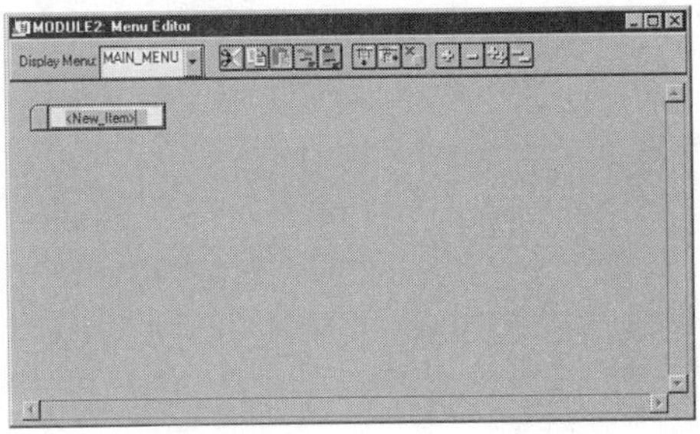


**FIG. 16.20**
The Menu Editor used to layout the menu options.

In the first block of buttons on the left of the editor are the preceding buttons: *cut*, *copy*, *paste*, *copy properties*, and *paste property* tools, respectively. These tools have the same functionality as buttons on other editors that have been discussed.

The middle three tools are the most commonly used on this screen.

The left tool with the downward pointing arrow is the *create down* tool and is used to create a new menu option below the currently selected option.

The middle tool with the right pointing arrow is the ***create right*** tool. It creates a new menu option to the right of the currently selected option.

The tool with the red X symbol is the ***delete option*** tool, which is used to delete the selected object.

The four tools on the left side of the menu editor are shown above. They are the ***expand***, ***collapse***, ***expand all***, and ***collapse*** tools respectively.

Change the label of an option, double-click the option. This will change the color of the label and allow the developer to edit the label.

Figure 16.21 displays the menu editor after the label was changed.

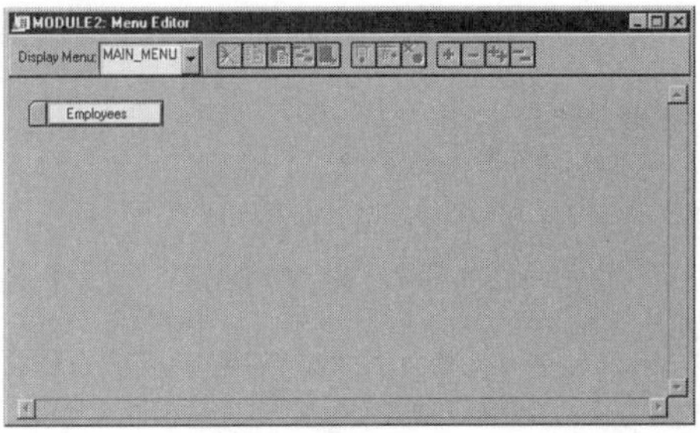


**FIG. 16.21**
The Menu Editor after the menu option label was changed.

Options placed on the menu become items under the menu object on the Object Navigator. Figure 16.22 shows the Employees item on the object navigator.

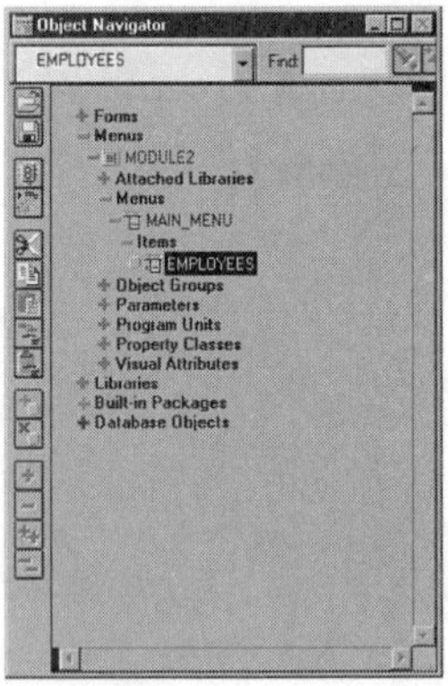


**FIG. 16.22**
The Employees option on the object navigator.

The last step in creating a menu is to add the PL/SQL script to the item. Double-clicking the icon next to the Employees item will open the menu option's PL/SQL editor. The PL/SQL code block can then be entered.

# Creating and Implementing an Employee System Menu

This section will illustrate the creation of a menu and its subsequent use in an Employee system. You may perform the following steps to create the Employee system menu:

The first step is to create a menu module.



1. Select the high-level menus module object on the Object Navigator.
2. Pressing the Create tool will set up a new module. Change the name of the menu module to Empmenu.
3. Select the Menus child object and click the Create tool. A menu module called Main_menu will appear.
4. Double-click the icon to the left of the Main_menu object. This will cause the menu editor to open. A "<New Item>" option will appear on the editor.
5. Change the name of this option to "Employees" by clicking on the item and changing the name.
6. Click the *create down tool* twice. This will create two new menu options below the "Employees" option.
7. Name the first option "Employee Directory" and the second option "Employee Update."
8. Re-select the "Employees" menu option. Press the *create right* tool twice. This will create two options to the right of the "Employees" option.
9. Label the first menu option "Miscellaneous."
10. Label the second menu option "Exit."
11. Select the "Miscellaneous" option. Click the *create down* icon twice.
12. Label the first option "Department."
13. Label the second option "Security."

    Figure 16.23 shows the layout after these steps are taken.

**FIG. 16.23**
The Employee Menu layout.

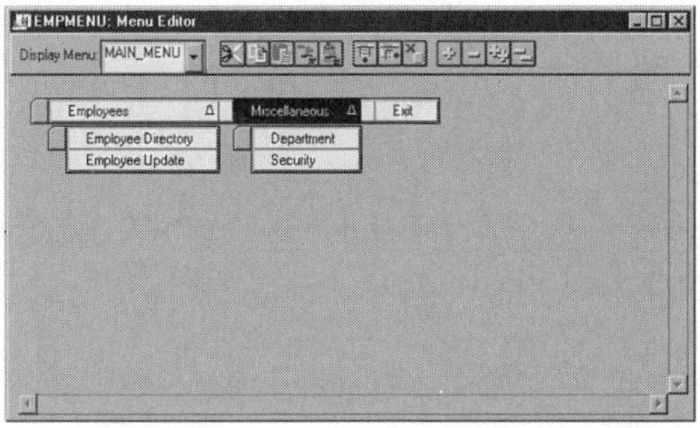


14. The next step is to enter the PL/SQL for each of the items. Figure 16.24 shows the Object Navigator and the newly created menu options.

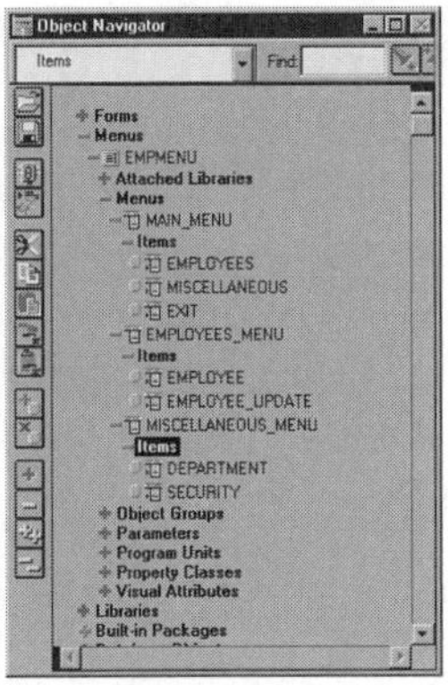


**FIG. 16.24**
The object navigator and the Employee menu options.

The "Employees" and "Miscellaneous" options do not need PL/SQL. Forms Designer places the PL/SQL into the command text when the option is the first option of a sublist. These types of menu options call another menu option. The developer only needs to populate the items that call a form or execute a subprogram. Table 16.1 lists the menu items that need PL/SQL code and the PL/SQL commands.

**Table 16.1 Menu Options That Require a PL/SQL Code Block**

| Menu | Item | Command |
|---|---|---|
| Main_menu | Exit | `exit_form;` |
| Employees_menu | Directory | `call_form ('d:\dirch16.fmx');` |
| Employees_menu | Employee_update | `call_form (d:\empch16a.fmx');` |
| Miscellaneous_menu | Department | `call_form ('d:\depch16.fmx', no_hide);` |
| Miscellaneous_menu | Security | `message ('Not available    yet');` |

15. Open the Object Navigator.
16. Double-click the button icon to the left of the each menu item listing in Table 16.1. Enter the command for the table into the displayed PL/SQL editor.

    Figure 16.25 displays the PL/SQL editor and the code block for the "Directory" option.

    After entering the PL/SQL code, the menu is completed.
17. Generate the menu.

**CAUTION**

Two common errors occur when developing menus. The first error is failing to generate the menu before using it. When developing a form, the developer does not have to generate the form because Designer usually generates it before executing the form. This is a Designer runtime option. This option does not apply to menus. Because they are never run like a form, there is not automatic generation. It is very common for a developer to make changes, run a form and corresponding menu, only to find the menu changes do not appear.

The second error is to forget to put PL/SQL code blocks in all of the items. The menu will not generate unless each option has code.



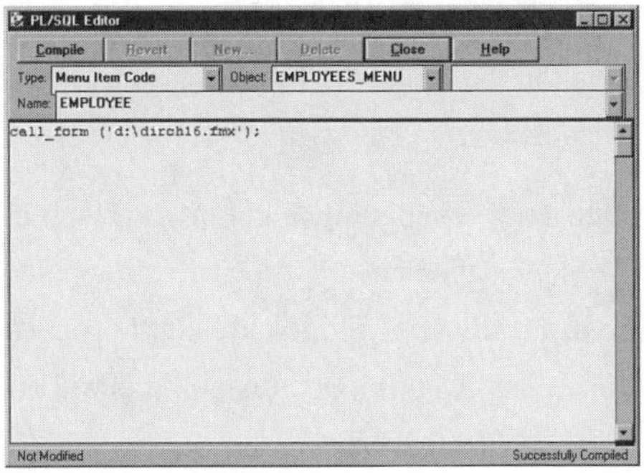


**FIG. 16.25**
The PL/SQL editor and code block for the Employee directory menu option.

A menu must be linked to an application in order to be executed. The menu is linked to a form by means of the form's *Menu Module* property. This property is located in the form object property sheet. It denotes the name and location of the menu that will be used with the form. Figure 16.26 shows a Form object property sheet. The *Menu Module* property specifies the menu file used for the form. The form uses the specified file when the *Use File* property is set to true.

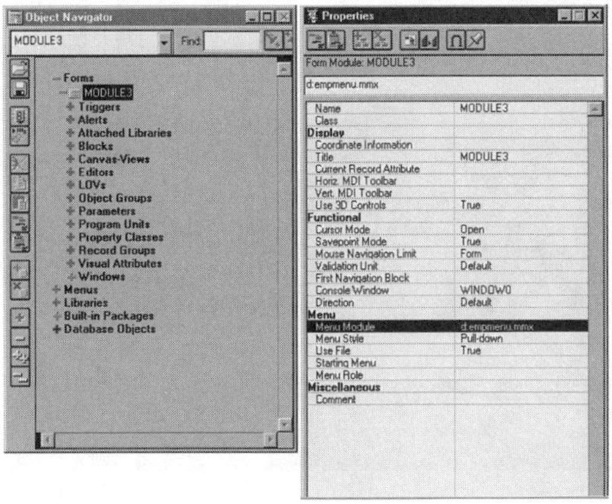

**FIG. 16.26**
A Form object property sheet.

## Developing a System Startup Application

A system menu is usually linked to a startup application. This application is a nonbase table form used to set up the system. It contains the name of the menu used in the system, initializes the global variables used in the system, logs the operator on the database, and accepts security values from the operator. This application often has a photo image of something representative of the system's entity displayed on the startup canvas.

As an example of the preceding, the following will describe the development of a startup application for the Employee system.

**NOTE** Some of these steps are condensed since we have performed them in numerous examples in previous sections.

1. The first step is to create a new form module in Forms Designer.
2. Create a nonbase table block called one.
3. Set the canvas and window properties width and height properties.
4. Open the Layout Editor. Select Edit, Import, Image. This will open the Import Image dialog box.
5. Select the WHITEH.PCX image from the CD. Figure 16.27 displays the canvas after the image was imported.
6. The image should be resized to cover the entire canvas by grabbing a handle and stretching the image.

**FIG. 16.27** The Startup Application canvas with the imported image before it is resized.

7. Create two text items that will allow the operator to enter the payroll number and password values used for system security. These items should be on block one and are called payroll_number and password respectively. Figure 16.28 displays the two text items as they appear on the canvas.

**FIG. 16.28**
The Startup Application canvas and the payroll number and password text items.

Each of the text items has post-change triggers. The payroll number item trigger assigns the value to the global variable payroll_number. The code for the password item is contained in Figure 15.10.

8. Create a post-change for the password item. Enter the code from Figure 15.10 into the trigger.
9. Create a post-change trigger for the payroll number item. The trigger should contain the following code:

   ```
   :global.payroll_number := :one.payroll_number;
   ```

10. Link the menu to the form by placing the menu name in the Form's *Menu Module* property. The menu module is "empmenu.mmx."

    Forms are usually executed in Forms Runtime. In order to avoid having the user log on the database, an `on-logon` trigger is generally created to log the operator on the database. Figure 16.29 shows this trigger. The first command logs the operator on the system. The first setting in the command is the database user account and the second is the password. Following the command, the system's global variables are initialized.

11. Create an `on-logon` trigger for the startup form. Use the script contain in Figure 16.29.
12. Generate and run the form.

This completes the Employee system. Figure 16.30 displays the startup form and the system menu. All system applications are now available from the menu.

**NOTE** The CD has the completed components of the Employee system. The startup application is called EMPSTART.FMX. It may be executed from Forms Runtime.

**Launching the Employee System from an Icon** The Employee system can be launched by opening Forms Runtime and specifying the start up application, EMPSTART.FMX. However, the number of steps to launch the system can be reduced by creating a Windows icon to launch the system.

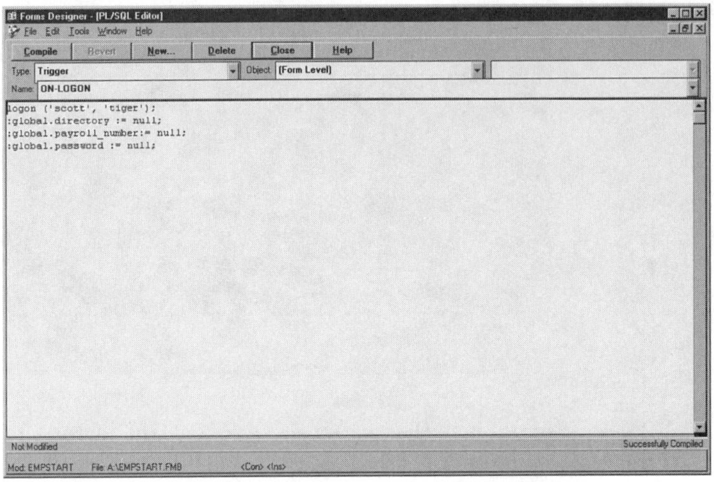


**FIG. 16.29** The on-logon trigger that logs the operator into the Oracle database.

**FIG. 16.30** The Employee System startup form displaying the Employees menu options.

The command line expression for the Windows icon consists of two parts. The first part of the expression launches Forms Runtime. The second part of the expression contains the name of the startup file. Figure 16.31 shows the command to launch the Employee system. It assumes Forms Runtime is loaded on the PC and the file is contained on the CD.

**Maximizing the Initial Screens** When a form is initially displayed, it is presented in the normal Window size. This window size does not cover the entire screen. Because I design for a maximized screen, the window does not display the entire canvas. The operator needs to click the Maximize window icon to properly see the form. I generally correct for this problem by maximizing the window size for the startup application. Once the window is maximized, all other forms displayed will use that window size unless the Windows size is changed.

In order to maximize the window, create a form When-new-form-instance trigger that contains the statement shown in Figure 16.32.



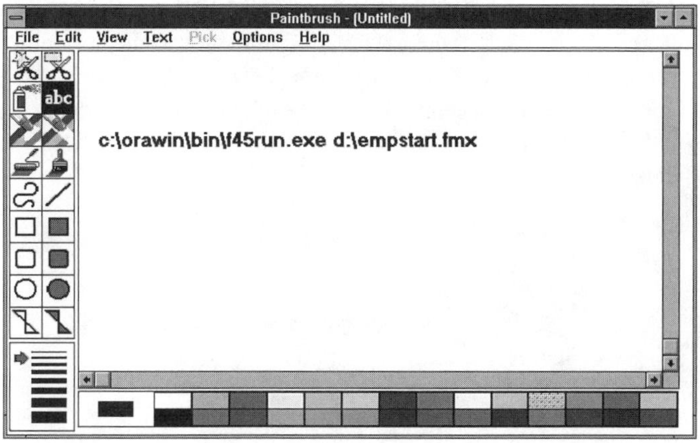


**FIG. 16.31**
The command to a launch the Employee System from a Windows icon.

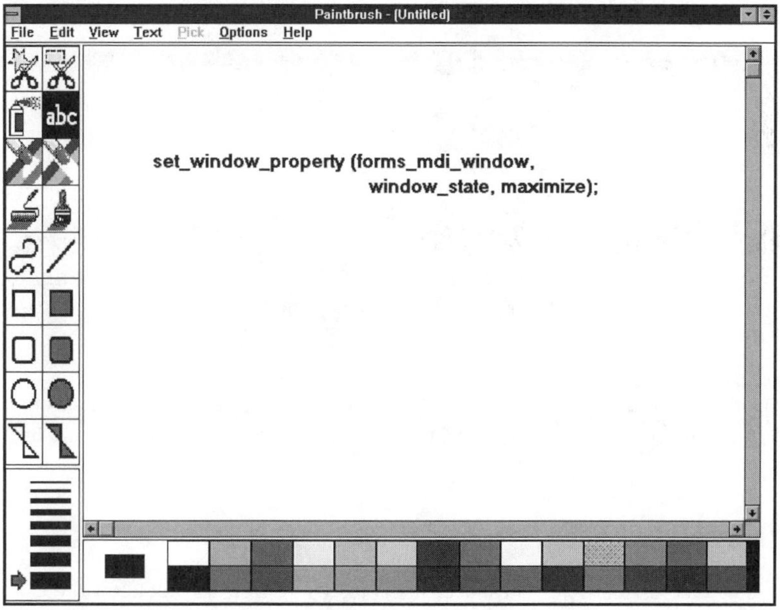


**FIG. 16.32**
The command to dynamically maximize a window.

**Calling Forms within the System** Throughout this chapter there have been PL/SQL commands that call another form. In the references the file path was included. In the case of this chapter, the file path used in the examples consists of "d:", the assumed CD drive. These path expressions are hard coded into the application. Each form and menu in the system would need to be modified and regenerated with a new file path if the applications are moved to another location. Hard coding the file path also causes problems when the applications are distributed on different servers. The applications may reside on different directories on different servers. The developer would have to have a different set of applications for each server.

In order to overcome this problem, I populate a global variable with the file path used throughout the system. The global variable is populated in a `When-new-form-instance` trigger on the startup application. Each of the `call_form` commands in the system must be changed to include the global variable as part of the concatenated expression denoting the location of the called form. Following this approach, the developer will only need to modify the When-new-form-instance trigger of the start up application when the code location is changed. Figure 16.33 illustrates this syntax.

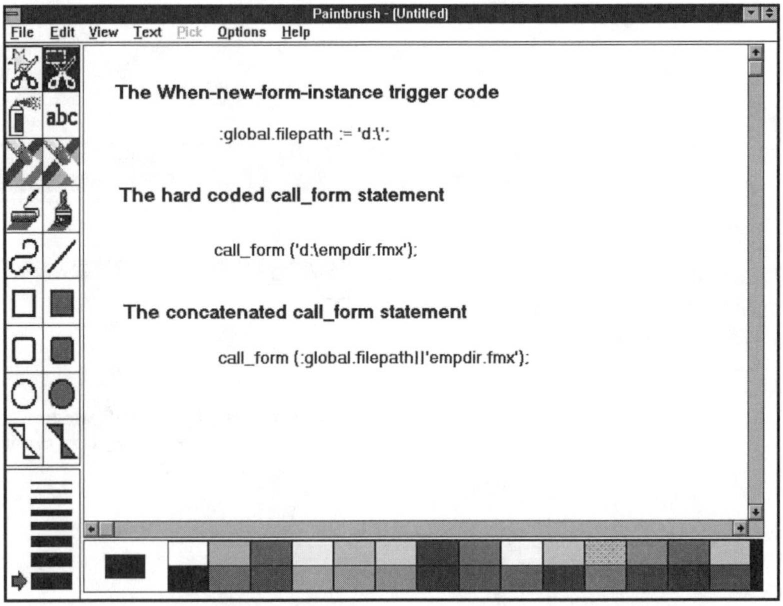


**FIG. 16.33**
The syntax of the `call_form` command using a concatenated global variable as part of the file path expression.

**NOTE** The location of the menu module is hard coded in the start up form's Menu Module property. This technique will not work on that value. It must remain hard coded.

# Creating a Toolbar

Toolbars are graphical user interface (GUI) objects that allow the user to poke at an image or icon to perform an action. We have seen numerous toolbars in this part of the chapter. The Object Navigator, screen painter, and the property sheet each contain a toolbar. A form can also have a toolbar. It consists of a set of iconified buttons on a form canvas. *Iconified* means the button has an image on it.

To create a horizontal toolbar follow these steps:

1. Open the Object Navigator and create a new canvas-view object.
2. Open the canvas's property sheet and modify the `Canvas-view Type` property. The developer has a choice between a vertical or horizontal toolbar.

   Figure 16.34 displays the `Canvas-view Type` picklist.
3. Select the *Horizontal Toolbar* value and set the *Height* property set to 20.



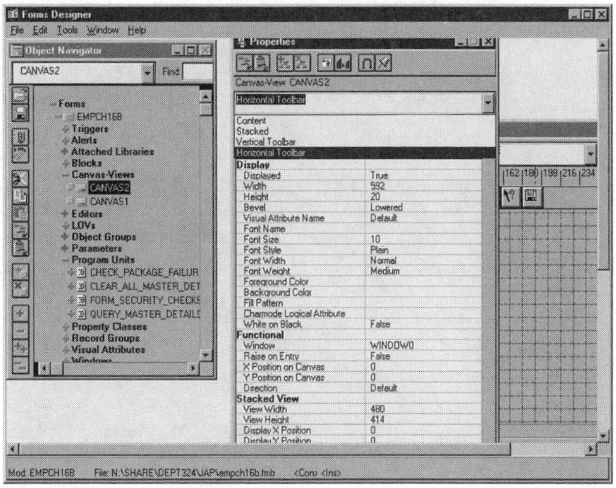


**FIG. 16.34**
The `Canvas-view type` values picklist.

4. Open the form's property sheet.

   This property sheet has two properties that pertain to toolbars. They are the `Vert. MDI Toolbar` and the `Horiz. MDI Toolbar` property. The properties contain the names of canvases that will be displayed as vertical or horizontal toolbars. Figure 16.35 displays the form property sheet for the Employee Update form (EMPCH16.FMB). The `Horiz. MDI Toolbar` is selected and the picklist displays the canvas toolbars available. `Canvas2` is selected.
5. Select the Horiz. MDI Toolbar and the canvas created in Step 1.

   Figure 16.36 contains the executed form that includes an unpopulated toolbar. The toolbar is located between the menu and the application. It has a height of 20 pixels and stretches across the screen.

The next step is to create the iconified buttons that will appear on the toolbar. This can be done on the Object Navigator. Add the buttons to the Button Palette Block or create a new nonbase table block. In the case of the Employee Update form, a new block called "Tools" is created.

1. Open the Object Navigator.
2. Select the Blocks object. Click the create button. This will open the New Block dialog.

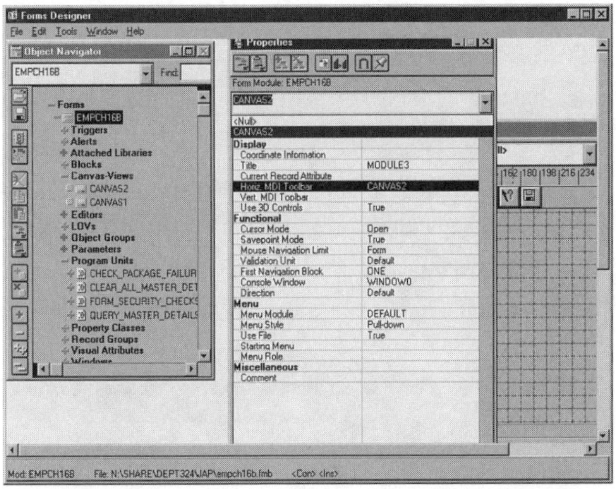

**FIG. 16.35**
The form property sheet and the `Horiz. MDI Toolbar` and `Vert. MDI Toolbar` properties.

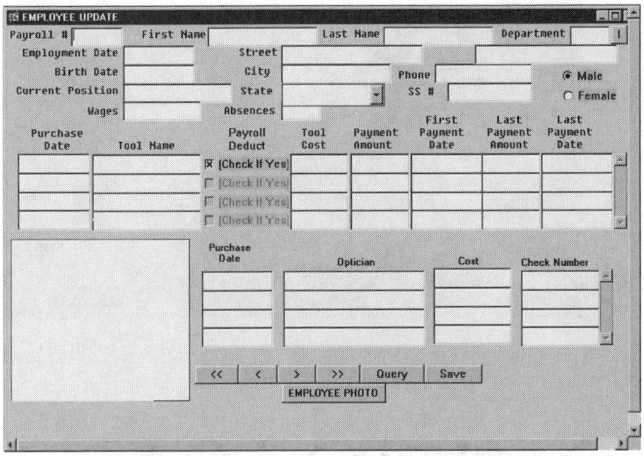

**FIG. 16.36**
The Employee Update form with a blank horizontal tool bar.

3. Change the name of the block to "Tools." Click the OK button.
4. Expand the Tools block object on the Object Navigator.
5. Select the Items object under the Tools block.
6. Click the Create button ten times. This will create ten items.
7. Rename the items to the names shown in Figure 16.37. You can do this by clicking on the item on the Object Navigator until it is highlighted. At that point, type over the old name. Figure 16.37 shows the Object Navigator and the tools.

   The next step is to set up a property class. The property class decreases the labor needed to populate the tool item properties.
8. Select the property class object on the Object Navigator. Click the Create button on the Tool Palette. This will create a property class object.

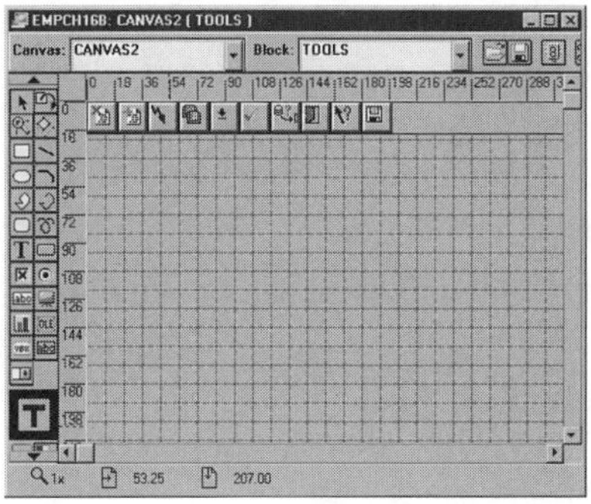


**FIG. 16.37**
The Object Navigator displaying the Tools block and the tool items after they have been renamed.



9. Add `item_type`, `canvas`, `width`, `height`, and `iconic` properties to the property class. You may use the add tool to accomplish this.
10. Populate the new property class with the settings shown in Figure 16.38.

    Figure 16.38 contains the property class that will be used by the buttons. This property class is assigned to each of the items.

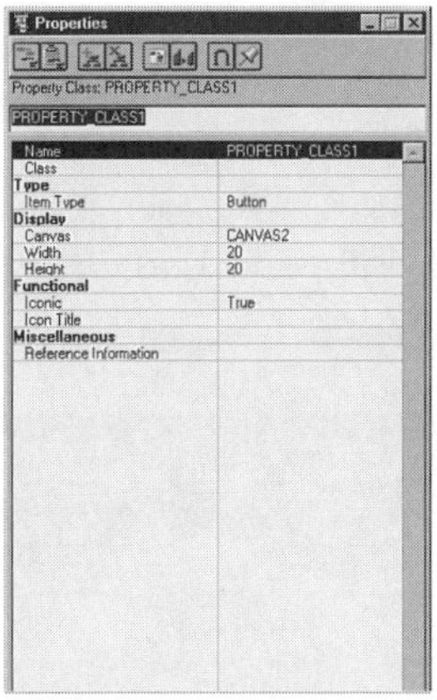


**FIG. 16.38**
The tool item property class.

After creating the property class:

11. Select and open the property sheet of each of the tool items.
12. The property class created in Step 13 should be added to the *class* property.

    This will change the values of several of the properties.
13. Change the value of the *X Position* property. The value for each tool should be 20 pixels more than the previous tool. For instance, the first tool on the toolbar has an *X Position* value of 0. The next tool has an *X position* value of 20. This will spread the tools across the toolbar.

    The last item property to change is the *Icon Name*. This value consists of the icon file name without the file path and file extension. Figure 16.39 illustrates the *Icon Name* property for the Save tool. The *Icon Name* property is "save." It will call the "save.ico" icon file in the \orawin\forms45\demos\icons directory. Oracle has placed the icons used in this example in that directory. Other icons can be created and used by a form. However, they must be moved to the this directory before the form will use them.

14. Add the name of the icon file to the Icon Name property.
15. Repeats Steps 11-14 for each item on the tool bar.

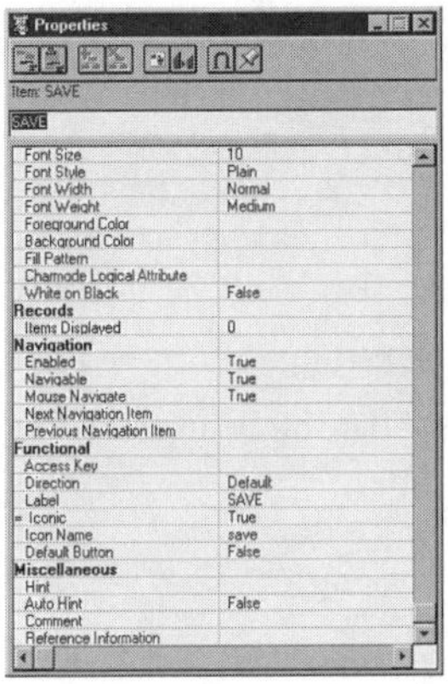

**FIG. 16.39**
The Save tool property sheet specifying the name of the Icon file.

The last step is to attach a `When-button-pressed` trigger to each of the buttons. This trigger will perform the actual function. Figure 16.40 displays the EMPCH16B.FMB form that contains a horizontal toolbar. This file is contained on the CD.

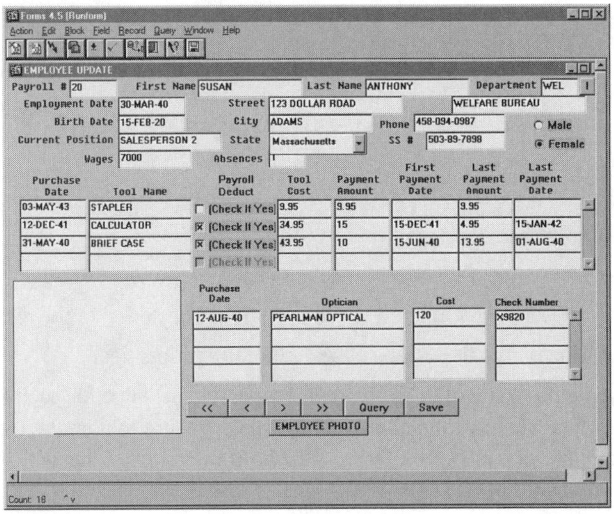

**FIG. 16.40**
The Employee Update form after a horizontal toolbar has been added.

# Summary

The `call_form` command calls another form from an existing form or menu. The command overlays the child form on top of the parent form. When closing the called form, the operator returns to the original form. The `new_form` command calls another form, but replaces it with the called form.

The `call_form` command entirely overlays the existing form with the new form. If the called form is smaller that the parent form, it covers the entire form. This can be prevented by using the `no_hide` option. Using this option makes Forms cover only the portion of the parent form taken up by the called form.

A directory is a special application used to search the database. It consists of a two-part form. The first part consists of search fields and the second part the results of the search. This application usually has a variety of buttons that allow the operator to navigate to other applications for additional information.

A menu is a `Forms` module attached to a form. A menu contains a number of options that allow the operator to execute functions or call other forms. The most common use of a menu is to tie a set of related applications into a system.

Menus are usually attached to a startup application. This is the application initially launched by the operator. It sets up the system. It contains the name of the system menu, the database log in passwords, records security values, and maximizes the screen.

Toolbars are `Forms` objects that consist of a vertical or horizontal row of iconified buttons that execute a When-button-pressed trigger when poked.



# From Here...

This chapter completes Part IV of the book. At this time you should have a grasp of how to develop a Forms system. The operator adds, deletes, and modifies records on these applications. The next part of the book covers Oracle's SQL *Reports product. It is a sophisticated tool for developing and executing reports. Chapter 17 will introduce you to the Reports Runtime and Designer products. In some respects they are similar to the Forms products. The chapter will cover the Reports object navigator and data model editor. The chapter will also describe how to create a simple employee listing using the product.

The tables were loaded and the data converted in Installment 3. The portion of the Employee Project will consist of creating the system that will be used by the user to maintain the database. Create the following modules:

Department Update Form

Employee Update Form

Employee Directory

Security Administration Form

Startup Application

Employee System Menu

The Department form is used to maintain the department table. It should be called from both the Employee Update form and the Main Menu. Only authorized users may update records by using this screen.

The Employee Update form is used to maintain the employee, tools, and glasses tables. It will consist of a three-part form. It has also been requested that the form display a photo of the employee. Liberal use of buttons, picklists, radio buttons, and check boxes should be used. This form should be called from the Employee Directory and the Main Menu. Only authorized users may update records by using this screen.

The Employee Directory is an application that will display sets of employee records based upon entered search criteria. The operator shall be able to select a record and navigate to the Employee Update screen from this application. This application should be called from the Main Menu.

The Security Administration form is used to maintain security and passwords on the security table. This application should be called from the directory, but only by authorized personnel.

The Startup application is the main system screen. As such it should contain an image appropriate to the firm. The screen should have fields that enable the operator to enter security values. This screen will maximize when first displayed.

The Main Menu is a menu module that calls each of the form applications. It should also have an exit selection.

PART V

# Oracle's Report Writer: Oracle Reports 2.5

CHAPTER 17

# Creating Your First Report

Reports REPCH17.RDF and DEPTEMP.RDF, used in this chapter to demonstrate the techniques, are on the CD in the back of this book. ■

**Launching Oracle Reports 2.5**

Covers how to execute Oracle Reports 2.5, and gives a brief overview of the product.

**Creating and running your first report**

Describes the basic steps needed to develop a report. It also describes how to run and view the report by using the previewer.

**The Object Navigator**

Discusses the Reports Object Navigator.

**The designer menu options**

Offers an overview of the Reports Designer menu options.

**Understanding the data model**

Discusses the data model designed to produce an employee listing, gives an overview of how the various objects interact, and covers the various tools available on the data model editor to create objects and perform file functions.

# Launching Oracle Reports 2.5

Oracle Reports 2.5 is Oracle's report writing tool and is a very important part of the Developer 2000 tool set. Users need reports from their databases and this tool can create reports.

**NOTE** I have used a variety of good report-writing tools over the years. The reports I produced generally accomplished their goal, but never with flair. To get a highly customized or complicated report, I generally had to resort to programming in C or some other difficult language. I produced the information with these products but never truly created nice-looking reports. After I learned Reports, I was able to take my C books and place them under the rain pipe outside my house and let them mildew. I could now do all of the difficult calculations and procedures and easily format the product, which really increased my productivity.

Oracle Reports 2.5 consists of two different tools. The first tool is Reports Designer. This is the product used to design and generate the report. The second product is Reports Runtime. It is used to run the compiled form of the report. Selecting the designated folder from the Developer 2000 palette will launch these products. The Developer 2000 palette and the Designer and Runtime selections are displayed in Figure 17.1.

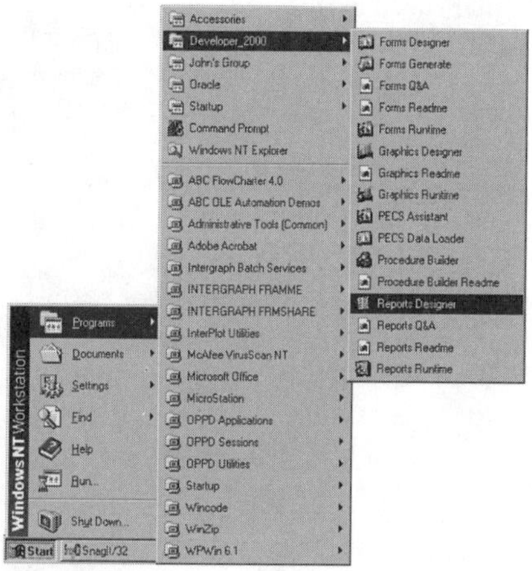


**FIG. 17.1**
The Developer 2000 palette containing the selections used to launch Reports Designer and Reports Runtime icons.

The products can also be launched from the operating system command line. The commands are listed in Figure 17.2. The *filepath* indicates the location of the run files on your PC's hard drive or server. The tools are normally located in the \orawin\bin directory.

## Launching Reports Runtime Without Specifying the Report Name

Reports Runtime executes the compiled version of a report. To execute a report, perform the following steps:

1. Select the Report Runtime tool to launch Reports Runtime.

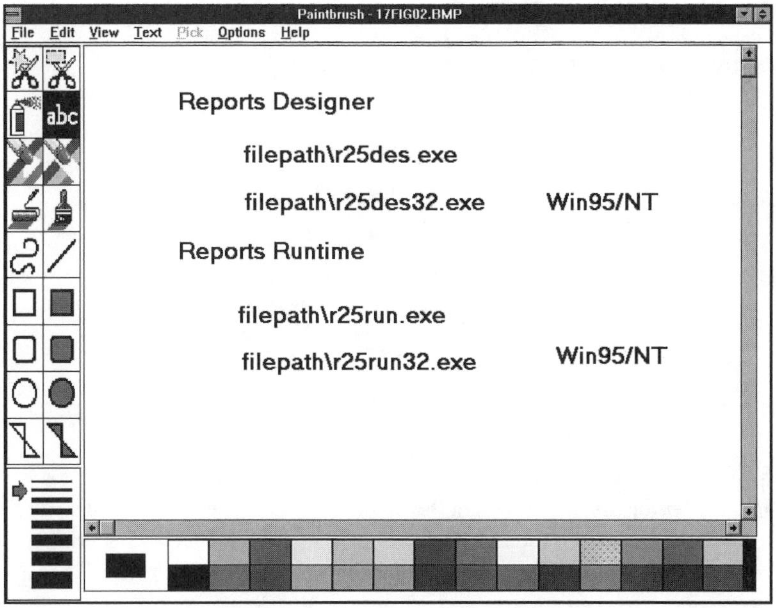


**FIG. 17.2**
The command line commands to launch Reports Designer and Reports Runtime.



When you launch Reports Runtime and the executable file is unidentified, the Reports Runtime window appears, as shown in Figure 17.3. The window is used to specify the report module (file) and the needed database.

The File menu options are displayed in Figure 17.3. The top option is *Connect*. This opens the same Connect Dialog box used for SQL Forms. It is used to log on to the database needed for the report. The dialog box has fields for the database username, password, and connect string. The *Disconnect* option breaks the connection to the database. The option is grayed out when an active database connection does not exist. The option is blackened when a connection exists. Conversely, the *Connect* option is blackened when a connection does not exist and grayed out when the database is connected.

2. Select the File, Connect menu option.
3. The Connect dialog box appears. Enter the requested database identification values. Press the Connect button.
4. Select the File, Run menu option. When you select the *Run* option, the Open File dialog box appears. The box initially displays .REP files (Reports executable files have an extension of .REP.) for the default Oracle directory. This dialog box helps the user identify the desired executable file. Reports Runtime executes the report when the report has been selected and the OK button clicked .
5. Locate the DEPTEMP.REP file on the CD.

Figure 17.4 displays the Open dialog box with the DEPTEMP.REP displayed.

**FIG. 17.3**
The Reports Runtime dialog box displaying File menu options.

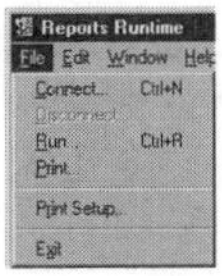


**FIG. 17.4**
The Open dialog box with the DEPTEMP.REP file displayed.

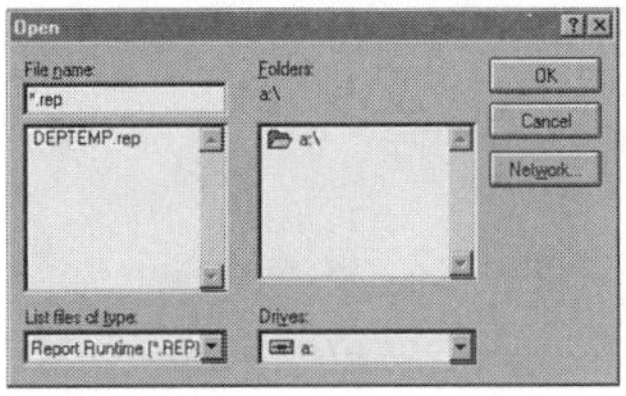


6. Select the DEPTEMP.rep file and click the OK button.

After you click the OK button, the Runtime Parameter Form appears. This form prompts the user for the destination of the output. Clicking the Destination Type picklist shows the other options: screen (default destination), file, printer, mail, and preview. Enter the Destination Name field when the report destination is *file*. The Parameter Form and destination type options are shown in Figure 17.5.

**FIG. 17.5**
The Runtime Parameter Form.

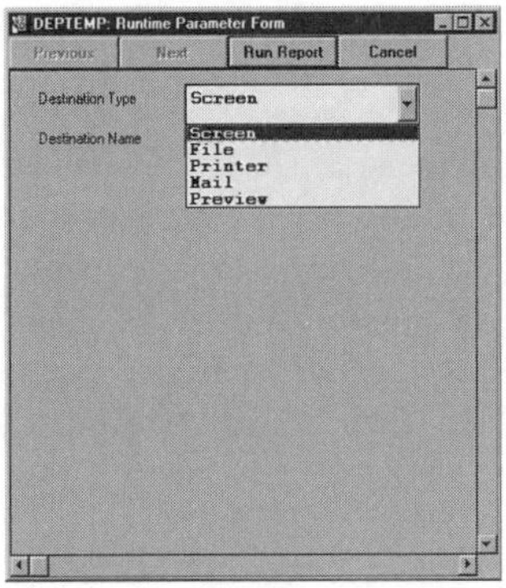


The report is run when the options are entered and the Run Report button clicked. The report output will be discussed later.

7. Click the Run Report button.

# Executing a Report From a Form

It is very common to execute a report from a form. Most of the systems that I have developed include a number of *canned reports*, which are reports that users run directly from the system. Users pick the report from a menu or push a button. Infrequent system users appreciate the ease of launching reports by using a menu or button.

When you execute a report from a form or menu, you must pass all of the necessary information to Reports Runtime. Without passing the information, the product will have to open the default dialog box and prompt the user for information. The command to launch Reports from a form is *Run_product,* followed by the parameters needed by Reports Runtime. The syntax of this command is contained in Figure 17.6.

**FIG. 17.6**
Run_product syntax.

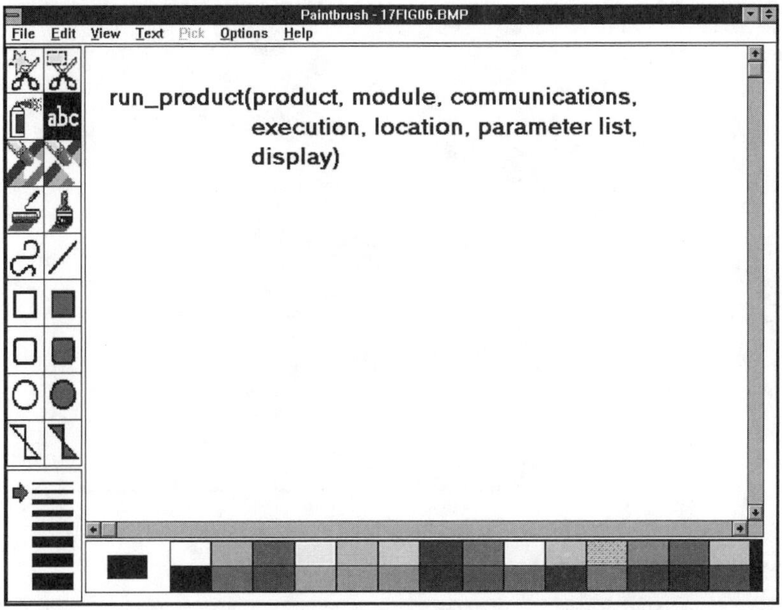


The *product* option refers to the Oracle product to be run. The available constants are GRAPHICS, REPORTS, FORMS, or BOOK. GRAPHICS refers to Oracle Graphics, FORMS to Forms Runtime, REPORTS to Reports Runtime, and BOOK to Oracle Book. The *module* value contains the name of the executable file that will be executed. Reports executable files have a file extension of .REP.

The *communications* option can contain one of two values. The first value is *Synchronous,* which means control returns to Forms only after the called product is closed. The second value is *Asynchronous,* which means control returns to the calling application immediately.

The *execution* option is used to determine the execution mode. The mode may be *Batch* or *Runtime*. Oracle Reports or Graphics can be executed in batch or runtime. Oracle Forms must always be runtime.

The *location* option determines where the *module* is stored. The options are *Filesystem* or *DB.* The latter refers to the database.

The *parameter list* option contains the name of a parameter list passed to the called product. The list usually contains objects such as print settings (landscape or portrait), input values, or print destination.

The *display* option specifies the name of the Forms chart item that contains the display.

Figure 17.7 illustrates an actual PL/SQL trigger that calls Reports and passes a parameter list.

**FIG. 17.7**
Actual code creating a parameter list and calling a report from a form.

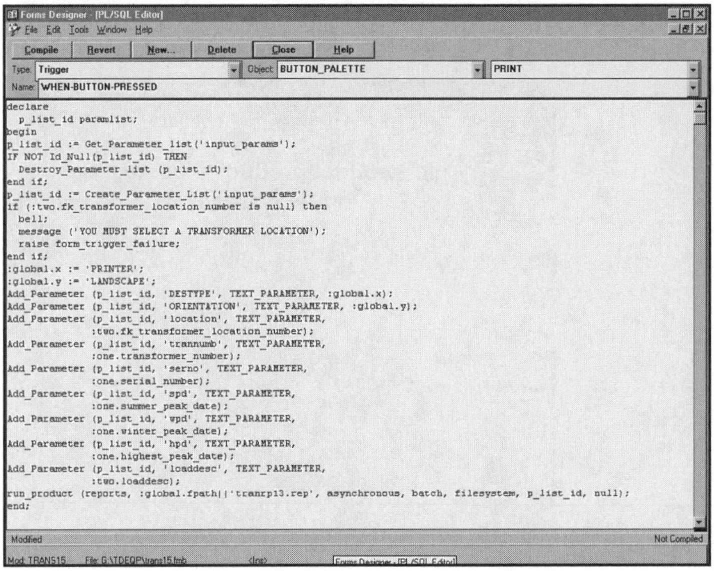


## Launching Reports Designer

Reports Designer is the Oracle product used to build reports. Double-clicking the Reports Designer selection on the Developer 2000 palette launches it. The Report Designer main window appears. The default screen will be the object navigator.

# Creating Your First Report

Reports Designer has three important windows used to develop a report. The first is the Object Navigator. It is a screen used to quickly locate and select any report object. It is very similar in nature to the object navigator used by SQL*FORMS. The second screen is the Data Model Editor. This is the screen used by the developer to document the queries or select statements used to retrieve records from the database. The third screen is the Layout Editor. This screen is used to format the report. It is a report painter that allows the developer to place boilerplate text, change fonts, realign columns, and perform a host of other functions.

## Steps to Create a Simple Report

Following are the steps to create a basic report. They may be used to create your initial reports before formatting and adding complexity.

1. Open the Object Navigator. Create a new report module by selecting the Reports object and clicking the Create button (green plus sign) on the tool bar.
2. Open the Data Model Editor by double-clicking the icon to the left of the Data Model object.
3. Activate the Query tool by clicking the SQL icon on the tool bar. Select a spot on the layout area and press the left mouse button. This creates a query box prefaced by the letter Q.
4. Open the Query dialog box by double-clicking it, and then enter a valid select statement into the Select Statement window. Click the Apply button when done to validate the Select statement. Click the Close button when done.
5. Double-click the default layout icon at the top of the Data Model editor to open the Default Layout dialog box. Click OK and Layout Editor appears.
6. Save the report by using the File/Save option. Run the report.



## Creating an Employee Listing

In this section, the steps outlined in the previous section will be used to actually create an Employee listing.

1. Open the Object Navigator.
2. Create a report module. This is done by selecting the Reports object and clicking the Create button, as shown in Figure 17.8.

**FIG. 17.8**
Selecting the Reports object on the Object Navigator.

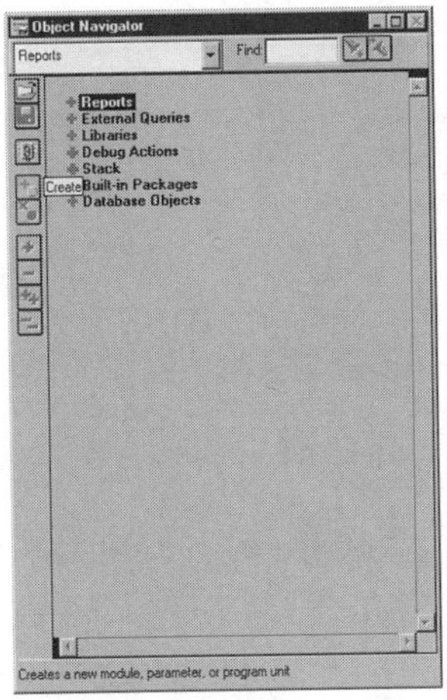


This step creates a default report module or file. The first object under the report object is the Data Model.

1. Double-click the Data Model button.

Figure 17.9 shows the Object Navigator and the Data Model object.

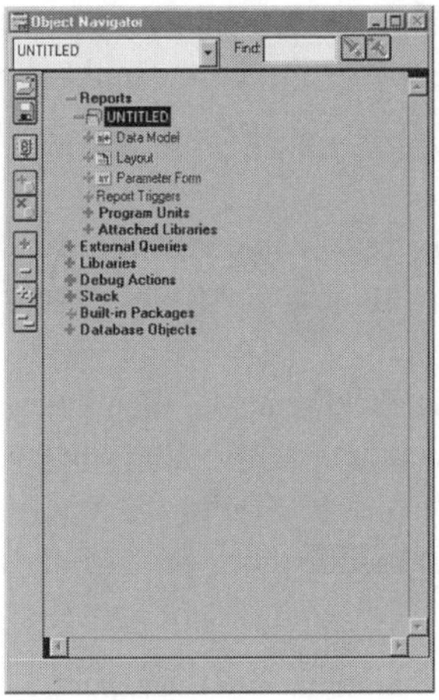


**FIG. 17.9**
The Object Navigator and the Data Model object used to open the Data Model editor.

The Data Model editor is used to document or model the queries used for the report.

2. Select the Query tool. It has the word SQL on it.
3. Select a spot on the Data Model editor and click the mouse to create a query box.

Figure 17.10 shows the Data Model editor after the first query box has been created.

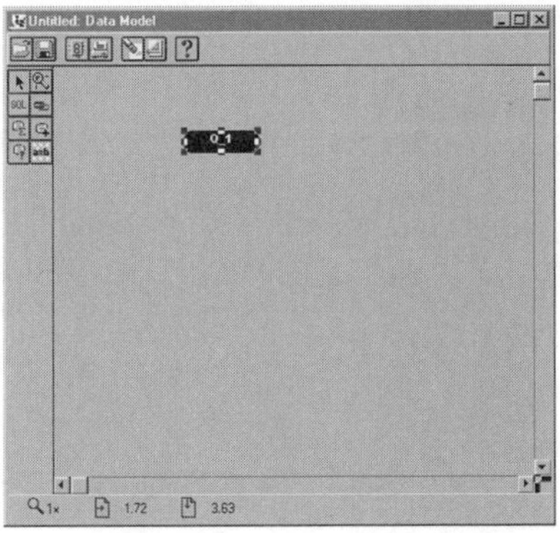


**FIG. 17.10**
The Data Model editor and a query box

The next step is to document the SQL statements that Reports will use to retrieve the report records.

1. Double-click the query group object on the Data Model editor to open the Query dialog box.

Figure 17.11 shows the filled-in dialog box for the example report. The dialog box contains four text items. The top item contains the name of the query. By default the queries begin with the letter Q, followed by a sequential number. The query name may be changed as necessary. The second item is Maximum Rows. This item can be used to limit the number of records retrieved by the query. *Null* is the default value for this text item. This value causes all records to be retrieved from the database.

The third item is External Query. It contains the name of an external query that will be used for the report in place of the query in the select window. The adjacent Browse button can be used to launch a standard Windows Open File dialog box. The dialog box is used to locate and identify the external query. The last item is the Select statement text item. This item is a multi-line text item used to enter or modify the SQL statement used to retrieve records

Any change made to the SQL statement in the Select window causes the Apply button to be activated. Clicking the Apply button causes Reports to validate the Select statement. The button will become grayed-out when the validation is successful. Click OK or Close to close the dialog box.



1. Enter the select statement displayed in Figure 17.11 into the Select statement text item.
2. Click the Apply button to validate the statement.
3. Click the OK button to close the dialog box.

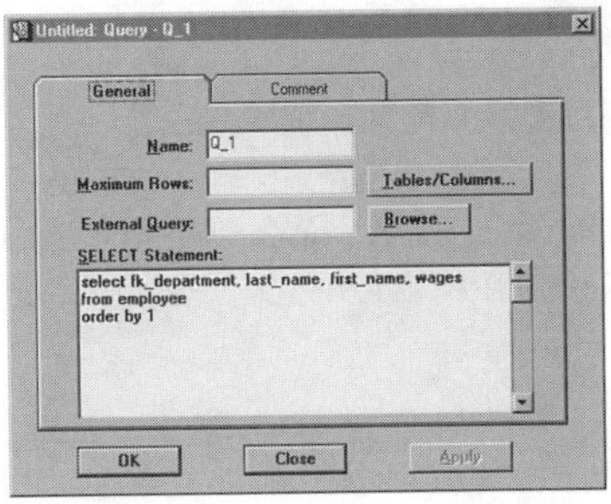


**FIG. 17.11** The Query dialog box containing the Select statement.

The Data Model editor now shows a group box containing the items or columns listed in the query select statement. The group box is attached to the query box by a thin black line. Figure 17.12 shows a group box that contains the query's columns.

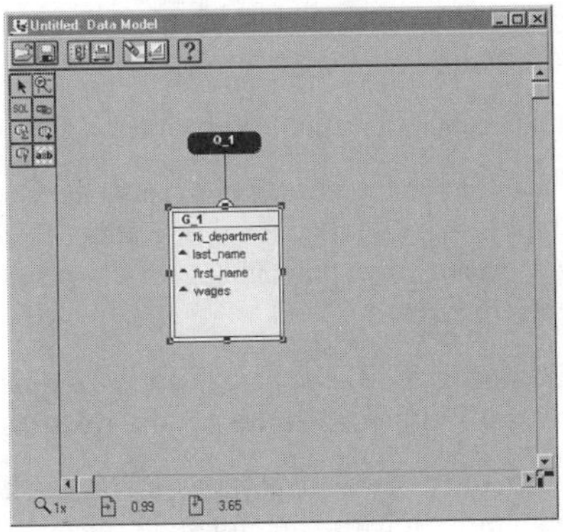


**FIG. 17.12** The Data Model editor displaying a group box.

The report cannot be executed until a layout is produced. The layout contains the placement specification of the report boilerplate and data items. The first step is to create a default layout by using one of two methods: select the Tools/Default Layout option, or click the default layout button at the top of the editor. The button shows an image of a T-square and triangle. Selecting either of these methods opens the Default Layout dialog box.

4. Click the Default Layout button.

The Default Layout dialog box is shown in Figure 17.13. The dialog box has two tabs: Style, and Data/Selection. Style determines the type of report and Data/Selection selects the columns for the report and modifies the item labels.

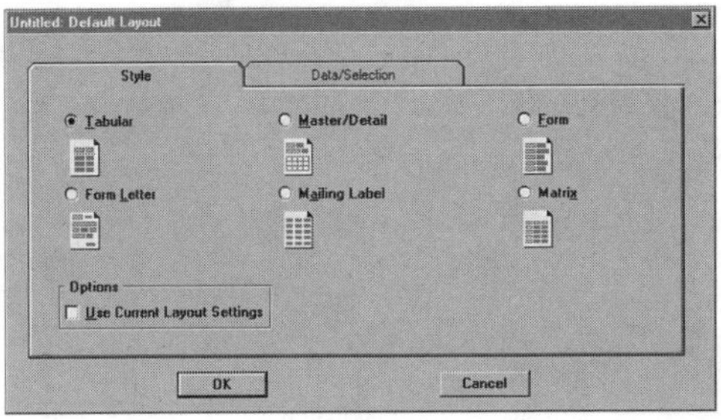


**FIG. 17.13** The Style tab of the Default Layout dialog box.

Style offers the developer six default style reports from which to choose. The style is selected by clicking the option button to the left of the Style description. Table 17.1 contains a description of each of the styles.

**Table 17.1 Report Styles**

| Style | Description |
|---|---|
| Form | Displays data in a format similar to a screen application. The fields are spread around the report and the field labels appear on the left of the item. |
| Form Letter | Intermixes text with fields. The text wraps onto multiple lines at word breaks. |
| Mailing Label | Prints records in multiple columns on the page. |
| Master/Detail | Consists of two or more sets of records. One set contains the master record and the remaining sets the detail records. Each time a master record is displayed, the related records in the detail sets are displayed. |
| Matrix | Similar to a grid, this style has a row of headings and a column of headings. The values in the middle relate to both columns. |
| Tabular | Displays the records in rows with column headings at the top of each column. It is the default style. |

5. Select the Tabular style.

At the bottom left-hand corner of the tab sheet is a check box. This check box is used when a layout already exists. Checking this box causes Reports to use the same settings as the layout it will replace.

6. Click the Data/Selection tab.

The Data/Selection tab is shown in Figure 17.14. The List box on the left displays the groups created on the model layout editor. The window on the right contains the columns for the currently selected group(s).

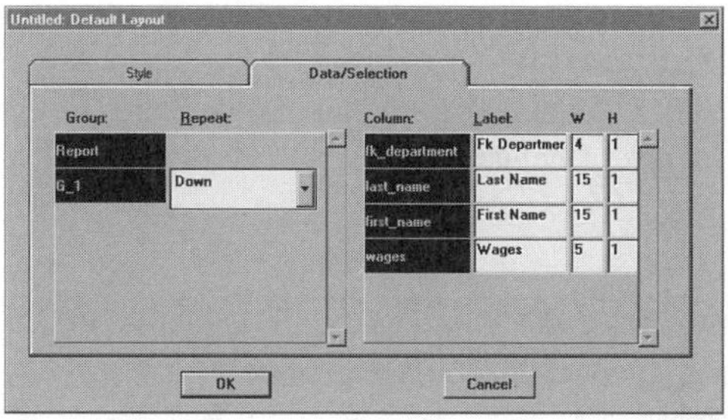


**FIG. 17.14**
The Data/Selection tab sheet.



The *repeat* window in the left box determines the print direction for the group. Table 17.2 contains descriptions of the various repeat settings.

**Table 17.2 Repeat Settings**

| Setting | Description |
|---|---|
| Across | Prints each record as a column to the left of the previous record. Each field is a row of the table. |
| Across/Down | Prints each record as a column to the left of the previous record. When the right edge of the page is reached, the next record is printed below the left—most record. |
| Down | Prints each record as a row below the previous record. Each field of the record is a column. |
| Down/Across | Prints each record as a row below the previous record until they cannot fit on the page. At that point, Reports prints the next record to the right of the top-most record on the logical page. This occurs only if enough horizontal space is available. |
| Matrix | The required setting for matrix reports. |

The dialog box window labeled "Column:" displays the columns or fields for the selected group(s). The "Label:"column of the dialog box contains the heading or field boilerplate. The labels can be changed before the default layout is created. The columns with the W and H headings are the width and height, respectively. These values can be modified. The columns and groups that are blackened are currently selected. Clicking on the column changes the selection. Gray columns are deselected. Only selected columns appear on the report layout.

7. Change a label value.
8. Press the OK button.

Clicking the OK button creates the report layout and displays the Layout editor. The default layout created is displayed in Figure 17.15. The Layout editor produces a more pleasing report format, and is discussed in Chapter 18. The report can now be executed and saved.

9. Save the report.
10. Generate the report.
11. Click the File, Run menu option or the Run button to run the report. (This is explained in greater detail in the next section).

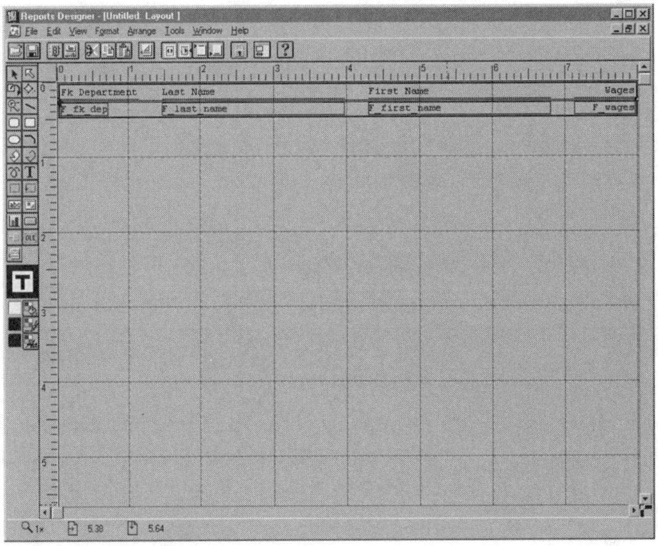


**FIG. 17.15**
The default layout for the Employee Listing

## Running the Employee Listing

The Employee Listing can be executed directly from Reports Designer. To run the report perform the following steps.

1. Select the File, Run menu option or the Run button on the Layout editor, Object Navigator, or the Data Model editor to execute the report. The Run button contains the image of a green light.

After launching the report, the Runtime Parameter Form appears, as shown in Figure 17.16. This screen is used to enter runtime parameters such as the destination type.

2. Click the Run Report to execute the report.

**FIG. 17.16**
The Default Runtime Parameter Form.

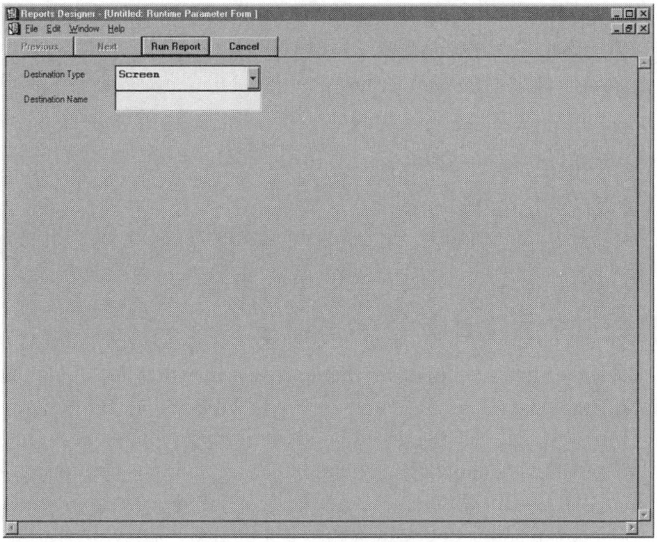




Figure 17.17 displays the Employee Listing contained in a window called a previewer, which allows the user to view the report before it is printed.

**FIG. 17.17**
The Employee Listing in the previewer window

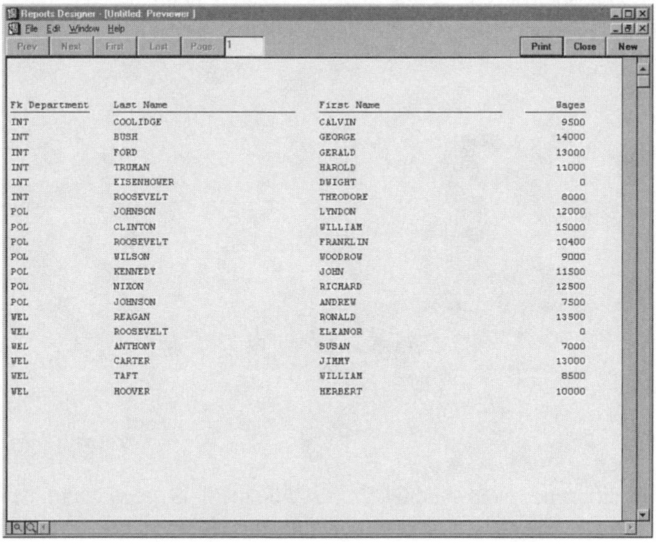


| Fk Department | Last Name | First Name | Wages |
|---|---|---|---|
| INT | COOLIDGE | CALVIN | 9500 |
| INT | BUSH | GEORGE | 14000 |
| INT | FORD | GERALD | 13000 |
| INT | TRUMAN | HAROLD | 11000 |
| INT | EISENHOWER | DWIGHT | 0 |
| INT | ROOSEVELT | THEODORE | 8000 |
| POL | JOHNSON | LYNDON | 12000 |
| POL | CLINTON | WILLIAM | 15000 |
| POL | ROOSEVELT | FRANKLIN | 10400 |
| POL | WILSON | WOODROW | 9000 |
| POL | KENNEDY | JOHN | 11500 |
| POL | NIXON | RICHARD | 12500 |
| POL | JOHNSON | ANDREW | 7500 |
| WEL | REAGAN | RONALD | 13500 |
| WEL | ROOSEVELT | ELEANOR | 0 |
| WEL | ANTHONY | SUSAN | 7000 |
| WEL | CARTER | JIMMY | 13000 |
| WEL | TAFT | WILLIAM | 8500 |
| WEL | HOOVER | HERBERT | 10000 |

On the top of the previewer are eight buttons that perform the following functions:

- *Prev*—Displays the previous page of the report.
- *Next*—Displays the next page of the report.
- *First*—Displays the first page of the report.
- *Last*—Displays the last page of the report.
- *Page*—Displays the page entered in the field to its right.
- *Print*—Opens a standard Windows Print dialog box that prompts the user to enter the number of pages to print.
- *Close*—Terminates the report.
- *New*—Reexecutes the query producing fresh results on the previewer.

# The Designer Menu Options

Report Designer has six pull-down menus available when the Object Navigator screen appears: File, Edit, Navigator, Tools, Window, and Help. Options on these menus are very close to the Forms Developer options discussed in previous chapters. Because there is such great similarity in the options, the following sections only cover options contained on these menus that did not exist in SQL Forms. If you need information on the common options, return to Chapter 12, "Using Object Navigator to Create Your First Oracle Form."

## File, Edit, and Navigator Menu Options

Figure 17.18 shows the File menu options. Only one option—*Report Doc*—is available on this menu that is not available on the SQL*Forms File menu options. Report Doc creates a report that lists the report settings in the database. This option is useful for creating a record of your reports.

**FIG. 17.18**
The File menu options.

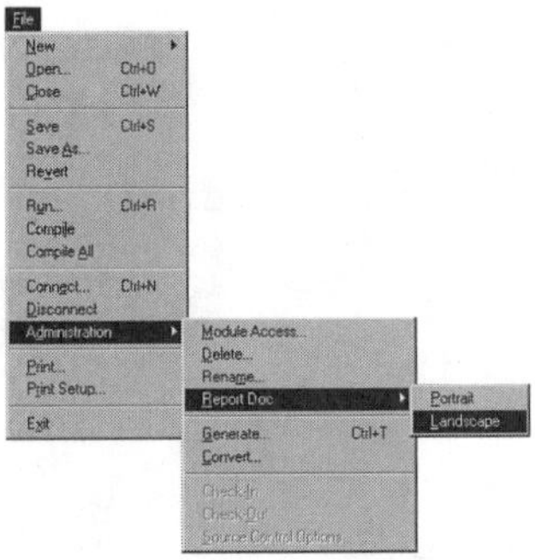


Another difference from the SQL*Forms File menu is the default file extension used in SQL*Reports. The source binary report file has a file extension of *.RDF.* This version of the report can only be read and modified by using Reports Designer. The *Administration/Convert*

option can be used to convert the file to a text file with an extension of *.REX*. This file can be read and modified by using a text editor. The compiled, or executable, version of the report has an .REP. file extension.

The Edit menu options are the same as those found on the Forms Edit menu in Chapter 12, as shown in Figure 17.19.

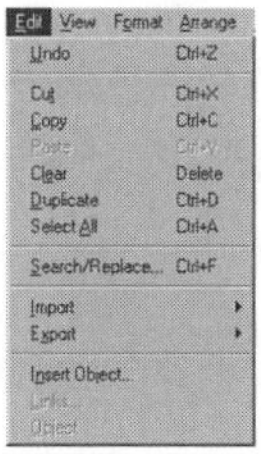


**FIG. 17.19**
The Edit Menu options.



Most of the options on the Navigator pull-down menu are also on the Forms menu. Two options are particular to this menu: *Toolbar and Navigator.* You can use Toolbar to remove the toolbar on the left side of the object navigator. This option is checked when the toolbar is displayed, and unchecked when it is removed. Navigator opens the Object Navigator Options dialog box. The dialog box and the *Navigator Options* pull-down menu are displayed in Figure 17.20.

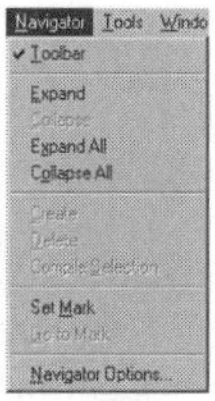


**FIG. 17.20**
The Navigator menu options and the General tab of the Object Navigator Options dialog box.

The General tab of the Object Navigator Options dialog box contains two check boxes. The *Show Object Icons* check box causes the buttons to the left of any report object to appear when it is checked. They will not appear when it is unchecked. The *Show PL/SQL Icons* check box causes the icons to the left of a PL/SQL object to appear when it is checked. They will not appear when it is unchecked.

The Groups tab of the dialog box also contains two check boxes *View by Structure* and *Show Columns in Groups* View by Structure causes the group objects to appear in a hierarchical structure. The child group of objects is indented below the parent. Show Columns In Groups causes the report columns to appear under the groups when the box is checked. Figure 17.21 shows the Object Navigator displaying the groups and columns in a hierarchical structure.

The Layout tab of the dialog box controls the objects displayed under the Layout object. Checking the View by Structure causes the structure to appear on the Object Navigator. The items will be rearranged when the checkbox is unchecked. The Layout Structure frame contains check boxes that allow the developer to view or not view layout items on the Object Navigator. These settings offer the developer a great deal of control over the number of objects that appear on the Object Navigator. Figure 17.22 shows the Layout section of the Object Navigator.

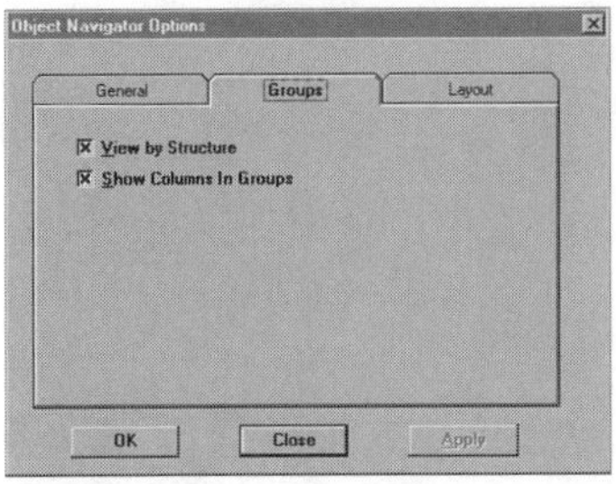


**FIG. 17.21**
The Object Navigator displaying groups and columns in a hierarchical structure.

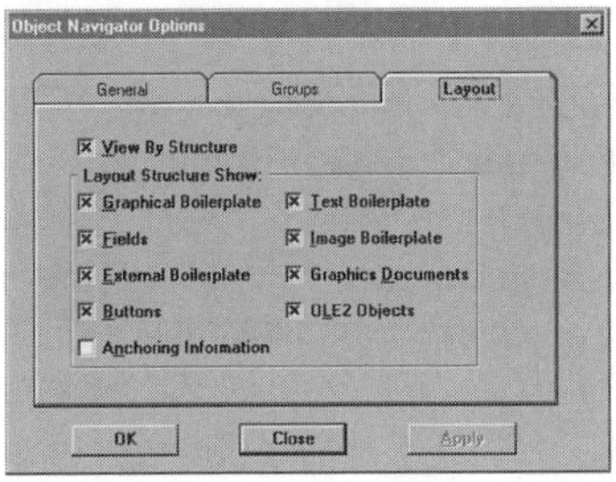


**FIG. 17.22**
The Layout tab of the Object Navigator Options dialog and various Layout objects on the object navigator.

**The Tool Menu Options** The Tools menu, as shown in Figure 17.23, contains menu options used to develop the report.

The *Properties* menu option opens the property sheet for the Reports objects. Most of the objects in Reports contain properties. You can open the property sheets by using this option, and then double-clicking on the object on the Object Navigator, or double-clicking on the item in the Layout editor.

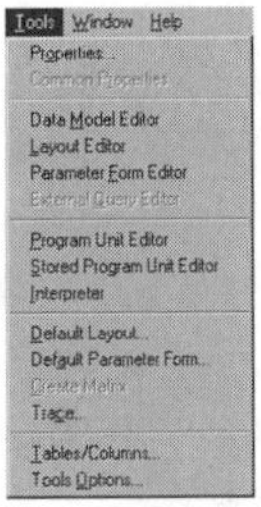


**FIG. 17.23**
The Tools menu options.

The *Common Properties* menu option changes the property values for multiple objects by using a common property sheet. Select the objects you want to modify and click the option, which opens a dialog box similar to the one in Figure 17.24. The Common Porperties dialog box has two tabs: Generic and Field. Generic contains the properties common to all of the objects, and the Field tab has properties common to the selected subset of the objects. The Field tab or page will only be displayed if one of the selected objects is a field.

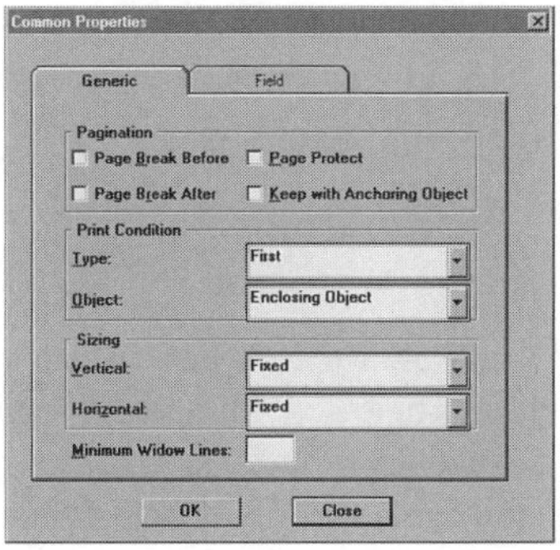


**FIG. 17.24**
The Common Properties dialog box.

The *Data Model editor*, *Layout editor*, and *Parameter Form editor* menu options display the editors with the name. The *External Query editor* menu option opens an editor used to modify a query stored in a database or file. The *Program Unit editor* menu option opens Oracle Procedure Builder. The *Stored Program Unit editor* menu option provides the tools to develop program units stored in the database. The *Interpreter* menu option opens Oracle Procedure Builder's central debugging workspace.

The *Default Layout* menu option is an important option that opens the Default Layout dialog box, and creates a report layout. A report cannot be generated and run unless a layout exists. The Default Layout option will replace any existing layouts with a new default.

The *Default Parameter Form* menu option opens the Default Parameter Form dialog box, which creates the initial report parameter form. A parameter form is a window that appears before the report is executed, and allows the user to specify values at runtime.

The *Create Matrix* menu option enables the developer to create a matrix object manually on the Layout editor. The *Trace* menu option opens the Trace Settings dialog box, as shown in Figure 17.25, which enables the developer to indicate what tracing information should be placed in a log file during execution of a report. Trace is useful for documenting runtime occurrences.

The Trace File box contains the name of the file that receives the tracing information. The dialog box also contains a combo box that allows you to specify the Trace Mode. There are two mode types. The first type is append. This option will cause the tracing information to be added or appended to the end of an existing file. The second mode type is replace. This option will override an existing file each time the report is executed.

The Trace Options contain an array of check boxes that determine the information that will be recorded in the file. Checking the All check box causes all of the occurrences to be recorded. You can achieve a customized selection by selecting individual check boxes.

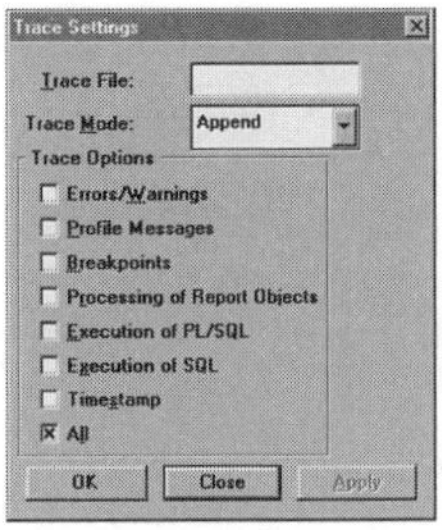


**FIG. 17.25**
The Trace Settings dialog box.

The *Tables/Columns* option opens the Table and Column Names dialog box as shown in Figure 17.26, which displays the tables and columns to which the developer has access. It can be used to identify the database object names and construct select statements. Selecting an object in the Database Objects list causes the Columns window to be populated with the tables columns.

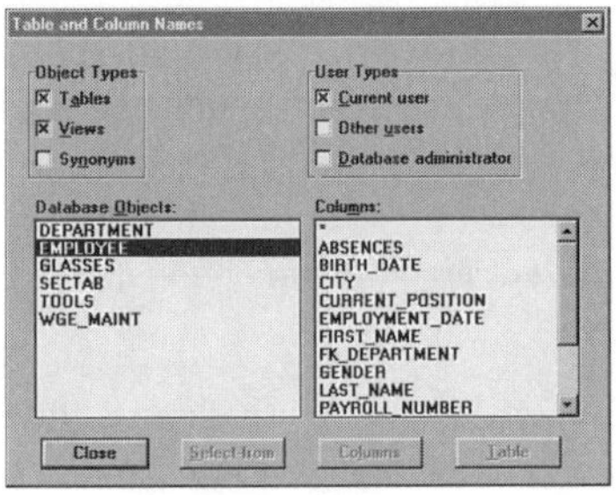


**FIG. 17.26**
The Table and Column Names dialog box.

The final option on the Tools Menu is the *Tools Options.* Selecting this option opens the Tools Options dialog box, which has three tabs: Preferences, Runtime Parameters, and Runtime Settings.

***The Tools Options Preferences Tab*** The *Tools Options Preferences* tab, as shown in Figure 17.27 (displaying its default settings), contains a number of settings that affect the design session. The *Disable PL/SQL Compilation* check box disables the compilation of PL/SQL constructs until the report is generated. The *Suppress Define Property Sheets* check box disables the automatic display of an item's property sheet when it is created in an editor. The *Suppress List Retrieval on Dialog Box Entry* suppresses lists when an action brings up a database dialog box.

The *Unit of Measurement* combo box specifies the units used in a report specification. The values are *centimeter, inch,* and *point.* The *Color Palette Mode* combo box determines how a report's color palette is implemented on your system.

The *Storage/Type* setting indicates the default location of the report modules. The *Reports, Queries, PL/SQL Libraries,* and *All* check boxes determine whether the named object should be included in objects/files list when the operation requires an object/file name.

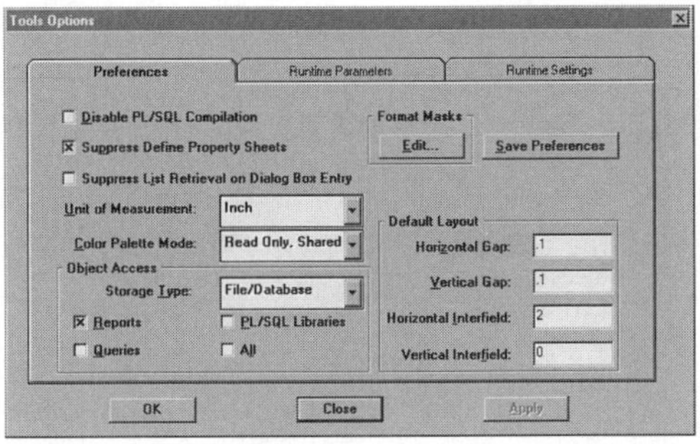


**FIG. 17.27**
The Preferences tab of the Tools Options Dialog box.

The *Format Masks Edit* button opens the Format Masks dialog box, which shows the various masks available. This option compiles a list of format masks that will appear in the list of values for the Format Mask field in the Field property and the Input Mask field in the Parameter property sheet. The *Save Preferences* button saves the preferences specified on the form.



The *Default Layout* frame contains four boxes that affect the layout. *Horizontal Gap* and *Vertical Gap* determine the amount of horizontal space Reports places between the object and the objects they enclose. *Horizontal Interfield* and *Vertical Interfield* determine the amount of space between fields created in the default layout. The greater the values, the easier it will be to read the objects in the layout editor. These options increase the white space in your report output.

***The Tools Options Runtime Parameters*** The *Tools Options Runtime Parameters* tab, as shown in Figure 17.28, contains settings that affect the execution of the report. The Destination frame contains three settings that control the report destination.

- The Type setting determines the default value used for the type of device that will receive the report. The options are Screen, File, Printer, Preview, and Mail.
- The Name setting determines the default value used for the name of the output file, printer, or Oracle*Mail userid.
- The Format setting specifies the printer driver to be used when the destination type is file.
- The Copies setting, which determines the default number of copies to print. The following settings determine the default format of numbers:
- The Currency Symbol, which specifies the currency character that will be used.
- The Thousands Separator, which specifies the separator that will be used.
- The Decimal Indicator, which specifies the decimal character that will be used.

The following settings are combo boxes located on the lower right corner of the dialog box.

- Orientation determines whether the report will be printed in landscape or portrait mode.
- Mode specifies whether to run the report in character mode or bitmap.
- Background determines whether the report should be run in the background.
- Print Job determines whether the Print Job dialog box will be displayed before running a report.

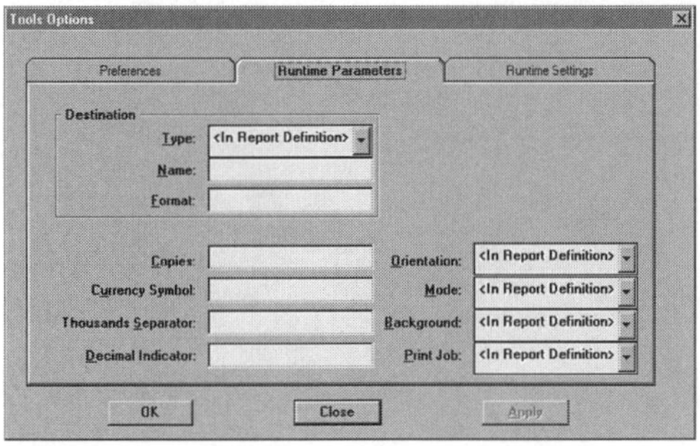


**FIG. 17.28**
The Tools Options Runtime Parameters tab sheet.

***The Tools Options Runtime Settings*** The third tab in the Tool Options dialog box is Runtime Settings, as shown in Figure 17.29 (showing the default settings). The following is a description of the Runtime Settings sheet text items and checkboxes.

- *Array Size* determines the size of the array in kilobytes Oracle uses for array processing.
- *Buffers* specifies the size of the virtual memory cache in kilobytes.
- *Long Chunk* is the size of the increments in which Reports retrieves a LONG column value.
- *Page Width* and *Height* determine the dimensions of the physical page size.
- *On Success* tells Oracle to perform a commit or rollback when the report is finished.
- *On Failure* determines whether a commit or rollback is performed when an error occurs.
- The *Parameter Form* check box tells Reports to display the parameter form when a report is executed.
- The *Read Only* check box tells Reports to read consistently across multiple queries in a report.
- The *Run Debug* check box causes extra runtime checking for logical errors. This procedure tries to identify items that are not errors, but could result in undesirable output.
- The *Auto Commit* check box causes Reports to automatically commit changes to the database.
- The *Non-blocking SQL* determines whether fetching data for a report will cause other programs to pause. A checked value allows the other program to execute during a fetch procedure. An unchecked value causes Oracle not to execute the other programs.

# Examining the Object Navigator

The Object Navigator, as shown in Figure 17.30, is a screen used to locate and retrieve Reports Designer objects. It serves the same function as the Object Navigator in Forms Designer. The Navigator has the following items.

**FIG. 17.29**
The Tools Options dialog box Runtime Settings tab.

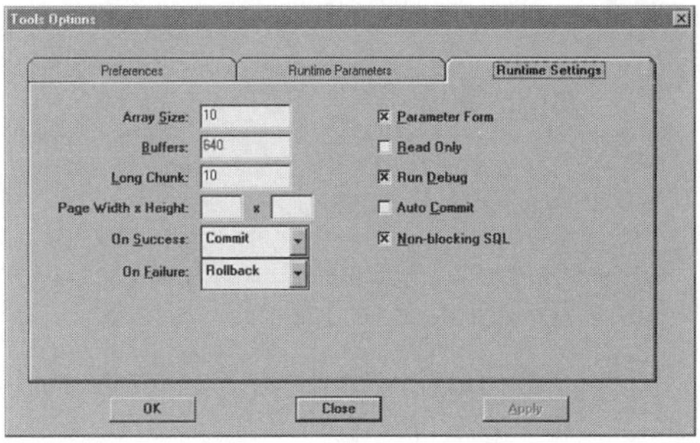


- The first, or main, part is an expandable list or report object tree, which is the central part of the window.
- The second, on the left of the object list, is a tool palette.
- The third, at the top of the screen, is a module list and a Find box.
- The module list is on the left side. Selecting the item opens a drop down-list containing all currently opened modules on the Navigator.
- The Find box is on the right side and is used to locate objects. The icons next to the Find box direct the search forward or backward from the currently selected object.



**FIG. 17.30**
The Reports Object Navigator.

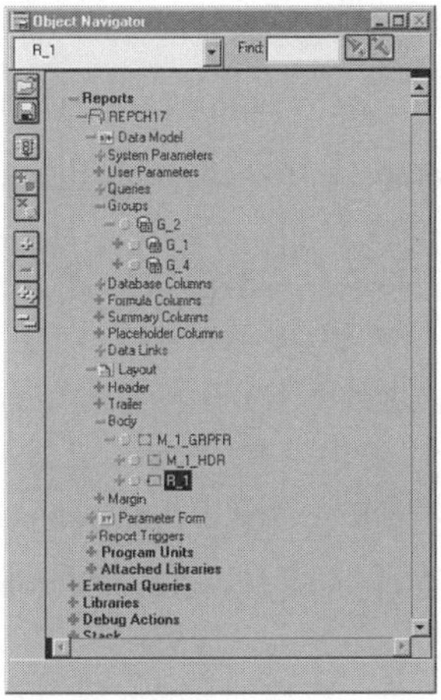

# Object Navigator Objects

The Object Navigator contains a large number of report objects. The definition of these objects is contained in Table 17.3

**Table 17.3 Report Objects**

| Object Name | Description |
|---|---|
| After Parameter Form | A report trigger that fires and executes a PL/SQL block after displaying a parameter form. |
| After Report | A report trigger that fires and executes a PL/SQL block after the report is completed. |
| Attached Libraries | A high-level object that lists libraries of PL/SQL code available for use in the report. |
| Background | A system parameter used to determine whether the report is run in the background or foreground. |
| Before Parameter Form | A report trigger that fires and executes a PL/SQL block before displaying the parameter form. |
| Before Report | A report trigger that fires and executes a PL/SQL block before the report is executed. |
| Between Pages | A report trigger that fires and executes a PL/SQL block after producing one page and before processing the following page. |
| Body | A layout object that groups the objects contained in the body of the report. The body is the main section of the report that contains the database records. |
| Built-in Packages | This object groups built-in packages developed by Oracle. |
| Copies | A system parameter to determine the number of reports to print. |
| Currency | A system parameter to determine whether the numeric values should be preceded by currency symbols. |
| Database Columns | A data model object that groups the names of the database columns used in the report. |
| Database Objects | Groups objects that exist in the connected database. |
| Data Links | A data model object that groups the defined links between queries. |
| Data model | A high-level report object which groups a variety of lower-level database objects that may be modified by using the Data Model screen. |
| Decimal | A system parameter to determine whether the decimal character should be used in number fields. |
| Desformat | A system parameter that specifies the print option to use when the report is sent to a file. Examples of valid values are: hpl, hplwide, dec, decwide, declared, dec180, dilt, and wide. |

| Object Name | Description |
|---|---|
| Desname | A system parameter to determine the name of the report destination. It can be printer, file, or mail. If the keyword is ignored, the destination will be screen. |
| Destype | A system parameter to specify the type of device that will receive the output. Options for this parameter are: screen, printer, file, previewer, or mail. |
| External Queries | Groups external queries available to the report. |
| Fields | A parameter form object that groups the fields or items contained on the parameter form. |
| Formula Columns | A Data Model object that groups the formula columns used in the report. Formula columns perform a computation on a database column. |
| Graphics Boilerplate | A parameter form object that groups graphics objects such as rectangles and ovals used on a parameter form. |
| Groups | A Data Model object that represents a set of data items or columns. |
| Header | A layout object used to group the report objects contained in the report header. A header is a report object that precedes the report. |
| Image Boilerplate | A parameter form object that groups image objects used on a form. |
| Layout | A high-level report object used to group report layout objects. These consist of the header, trailer, body, and margin. Double-clicking the button next to this item will launch the Layout Editor. |
| Libraries | Groups libraries of PL/SQL code contained in the file system. |
| Margin | A layout object used to group the objects contained in the report margin. The margin appears at the top or bottom of each report page. |
| Mode | A system parameter to specify whether to run the report in character mode or bitmap. |
| Orientation | A system parameter to specify whether to print the report in landscape or portrait mode. |
| Parameter Form | A high-level report object that groups parameter forms objects. A parameter form contains items or fields that pass runtime values to the report. The parameter form can also be used to include graphics in the report. Double-clicking the the button to the left of the object will invoke the Parameter Form editor. |

**Table 17.3 Continued**

| Object Name | Description |
|---|---|
| Placeholder Columns | A data model object that groups columns that receive their values through a PL/SQL routine. |
| Printjob | A system parameter used to determine whether the Print Job dialog box is displayed before running the report. |
| Program Units | A high-level object to group blocks of PL/SQL code that can be referenced by the report. |
| Queries | A Data Model object that contains an SQL statement used to retrieve records from the database. |
| Reports | The names of the report source code files currently open in the object navigator. |
| Report Triggers | A high-level report object to group the five report triggers. These triggers are: Before Report, After Report, Between Pages, Before Parameter Form, and After Parameter Form. |
| Summary Columns | A Data Model object which groups columns that compute summary values based on group data. Calculations types are: average (avg), first record in the set (first), last record in the set (last), the greatest value in the set (maximum), the smallest value in the set (minimum), the percent of the total group (% of total), standard deviation (std deviation), sum of the values in the set (sum), and variance of the values (variance). |
| System Parameters | A lower-level Data Model object to group parameters that control a function or attribute of the report. Values can be passed to these parameters. |
| Text Boilerplate | A parameter form object that groups text used on a parameter form. |
| Thousands | A system parameter used to specify whether to use the thousands character to format numbers. |
| Trailer | A layout object that contains the object placed in a report trailer. A trailer is an object that follows the report. |
| User Parameters | A lower-level Data Model object to group parameters or variables created by the developer. These parameters allow the user to pass information to the report. |

## Object Navigator Tool Bar

- The Reports object navigator has a vertical tool bar on the left side of the window. It has a set of nine buttons. Placing your cursor point over a button will cause Reports to display the tool label.
- The top button is the Open file tool. Selecting this tool brings up a standard Windows Open File dialog box.
- The second button contains an image of a floppy disk. Selecting this button saves changes to the current report file.
- The third button is the Run tool, which contains the image of a green light and will execute the selected report module.
- The next two buttons are the Create and Delete object tools.
- The Create button contains an image of a plus sign. Pressing this button causes a new object to be created beneath the currently selected object.
- The Delete button contains a red minus sign and will delete any selected object.
- The next four tools expand and collapse items on the Object Navigator.
- The tool with the single-plus expands the currently selected object. It will not expand any of the item's children objects.
- The tool with the double-plus signs expand the marked object and all of the object's children.
- The tool with the minus sign collapses the currently selected object.
- The tool with the double minus signs collapses the currently marked object and all of the object children.
- Expanding and collapsing objects is discussed in greater depth in Chapter 12.



# Understanding the Data Model

The Data Model Editor is a major Reports Designer screen used to model the queries, groups, data links, and parameters in a report. The data model is a graphical representation of how the data will be retrieved and how it will be combined. Figure 17.31 illustrates a data model and some of the various model objects. Pointers tipped by arrowheads are used in the figure to identify these objects. Do not be confused by the datalink symbol. It consists of a line between two query boxes with an arrow on the end.

The first object placed in the data model is a query box, which has a SELECT statement that executes during runtime. The object, represented by a round black box, is placed on the editor by selecting the Query tool on the tool palette. The Query tool is labeled with the letters SQL. When the tool is activated, the cursor turns into a set of crosshairs. Place the Query box by clicking the active tool over the model area. You can size and position the query box by dragging it with the cursor. Double-clicking the Query box opens a Query dialog box (refer to Figure 17.11), which records the SELECT statement.

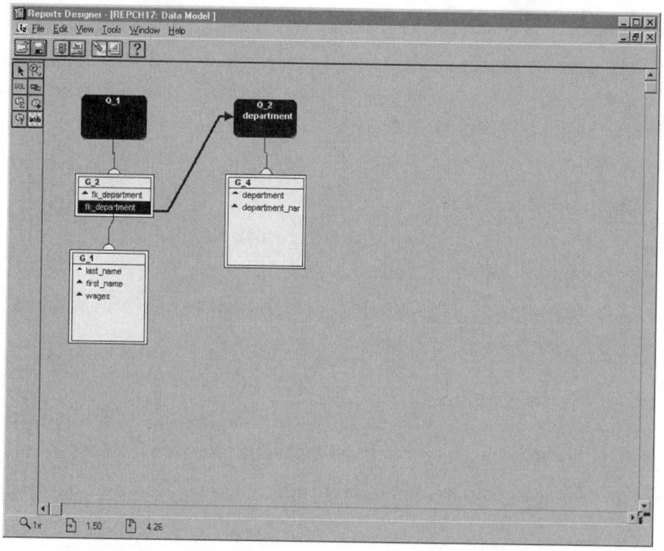


**FIG. 17.31**
A data model containing two queries, three groups, and a data link.

Clicking the Apply button on the Query dialog box validates the Select statement and creates a group box. Square corner boxes identify group boxes, which display the columns contained within the group. The group box is also attached to its query by a thin line.

Below query Q_1 are two group boxes. Originally, the columns in both boxes were part of one box. When groups are created, all query columns are contained in one group. Within the group some of the column values may be repeated. In the case of query Q_1, the value in the department column is repeated for each employee in the department. Printing the department number only when it changes enhances the report. This effect is called a break. The second group under the Q_1 query was created to produce this effect. The columns that contain non-repeating values for each row were selected and dragged outside the G_2 box. This caused Reports Designer to create a new group box for these columns. The new group box is attached to the original group by a thin line.

When Reports encounters two independent queries in the data model, it executes the first query then executes the second query. The results of the first query will be printed above the results of the second query. The effect of having two independent queries is the same as producing two independent reports on the same listing. This doesn't usually produce meaningful results because the queries are not coordinated.

Queries can be linked by using a data link. The black line from the G_2 group to the Q_2 query is a graphical representation of a data link. The G_2 and Q_2 objects are linked by common values in the department and fk_department columns. Query Q_2 is executed once for each record returned to the G_2 group. The Q_2 query returns the corresponding department name for each record in the G_2 group.

The effect of this data model is to produce a listing of the employees in the Employee table. The records will be ordered by department. The department number and name will only be printed when the values change. Figure 17.32 displays the report produced by this model.

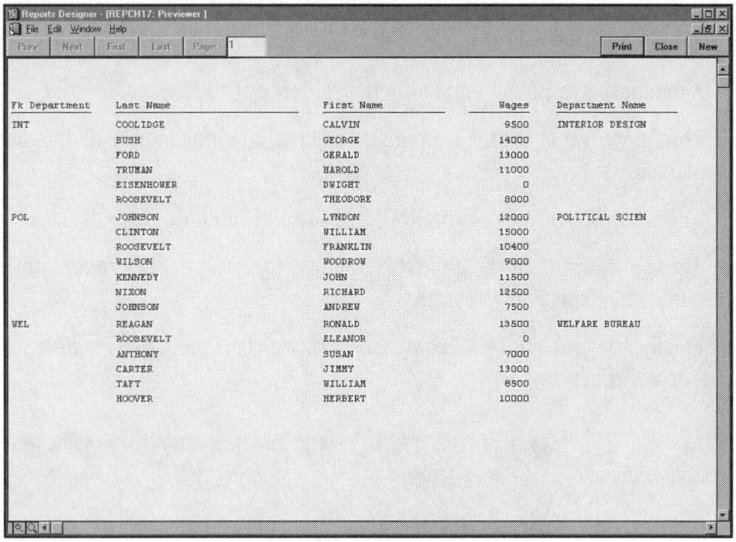


| Fk Department | Last Name | First Name | Wages | Department Name |
|---|---|---|---|---|
| INT | COOLIDGE | CALVIN | 9500 | INTERIOR DESIGN |
| | BUSH | GEORGE | 14000 | |
| | FORD | GERALD | 13000 | |
| | TRUMAN | HAROLD | 11000 | |
| | EISENHOWER | DWIGHT | 0 | |
| | ROOSEVELT | THEODORE | 8000 | |
| POL | JOHNSON | LYNDON | 12000 | POLITICAL SCIEN |
| | CLINTON | WILLIAM | 15000 | |
| | ROOSEVELT | FRANKLIN | 10400 | |
| | WILSON | WOODROW | 9000 | |
| | KENNEDY | JOHN | 11500 | |
| | NIXON | RICHARD | 12500 | |
| | JOHNSON | ANDREW | 7500 | |
| WEL | REAGAN | RONALD | 13500 | WELFARE BUREAU |
| | ROOSEVELT | ELEANOR | 0 | |
| | ANTHONY | SUSAN | 7000 | |
| | CARTER | JIMMY | 13000 | |
| | TAFT | WILLIAM | 8500 | |
| | HOOVER | HERBERT | 10000 | |

**FIG. 17.32**
The Employee Listing produced from the data model.



# Understanding Data Model Editor Tools

The Data Model Editor contains a variety of tools, as shown in Figure 17.33. The tool buttons are located in the top-left corner of the editor. The button with the Open file opens a standard Windows Open file dialog box. It is used to locate and bring a file into the Designer. The adjacent icon is the *Save* tool, which, when clicked, permanently saves the latest modifications to the currently selected module. The icon with the green stoplight is the *Run* tool, which executes the report. Pictures of these buttons can be seen in the previous section "Object Navigator Tools."

The printer symbol indicates the *Print* tool, which you use to print the report. The *Clear* tool symbol is the pencil eraser, which removes objects from the editor. Select the object and click the tool to remove the object. The delete key may also be used to remove the object.

The *Default Layout* tool (triangle and T-square symbol) launches the Default Layout dialog box.

The tool with the question mark launches Reports help facilities.

The left horizontal toolbar contains the tools to place objects on the editor.

The tool symbolized by the black arrow is the *Selection* tool. Clicking this icon deactivates the current tool and allows the developer to select an object.

The *Query* tool is symbolized by the words SQL.

Beneath the query tool is the *Summary* column tool. It is symbolized by the summation symbol. It places special objects on the form used to contain the result of a calculation.

A database symbol and question mark identify the *Placeholder* tool.

The *Magnify* tool contains an image of a magnifying glass. This tool can be used to zoom in on objects.

The *Data Link* tool is symbolized by blue and red link symbols.

The tool with the plus sign is the *Formula* tool. It creates a report object that contains a formula and displays the results.

Finally, the tool symbolized with the axb words is the *Cross Product* tool. It is used to produce matrix reports.

**FIG. 17.33**
The Data Model Editor tools.

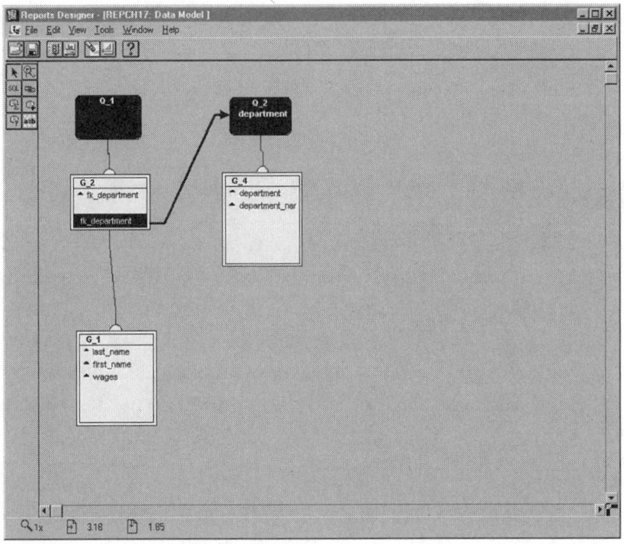


# Summary

Oracle Reports 2.5 is Oracle's report writing tool. It consists of two products: Reports Designer and Reports Runtime. Designer develops the report and Runtime executes the report. The products can be launched by double-clicking the respective icons in the Developer 2000 program group Reports Runtime can also be launched from a form by using the run_product built-in subprogram.

Reports Designer consists of three screens. The first is the Object Navigator, which locates and identifies report objects. Second is the Data Model editor, which documents the queries, groups, data links, and columns used to retrieve the data for the report. Third is the Layout Editor, which is a report painter that formats the presentation of the report.

To create a report, open a new report module. Document the report data model on the data model editor. Finally, create a default layout. The report will now be ready to run.

## From Here...

The next chapter covers the Layout Editor, a Reports Designer tool that has a number of features for customizing a report. The chapter covers the various formatting tools available on the Layout Editor. It also covers procedures such as moving columns, changing fonts, adding images, and adding boilerplate. Finally, the chapter describes how to add summary and formula columns to the report.



## Review Exercises

1. Create a report that lists employees within the Employee database. The report is to be sorted by department number.
2. Put a break on the report on the department column.
3. Add the department name for the Department table to the report.

CHAPTER 18

# Customizing Reports and Advanced Report Functions

**Understanding the Layout Editor**

This section discusses the objects created when you use the Default Layout Editor tool. It will show how the objects interact.

**The Layout Editor menu options**

This section provides an overview of the Layout Editor Menu options.

**The Layout Editor tools**

This section provides an overview of the Layout Editor Tools including the toolbar and Tool Palette.

**Layout object properties**

This section describes the properties of the different layout objects.

**Making a report presentable**

This section describes how to use the menu options, tool palette, and layout objects to create a good looking report.

**Creating a report layout from scratch**

This section describes how to create a layout from scratch.

**Summary columns and formula columns**

This section describes summary and formula columns and how to add them to a report.

Oracle Reports 2.5 is a frame-based report writer. There are two kinds of report writers: frame-based and banded. A banded report writer such as Powersoft's Infomaker places fields or database columns in *bands*, which represent the header, body, and footer of a report. A frame-based report writer gives you much more flexibility because frames correspond to actual groups from the query, not sections of the report. Frames hold all of the fields that are in one group from the query. You can manipulate frames in any number of ways in the layout, whereas bands can be expanded only vertically to fit more fields.

It is also very helpful to use the Object Navigator, discussed in the previous chapter, when creating a layout. The Object Navigator gives you a way to keep track of your objects and be sure that they are in their proper sequence. So, keep the Object Navigator open when creating a layout. ■

# Description of Layout Editor Objects

This discussion is based on the default layout of the employee listing from Chapter 17. The objects will be explained in the order they appear in the Object Navigator, to make it easier to understand the objects' interaction. Take notice in Figure 18.1 that the Object Navigator window expanded to show the layout objects.

**FIG. 18.1**
Default Layout for employee listing report, with expanded Object Navigator window.

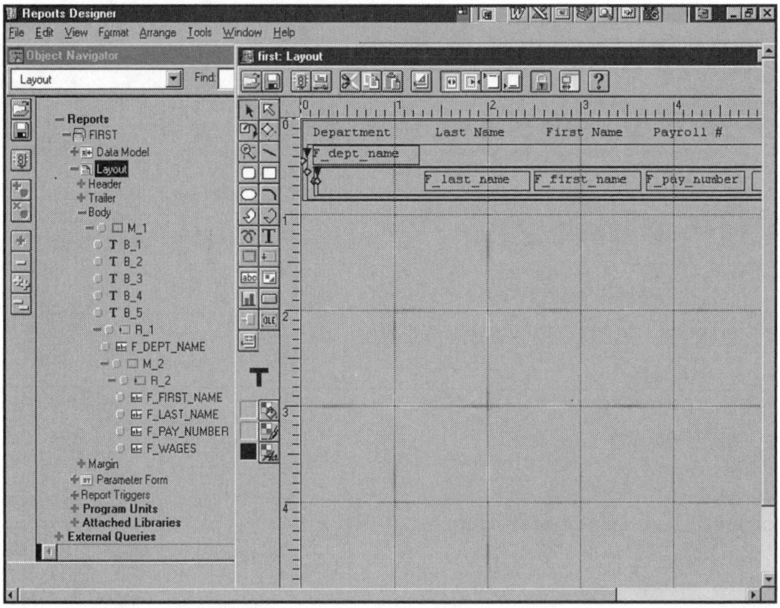

Open the report file from the CD or refer to the preceding figure. Click the outermost frame from the layout editor or select the first frame whose name ends with GRPFR. This is the first object created by the default layout tool described in the previous chapter. This frame gets created every time a repeating frame is created. Its purpose is to group all the objects that belong to a group in the query, therefore it is called a group frame. Any other frames that you create will begin with an M_ and the name will be a number, unless you name!them and they will not end with GRPFR.

The second object is another frame. This frame's name ends with an _HDR. This is a header frame and it contains two other objects: boilerplate text and line. These objects' names start with a B_. The frame's purpose is to group the boilerplate text and line objects to form the column headings for the report. This frame is not necessary, although it is helpful if you want to perform any operations on the header, such as a certain print condition or format trigger. There is also another frame with an _EXP at the end of its name. (This third frame isn't represented here because we did not define any summary columns.) Again, this frame isn't necessary; it's just useful for print conditions and format triggers.

The next object is the repeating frame. You can tell repeating frames in two different ways: they always have an arrow on the frame signifying the print direction of the frame, and their names start with an R_. A repeating frame represents a group in the query. There is a one-to-one relationship. If you have a group, you must have a repeating frame. It is very helpful to name the groups in your query, because when the Default Layout Editor creates the repeating frames it names them the same as the groups. You may have multiple groups in a query in which case the layout will have group frames (GRPFR) and repeating frames inside of other group and repeating frames. The way they are laid out is the uppermost group from the query is the outermost set of frames (group and repeating)and as you move down the query the frames go inside one another. So the last group is the innermost frame.

The last objects are the Field objects. These objects reside inside the repeating frame. Field objects display database columns and formula columns. The Fields' names start with an F_. The fields must be displayed in the repeating frame that corresponds to the group they are in, in the query. This will be stressed a number of times in this chapter because if you are moving objects around in the layout, they sometimes can be moved outside of their correct repeating frame and you get an error when you try to run the report. If you are creating the layout from scratch you have to be very careful that the fields are placed in the correct repeating frames corresponding to the query. That is why it is very helpful to name your groups.



# Layout Editor Menu Options

The File, Tools, Window, and Help menus are the same as previously discussed in Chapter 17, in this book.

## Edit Menu Options

The Edit menu has standard windows editing options, as shown in the following minitable and Figure 18.2:

| | |
|---|---|
| *Undo* | Undoes the last change you made. |
| *Cut* | Cuts a selection to the clipboard. |
| *Copy* | Copies a select to the clipboard. |
| *Paste* | Pastes a selection from the clipboard. |
| *Clear* | Deletes a selection from the layout. |
| *Duplicate* | Duplicates a selection and keeps all of its properties. |
| *Select All* | Selects all layout objects. |
| *Search/Replace* | Searches and replaces text in a PL/SQL editor. |
| *Import* and *Export* | Imports and export stext, drawings, or images. |
| *Insert Object* | Allows you to insert any variety of different objects into the report from Excel spreadsheets to sound files. |

| | |
|---|---|
| *Links* | Provides a list of any OLE2 objects linked to the report. |
| *Object* | Provides a menu for an OLE2 server when there are OLE2 objects linked to the report. |

Figure 18.2 shows the Edit menu options.

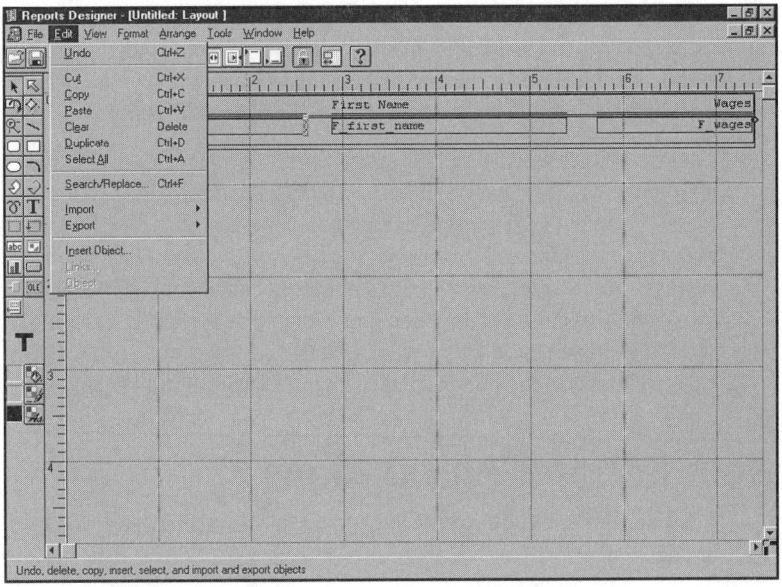


**FIG. 18.2**
Edit Menu Options.

# View Menu Options

The View menu options govern the way things appear as well as what appears on the Layout Editor. Figure 18.3 shows the View Menu options.

The first set of options changes the way objects appear in the Layout Editor. The first option, *Zoom In*, magnifies the objects to twice their original size. *Zoom Out* resizes the objects to one half their original size. *Normal Size* returns the objects to their original size. *Fit to Window* sizes the layout window to fit the entire Report Designer window. These options only change the way the objects appear when viewed in the layout editor; it does not change the actual sizing of the objects.

The next section of options are all things that you can have displayed on the Layout Editor. The options being displayed have a check mark next to them, and things not displayed do not have a check mark next to them. *Rulers* are the rulers that display at the top and along the side of the layout. Their purpose is to help with the positioning of objects on the layout. *Ruler Guides* are dotted lines that you can activate by clicking the ruler and dragging either down or to the right. These help with the aligning of objects on the layout. *Grid* either displays the grid lines or doesn't display them. The grid is most helpful when doing character-mode reports. *Snap to*

*Grid* causes objects to snap to the closest grid points to them. This is used when you are using the grid. *Page Breaks* displays where the physical page breaks are on the layout. *Tool Palette, Status Line* and *Toolbar* can be displayed for ease of use or you can turn them off. The Status Line displays the zoom status of the layout editor as well as the X and Y coordinates of the cursor.

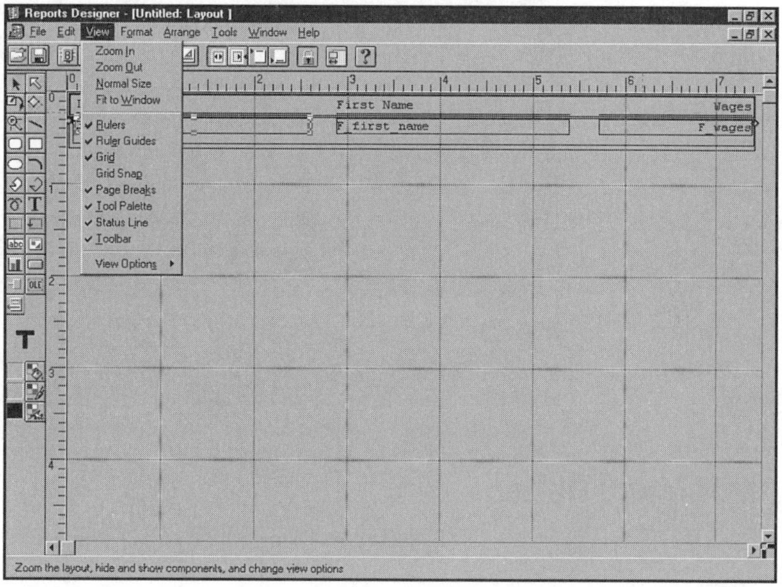


**FIG. 18.3**
View Menu options.

The last section, *View Options,* has two choices: *Rulers* and *Layout.* Figure 18.4 shows the two dialog boxes for these options.

Rulers enable you to set specifics for the grid. You can specify its units of measure, Size, Spacing, and Snap Points. The units of measure should be the same as the reports' units of measure. Size is the vertical and horizontal space between the grid lines. Snap Points are the number of points between the grid lines to which objects can snap.

Layout enables you to set specific properties for the layout in general. There are four views that you can look at when editing the layout of the report. Each view controls a part of the report. The views are Body, Margin, Header, and Trailer. Body is where you create the body of the report. Margin is where you can visually set the margins of the report as well as add fields for display. Header and Trailer are where you create header or trailer pages for the report. You can chose to display fields as their masks, or just an outline. You can also set the layout to be in either *confine* or *flex* modes. Confine mode does not allow you to move any objects in a way that would cause the layout not to work. You can't move a field out of its parent-repeating frame. Flex mode allows you to move an object, its parent object, and all objects in the direction of the move, its push path. This ensures that the layout stays in working order.

**FIG. 18.4**
Rulers and Layout Dialog boxes from the View Options menu.

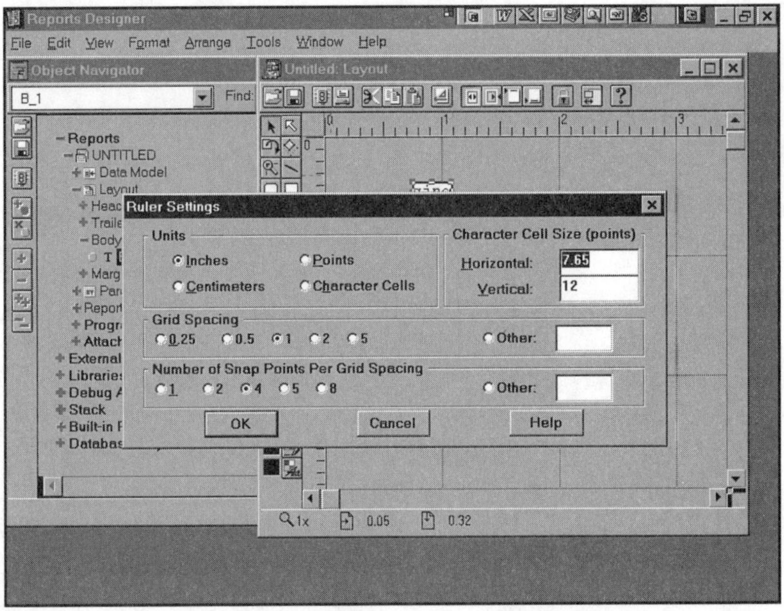

## Format Menu Options

The Format Menu enables you to change the display properties of objects. Figure 18.5 shows the Format Menu options.

**FIG. 18.5**
Format Menu options.

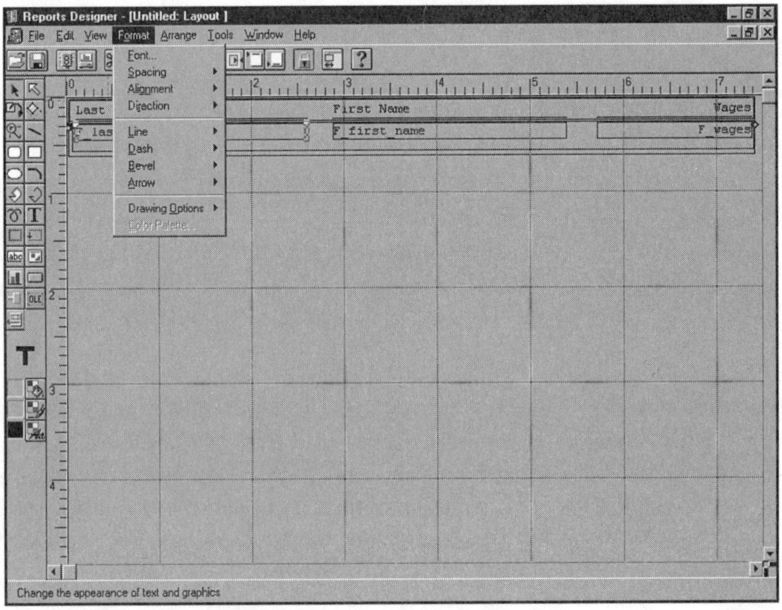

The first option is *Font*. It opens a standard windows font dialog box shown in Figure 18.6. The dialog box enables you to choose a font style, size, and color.

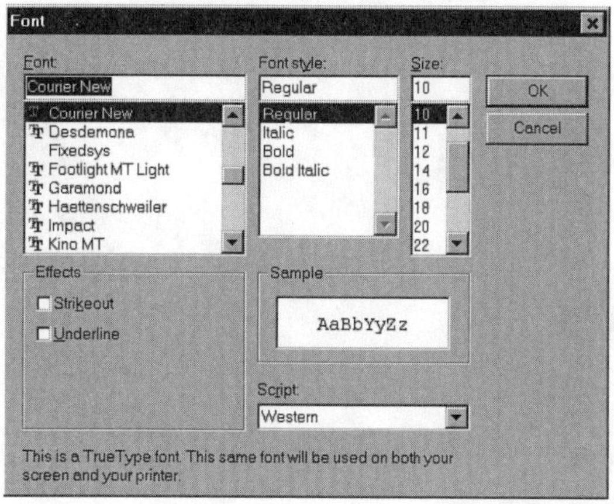


**FIG. 18.6**
Font dialog box.

*Spacing* enables you to select a line spacing for the report, either single, double, one and a half, or custom.

- *Alignment* enables you to justify field and boilerplate objects, either left, center, right, start, or end. Start alignment aligns the text at the start of the box that surrounds the field and end aligns the text at the end of the box that surrounds the field.
- *Direction* specifies the way a field is read. This is used only on bi-directional platforms. Your choices are Default, Left to right, or Right to left.
- *Line* enables you to select a thickness for a line. You have six point-size choices.
- *Dash* enables you to chose a style for a dashed line. *Bevel* enables you to turn on a bevel for an object. You have four choices: Inset, Outset, Raised, or Lowered.
- *Arrow* enables you to select a style of arrow to use.
- *Drawing Options* gives you another way to add a drawing object to the layout, besides using the tool palette. The grayed out Color Palette would allow you to select a different color palette from the one that is being used.



## Arrange Menu Options

The Arrange Menu gives you the ability to arrange and size the objects on the layout. Figure 18.7 shows the Arrange Menu options.

The first set of options gives you control over the objects on the layout and how they are displayed.

- *Bring to Front* brings an object to the front that has other objects that overlap it, making the object not appear correctly on the layout.

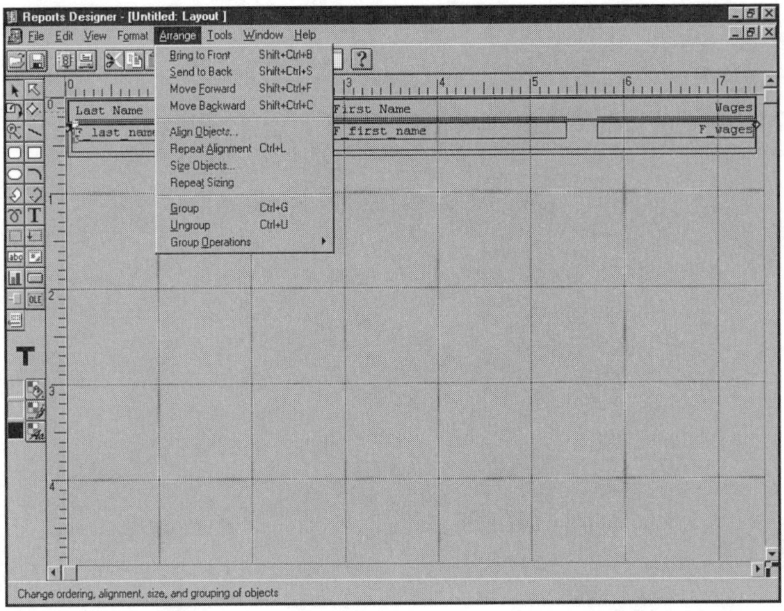


**FIG. 18.7**
Arrange Menu options.

- *Send to Back* sends an object behind other objects previously behind the object you are sending back.
- *Move Forward* and *Move Backward* do the same except they work when only one other object is obscuring the object you want to display.
- *Align Objects* enables you to select a group of objects on the layout and align them in a number of different ways. Figure 18.8 displays the Align Objects dialog box. You can align the objects to each other or to the grid if you are using one. You also chose either to Horizontally or Vertically align the objects.

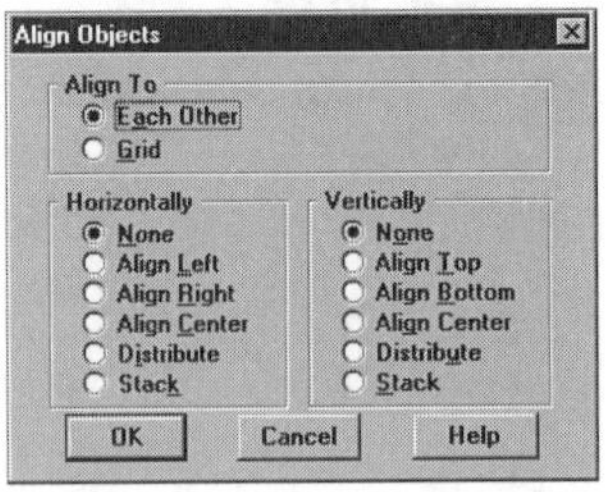


**FIG. 18.8**
Align Objects dialog box.

- *Distribute* spaces the objects out evenly and Stack stacks the objects one right next to the other, either on top of one another, or next to one another depending if it is horizontal or vertical.
- *Align Left* aligns the objects so their left-most sides are in line.

That is how the alignment options work; whichever way you chose, the objects are aligned based on that side on the objects. Be careful if you chose an alignment because objects are aligned based on the object that is the most of whatever direction you chose. What this means is that if you set up a field in the position that you want the rest of the objects to align to, say the top, but there is another object that is above your object on the layout, the objects selected to align will align to that higher object not to yours. Be careful of this.

- *Repeat Alignment* repeats the last alignment setting that you did.
- *Size Objects* enables you to size or resize a group of objects at the same time. Figure 18.9 shows the Size Objects dialog box. You can set the height or width of the objects based on one of the objects selected. This assumes that you have already created one field the size that you want. There is also the capability to set the fields based on a custom size that you have determined. You can also set the units of measure for the sizing, this should be the same as the units of measure for the report.

**FIG. 18.9**
Size Options dialog box.

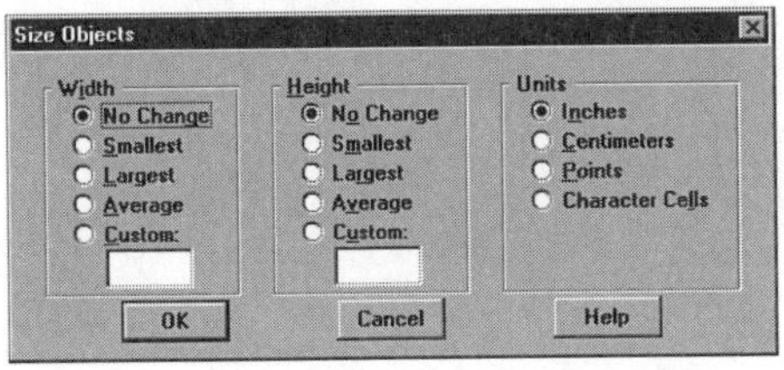




- The last set of options on the Arrange menu are the group options. *Group, Ungroup,* and *Group Operations* are used to group, ungroup, or modify the grouped objects on the layout. Any operation performed on one of the grouped objects will be applied to all of the objects in the group. This is not a commonly used feature.

# Layout Editor Tools

The Layout Editor has two sets of tools. Along the top is the toolbar with standard icons for formatting and some special layout icons. Figure 18.10 shows the toolbar. Along the side of the Layout Editor is the Tool Palette. The tool palette is all of the icons for all of the objects to building a report.

## The Toolbar

The standard icons are Open, Save, Run, Print, Cut, Copy, and Paste. The next icon is the Default Layout tool icon; it has a triangle and a T-square on it. This launches the Default Layout dialog box.

The next four icons are for the different parts of the report. The first is for the body of the report, which is where the data is displayed. The icon has two arrows pointing out. The second is for the margins of the report. This icon has an arrow on the outside pointing in and an arrow on the inside pointing out. The next icon is for the header page of the report. It has an arrow at the top. The last icon is for the trailer page of the report. It has an arrow at the bottom.

**FIG. 18.10**
The toolbar for the Layout Editor.

The next icon, with the padlock, shows that the report is in confine mode. The lock is open when confine mode is off. The next icon with the arrows and the blue box shows that flex is off. The arrows point away from the box if flex is on. The last icon is the Help icon.

## The Tool Palette

The tool palette contains all of the tools necessary for creating a report layout. Figure 18.11 shows the tool palette. It has icons for all of the objects that can be added to the layout and some properties for those objects.

**FIG. 18.11**
Layout Editor tool palette.

The first 13 icons are standard drawing tools. They are, from right to left: Select, Frame Select, Rotate, Reshape, Magnify, Line, Rounded Rectangle, Rectangle, Ellipse, Arc, Polygon, Polyline, and Freehand. These objects can be added anywhere in the report.

The next four icons are the layout building icons. The first icon is the text icon, showing the capital T, which adds boilerplate text to the report. The icon with the broken line square is the frame icon. The icon with the broken square with the arrow is the repeating frame icon. The next icon with abc in a white box is the field icon. You create fields for database, formula and summary columns with this icon.

The next set of icons is for adding special objects to the report. The icon with the triangle and the square links files to the report. The icon with what looks like a bar chart adds graphics to the report. The tool that looks like a button adds a button to the report. The button executes a PL/SQL block of code. The next icon is the anchor icon, which anchors two objects together on the layout. The icon with OLE links an OLE2 object to the report. The last icon is the Additional Default Layout icon. This is used to create another layout along with the one that you have already designed, if you add another query to your report.

The last set of icons separated by the big capital T, or the text symbol, are the icons that control the properties for the drawing objects, the boilerplate objectss and the field objects. The first icon is the Fill Color icon. This gives the background of an object a color. The second is the Line Color icon. If you have line objects, or borders, you can give them color. The last icon is the Text color icon. Your text can have different colors, to illustrate different parts of the report.

# Layout Object Properties

To access an object's properties when the object is selected, right-click it and select Properties, or on the Tools menu select Properties.

To access an object's properties, select the object then right-click it and select Properties, or from the tool bar select the Tools menu and the Properties option.



## Common Tabs

Some objects in the Layout Editor have the same properties on their property sheets. The properties are separated onto different tabs. The tabs are General Layout, Printer Codes, and Comments. The tabs are used to group similar properties together.

**General Layout Tab** The General Layout tab has four sections. Figure 18.12 shows the General Layout tab. The first section is *Pagination*, with four check boxes. The first two are for creating page breaks before and after an object. These are usually placed on outside frames to cause separation of different sections of the report. *Page Protect* enables you to keep child records from separating onto different pages. If the records won't fit on the current page the report won't print them; it will go to the next page and print them. You have to be careful using this feature because if you have child records that won't fit on a single page, Reports will give you an error. The Keep with Anchoring Object checkbox prevents an anchored or child object from printing on a different page from the object it is anchored to, or its parent. This makes reports much easier to read and understand in many cases.

The next section is Format Trigger. This button launches a program unit editor window, as shown in Figure 18.13. A *format trigger* is a Boolean function that, when it is true, prints the object and, when it is false, won't. The CD has code examples of how to use format triggers. They are most useful for suppressing information from printing. For example, in a numeric column you might not want to print zeros or negative numbers, only whole, nonzero numbers. You can write code to suppress those numbers from being printed on the report even if they are returned from the query.

**FIG. 18.12**
The General Layout tab.

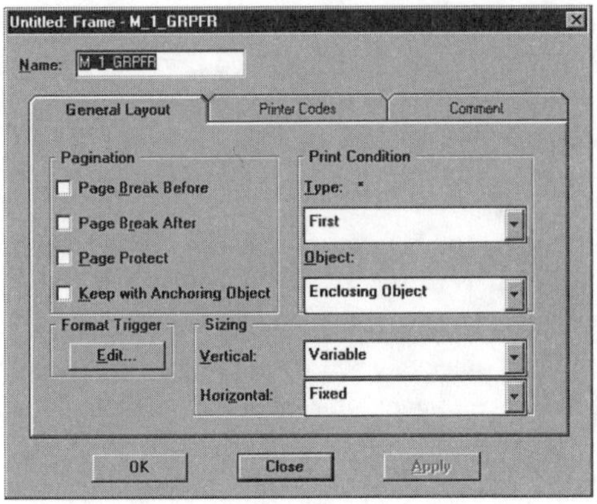


**FIG. 18.13**
Program Unit editor window.

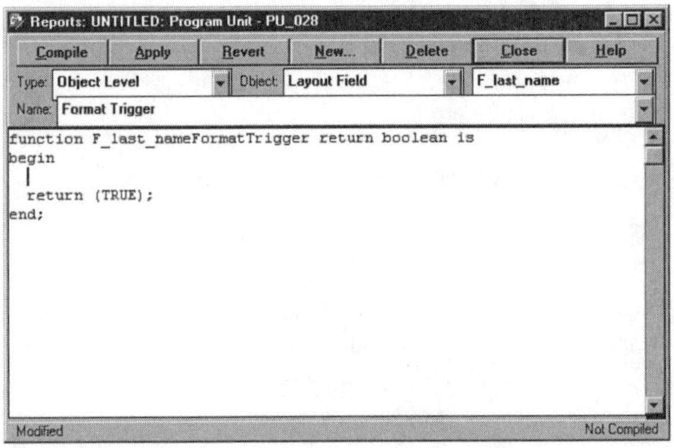


To use the program unit editor window, type in the code you want for the format trigger then press the Compile button. This verifies that your code is syntactically correct. If you make a change then decide that it isn't what you want you can click the Revert Button and revert the code back to the way that it was before you put in the new code. After you compile, click the Close button to go back to the Layout Editor.

The next section is the Print Condition section, which governs how and when objects print. Type is when an object prints, and Object is how the object prints. The choices for Type are: First, All But First, All But Last, All, and Default.

- Default is either First or All. Reports itself chooses which First or All based on the object's position on the layout.
- First means the object will only print on the first page; however, this option can overflow to the next page if the data is that lengthy.
- All But First means it will print on all pages except the first.

- All But Last means that the object will print on all pages except the last.
- All means the object will print on all pages; however, it will not overflow to the next page. If the data is too long, it will be truncated. The Object is how the object should print, either with its Enclosing Object or with it's Anchoring Object.

The last section is the Sizing section. The Sizing of an object determines how an object sizes depending on the data returned to it. You have four choices for Horizontal and *Vertical*: *Contract*, *Expand*, *Fixed*, and *Variable*.

- Variable is the most flexible and all repeating frames should have this sizing. It is the most flexible because it allows the objects to shrink and grow as necessary so the data will fit.
- Fixed sizing never changes.
- Contract means that the size of the object is the biggest it can ever be, but the object can shrink to fit smaller records of data.
- Expand is the opposite. The size of the object is the minimum size the data can be, but the object can grow to fit more data.

Boilerplate objects should never have any sizing other than Fixed both Horizontal and Vertical. All objects contract from the bottom right to the upper left. This is very important when you are dealing with the space in a report.



**Printer Codes and Comments Tabs** The Printer Codes tab allows you to send special printer instructions before and after the object is printed. Figure 18.14 shows the tab.

For specifics on the codes, refer to your printer manual, as each printer has different codes. This is only suggested for advanced users that need other fonts or print styles.

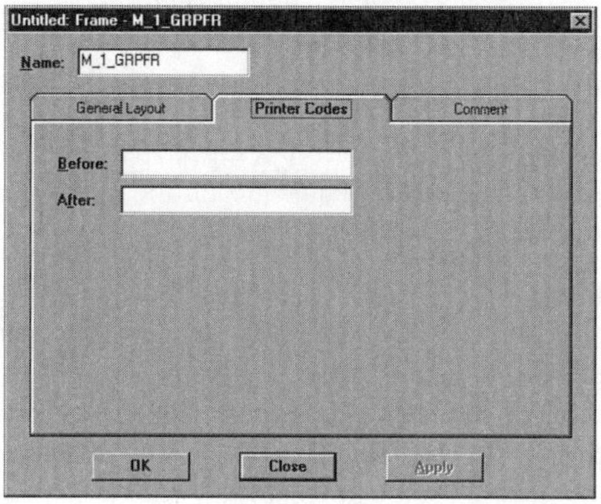


**FIG. 18.14**
Printer Codes tab.

The Comment tab is a large text field in which you can document the object. Figure 18.15 shows the tab.

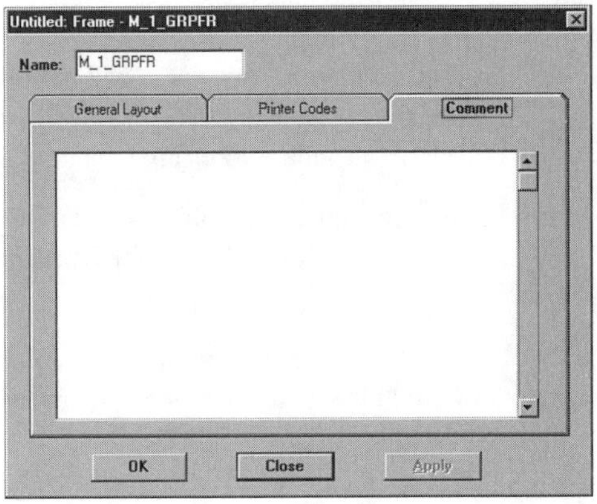


**FIG. 18.15**
Comment tab.

# Special Tabs

Repeating frames and fields have another tab, the Object tab. This tab allows you to set specific properties for the objects.

**Repeating Frame Object Tab** Source is where you assign a frame to a group in the query.

- Print Direction governs in what direction the frame will print. The choices are Across, meaning from left to right; Across/Down, meaning from left to right then down to the next line; Down, meaning top to bottom; and Down/Across, meaning top to bottom left to right.
- Maximum Records Per Page specifies how many instances of the repeating frame should print on each page.
- Minimum Widow Records specifies the minimum number of records that should display where the repeating frame starts to print.
- Column Mode controls how reports gets and formats data for a repeating frame.

The last section is Spacing. You can set in units how much space should print between instances of the repeating frame. The units are the units for the report. You can set both horizontal and vertical spacing. Figure 18.16 shows the dialog box.

**Field Object Tab** The Field Object tab (see Figure 18.17) has two sections: Source and Display. In the Source section, you specify from the drop-down list which database, formula, or summary column the field should display. In the Display section, you can select a format mask for a field if it is of type number. You can set the Minimum Widow Lines, if you only want a certain number of lines to print on a page initially. By clicking the box next to Hidden, you are saying that the field should not print when the report is run.

**FIG. 18.16**
Repeating Frame Object tab.

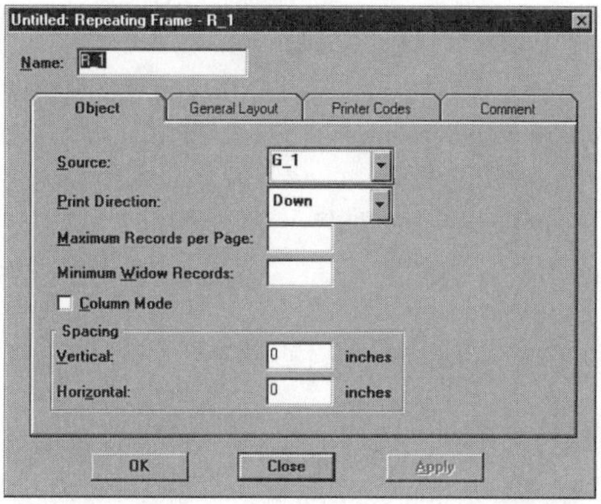


**FIG. 18.17**
Field Object tab.

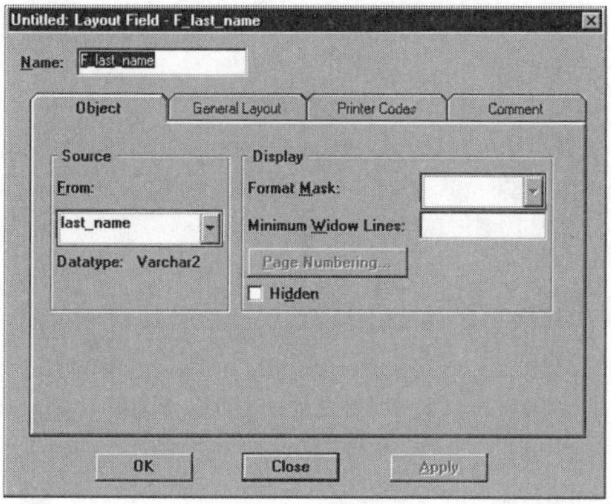




The Page Number button is unavailable unless you give the field a source of `&Logical Page Number`, `&Panel Number`, or `&Physical Page Number`. These are report functions that return the logical page number, the panel number, or the physical page number. Figure 18.18 shows the Page Number dialog box. You can select by clicking the check boxes to include the header page, the body pages, and the trailer pages. You can set what number the pages should start at as well as how they should increment. You can also set a reset point for the numbering. This is useful if you want each break section of a report to have its own page number sequence.

**FIG. 18.18**
Page Number dialog box.

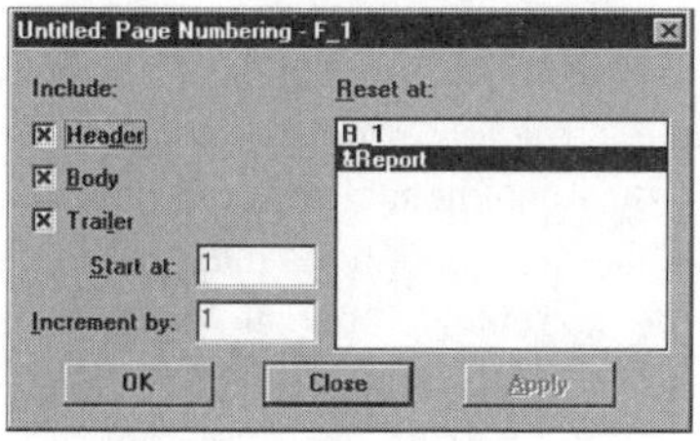

# Making a Report Presentable

The Default Layout Editor is the best place to start a report. The default layout is very basic and generally considered ugly when it comes to presentation, but because of the frames it is the best place to start. Until you fully understand how frames work it is best to start the report from the default and then make improvements from there.

Some of the improvements that you might want to make include the following.

## Changing the Fonts of Different Objects

To change the font of an object or several objects, select the object(s) by clicking the first and shift-clicking any others. Then from the Format menu, select Font. Select the font style, size, or color that you want and click OK to apply the changes.

## Changing the Text of the Column Headings

To change the text or boilerplate labels that were created, select the object, then click the Text tool on the Tool Palette (the capital T), and then click inside the boilerplate object. This opens up the object for changes. Type whatever you want, even if the boxes don't appear big enough; you can resize it later. Then click outside the box to close it. To make the boilerplate bigger, click on the handles and drag to the appropriate size.

## Removing the Dotted Line or Changing the Line

To remove the dotted line that serves as a separator between the column headings and the data, click the object and then click the Delete key. If you want to change it or resize it, it is a boilerplate text object so follow the preceding steps.

## Adding a Report Title

To add a report title that will appear on every page, you need to switch to the margin view of the report by clicking the Margin button on the toolbar. To create space to add your report title, click inside the body outline then drag the handle down until you have enough space. Now you can add whatever you want for the title. Figure 18.19 shows the margin window for the report.

## Adding Page Numbers or a Report Date

In the margin of the report, you may also want to add page numbers or a report date. To do this, create a field by using the field tool from the tool palette (the abc icon). Open the property sheet and give the field a source of one of the following: `&Logical Page Number`, `&Panel Number`, or `&Physical Page Number`. You will almost always use `&Logical Page Number`. The Page Numbering button is now available. Set any options in the dialog box then click OK to apply them. To add a report date of the current system date, create a field, give the field a source of `&Current Date`, and then select a format mask for the date. These two examples may be added anywhere in the report; they don't have to be in the margin.

FIG. 18.19
Margin window of Layout Editor.

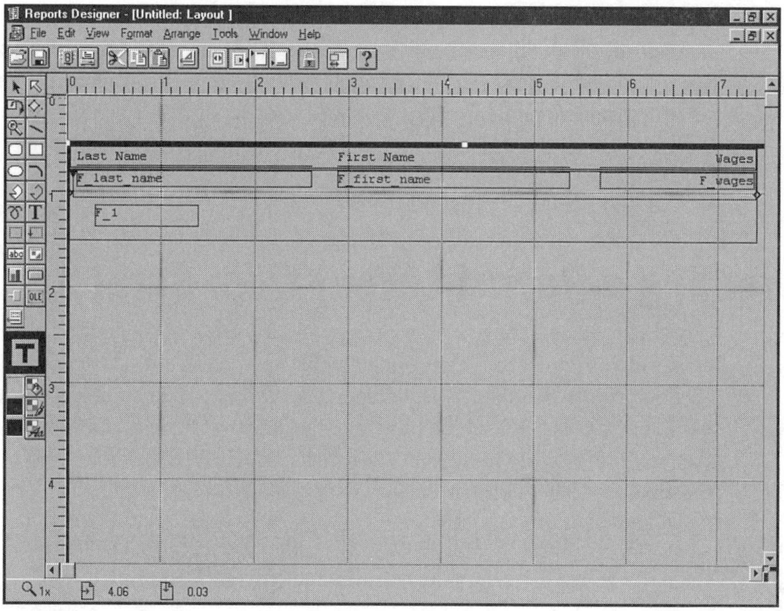




## Changing the Positioning of Fields

To change the positioning of a field, click and drag the field to where you want it. However, remember that any database, formula, or summary columns that belong to a group in the query must remain inside the repeating frame for that group. The only way to reference a column outside its group is if you are doing a summary or another function using the Summary Column tool in the Data Model. To help keep objects in their correct placements, make sure you keep Confine turned on.

## Formatting Fields and Resizing Fields

Formatting fields means giving number fields format masks. Open their property sheets and select the mask you want. You can justify the fields differently by using the Format menu, Alignment option. You can also align the fields by selecting the fields you want to align then selecting the Arrange menu Align Objects option. You can resize objects by using the Size Objects option from the Arrange menu.

## Add Header or Trailer Pages

You can design header or trailer pages for your report by selecting the Header or Trailer icons from the toolbar. You can then design the pages however you want. They work exactly the same as the body of the report; you can put the same objects as in the body in the header and trailer.

There are other things that you can do to make a report look better. You can add graphics, or images, or use the drawing objects to illustrate a part of the report. To do any of these things, you should either first create a frame to hold the objects, or place the drawing objects in an exisitng frame depending on how or when you want the new object to print. Then use the tool palette to select the tool you want and then use the mouse to place the object on the layout.

After doing some or all of these things you should have a pretty decent looking report.

# Creating a Report Layout from Scratch

You always need to have a query defined in the Data Model editor before you start this process. I also suggest that you create a default layout as a starting point, as mentioned in the section prior to this one. This is important until you really understand frames and how they work. I am going to describe how to create a layout from scratch, although I highly suggest that you don't do it. The reason I will describe it is in hopes that it helps you to understand how the objects relate to each other.

1. Open the Layout Editor and select the frame tool from the Tool Palette (the broken box).
2. Click and drag the mouse so that it creates a large box.
3. Right-click inside the frame, and from the menu select the Properties option. On the General Layout tab select a Sizing of Vertical Variable. Then click OK to close the dialog box. Figure 18.20 shows this step.

**FIG. 18.20**
What the frame looks like in the layout.

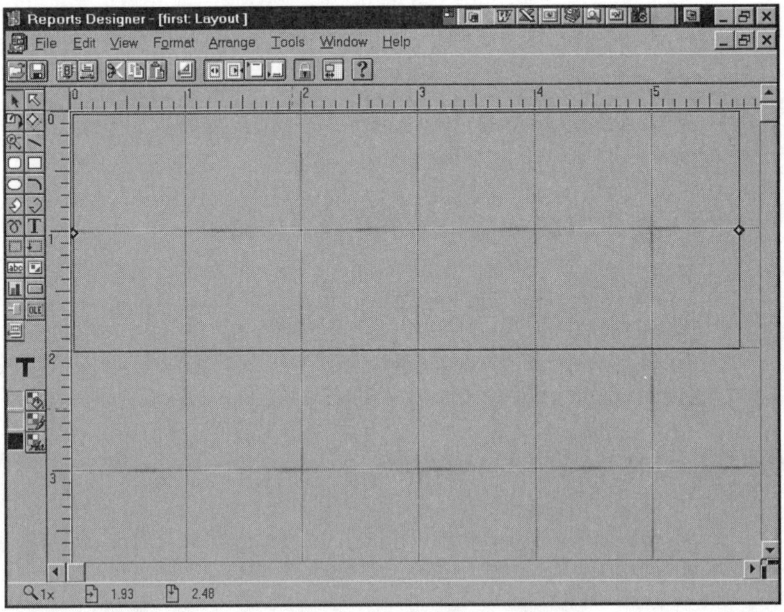

## Adding a Repeating Frame

1. Select the repeating frame tool from the Tool Palette (the broken box with the arrow).
2. Click and drag inside the frame created in Step one.
3. Right-click inside the new repeating frame. On the Object tab, name the frame and select a source for the frame. On the General Layout tab give the frame a Sizing of Vertical Variable. Then click OK to close the dialog box. Figure 18.21 shows this step.

**FIG. 18.21**
The layout with a frame and a repeating frame with vertical variable sizing, shown by the diamonds on the frames.

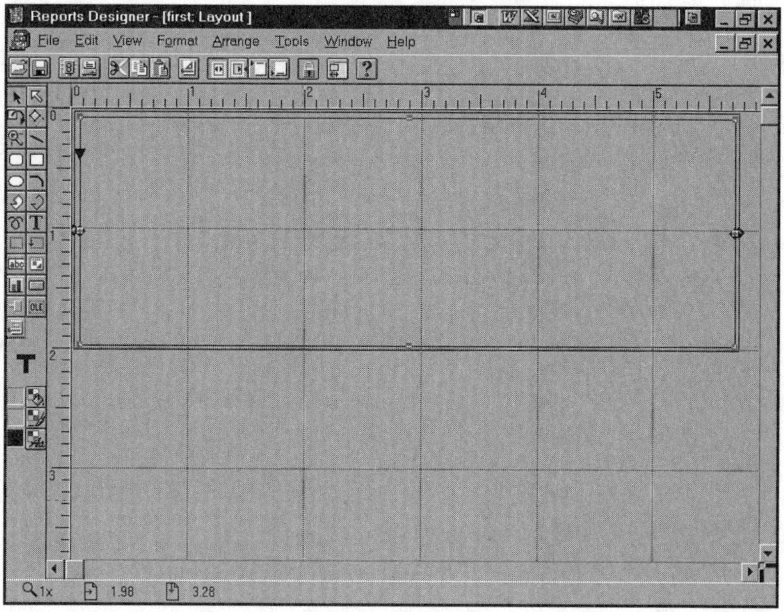




Repeat Steps 1 and 2 for all groups in the query. Make sure that the frames and repeating frames of subsequent groups are added inside the repeating frame of the group above it in the data model. In other words, as you build you should be working down the data model and inside of previous repeating frames.

## Adding Fields to the Layout

1. Select the Field tool from the tool palette (the abc button).
2. Click and drag the mouse to create a box with an appropriate length and width. Make sure that the field is inside the repeating frame that corresponds to its group in the query. If you put the field in the wrong repeating frame, you will get an error.

   Hint: If you need to move a field from one frame to another a trick is to cut(Ctrl+X) the field then paste(Ctrl+V) the field back in the layout. It will paste the field in the middle of the screen, click on it and place it inside the new frame.

3. Right-click the field and on the Object tab give the field a source and a format mask if the field is of type number. If the field needs to have a Sizing specified, go to the General Layout tab and select it, and then click OK and close the dialog box. Figure 18.22 shows fields added to the layout.

**FIG. 18.22**
Notice that the field for department is in the department repeating frame and the employee fields are in the employee repeating frame.

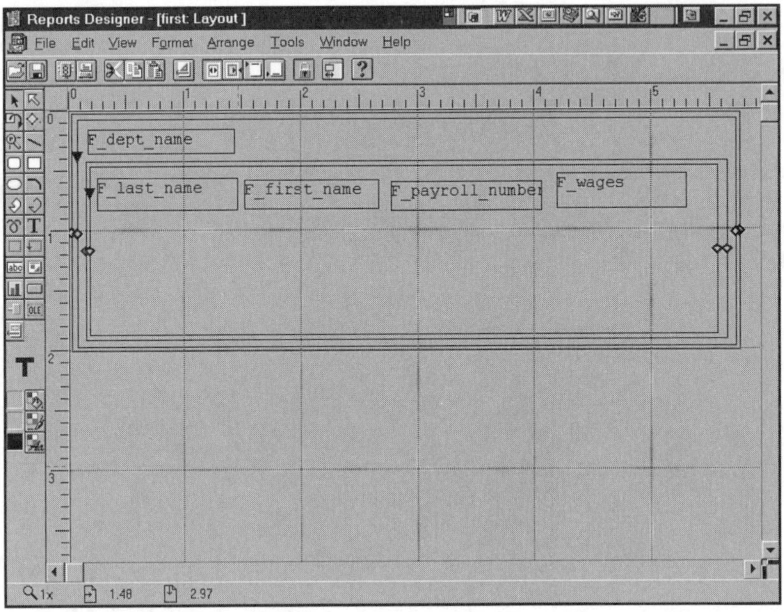


Repeat Step 3 for all database columns that are to be displayed as well as any formula columns or summary columns.

## Adding Boilerplate Text to a Layout

1. Select the Text tool from the tool palette (the big T). In the frame that surrounds the first repeating frame, click and drag the mouse to create a box. When you release the mouse button, the cursor appears in the box. Type the text that you want to appear. Click outside the box to close it.
2. To edit the text later, click the Text tool and then click inside the boilerplate object on the layout. Figure 18.23 shows the boilerplate text labels added to the report.

   Use Step 1 to create any boilerplate text anywhere on the report. Other places you may want boilerplate text are in the report Header, Footer, or in the Margin.

   You also can add any OLE2 links or images to the report by selecting the appropriate tool from the tool palette, click-dragging the mouse on the layout to create a box, and then selecting the image or file. To add a drawing object, it is best to first create a frame, then select the tool from the tool palette, and then inside the frame draw what you desire.

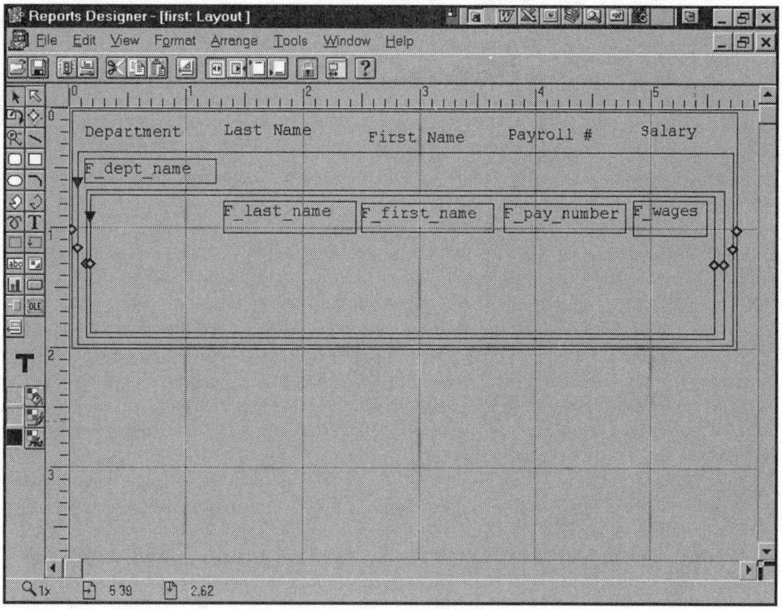


**FIG. 18.23**
Boilerplate text has been added to the report to make it easy to understand.



## Perfecting the Layout

The last step will be the most time consuming and frustrating step in the whole process of creating a report. In this step, you work out the exact layout and look of the report. You will preview the report many times in this step until you get the report looking how you want it to look.

1. To get the correct spacing and positioning of the objects that you created, or that the Default Layout Editor tool created, move objects closer together; use the spacing options on the repeating frame Object tab; resize objects by clicking the handles and dragging. This process will take time to learn and there are really no suggestions on how to do it because each report is different. You will learn by trial and error. Be patient. Figure 18.24 shows the finished layout.

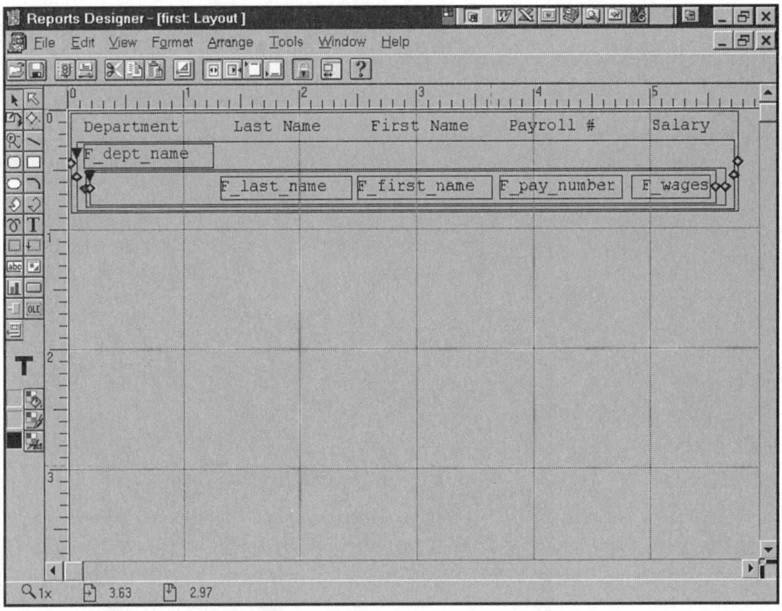


**FIG. 18.24**
The finished report layout with fields aligned and justified with appropriate labels.

# Adding Formula and Summary Columns

Summary and Formula Columns are added to the report in the Data Model Editor. To add them, click the icon for the column that you want then click in the data model where you want the column to be. These columns can be added inside the query or outside the query. However, with formula columns if you are going to reference a database column, you must put the formula column in the same group as the database column.

## Summary Columns

Summary columns are really more than just sums. As discussed in Chapter 17, they can perform many different functions. Figure 18.25 shows the General tab of the summary column dialog box. The most common uses of this column are for sums of records and counts of records returned. To create a summary column, follow these steps:

1. Give the column a meaningful name.
2. Select a function to perform.
3. Select the source column for the function. The Datatype and Width automatically fill in based on the source columns type and width. You may enter a value for the column to return in the case that the function return a null value.

The next step, selecting the Reset group for the function, is very important. This corresponds to the group the summary is in, if it is, otherwise you should select either report, meaning it is a function for the whole report, or page, meaning perform the function for a page worth of data.

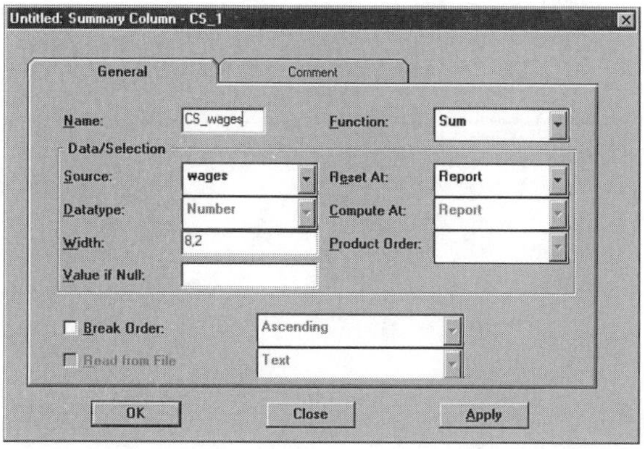


**FIG. 18.25**
General tab of Summary Column.

The next two settings are available only in certain cases, but in those cases they are very important. If they are not set right, you will get errors. The first is Compute At, which is used when you use a function of `% of Total`. The group you select is the group the total is computed for. Product Order is used with matrix reports. The product order dictates the order in which the function will be computed when the summary column is inside the matrix. If this is not set the same as the Reset At, you will get an error.

The last setting that is available is Break Order. If the function that you are performing is distinct, you may use it as a break column. You can then also select the direction of the break.



## Formula Columns

Formula Columns are functions that execute blocks of PL/SQL code. Figures 18.26 and 18.27 show the General tab of a formula column and the program unit editor window where the code is placed.

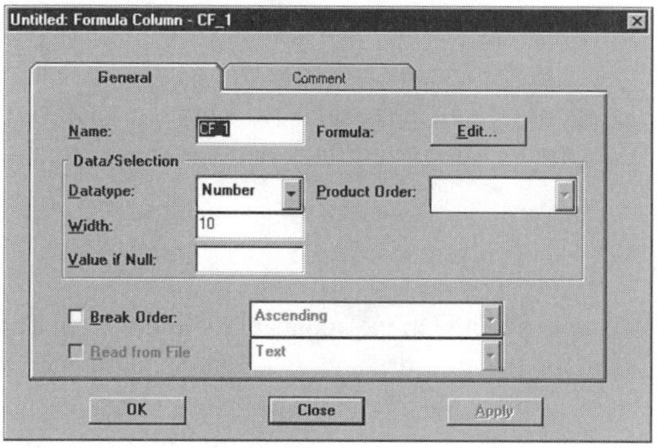


**FIG. 18.26**
General tab of a Formula Column.

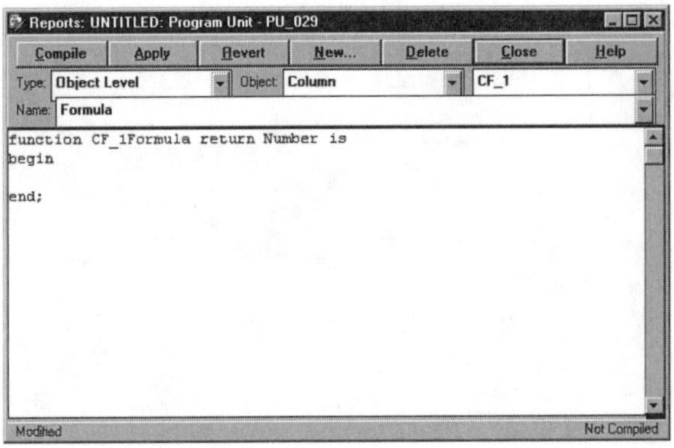


**FIG. 18.27** Program Unit editor window for formula columns.

The first thing you need to do is name the column with a meaningful name. Then you should select a Datatype and a Width. You can enter a value for the column to return if the code that you write returns null. Product Order is available only in a matrix report if the formula column is inside the matrix group in the data model. Break Order is available if the column will be returning a distinct value; otherwise, if you select it, you will get an error. Now you can click the Edit button. This will open a Program Unit editor window, as shown in Figure 18.27. This is where you enter a computation such as `:salary*1.10` to calculate each person's salary, whether they were given a 10 percent raise. You can also enter PL/SQL code that you wany to execute for each record. The most popular use for formula columns using PL/SQL code is writing `if` statements to do certain calculations on a record based on the `if` statement. See the CD for more complex code examples for Formula Columns.

# Summary

The Layout Editor of Oracle Reports is very complex and at times will be very frustrating. At the same time there is almost nothing you can't do in the layout with this tool.

You start with a very basic default layout and then through the use of the tool palette you can add and change the layout objects to make the report presentable. You can also add complex computations to the data model through formula and summary columns.

# From Here...

The next chapter discusses moving Oracle applications to the Web. That chapter covers what software is required to make this all work and give details on configuration, running Web applications, and identify quirks and confusing items that I ran into along the way.

# Review Exercises

These exercises use the exercises from Chapter 17 and build on them.

1. Rearrange the columns in the report. Display them in an order that makes sense to you.
2. Add a summary column to the data model to sum salary at the department level. Also add the column to the layout and format it properly.
3. Add a formula column to the report to count the number of employees in a department. Add the column to the layout with a boilerplate text label describing the column.

PART VI

# Moving Your Application to the Web

CHAPTER 19

# Moving Oracle Applications to the Web

With the advent of Microsoft Windows NT and Web servers that run on that platform, setting up and configuring Web servers has become much easier. I have attempted to write this chapter for the novice, but as with any technology it is always desirable to get as much information as possible before diving right into the fray. I recommend reading and understanding the available documentation for your Web before proceeding with this chapter. Although I have found the documentation that comes with Web servers I have configured to usually be adequate, there are additional books that may help. I am told that the Que Special Edition book on the Oracle WebServer is quite good.

Now that you have created your application system in Oracle Developer 2000, wouldn't it be nice if you could just push a button and move the application to the World Wide Web? Well, it is not quite as simple as that yet, but with Oracle Developer 2000, it is surprisingly easy to get the Forms and Reports to run from the Web once a few configuration snags are removed. In this chapter, I will cover what software is required to make this all work and give details on configuring and running Web applications, and identifying quirks and confusing items that I ran into along the way. ■

**How does the Web implementation work?**

Oracle describes the Web implementation as a three-tiered approach to delivering an application.

**Required software and where it may be installed**

Some detail on the software requirements for moving Oracle Designer 2000 forms and reports to the Web.

**Setting up Oracle Forms on the Web**

Now it is time to make the application available on the Web server. To do this there are two options available.

**Setting up Oracle Reports on the Web**

Oracle implements the reports part of Developer 2000 via a reports CGI program loaded onto the Web server CGI directory.

# How Does the Web Implementation Work?

Before we dive into all the messy details about configuring Developer 2000 applications to run on the Web, I thought it would be helpful to give a high-level description of what makes all this magic work. Oracle describes the Web implementation as a three-tiered approach to delivering an application (as opposed to the two-tiered approach of client/server).

## The Three-Tiered Web Approach Described

So what exactly is the three-tiered approach, and how does it differ from the common two-tiered client/server implementation are two questions you may have. On a two-tiered configuration, an application runs on the end-user desktop and accesses data located on the database server. The three-tiered approach inserts an additional layer, as its name implies. The end-user desktop is used only for the application presentation and input retrieval. The application actually runs on an application, or in this case Web, server. Table 19.1 briefly explains where each piece may be loaded and its function as follows:

**Table 19.1 Three-Tiered Architecture**

| Tier | Installed On | Function |
|---|---|---|
| Front-End | Any number of client desktop machines | Application presentation and input |
| Middle | One or more application servers | Execution of the application |
| Back-End | One or more database servers | Database management |

# Advantages of the Web Approach

There are several advantages to delivering applications via the Web. First, the client or front-end piece of the implementation does not require a heavily configured workstation to run these applications. All that is required is a Java-enabled Web browser (see the following section on required software for details on the Java version requirements). As mentioned before, the front-end handles mainly the presentation or display of the forms and reports, along with gathering user input.

Second, deployment of applications to the user community should be greatly eased. This is one feature that I personally am interested in. Currently, to move client/server systems out to the user community, I have to do the following:

- Copy the forms or reports out to all of the LAN/Application servers. Presently, I am using a mix of NetWare v.3.12 and Windows NT v.4.0.
- Ensure that users wanting to access those forms or reports have access to the proper runtime executables and that they are properly configured on their PC.
- Finally, create an icon on the desktop pointing to the forms or reports.

With a Web deployment, I configure the Web or Application server with the proper versions of the runtime executables, move over the necessary FMX files (for forms) and RDF files (for reports), and set up HTML hyperlinks on my Web site. True, these steps are the same or at least similar to the steps outlined earlier for the individual desktops, but the main difference here is that I do these steps in one place (on the Web/Application server) as opposed to many times (possibly thousands of times) with the two-tiered client/server approach.

# Required Software and Where It May Be Installed

And now for some detail on the software requirements for moving Oracle Designer 2000 forms and reports to the Web. Just because the implementation is called three-tiered does not mean that it must reside on three different machines; the configuration I used for this chapter loaded all components (browser, application, and database) onto one machine. While the front-end piece will be via a Java-capable browser usually on the end-user desktop, the middle and back-end pieces may be on the same or different machines. If multiple application servers are to be used, each application server must have a Web server (also called a Web Listener) installed.

## Software for the Front-End

This piece of the three-tiered puzzle is at the end-user's workstation. As mentioned before, a Java-enabled browser is all that is required here. However, the Java requirements for the Oracle Web implementation is version 1.1.2. The problem with this is that, as of the writing of this chapter, no available Web browser supports this version of Java.

Oracle informed me that they are currently working with the major browser vendors (Netscape and Microsoft) to get this version of Java into the new versions of their products. To Oracle's credit, they have worked with Sun on making their additions to Java part of the standard version of Java. Hopefully, this Java release will be the version that all browser vendors will implement in their products, or at least include as a minimum set of functionality. As for when you will be able to get your hands on one of the new browsers, Oracle said it is hoping that these browsers will be on the market by October 1997. For an exact date of Web browser availability supporting Java version 1.1.2, bug Netscape and Microsoft. To keep track of browser advances yourself, Cnet provides an excellent site that keeps track of the various browser advances at **http://www.cnet.com/Content/Browser/?ctb.browser**.



So until a Java 1.1.2 browser is available, what does this mean to you when looking at implementing Developer 2000 on the Web? It means you will not likely be doing the forms piece until Java 1.1.2 browsers are available. The reports piece will work fine without the Java 1.1.2 support in a browser (I used Microsoft Internet Explorer 3.0 during my experimentation).

You are probably asking yourself, "Just how are you going to tell me how the forms piece works if you cannot use a browser?" For this chapter, I used the Java Development Kit and the appletviewer application that is included. This development kit is included on the Developer 2000 CD-ROM, or a more recent version of the kit may be downloaded from Oracle's Developer 2000 page on the Internet at ***http://www.oracle.com/products/tools/dev2k/***.

This product comes with a README file that outlines how to install the kit. After performing the installation on my Windows NT 4.0 Workstation, I had to define three variables (HOMEDRIVE, HOMEPATH, and HOME) as outlined in the Windows Installation Troubleshooting section. Additionally, I had to remove the CLASSPATH variable even though the Oracle version of the README said to use it. These variables can be defined by right-clicking the My Computer icon on the Windows NT 4.0 desktop and selecting Properties from the pop-up menu. On the properties page, select the Environment tab and enter the variables. After installation, the appletviewer is started up from a Command Prompt in Windows NT by entering the command APPLETVIEWER followed by the URL of the Web page to display.

## Software for the Middle or Application Server

According to the Windows NT version of the Developer 2000 documentation, the application server needs to be running either Windows NT 4.0 server and later or Sun Solaris version 2.4 and later for its operating system. Once the appropriate machine is available, the Designer 2000 products that you will be implementing need to be installed.

Next, a Web server should be loaded onto the application server. While the documentation says that Developer 2000 will support any Web server, I was informed by Oracle support that there were some bugs in the Web cartridge forms implementation when using a Web server other than Oracle's. I did successfully run the non-cartridge forms implementation with Microsoft's Internet Information Server (IIS) Web server.

Whether you choose to load the Oracle Web server or not, you are required to load the Oracle Web Request Broker if implementing forms with the Web Cartridge. I will explain later in this chapter the difference between cartridge and non-cartridge forms implementations in the section titled Cartridge versus Non-Cartridge. One important note, when installing the Oracle Web Request Broker or Oracle Web server, you will be prompted for a configuration port (default is 9999), and a username and password. Remember the username and password for later for they will be required to enter the Web page for configuring the Oracle Web Request Broker.

Finally, if connecting to a database on another machine, the SQL*Net or other remote database access software will need to be loaded onto the application server.

## Software for the Back-End or Database Server

The back-end piece may be any Oracle 7.1 or later database server or an ODBC-compliant RDBMS. If the back-end/database is on a machine other than the application server, then the necessary remote database access software will need to be installed (SQL*Net, for example).

## Software Configuration Used for This Article

As mentioned before, for my experimentation for writing this chapter, I loaded all the pieces for implementing Designer 2000 forms and reports via the Web on my NT 4.0 workstation. Table 19.2 shows a breakdown of the complete configuration:

**Table 19.2 Software Configuration**

| Tier | Component | Software Installed |
|---|---|---|
| Front-End | Operating system | Windows NT v.4.0 Workstation |
| | Web Browser | Internet Explorer 3.02 (used for reports) |
| | Appletviewer | JDK v.1.1.1.o7 from Oracle (used for forms) |
| Middle | Operating system | Windows NT v.4.0 Server |
| | Web Server | Microsoft IIS and Oracle WebServer |
| | Developer 2000 v.1.4W | Forms and Reports |
| | Other Software | Oracle Web Request Broker (used for forms Cartridge) |
| Back-End | Database | Oracle Workgroup Server for Windows NT |

Throughout the remainder of this chapter, configuration details will be given for the Windows NT installation. There will be references in the chapter to the ORACLE_HOME directory. This variable points to the directory into which you install the Oracle products (Developer 2000 or Web server components).

# Setting Up Oracle Forms on the Web



Now comes the fun part, taking a fully developed Oracle client/server system and moving the forms to a Web server. The first step is relatively simple and mundane. Take the forms Binaries (FMX files) and move them to a directory on the Web server. The forms should be re-generated by using the Developer 2000 v.1.4W for Windows NT version (or later) of forms before moving them to the Web server.

It would be wise to create a common forms and reports product directory into which you would copy all forms and reports that will be accessed via the Web interface. For my purposes I created a directory called *oraprod*. This directory could be further subdivided into directories for each system implemented.

Next, start the Forms Server Listener process. For NT, this was installed as part of the Developer 2000 forms installation. There should be an icon in the Developer 2000 group for the Forms Server Listener. You can verify that the Forms Server Listener is started by going to the Task Manager and looking for the process *F45srv32.exe*.

Now it is time to make the application available on the Web server. To do this, there are two options available.

## Cartridge versus Non-Cartridge Implementation

Oracle gives you two options for implementing forms, via the Web Cartridge or Non-Cartridge. Both of the implementations require Java v.1.1.2. The main difference between the two options is that the Cartridge implementation can be set up once and used with many different Developer 2000 Web applications by just changing the URL that calls the application.

The Non-Cartridge application will require a unique static HTML file for each application. An additional difference between the Cartridge and Non-Cartridge implementations was mentioned earlier in the chapter. That difference is that the Cartridge configuration requires the additional Oracle Web Request Broker software.

## Setup Common to Both Implementations

Regardless of which Web forms implementation you will be using, there are some Virtual directories that should be configured upon the Web Server. It is important to note that the virtual directory names can be anything you want; however a virtual directory should be set up for each of the following:

**NOTE** If you are not familiar with configuring a Web server, you may be unfamiliar with the term Virtual Directory. A Virtual Directory is a sort of shortcut to or alias for a directory on a Web server. It is a way of cleaning up the URL or link that is used to navigate the various information on a Web server. ■

The **Applet codebase** directory points to the absolute directory where the forms client will search for the Java Class files. These files are located in the *ORACLE_HOME\forms45\java* directory. This virtual directory must point to this directory for the forms to run on the Web. In my examples, I use the virtual directory */Web_code/*.

The **HTML files** directory points to the absolute directory where the Cartridge and static HTML files are located. In my examples, I use the virtual directory called */Web_html/* which will point to the absolute directory *D:\ORAPROD\WEB\HTML* (another location may be substituted for this directory).

The **JAR files** directory points to the absolute directory where the Oracle JAR files are stored. In my examples, I use the virtual directory called */Web_jars/* which will point to the absolute directory *D:\ORAPROD\WEB\JARS* (another location may be substituted for this directory). A jar file is a bundle of multiple files (Java class files, images, and so on) that because it contains many files, accomplishes in a single download what would take many downloads if the files were unbundled. These jar files are downloaded at the startup of the application. This is supposed to increase the speed of the forms applet due to its compression and the fact that it takes only a single transaction to download. This directory can be used to hold any custom jar files that you create for your forms.

To set up the virtual directories, go to your Web server's configuration page and add entries for the virtual directories noted earlier. These steps will vary from Web server to Web server. Following is a setup screen from the Microsoft IIS Web server (see Figure 19.1) that is used to configure the virtual directories.

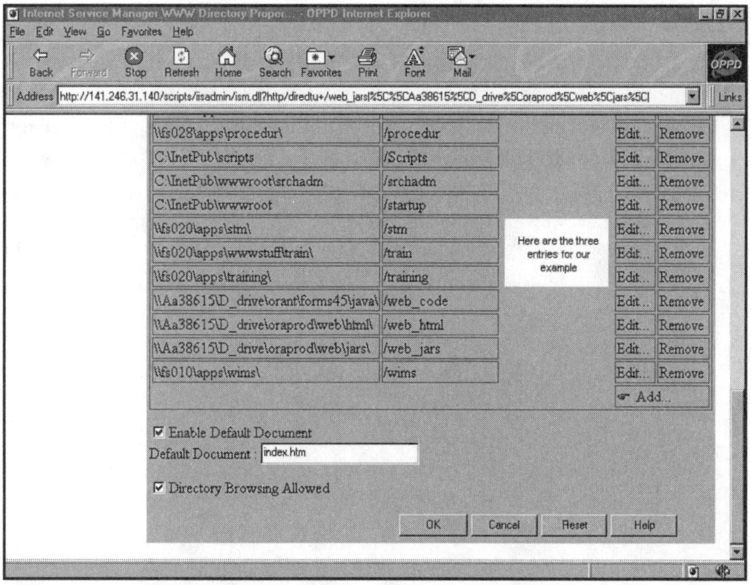


**FIG. 19.1**
Defining virtual directories for the Microsoft IIS Web server.

After defining the virtual directories, the Web server will most likely have to be stopped and then started to get the Web listener to recognize the new configuration. This can usually be done through the Web server's browser administration interface or in the Windows NT control panel. Web servers are normally running as services under NT, so going to the Services applet under the NT Control panel and stopping the service and restarting the service will load the modified configuration.

**CAUTION**

While stopping and restarting the Web server is a quick way to reinitialize a Web server after configuration changes, this is not necessarily a task for the novice. Some servers such as Microsoft's IIS should be stopped and started only via their administrative utilities. The safest way to reinitialize a Web server is to shut down the NT server and restart it.

**CAUTION**

When configuring virtual directories, make sure the syntax for the definition is correct for the Web server you are using. When I was configuring the virtual directories on the Oracle Web server, just leaving out a slash at the end of the virtual directory definition prevented the Web server from restarting until the entry was corrected.

## Cartridge Implementation Requirements

To set up a Web cartridge forms implementation, the following steps need to be performed. Remember, that the cartridge implementation of Web forms requires that the Oracle Web Broker be installed. If this software is not installed on your Web server, it will need to be installed before the following steps can be performed:

- Create the Cartridge for the Web form.
- Register the Web form Cartridge with the forms cartridge handler.
- Create a virtual directory for the Web form Cartridge.
- Create a base HTML file for the Cartridge.

Once the Oracle Web Request Broker is installed, an Oracle WebServer Administration Icon is placed in the Oracle for NT group. Selecting this icon will start your Web Browser, loading the Oracle WebServer configuration page (see Figure 19.2). This page connects to the Oracle WebServer configuration port. You will be prompted for the username and password that you entered during the products installation.

**FIG. 19.2**
The Oracle WebServer configuration page.

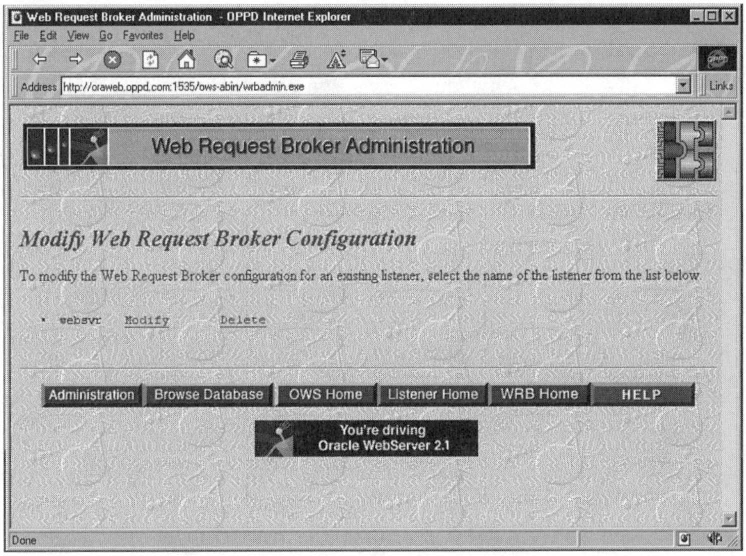


Selecting the WebServer Manager link will take you to the WebServer Administration page shown in Figure 19.3 where you have several options. Two of these options, Oracle Web Listener and Web Request Broker, are used to configure the Web-related areas.

The Oracle Web Listener selection configures the Webserver, whether it is an Oracle, Microsoft, or Netscape server. Selecting this link will take you to a page that identifies the Webserver presently running and will allow you to modify the listener configuration (by calling up the corresponding server's Web-based configuration page). This is where virtual directories and other Web server configuration items are set.

The Web Request Broker selection configures Cartridge configuration for Oracle's Web forms implementation. This is the section that will be used to perform most of the Cartridge configuration steps that follow.

Following is a list of all of the items that are available on the Oracle WebServer Manager page shown in Figure 19.3:

- Oracle 7 Server—Configures the databases to use with the Oracle WebServer.
- PL/SQL Agent—Allows the Oracle Web Listener to access Oracle 7 Databases and access PL/SQL code in response to an HTTP request.
- External Listener Registration—Used to configure a third-party Web server. Presently only Microsoft's and Netscape's Web servers are the only supported third-party Web servers.
- Oracle Web Listener—Configures various Webserver options.
- Web Request Broker—Used to configure Oracle Web Cartridge Interface.

Throughout the configuration of the cartridge, while modifying the parameters, it was not uncommon to have connections failures to the Webserver. When these errors would occur, simply resubmitting the modification by selecting the Modify Cartridge Configuration button shown in Figure 19.4 again would correct the situation.

**FIG. 19.3**
Oracle WebServer Administration Page.

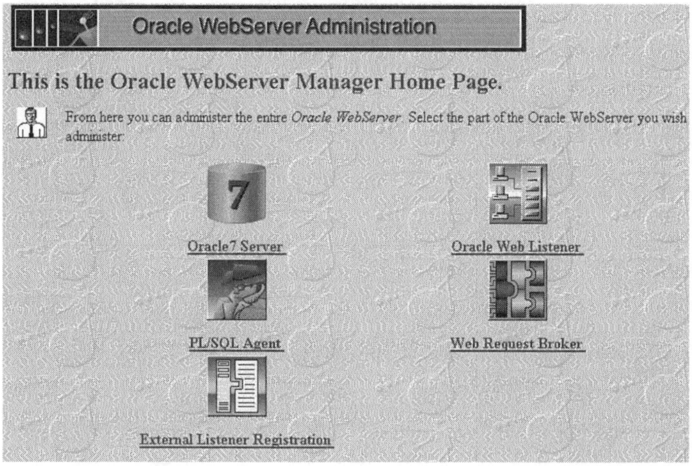




**Creating the Cartridge for Web Forms** From the Web Request Broker Administration screen, select the MODIFY link. This will take you to the WRB Cartridge Administration screen. From here, go to the Cartridges section of the page and in the text entry box next to the Create Cartridge button, enter the name for your new cartridge. For our example, we will use Web_cart.

Select the Create Cartridge button and the WRB Cartridge Configuration page will be displayed. In the Cartridge parameters section, enter the desired Cartridge parameters. I found using the following parameters were sufficient to configure the cartridge and yet leave it generic enough to allow the one cartridge to be used for all Web forms. The parameters' names are case-sensitive, so remember how they are entered here in the cartridge because the same names will be used in the base HTML file (see Figure 19.4).

The first parameter entered is *baseHTML*. This is the absolute path and file name of the base HTML file that the cartridge will use when calling up the form.

Next, the *HTMLdelimiter* is input. This is the special character that acts as a delimiter for variables in the base HTML file defined earlier.

Next, the *Code* variable is defined. This is a case-sensitive variable that points to the Java code that executes the Oracle form within the Web browser. This variable MUST be entered as defined in Table 19.3.

Finally *Codebase* is defined. This is the virtual directory for the Oracle application code for the Java class files defined earlier.

**FIG. 19.4**
The Create Cartridge Parameters Screen after successful modification.

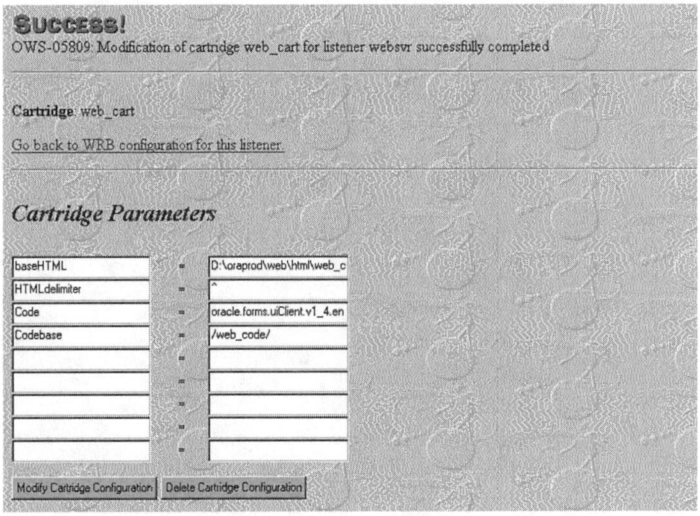


When using a Cartridge, I found it useful to keep the configuration nonspecific to an individual forms application. In other words, do not use the options that allow you to hard code userid information, or forms module information. Not hard-coding this information will allow you to use one cartridge for all your forms Web applications by modifying the URL that calls the application.

The following table details the values used in my examples for the values of these Cartridge parameters:

**Table 19.3 Web Cartridge Configuration**

| Parameter | Value |
|---|---|
| baseHTML | D:\ORAPROD\WEB\HTML\WEB_CART.HTM |
| HTMLdelimiter | ^ |
| Code | oracle.forms.uiClient.v1_4.engine.Main |
| Codebase | /Web_code/ |

Once you've finished entering these parameters, select the Modify Cartridge Configuration button. When this modification is completed, a success message will appear at the top of the page. After this, select the "Go back to WRB Configuration for this Listener" link to continue on with the next step. Note, if your cartridge does not appear in the list of existing WRB Cartridges, do not panic. A refresh of the Web page may be required to get the list to update.

**Register the Web Form Cartridge** Now that we have created the cartridge, the next step is to register the Cartridge we just created with the Web forms handler. This is done by scrolling down the WRB Cartridge Administration page to the *Applications and Objects* section as shown in Figure 19.5.

Enter the following values for your Cartridge as shown in Figure 19.5:

- For the Applications, enter the Web Cartridge name created in the creating a cartridge for Web forms section. In my example, this would be *Web_cart*.
- For the Object Path, enter the absolute path and file name of the Oracle Web forms cartridge handler. This would be *ORACLE_HOME\bin\f45webc.dll* for Windows NT.
- For Entry Point, enter *form_entry*.
- For Minimum and Maximum, enter the minimum and maximum number of users to be allowed to connect to the cartridge at a single time. This should be dictated by the size of processor and amount of memory installed on the Web server. Oracle recommends for a 2- to 6-megabyte application (which is the total size of all FMX and PLL files for the application) that you have 3 to 4 megabytes of RAM and 12 megabytes of swap space per user. It is a good thing that memory and disk drives are relatively cheap.
- The last field is for whether the cartridge is to run as a Thread or Process. I set it up as a Process by entering a *P*.

When completed, select the Modify WRB Configuration button to update the Broker configuration. Success is indicated at the top of the page once the configuration is completed and the page is reloaded by the Broker.

**Create a Virtual Directory for the Web Form Cartridge** The next step is to create a virtual directory for the Web Cartridge. This is again performed on the WRB Cartridge Administration page by scrolling down to the *Applications and Directories* section of the page as shown in Figure 19.6.

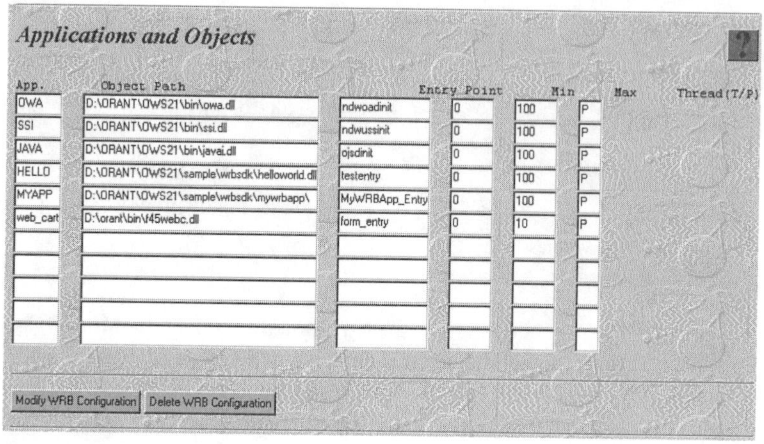

**FIG. 19.5**
Web Cartridge
Applications and
Objects Section.

*Applications and Objects*

| App. | Object Path | | Entry Point | | Min | Max | Thread(T/P) |
|------|-------------|--|-------------|--|-----|-----|-------------|
| OWA | D:\ORANT\OWS21\bin\owa.dll | ndwoadinit | 0 | 100 | P | | |
| SSI | D:\ORANT\OWS21\bin\ssi.dll | ndwussinit | 0 | 100 | P | | |
| JAVA | D:\ORANT\OWS21\bin\javai.dll | ojsdinit | 0 | 100 | P | | |
| HELLO | D:\ORANT\OWS21\sample\wrbsdk\helloworld.dll | testentry | 0 | 100 | P | | |
| MYAPP | D:\ORANT\OWS21\sample\wrbsdk\mywrbapp\ | MyWRBApp_Entry | 0 | 100 | P | | |
| web_cart | D:\orant\bin\if45webc.dll | form_entry | 0 | 10 | P | | |

Modify WRB Configuration | Delete WRB Configuration

Enter the following values:

- For the Virtual Path, enter the virtual path directory name for the cartridge. This may be whatever you want to call it; however do not include the trailing slash in its definition. In my example, I use */Web_cart.*

- For the Application, enter the name of the Cartridge the WRB will execute. This should be the name of the cartridge we created in the creating a cartridge for Web forms section (*Web_cart* for my example).

- For the Physical Path, enter the directory path for the Oracle forms cartridge handler. This would be *ORACLE_HOME\bin* on Windows NT.

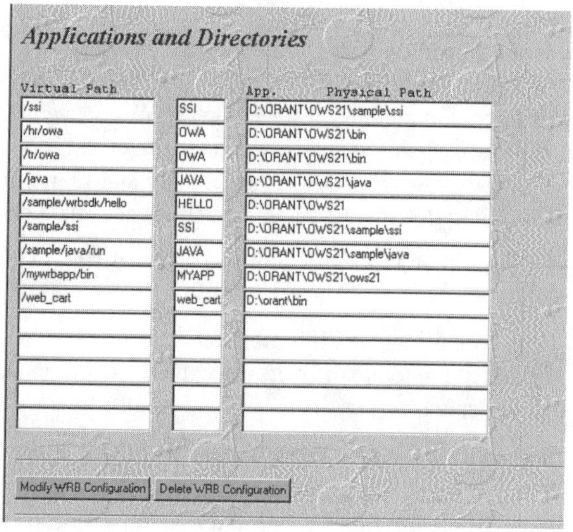

**FIG. 19.6**
Creation of a virtual
directory for the
cartridge.

*Applications and Directories*

| Virtual Path | App. | Physical Path |
|--------------|------|---------------|
| /ssi | SSI | D:\ORANT\OWS21\sample\ssi |
| /hr/owa | OWA | D:\ORANT\OWS21\bin |
| /tr/owa | OWA | D:\ORANT\OWS21\bin |
| /java | JAVA | D:\ORANT\OWS21\java |
| /sample/wrbsdk/hello | HELLO | D:\ORANT\OWS21 |
| /sample/ssi | SSI | D:\ORANT\OWS21\sample\ssi |
| /sample/java/run | JAVA | D:\ORANT\OWS21\sample\java |
| /mywrbapp/bin | MYAPP | D:\ORANT\OWS21\ows21 |
| /web_cart | web_cart | D:\orant\bin |

Modify WRB Configuration | Delete WRB Configuration

Once these values are entered, select the Modify WRB Configuration button to update the Broker configuration. As before, success is indicated at the top of the Web page once the configuration is updated and the page refreshed by the broker.

**Create a Base HTML File** Finally, the last step for a Cartridge implementation is to create the base HTML file. This file should be saved into the virtual directory created for HTML code earlier. Oracle includes a sample base HTML file if you load the Forms demos. This base HTML file is located in *ORACLE_HOME\forms45\demos\webdemos* and is called *cartridg*. I took this file and modified its content to get the following generic base HTML file in Listing 19.1:

**Listing 19.1 WEB_CART.HTM—Sample of a Base HTML File for the Web Forms Cartridge Implementation**

```
<HTML>
<!-- FILE: Cartridge.html -->
<!-- Oracle Cartridge File Template (Windows NT) -->
<!-- Rename, and modify tags and parameter values as needed -->
<HEAD><TITLE>Developer/2000 for the Web</TITLE></HEAD>
<BODY><BR>Please wait while the Forms Client class files download and run.
      <BR>This will take a second or two...
<P>
<!-- applet definition (start) -->
<APPLET CODEBASE="^Codebase^"
        CODE="^Code^"
        ARCHIVE="/Web_jars/f45web.jar"
        HEIGHT=20
        WIDTH=20>
<PARAM NAME="serverPort" VALUE="9000">
<PARAM NAME="serverArgs" VALUE="module=^Module^">
</APPLET>
<!-- applet definition (end) -->
</BODY>
</HTML>
```



Note that the variables defined in the Cartridge are in place for Code and Codebase and they are delimited by the character defined as the HTML delimiter in our cartridge definition. There is one variable left in the HTML file that is not defined. The Module variable will be entered on the URL when the application is called. Leaving this variable for definition on the URL will allow this cartridge to be used for many different Web forms implementations. Any variables not defined in the cartridge but referenced in the base HTML file for the cartridge must be input on the URL as defined in the following section for running the forms.

Having completed this step, the cartridge is now fully configured and ready for use. Before calling the Web form, the Web server should be stopped and then restarted. This can usually be done from the Services applet on the Windows NT Control Panel.

## Non-Cartridge Implementation Requirements

The only setup requirement for the noncartridge implementation of the Oracle Web forms is that a static file be created for each Web application to be implemented. This file should be placed in the virtual directory created earlier for the HTML code. As with the Cartridge type implementation, Oracle includes a sample base HTML file if you load the Forms demos. This HTML file is located in *ORACLE_HOME\forms45\demos\webdemos* and is called *static.html.* I took this file and modified its contents to get the following static HTML file for my demo in Listing 19.2:

**Listing 19.2 STATIC.HTM—A Static HTML File for Use with Oracle Web Forms Non-Cartridge Implementation**

```
<HTML>
<!-- FILE: static.html -->
<!-- Oracle Static (Non-Cartridge) HTML File Template (Windows NT) -->
<!-- Rename, and modify tags and parameter values as needed -->
<HEAD><TITLE>Developer/2000 for the Web</TITLE></HEAD>
<BODY><BR>Please wait while the Forms Client class files download and run.
      <BR>This will take a second or two...
<P>
<!-- applet definition (start) -->
<APPLET CODEBASE="/Web_code/"
        CODE="oracle.forms.uiClient.v1_4.engine.Main"
        ARCHIVE="/Web_jars/f45web.jar"
        HEIGHT=20
        WIDTH=20>
<PARAM NAME="serverPort"
       VALUE="9000">
<PARAM NAME="serverArgs"
       VALUE="module=a:\Empch16a.fmx userid=system/manager">
<PARAM NAME="serverApp"
       VALUE="default">
</APPLET>
<!-- applet definition (end) -->
</BODY>
</HTML>
```

With a non-cartridge implementation, you cannot use variables in the HTML file so all values need to be hard-coded, thus the requirement for an HTML file for each application is implemented via the noncartridge method.

## Running the Forms from the Web

Until Web browsers that support Java version 1.1.2 are available, the only option available to run the forms is the appletviewer from the Java development kit. The format of the URL that is entered depends on the Web forms implementation (cartridge or noncartridge).

**Entering the URL** First, we will cover the format of the URL for the Cartridge implementation. The cartridge URL must include the virtual directory that was created for the Web cartridge. Also included in the URL are any variables for the base HTML file that were not defined by the cartridge. These variables are entered in the URL following a question mark that is placed after the virtual directory. Below is the URL for my example cartridge Web forms implementation (note: the following command should be entered on one line):

**appletviewer http://localhost/Web_html/static.htm**

Because userid information was not specified in my example, a prompt to log in to the database will be displayed first, followed by the starting up of the form under Java.

The static version of the Web form implementation will require a call to the virtual directory that contains the static HTML file. Because no variables can be used with the static implementation, the URL is potentially much shorter and straightforward. Following is the URL for my example noncartridge Web forms implementation:

**appletviewer http://localhost/Web_html/static.htm**

Because the userid information was included in the static HTML file, the Web form is immediately displayed in the Java applet (see Figure 19.7).

**FIG. 19.7**
The Web form running under Java.

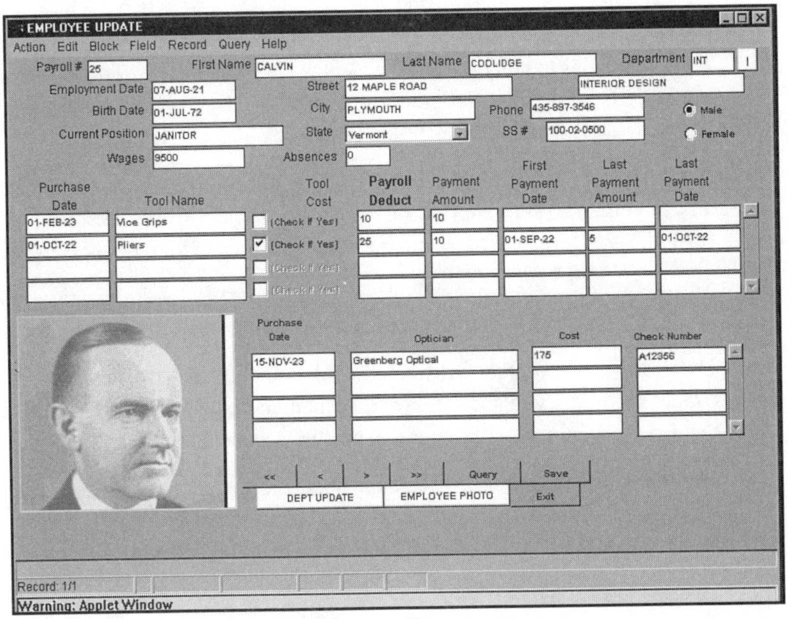


Regardless of which implementation is used, the display of the form looks and behaves remarkably similar to the client/server version of the form.

**Things to Watch Out For** The first couple times I tried to get an Oracle form to work, I ran into problems with the system finding my form. I started out with a noncartridge implementation and, after double- and triple-checking my implementation, I finally called Oracle. After a few minutes on the phone, it was determined that a line break between the module and userid variables in the static HTML file should be removed and replaced with a single space. This worked! The moral of this story is start out simple, and add complexity to the static or cartridge implementation once you get the basics working.

I found the appletviewer to be quite quirky. After making changes to the configuration, I usually had to restart the appletviewer after its initial startup to get it to acknowledge my changes in the configuration. The only sure way to get the appletviewer to recognize my changes on initial startup of the forms applet was to restart the NT workstation.

# Setting Up Oracle Reports on the Web

Oracle implements the reports part of Developer 2000 via a reports CGI program loaded onto the Web server CGI directory. This CGI engine working in combination with the reports engine is capable of displaying reports in either HTML or Adobe Acrobat PDF format. If you are planning to implement reports via the PDF format, you will have to ensure your browsers are all configured with the Adobe Acrobat plug-in.

## Configuring the Web Server for Web Reports

The first step is to copy the RDF files onto the Web server. The location to which these reports are copied should be included in the REPORTS25_PATH variable that Oracle uses (setup of this variable is detailed later in this section).

Next the CGI engine, *R25CGI32.EXE*, should be copied from the *ORACLE_HOME\bin* directory to your Web server's CGI directory. For Oracle Web server v.2.1, the CGI directory was in *ORACLE_HOME\ows21\bin* and had the virtual directory */ows-bin/* defined.

Now define the necessary variables for the Reports CGI. Following are the variables that are necessary for the CGI and their suggested values:

The first required value, ORACLE_HOME, should already be defined if you have installed any Oracle products (you should have at least installed Developer 2000). This key should point to the directory into which the Oracle products were installed.

The REPORTS25_WEBLOC variable specifies the virtual directory that is set up on the Web server for runtime reports output file. Set this virtual directory up on your Web server like any other virtual directory. For my example, I used /report_out/.

The REPORTS25_WEBLOC_TRANSLATED variable specifies the absolute path of the virtual directory specified by REPORTS25_WEBLOC variable. For my example, I used D:\temp.

The REPORTS25_PATH variable should include an absolute path to the location of the reports files (A:\ for my example).

These variables must be defined in the Windows Registry by adding values under the Oracle key for the local machine key (see Figure 19.8). Following is an outline of the steps necessary to make these modifications:

> **CAUTION**
>
> Using the Registry editor incorrectly can cause serious, system-wide problems that can corrupt your Windows NT installation. Microsoft does not guarantee that any problems resulting from use of the Registry editing tools can be corrected (except by reinstall). So the moral of this story is use caution when modifying the Registry.

- To start up the Windows NT Registry editor, enter **REGEDT32** in the Open dialog box displayed by the RUN command on the NT Start menu.
- Find the HKEY_LOCAL_MACHINE hive window.

Under the Software key, there is an Oracle key. Select this key by clicking it once.

- From the Edit pull-down menu, select the Add Value option.
- For the Value name, enter one of the variable names noted before.
- For the Data type, select REG_EXPAND_SZ, then select OK.
- Finally, enter the variable value in the string window and select OK.

Enter or ensure that all variables are defined and then exit out of REGEDT32.

**FIG. 19.8**
Modifying the Oracle variables for the Reports CGI.

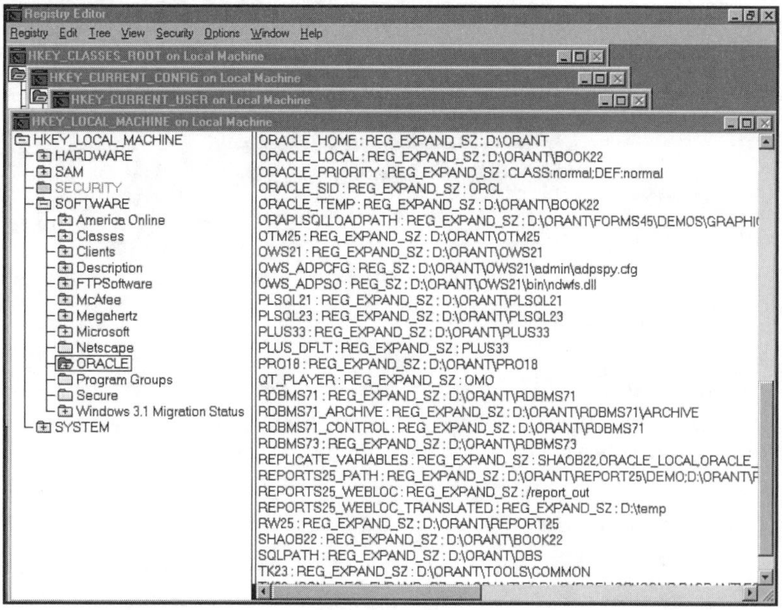




Finally, set the Web listener service up to use an account other than the system account. And verify that the account has a default printer defined.

To redefine the account that executes the Web listener service, start up the Services applet from the NT Control Panel. Select the service for your Web server and select the Startup button to modify the Login account. The login account should be a local account on the NT machine, and this account MUST have a printer defined or the reports will not print. After the login account has been modified, the Web server service must be stopped and started to make the changes effective (see Figure 19.9).

**NOTE** The account used here must have the "Log on as a service" right assigned to it. Without this right, the listener will not start. This right is set in the User Manager for NT. For more details on setting rights, see the online help for NT user manager.

I used the local Administrator account because it already existed, had a printer defined, and I was sure that it would not run into problems with having the proper right to execute the CGI. You may or may not want to use this account for your site. If you use another account, make sure the account has the proper rights to execute the CGI.

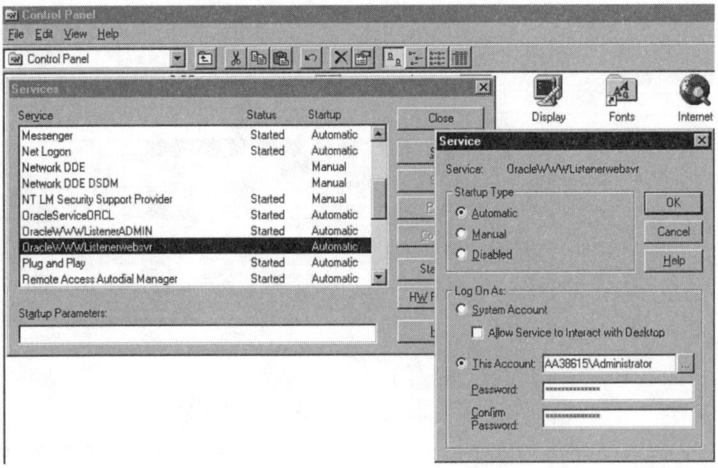


**FIG. 19.9**
Modifying the Web server service's login account.

Now you must ensure that the account you entered has a default printer. The best way to do this is to log on to the NT machine with the local account that you entered for the Web server service to use to log in and define a default printer for that account.

## Running the Reports

To run the reports, enter the path to the reports CGI on your Web server in the URL address space of your Web browser and include at least two parameters (REPORT and USERID are required at a minimum). The parameters are command-line reports parameters; others may be included on the URL in addition to the two required parameters. For the reports part, Java is not required so you may use the Web browsers that are currently available (I used the Microsoft Internet Explorer v.3.02).

**Entering the URL** To run a report from the Web, the URL calling the reports CGI engine is called in the following fashion via a Web browser:

**http://localhost/ows-bin/r25cgi32.exe?report=a:\A_17_03.rdf+userid=system/manager+desformat=HTML**

It is important to note that the r25cgi32.exe portion of the URL is case-sensitive. The preceding command will output the report in an HTML format. To output the report in a PDF format, I entered the following URL in my Web browser:

**http://localhost/ows-bin/r25cgi32.exe?report=a:\A_17_03.rdf+userid=system/manager+desformat=PDF**

The PDF option will require that the Adobe Acrobat reader plug-in is configured for your browser.

**Reports URL Mapping Feature** The reports mapping feature documented in the books for Developer 2000 does not function at all in the 1.4W release. This feature is supposed to let you hard-code in various reports parameters while allowing others to be entered dynamically on the URL line. I was told by Oracle support that this feature currently does not work. After finding this out, I removed the variable (REPORTS25_CGIMAP) from the system registry. However, I was still having problems getting the reports to run again afterward. After carefully reading the documentation, I discovered that this feature is enabled by either using the fore-mentioned variable or by placing a file called CGICMD.DAT in the ORACLE_HOME\report25 directory. That was where I put this file and the name that I used (see Figure 19.10). After renaming the file, the Web reports started working again.

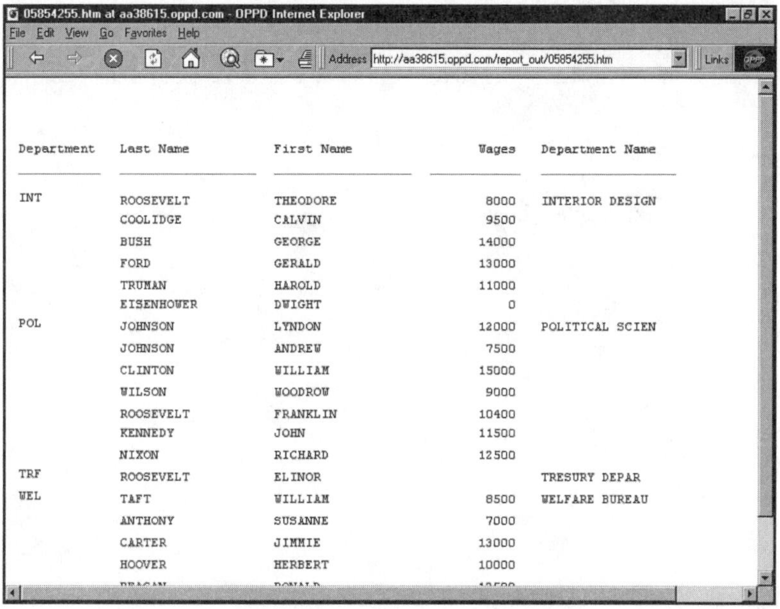


| Department | Last Name | First Name | Wages | Department Name |
|---|---|---|---|---|
| INT | ROOSEVELT | THEODORE | 8000 | INTERIOR DESIGN |
| | COOLIDGE | CALVIN | 9500 | |
| | BUSH | GEORGE | 14000 | |
| | FORD | GERALD | 13000 | |
| | TRUMAN | HAROLD | 11000 | |
| | EISENHOWER | DWIGHT | 0 | |
| POL | JOHNSON | LYNDON | 12000 | POLITICAL SCIEN |
| | JOHNSON | ANDREW | 7500 | |
| | CLINTON | WILLIAM | 15000 | |
| | WILSON | WOODROW | 9000 | |
| | ROOSEVELT | FRANKLIN | 10400 | |
| | KENNEDY | JOHN | 11500 | |
| | NIXON | RICHARD | 12500 | |
| TRF | ROOSEVELT | ELINOR | | TRESURY DEPAR |
| WEL | TAFT | WILLIAM | 8500 | WELFARE BUREAU |
| | ANTHONY | SUSANNE | 7000 | |
| | CARTER | JIMMIE | 13000 | |
| | HOOVER | HERBERT | 10000 | |

**FIG. 19.10**
An Oracle Web Report displayed in HTML format.

# Summary

That is all there is to it. Now that all of the initial configuration hurdles have been overcome, moving more forms and reports to the Web will be as simple as creating an HTML file or a hyperlink on a Web page (depending on your forms and reports implementation). Oracle had a good suggestion in their Designer 2000 documentation, which was to have a predefined page on your Web site that contains links to all the Web-enabled systems. This way, you do not have to send out cryptic URLs to end users that may be misentered. Additionally, URLs may be changed at any time on this page and not impact user bookmarks.

To wrap things up, here is a quick outline of the tasks performed to Web-enable Oracle forms and reports:

- Install Web server and Designer 2000 software on the application server.
- Determine type of Web forms implementation (Cartridge or Non-Cartridge).
- Set up the virtual directories.
- Configure the Web Cartridge (if using a cartridge implementation).
- Create the Cartridge for the Web Form.
- Register the Web with the Cartridge handler.
- Configure a virtual directory for the Web form Cartridge.
- Create an HTML file for the form.
- Copy the RDF files to the Web server for the reports.
- Copy the CGI Reports engine from ORACLE_HOME/BIN to the CGI directory for the Web server.
- Define the necessary Reports variables.
- Modify the Web listener service to use an ID that has a defined printer.

# From Here...

The next chapter shows you how to develop a template employee information system.

PART VII

# Complete Template System

CHAPTER 20

# Developing a Template Employee Information System

This chapter describes the processes and methodology used to fulfill the requirements outlined in the various installments at the end of key portions of the book. Each installment covers a portion of the tasks needed to design and implement a working system. The installments are based upon real-life requirements of a system developed at my company. The result of performing the installments is a system that can be used as a guide for other Oracle databases. ■

**Installment 1—data normalization and database design**

This section describes the process of designing a normalized relational database to replace an existing unnormalized employee database. The installment is presented at the end of Chapter 2, "Designing Your Database."

**Installment 2—Creating the database objects**

This section describes the steps needed to create the employee system database objects. These consist of a number of objects such as tablespaces, user accounts ids, tables, indexes, and sequences.

**Installment 3—Loading the data into the tables**

This section describes the tasks needed to load the database tables. The data from the old system resides in a comma-separated value file. This data will be loaded into the Oracle tables and a PL/SQL program used to modify the data.

**Installment 4—Designing and building the user interface**

This section describes the design and special features of the forms and menu that will be used in the employee system.

# Installment 1—Data Normalization and Database Design

The purpose of this installment is to produce and document a design for a normalized set of relational tables for a new employee information system. This system will replace an existing system that contains unnormalized data. The attributes contained in the new set of tables are to be based upon the existing employee table and future requirements. To perform this task, you will use the normalization model to normalize the data in the existing tables to the third normal form. The first principle or step in the normalization methodology is to place all repeating fields in a table of their own. This will place the data in first normal form.

The existing employee database consists of one table. It contains repeated sets of fields for eyeglass purchases, tool purchases, and historic employee classifications. These sets of fields need to be placed in their own tables. The payroll number is the piece of information that can be used to relate the sets of records to the main entity, the employee. Payroll numbers should be included in the new tables as a foreign key. Table 20.1 illustrates the new tables and fields:

**Table 20.1 The Employee Database Tables and Fields In the First Normal Form**

| Employees | Eyeglasses | Tools | Classifications |
|---|---|---|---|
| Payroll number | Payroll number | Payroll number | Payroll number |
| Last name | Purchase Date | Purchase Date | Department |
| First name | Optician | Payroll Deduct | Classification |
| Absences | Cost | Tool Name | Classification Date |
| Wages | Check Number | Tool Cost | Wages |
| Street | Payment | Comments | |
| City | Last Payment Amount | | |
| State | First Payment Date | | |
| Phone | Last Payment Date | | |
| Social Security Number | | | |
| Employment Date | | | |

| Employees | Eyeglasses | Tools | Classifications |
|---|---|---|---|
| Birth Date | | | |
| Classification | | | |
| Classification Date | | | |
| Department | | | |
| Department Name | | | |

Normalizing the data to the first normal form allows the developer to reduce the size of the database. The extra fields placed in the original file for repeating records are eliminated. These fields consume disk space even when empty. Eliminating them reduces the size of the table record. Any values contained in these fields will exist in their own tables. The three new tables will take disk space only when actual records exist in the table. The next step is to place the database in the second normal form.

To place the data in the second normal form, you must first look at the keys to each table. Each nonkey field in the table must be fully dependent upon the primary key. The primary key to the employees table is the Payroll Number. One field in the table, the Department Name, is not dependent upon the Payroll Number. The field is fully dependent upon the Department field. This means Department Name should be removed from the employee table and a new department table created. Department will be the key to the new table. It will also be a foreign key in the employees table. The fields in the remainder of the tables are dependent upon their primary key.

Normalizing a database to the third normal form requires that all nonkey fields be fully dependent upon the primary key and not dependent upon any other field in the table. The database fulfills this requirement.

Two additional changes need to be made in order to satisfy user requirements. The first, a new requirement, is to add a table to track past performance appraisals. The old system did not track these items. It will require a new table because multiple appraisal dates must be tracked. The second change is to add a department name column in the classification table. This violates the second normal form principle of having columns not fully dependent upon the key. It is necessary because this is a historical table. Throughout the career of the employee, the name of a department may change or a department may be eliminated. In order to retain this information the column must be added.



Table 20.2 illustrates the file design for the new employee system.

**Table 20.2 The Employee Database Tables and Fields In the First Normal Form**

| Employees | Eyeglasses | Tools | Classifications | Security | Appraisals | Departments |
|---|---|---|---|---|---|---|
| Payroll number | Payroll number | Payroll number | Payroll number | Payroll Number | Payroll Number | Department |
| Last name | Purchase Date | Purchase Date | Department | Security Option | Appraisal Date | Dept Name |
| First name | Optician | Payroll Deduct | Classification | | | |
| Absences | Cost | Tool Name | Classification Date | | | |
| Wages | Check Number | Payment | Department Name | | | |
| Street | | Last Payment Amount | Wages | | | |
| City | | First Payment Date | Comments | | | |
| State | | Last Payment Date | | | | |
| Phone | | Tool Name | | | | |
| SocialSecurity Number | | | | | | |
| Employment Date Date | | | | | | |
| Birth Date | | | | | | |
| Classification | | | | | | |
| Classification Date Number | | | | | | |
| Class Comments | | | | | | |
| Gender | | | | | | |
| Department | | | | | | |

Figure 20.1 contains the employee system table relationship. The chart indicates the primary and foreign keys to the various tables.

**FIG. 20.1**
The Employee System Table Relationship diagram.

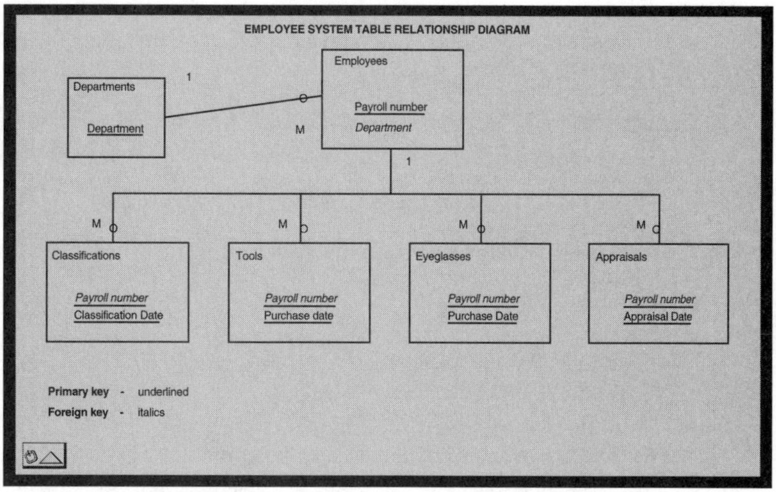


# Installment 2—Creating the Database Objects

This installment creates the Oracle7 database objects that will be used in the employee system. This installment also creates the tables and table constraints identified in the previous installment. The design in Figure 20.1 consists of seven tables. Before these objects can be created, however, a tablespace must be created. A tablespace consists of a file(s) that has a predetermined size. It holds the database objects and is the first object the database administrator needs to create. The script to create the employee system is contained in Listing 20.1. The script is executed in SQL *Plus from the database administrator's id.



**Listing 20.1 L_20_01.SQL—The Employee System's Create Tablespace Script**

```
SQL> create tablespace emp datafile 'emp_sys.tab' size 3 m
 2  default storage (pctincrease 1);

Tablespace created.

SQL>
```

**NOTE** If you are using a trial copy of Personal Oracle7, the default database administrator id is *system* and password is *manager*.

The next step is to create a user account or id. This must also be done from the data administrator's id. The user account determines the ownership of the object. Objects are created from the user id. Oracle will then subscribe ownership of the object to that account. The script to create the employee system user id is contained in Listing 20.2. This script creates a user account called emp_sys_user with a password of welcome.

**Listing 20.2 L_20_02.SQL—Creating the User Id Emp_sys_user for the Employee System**

```
SQL> create user emp_sys_user identified by welcome
 2  default tablespace emp
 3  temporary tablespace temporary_data
 4  quota unlimited on emp;

User created.

SQL>
```

After the user acccount is created, it must be granted privileges. Without privileges, the account cannot log on to Oracle. The emp_sys_user account is the main account that will be used for the employee system. It has the ability to modify the systems data. The system administrator will likely be the only person outside the DBA who knows the password. This account is given a broader range of privileges than an ordinary user. The granting of privileges to emp_sys_user account must also be done by the DBA. Listing 20.3 contains the script used to grant privileges to the id.

**Listing 20.3 L_20_03.SQL—Granting Privileges to the "Emp_sys_user" Id**

```
SQL> grant create session, alter session, create table,
 2  create any table, drop any table, create view, drop any view,
 3  create synonym, drop any synonym, create any index, drop any index,
 4  create public synonym, drop public synonym, create any sequence,
 5  drop any sequence
 6 to emp_sys_user;

Grant succeeded.

SQL>
```

The system's tables can be created after the emp_sys_user has been granted privileges. These tables should be created by using the new user id. Seven tables need to be created. Because there are constraints between the tables, they must be created in a specific order. The parent table must be created before the children tables, which means that the Departments table must be created first. The storage clause is used to specify the initial size of the file. Listing 20.4 contains the script used to create the Departments table. The Department field is the primary key to the table. The field contains a Primary Key column constraint used to ensure that the field always has a value and the value is unique.

**Listing 20.4 L_20_04.TXT—Creating the Departments Table**

```
SQL> create table departments
  2  (department char(4) primary key,
  3   department_name varchar(15))
  4  storage (initial 10k next 10k pctincrease 1);

Table created.

SQL>
```

The next table created is the Employees table (see Listing 20.5). The primary key to this table is the Payroll_Number field. The Department field is a foreign key to the same field on the Departments table. Column constraints will be placed on both of these fields. A Check constraint will be placed on the Gender field. The constraint will ensure that the values in the field will be either M or F. The Last name, First name, Employment Date, Classification, and Classification Date fields must always contain a value that is not a null. A Not Null constraint will be placed on each of these fields. The Default constraint is placed on the Absences and Wages fields. This will ensure that these numeric fields contain a value of 0 rather than a null value. This means the value can be used in calculations without the worry of nulls. The letters *fk* precede the Department field name to denote that the field is a foreign key. Figure 20.5 illustrates the create table statement for the Employees table.

**Listing 20.5 L_20_05.SQL—Creating the Employees table**

```
SQL> create table employees
  2  (payroll_number number primary key, last_name varchar(15) not null,
  3   first_name varchar(15) not null,
  4   absences number(2) default (0), wages number(8) default (0),
  5   street varchar(20), city varchar(15), state char(2), phone varchar(13),
  6   social_security_number char(11), employment_date date not null,
  7   birth_date date, classification varchar(15) not null,
  8   classification_date date not null, class_comments varchar2(20),
  9   gender char(1) check (gender in ('M', 'F')),
 10    fk_department char (4) references departments)
 11   storage (initial 100k next 10k pctincrease 1);

Table created.

SQL>
```



The remainder of the tables can be created once the Employees table is created. Each of these tables contains the Payroll Number field. This field is a foreign key that relates the tables to the Employees table. This field will have a foreign key constraint placed upon it in each of the tables. The tables also have composite primary keys. This means the primary key constraint must be specified as a table constraint. The tables use the same types of constraints as used on the Employees table. They have one additional constraint option. The tables will use the `on delete cascade` option. When this option is specified, the child records in the table will be deleted when the parent record is deleted in the Employees table.

Listing 20.6 illustrates the script used to create the Classifications table.

**Listing 20.6 L_20_06.SQL—Creating the Classifications Table**

```
SQL> create table classifications
  (fk_payroll_number number, classification_date date,
   classification varchar(15) not null, wages number(8) default(0),
   comments varchar(20), department char(4), department_name varchar(15),
   primary key (fk_payroll_number, classification_date),
   foreign key (fk_payroll_number) references employees
    on delete cascade)
  storage (initial 100k next 10k pctincrease 1);

Table created.

SQL>
```

Listing 20.7 illustrates the script used to create the Eyeglasses table.

**Listing 20.7 L_20_07.SQL—Creating the Eyeglasses Table**

```
SQL> create table eyeglasses
  (fk_payroll_number number, purchase_date date,
   optician varchar2(20) not null, cost number(6,2) default(0) not null,
   check_number varchar2(10),
   primary key (fk_payroll_number, purchase_date),
   foreign key (fk_payroll_number) references employees
    on delete cascade)
  storage (initial 50k next 10k pctincrease 1);

Table created.

SQL>
```

Listing 20.8 illustrates the script used to create the Tools table.

**Listing 20.8 L_20_08.SQL—Creating the Tools Table**

```
SQL> create table tools
  (fk_payroll_number number, purchase_date date,
   payroll_deduct char (1) default('N') check (payroll_deduct in ('N', 'Y')),
   tool_name varchar(15), tool_cost number (6,2) default(0),
   payment number(6,2) default(0),
   last_payment_amount number(6,2) default(0), first_payment_date date,
   last_payment_date date,
   primary key (fk_payroll_number, purchase_date),
   foreign key (fk_payroll_number) references employees
```

```
 10    on delete cascade)
 11  storage (initial 50k next 10k pctincrease 1);

Table created.

SQL>
```

Listing 20.9 shows the script used to create the Appraisals table.

**Listing 20.9 L_20_09.SQL—Creating the Appraisals Table**

```
SQL> create table appraisals
  2  (fk_payroll_number number, appraisal_date date,
  3   primary key (fk_payroll_number, appraisal_date),
  4   foreign key (fk_payroll_number) references employees
  5    on delete cascade)
  6  storage (initial 10k next 10k pctincrease 1);

Table created.

SQL>
```

The last table created is the Security table. This table will be used to validate security before the form allows records to be inserted, updated, or deleted (see Listing 20.10).

**Listing 20.10 L_20_10.SQL—Creating the Security Table**

```
SQL> create table security
  2  (payroll_number  number,
  3   security_option  varchar2(4));

Table created.

SQL>
```



The last database object to be created is a sequence. The sequence will be used in the Employee system to generate a unique number for new employees (see Listing 20.11).

**Listing 20.11 L_20_11.SQL—Creating the Next_payroll_number Sequence**

```
SQL> create sequence next_payroll_number
  2  increment by 1 start with 1;

Sequence created.

SQL>
```

# Installment 3—Loading the Data into the Tables

The goal of this installment is to load the data from the original Employee system into the Oracle tables created in Installment 2. The data from the original system was converted into a comma-separated value file called RAWDATA.CSV. The records in this file are not normalized and need some reformatting. In order to accomplish this, the data will be loaded into a temporary table. A PL/SQL program is then executed against the data in the temporary table. This program scrubs the data and places the fields into the normalized tables of the Employee database.

Listing 20.12 contains the Create table file for the temporary load table. The name of the table is "Temptable."

**Listing 20.12 L_20_12.SQL—Creating the Temporary Load Table Called Temptable**

```
SQL> create table temptable
(last_name varchar2(15),first_name varchar2(15), absences number(2),
wages number(8,2), street varchar2(20), city varchar2(15), state char(2),
phone char(13), social_security_number char(11), employment_date char(9),
birth_date char(9), current_position varchar2(15), position_date char(9),
department char(4), department_name varchar2(15),
department_1 char(4), historic_position_1 varchar2(15),
position_date_1 char(9), wages_1 number(8), comments_1 varchar2(20),
department_2 char(4), historic_position_2 varchar2(15),
position_date_2 char(9), wages_2 number(8), comments_2 varchar2(20),
department_3 char(4), historic_position_3 varchar2(15),
position_date_3 char(9), wages_3 number(8), comments_3 varchar2(20),
department_4 char(4), historic_position_4 varchar2(15),
position_date_4 char(9), wages_4 number(8), comments_4 varchar2(20),
department_5 char(4), historic_position_5 varchar2(15),
position_date_5 char(9), wages_5 number(8), comments_5 varchar2(20),
department_6 char(4), historic_position_6 varchar2(15),
position_date_6 char(9), wages_6 number(8), comments_6 varchar2(20),
purchase_date_1 char(9), optician_1 varchar2(20),
cost_1 number(5), check_number_1 char(10),
purchase_date_2 char(9), optician_2 varchar2(20),
cost_2 number(5), check_number_2 char(10),
purchase_date_3 char(9), optician_3 varchar2(20),
cost_3 number(5), check_number_3 char(10),
tool_purchase_date_1 char(9), payroll_deduct_1 char(1),
tool_name_1 varchar2(15), tool_cost_1 number(5),
payment_amount_1 number(5), last_payment_amount_1 number(5),
first_payment_date_1 char(9), last_payment_date_1 char(9),
tool_purchase_date_2 char(9), payroll_deduct_2 char(1),
tool_name_2 varchar2(15), tool_cost_2 number(5),
payment_amount_2 number(5), last_payment_amount_2 number(5),
first_payment_date_2 char(9), last_payment_date_2 char(9),
tool_purchase_date_3 char(9), payroll_deduct_3 char(1),
```

```
 34  tool_name_3 varchar2(15), tool_cost_3 number(5),
 35  payment_amount_3 number(5), last_payment_amount_3 number(5),
 36  first_payment_date_3 char(9), last_payment_date_3 number(5))
 37 storage (initial 100k next 10k pctincrease 1);

Table created.

SQL>
```

The next step is to load this table with the values from the RAWDATA.CSV load file. This is performed by using SQL*LOADER. Listing 20.13 contains the control file used to load the Temptable file. The control file contains two important settings. The `field terminated by` expression tells Oracle what terminates the field. Because this is a comma-separated value file, the statement must be used. The TRAILING NULLCOLS option must also be used because some of the load records contain null values. This option tells Oracle to load the table's fields with nulls when a value does not exist rather than generating an error. The command on line 2 specifies that the data is on the d drive. This is the assumed CD. Please change this command if it does not match the actual file path.

**Listing 20.13 L_20_13.CTL—The Control File Used by SQL*LOADER to Populate the Temporary File**

```
load data
infile 'd:\rawdata.csv'
into table temptable
replace
fields terminated by "," TRAILING NULLCOLS
 (last_name, first_name, absences, wages, street, city, state,
 phone, social_security_number, employment_date,
 birth_date, current_position, position_date,
 department, department_name, department_1, historic_position_1,
 position_date_1, wages_1, comments_1, department_2, historic_position_2,
 position_date_2, wages_2, comments_2, department_3, historic_position_3,
 position_date_3, wages_3, comments_3, department_4, historic_position_4,
 position_date_4, wages_4, comments_4, department_5, historic_position_5,
 position_date_5, wages_5, comments_5, department_6, historic_position_6,
 position_date_6, wages_6, comments_6,
 purchase_date_1, optician_1,
 cost_1, check_number_1, purchase_date_2, optician_2,
 cost_2, check_number_2, purchase_date_3, optician_3,
 cost_3, check_number_3, tool_purchase_date_1, payroll_deduct_1,
 tool_name_1, tool_cost_1, payment_amount_1, last_payment_amount_1,
 first_payment_date_1, last_payment_date_1,
 tool_purchase_date_2, payroll_deduct_2,
 tool_name_2, tool_cost_2, payment_amount_2, last_payment_amount_2,
 first_payment_date_2, last_payment_date_2,
 tool_purchase_date_3, payroll_deduct_3, tool_name_3, tool_cost_3,
 payment_amount_3, last_payment_amount_3,
 first_payment_date_3, last_payment_date_3)
```

The next step is to execute a conversion program that will modify and normalize the values. This program is shown in Listing 20.14. The first part of the program contains the cursors that will be used to retrieve the data for the program. The program uses the `Cursor For` loop because of its built-in functionality. The developer does not have to define the local variables, fetch statements, and other cursor commands. The program contains a large number of variables. The `Cursor For` loop dramatically reduces the amount of code that must be written.

The first section of the program populates the Departments table. This table must be populated first since it is the parent table to the Employees table. This is mandated by the foreign key constraint that exists on the fk_department field of the Employees table. The section contains a cursor that retrieves the unique Department values from Temptable. As each value is retrieved, a record is inserted into the Departments table.

The next section populates the Employees, Classifications, Eyeglasses, and Tools tables. The section is controlled by a `Cursor For` loop that retrieves each record in the load table, Temptable. The physical record from Temptable is changed into logical records. The logical records are inserted into the proper table. Before the records are placed into their tables, a value is generated from the sequence Next_payroll_number. This value is assigned to a local variable (pay_number) to be used to populate the payroll number fields in all of the tables. One payroll_number is generated for each record in Temptable. As the records are inserted into the tables, the Upper function is used to make an alpha character uppercase.

In addition, the historic classification fields do not contain a value for the Department name. The records only contain the department id. The Classifications table contains the Department Name for reasons mentioned earlier. In order to populate the Department Name field, a cursor is opened to retrieve the Department Name value from the Departments table before records are inserted into the Classifications table.

**Listing 20.14 L_20_14.SQL—The Data Conversion Program for the Employee System**

```
declare
pay_number   number;
dept      varchar2(4);
dept_name    varchar2(15);
cursor a is select distinct department, department_name
      from temptable;
cursor b is select * from temptable;
cursor c is select department_name from departments
       where department = dept;
begin
delete from appraisals;
delete from tools;
delete from eyeglasses;
delete from classifications;
delete from employees;
delete from departments;
```

```
/* The Departments table is the parent table to Employees table.
  The valid departments must reside on this table before the Employee
  table is populated. Cursor a select the distinct department,
  department name combinations from the load data. These values
  are inserted as records in the Departments table*/

for loc in a loop
  insert into departments (department, department_name)
   values (rtrim(upper(loc.department)), upper(loc.department_name));
end loop;

/* This section populates the Employee, Classifications, Tools, and
  Eyeglasses tables. A payroll number was needed as part of the primary
  key for each of these tables. Since it did not exist in the original
  data, the number needed to be generated. Cursor b is used to select
  the entire record from the Temptable table.*/
for loc1 in b loop

  /* The following line generates the payroll number for each
    employee*/

  select next_payroll_number.NextVal into pay_number from dual;

  /* The following insert statement populates the Employees table*/

  insert into employees (payroll_number, last_name, first_name,
   absences, wages, street, city, state, phone,
   social_security_number, employment_date,
   birth_date, classification, classification_date, fk_department)
  values (pay_number, upper(loc1.last_name), upper(loc1.first_name),
   loc1.absences, loc1.wages, upper(loc1.street),
   upper(loc1.city), upper(loc1.state), loc1.phone,
   loc1.social_security_number, upper(loc1.employment_date),
   upper(loc1.birth_date), upper(loc1.current_position),
   upper(loc1.position_date), rtrim(upper(loc1.department)));

  /* The following section populates the Classifications table. The
    original data consists of six sets of fields. The following
    six if-then-else statements evaluate the fields. A record will
    be created for each set that contains values */

  if (loc1.position_date_1 is not null) then
   dept := rtrim(upper(loc1.department_1));
   open c; fetch c into dept_name; close c;
   insert into classifications (fk_payroll_number, department,
    classification, classification_date, wages, comments,
    department_name)
   values (pay_number, rtrim(upper(loc1.department_1)),
    upper(loc1.historic_position_1), upper(loc1.position_date_1),
    loc1.wages_1, upper(loc1.comments_1), dept_name);
  end if;
  if (loc1.position_date_2 is not null) then
   dept := rtrim(upper(loc1.department_2));
```

Part VII Ch 20

*continues*

**Listing 20.14 Continued**

```
  open c; fetch c into dept_name; close c;
  insert into classifications (fk_payroll_number, department,
   classification, classification_date, wages, comments,
   department_name)
  values (pay_number, rtrim(upper(loc1.department_2)),
   upper(loc1.historic_position_2), upper(loc1.position_date_2),
   loc1.wages_2, upper(loc1.comments_2), dept_name);
 end if;
 if (loc1.position_date_3 is not null) then
  dept := rtrim(upper(loc1.department_3));
  open c; fetch c into dept_name; close c;
  insert into classifications (fk_payroll_number, department,
   classification, classification_date, wages, comments,
   department_name)
  values (pay_number, rtrim(upper(loc1.department_3)),
   upper(loc1.historic_position_3), upper(loc1.position_date_3),
   loc1.wages_3, upper(loc1.comments_3), dept_name);
 end if;
 if (loc1.position_date_4 is not null) then
  dept := rtrim(upper(loc1.department_4));
  open c; fetch c into dept_name; close c;
  insert into classifications (fk_payroll_number, department,
   classification, classification_date, wages, comments,
   department_name)
  values (pay_number, rtrim(upper(loc1.department_4)),
   upper(loc1.historic_position_4), upper(loc1.position_date_4),
   loc1.wages_4, upper(loc1.comments_4), dept_name);
 end if;
 if (loc1.position_date_5 is not null) then
  dept := rtrim(upper(loc1.department_5));
  open c; fetch c into dept_name; close c;
  insert into classifications (fk_payroll_number, department,
   classification, classification_date, wages, comments,
   department_name)
  values (pay_number, rtrim(upper(loc1.department_5)),
   upper(loc1.historic_position_5), upper(loc1.position_date_5),
   loc1.wages_5, upper(loc1.comments_5), dept_name);
 end if;
 if (loc1.position_date_6 is not null) then
  dept := rtrim(upper(loc1.department_6));
  open c; fetch c into dept_name; close c;
  insert into classifications (fk_payroll_number, department,
   classification, classification_date, wages, comments,
   department_name)
  values (pay_number, rtrim(upper(loc1.department_6)),
   upper(loc1.historic_position_6), upper(loc1.position_date_6),
   loc1.wages_6, upper(loc1.comments_6), dept_name);
 end if;

 /* This section populates the Eyeglasses fields. It evaluates three
   sets of records*/
```

```
if (loc1.purchase_date_1 is not null) then
 insert into eyeglasses (fk_payroll_number, purchase_date,
  optician, cost, check_number)
 values (pay_number, upper(loc1.purchase_date_1),
  upper(loc1.optician_1), loc1.cost_1, upper(loc1.check_number_1));
end if;
if (loc1.purchase_date_2 is not null) then
 insert into eyeglasses (fk_payroll_number, purchase_date,
  optician, cost, check_number)
 values (pay_number, upper(loc1.purchase_date_2),
  upper(loc1.optician_2), loc1.cost_2, upper(loc1.check_number_2));
end if;
if (loc1.purchase_date_3 is not null) then
 insert into eyeglasses (fk_payroll_number, purchase_date,
  optician, cost, check_number)
 values (pay_number, upper(loc1.purchase_date_3),
  upper(loc1.optician_3), loc1.cost_3, upper(loc1.check_number_3));
end if;

/*This section of the program populates the Tools table*/

if (loc1.tool_purchase_date_1 is not null) then
 insert into tools (fk_payroll_number, purchase_date,
  payroll_deduct, tool_name, tool_cost, payment,
  last_payment_amount, first_payment_date, last_payment_date)
 values (pay_number, upper(loc1.tool_purchase_date_1),
  upper(loc1.payroll_deduct_1), upper(loc1.tool_name_1),
  loc1.tool_cost_1, loc1.payment_amount_1,
  loc1.last_payment_amount_1, upper(loc1.first_payment_date_1),
  upper(loc1.last_payment_date_1));
end if;
if (loc1.tool_purchase_date_2 is not null) then
 insert into tools (fk_payroll_number, purchase_date,
  payroll_deduct, tool_name, tool_cost, payment,
  last_payment_amount, first_payment_date, last_payment_date)
 values (pay_number, upper(loc1.tool_purchase_date_2),
  upper(loc1.payroll_deduct_2), upper(loc1.tool_name_2),
  loc1.tool_cost_2, loc1.payment_amount_2,
  loc1.last_payment_amount_2, upper(loc1.first_payment_date_2),
  upper(loc1.last_payment_date_2));
 end if;
 if (loc1.tool_purchase_date_3 is not null) then
 insert into tools (fk_payroll_number, purchase_date,
  payroll_deduct, tool_name, tool_cost, payment,
  last_payment_amount, first_payment_date, last_payment_date)
 values (pay_number, upper(loc1.tool_purchase_date_3),
  upper(loc1.payroll_deduct_3), upper(loc1.tool_name_3),
  loc1.tool_cost_3, loc1.payment_amount_3,
  loc1.last_payment_amount_3, upper(loc1.first_payment_date_3),
  upper(loc1.last_payment_date_3));
 end if;
end loop;
end;
/
```

After this program has been completed, the tables used in the system are populated. The system is ready for forms to be developed.

# Installment 4—Designing and Building the User Interface

This installment is to develop the menu and forms that will be used to maintain the Employee system data. These forms consist of a Department Update form, an Employee Update form, an Employee Directory, and a Security Administration form. The system will also have a main menu that is used to call any form in the system.

**NOTE** This section will not describe each step in the creation of the forms and menus. This was covered in Chapters 11 to 16. The forms and menus are similar to those covered in these chapters. This chapter only discusses the design and special features of the applications. The steps to achieve the design are covered in the indicated chapters.

## The Department Update Form (Deptupd.fmb)

The first application to create is the Department Update application, which will be used to maintain the Departments table. This form only contains two columns. It will be designed with a partial screen-size canvas. This means the form will not entirely overlay other applications. Table 20.3 contains some of the key triggers and form attributes used in the Department Update form.

**Table 20.3 Department Update Form Triggers and Key Attributes**

| Item | Purpose/Setting |
|---|---|
| Canvas Height | 287 |
| Canvas Width | 336 |
| Security triggers | The form should have form-level preinsert, preupdate, and predelete triggers that prevent unauthorized users from modifying the records. |
| When-new-form-instance | This trigger will contain the execute-query built-in. This will enable the form to display the table's records as it is displayed. |
| Window Height | 287 |
| Window Width | 336 |

Figure 20.2 shows the executed Department Update form. The source code for this application is in file Deptupd.fmb.

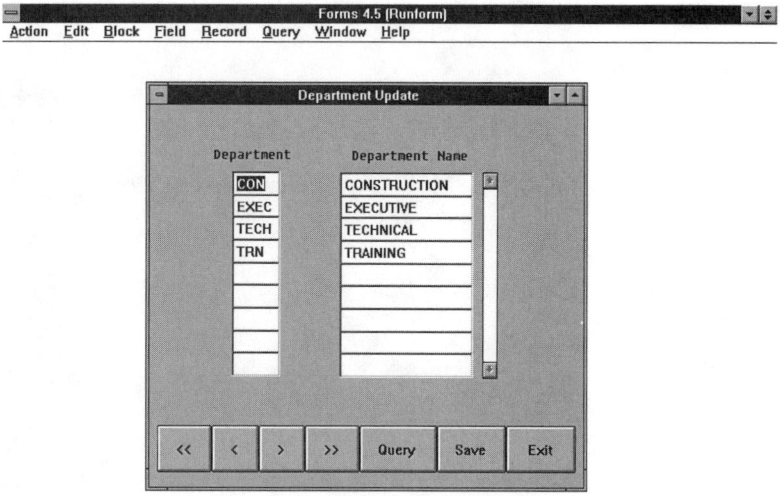


**FIG. 20.2**
The Department Update screen used in the Employee system.

## The Employee Update Form (Empupd.fmb)

The next form to create is the Employee Update form. This form will be the most sophisticated in the system. It is similar to the Employee Update form discussed in Chapters 11 to 16 except that it will have added functionality.

One of the new features is the ability to generate payroll numbers for new employees. The Next_payroll_number sequence is added to the form in a block "one" pre-insert trigger. The trigger is fired before a record is inserted into the Employees table. The trigger populates the Payroll_number item with the next value generated by the sequence. The Payroll_number item's Insert Allowed, Update Allowed, and Navigable properties will also be changed to value of false. This will preclude the operator from changing the item's value. Figure 20.3 illustrates the trigger used to generate the payroll number.

This form differs from the other Employee Update form in that it must have blocks for two additional tables. This form displays historical classification records contained in the Classification table. It will also display historical appraisal records contained in the Appraisal record. The form does not contain enough room to display the four child blocks that will display the records for the Appraisals, Classifications, Tools, and Eyeglasses tables. This will require the form to have stacked canvases. These canvases will overlay the original content canvas. The Tools and Eyeglasses table records will be displayed on one stacked canvas. The Appraisals and Classifications tables will be displayed on another stacked canvas.



The records for the Employees table is displayed in block one. The canvas for this block is "canvas2." Canvas2 and the block "one" layout are shown in Figure 20.4. The block uses a post-query trigger to populate the name of the nonbase table Department item. The State item was changed to a picklist and the Gender item to a radio group button. A LOV for the fk_department item is also created. A button adjacent to the item initiates the LOV.

**FIG. 20.3**
The Block One Preinsert trigger used to generate the new payroll number for added records.

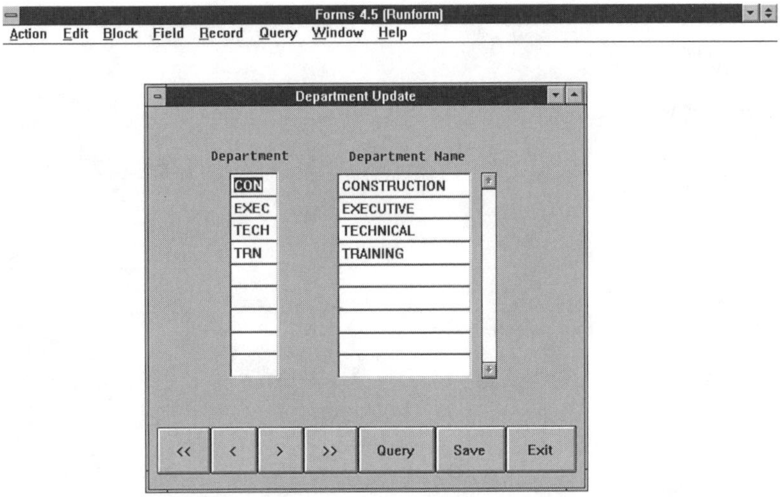


**FIG. 20.4**
Canvas2 and the block-one item layout.

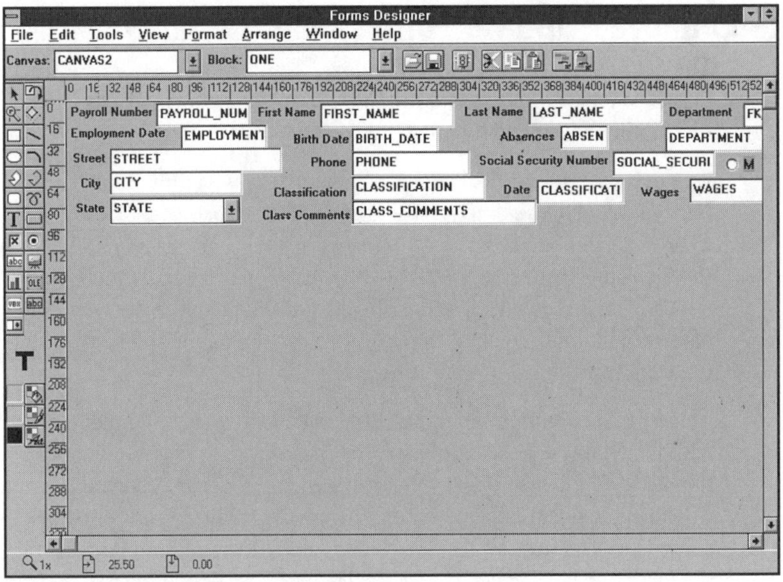


Canvas4 is the next canvas created. It contains the records for the Tools and Eyeglasses tables. They are contained on blocks "five" and "six." Figure 20.5 shows this layout.

Canvas5 displays the records for the Appraisals and Classifications tables. These records are contained on blocks "two" and "three." The Payroll_deduct item on block two was changed to a check box. Figure 20.6 shows this layout.

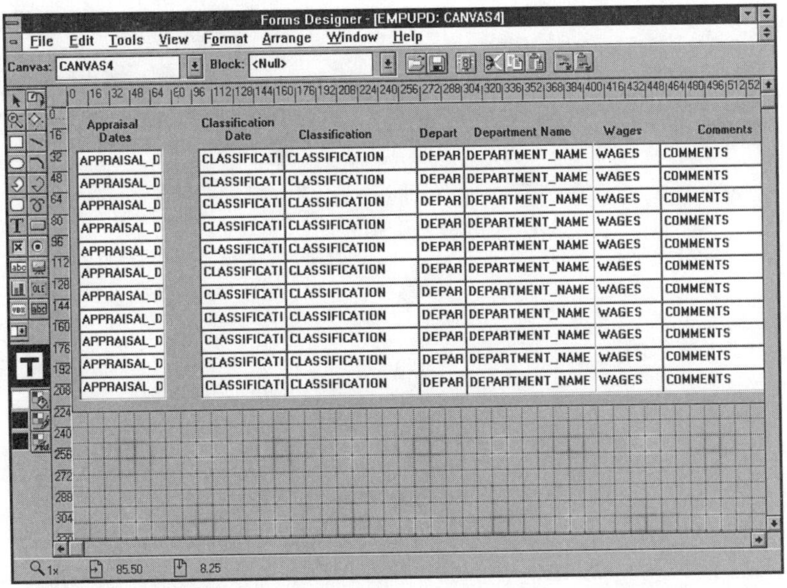


**FIG. 20.5**
Canvas4 and the block "five" and "six" layout.

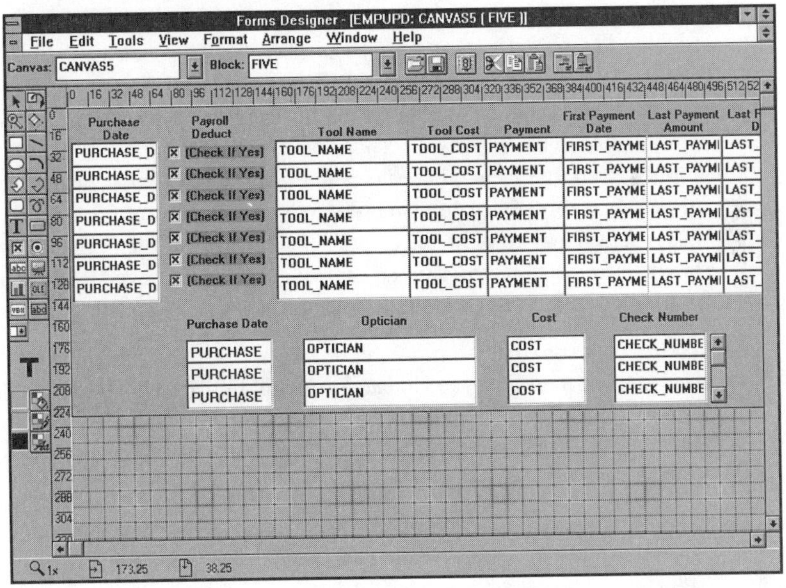


**FIG. 20.6**
Canvas5 and the block "two" and "three" layout.

Two buttons were placed on the Button Palette to enable the operator to change the displayed canvases. Clicking the "Tools/Eyeglasses" button brings up canvas4. Clicking the "Class/ Appraisals" button brings up canvas5. Figure 20.7 shows the Employee Update button palette.

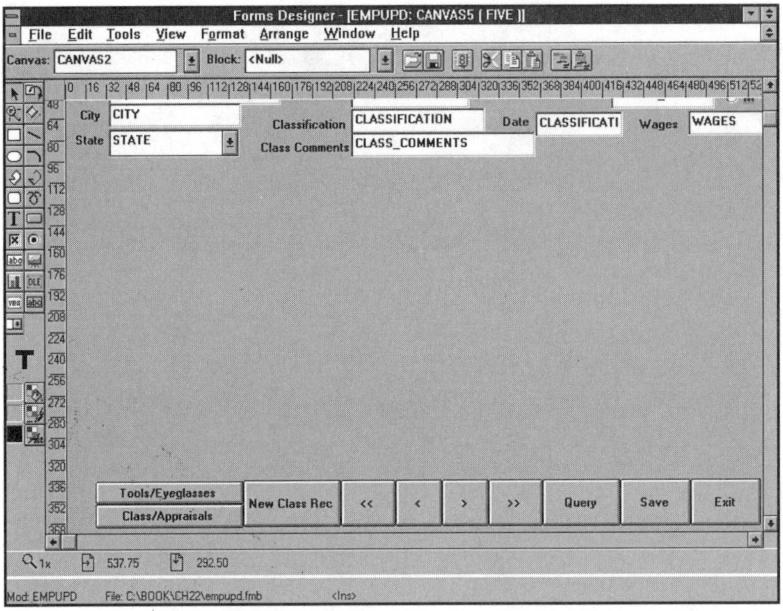


**FIG. 20.7**
The Employee Update button palette that contains the buttons to change canvases.

**Creating Classification Records** The Classifications table contains historic classification records. The current classification attributes are retained on the Employees table. These columns are redundant to the columns on the Classifications table. They were placed on the Employees table so the secretary responsible for the database would not have to create a join to produce a report. Placing these fields in the Employees table violates the table normalization rules. This is sometimes done in order to increase the user friendliness of the database. The redundancy does cause the developer some problems. The developer must make sure the current classification values in the Employees table are saved in the Classifications table before the new values are placed in the Employees table.

In order to ensure that the proper updates and inserts occur, some special programming was developed for the Employee Update form. A button, called New Class Rec, was placed at the bottom of the form. Clicking this button opens a new window called New Classification Record Entry. Canvas3 and nonbase table block "four" are displayed in this window, as shown in Figure 20.8.

The new values are placed in the fields in this window. Clicking the Save button fires a trigger. This trigger inserts a record into the Classifications table. The record contains the values currently in the classification items on the Employees table. The trigger then moves the new values from the window to the corresponding items on block "one." A commit is then issued to save the block "one" changes. The trigger then causes the input focus to change to block "three." This will close down the New Classification Record Entry window. Finally, the trigger causes block "three" to execute a query. This will return the inserted Classifications record to the screen. Figure 20.9 shows the trigger.

**FIG. 20.8**
The New Classification Record Entry window.

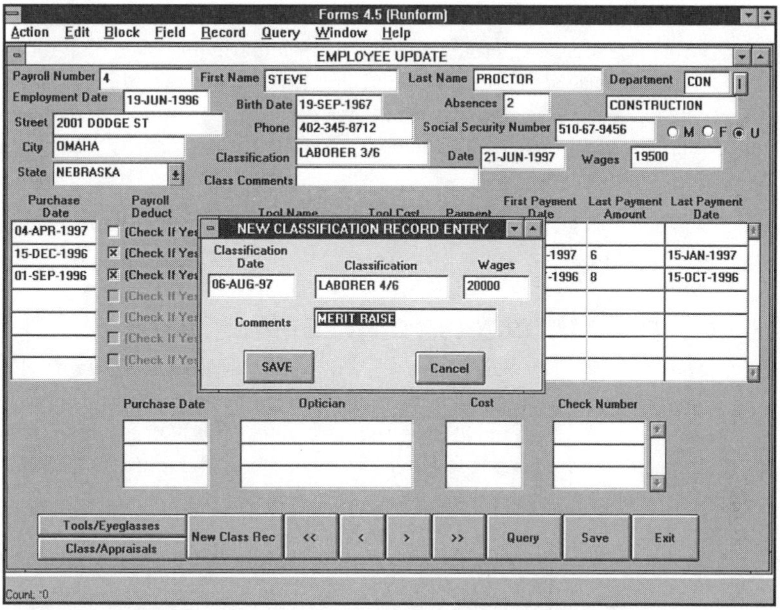


**FIG. 20.9**
The When-button-pressed trigger that creates the Classifications Record and updates the Employees table with classification changes.

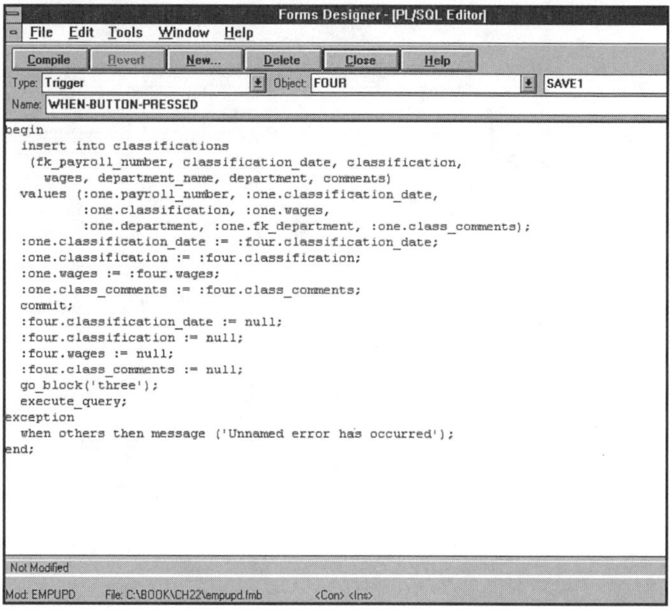


Part VII
Ch 20

**Remaining Changes** The Employees form needs some remaining standard changes. The form-level preinsert, preupdate, and predelete triggers used on the Department Update screen should be placed in the form. The easiest way to perform this is to open the Department Update form and drag the items to the proper location on the Employee Update form. Designer will then copy these items into the form. The Form_Security_Checks procedure is also copied into the form.

A When-new-form-instance trigger is created. This trigger has the same code as the trigger outlined in Chapter 16.

## The Employee Directory Form (Empdir.fmb)

The Employee Directory has the same design as the directory described in Chapter 16, except for two minor additions: The number of records displayed was changed to 14 and a LOV was added for the Department item on block "one." The LOV will help the user in determining the proper department code to enter in the search field. Figure 20.10 contains the final Employee Directory.

**FIG. 20.10**
The Employee Directory.

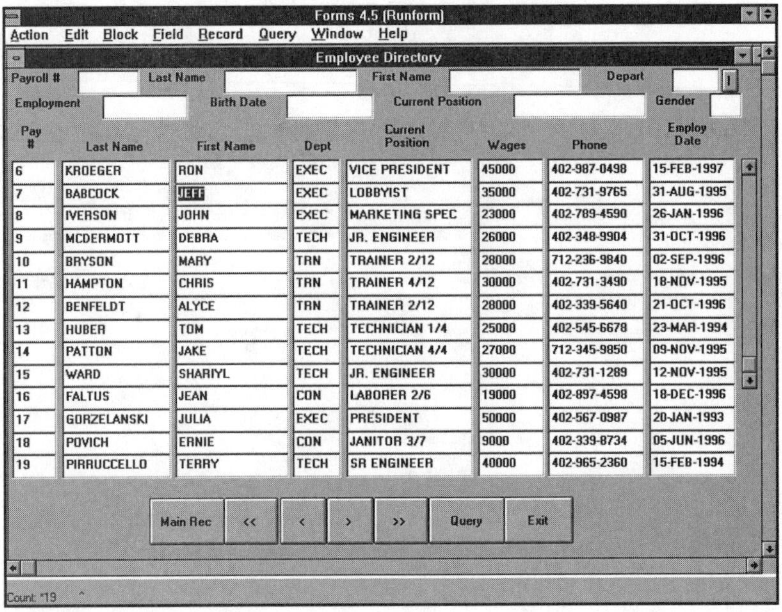


## The Security Update Form (Empsec.fmb)

The Employee system is a secured system. The user must have a valid payroll number, password combination, and security option value of AUD to modify the database. These security values are contained in the Security table. Normally in a production system, the security table is not available for modification or viewing. The table is accessible only through a secured application by a security administrator. The Security Update form described in this section is such an application. It is the form used by the security administrator to manage the Security table. Triggers are placed within the system to ensure that the security administrator is the only operator who may access this form. This requires the security administrator to have a special security option of “SEC.” A trigger will be placed in the menu checking whether the operator has a security option of “SEC.” If the operator does not this option, access to the Security Update form will be denied.

The Security table is the only table displayed on the Security Update form. The table contains two columns: payroll_number and security option. A one-block form that does not encompass the entire screen will be adequate for this data. Figure 20.11 displays the form with several security records displayed.

**FIG. 20.11**
The Security Update form displaying security records.

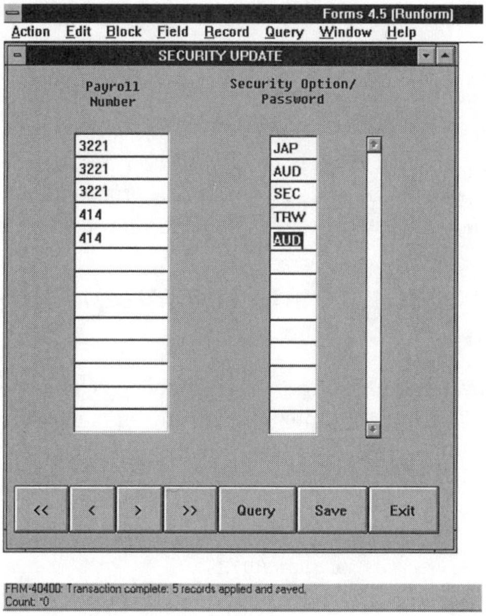


The form must also have the same form-level preinsert, preupdate, and predelete triggers used as security control throughout the book. The form must also have the Form_security_checks procedure. This option has been modified to check for the SEC security option rather than the AUD. Figure 20.12 shows this procedure.

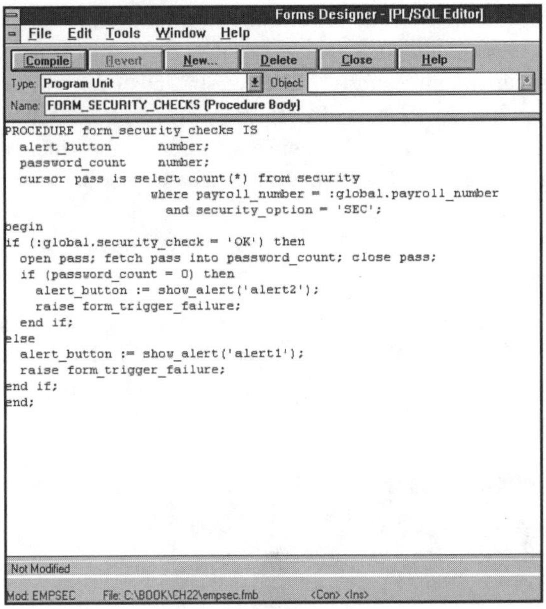
Forms Designer - [PL/SQL Editor]
File Edit Tools Window Help
Compile Revert New... Delete Close Help
Type: Program Unit
Object:
Name: FORM_SECURITY_CHECKS (Procedure Body)
PROCEDURE form_security_checks IS
alert_button number;
password_count number;
cursor pass is select count(*) from security
where payroll_number = :global.payroll_number
and security_option = 'SEC';
begin
if (:global.security_check = 'OK') then
open pass; fetch pass into password_count; close pass;
if (password_count = 0) then
alert_button := show_alert('alert2');
raise form_trigger_failure;
end if;
else
alert_button := show_alert('alert1');
raise form_trigger_failure;
end if;
end;
Not Modified
Mod: EMPSEC File: C:\BOOK\CH22\empsec.fmb <Con> <Ins>

**FIG. 20.12**
The Form_security_checks procedure used in the Security form.

Access to the screen will also be controlled by using this procedure in the menu command that calls the form. This trigger will be discussed in the following section.

## The Employee System Startup Form (Eemptup.fmb) and System Menu (Esysmenu.mmb)

The design of the Employee System startup form and menu is fundamentally the same as discussed in Chapter 16. The main changes are the name of the forms called by the menu, a security check trigger in the Security form option, and a new image on the startup form. You can use the image file factory.pcx. The on-logon trigger must use the new user id created in installment 2.

The major change is to the Security form menu option. A trigger is placed in the menu command, which prevents unauthorized operators from calling the form. The modified security trigger is shown in Figure 20.13.

After compiling all the forms, the Employee system is ready for use. It is executed by launching Forms Runtime and the startup application Empstup.fmx.

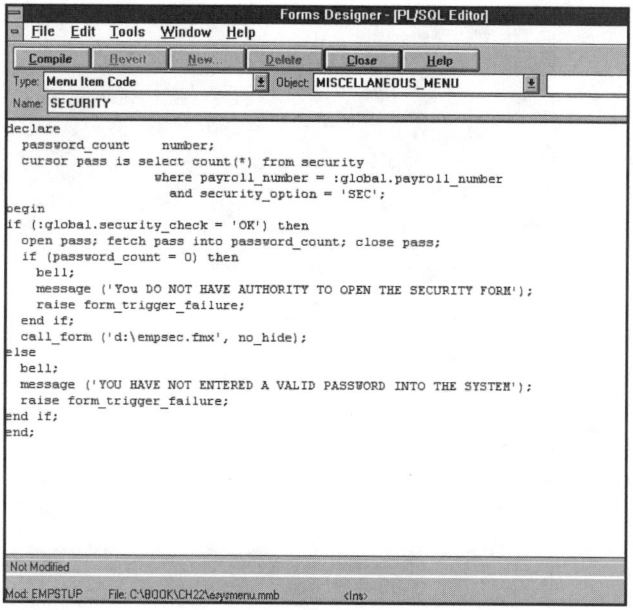

**FIG. 20.13**
The Security Form menu option command used to validate security.

```
                                        Forms Designer - [PL/SQL Editor]
  File  Edit  Tools  Window  Help
  Compile    Revert    New...    Delete    Close    Help
Type: Menu Item Code            ▼  Object: MISCELLANEOUS_MENU          ▼
Name: SECURITY
declare
  password_count    number;
  cursor pass is select count(*) from security
                    where payroll_number = :global.payroll_number
                    and security_option = 'SEC';
begin
if (:global.security_check = 'OK') then
  open pass; fetch pass into password_count; close pass;
  if (password_count = 0) then
    bell;
    message ('You DO NOT HAVE AUTHORITY TO OPEN THE SECURITY FORM');
    raise form_trigger_failure;
  end if;
  call_form ('d:\empsec.fmx', no_hide);
else
  bell;
  message ('YOU HAVE NOT ENTERED A VALID PASSWORD INTO THE SYSTEM');
  raise form_trigger_failure;
end if;
end;

Not Modified

Mod: EMPSTUP    File: C:\BOOK\CH22\esysmenu.mmb          <Ins>
```

# Installment 5—Developing and Adding Reports to the System

The goal of this installment is to develop several reports by using SQL*Reports. These reports will be linked to the menu created in installment 4. This will allow the operator to launch the form from the system's menu. The first report (empewp1.rdf) is a listing of employees who need an appraisal performed within the next 30 days. The query for this report identifies the employees who have not had an appraisal in more than 335 days. Figure 20.14 shows the query used to retrieve the records for the report.

After the report is properly formatted and an executable file generated, a menu option to launch the report is placed on the Employee system menu. The command to launch the report is shown in Figure 20.15. This command launches Reports Runtime and passes it the name of the report file, database logon information, and disables the default parameter list displayed before the report is executed. This command initiates the report immediately. The report will appear in the Reports Previewer upon completion.

Part
**VII**

Ch

**FIG. 20.14**
The query used to identify employees that require an appraisal.

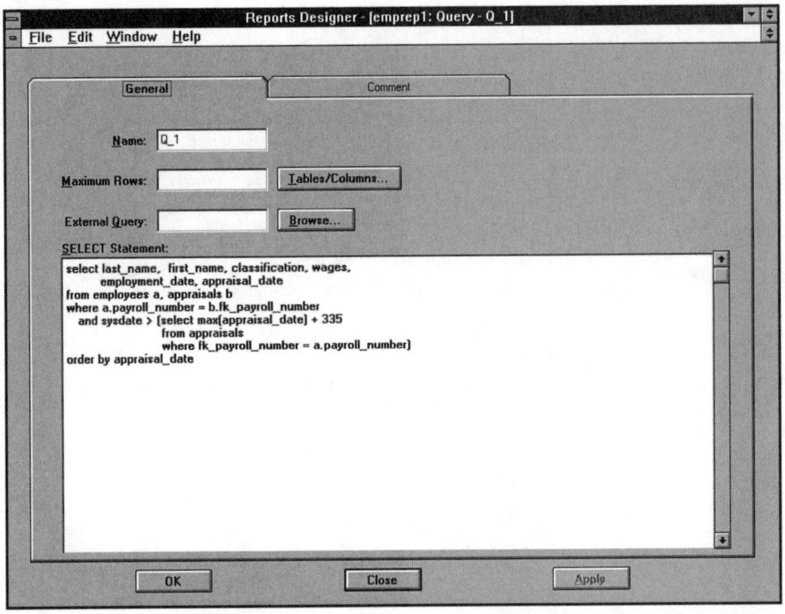


**FIG. 20.15**
The command to launch the Appraisal Due report from the Employee System menu.

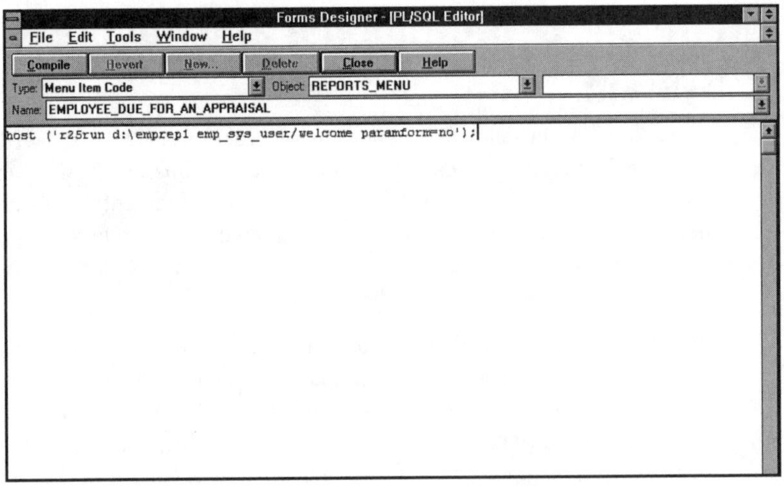


The second system report compiles a list of employees who require a tool payroll deduction for the specified pay date. The report is initiated from a menu option on the system's menu. Before the report is executed, a parameter form is displayed that requests the operator to specify a pay date. This date is used to evaluate dates in the query. The query searches for employees who have purchased a tool on payroll deduction. The specified pay date must be greater-than-or-equal-to the value in the first_payment_date and less-than-or-equal to the last_payment_date to be included on the list. If the pay date is equal to the last_payment_date, the payroll deduction amount is equal to the last_payment_amount rather than the payment. Figure 20.16 shows the query that will produce this report.

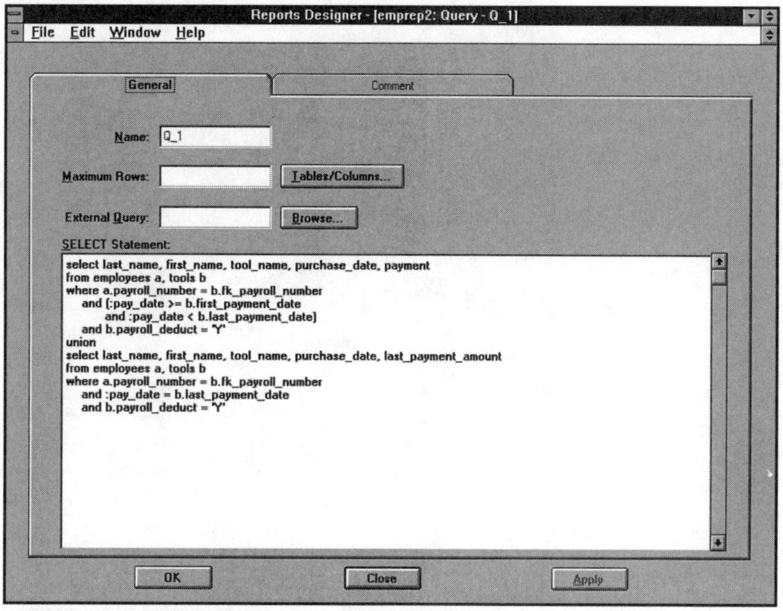


**FIG. 20.16**
The query to produce the Payroll Deduction for Tools report.

The command to execute the report is displayed in Figure 20.17. Because this report requires a parameter list to be displayed, the paramlist option is yes.

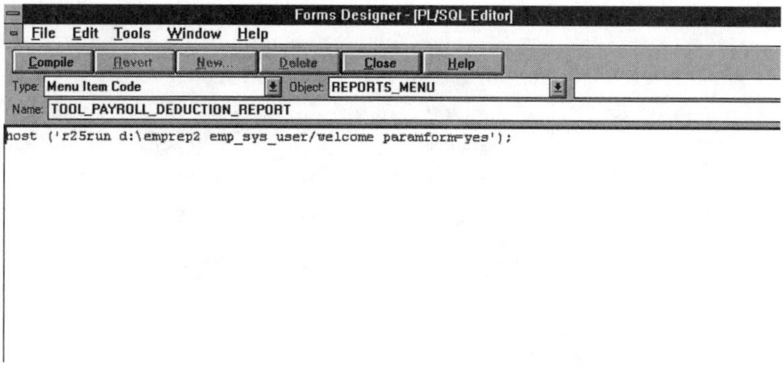


**FIG. 20.17**
The command to launch the Payroll Deduction report.

Figure 20.18 shows the two report options as they appear to the operator on menu.

**FIG. 20.18**
The report options as they appear on the system menu.

# Summary

The purpose of this chapter is to offer you an approach to developing an actual application by using Oracle Developer 2000 on the front end and the Oracle database on the back end. The book presented a variety of tasks and tools used in one manner or another. This chapter is an attempt to place the tools and tasks in their logical order and show how the tools are used to develop a system.

This chapter is also an attempt to give you a place to answer your development questions. When I have a problem with a system, I generally ask myself whether I had performed the procedure before. If I have, I look at the code and try to emulate it. Sometimes when I try to use commands and procedures described in the Help section or a reference manual I have problems. It is always nice to be able to look at a working application. This chapter is an attempt to give you a working application that can be used by you to solve development products.

Finally, I find Oracle an excellent product for developing systems. I hope that you find Oracle a good product also, and that this book helps in your development work. ●

# Appendixes

APPENDIX A

# Built-In Subprograms

Oracle Forms 4.5 contains a large variety of built-in subprograms that PL/SQL scripts use in objects such as triggers and user-defined subprograms. Developers use these subprograms to perform various functions, such as dinging a bell, executing a query, navigating to the next record, or inserting records into the database. Table A.1 defines the built-in subprograms available to you.

The first column contains the name of the built-in subprogram and lists any parameters that may be needed. The second column determines whether the subprogram is restricted.You cannot use restricted subprograms in all triggers because they affect form navigation and cannot be used from a trigger that is causing navigation to occur in the form. Examples of triggers that cannot contain restricted subprograms are the Pre_text_item and Post_change_item triggers. They fire on moving the cursor into and out of an item, respectively. These triggers that cannot contain "Restricted" subprograms because they are fired during a navigation procedure. Subprograms with a Yes in the Restricted column are restricted.

Some of the subprograms cannot be fired in the *Enter Query* mode. This mode occurs when the form is prompting the user to enter a query value. Each subprogram in the table is marked with a Yes in the Enter Query column if is used in the Enter Query mode. ■

**Table A.1 Built-In Subprograms**

| Built-In Name/ Parameter Syntax | Restricted | Enter Query | Description |
|---|---|---|---|
| `abort_query;` | No | Yes | Stops the execution of a query. |
| `add_group_column` (*record group id* or *name, group column name, column type, column width*); | No | Yes | Adds a column to a record group. Record group id is the unique name Oracle assigns the group. Record group name is the user-defined name of the group. Group column name is the name of the column. Column type indicates the data type. The allowable column types are: `char_column`, `date_column`, `long_column`, and `number_column`. |
| `add_group_row` (*record group id* or *name, row number*); | No | Yes | Adds a row to the record group. Record group id is the unique name Oracle assigns the group. Record group name is the user-defined name of the group. Row number specifies the row in the group. |
| `add_list_element` (*list name* or *list id, list index, list label, list value*); | No | Yes | Adds an item to a pick list. List id is the unique Oracle id for the list. List name is the user-defined name of the list. List index indicates the list position of the element. List label specifies the string value to place in the list. List value contains the list label's corresponding database value. |
| `add_parameter` (*list* or *name, parameter, parameter type, value*); | No | Yes | Adds a parameter to a parameter list. A parameter list is a list of variables that will be passed to another object. List or name specifies the identifier of the list. Parameter type holds two acceptable values: `Text_type`, which is a string literal; and `data_parameter`, which is a string specifying a record group defined in the form. Value is the actual value passed to the called module. |

| Built-In Name/ Parameter Syntax | Restricted | Enter Query | Description |
|---|---|---|---|
| `application_parameter;` | No | Yes | Causes Oracle to display the Enter Parameter Values dialog box. The parameters associated to the current menu form are displayed along with their values. |
| `background_menu` (*1 .... 10*); | No | Yes | Displays a menu item from a background menu. |
| `bell;` | No | Yes | Causes the terminal bell to sound. |
| `block_menu;` | Yes | Yes | Displays a list of values that contains the valid block names and their sequence number. |
| `break;` | No | Yes | Stops the execution of the form and displays the Debugger. This occurs only when the form is running in Debug mode. |
| `call_form` (*form name, how to display, switch menu, query mode, parameter list*, or *parameter name*); | No | Yes | Executes the called form while keeping the current form in the background. Form name is the name of the form. The how to display parameter has two values: `hide` or `no_hide`. `Hide` causes Oracle to clear the calling screen and `no_hide` does not clear the screen. Switch menu has two settings: `no_replace`, which causes the called form to keep the default menu of the calling form active; and `do_replace`, which replaces the default menu. Placing a value of `query_only` in the Query mode parameter causes the called application to be run in Query mode only. Placing the `no_query_only` value in this parameter enables the user to insert, update, and delete records on the form. Parameter list id or name is the unique ID Forms Designer assigns a parameter list. Parameter list name is the user-defined name for a parameter list object. |

*continues*

**Table A.1 Continued**

| Built-In Name/ Parameter Syntax | Restricted | Enter Query | Description |
|---|---|---|---|
| `call_input;` | Yes | No | Accepts and processes function key input. |
| `checkbox_checked;` | Yes | No | Returns a true or false value indicating the state of the checkbox. |
| `check_record` ➥`_uniqueness;` | No | Yes | Initiates the Forms processing for checking primary key uniqueness when called from an On-Check-Unique trigger. |
| `clear_block;` | Yes | No | Clears the records from the current block. |
| `clear_eol;` | Yes | No | Clears a text item's value from the current cursor position to the end of the line. |
| `clear_form` (*commit mode, rollback mode*); | Yes | No | Clears the form of all records. The commit mode parameter has several parameters: `Ask_commit`, which prompts the operator to commit the records; `Do_commit`, which performs the commit; `No_commit`, which clears the form and does not commit the data; and `No_validate`, which commits the data without validating. |
| clear_item; | Yes | Yes | Changes the current text item to null. |
| `clear_list` (*list id* or *name*); | No | Yes | Clears the values in a pick list. List id is the list's Oracle ID. List name is your name for the list. |
| `clear_message;` | Yes | Yes | Clears the message area of any existing message. |
| `clear_record;` | Yes | Yes | Removes all values in the current record. |
| `close_form` (*form name* or *id*); | Yes | No | Shuts the current form. A different form may be closed by specifying the form name or id. |

| Built-In Name/ Parameter Syntax | Restricted | Enter Query | Description |
|---|---|---|---|
| `commit_form;` | Yes | No | Modifies the database tables with the values on the form. |
| `convert_other_value` (*list name* or *id*); | Yes | Yes | Changes the value of a pick list, radio group, or check box to the value associated with the current state of the item. |
| `copy` (*variable 1, variable 2*); | No | Yes | Copies the value from variable 1 to variable 2. |
| `copy_region;` | Yes | Yes | Copies text from the current screen and saves it in the clipboard buffer for later use. |
| `count_query;` | Yes | Yes | Identifies the number of records a query retrieves when used in an On-count trigger. |
| `create_group` (*record group name*); | No | Yes | Creates a static or nonquery record group. Records are added to the group using the `populate_group_with_query`, `add_group_column`, and `add_group_row` subprograms. |
| `create_group_from_query` (*record group name, select statement,*); | No | Yes | Creates a record group based on the specified select statement |
| `create_parameter_list` (*list name*); | No | Yes | Creates a parameter list. Parameters can be added by using the `add_parameter` subprogram. Parameter lists are often passed as arguments to the `run_product`, `call_form`, and `new_form` subprograms. |
| `create_queried` ➥`_record;` | Yes | No | Creates a record in a block's record buffer when used in an On-Fetch trigger. The buffer contains records that have been retrieved but not displayed. |
| `create_record;` | Yes | No | Places the current block into the input record mode. |

*continues*

**Table A.1 Continued**

| Built-In Name/ Parameter Syntax | Restricted | Enter Query | Description |
|---|---|---|---|
| `create_timer` (*timer name, milliseconds, iterate*); | No | Yes | Creates a timer. Milliseconds determines the allotted time of each cycle. The iterate parameter has two options: repeat, the default setting that tells the timer to repeat on completion; and no_repeat, which tells the timer to stop on completion. |
| `cut_region;` | Yes | No | Cuts the selected text and stores it in the clipboard buffer. |
| `dbms_error_code;` | No | Yes | Traps and displays the last database error code. |
| `dms_error_text;` | No | Yes | Displays the database error message type and text. |
| `debug_mode;` | No | Yes | Turns the Debug mode on and off. This mode applies only to menu modules. |
| `default_value` (*literal, variable*); | No | Yes | Places the string literal into the variable if its current value is null. |
| `delete_group` (*record group id* or *name*); | No | Yes | Deletes a record group created by a program. |
| `delete_group_row` (*record group id* or *name, row number*); | No | Yes | Removes the indicated row from the record group. Record group id is the unique name Oracle assigns the group. Record group name is the user-defined name of the group. Row number specifies the row in the group. |
| `delete_list_element` (*list name* or *list id, list index*); | No | Yes | Removes the indicated pick list item. List name is the user-defined name of the list. List index indicates the list position of the element. |
| `delete_parameter` (*list* or *name, parameter*); | No | Yes | Removes the specified parameter from the parameter list. List and name refer to the name of the parameter list. Parameter refers the deleted parameter. |
| `delete_record;` | Yes | No | Deletes the current record on the form. |

| Built-In Name/ Parameter Syntax | Restricted | Enter Query | Description |
|---|---|---|---|
| `delete_timer` (*timer id* or *time name*); | No | Yes | Eliminates the specified timer. Timer id or time name contain the name of the timer. |
| `destroy_parameter` ➥`_list` (*list* or *name*); | No | Yes | Removes a programmatically called parameter list. List or name refer to the name of the list. |
| `display_error;` | No | Yes | Activates the Display Error screen if an error has been logged. |
| `display_item` (*item name* or *id*, *attribute*); | No | Yes | Alters an item's appearance by assigning it a different attribute. Item name or id refers to the name of the displayed item. Attribute refers to the attribute that is to be changed. |
| `down;` | Yes | No | Displays or navigates to the next record in the record buffer. |
| `do_key` (*built-in subprogram name*); | Yes | Yes | Simulates the pressing of the function key defined with the name of the subprogram. (See Appendix B for a list of function key trigger names). |
| `duplicate_item;` | Yes | No | Copies the value of the same item from the previous record into the current item. |
| `duplicate_record;` | Yes | No | Copies the values from each item on the previous record into the corresponding items on the current record. |
| `edit_text_item` (*x*, *y*, *width*, *height*); | Yes | Yes | Causes the form to display the Runform text editor for the current item. The x parameter specifies the horizontal position of the editor. The y parameter specifies the vertical position. The built-in subprogram also has provisions for specifying height and width. |
| `enforce_column` ➥`_security;` | No | Yes | Causes the application to check column security. |
| `enter;` | Yes | No | Performs validation checks on the current item. |

*continues*

**Table A.1 Continued**

| Built-In Name/ Parameter Syntax | Restricted | Enter Query | Description |
|---|---|---|---|
| `enter_query;` | Yes | Yes | Changes the form mode to Enter Query. |
| `erase` (*global variable name*); | No | Yes | Eliminates the specified global variable from memory. |
| `error_code;` | No | Yes | Traps and displays the number of the Oracle Forms error. |
| `error_text;` | No | Yes | Displays message text explaining the Forms error. |
| `error_type;` | No | Yes | Displays the type of error. FRM indicates it is a Forms error. ORA indicates it is a database error. |
| `execute_query;` | Yes | Yes | Causes Oracle to fetch records to the form, and to place the form into the Update mode. |
| `execute_trigger` (*trigger name*); | Yes | Yes | Performs the specified trigger. |
| `exit_form` (*commit mode, roll_back mode*); | Yes | Yes | Changes the mode to the Input mode when the form is in the Enter Query mode. It closes the form in all other modes. The Commit mode parameter has several parameters: `Ask_commit`, which prompts the operator to commit the records; `Do_commit`, which performs the commit; `No_commit`, which clears the form and does not commit the data; and `No_validate`, which commits the data without validating. The rollback mode tells Oracle the point to rollback the changes. The settings are: To_savepoint, Full_rollback, and No_rollback. |
| `fetch_records;` | No | No | Initiates the fetching of records to the form. |
| `find_alert` (*alert name*); | No | Yes | Identifies the ID of the alert. The ID must be returned to a defined variable. |

| Built-In Name/ Parameter Syntax | Restricted | Enter Query | Description |
|---|---|---|---|
| `find_block` (*block name*); | No | Yes | Identifies the ID of the block. The ID must be returned to a defined variable. |
| `find_canvas` (*canvas name*); | No | Yes | Identifies the ID of the canvas. The ID must be returned to a defined variable. |
| `find_column` (*record group, group column name*); | No | Yes | Identifies the ID of the record group column. The ID must be returned to a defined variable. |
| `find_editor` (*editor name*); | No | Yes | Identifies the ID of the editor. The ID the editor. The ID must be returned to a defined variable. |
| `find_form` (*form name*); | No | Yes | Identifies the ID of the form. The ID must be returned to a defined variable. |
| `find_group,` (*record group name*); | No | Yes | Identifies the ID of the record group. The ID must be returned to a defined variable. |
| `find_item` (*block_name, item_name*); | No | Yes | Identifies the ID of the item. The ID must be returned to a defined variable. |
| `find_lov` (*list of values name*); | No | Yes | Identifies the ID of the list of values. The ID must be returned to a defined variable. |
| `find_menu_item` (*menu_name, item _name*); | No | Yes | Identifies the ID of the menu item. The ID must be returned to a defined variable. |
| `find_relation` (*relation name*); | No | Yes | Identifies the ID of the relation. The ID must be returned to a defined variable. |
| `find_timer` (*timer name*); | No | Yes | Identifies the ID of the timer. The ID must be returned to a defined variable. |
| `find_view` (*canvas-view name*); | No | Yes | Identifies the ID of the canvas-view. The ID must be returned to a defined variable. |
| `find_window` (*window name*); | No | Yes | Identifies the ID of the window. The ID must be returned to a defined variable. |

*continues*

**Table A.1 Continued**

| Built-In Name/ Parameter Syntax | Restricted | Enter Query | Description |
|---|---|---|---|
| `first_record;` | Yes | No | Displays the first record in the set of records fetched to the form. |
| `form_failure` | No | Yes | Returns a Boolean value indicating the outcome of the last form action. |
| `form_fatal;` | No | Yes | Returns a Boolean expression indicating the result of the last action performed. Outcomes that were successful or failed return a value of false. Fatal errors return a value of true. |
| `form_successs;` | No | Yes | Returns a Boolean expression indicating the result of the last action performed. Outcomes that fail or are fatal errors return a value of false. Success returns a value of true. |
| `forms_ddl` (*statement*); | No | Yes | Issues SQL commands while operating the form. The statements may be a literal, dml, or ddl statement or an expression representing a block of PL/SQL code. |
| `forms_ole.activate_server` (*item id* or *item name*); | No | No | Initiates an OLE server and prepares it to receive OLE automation events. |
| `forms_ole.close_server` (*item id* or *name*) | No | No | Shuts down the OLE server and breaks the connection between the server and the container. |
| `forms_ole.exec_verb` (*item id* or *name*, *verb index* or *verb name*); | No | No | Tells the OLE server to perform the command identified by the verb id or name. |
| `forms_ole.find_ole_verb` (*item id* or *item*, *verb name*); | No | No | Returns the index value of an OLE verb. |
| `forms_ole.get_interface_pointer` (*item id* or *name*); | No | No | Identifies the handle of an OLE2 automation object. |

| Built-In Name/ Parameter Syntax | Restricted | Enter Query | Description |
|---|---|---|---|
| `forms_ole.get_verb _count` (*item id* or *name*); | No | No | Identifies the quantity of commands the OLE server recognizes. |
| `forms_ole.get_verb _name` (*item id* or *name, verb index number*); | No | No | Captures and returns the name of the verb associated to the verb index number. |
| `forms_ole.initialize_ container` (*item id* or *name, file name*); | No | No | Adds an OLE object into an OLE container when it is server compatible. |
| `forms_ole.server _active` (*item id* or *item name*; | No | No | Returns a Boolean value indicating the server associated with the container is running. True indicates it is running, and false indicates it is not. |
| `generate_ sequence_number;` | No | Yes | Initiates the generation of a sequence number when a sequence is defined as the default value in an item property. |
| `get_application_property` (*property name*) | No | Yes | Identifies property values for the current form. |
| `get_block_property` (*block id* or *block name, property*); | No | Yes | Returns the value of various block properties. |
| `get_canvas_property` (canvas name or id, property). | No | Yes | Returns the value of the specified canvas property. The properties are: height, width, and visual_attribute. |
| `get_form_property` (form id or property); | No | Yes | Returns the value of the specified form property. name, |
| `get_group_char_cell` (*group column id* or *name, row number*); | No | Yes | Identifies the character or long value of a record group cell. A cell is a row/column intersection. |
| `get_group_date_cell` (*group column id* or *name, row number*); | No | Yes | Identifies the date value of a record group cell. A cell is a row/column intersection. |
| `get_group_number_cell` (*group column id* or *name, row number*); | No | Yes | Identifies the numeric value of a record group cell. A cell is a row/column intersection. |

*continues*

**Table A.1 Continued**

| Built-In Name/ Parameter Syntax | Restricted | Enter Query | Description |
|---|---|---|---|
| `get_group_row_count` (*record group id*, or *name*); | No | Yes | Identifies the number of rows in a specified record group. |
| `get_group_selection` (*record group id* or *name*, *selection number*); | No | Yes | Identifies the numeric position of the selected row in a record group. |
| `get_group_selection _count` (*record group id* or *name*); | No | Yes | Identifies the total number of rows programmatically marked as selected. |
| `get_item_property` (*item id* or *name*, *property*); | No | Yes | Identifies the value of the specified item property setting. |
| `get_list_element_count` (*list id* or); | No | Yes | Identifies the total number of values in a pick list. |
| `get_list_element_label` (*list id* or *name*, *list_index*); | No | Yes | Identifies the list label name value of the specified pick list item. |
| `get_list_element_value` (*list id* or *name*, *list index*); | No | Yes | Identifies the actual value of the specified pick list item. |
| `get_lov_property` (*list of values id* or *name*, *property*); | No | Yes | Identifies various list of values property settings. The properties are: *auto_refresh*, *group_name*, *height*, *width*, *x_pos*, and *y_pos*. |
| `get_menu_item_ property` (*menu item id* or *name*, *property*) | No | Yes | Identifies the state of the specified menu item. The properties are: *checked*, *enabled*, and *labeled*. |
| `get_message`; | No | Yes | Displays the current message. |
| `get_parameter_attr` (*list* or *name*, *parameter name*, *parameter type*, *value*); | No | Yes | Identifies the type and value of the specified parameter in a parameter list. The parameter types are: `data_parameter`, which indicates the value is the name of the group; and `text_parameter`, which indicates the parameter value is an actual data value. |

| Built-In Name/ Parameter Syntax | Restricted | Enter Query | Description |
|---|---|---|---|
| `get_parameter_list` (*list name*); | No | Yes | Identifies the parameter list ID for the specified list. |
| `get_radio_button_property` (*item name* or *id*, *button name*, *property*); | No | Yes | Identifies the value of the specified radio button property. The properties are: `displayed`, `enabled`, `height`, `label`, `visual_attribute`, `width`, `window_handle`, `x_pos`, and `y_pos`. |
| `get_record_property` (*record number*, *block name*, *property*); | No | Yes | Identifies the status of the specified record. The property that is supported is `status`. The various status values are: `new`, `changed`, `query`, and `insert`. |
| `get_relation_property` (*relation id* or *name*, *property*); | No | Yes | Identifies the state of the specified property. The properties are: `autoquery`, `deferred_coordination`, `detail_name`, `master_deletes`, `master_name`, `next_detail_relation`, `next_master_relation`, and `prevent_masterless_operation`. |
| `get_view_property` (*view id* or *name*, *property*); | No | Yes | Identifies the value of the specified view property. The properties are: `display_x_pos`, `display_y_pos`, `height`, `visible`, `width`, `window_name`, `x_pos_on_canvas`, and `y_pos_on_canvas`. |
| `get_window_property` (*window id* or *name*, *property*); | No | Yes | Identifies the value of the specified window property. The properties are: `height`, `remove_on_exit`, `title`, `visible`, `width`, `window_handle`, `window_size`, `window_state`, and `x_pos`. |
| `go_block` (*block name*); | Yes | No | Navigates to the specified block. |
| `go_form` (*form id* or *name*); | Yes | No | Navigates to the specified form in a multiform application. |
| `go_item` (*item name* or *id*) ; | Yes | Yes | Navigates to the specified item. |

*continues*

**Table A.1 Continued**

| Built-In Name/ Parameter Syntax | Restricted | Enter Query | Description |
|---|---|---|---|
| `go_record` (*record number*); | Yes | No | Navigates to the specified record. |
| `help;` | Yes | Yes | Shows the current item's hint message. |
| `hide_menu;` | No | Yes | Causes the current menu to disappear when operating on Character mode platforms. |
| `hide_view` (*view name* or *id*); | No | Yes | Causes the specified view to disappear. |
| `hide_window` (*window name* or *id*); | No | Yes | Causes the specified window to disappear. |
| `host` (*system command, screen action*); | No | Yes | Performs the specified operating system command. |
| `id_null` (*object id*); | No | Yes | Returns true if the specified object is available and false if not. |
| `image_zoom` (*image_id* or *name, zoom type, zoom factor*); | No | Yes | Changes the amount of the image seen by zooming in or out. Zoom types consist of: `adjust_to_fit`, `selection_rectangle`, `zoom_in_factor`, and `zoom_percent`. The zoom factor is a percentage. |
| `insert_record;` | Yes | No | Adds the current record to the database. |
| `issue_rollback` (*savepoint name*); | No | No | Issues the Rollback command. The *savepoint name* refers to the last time the data was committed. |
| `issue_savepoint` (*savepoint name*); | No | No | Issues a savepoint. |
| `item_enabled` (*menu name, item name*); | No | Yes | Returns a value of true when the menu item is enabled, and false when not. |
| `last_record;` | Yes | No | Displays the last record in the record buffer. |

| Built-In Name/ Parameter Syntax | Restricted | Enter Query | Description |
|---|---|---|---|
| `list_value` (*parameter value*); | Yes | No | Displays the list of values for the current item. The parameter values are: `no_restrict`, which tells Forms not to use the automatic search and complete feature; and `restrict`, which does the opposite. |
| `lock_record;` | No | No | Causes Forms Runtime to lock the corresponding row in the database. |
| `logon` (*user name, password, display logon screen on error*); | No | Yes | Causes the form to connect to the Oracle database. Specifying true in the display logon screen parameter causes Oracle to show the logon screen when the subprogram fails to connect with the database. |
| `logon_screen;` | No | Yes | Displays the database logon screen. |
| `logout;` | No | Yes | Logs off the database. |
| `main_menu;` | Yes | Yes | Displays the application's main menu. |
| `menu_clear_field;` | No | Yes | Removes characters in the current field to the right of the cursor position. |
| `menu_next_field;` | Yes | Yes | Moves the cursor to the next field in an Enter Parameter Values dialog box. |
| `menu_parameter;` | No | Yes | Shows all the current menu's parameters in the Enter Parameter Values dialog box along with their values. |
| `menu_previous_field;` | No | Yes | Moves the cursor to the previous field in the Enter Parameter Values dialog box. |
| `menu_redisplay;` | No | Yes | Redraws the screen in a menu. |
| `menu_show_keys;` | No | Yes | Displays the Function Keys dialog box. |

*continues*

**Table A.1 Continued**

| Built-In Name/ Parameter Syntax | Restricted | Enter Query | Description |
|---|---|---|---|
| `message` ( *message literal, response* ); | No | Yes | Places the specified message on the message line. The response parameter has two values: `acknowledge`, which displays a modal alert the operator must dismiss; or `no_acknowledge`, which tells Oracle that no response is necessary when two messages are issued. |
| `message_code`; | No | Yes | Identifies the number of the most recently generated message. |
| `message_text`; | No | Yes | Returns the text for the most recently generated message. |
| `message_type`; | No | Yes | Identifies the type of message. Valid types are: `Ora`, Oracle database message; `FRM`, Forms error; or `Null`, no message was issued. |
| `move_window` (*window id* or *name, x, y*); | No | Yes | Changes the location of the window. The `x` parameter is the horizontal setting and y the vertical setting. |
| `name_in` (*variable*); | No | Yes | Identifies the value of the specified variable. |
| `new_form` (*form name, rollback mode, query mode, parameter list id* or *parameter list name* ); | Yes | No | Closes the existing form and initiates a `to_savepoint`, all the current form's changes are rolled back to the last savepoint; `no_rollback`, no rollback occurs on the current form; and `full_rollback`, all uncommitted changes are rolled back. Form name refers to the name of the form. The Query mode setting determines whether the form is executed in query only mode. The parameter list name identifies the list of parameters passed to the new application. |

| Built-In Name/ Parameter Syntax | Restricted | Enter Query | Description |
|---|---|---|---|
| `next_block;` | Yes | No | Moves the cursor to the next block. This block is determined by the sequence setting. |
| `next_form;` | Yes | No | Navigates to the next form in a multiform application. |
| `next_item;` | Yes | Yes | Moves the cursor to the next item as determined by the item sequence. |
| `next_key;` | Yes | Yes | Moves the cursor to the next item that is a primary key item. The primary key must be enabled and navigable. |
| `next_menu_item;` | Yes | Yes | Moves the cursor to the next menu item. |
| `next_record;` | Yes | No | Displays the next record in the record buffer. |
| `next_set;` | Yes | No | Retrieves the next set of records from the database and moves the cursor to the first record. |
| `open_form` (*form name*, *activate*, *session*, *parameter id* or *parameter list*); | Yes | No | Opens the specified form. The activate parameter settings are: `activate`, makes the opened form the current form; `no_activate`, leaves the current form the focus. The session parameters are: `no_session`, tells Oracle the opened form will use the same database as the other forms; `session`, tells Oracle a new database session needs to be created. |
| `paste_region;` | Yes | Yes | Pastes the contents of the clipboard buffer at the cursor location. |
| `pause;` | No | Yes | Halts form processing until the user presses a function key. |
| `populate_group` (*group name* or *id*); | No | Yes | Runs the record group query, returning a number indicating success (0) or failure (not 0). |

*continues*

**Table A.1 Continued**

| Built-In Name/ Parameter Syntax | Restricted | Enter Query | Description |
|---|---|---|---|
| populate_group _with_query (*record group id* or *name, query*); | No | Yes | Replaces the rows of a record group with the results of the query. |
| populate_list (*list id* or *name, record group id* or *name*); | No | Yes | Replaces the contents of a picklist with the values from the specified record group. |
| post; | Yes | No | Sends the data from the form to the database without committing it. |
| previous_block; | Yes | No | Moves the cursor to the previous block. This block is determined by the sequence setting. |
| previous_form; | Yes | No | Navigates to the previous form in a multiple form application. |
| previous_item; | Yes | Yes | Moves the cursor to the previous item as determined by the item sequence. |
| previous_menu; | Yes | Yes | Moves the cursor to the previously active menu. |
| previous_menu _item; | Yes | Yes | Moves the cursor to the previous menu item. |
| previous_record; | Yes | No | Displays the previously displayed record in the record buffer. |
| print; | No | Yes | Performs a screen print of the current window. |
| query_parameter (*parameter literal*); | No | Yes | Shows the Query Parameter dialog box, which shows the values of the specified parameters. |
| read_image_file (*file name, file type, item name* or *id*); | No | Yes | Displays an image from the specified file in a Forms image item. |
| redisplay; | No | Yes | Clears existing messages and reinitiates the screen. |

| **Built-In Name/ Parameter Syntax** | **Restricted** | **Enter Query** | **Description** |
|---|---|---|---|
| `replace_content view` (*window name* or,*view name* or *id*); | No | Yes | Changes the content canvas_view in the current window. |
| `replace_menu` (*menu file name, menu type, initial menu name, group name, use_file* ; | No | Yes | Substitutes the new menu for the current menu. |
| `reset_group_ selection` (*record group id* or *record group name*); | Yes | No | Unselects rows currently selected in a group. |
| `resize_window` (*window id* or *name, width, height*); | No | Yes | Changes the size of the window to the specified dimensions. |
| `retrieve_list` (*list id* or *name, record group id* or *name*); | No | Yes | Places the current list into the specified record group. |
| `run_product` (*Oracle product, file, communications* style, execution style, *location, list* or *name, display*); | No | Yes | Starts the specified Oracle product and executes the file. The communications settings are: synchronous, which tells Oracle to return control to Forms after the new product has closed; and asynchronous, which tells Oracle to return control immediately. The execution settings are: batch or runtime. The location setting determines where the file the product will execute is located. The list or name variable specifies the parameter list to be passed to the product. The display variable specifies the name of the Forms chart item that will display the chart generated by Graphics. |
| `scroll_down;` | Yes | No | Displays the next set of records from the record buffer. |

*continues*

**Table A.1 Continued**

| Built-In Name/ Parameter Syntax | Restricted | Enter Query | Description |
|---|---|---|---|
| `scroll_up;` | Yes | No | Displays the previously displayed set of records from the record buffer. |
| `scroll_view` (*view name* or *id*, *x*, *y*); | No | Yes | Repositions the view by changing the horizontal (x) and vertical (y) canvas property settings. |
| `select_all;` | Yes | Yes | Grabs or selects the text in the current item. |
| `select_records;` | Yes | No | Starts the Forms select processing. |
| `set_alert_property` (*alert id* or *name*, *alert_message_text*, *message*); | No | Yes | Changes the message text displayed in the alert. The alert message property (second parameter) is `alert_message _text`. |
| `set_application _property` (*property*, *setting*); | No | Yes | Changes a property of the current application. The property used is `cursor_style`. The values for this property are: `busy`, `crosshair`, `default`, `help`, and `insertion`. |
| `set_block_property` (*block name* or *id*, *property*, *value*); | No | Yes | Changes a block property setting. |
| `set_canvas_property` (*canvas id* or *name*, *property*, *value* or [*x*, *y*]); | No | Yes | Changes the value of a canvas property. The properties are: `height`, `width`, and `visual_ attribute`. |
| `set_form_property` (*form name* or *form id*, *property*, *value*); | No | Yes | Changes a form property. |
| `set_group_char_cell` (*group column name* or *id*, *row number*, *value*); | No | Yes | Changes the value of a character group cell. |
| `set_group_date_cell` (*group column name* or *id*, *row number*, *value*); | No | Yes | Changes the value of a date group cell. |

| Built-In Name/ Parameter Syntax | Restricted | Enter Query | Description |
|---|---|---|---|
| set_group_number _cell (*group column name* or *id*, *row number*, *value*); | No | Yes | Changes the value of a numeric group cell. |
| set_group_ selection (*record group name* or *id*, *row number*); | No | Yes | Selects or tags the specified row of a record group. |
| set_input_focus (*menu*); | No | Yes | Changes the input focus to the current form's menu. |
| set_item_property (*item id* or *name*, *property*, *value* or [*x*, *y*]); | No | Yes | Changes an item's property setting. |
| set_lov_property (*list-of-values id* or *name*, *property*, *value* or [*x*, *y*]); | No | Yes | Changes the specified list-of-values property. |
| set_menu_item _property (*menu item id*, *property*, *value*); | No | Yes | Changes the value of a menu property. The properties are: checked, displayed, enabled, and label. The value parameters consist of: property_true and property_false. |
| set_parameter attr (*list* or _ *name*, *parameter name*, *parameter type*, *value*); | No | Yes | Changes the type and value of the specified parameter in a parameter list. |
| set_radio_button _property (*item id* or *name*, *button name*, *property*, *value* or [*x*, *y*]); | No | Yes | The properties are: displayed, enabled, height, label, visual_ attribute, width, window_handle, x_pos, and y_pos. |
| set_record_ property (*record number*, *block name*, *property*, *value*); | No | Yes | Changes the specified record status property. The values are: changed_ status, insert_status, new_status, and query_status. |

*continues*

**Table A.1 Continued**

| Built-In Name/ Parameter Syntax | Restricted | Enter Query | Description |
|---|---|---|---|
| `set_relation_property` (*relation id* or *name*, *property*, *value*); | No | Yes | Changes the specified relation property. |
| `set_timer` (*timer id* or *name*, *milliseconds*, *iterate*); | No | Yes | Modifies the setting of a timer. The millisecond parameter can be set between `1` to `2147483648`. The `no_change` value keeps the current setting. The iterate values are: `repeat`, `no_repeat`, and `no_change`. |
| `set_view_property` (*view id* or *name*, *property*, *value* or [*x*, *y*]; | No | Yes | Changes a `canvas-view` property. |
| `set_window_property` (*window id* or *name*, *property*, *value* or [*x*, *y*]); | No | Yes | Changes a window property setting |
| `show_alert` (*alert id* or *name*); | No | Yes | Initiates the specified alert, and returns a value that corresponds to the chosen button. |
| `show_background _menu;` | No | Yes | Exhibits the background menu. |
| `show_editor` (editor id or name, text in, [x, y] optional, text out, result); | No | Yes | Initiates the editor at the specified location. It passes a text string in and out of the editor. |
| `show_keys;` | No | Yes | Exhibits the Forms function key dialog. |
| `show_lov` (*list-of-values id* or *name*, [*x*, *y*]); | Yes | Yes | Exhibits the specified list of values. This built-in subprogram returns a Boolean value. It should be included as part of an equality expression (such as `a = show_lov (lov name);` |
| `show_menu;` | No | Yes | Activates and exhibits the current menu. |

| Built-In Name/ Parameter Syntax | Restricted | Enter Query | Description |
|---|---|---|---|
| `show_view` (*view id* or *name*); | No | Yes | Exhibits the specified `canvas-view`. |
| `show_window` (*window id* or *name*, [*x*, *y*] ); | No | Yes | Exhibits the specified window at the `x`, `y` coordinates. |
| `synchronize`; | No | Yes | Allows Oracle to update the display only if two conditions are met: Navigation to a new `canvas-view` has occurred and Forms is at the item level. |
| `terminate`; | Yes | No | Stops entry of values into the form or dialog box. |
| `unset_group_selection` (*record group id* or *name*, *row number*); | No | Yes | Unselects rows that were marked by the `set_group_selection`. |
| `up`; | Yes | No | Displays the previous record from the record buffer. |
| `update_record`; | Yes | No | Causes Forms to update the database with the form modifications. |
| `user_exit` (*expression*, *error text* ); | No | Yes | Initiates the user exit contained in the expression parameter. |
| `validate` (*parameter*); | No | Yes | Causes Forms to execute validation processing based on the scope of the parameter value. The values are: `default_scope`, `form_scope`, `record_scope`, and `item_scope`. |
| `vbx.fire_event` (*item id* or *name*, *event*, *parameter list id* or *name*); | No | Yes | Initiates an event for a VBX control. |
| `vbx.get_property` (*item id* or *name*, *property*); | No | Yes | Identifies the value of a VBX control property. |
| vbx.get_value_property (*item id* or *name*); | No | Yes | Obtains the VBX control value property of a VBX control. |

*continues*

**Table A.1 Continued**

| Built-In Name/ Parameter Syntax | Restricted | Enter Query | Description |
|---|---|---|---|
| `vbx.invoke_method` (*item id* or *name*, *method name*, *w*, *x*, *y*, *z*); | No | Yes | Performs the argument contained in the method name on the item. |
| `vbx.set_property` (*item id* or *name*, *property*, *value*); | No | Yes | Changes the specified VBX control property. |
| `vbx.set_value_ property` (*item id* or *name*,*property*); | No | Yes | Changes the specified VBX control value property. |
| `where_display;` | No | Yes | Changes the value of the Where menu navigation option. The values are on or off. |
| `write_image_file` (*image file*, *file type*, *item id* or *name*); | No | Yes | Places the image from an Oracle Forms image item into a file. |

APPENDIX B

# Triggers

Triggers are procedures performed when a particular event occurs. A myriad of events can fire the trigger. The names of the triggers in Oracle Forms mirror the event that initiates them. This appendix describes the various available triggers.

Oracle Forms has nine different types of triggers. The types are discussed in the following bullet list. Each type also has a code that will be used in Table B.1 to denote the trigger type. ■

- *Block processing*—These triggers are initiated when an event happens on a block. The trigger type code is "B."
- *Interface event*—These triggers are initiated through an action by a user. The trigger type code is "I."
- *Key*—These triggers are initiated by the actual or simulated pressing of a keyboard key. The trigger type code is "K."
- *Master-detail*—These triggers are used to keep multiple blocks on a form in sync. They are fired when conditions occur on the form that require Forms to synchronize actions. The trigger type code is "MD."
- *Message-handling*—These triggers are fired when messages are sent to the form. The trigger type code is "MH."
- *Navigation*—These triggers are fired during a form navigation procedure. The trigger type code is "N."
- *Query*—These triggers are fired as a result of a form query. The trigger type code is "Q."
- *Transaction*—These triggers are fired during an Oracle Form transaction or procedure. The trigger type code is "T."
- *Validation*—These triggers are fired as a result of an Oracle Form validation procedure. The trigger type code is "V."

Triggers may also be defined at the form, block, or item level. You can determine the trigger's usage by looking for "FRM," "BLK," and "ITM" codes in the Usage or "USG" column. These codes mean Form, Block, and Item, respectively.

Some of the triggers may not be fired in the Query mode. This quality is contained by a value of "Yes" or "No" in the Query or "QRY" column.

Finally, triggers accept only certain commands. These are Select statements, restricted built_in subprograms, unrestricted built-in subprograms, PL/SQL, or data manipulation language (DML) commands. The appendix carries values of "SEL" (Select), "RES" (Restricted), "UNRES" (Unrestricted), "PL/SQ" (PL/SQL), "DML" (Data Manipulation Language), or "All" in the Restricted or "RES" column to denote these qualities. The "ALL" designation means that you can use all the commands.

**Table B.1—Valid Triggers and Trigger Characteristics**

| Name | TYP | USG | QRY | RES | Description |
|---|---|---|---|---|---|
| Key-Clrblk | K | FRMBLKITM | No | SELRESUNRES | Simulates the pressing of the Clear Block function key. This executes the clear_block built-in subprogram. Clears the current block of values. |

| Name | TYP | USG | QRY | RES | Description |
|---|---|---|---|---|---|
| Key-Clrfrm | K | FRMBLKITM | No | SELRESUNRES | Simulates the pressing of the Clear Form function key. This executes the clear_form built-in subprogram, which clears the current form of values. |
| Key-Clrrec | K | FRMBLKITM | No | SELRESUNRES | Simulates the pressing of the Clear Record function key. This executes the clear_record built-in subprogram, which clears the current record of values. |
| Key-Commit | K | FRMBLKITM | No | SELRESUNRES | Simulates the pressing of the Accept function key. This executes the commit built-in subprogram, which permanently saves the data changes. |
| Key-Cquery | K | FRMBLKITM | Yes | SELRESUNRES | Simulates the pressing of the Count Query Hits function key. This executes the count_query built-in subprogram, which counts the number of records a query will return. |
| Key-Crerec | K | FRMBLKITM | No | SELRESUNRES | Simulates the pressing of the Insert Record function key. This executes the create_record built-in subprogram, which places the current record in the input mode. |

*continues*

**Table B.1 Continued**

| Name | TYP | USG | QRY | RES | Description |
|---|---|---|---|---|---|
| Key-Delrec | K | FRMBLKITM | No | SELRESUNRES | Simulates the pressing of the Delete Record function key. This executes the delete_record built-in subprogram, which removes the current record from the screen and marks the database record for permanent removal. |
| Key-Down | K | FRMBLKITM | No | SELRESUNRES | Simulates the pressing of the Down function key. This executes the down built-in subprogram, which navigates to the next record. |
| Key-Dup-Item | K | FRMBLKITM | No | SELRESUNRES | Simulates the pressing of the Duplicate Item function key. This executes the duplicate_item built-in subprogram, which copies the value from the same item in the previous record into the item in the current record. |
| Key-Duprec | K | FRMBLKITM | No | SELRESUNRES | Simulates the pressing of the Duplicate Record function key. This executes the duplicate_record built-in subprogram, which copies the values from the previous record into the current record. |

| Name | TYP | USG | QRY | RES | Description |
|---|---|---|---|---|---|
| Key-Edit | K | FRMBLKITM | Yes | SELRESUNRES | Simulates the pressing of the Edit function key. This executes the edit_text_item built-in subprogram, which displays the item's defined text editor. |
| Key-Entqry | K | FRMBLKITM | Yes | SELRESUNRES | Simulates the pressing of the Enter Query function key. This executes the enter_query built-in subprogram, which places the current block in the Enter Query mode. |
| Key-Exeqry | K | FRMBLKITM | Yes | SELRESUNRES | Simulates the pressing of the Execute Query function key. This executes the execute_query built-in subprogram, which executes a database query and places the form in the Input mode. |
| Key-Exit | K | FRMBLKITM | Yes | SELRESUNRES | Simulates the pressing of the EXIT function key. This executes the exit_form built-in subprogram, which closes the current form. When the form is in the input mode, this trigger places the block in the input mode. |
| Key-*[F0 .......F9]* | K | FRMBLKITM | Yes | SELRESUNRES | Fires when the associated function key [F0, F1, F2, F3, F4, F5, F6, F7, F8, or F9] is pressed. |

*continues*

**Table B.1 Continued**

| Name | TYP | USG | QRY | RES | Description |
|---|---|---|---|---|---|
| Key-Help | K | FRMBLKITM | Yes | SELRESUNRES | Simulates the pressing of the HELP function key. This executes the help built-in subprogram, which displays the current item's hint message. |
| Key-Listval | K | FRMBLKITM | Yes | SELRESUNRES | Simulates the pressing of the List of Values function key. This executes the show_lov built-in subprogram, which displays this list of values for the current item. |
| Key-Menu | K | FRMBLKITM | No | SELRESUNRES | Simulates the pressing of the Block Menu function key. This executes the show_menu built-in subprogram, which displays the current menu. |
| Key-Nxtblk | K | FRMBLKITM | No | SELRESUNRES | Simulates the pressing of the Next Block function key. This executes the next_block built-in subprogram, which navigates to the next block in the form. |
| Key-Nxt-Item | K | FRMBLKITM | Yes | SELRESUNRES | Simulates the pressing of the Next Item function key. This executes the next_item built-in subprogram, which navigates to the next item in the form. |
| Key-Nxtkey | K | FRMBLKITM | No | SELRESUNRES | Simulates the pressing of the Next Primary Key function key. This executes the next_key |

| Name | TYP | USG | QRY | RES | Description |
|---|---|---|---|---|---|
| | | | | | built-in subprogram, which navigates to the next item defined as a primary key. |
| Key-Nxtrec | K | FRMBLKITM | No | SELRESUNRES | Simulates the pressing of the Next Record function key. This executes the next_record built-in subprogram, which navigates to the next record in the record buffer. |
| Key-Nxtset | K | FRMBLKITM | No | SELRESUNRES | Simulates the pressing of the Next Set Of Records function key. This executes the next_set built-in subprogram, which displays the next set of records from the record buffer. |
| Key-Others | K | FRMBLKITM | Yes | SELRESUNRES | Fires when a function key not currently defined by the form or by Oracle is pressed. |
| Key-Print | K | FRMBLKITM | Yes | SELRESUNRES | Simulates the pressing of the Print function key. This executes the print built-in subprogram, which screen prints the current form. |
| Key-Prvblk | K | FRMBLKITM | No | SELRESUNRES | Simulates the pressing of the Previous Block function key. This executes the previous_block built-in subprogram, which navigates to the previous block in the current form. |

*continues*

**Table B.1 Continued**

| Name | TYP | USG | QRY | RES | Description |
|---|---|---|---|---|---|
| Key-Prv-Item | K | FRMBLKITM | Yes | SELRESUNRES | Simulates the pressing of the Previous Item function key. This executes the previous_item built-in subprogram, which navigates to the previous item in the form. |
| Key-Prvrec | K | FRMBLKITM | No | SELRESUNRES | Simulates the pressing of the Previous Record function key. This executes the previous_record built-in subprogram, which navigates to the previously displayed record in the record buffer. |
| Key-Scrdown | K | FRMBLKITM | No | SELRESUNRES | Simulates the pressing of the Scroll Down function key. This executes the scroll_down built-in subprogram, which displays the next set of records from the record buffer. |
| Key-Scrup | K | FRMBLKITM | No | SELRESUNRES | Simulates the pressing of the Scroll Up function key. This executes the scroll_up built-in subprogram, which displays the previously displayed set of records from the record buffer. |
| Key-Up | K | FRMBLKITM | No | SELRESUNRES | Simulates the pressing of the UP function key. This executes the up built-in subprograms, which display the |

| Name | TYP | USG | QRY | RES | Description |
|---|---|---|---|---|---|
| | | | | | previously displayed record from the record buffer. |
| Key-Updrec | K | FRMBLKITM | No | SELRESUNRES | Executes the lock_record built-in subprogram, which locks the form's associated database record. |
| On-Check-Delete-Master | MD | FRMBLK | No | SELDMLUNRES | This trigger is created by Forms when multiple blocks are created. It fires when an attempt is made to delete a record from the master block. |
| On-Check-Unique | T | FRMBLK | No | SELPL/ SQUNRES | This trigger fires previous to a database commit. It checks the database to ensure that values contained in items marked in Oracle Forms as primary keys do not exist in the associated database columns. |
| On-Clear-Details | MD | FRMBLK | No | ALL | This trigger fires when an event occurs on the master block that dictates the need for form coordination. An example would be navigating to the next record. |
| On-Close | T | FRM | No | SELPL/ SQUNRES | This trigger fires when the last record in a query has been displayed or the query has been aborted. |

*continues*

**Table B.1 Continued**

| Name | TYP | USG | QRY | RES | Description |
|---|---|---|---|---|---|
| On-Column-Security | T | FRMBLK | No | SELPL/ SQUNRES | This trigger fires when Forms enforces column-level security. The block level Column Security property must be set to on. |
| On-Commit | T | FRM | No | SELPL/ SQUNRES | This trigger fires when Oracle Forms attempts to commit records in the database. |
| On-Count | T | FRMBLK | Yes | SELPL/ SQUNRES | This trigger fires when Oracle counts the number of rows that will be returned in a query. |
| On-Delete | T | FRMBLK | No | SELDMLUNRES | This trigger fires when Oracle is marking the database record for delete. It fires after the Pre-Delete trigger and before the Post-Delete trigger. |
| On-Error | MH | FRMBLKITM | Yes | SELUNRES | This trigger fires when Oracle Forms would display an error message. |
| On-Fetch | T | FRMBLK | No | SELPL/ SQUNRES | This trigger is fired each time a record is fetched from the table to the form. |
| On-Insert | T | FRMBLK | No | SELDMLUNRES | This trigger fires when Oracle inserts or adds a record to the database. |

| Name | TYP | USG | QRY | RES | Description |
|---|---|---|---|---|---|
| On-Lock | T | FRMBLK | No | SELUNRES | This trigger fires when Oracle tries to lock a table record. This occurs when the user updates the first item on the form. |
| On-Logon | T | FRM | No | UNRES | This trigger fires when the Form tries to connect to the database. |
| On-Logout | T | FRM | No | SELUNRES | This trigger fires when the Form tries to break connection with the database. |
| On-Message | MH | FRMBLKITM | Yes | SELUNRES | This trigger fires when the form displays a message. |
| On-Populate-Details | MD | FRMBLK | No | SELPL/SQUNRESRES | This trigger fires when the form needs to populate the detail block in a multiple block form. |
| On-Rollback | T | FRM | No | SELPL/SQ | This trigger fires when a Rollback command is issued. |
| On-Savepoint | T | FRM | No | SELPL/SQUNRES | This trigger fires when a Savepoint command is issued. |
| On-Select | T | FRMBLK | No | SELPL/SQUNRES | This trigger fires when the Form tries to select records as a result of a query. |
| On-Sequence-Number | T | FRMBLKITM | No | SELUNRES | This trigger fires when the Form attempts to generate the next number from a database sequence. |

*continues*

**Table B.1 Continued**

| Name | TYP | USG | QRY | RES | Description |
|---|---|---|---|---|---|
| On-Update | T | FRMBLK | No | SELDMLUNRES | This trigger fires when the Form updates the database record. |
| Post-Block | N | FRMBLK | No | SELUNRES | This trigger fires when you navigate from the current block. |
| Post-Change | T | FRMBLKITM | No | SELUNRES | This trigger fires when Oracle determines the item was changed and is not null, a LOV item value is placed in the item, or a value is fetched into the item as a result of a query. |
| Post-Database-Commit | T | FRM | No | SELDMLUNRES | This trigger fires after changes have been permanently committed in the database. |
| Post-Delete | T | FRMBLK | No | SELDMLUNRES | This trigger fires when the deleted record is permanently removed from the table by a commit. |
| Post-Form | N | FRM | No | SELUNRES | This trigger fires when exiting a form. |
| Post-Forms-Commit | T | FRM | No | SELDMLUNRES | This trigger fires after the form changes have been made in the database and before they are committed. |
| Post-Insert | T | FRMBLK | No | SELDMLUNRES | This trigger fires after the record is added to the table during the commit phase. |
| Post-Logon | T | FRM | No | SELUNRES | This trigger fires after connecting to the database or after a successful on-logon trigger execution. |

| Name | TYP | USG | QRY | RES | Description |
|---|---|---|---|---|---|
| Post-Logout | T | FRM | No | SELUNRES | This trigger fires after the connection to the database is broken or after the on-logout trigger. |
| Post-Query | QT | FRMBLK | No | SELUNRES | This trigger fires each time a record is fetched or returned to the form. |
| Post-Record | N | FRMBLK | No | SELUNRES | This trigger fires whenever the input focus is moved to another record. |
| Post-Select | T | FRMBLK | No | SELUNRES | This trigger fires after the selection phase of the query or upon successful performance of the extra trigger. |
| Post-Text-Item | N | FRMBLKITM | No | SELUNRES | This trigger fires when the input focus leaves the current item. |
| Post-Update | T | FRMBLK | No | SELDMLUNRES | This trigger fires when the record is updated and committed in the database. |
| Pre-Block | N | FRMBLK | No | SELUNRES | This trigger fires prior to the cursor entering a new block. |
| Pre-Commit | T | FRM | No | SELDMLUNRES | This trigger fires after Forms determines there are changes to process and they are processed. |
| Pre-Delete | T | FRMBLK | No | SELDMLUNRES | This trigger fires before a row is deleted from the database. |
| Pre-Form | N | FRM | No | SELUNRES | This trigger fires upon entry into the form, at the form startup. |

*continues*

**Table B.1 Continued**

| Name | TYP | USG | QRY | RES | Description |
|---|---|---|---|---|---|
| Pre-Insert | T | FRMBLK | No | SELDMLUNRES | This trigger fires before a row is added to the database. |
| Pre-Logon | T | FRM | No | SELUNRES | This trigger fires prior to attempting to connect to the database. |
| Pre-Logout | T | FRM | No | SELUNRES | This trigger fires before disconnecting from the database. |
| Pre-Query | QT | FRMBLK | No | SELUNRES | This trigger fires prior to Forms executing a query. |
| Pre-Record | N | FRMBLK | No | SELUNRES | This trigger fires prior to navigation to another record. |
| Pre-Select | T | FRMBLK | No | SELUNRES | This trigger fires before Forms executes the Select statement that performs the query. |
| Pre-Text-Item | N | FRMBLKITM | No | SELUNRES | This trigger fires before the entry of the cursor into an item. |
| Pre-Update | T | FRMBLK | No | SELDMLUNRES | This trigger fires prior to the update of a database record. |
| User-Named | N | FRMBLKITM | No | All | This trigger fires when you call it explicitly from another trigger. |
| When-Button-Pressed | I | FRMBLKITM | Yes | SELRESUNRES | This trigger is fired when the user clicks a button. |
| When-Checkbox-Changed | I | FRMBLKITM | Yes | SELRESUNRES | This trigger fires when the user changes the state of the check box. |

| Name | TYP | USG | QRY | RES | Description |
|---|---|---|---|---|---|
| When-Clear-Block | B | FRMBLK | Yes | SELUNRES | This trigger fires prior to Forms clearing the block of values. |
| When-Create-Record | B | FRMBLK | No | SELUNRES | This trigger fires when Forms creates a new record. |
| When-Custom-Item-Event | I | FRMBLKITM | Yes | UNRES | This trigger fires when Forms encounters an event sent from a custom item. |
| When-Database-Record | B | FRMBLK | No | SELUNRES | This trigger fires when Forms marks a record for insert or update. |
| When-Image-Activated | I | FRMBLKITM | No | SELUNRES | This trigger fires when the user double-clicks an image item. |
| When-Image-Pressed | I | FRMBLKITM | Yes | SELRESUNRES | This trigger fires when the user single- or double-clicks on an image item. |
| When-List-Activated | I | FRMBLKITM | Yes | SELRESUNRES | This trigger fires when the user displays a pick list. |
| When-List-Changed | I | FRMBLKITM | Yes | SELRESUNRES | This trigger fires when the user selects a different item from a pick list. |
| When-Mouse-Click | I | FRMBLKITM | Yes | SELRESUNRES | This trigger fires when the mouse is clicked |
| When-Mouse-Doubleclick | I | FRMBLKITM | Yes | SELRESUNRES | This trigger fires when the mouse is double-clicked. |
| When-Mouse-Down | I | FRMBLKITM | Yes | SELUNRESRES | This trigger fires when the mouse is de-pressed. |
| When-Mouse-Enter | I | FRMBLKITM | Yes | SELRESUNRES | This trigger fires when the mouse enters an item or canvas. |

*continues*

**Table B.1 Continued**

| Name | TYP | USG | QRY | RES | Description |
|---|---|---|---|---|---|
| When-Mouse-Leave | I | FRMBLKITM | Yes | SELRESUNRES | This trigger fires when the mouse leaves the item or canvas. |
| When-Mouse-Move | I | FRMBLKITM | Yes | SELRESUNRES | This trigger fires when the mouse moves. |
| When-Mouse-Up | I | FRMBLKITM | Yes | SELRESUNRES | This trigger fires when the operator releases the mouse button after it has been depressed. |
| When-New-Block-Instance | N | FRMBLK | No | SELRESUNRES | This trigger fires when the cursor or input focus moves to an item in a different block. |
| When-New-Form-Instance | N | FRM | No | SELRESUNRES | This trigger fires when the cursor enters the first navigable item as the form is first initiated. |
| When-New-Item-Instance | N | FRMBLKITM | Yes | SELRESUNRES | This trigger fires when the cursor or input focus moves to another item. |
| When-New-Record-Instance | N | FRMBLK | Yes | SELRESUNRES | This trigger fires when the cursor or input focus is moved to a different record. |
| When-Radio-Changed | I | FRMBLKITM | Yes | SELRESUNRES | This trigger fires when the selected radio group button is changed. |
| When-Remove-Record | B | FRMBLKITM | No | SELUNRES | This trigger fires when the operator deletes a record. |
| When-Timer-Expired | I | FRM | Yes | SELRESUNRES | This trigger fires when a timer runs out of time. |
| When-Validate-Item | V | FRMBLKITM | No | SELUNRES | This trigger fires when Forms performs the item validation process. |

| Name | TYP | USG | QRY | RES | Description |
| --- | --- | --- | --- | --- | --- |
| When-Validate-Record | V | FRMBLK | No | SELUNRES | This trigger fires when Forms performs the record validation process. |
| When-Window-Activated | I | FRM | Yes | SELRESUNRES | This trigger fires when a window is made the current window. |
| When-Window-Closed | I | FRM | Yes | SELRESUNRES | This trigger fires when the window is closed by the operator. |
| When-Window-Deactivated | I | FRM | Yes | SELRESUNRES | This trigger fires when the window is deactivated. |
| When-Window-Resized | I | FRM | Yes | SELRESUNRES | This trigger fires when the window is resized. |

APPENDIX C

# System Variables

System variables are Oracle attributes that exist throughout a Form's runtime session. Variables contain important bits of information about various attributes that concern the Form. Some variables indicate current status and some have settings that tell the Form how to act. You can modify the behavior of your form by changing some of the variables.

A colon precedes the variables when it is used in an expression. The first part of the variable name, system, tells Oracle the variable is a system variable. The second part of the name following the dot notation is the variable name. Both the qualifier and the variable name must be used. The following is an example of a typical statement containing a system variable. The statement is assigning a value of 25 to the system variable :system.message_level.

```
:system.message_level = '25';
```

| Variable Name | Description |
|---|---|
| system.block_status | Contains the current status of the block. Three values can exist. The first is CHANGED, which indicates the block is holding at least one record that has been modified. The second is NEW, which indicates the block contains only unmodified records. The third value is QUERY, which indicates the block is in the Query mode. |
| system.coordination_operation | Used during block synchronization procedures. It is used in conjunction with the system.master_block variable. During the clearing phase of a block synchronization, the system.master_block contains the name of the master block, and the system.coordination_operation contains the name of the event that occurred on the master block that caused the on-clear-details trigger to fire. |
| system.current_block | Determines the position of the input focus. When it is in a block, record, or item, the value of this variable will be a block name. It will be Null when pre- and post-form triggers are firing. |
| system.current_datetime | Contains a character value of the current operating system date and time. The default format is DD-MON-YYYY HH24:MI:SS. |
| system.current_form | Contains the name of the current form. |
| system.current_item | Contains the name of the current field. The value will be Null when the cursor is moving from one item to another. |
| system.current_value | Contains the value of the item that is represented by the system.current_item variable. |
| system.cursor_block | Contains the name of the block in which the cursor is currently located. |
| system.cursor_item | Contains the name of the block and item in which the cursor is currently located. |
| system.cursor_record | Contains the number of the record in which the cursor is currently located. |
| system.cursor_value | Contains the value of the item in which the cursor is currently located. |
| system.custom_item_event | Contains the name of an event that was caused by a VBX control. |
| system.custom_item_event _parameters | Holds supplementary event arguments for a VBX control. |

| Variable Name | Description |
|---|---|
| system.date_threshold | Holds the database date requery threshold. The variable works with the $$DBDATE$$, $$DBDATETIME$$, and $$DBTIMES$$ variables to control how often Forms synchronizes the database date with the RDBMS. The format of the value is mi:ss. |
| system.effective_date | Sets the effective database date. The value has the following format: DD-MON-YYYY. HH24:MI:SS. |
| system.event_window | Holds the name of the last window affected by an action that resulted from a window event trigger firing. |
| system.form_status | Holds the status of the form that contains the cursor. The value can be one of the following: CHANGED, NEW, or QUERY. |
| system.last_query | Contains the Select statement used to populate a form block during the current session. |
| system.last_record | Contains a Boolean value indicating whether the current record is the last record in a block's set of records. |
| system.master_block | Works in conjunction with the system.coordinations_operation variable to determine the type of operation fired by the on-clear-details trigger. |
| system.message_level | Controls the display of error messages. Oracle error messages are assigned a value from 0 to 25, in increments of 5. Messages with a value less than this variable will not be displayed. The value should be enclosed by single quotes. |
| system.mode | Determines whether the form is in the Normal, Enter-Query, or Query processing mode. |
| system.mouse_button_pressed | Contains the number of the mouse button clicks. The far-left button has a value of one. The buttons increment by a value of one from left to right. |
| system.mouse_button_shift_state | Indicates the key pressed during the click. Examples of the value are SHIFT, CONTROL, or ALT. |
| system.mouse_canvas | Contains the name of the canvas in which the mouse input focus resides. |
| system.mouse_form | Contains the name of the form in which the mouse input focus resides. |

*continues*

*continued*

| Variable Name | Description |
|---|---|
| system.mouse_item | Contains the name of the item in which the mouse input focus resides. |
| system.mouse_record | Contains the number of the record in which the mouse input focus resides. |
| system.mouse_record_offset | Contains the number of the visible record in which the mouse input focus resides. |
| system.mouse_x_pos | Contains the value of the mouse x-coordinate position. |
| system.mouse_y_pos | Contains the value of the mouse y-coordinate position. |
| system.record_status | Contains the status of the record in which the mouse is located. The values are CHANGED, INSERT, NEW, and QUERY. |
| system.suppress_working | Contains a Boolean value that suppresses the `working...` message displayed by the form during runtime. True will prevent the display of the message. False will not prevent the message. |
| system.trigger_block | Contains the name of the block where the cursor was located when the current trigger was fired. |
| system.trigger_item | Contains the name of the block and item where the cursor was located when the current trigger was fired. |
| system.trigger_record | Contains the number of the record that Forms is processing. |

APPENDIX D

# Practice Database Installation Instructions

The examples used in this book require an Oracle7 database and the Developer 2000 tool products. If you do not have access to this database or the tools, a trial version may be obtained from Oracle. This trial version contains a copy of Personal Oracle7 and the complete Developer 2000 tool kit. At the time of this writing, Oracle allows interested parties to download the products from their Web site for a 60-day evaluation at no cost. For $15, Oracle will send a CD to you. I received a trial copy and installed it on my PC with no trouble. I would like to caution that this offer may be withdrawn at any time by Oracle and may not be available to you. Oracle's Web site address is **http//www.oracle.com/**. I strongly urge you to visit the site and check the availability of trial products.

If you do not have access to Personal Oracle7 and the Developer 2000 tools on your PC, you may be able to access the products at your place of employment. Oracle7 is normally used in the client/server environment. Your place of employment is probably using Oracle7 and the Developer 2000 tool set on a server. Contact your database administrator (DBA) to see if a user id and tablespace can be set up for the practice database. The database can be easily installed on the server by your DBA.

The database used for practice throughout this book consists of seven tables. The tables are identified in Table D.1. ■

**Table D.1 Practice Database Tables**

| Table Name | Description |
|---|---|
| Department | Contains employee department attributes. |
| Employee | Contains employee attributes. |
| Glasses | Contains records on employee eyeglass purchases. |
| Sectab | Used for security examples. This table is normally empty. |
| Tools | Used for employee tool purchase records. |
| Wge_maint | A wage maintenance table. It is normally empty. |

The database can be installed in your Oracle7 database by using either one of two methods. The first is to import the tables by using Oracle's import/export facilities. This is the quickest and easiest method. The second is to create the tables and load them by using SQL*LOADER. The CD has the files and data for both options. The following describes each of the methods.

# Importing the Database

Personal Oracle7 comes with import and export facilities. The import facility is used to put the tables into the database. This icon is located in the Personal Oracle7 group. Figure D.1 displays the Personal Oracle program group icons and among them is the Import tool icon.

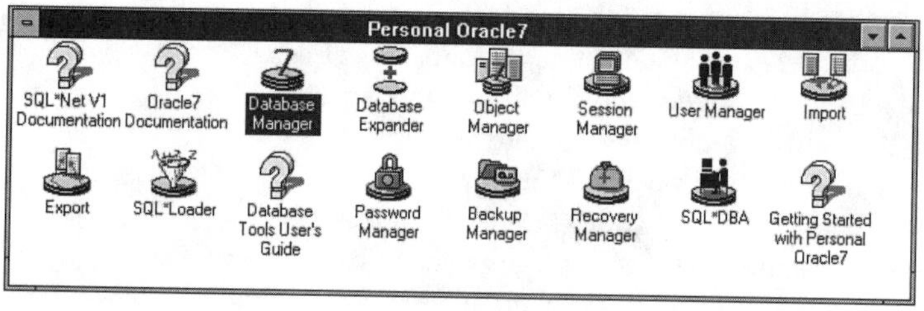


**FIG. D.1**
The Personal Oracle7 icon group and the Import facility.

Double-clicking this icon opens the Import dialog box. A modal dialog box requesting Database Logon information appears. Enter the values of a user id with DBA privileges. The default Personal Oracle user id and password is "system/manager." Click OK when done. The Database Importer dialog box appears, as shown in Figure D.2.

The dialog box has three settings. The first is the name of the Import file. It is called EMPEXP.DMP and is on the CD. The Users radio button should be clicked within the Import mode. The User to Import window should contain the name of the user id that will receive the tables. In Figure D.2 the user id is test_user. The default user_id in Personal Oracle7 is "scott." If a different user id is used, it must be created. The window should contain the name of the id that is sending the data. This id is "scott." The Specify button can be used to call a dialog box that will allow you to input the proper user ids.

**FIG. D.2**
The Database Importer dialog box.

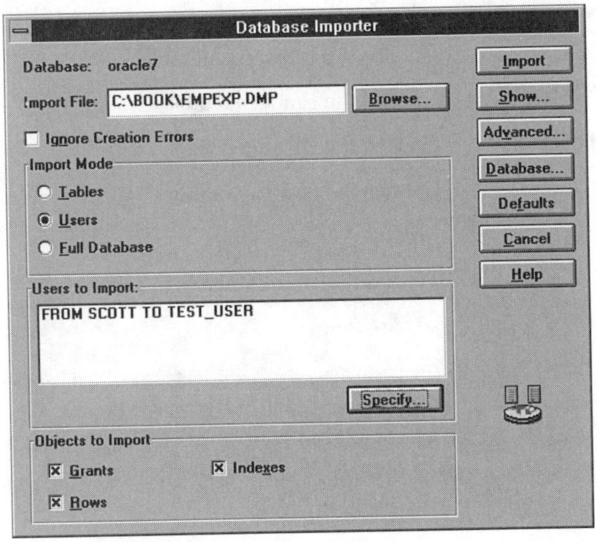




Click the Import button to import the tables into the user id. The server will process the Import request, then, if it is successful, a dialog box will appear stating that the Import procedure was successful. A dialog box will appear stating that the import procedure was successful. If the process is not successful, the server sends an exception (error) message to the user interface.

**NOTE** If you are using Personal Oracle7, be sure to start the database before employing either of the two methods. The Personal Oracle7 icon group has a Database Manager tool that can be used to start the database. The default password is oracle. The password does not include parentheses.

If you are using Personal Oracle7 for Win95, Oracle7 version 7.2, or Oracle8, the tool icons or folders have changed. The procedure to import the data has remained fundamentally the same.

# Creating and Loading Your Tables

The second method is to create and load the tables. If you are using Oracle7 on a server, have a DBA establish user id and tablespace for you. You must have the ability to create tables and to add, update, and delete records. The DBA must also grant you these privileges. If you are using Personal Oracle7, you can use the "scott/tiger" user account id. This is the default user id and has all of the needed privileges.

Log on to SQL*PLUS. Chapter 3, "Acquiring Data by Using the Select Statement," describes this process. Run the PL/SQL scripts listed in Table D.2, which are located on the CD.

**Table D.2 Table Create Programs**

| File Name | Description |
|---|---|
| DEPART.DDL | Creates the Department table. |
| EMPLOYEE.DDL | Creates the Employee table. |
| GLASSES.DDL | Creates the Glasses table. |
| SECTAB.DDL | Creates the Security table. |
| TOOLS.DDL | Creates the Tools table. |
| WGEMNT.DDL | Creates the Wage Maintenance Table. |

**NOTE** The tables should be created in the order in which they are listed in Table D.2. The files are executed by using the following syntax: run *drive\filepath\filename.*

The following command executes the first create file in Table D.2. It assumes the file is located on the CD drive or d drive: run d:\depart.ddl. Review Chapter 3, "Acquiring Data by Using the Select Statement," for further help in executing files.

After the tables have been created, the data may be loaded into them by using the SQL*LOADER product. If you are using Personal Oracle7, SQL*Loader is launched by clicking the icon located in the Personal Oracle7 group (see Figure D.1).

If the database is located on the server, SQL*Loader is launched by executing the sqlldr71.exe, sqlldr72.exe, sqlldr73.exe, or sqlldr80.exe files. The last two digits of the file name refer to the version of the Oracle database. The file is normally located in the \orawin\bin directory. If you cannot find the tools, contact your DBA.

Table D.3 contains the names of the load programs.

**Table D.3 Load Programs for the Practice Database**

| File Name | Description |
|---|---|
| LOADDEPT.CTL | Loads the Department table |
| EMP1.DAT | Loads the Employee table |
| GLA1.DAT | Loads the Glasses table |
| TOOL1.DAT | Loads the Tools table |

**NOTE** The tables should be loaded in the order in which they are listed in Table D.3. Review Chapter 10, "Using SQL*LOADER," to determine how to execute the files.

If you are unable to locate the SQL*LOADER icon, you may load the table by using line commands. To do so, perform the following:

1. Locate the SQL*LOADER executive program. This can be done by performing a hard drive search on the following character set: "sqlldr*.exe".
2. After locating the sqlldr72.exe, sqlldr73.exe, or sqlldr80.exe file, open the DOS Prompt window.
3. Change to the directory that contains SQL*LOADER.
4. Use the following line command to start SQL*LOADER: sqlldr72 scott. (This assumes the name of the SQL*LOADER program and the name of the Oracle user account.)
5. You will be prompted for the name of the control file. Use the name from table D3 (i.e., d:\loaddept.ctl, d:\emp1.dat, d:\gla1.dat, or d:\tool1.dat).
6. You will be prompted for the user account password. Enter the password. The default password for the scott user id is *tiger*.

APPENDIX E

# Answers to Practice Problems

At the end of most of the chapters are exercises for you to practice. This appendix contains the answers to those exercises. ■

# Chapter 2

## TRANSFORMER DATA FILE

| TRF# | DATE | MFG | TEST MODEL | TEST STATUS | TEST WEIGHT | TEST LOCATION | DATE1 | RESULT1 | DATE2 | RESULT2 |
|---|---|---|---|---|---|---|---|---|---|---|
| A100 | 09-JUL-85 | W | GO-5 | AHISTORY | 1000 | 9311Monroe | 08-JUL-85 | 70 | | |
| B670 | 10-SEP-86 | GE | W-97 | CURRENT | 2000 | 1719 Taylor | | | | |
| A101 | 12-SEP-91 | W | GO-5 | CURRENT | 1000 | 9311Monroe | 10-SEP-91 | 72 | | |
| A100 | 12-SEP-91 | W | GO-5 | CURRENT | 100 | STORES | 12-SEP-91 | 73 | | |
| B979 | 12-SEP-91 | GE | W-97 | CURRENT | 2000 | 8742 Pine | 11-SEP-91 | 94 | 11-OCT-91 | 76 |

After analyzing the database, you might have noticed a variety of problems. The most glaring is the need to create a new record for every transformer move. Not only is this time consuming, but also the clerk has made a mistake transfering the data to the new record. This is evident when looking at the weight attribute for transformer A100. The current weight is 100 and the previous weight was 1000. The clerk forgot to enter the last digit on the weight value when it was entered. Another mistake the clerk made was placing a letter A at the end of the model number in the first record. This mistake was corrected when the current record was created. However, during the time the A100 transformer was at the location, it had the wrong model number on the record. The model number is important information and the database does not have a mechanism to validate it.

Another problem with the database is the tests results. Each record has space for two test results. This causes several problems. When no tests have occurred, the database reserves space for the values. If you perform three or more tests on transformer you do not have any place to record the results unless you create a new record for the transformer. It is very difficult to compare the results of the tests because they are in different records in different fields.

The final problem was the manufacturer attribute. The data base contains codes for the various values. This was done so the clerk would not have as much data entry. But users not familiar with the values may have a hard time determining which manufacturers the values represent.

For instance, does the W manufacturer value refer to Wagner or Westinghouse.

*The next step is to identify the fields not dependent on the keys. Three fields meet this criteria: mfg, model, and status. You need to create three related tables. One will contain the mfg field and the manufacturer's full name. Use the model table as a validation table. Finally, a transformer history table will be created to hold historic transformer records. The final model is shown in Figure E.1.*

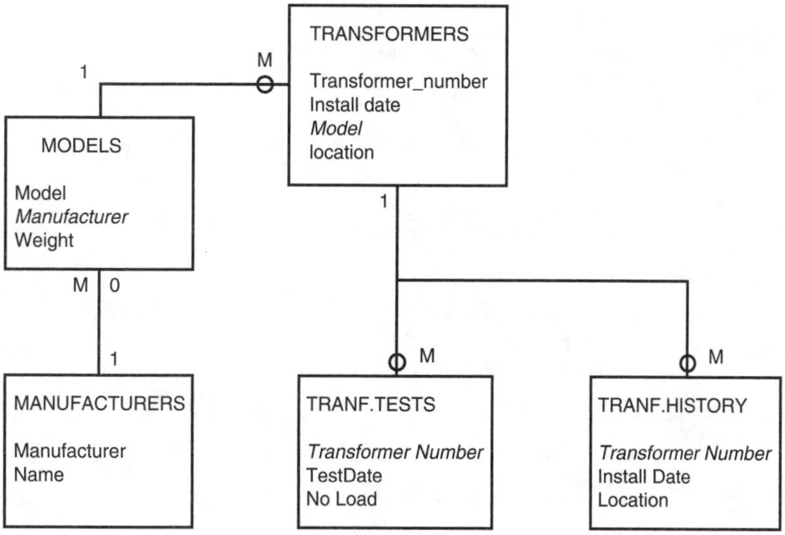


**FIG. E.1**
The Transformer history Table.

# Chapter 3

1. --a_03_01.sql--

```
describe department
desc employee
```

2. --a_03_02.sql--

```
select * from department;
```

3. --a_03_03.sql--

```
c\department\employee
l
```

4. --a_03_04.sql--

```
select last_name, first_name
from employee
order by last_name desc, first_name;
```

5. --a_03_05.sql--

```
select decode(gender, 'M', 'MALE', 'F', 'FEMALE', 'UNKNOWN'),
last_name, first_name
from employee;
```

6. --a_03_06.sql--

```
select last_name, first_name, gender
from employee
where gender = 'M';
```

7. --a_03_07.sql--

```
select last_name, gender, birth_date
from employee
where substr(birth_date, 4,3) = 'JUL'
and gender = 'M';
```

8. --a_03_08.sql--

```
select avg(nvl(wages, 0))
from employee;
```

9. --a_03_09.sql--

```
select fk_department, avg(nvl(wages,0)) "AVG WAGES"
from employee
group by fk_department;
```

10. --a_03_10.sql--

```
select last_name, first_name, wages, (((wages*.9)-150)/52) weekly
from employee
where fk_department ='INT';
```

11. --a_03_11.sql--

```
select last_name, first_name,
round(months_between(sysdate, employment_date)/12, 1) years
from employee
where fk_department = 'POL'
order by 3 desc;
```

12. --a_03_12.sql--

```
select fk_department, last_name, first_name, sysdate, employment_date,
round(months_between(sysdate, employment_date)/12, 1) seniority
from employee
where fk_department = 'POL'
and sysdate-employment_date = (select max(sysdate-employment_date)
from employee
where fk_department = 'POL');
```

13. --a_03_13.sql--

```
select fk_department, last_name, first_name
from employee
where wages > (select wages from employee
where last_name = 'TRUMAN')
and fk_department in ('INT', 'WEL');
```

14. --a_03_14.sql--

```
select first_name, last_name
from employee
where first_name like '_W%';
```

15. --a_03_15.sql--

```
select last_name, first_name
from employee
where last_name like '%V%T%';
```

16. --a_03_16.sql--

```
select fk_department, sum(nvl(wages, 0))
from employee
where fk_department != 'WEL'
group by fk_department;
```

17. --a_03_17.sql--

```
select initcap('mr. '|| rtrim(first_name)||' '||last_name) "NAME"
from employee;
```

18. --a_03_18.sql--

```
desc tab
select tname from tab;
```

# Chapter 4

1. --a_04_01.sql--

```
ttitle left tday center 'EMPLOYEES BY BIRTHDATE'
btitle newline left 'PAGE: ' sql.pno
column b heading 'BIRTH DATE' format a20
column a new_val tday noprint
select sysdate a, last_name, first_name,
       to_char(birth_date, 'dd-MON-YYYY') b
from employee;
ttitle off
btitle off
```

2. --a_04_02.sql--

```
ttitle left tday center 'EMPLOYEE WAGES' right 'PAGE: ' sql.pno skip 1 -
center 'BY' skip 1 center 'GENDER, WAGES'
column gender format a6 justify center
column a new_val tday noprint
column last_name heading 'LAST|NAME'
column wages center format '$99,999.99'
select sysdate a, gender, last_name, wages
from employee;
ttitle off
clear columns
```

3. --a_04_03.sql--

```
ttitle left tday center 'EMPLOYEE WAGES' right 'PAGE: ' sql.pno skip 1 -
       center 'BY' skip 1 center 'DEPT, GENDER, WAGES'
break on fk_department skip 2
column a new_val tday noprint
       column gender format a6
       column last_name heading 'LAST|NAME'
       column wages center format '$99,999.99'
       column fk_department heading 'DEPARTMENT' format a10
       select sysdate a, fk_department, gender, last_name, wages
       from employee
       order by 1, 4 desc;
       ttitle off
       clear columns
       clear breaks
```

App E

4. --a_04_04.sql--

```
ttitle left tday center 'EMPLOYEE WAGES' '   PAGE: ' sql.pno skip 1 -
center 'BY' skip 1 center 'GENDER, WAGES FOR DEPARTMENT ' dpt
break on fk_department page
column gender format a6
column a new_val tday noprint
column last_name heading 'LAST¦NAME'
column wages center format '$99,999.99'
column fk_department new_val dpt noprint
select sysdate a, fk_department, gender, last_name, wages
from employee
order by 2, 5 desc;
ttitle off
clear columns
clear breaks
```

5. --a_04_05.sql--

```
ttitle left tday center 'EMPLOYEE WAGES' '   PAGE: ' sql.pno skip 1 -
center 'BY' skip 1 center 'GENDER, WAGES FOR DEPARTMENT ' dpt
break on fk_department page
compute avg sum of wages on fk_department
column gender format a6
column a new_val tday noprint
column last_name heading 'LAST|NAME'
column wages center format '$99,999.99'
column fk_department new_val dpt noprint
column a new_val tday noprint
select sysdate a, fk_department, gender, last_name, wages
from employee
order by 2, 5 desc;
ttitle off
clear columns
clear breaks
```

6. --a_04_06.sql--

```
set termout off
ttitle left tday center 'EMPLOYEE WAGES' '   PAGE: ' sql.pno skip 1 -
center 'BY' skip 1 center 'GENDER, WAGES FOR DEPARTMENT ' dpt
break on fk_department page
compute avg sum of wages on fk_department
column gender format a6
column a new_val tday noprint
column last_name heading 'LAST|NAME'
column wages center format '$99,999.99'
column a new_val tday noprint
column fk_department new_val dpt noprint
spool a:a_04_06.txt
select sysdate a, fk_department, gender, last_name, wages
from employee
order by 2, 5 desc;
spool off
ttitle off
clear columns
clear breaks
set termout on
```

# Chapter 5

1. --a_05_01.sql--

```
select last_name, first_name, purchase_date, tool_name, tool_cost
from employee, tools
where payroll_number = fk_payroll_number;
```

2. --a_05_02.sql--

```
break on department_name on last_name on first_name page
column last_name noprint new_val ln
column first_name noprint new_val fn
column department noprint new_val dpt
column tool_name heading "TOOL NAME"
column purchase_date heading "PURCHASE|DATE" center format a8
column tool_cost heading "TOOL|COST" format $999.99
ttitle left sysdate center "TOOL PURCHASES FOR " ln', 'fn skip 1 -
  center "DEPARTMENT " dpt
select department_name, last_name, first_name, purchase_date, tool_name,
tool_cost,
       department
from employee, department, tools
where department = fk_department
    and payroll_number = fk_payroll_number(+)
order by 1,2, 3 desc;
ttitle off
clear break
clear columns
```

3. --a_05_03.sql--

```
select department_name, sum(cost)
from department, employee, glasses
where department = fk_department(+)
    and payroll_number = fk_payroll_number(+)
group by department_name
order by 2 desc;
```

4. --a_05_04.sql--

```
     select last_name, first_name, max(tools.purchase_date),
max(glasses.purchase_date)
from employee, glasses, tools
where payroll_number = tools.fk_payroll_number(+)
    and payroll_number = glasses.fk_payroll_number(+)
group by last_name, first_name;
```

5. --a_05_05.sql--

```
break on department_name on last_name on first_name page
column last_name noprint new_val ln
column first_name noprint new_val fn
column department noprint new_val dpt
column tool_name heading "TOOL/GLASSES NAME"
column purchase_date heading "PURCHASE|DATE" center format a8
column tool_cost heading "COST" format $999.99
ttitle left sysdate center "TOOL AND GLASSES PURCHASES FOR " ln || ' ' || fn
skip 1-
  center "DEPARTMENT " dpt
```

```
select department_name, last_name, first_name, purchase_date, tool_name,
tool_cost
from employee, department, tools
where department_number = fk_department_number
    and payroll_number = fk_payroll_number(+)
union
select department_name, last_name, first_name, purchase_name, optician, cost
from employee, department, glasses
where department_number = fk_department_number
   and payroll_number = fk_payroll_number(+)
order by 1,2, 3 desc;
ttitle off
clear break
clear columns
```

6. --a_05_06.sql--

```
select last_name, first_name
from employee, tools
where payroll_number = fk_payroll_number
minus
select last_name, first_name
from employee, glasses
where payroll_number = fk_payroll_number;
```

7. --a_05_07.sql--

```
break on department_name
select department_name, last_name, first_name
from department, employee
where department = fk_department
    and payroll_number in (select fk_payroll_number from glasses
      minus
      select fk_payroll_number from tools)
order by 1, 2;
clear break
```

8. --a_05_08.sql--

```
break on department_name
select department_name, last_name, first_name
from department, employee
where department = fk_department
    and payroll_number in (select fk_payroll_number from glasses
                                   intersect
                                       select fk_payroll_number from
➥tools)
order by 1, 2;
clear break
```

# Chapter 6

1. --a_06_01.sql--

```
create table transformer (serial_number char(10) , location varchar2(30),
           purchase_date date, cost number(6,2),
           manufacturer varchar2(15));
```

2. --a_06_02.sql--

```
alter table transformer modify (serial_number char(15));
alter table transformer add primary key (serial_number);
alter table transformer add (oil number(4));
```

3. --a_06_03.sql--

```
create index addind on transformer (location);
```

4. --a_06_04.sql--

```
create table transformer_tests (fk_serial_number char(15), test_date date,
          voltage number(3), amps number(3),
   overhauled char(1) check(overhauled in ('Y', 'N')),
   primary key (fk_serial_number, test_date),
          foreign key (fk_serial_number) references transformer on delete
➥cascade);
```

5. --a_06_05.sql--

```
create public synonym trf for transformer;

or

create synonym trf for transformer;

Note: The "scott" user account on Personnel Oracle7 does not have the
privileges to create public synonyms. You can use the system account to
perform this or create a synonym used on the "scott" user account only.
```

6. --a_06_06.sql--

```
create view glassescost as
          select payroll_number, last_name,
             first_name, fk_department, sum(cost) cost
            from employee, glasses
    where payroll_number = fk_payroll_number(+)
        group by payroll_number, last_name, first_name,
        fk_department;
create view deptcost1 as
          select department, sum(cost) deptcost
           from department, employee, glasses
           where payroll_number = fk_payroll_number(+)
               and department = fk_department
           group by department;
 select department, last_name, first_name,
  cost, deptcost, (cost/deptcost)*100 percent
  from glassescost, deptcost1
  where department = fk_department;
```

7. --a_06_07.sql--

```
drop table transformer_tests;
drop table transformer;
drop index addind;
drop view glassescost;
drop view deptcost1;
drop table t_and_d_cable_terminal_poles;
```

# Chapter 7

1. --a_07_01.sql--

```
insert into employee
 (payroll_number, last_name, first_name, birth_date, wages, street, city,
➥state,
              employment_date, social_security_number, current_position,
              phone, fk_department)
values (40, 'GORE', 'AL', '01-APR-48', 18567, '444 S. MAIN ST', 'NASHVILLE',
                       'TN', '20-JAN-92', '508-34-8912', 'BILL COLLECTOR',
                        '894-123-8765', 'POL');
```

2. --a_07_02.sql--

```
     insert into employee
 (payroll_number, last_name, first_name, birth_date, wages, street, city,
➥state,
    employment_date, social_security_number, current_position, phone,
fk_department)
values (41, 'QUAYLE', 'DAN', '04-DEC-47',  20456, '1600 PENNSYLVANIA AV',
                       'WASHINGTON', 'DC', to_date('20-JAN-2000',
➥'DD-MON-YYYY'),
                       '405-39-1212', 'CHIEF EXECUTIVE', '100-100-0001',
➥'POL') ;
```

3. --a_07_03.sql--

```
create table temp_employee as
  select * from employee;
delete from temp_employee;
insert into temp_employee
  select * from employee where fk_department = 'WEL';
```

4. --a_07_04.sql--

```
update temp_employee
  set wages = wages * 1.15;
```

5. --a_07_05.sql--

```
update temp_employee
      set wages = wages * 1.01
     where payroll_number not in (select fk_payroll_number from glasses);
```

6. --a_07_06.sql--

```
delete from employee where last_name = 'GORE' and first_name = 'AL';
select * from employee where last_name = 'GORE' and first_name = 'AL';
rollback;
delete from employee where last_name = 'GORE' and first_name = 'AL';
commit;
rollback;
select * from employee where last_name = 'GORE' and first_name = 'AL';
YES
```

7. --a_07_07.sql--

```
update employee a
set wages = (select wages from temp_employee
              where temp_employee.payroll_number = a.payroll_number)
where payroll_number in (select payroll_number from temp_employee);
```

8. --a_07_08.sql--

```
truncate table temp_employee;
rollback;
No
```

9. --a_07_09.sql--

```
drop table temp_employee;
```

# Chapter 8

1. --a_08_01.sql--

```
set serveroutput on;
begin
        dbms_output.put_line ('I am a PL/SQL guru');
end;
/
```

2. --a_08_02.sql--

```
set serveroutput on;
declare
  age       number;
begin
  select avg((employment_date - birth_date)/365)
     into age
  from employee;
  dbms_output.put_line (age);
end;
/
```

3. --a_08_03.sql--

```
set serveroutput on;
declare
  fname             employee.first_name%type;
  lname              employee.last_name%type;
  cursor a is select first_name, last_name from employee;
begin
  open a;
  loop
    fetch a into fname, lname;
    exit when a%notfound;
    dbms_output.put_line (lname||', '||fname);
  end loop;
end;
/
```

4. --a_08_04.sql--

```
set serveroutput on;
  declare
  e_rec               employee%rowtype;
  leap_yes_no                number;
  cursor a is select * from employee;
```

```
begin
  open a;
  loop
  fetch a into e_rec;
  if (a%notfound) then exit;
    end if;
  leap_yes_no := mod(to_number(to_char(e_rec.birth_date,'yy')),4);
  if leap_yes_no = 0 then
     dbms_output.put_line (e_rec.first_name||' '||e_rec.last_name||'was born
➥in'|| a leapyear');
  end if;
  end loop;
  close a;
end;
/
```

5. --a_08_07.sql--

```
set serveroutput on;
declare
  lname              employee.last_name%type;
begin
  select last_name into lname from employee
     where last_name = 'CLINTON' and first_name = 'HILLARY';
  dbms_output.put_line (lname);
exception
  when no_data_found then dbms_output.put_line ('No Records Found');
  end;
/
```

6. --a_08_06.sql--

```
set serveroutput on;
declare
  No_Record_Found           exception;
  Pragma excep_init      ('No_Record_Found', -1403);
  lname              employee.last_name%type;
begin
  select last_name into lname from employee
    where last_name = 'CLINTON'  and first_name = 'HILLARY';
exception
   when No_Record_Found then dbms_output.put_line ('No Records Found');
end;
/
```

7. --a_08_07.sql--

```
set serveroutput on;
declare
  emp_record              employee%rowtype;
  franklin_excep         exception;
  cursor a is select * from employee
    order by first_name;
begin
  open a;
  loop
    fetch a into emp_record;
    exit when a%notfound;
```

```
    if emp_record.first_name = 'FRANKLIN' then
      raise franklin_excep;
    end if;
  end loop;
  close a;
exception
  when franklin_excep then
    dbms_output.put_line('Encountered the Name Franklin');
end;
/
```

# Chapter 9

1. --a_09_01.sql--

```
serveroutput on;
declare
  e_rec      employee%rowtype;
  tot_tools      number;
  cursor emp is select payroll_number, last_name, first_name from employee;
  cursor tool is select count(*) from tools
                 where fk_payroll_number = e_rec.payroll_number;
begin
  open emp;
  fetch emp into e_rec.payroll_number, e_rec.last_name, e_rec.first_name;
  while (emp%found) loop
    open tool; fetch tool into tot_tools; close tool;
    dbms_output.put_line(e_rec.first_name||' '||e_rec.last_name||' '||
➥'purchased '||tot_tools||' tools');
    fetch emp into e_rec.payroll_number, e_rec.last_name, e_rec.first_name;
  end loop;
  close emp;
end;
/
```

2. --a_09_02.sql--

```
serveroutput on;
declare
  e_rec      employee%rowtype;
  tot_tools      number;
  cursor emp is select payroll_number, last_name, first_name from employee;
  cursor tool is select count(*) from tools
                 where fk_payroll_number = e_rec.payroll_number;
begin
  open emp;
  fetch emp into e_rec.payroll_number, e_rec.last_name, e_rec.first_name;
  while not emp%notfound loop
    open tool; fetch tool into tot_tools; close tool;
    dbms_output.put_line(e_rec.first_name||' '||e_rec.last_name||' '||
➥'purchased '||tot_tools¦¦' tools');
    fetch emp into e_rec.payroll_number, e_rec.last_name, e_rec.first_name;
  end loop;
  close emp;
end;
/
```

3. --_09_03a.sql--

```
serveroutput on;
declare
  e_rec     employee%rowtype;
  tot_tools     number;
  cursor emp is select payroll_number, last_name, first_name from employee;
  cursor tool is select count(*) from tools
                where fk_payroll_number = e_rec.payroll_number;
begin
  open emp;
  fetch emp into e_rec.payroll_number, e_rec.last_name, e_rec.first_name;
  while not emp%notfound loop
    open tool; fetch tool into tot_tools; close tool;
    open emp;
    dbms_output.put_line(e_rec.first_name||' '||e_rec.last_name||' '||'pur-
chased '||tot_tools||' tools');
    fetch emp into e_rec.payroll_number, e_rec.last_name, e_rec.first_name;
  end loop;
  close emp;
end;
/
--a_09_03b.sql--
serveroutput on;
declare
  e_rec     employee%rowtype;
  tot_tools     number;
  cursor emp is select payroll_number, last_name, first_name from employee;
  cursor tool is select count(*) from tools
                where fk_payroll_number = e_rec.payroll_number;
begin
  open emp;
  fetch emp into e_rec.payroll_number, e_rec.last_name, e_rec.first_name;
  while not emp%notfound loop
    open tool; fetch tool into tot_tools; close tool;
    if not emp%isopen then open emp; end if;
    dbms_output.put_line(e_rec.first_name||' '||e_rec.last_name||' '||'pur-
chased '||tot_tools||' tools');
    fetch emp into e_rec.payroll_number, e_rec.last_name, e_rec.first_name;
  end loop;
  close emp;
end;
/
```

4. --a_09_04.sql--

```
serveroutput on;
declare
  e_rec     employee%rowtype;
  tot_tools     number;
  cursor emp is select payroll_number, last_name, first_name from employee;
  cursor tool is select count(*) from tools
                where fk_payroll_number = e_rec.payroll_number;
begin
  open emp;
  fetch emp into e_rec.payroll_number, e_rec.last_name, e_rec.first_name;
```

```
  while emp%rowcount < 6 loop
    open tool; fetch tool into tot_tools; close tool;
    if not emp%isopen then open emp; end if;
    dbms_output.put_line(e_rec.first_name¦¦' '¦¦e_rec.last_name¦¦' '¦¦'pur-
chased '¦¦tot_tools¦¦' tools');
    fetch emp into e_rec.payroll_number, e_rec.last_name, e_rec.first_name;
  end loop;
  close emp;
end;
/
```

5. --a_09_05.sql--

```
set serveroutput on;
declare
  e_rec         employee%rowtype;
  age           number(4,0);
  cursor emp is select last_name, first_name, birth_date
                   from employee
                 order by birth_date;
begin
open emp;
for emp_num in 1..3
  loop
   fetch emp into e_rec.last_name, e_rec.first_name, e_rec.birth_date;
   age := (sysdate - e_rec.birth_date)/365;
   dbms_output.put_line (e_rec.first_name||' '||e_rec.last_name||' is
'||age);
  end loop;
close emp;
end;
/
```

6. -a_09_06.sql--

```
set serveroutput on;
declare
  ret_date         date;
begin
for retire in (select last_name, first_name, birth_date from employee
                    where fk_department = 'INT')
  loop
  ret_date :=  retire.birth_date + (65 * 365);
  dbms_output.put_line (retire.first_name||' '||retire.last_name||' retires
on '||ret_date);
  end loop;
end;
/
```

7. -a_09_07.sql--

```
set serveroutput on;
declare
  ret_date         date;
  t_rec            tools%rowtype;
  cursor tool is select tool_name from tools where fk_payroll_number =
t_rec.fk_payroll_number;
begin
```

App E

```
for retire in (select payroll_number, last_name, first_name, birth_date from
➥employee
                        where fk_department = 'INT')
  loop
  ret_date :=  retire.birth_date + (65 * 365);
  dbms_output.put_line (retire.first_name||' '||retire.last_name||' retires
on '||ret_date);
  t_rec.fk_payroll_number := retire.payroll_number;
  open tool;
  fetch tool into t_rec.tool_name;
  while tool%found loop
    dbms_output.put_line ('      Purchased a '||t_rec.tool_name);
    fetch tool into t_rec.tool_name;
  end loop;
  close tool;
  end loop;
end;
/
```

8. –a_09_08.sql--

```
set serveroutput on;
create function tot_dept_wages (dept in char)
return number
is
tot_wages  number;
begin
  select sum(wages)
  into tot_wages
  from employee
  where fk_department = dept;
  return tot_wages;
end;
/
```

9. –a_09_09.sql--

```
set serveroutput on;
create procedure total_dept_wages (dept in char)
is
e_rec      employee%rowtype;
perc       number(3,2);
cursor wage is select first_name, last_name, wages
       from employee
       where fk_department = dept;
begin
open wage;
fetch wage into e_rec.first_name, e_rec.last_name, e_rec.wages;
while wage%found loop
  perc := e_rec.wages/tot_dept_wages(dept);
  dbms_output.put_line (e_rec.first_name||' '||e_rec.last_name||' wages are
'||perc||' of the total');
  fetch wage into e_rec.first_name, e_rec.last_name, e_rec.wages;
end loop;
close wage;
end;
/
```

10. –a_09_10.sql--

```
set serveroutput on;
begin
  total_dept_wages ('INT');
end;
/
```

11. --a_09_11a.sql--

```
set serveroutput on;
create package ans11
is
  cursor emp return employee%rowtype;
  function tot_dept_wages (dept in char) return number;
  procedure total_dept_wages (dept in char);
end ans11;
/
       --a_09_11b.sql--
set serveroutput on;
create package body ans11
is
cursor emp return employee%rowtype
  is select *
     from employee
     order by birth_date;
procedure total_dept_wages (dept in char)
is
perc       number(3,2);
e_rec   employee%rowtype;
begin
open ans11.emp;
fetch ans11.emp into e_rec;
while ans11.emp%found loop
  perc := e_rec.wages/tot_dept_wages(dept);
  dbms_output.put_line (e_rec.first_name||' '||e_rec.last_name||' wages are
'||perc||' of the total');
  fetch ans11.emp into e_rec;
end loop;
close ans11.emp;
end;
function tot_dept_wages (dept in char)
return number
is
tot_wages  number;
begin
  select sum(wages)
  into tot_wages
  from employee
  where fk_department = dept;
  return tot_wages;
end;
end ans11;
/
    --a_09_11c.sql
set serveroutput on;
```

```
begin
   for employees in ans11.emp
    loop
       dbms_output.put_line (employees.last_name);
    end loop;
end;
/
    --a_09_11d.sql
begin
  ans11.total_dept_wages ('POL');
end;
/
```

# Chapter 10

1. –a_10_01.sql--

```
delete from glasses;
delete from tools;
delete from employee;
delete from department;
commit;
```

2. –a_10_02.ctl--

```
load data
infile 'd:\dept.dat'
into table department
(
department      position(01:04) char(4),
department_name position(06:20) char(15)
)
```

3. –a_10_03.ctl--

```
load data
infile *
into table employee
fields enclosed by '"'
(payroll_number, last_name, first_name, absences, wages,
 street, city, state, phone, social_security_number, employment_date date
➥"dd-mon-yyyy",
 birth_date date "dd-mon-yyyy", current_position, fk_department)
begindata
"25" "COOLIDGE"        "CALVIN"                    "0"      "9500" "12 MAPLE
ROAD"          "PLYMOUTH"        "VT" "435-897-3546"  "100-02-0500" "07-AUG-
1921" "01-JUL-1972" "JANITOR"         "INT"
"31" "JOHNSON"         "LYNDON"                    "3"      "12000" "RR #1"
"STONEWALL"       "TX" "560-456-9876"  "456-91-2345" "23-NOV-1963" "27-AUG-
1908" "TREASURER CLERK" "POL"
"35" "REAGAN"          "RONALD"                    "5"      "13500" "10 RODEO
LANE"          "TAMPICO"         "IL" "721-898-0987"  "101-11-9832" "03-MAR-
1980" "01-OCT-1924" "PRESIDENT"       "WEL"
"36" "BUSH"            "GEORGE"                    "0"      "14000" "1456
PLEASANT"          "FALL HARBOR"     "ME" "409-339-9087"  "459-98-3456"
"05-JAN-1988" "06-FEB-1911" "CLERK 2"         "INT"
"21" "JOHNSON"         "ANDREW"                    "2"      "7500"  "1233
```

```
TABACCO RD"        "RALEIGH"           "NC" "640-789-3450"  "267-88-9876"
"13-APR-1965" "29-DEC-1908" "SALESPERSON 1"    "POL"
"37" "CLINTON"           "WILLIAM"                  "2"      "15000" "1234 OAK
DALE"        "HOPE"                "AR" "402-731-2489"  "456-98-9987" "01-JAN-
1992" "03-APR-1940" "CLERK 1"          "POL"
"34" "CARTER"            "JIMMIE"                   "1"      "13000" "RR #3"
"PLAINS"           "GE" "432-987-0987"  "563-99-7765" "10-JUL-1976" "14-JUL-
1913" "LABORER 3"        "WEL"
"33" "FORD"              "GERALD"                   "0"      "13000" "3301
CENTER ST"         "OMAHA"             "NE" "408-765-3487"  "456-33-9801"
"20-MAY-1973" "09-JAN-1913" "LABORER 2"         "INT"
"32" "NIXON"             "RICHARD"                  "6"      "12500" "12 PASA-
DENA AVE"     "YORBA LINDA"     "CA" "402-636-3171"  "555-45-2345" "15-DEC-
1968" "27-AUG-1908" "TREASURER"        "POL"
"30" "KENNEDY"           "JOHN"                     "2"      "11500" "1230 N
OCEAN"        "BROOKLINE"          "MA" "345-908-8765"  "234-66-2356" "01-JAN-
1961" "29-MAY-1917" "PROGRAMMER 1"     "POL"
"29" "EISENHOWER"        "DWIGHT"                   "1"      "0"     "12 SOLDIER
WAY"            "DENISON"          "TX" "367-098-0002"  "876-99-1201" "20-
MAR-1953" "14-OCT-1890" "GUARD 4"          "INT"
"28" "TRUMAN"            "HAROLD"                   "0"      "11000" "RRT #7"
"LAMAR"            "MO" "546-987-6512"  "345-09-0191" "15-APR-1945" "08-MAY-
1884" "COUNSELER 2"      "INT"
"27" "ROOSEVELT"         "FRANKLIN"                 "3"      "10400" "12 CHERRY
LANE"        "HYDE PARK"         "NY" "983-097-8734"  "001-01-0001" "26-MAR-
1933" "30-JAN-1882" "CLERK 1"          "POL"
"26" "HOOVER"            "HERBERT"                  "2"      "10000" "1234 MAIN
ST"          "WEST BRANCH"       "IA" "213-467-0932"  "100-02-0004" "06-APR-
1928" "10-AUG-1874" "MAINT. MAN 2"     "WEL"
"24" "WILSON"            "WOODROW"                  "1"      "9000"  "123 SMOKEY
ROAD"        "STAUTON"           "VA" "567-123-9867"  "200-05-9879" "05-SEP-
1912" "28-DEC-1856" "MAINT. MAN 3"     "POL"
"23" "TAFT"              "WILLIAM"                  "2"      "8500"  "1234
RIVERFRONT RD"    "CINCINNATI"     "OH" "234-632-7806"  "340-90-9856"
"01-JUN-1908" "15-SEP-1857" "VICE PRESIDENT"   "WEL"
"22" "ROOSEVELT"         "THEODORE"                 "0"      "8000"  "12 BROAD-
WAY"            "NEW YORK"         "NY" "389-329-0418"  "378-66-9854" "20-NOV-
1902" "27-OCT-1858" "CONTROLLER"       "INT"
"20" "ANTHONY"           "SUSAN"                    "1"      "7000"  "123 DOLLAR
ROAD"        "ADAMS"             "MA" "458-094-0987"  "503-89-7898" "30-MAR-
1840" "15-FEB-1820" "SALESPERSON 2"    "WEL"
"19" "ROOSEVELT"         "ELEANOR"                  "0"      "0"     "123 W 57
TH"               "NEW YORK"       "NY" "120-234-9876"  "509-66-8999"
"20-MAR-1932" "11-OCT-1884" "SYSTEM ANALYST"   "WEL"
```

4. –a_10_04.ctl--

```
load data
infile *
into table glasses
fields terminated by ","
(fk_payroll_number, purchase_date date "dd-mon-yy",
 optician, cost, check_number)
begindata
34,12-AUG-79,Greenberg Optical,175,N8754
25,15-NOV-23,Greenberg Optical,175,A12356
31,31-JAN-64,Peralman Optical,170,B9054
```

App E

```
35,23-OCT-83,Greenberg Optical,165,X6789
21,31-MAY-67,Greenberg Optical,165,B7865
34,08-SEP-77,Pearlman Optical,164,B9087
33,01-FEB-74,Downtown Optical,145,B9876
32,23-JUN-70,Downtown Optical,123,B897
19,01-JUL-33,TROIA OPTICAL,134,BV12798
19,20-JUL-35,TROIA OPTICAL,143,BN9876
20,12-AUG-40,PEARLMAN OPTICAL,120,X9820
22,12-MAR-03,GREENBERG OPTICAL,123,X9812
22,06-MAY-04,WYOMING OPTICAL,145,Y1245
29,31-MAR-53,GREENBERG OPTICAL,15,V8762
28,12-OCT-47,LAMAR OPTICAL,110,Z9876
27,03-JUN-33,HYDE PARK OPTICAL,129,C9876
24,01-JAN-17,STERLING OPTICAL,123,C8734
23,08-NOV-10,WAL-MART,145,N8762
```

4. –a_10_05.ctl--

```
load data
infile *
into table tools
fields terminated by "," optionally enclosed by '"'
(fk_payroll_number, purchase_date date "dd-mon-yy",
 payroll_deduct, tool_name, tool_cost, payment_amount, last_payment_amount,
 first_payment_date date "dd-mon-yy", last_payment_date date "dd-mon-yy")
begindata
25,01-OCT-22,Y,Pliers,"25",10,"5",01-SEP-22,"01-OCT-22"
25,01-FEB-23,N,Vice Grips,"10",10,,,
35,04-JUN-80,Y,3/4" Wrench,"4",2,"2",01-JUL-80,"15-JUL-80"
35,06-NOV-82,Y,Tool Chest,"16.75",6,"4.75",01-DEC-80,"01-JAN-81"
35,24-APR-81,N,Knife,"7.95",7.95,,,
36,23-SEP-88,,Drill Bit,"2.75", 2.75,,,
36,10-NOV-88,Y,Drill,"35.95",10,"5.95",01-DEC-88,"15-JAN-89"
36,23-FEB-89,Y,Hack Saw,"7.5",4,"3.5",01-MAR-89,"15-MAR-89"
21,01-FEB-66,Y,Fountain Pen,"5.95",3,"2.95",01-MAR-66,"15-MAR-66"
21,10-MAY-67,Y,Shovel,"10.75",5.75,"5",01-JUN-67,"15-JUN-67"
33,01-JAN-74,Y,Golf Balls,"12",5,"2",01-FEB-74,"15-MAR-74"
33,10-AUG-74,N,1st Aid Kit,"0",,,,,
33,23-MAR-77,N,1st Aid Kit,"0",,,,,
32,14-FEB-69,Y,Hack Saw,"12.75",6,"6.75",01-MAR-68,"15-MAR-69"
32,21-OCT-69,Y,Pliers,"5.75",5.75,"5.75",01-NOV-69,"01-NOV-69"
19,01-MAY-33,Y,CALCULATOR,"55",10,"5",15-MAY-33,"15-JUL-33"
19,06-SEP-34,N,FOUNTAIN PEN,"1.95",1.95,"1.95",,
19,30-NOV-34,Y,PLIERS,"5",5,"5",01-DEC-34,"01-DEC-34"
20,31-MAY-40,Y,BRIEF CASE,"43.95",10,"13.95",15-JUN-40,"01-AUG-40"
20,12-DEC-41,Y,CALCULATOR,"34.95",15,"4.95",15-DEC-41,"15-JAN-42"
20,03-MAY-43,N,STAPLER,"9.95",9.95,"9.95",,
22,01-FEB-03,N,BIG STICK,"34",34,,,
22,10-MAR-05,Y,RIFLE,"290",70,"10",15-MAR-05,"15-MAY-05"
29,31-MAR-53,Y,UNIFORM,"200",50,"50",15-APR-53,"15-JUN-53"
29,31-MAR-53,Y,RIFLE,"150",50,"50",01-JUN-53,"01-JUL-53"
29,01-MAR-53,N,BOOTS,"25",25,"25",,
27,01-MAY-33,N,CIGARETTE HOLDE,"12",12,"12",,
27,10-SEP-34,N,STAPLER,"8",8,"8",,
26,12-MAR-29,Y,BROOM,"8",4,"4",15-MAR-29,"01-APR-29"
26,31-MAY-29,Y,TIN SNIPS,"16",8,"8",15-JUN-29,"01-JUL-29"
24,04-NOV-13,N,DUST PAN,"4.95",4.95,"4.95",,
```

```
24,04-NOV-13,Y,VACUUM,"100",25,"24",15-NOV-13,"15-JAN-14"
24,10-SEP-15,Y,VISE GRIPS,"12",6,"6",15-SEP-15,"01-SEP-15"
23,01-AUG-09,N,FOUNTAIN PEN,"23",23,"23",,
```

# Chapter 11

1. Double-click the Run Forms icon in the Developer 2000 icon grouping. The database should also be entered.
2. Click the query button. Enter **WEL** in the department field. Click the query button again. Click the down keyboard arrow several times. Click the up keyboard arrow several times.
3. Click the F7 function key. Click the quit button. Enter a record into the form. Click the F10 function key.
4. Click the down keyboard arrow button. Click the Ctrl+F1 buttons. Identify the duplicate record button. Close the Function key dialog box. Click the duplicate record button. Click the Save button. An error should occur. Select Help, Display error from the menu. The error will appear. Close the error dialog box. Change the value in the Payroll number field. Click the save button.
5. Press the F7 function key. Enter **#is null or wages > 12000** into the Wages field. Click the F8 function key.

# Chapter 12

1. –A_12_01.fmb-

   Open the Object Navigator. Select the Forms object. Click the Create tool. A new form file will be created. Select the blocks object. Click the Create tool. The New Block Options dialog box will appear.

   On the General Tab sheet enter **Department** in the Base Table item. Enter **one** in the Block Name item. Select the Items tab.

   On the Items Tab sheet, click the Select Columns button. This will display the available columns from the Department table. Click the Layout button.

   On the Layout Tab sheet, enter **Tabular** in the Style pick list, **Vertical** in the Orientation picklist, and **12** in the Records item. Check the Button Palette and Scrollbar checkboxes. Press the OK button. The form has now been created. Save, generate, and run the form.

2. –A_12_02.fmb-

   Open the Object Navigator. Select the Forms object. Click the Create button.

   Select the Blocks object. Click the Create button. The New Block Options dialog box will appear. The General Tab sheet will appear.

   Enter **employee** in the Base Table item and **one** in the Block Name item. Click the Items tab.

On the Items Tab sheet, click the Select Columns button. Click the Layout Tab.

On the Layout Tab sheet, select "Form" on the Style picklist, "Vertical" on the Orientation picklist, and "1" in the Records item. Press OK to create the block.

Save, generate, and run the form.

# Chapter 13

1. -A_13_01-

   Open the Object Navigator. Click the File Open button. Open the Employee form created in the exercises in Chapter 12 or form A_12_01.fmb on the CD.

   Select the Tools, Layout Editor menu option. Select each part of the block frame one. Delete each of the selected frame items.

   Select the Payroll Number item. Hold the shift key and select the Payroll Number item boilerplate. Both items should now be selected. Drag the items to the proper form location.

   Repeat this procedure for each of the items on the form.

   Use the Arrange|Align Object menu option to align the various items.

   Select all of the text items. Set the fill color to white using the Fill color tool.

   Open the Object Navigator. Select the canvas object. Select the Tools, Properties menu option. Set the Width to "592," the Height to "378," and the background color to "cyan." Close the canvas property sheet.

   Select and expand the Windows object. Double click the button to the left of the window object. This will open the item's property sheet. Change the Width property to "592," the Height to "378," and the Title to "Employee Update."

   Save, generate, and run the form.

2. -A_13_02.fmb-

   Open the Object Navigator. Click the File Open button. Open the Employee form created in the exercises in Chapter 12 or form A_12_02.fmb on the CD.

   Select the Tools|Layout Editor menu option. Select each part of the block frame one. Delete each of the selected frame items.

   Select the Department_name item. Hold the shift key down and select the items boilerplate. Drag the two selected items to the right. Repeat this procedure for the Department item and the scroll bar. Arrange the items.

   Select the each text item and set the fill color to white by using the Fill tool.

   Click the Text tool. Select the Department boilerplate. Enter the missing boilerplate characters.

   Open the Object Navigator. Select the canvas object. Select the Tools|Properties menu option. Set the Width property to "320," the Height to "304," and Background to "r50g75b50." Close the property sheet.

Open the Object Navigator. Select and expand the Windows object. Double-click the button next to the window object. Set the following properties:

| | |
|---|---|
| X position | 100 |
| Y position | 30 |
| Width | 320 |
| Height | 304 |
| Title | Department Update |

Save, generate, and run the form.

# Chapter 14

You may use the a_13_01.fmb file to practice these steps.

1. Open the Object Navigator. Select the blocks object. Click the create icon on the tool bar. The New Block Options dialog box opens.
2. The settings for the General Tab are: Base Table–tools, Block Name–two, Canvas–use default, and Sequence id–2.
3. Click the Items tab. Click the Select Columns button to populate the list box. Change the Label settings to suit. Include all items.
4. Click the Layout tab. Change the Records setting to 4. Check the Scrollbar check box.
5. Click the Master/Detail tab. Enter **one** in the Master Block setting. Enter **one.payroll_number = two.fk_payroll_number** in the join condition. Click the OK button to create the block.
6. Format the block in the middle of the screen.
7. Open the Object Navigator. Select the block object. Click the create icon on the tool bar. The New Block Option dialog box opens.
8. The settings for the General Tab are: Base Table–glasses, Block Name–three, Canvas–default, and Sequence id–3.
9. Click the Items tab. Click the Select Columns button to populate the list box. Change the Label settings to suit. Include all items.
10. Click the Layout tab. Change the Records setting to 4. Check the Scrollbar and Button Palette check boxes.
11. Click the Master/Detail tab. Enter **one** in the Master Block setting. Enter **one.payroll_number = three.fk_payroll_number** in the join condition. Click the OK button to create the block.
12. Format the block.
13. Open the Object Navigator. Select the Visual Attributes object. Click the create icon. Double-click the icon next to the newly created visual attribute to open its property sheet. Change the Foreground property to red.

14. Open the property sheets for block two and three. Place the name of the visual attribute in the Current Record Attribute properties.
15. Open the Object Navigator. Select the LOV object. Click the create button to open the New LOV dialog box. Enter the following query: **select department, department_name from department order by department**. Click the OK button. Change the name of the LOV and record group to DEPT.
16. Open the Dept LOV's property sheet. Change the title property to Valid Departments. Change the Background color to r100h100b50. Change the X Position property to 160 and the Y Position property to 100. Select the Column mapping property and press the More button. Enter **one.fk_department' into the department column Return Item property**. Click OK.
17. Open the property sheet for the fk_department item on block one. Enter **DEPT** in the LOV property. Enter **true** in the LOV for Validation property.
18. Open the Layout Editor. Select the push button tool. Place a default button on the canvas. Resize the button and place it adjacent to the department item. Double-click the button to open its property sheet. Change the Name of the item to Deptlov and the Label to a pipe symbol (|). Open the Object Navigator. Locate and expand the Deptlov button item. Select the Trigger child object and click the create button. Select the When-Button-Pressed trigger from the dialog box. Enter the following in the PL/SQL editor:

```
Go_item ('one.fk_department');
List_values;
```

19. Open the Layout Editor. Double-click the payroll_deduct item to open its property sheet. Change the Item Type to Check Box. Change the Default Value to Y. Change the Label to (Check if Yes). Change the Background Color to Cyan. Resize the item on the Layout Editor. Change the Check property to Y and the Unchecked property to M.
20. Open the Object Navigator. Select the gender item. Open its property sheet. Change the Item Type to radio group. Change the default value to M. Change the Background to Cyan. Navigate to the Object Navigator. Expand the gender item. Select the Radio Buttons object. Click the create icon twice. Open the first radio button's property sheet. Change the Label to Male and the Value to M. Open the second radio button's property sheet. Change the Label to Female and the Value to F. Open the Layout Editor. The radio buttons will be located in the top left-hand corner. Select and drag them to the proper location.
21. Open the Layout Editor. Double-click the state item. Change the Item Type to List Item. Select the List Elements property. Click the More button. Enter the State values and their descriptions. Create a blank description with a null value. This will be the default. Resize the list on the layout editor.
22. Open the Layout Editor. Select the image tool. Place an image on the canvas. Be sure it is a block-one item. You may use the Object Navigator to drag the item there. Open the image item's property sheet. Change the Base Table Item to false and the Navigable property to false. Change the Sizing Style to adjust. Open the Layout Editor. Select the push button tool. Place the button on the canvas. Double-click the button to open the button's property sheet. Change the Name to photo and the Label to Employee Photo.

Open the Object Navigator. Drag the Photo button item to the Button Palette block. Expand the Photo item. Select the triggers child object. Click the create icon. Select When-button-pressed from the dialog. Enter the following in the PL/SQL editor for the trigger:

```
declare
filename       varchar2(25);
Begin
Filename := 'd:\'||to_char(:one.payroll_number)||'emp.tif';
Read_file_image (filename, 'TIF', 'one.imageitem');
End;
```

# Chapter 15

1. -a_15_01.fmb-

   Open the Object Navigator. Select and expand block two. Select and expand the items object. Select and expand the last_payment_date item. Create a trigger by clicking the Create icon. Select the When-validate-item trigger from the dialog box. Enter the following PL/SQL code block into the PL/SQL editor:

```
If (:two.last_payment_date < sysdate) then
      Message ('You Must Enter A Future Date');
      Raise form_trigger_failure;
 End if;
```

2. -a_15_01.fmb-

   Open the Object Navigator. Select and expand the form level triggers object. Click the create tool. Select the key-entqry trigger. Enter the following into the PL/SQL editor:

```
Go_block ('one');
Enter_query;
```

   Select and expand the button_palette block. Select and expand the items object. Select and expand the Query button object. Expand the triggers object. Open the When-button-pressed trigger object. Enter the following in the first section of the `if` statement before the statement "do_key ('enter_query');":

```
Go_block ('one');
```

3. -a_15_01.fmb-

   Open the Layout Editor. Move the social_security_number text item and boilerplate below the state text item. Select the street text item. Select Edit, Copy, select Edit, Paste. Drag the new item to the second row below the department text item. Double-click the new text item to open the property sheet. Change the name property to department_name, the navigable property to false, maximum_length property to 30, query_length to 30, and the base table property to false.

   Open the Object Navigator. Select the triggers object under block one. Click the create tool. Select the post-query trigger. Enter the following in the PL/SQL editor:

```
Begin
   Select department_name into :one.department_name from
➥department
```

```
                    Where uppert(rtrim(department,' ')) =
upper(rtrim(:one.fk_department,' '));
               exception
                  when others then :one.department_name := 'UNKNOWN';
               end;
```

Re-sequence the items on block one by opening the object navigator and dragging the objects.

4. -a_15_01.fmb-

   Open the Object Navigator. Select the alerts object. Click the Create tool. Change the name of the alert to "bad_date." Open the alerts' property sheet. Set the Button2 property to Null. Set the Message property to You May Only Enter Future Dates Into the Last Payment Date field. Select the When-validate-item trigger under the last_payment_date item. Double-click the item to open the PL/SQL editor. Change the trigger script to:

```
Declare
  Alert_value          number;
Begin
If (:two.last_payment_date < sysdate) then
         Alert_value := show_alert('bad_date');
         Raise form_trigger_failure;
 End if;
         End;
```

5. -a_15_02.fmb-

   Open the Object navigator. Select the canvas-view object. Click the Create item twice. Change the names of the new canvases to canvas2 and canvas3. Change the properties on canvas2 and canvas3 to the following:

| | |
|---|---|
| Canvas-view type | stacked |
| Width | 592 |
| Bevel | none |
| Background | cyan |
| Stacked View Width | 592 |
| Stacked View Height | 210 |
| Display Y Position | 90 |

Open the Layout Editor. Select each of the items on block three. Open the multi-item property sheet. Change the canvas property to canvas2. Select the image item. Double-click the item to open the property sheet. Change the canvas property to canvas3. Select all of the boilerplate for block2. Select Edit, Cut. Open the Object Navigator. Double-click canvas2. Position the cursor on the layout. Select Edit, Paste. Format the items on the form. Open the canvas3 layout editor. Position the image item.

Open the Object Navigator. Open the block-two property sheet. Change the records displayed property to 10. Open the block-three property sheet. Change the records displayed property to 10. Open the Layout Editor. Select the Employee Photo button. Select Edit, Copy menu option. Select Edit, Paste. Drag and position the new button.

Double-click the new button item. Change the name property of the item to glasses. Change the label property of the item to GLASSES. Select Edit, Paste. Drag and position the new button. Double-click the new button item. Change the name property of the item to tools. Change the label property of the item to TOOLS.

Open the Object Navigator and locate the When-button-pressed trigger for the glasses button. Open the trigger's PL/SQL editor. Change the code block to go_block ("three"). Locate the When-button-press trigger for the tools button. Open the trigger's PL/SQL editor. Change the code block to go_block ("two"). Open the When-button-pressed PL/SQL editor for the Photo button. Place the following two statements on the first line of the executable code:

```
Go_block ('one');
Go_item ('image37');
```

# Chapter 17

1. -a_17_01.rdf-

   Open the Object Navigator. Create a new report module. Open the data model editor by double-clicking the data model object. Select the query tool. Place a query box on the model layout area. Double-click the query box. Enter the following query into the box: **Select fk_department, last_name, first_name, wages from employee order by fk_department**. Click the Apply button. Press the Close button. Click the default layout icon at the top of the data model editor. Select the tabular style and modify the column labels. Click OK when done. Save the file. Execute the file by double-clicking the run icon.

2. -a_17_02.rdf-

   Open the file created in exercise one in Reports Designer. Open the data model editor by double-clicking the data model icon or selecting Tools, Data Model Editor menu option. Select the last_name column. Create a new group by dragging the item beneath the existing group box. Select the first_name column. Drag it into the new group box. Select the wages column. Drag it into the new group box. Create a new default layout by double-clicking the default layout icon. Click OK when done. Save the file. Execute the file by double-clicking the run icon.

3. -a_17_03.rdf-

   Open the file create in exercise two in Reports Designer. Open the data model editor by double-clicking the data model icon or selecting Tools, Data Model Editor menu option. Select the query tool. Create a new query box on the model layout area. Double-click the new query box. Enter the following in the Select statement window: **Select department, department_name from department**. Click the Apply button to validate the statement. Click the Close button when done. Activate the data link tool by clicking the data link icon. Select the fk_department column. Hold down the mouse button. Drag the data link line to the department column. Click the default layout icon. Open the Data/Selection tab of the dialog box. Deselect the department column. Click OK. Save the file. Execute the file by double-clicking the run icon.

# Index

## Symbols



## A

## D

## F

## G



## H

## I



## J-K

## L

## M



## N

## O

## P

## Q



## R

## S

## T

## U

## X-Y-Z

# Complete and Return This Card for a *FREE* Computer Book Catalog

Thank you for purchasing this book! You have purchased a superior computer book written expressly for your needs. To continue to provide the kind of up-to-date, pertinent coverage you've come to expect from us, we need to hear from you. Please take a minute to complete and return this self-addressed, postage-paid form. In return, we'll send you a free catalog of all our computer books on topics ranging from word processing to programming and the Internet.

☐ Mrs. ☐ Ms. ☐ Dr. ☐

me (first) ☐☐☐☐☐☐☐☐☐☐☐ (M.I.) ☐ (last) ☐☐☐☐☐☐☐☐☐☐☐☐☐☐☐

dress ☐☐☐☐☐☐☐☐☐☐☐☐☐☐☐☐☐☐☐☐☐☐☐☐☐☐☐☐☐☐☐☐☐☐☐

☐☐☐☐☐☐☐☐☐☐☐☐☐☐☐☐☐☐☐☐☐☐☐☐☐☐☐☐☐☐☐☐☐☐☐

y ☐☐☐☐☐☐☐☐☐☐☐☐☐☐☐ State ☐☐ Zip ☐☐☐☐☐ ☐☐☐☐

one ☐☐☐ ☐☐☐ ☐☐☐☐ Fax ☐☐☐ ☐☐☐ ☐☐☐☐

mpany Name ☐☐☐☐☐☐☐☐☐☐☐☐☐☐☐☐☐☐☐☐☐☐☐☐☐☐☐☐☐☐☐☐☐

nail address ☐☐☐☐☐☐☐☐☐☐☐☐☐☐☐☐☐☐☐☐☐☐☐☐☐☐☐☐☐☐☐☐☐

**lease check at least three influencing factors for purchasing this book.**

- nt or back cover information on book ........................ ☐
- cial approach to the content ........................ ☐
- mpleteness of content ........................ ☐
- thor's reputation ........................ ☐
- lisher's reputation ........................ ☐
- ok cover design or layout ........................ ☐
- ex or table of contents of book ........................ ☐
- ce of book ........................ ☐
- cial effects, graphics, illustrations ........................ ☐
- er (Please specify): ______________________ ☐

**How did you first learn about this book?**

- v in Macmillan Computer Publishing catalog ........... ☐
- commended by store personnel ........................ ☐
- v the book on bookshelf at store ........................ ☐
- commended by a friend ........................ ☐
- ceived advertisement in the mail ........................ ☐
- v an advertisement in: ______________________ ☐
- ad book review in: ______________________ ☐
- er (Please specify): ______________________ ☐

**How many computer books have you purchased in the last six months?**

- is book only ....... ☐ 3 to 5 books ..................... ☐
- ooks .................. ☐ More than 5 ..................... ☐

**4. Where did you purchase this book?**

- Bookstore ........................ ☐
- Computer Store ........................ ☐
- Consumer Electronics Store ........................ ☐
- Department Store ........................ ☐
- Office Club ........................ ☐
- Warehouse Club ........................ ☐
- Mail Order ........................ ☐
- Direct from Publisher ........................ ☐
- Internet site ........................ ☐
- Other (Please specify): ______________________ ☐

**5. How long have you been using a computer?**

☐ Less than 6 months ☐ 6 months to a year
☐ 1 to 3 years ☐ More than 3 years

**6. What is your level of experience with personal computers and with the subject of this book?**

| | With PCs | With subject of book |
|---|---|---|
| New | ☐ | ☐ |
| Casual | ☐ | ☐ |
| Accomplished | ☐ | ☐ |
| Expert | ☐ | ☐ |

Source Code ISBN: 0-7897-1419-1

**7. Which of the following best describes your job title?**

Administrative Assistant ☐
Coordinator ☐
Manager/Supervisor ☐
Director ☐
Vice President ☐
President/CEO/COO ☐
Lawyer/Doctor/Medical Professional ☐
Teacher/Educator/Trainer ☐
Engineer/Technician ☐
Consultant ☐
Not employed/Student/Retired ☐
Other (Please specify): ________ ☐

**8. Which of the following best describes the area of the company your job title falls under?**

Accounting ☐
Engineering ☐
Manufacturing ☐
Operations ☐
Marketing ☐
Sales ☐
Other (Please specify): ________ ☐

**9. What is your age?**

Under 20 ☐
21-29 ☐
30-39 ☐
40-49 ☐
50-59 ☐
60-over ☐

**10. Are you:**

Male ☐
Female ☐

**11. Which computer publications do you read regularly? (Please list)**

________
________
________
________
________
________
________
________
________

***Comments*:** ________

Fold here and tape to mail

NO POSTAGE NECESSARY IF MAILED IN THE UNITED STATES

**BUSINESS REPLY MAIL**

FIRST-CLASS MAIL PERMIT NO. 9918 INDIANAPOLIS IN

POSTAGE WILL BE PAID BY THE ADDRESSEE

ATTN MARKETING
MACMILLAN COMPUTER PUBLISHING
MACMILLAN PUBLISHING USA
201 W 103RD ST
INDIANAPOLIS IN 46290-9042

## Licensing Agreement

By opening this package, you are agreeing to be bound by the following:

This software product is copyrighted, and all rights are reserved by the publisher and author. You are licensed to use this software on a single computer. You may copy and/or modify the software as needed to facilitate your use of it on a single computer. Making copies of the software for any other purpose is a violation of the United States copyright laws.

This software is sold *as is* without warranty of any kind, either expressed or implied, including but not limited to the implied warranties of merchantability and fitness for a particular purpose. Neither the publisher nor its dealers or distributors assumes any liability for any alleged or actual damages arising from the use of this program. (Some states do not allow for the exclusion of implied warranties, so the exclusion may not apply to you.)